Silos

Silos
Fundamentals of theory, behaviour and design

Edited by C.J. Brown and J. Nielsen

CRC Press
Taylor & Francis Group
Boca Raton London New York

CRC Press is an imprint of the
Taylor & Francis Group, an **informa** business

A TAYLOR & FRANCIS BOOK

CRC Press
Taylor & Francis Group
6000 Broken Sound Parkway NW, Suite 300
Boca Raton, FL 33487-2742

First issued in paperback 2019

© 1998 by Taylor & Francis Group, LLC
CRC Press is an imprint of Taylor & Francis Group, an Informa business

No claim to original U.S. Government works

ISBN-13: 978-0-419-21580-6 (hbk)
ISBN-13: 978-0-367-86369-2 (pbk)

Typeset in 10/12 Sabon by Best-set Typesetter Ltd., Hong Kong

This book contains information obtained from authentic and highly regarded sources. Reasonable efforts have been made to publish reliable data and information, but the author and publisher cannot assume responsibility for the validity of all materials or the consequences of their use. The authors and publishers have attempted to trace the copyright holders of all material reproduced in this publication and apologize to copyright holders if permission to publish in this form has not been obtained. If any copyright material has not been acknowledged please write and let us know so we may rectify in any future reprint.

Except as permitted under U.S. Copyright Law, no part of this book may be reprinted, reproduced, transmitted, or utilized in any form by any electronic, mechanical, or other means, now known or hereafter invented, including photocopying, microfilming, and recording, or in any information storage or retrieval system, without written permission from the publishers.

For permission to photocopy or use material electronically from this work, please access www.copyright.com (http://www.copyright.com/) or contact the Copyright Clearance Center, Inc. (CCC), 222 Rosewood Drive, Danvers, MA 01923, 978-750-8400. CCC is a not-for-profit organization that provides licenses and registration for a variety of users. For organizations that have been granted a photocopy license by the CCC, a separate system of payment has been arranged.

Trademark Notice: Product or corporate names may be trademarks or registered trademarks, and are used only for identification and explanation without intent to infringe.

British Library Cataloguing in Publication Data
A catalogue record for this book is available from the British library

Publisher's Note
The publisher has gone to great lengths to ensure the quality of this reprint but points out that some imperfections in the original may be apparent.

Visit the Taylor & Francis Web site at
http://www.taylorandfrancis.com

and the CRC Press Web site at
http://www.crcpress.com

Contents

Contributors	xi
Foreword	xvi
C.J. Brown and J. Nielsen	

Part One   Silo Flow   1

1 Introduction   3
J. Schwedes and H. Wilms

2 Bulk solids testing   5
  2.1 Flow property measurements   6
       J. Schwedes
  2.2 Measurement of the flowability of bulk solids   18
       D. Schulze
  2.3 Flow property testing of particulate solids by uniaxial
       and biaxial testers   53
       G.G. Enstad and H. Feise
  2.4 Reflections on triaxial testing, rheology and flowability   65
       M.P. Luong
  2.5 Wall friction and wear testing   76
       G. Haaker
  2.6 The relevance of aeration and fluidization   88
       D. Höhne and B. Scarlett
  2.7 The application of bulk solids testers in industry   98
       E.J. Puik, J. Kater and P.J. Reuderink
  2.8 Classification of bulk solids   104
       H. Wilms and B. Kühnemund

vi   *Contents*

3   Flow in silos   **111**
    3.1   Flow patterns   112
           J. Schwedes
    3.2   Wall stress distributions in silos with inserts, and loads on inserts   118
           J. Strusch and J. Schwedes
    3.3   Inserts in silos for blending   131
           H. Wilms
    3.4   Simulation of blending silos   142
           D. Schulze
    3.5   Segregation of particulate solids in silos   160
           G.G. Enstad and J. Mosby
    3.6   Silo quaking   171
           D. Schulze
    3.7   Purge bin design requirements   183
           H. Wilms
    3.8   Flow patterns and velocity distributions in silos   192
           E.J. Puik and P.J. Reuderink

4   Discharge, feeding and metering equipment   **199**
    4.1   Feeders and flow-promoting devices   200
           D. Schulze
    4.2   Discharge of bulk solids from silos – description of discharge systems   221
           H. Heinrici
    4.3   Continuous feeding of bulk solids   231
           H. Heinrici
    4.4   Level control in silos   240
           H. Wilms

5   Silo fabricator's and system supplier's view   **250**
    H. Wilms

6   Summary   **255**
    J. Schwedes and H. Wilms

Part Two   Concrete Structures   259

7   Introduction and scope   **261**
    J. Eibl

8   Actions   **262**
    J. Eibl
    8.1   Pressure   262
    8.2   Temperature   266

Contents   vii

	8.3 Differential settlement	268
	8.4 Earthquakes	272
	8.5 Dust explosions	274
	Appendix 8.A	277
9	**Reinforcement** *J. Eibl*	312
10	**Concreting** *J. Eibl*	317
11	**Concluding remarks** *J. Eibl*	322

Part Three   Metal Structures   323

	Foreword *J.M. Rotter*	325
12	**Overview of metal silos** *J.M. Rotter*	327
13	**Structural forms of silos** *M.J. Blackler*	334
14	**Effects of silo loads** *J.M. Rotter*	337
15	**Cylindrical shells: symmetrical solids loadings** *J.M. Rotter*	346
16	**Cylindrical shells: unsymmetrical solids loadings and supports** *J.M. Rotter*	367
17	**Cylindrical shells: wind loading** *R. Greiner*	378
18	**Cylindrical shells: other actions** *D. Briassoulis*	400
19	**Conical hopper shells** *J.M. Rotter*	415
20	**Rectangular silo structures** *C.J. Brown*	426

21	Internal structures (ties and internals) A. Khelil	443
22	Finite element analysis of the stress state and stability of metal silo structures T. Ummenhofer	452
23	Challenges for the future and concluding comments J.M. Rotter	461

Part Four Numerical Simulation of Particulate Solids 469

24	Introduction and scope G. Rombach and J. Martinez	471
25	Comparison of existing programs G. Rombach	476
26	A dynamic finite element model for silo pressures and solids flow G. Rombach and J. Eibl	481
27	Finite element models for specific applications E. Ragneau, J.Y. Ooi and J.M. Rotter	495
28	Stochastic finite element analysis of filling pressures F. Dahlhaus and J. Eibl	509
29	Pressures under earthquake loading A. Braun and J. Eibl	518
30	Constitutive laws for granular materials H. Feise and J. Schwedes	528
31	The choice of constitutive laws for silo media J. Nielsen and J. Weidner	539
32	Numerical simulations based on discrete particle models U. Tüzün	551
33	Lattice grain models J. Martinez and S. Masson	556
34	Relationship between finite element and distinct element simulations J. Martinez and S. Masson	564

35 Evaluation of applications of FEM and DPM P.J. Reuderink	580
36 Challenges for the future in numerical simulation J.M. Rotter	584
37 Concluding comments J. Martinez	605

Part Five   Silo Tests   607

38 Introduction and scope H. Stoffers	609
39 Classification of silo tests J. Garnier	612
40 Test design	621
40.1 Tests for pressures H. Stoffers	622
40.2 Tests for flow H. Stoffers	630
40.3 Tests for vibrations H. Stoffers	635
40.4 Tests for structural buckling P. Knoedel	642
41 Test documentation	645
41.1 Test conditions J. Munch-Andersen	646
41.2 Properties of the stored granular solid J.M. Rotter, J. Munch-Andersen and J. Nielsen	650
41.3 Data presentation J. Munch-Andersen	673
42 Concluding remarks H. Stoffers	682

Part Six   Experimental Techniques   683

43 Introduction J. Garnier	685

44	Normal and shear stress on a silo wall, and stress and strain state in a silo medium V. Askegaard	686
45	Strain in a silo wall J.Y. Ooi, J.F. Chen and J.M. Rotter	699
46	Displacements, crack openings and total volume J. Nielsen	716
47	Local density measurements J. Garnier	719
48	Interstitial and atmospheric air pressure measurement G. Dau	729
49	Flow visualization J.Y. Ooi and J.M. Rotter	745
50	Measurement of moisture in silos J.M. Fleureau	761
51	Model laws and scale errors J. Nielsen	774
52	Gamma-ray tomographic techniques in granular flows in hoppers U. Tüzün and M.S. Nikitidis	781
53	Silo test facilities in Europe C.J. Brown	792
54	Concluding comments and research requirements J. Garnier	802

Part Seven Research for Industry 805

55	Industrial requirements C.J. Brown and J. Nielsen	807
56	Prenormative research J. Nielsen	817

Contributors

V. Askegaard
Technical University of Denmark
ABK DTH
Bygning 118
DK-2800 Lyngby
Denmark
Tel. (+45) 45 93 43 31
Fax (+45) 45 88 32 82

M.J. Blackler
Mott MacDonald
St Anne House
20–26 Wellesley Rd
Croydon
Surrey CR9 2UL
UK
Tel. (+44) 181 686 5041
Fax (+44) 181 681 5706

A. Braun
c/o Prof J. Eibl

D. Briassoulis
Agricultural University of Athens
Agricultural Engineering Dept
75 Iera Odos Str.
11855 Athens
Greece
Tel. (+30) 1 52 94 011
Fax (+30) 1 52 94 023
e-mail: briassou@auadec.aua.
    ariadne-t.gr

C.J. Brown
Brunel University
Dept of Mechanical Engineering
Uxbridge
Middlesex UB8 3PH
UK
Tel. (+44) 1895 274000 ext. 2206
Fax (+44) 1895 256392
e-mail: Chris.Brown@brunel.ac.uk

J.F. Chen
University of Edinburgh
The King's Buildings
Edinburgh EH9 3JN
UK
Tel. (+44) 131 650 5733
Fax (+44) 131 650 6781
e-mail: Chen@civ.ed.ac.uk

F. Dahlhaus
c/o Prof J. Eibl

G. Dau
University of Kaiserslautern
Erwin-Schroedinger-Strasse
D-67663 Kaiserslautern
Germany
Tel. (+49) 631 205 2560
Fax (+49) 631 205 3600
e-mail: dau@mv.uni-kl.de

J. Eibl
Institut für Massivbau und
 Baustofftechnologie
University of Karlsruhe
Abteilung Massivbau
Postfach 6980
D-7500 Karlsruhe 1
Germany
Tel. (+49) 721 608 2277
Fax (+49) 721 693 075

G.G. Enstad
Tel-Tek
Dept of POSTEC
Kjølnes Ring
N-3914 Porsgrunn
Norway
Tel. (+47) 35 57 40 00
Fax (+47) 35 57 40 10

H.J. Feise
current work address:
E.I. du Pont de Nemours
CR&D – PARSAT E304/A207
PO Box 80304
Wilmington
DE 19880-0304
USA
e-mail: feise@a1.esvax.umc.dupont.com

J.M. Fleureau
Laboratoire de Mécanique
Ecole Centrale de Paris
Grande Voie des Vignes
F-92295 Chatenay-Malabry
France
Tel. (+33) 1 41 13 13 20
Fax (+33) 1 41 13 14 42
e-mail: fleureau@mss.ecp.fr

J. Garnier
Laboratoire Central des Ponts et
 Chaussées
Route de Pornic
BP 19
F-44340 Bouguenais
France
Tel. (+33) 2 40 84 58 19
Fax (+33) 2 40 84 59 97
e-mail: garnier@lcpc.inrets.fr

R. Greiner
Institut für Stahlbau, Holzbau und
 Flächentragwerke
Technische Universität Graz
Lessingstrasse 25
A-8010 Graz
Austria
Tel. (+43) 316 873 6200
Fax (+43) 316 873 6707

G. Haaker
University of Twente
Dept of Mechanical Engineering
PO Box 217
NL-7500 AE Enschede
The Netherlands
Tel. (+31) 53 489 24 87
Fax (+31) 53 489 36 63
e-mail: g.haaker@wb.utwente.nl

H. Heinrici
Schenck Process GmbH
D-64273 Darmstadt
Germany
Tel. (+49) 6151 32 2717
Fax (+49) 6151 32 1336

D. Höhne
TU Bergakademie Freiberg
Institut für Mechanische
　Verfahrenstechnik und
　Aufbereitungstechnik
Agricolastr. 1
D-09599 Freiberg
Germany
Tel. (+49) 3731 39 3281
Fax (+49) 3731 39 2947

J. Kater
Shell Research and Technology
　Centre, Amsterdam
PO Box 38000
1030 BN Amsterdam
The Netherlands
Tel. (+31) 20 630 2873
e-mail: j.kater@siop.shell.nl

A. Khelil
LPMM UA CNRS 1215 (GRRS)
IUT Genie Civil
F-54601 Villers-les-Nancy
France
Tel. (+33) 83 91 22 20
Fax (+33) 83 91 22 21
e-mail: khelil@iutnb.u-nancy.fr

P. Knoedel
Boeckhstr. 52
D-76137 Karlsruhe
Germany

B. Kühnemund
Buhler A.G.
CH-9240 Uzwil
Switzerland
Tel. (+41) 71 955 2102
Fax (+41) 71 955 1251

M.P. Luong
Ecole Polytechnique
(LMS)
F-91128 Palaiseau
France
Tel. (+33) 1 69 33 33 68
Fax (+33) 1 69 33 30 26
e-mail: MEC@FRPOLY11.BITNET

J. Martinez
INSA Rennes
20 Avenue des Buttes de Coesmes
F-35043 Rennes
France
Tel. (+33) 2 99 28 66 21
Fax (+33) 2 99 28 66 21
e-mail: Martinez@insa-rennes.fr

S. Masson
c/o Prof J. Martinez

J. Mosby
Norton-Lillesand
PO Box 113
N-4791 Lillesand
Norway

J. Munch-Andersen
Danish Building Research Institute
PO Box 119
DK-2970 Hørsholm
Denmark
Tel. (+45) 45 86 55 33
Fax (+45) 45 86 75 35
e-mail: JMA@sbi.dk

J. Nielsen
Danish Building Research Institute
PO Box 119
DK-2970 Hørsholm
Denmark
Tel. (+45) 45 86 55 33
Fax (+45) 45 86 75 35
e-mail: JN@sbi.dk

M.S. Nikitidis
c/o Prof U. Tüzün

J.Y. Ooi
Dept of Civil and Environmental
  Engineering
University of Edinburgh
The King's Buildings
Edinburgh EH9 3JN
UK
Tel. (+44) 131 650 5725
Fax (+44) 131 667 9238
e-mail: J.Ooi@ed.ac.uk

E.J. Puik
Shell Research and Technology
  Centre, Amsterdam
PO Box 38000
1030 BN Amsterdam
The Netherlands
Tel. (+31) 20 630 3891
e-mail: e.j.puik@siop.shell.nl

E. Ragneau
INSA Rennes
20 Avenue des Buttes de Coesmes
F-35043 Rennes
France
Tel. (+33) 2 99 28 66 55
Fax (+33) 2 99 28 66 64

P.J. Reuderink
Shell Nederland Raffinaderij B.V.
PO Box 7000
3000 HA Rotterdam
The Netherlands
Tel. (+31) 10 431 1622

G. Rombach
Technische Universität Hamburg-
  Harburg
Arbeitsbereich Massivbau 3-07
Denickestr. 17
21073 Hamburg
Germany
Tel. (+49) 40 7718 3122
Fax (+49) 40 7718 2968

J.M. Rotter
Dept of Civil and Environmental
  Engineering
University of Edinburgh
Crew Building
The King's Buildings
Edinburgh EH9 3JN
UK
Tel. (+44) 131 650 5719
Fax (+44) 131 650 7170
e-mail: J.Rotter@ed.ac.uk

B. Scarlett
Faculty of Chemical Technology
  and Materials Science
Technical University Delft
Julianalaan 136
2628 BL Delft
The Netherlands
Tel. (+31) 15 78 35 77
Fax (+31) 15 78 44 52

D. Schulze
Fachhochschule Braunschweig/
  Wolfenbüttel
Institute for Recycling
Robert-Koch-Platz 12
D-38440 Wolfsburg
Germany
Tel. (+49) 5361 83 1412
Fax (+49) 5361 83 1402

Contributors

J. Schwedes
Institut für Mechanische
　Verfahrenstechnik
Technische Universität
　Braunschweig
Volkmaroder Strasse 4–5
D-38104 Braunschweig
Germany
Tel. (+49) 531 391 9610
Fax (+49) 531 391 9633

H. Stoffers
TNO Building and Construction
　Research
Lange Kleiweg 5
Rijswijk
PO Box 49
NL-2600 AA Delft
The Netherlands
Tel. (+31) 15 284 21 47
Fax (+31) 15 284 39 76

J. Strusch
Bayer AG
Alt ZT-TE 4.4
D-51368 Leverkusen
Germany

U. Tüzün
Surrey University
Dept of Chemical and Process
　Engineering
Guildford GU2 5XH
UK
Tel. (+44) 1483 300800 ext. 2188
Fax (+44) 1483 259510
e-mail: u.tuzun@surrey.ac.uk

T. Ummenhofer
Herzogin-Elisabeth-Strasse 32
D-38104 Braunschweig
Germany
Tel. (+49) 531 270 2390
Fax (+49) 531 270 2391
e-mail: ipp-bs@t-online.de

J. Weidner
Theodor-Hoerner-Strasse 12c
76275 Ettlingen
Germany

H. Wilms
Zeppelin Schüttguttechnik GmbH
Birkenweg 4
D-88250 Weingarten
Germany
Tel. (+49) 751 40090
Fax (+49) 751 400920

Foreword

This book is the collection of the state-of-the-art reports from various researchers and specialists who have been brought together by a research project on silos, the CA-Silo Project.

Through collaborative activity it represents an attempt to reach a common European understanding in the very complex field of silo research, and to present up-to-date information on many aspects of silo behaviour in a collected form.

The work is intended for use as a primer for silo researchers and aims to help avoid duplication of future research effort and hence optimize limited resources. It provides background material to textbooks, codes and other specifications relevant to both silo designers and silo users. As the title of the book suggests, it focuses on fundamentals and addresses the challenging problems related to theory, behaviour and design of silos. The book is not aimed at the beginner, and should be read as a natural sequel to textbooks that provide a more systematic introduction to the design of silos.

The CA-Silo Project was a Concerted Action, funded under the auspices of the BRITE EuRam Programme (Framework II) by the European Commission (Project 5021). It was started in September 1992, and was brought to a conclusion in the spring of 1997.

Silo problems are multidisciplinary with their backgrounds in civil engineering (safety of structures), mechanical engineering (equipment for handling and transportation), chemical engineering (processes involving storage in silos), and specialist areas such as experimental mechanics, dust explosion, simulations, etc. Silo problems are of interest to users of silos within all sectors of our society, and to the manufacturers of silos.

In relation to the importance of those structures and the complexity of the problems it is remarkable how little attention has been paid to research within this area, and how scattered the international research community has been in the area.

CA-Silo has thus been a much needed effort in establishing some common understanding of the practical use of existing knowledge, and of the research needs. Working Groups set up within CA-Silo have examined different aspects of silo technology. An important objective was to collaborate in establishing the state of the art in the specialist areas of the Working Groups. A workshop at Delft allowed identification of potential contributors. At later workshops at Paris and Braunschweig, and through correspondence, researchers and specialists from industry presented their findings for group discussion. When key aspects had been identified, the separate contributions to the state of the art were then written by contributors from that specialist area.

These contributions are collected here. Some authors have listened more than others to group opinions and the working styles of the groups have also been somewhat different, resulting in contributions of very different nature. These range from views of the individuals, to presentation of research projects, to well-documented recommendations and guidelines. As a result, the reader must assess the relevance and force of each contribution for their purposes.

The views expressed by the authors represent those of different schools of thought, from researchers with different philosophies. No attempt has been made by the editors to 'conform' the contributions to a particular school of thought.

Not all relevant papers are quoted, and the authors have often been selective from the wide range of literature available. Nevertheless the reference list is extensive and will prove sufficient for most needs.

Nomenclature used in the different sections of the book varies; this is representative of the different use of symbols in their areas of application.

Working Groups were established in silo flow, concrete structures, metal structures, numerical modelling (and associated constitutive laws), silo testing, experimental techniques, and finally the scientific basis for Eurocodes. The Chairmen of the Working Groups have each been responsible for developing a Part of the book. They are: Prof. J. Schwedes and Dr H. Wilms for Part One, Prof. J. Eibl for Part Two, Prof. J.M. Rotter for Part Three, Prof. G. Rombach and Prof. J. Martinez for Part Four, Dr H. Stoffers for Part Five, Prof. V. Askegaard and Dr J. Garnier for Part Six, and Dr J. Nielsen for Part Seven. The editors would like to express their sincere thanks to the Chairmen of the Working Groups and all the other authors for their contributions and cooperation.

The contents of this book follow the pattern of the Working Groups. Each Part can be read on its own but many items are dealt with in several Parts. For example, Part Four on computer simulations presents interesting results for problems concerning flow in silos, loads, and structural design.

Research needs and visions for future work are integrated in contributions in all chapters. Parts Five and Six should be read together since planning and reporting of silo tests are very closely related to the experimental techniques that are available. In Parts One to Six, generally the first and last chapters refer to the entire Part, serving as an Introduction and Conclusion respectively, and these chapters should be read in that context.

The editors would especially like to thank those who replied to the industry questionnaire for their efforts, and acknowledge the generosity of those who have given their time to such direct industrial input.

There have been many typists and graphics artists in the different EU countries who have helped enormously, and who are unknown to us; we hope they will accept our grateful thanks.

We would like to thank Ms Gayatri Bose for pulling the contributions into a final form, and for saving us from an avalanche of paper!

Finally, we would like to recognize the supportive nature of the EC Project Officers involved with the Project, and in particular Dr Lellis Braganza and Dr Susanna Becker, without whose support this book would not have been brought to fruition.

Chris Brown and Jørgen Nielsen
Spring 1997

Disclaimer

The opinions expressed are those of the authors and not necessarily those of the editors. Every effort has been made to ensure the accuracy in this book, but the publisher, the editors and the authors cannot accept responsibility for any loss, damage or other consequence resulting from the use of this material. Anyone making use of the information or material contained in this book, in whole or in part, does so at his own risk and assumes any and all liability from such use.

Part One

Silo Flow

1

Introduction

J. Schwedes and H. Wilms

Part One of this volume has been compiled by participants of the CA-Silo Project Working Group on Silo Flow. The participants are involved in the areas of silo design for flow, consulting, research and flow property testing. Thus, the authors are front-end engineers and scientists dealing with the practical daily problems occurring during silo operation. Research in this field involves silo experiments in order to derive and verify design principles and to understand the observed phenomena as well as to test simulation techniques based on sophisticated constitutive laws.

The major influencing factor on the flow of bulk solids from silos is the flow behaviour of the bulk solid itself. Since so many different bulk solids are to be stored in silos, it is very important to describe and determine the flow properties of the respective bulk solids. The flowability is usually determined by shear tests or similar procedures. Calibration of constitutive laws requires more information which can only be determined from stress–strain relationships measured in more sophisticated shear testers.

All these flow property data closely relate to the required silo geometry for trouble-free operation, usually obtained by mass flow. There is a lot of interaction between the flow of solids from silos and the silo structure, especially in funnel flow silos with asymmetric flow channels. Another important area of interest is the interface between the silo outlet and the inlet to a feeder underneath the silo. Feeders and flow-promoting devices have to be evaluated in more detail with respect to their applicability for bulk solids with certain flow properties. Thus, new discharge equipment can be developed. A lot of industrial input is required for this work. The operating conditions such as storage time, flow rates, ambient conditions and cyclic climatic changes do have an influence on reliable silo operation techniques.

Thus, there is interaction between the bulk solids under consideration, the silo structure itself, the operating and the ambient conditions. The aim of the work is therefore to broaden the knowledge on flow property testing, to define characterization procedures, to evaluate testing methods and to describe the design requirements for trouble-free silo operation.

This becomes even more important with additional unit operations being carried out in silo-like structures, such as blending, purging, de-aeration and drying. Especially for these processes, two-phase flow phenomena may become important. Respective design requirements and testing procedures need to be defined.

Writing a state-of-the-art report with individual experts from academia and industry does not guarantee to cover all aspects and thus can never give a complete picture. By inviting many experts to participate in CA-Silo, we have tried to overcome this deficiency. This report is the result of several intensive discussions with permanent and corresponding members of the Working Group. All participants have been involved in drafting and editing the report. From these discussions, individual members then volunteered to write the different sections of Part One. Their work and the discussions with all the participants are highly appreciated and form the basis for this book.

2
Bulk solids testing

2.1 Flow property measurements
J. Schwedes

2.1.1 Introduction

Many ideas, methods and testers exist to measure the flowability of bulk solids. People running those tests are seldom interested in exclusively characterizing the flow properties of the bulk solid in question. More often they want to use the measured data to design equipment, where bulk solids are stored, transported or otherwise handled, to decide which one out of a number of bulk solids has the best or the worst flowability, to fulfil the requirement of quality control, to model processes with the finite element method or to judge any other process in which the strength or flowability of bulk solids plays an important role. Many testers are available which measure some value of flowability, but only some of these will be mentioned here without claiming completeness: the Jenike shear cell, annular shear cells, triaxial tester, true biaxial shear tester, Johanson indicizer, torsional cell, uniaxial tester, oedometer, lambdameter, Jenike and Johanson quality control tester, Hosokawa tester and others. It is beyond the scope of this section to describe all testers in detail and to compare them one by one. Instead it will be attempted first to define flow properties. Secondly applications are mentioned. Here the properties which are needed for design are described and the testers able to measure these properties are mentioned. Finally a comparison with regard to application will be attempted.

2.1.2 Flow function

The flow function was first introduced by Jenike and first measured with the help of the Jenike shear cell (Jenike, 1964). Therefore a short explanation of the flow function and the relevant procedure will be given here. The main part of the Jenike shear tester is the shear cell (Fig. 2.1.1). It consists of a base A, a ring B resting on top of the base and a lid C. The base and ring are filled with a sample of the bulk solid. A vertical force is applied to the lid. A horizontal shearing force is applied on a bracket attached to the lid. Running shear tests with identically preconsolidated samples under different normal loads gives maximum shearing forces S for every normal force N. Division of N and S by the cross-sectional area of the shear cell leads to the normal stress σ and the shear stress τ. Figure 2.1.2 shows a σ,τ-diagram. The curve represents the maximum shear stress τ the sample can support under a certain normal stress σ; it is called the yield locus. The yield locus depends on a parameter – the bulk density ρ_b. With higher preconsolidation loads the bulk density ρ_b increases and the yield loci move upwards. Each yield locus terminates at point E in the direction of increasing normal stresses σ. Point E characterizes the steady-state flow, which is the flow with no change in stresses and bulk density. Two Mohr stress circles are shown. The major principal stresses of the two Mohr stress circles are characteristic of a yield locus. σ_1 is the major principal stress at steady-state flow, called the major consolidation stress, and σ_c is the unconfined yield strength of the sample. Each yield locus gives one pair of values of the unconfined yield strength σ_c and the major consolidation stress σ_1. Plotting σ_c versus σ_1 leads to the flow function (see later, Figs 2.1.5 and 2.1.7). The angle φ_e between the σ-axis and the tangent to the greatest Mohr circle – called the effective yield locus – is a measure of the inner friction at steady-state flow and is very important in the design of silos for flow.

Very often a theoretical experiment is used to show the relationship between σ_1 and σ_c (Fig. 2.1.3). A sample is poured into a cylinder with

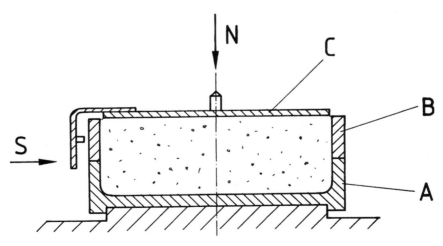

Fig. 2.1.1 Jenike shear cell (schematic); A: base, B: ring, C: lid.

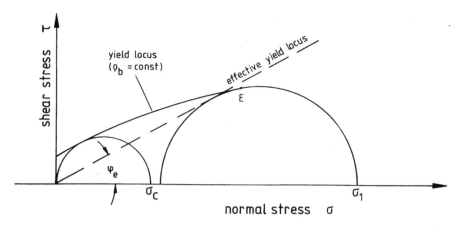

Fig. 2.1.2 Yield locus and effective yield locus.

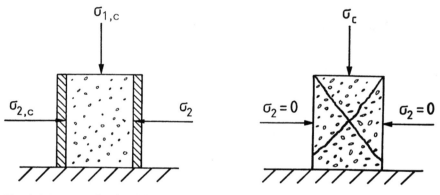

Fig. 2.1.3 Unconfined yield strength.

frictionless walls and is consolidated under a normal stress $\sigma_{1,c}$ leading to a bulk density ρ_b. After removal of the cylinder, the sample is loaded with an increasing normal stress up to the point of failure. The stress at failure is the unconfined yield strength σ_c. Contrary to results of shear tests steady-state flow cannot be reached during consolidation, i.e. the Mohr circle will be smaller. As a result density ρ_b and unconfined yield strength σ_c will also be smaller compared to the yield locus gained with shear tests (Schwedes and Schulze, 1990).

A tester in which both methods of consolidation – either steady-state flow (Figs 2.1.1 and 2.1.2) or uniaxial compression (Fig. 2.1.3) – can be realized is the true biaxial shear tester (Schwedes and Schulze, 1990; Harder, 1986; Nowak, 1994) (Fig. 2.1.4). The sample is constrained in the lateral *x*- and *y*-directions by four steel plates. Vertical deformations of the

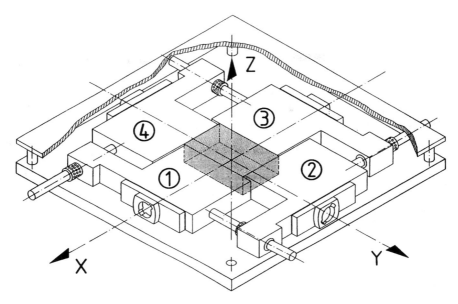

Fig. 2.1.4 True biaxial shear tester.

sample are restricted by rigid top and bottom plates. The sample can be loaded by the four lateral plates which are linked by guides so that the horizontal cross-section of the sample may take different rectangular shapes. In deforming the sample, the stresses σ_x and σ_y can be applied independently of each other in the x- and y-directions. To avoid friction between the plates and the sample the plates are covered with a thin rubber membrane. Silicone grease is applied between the steel plates and the rubber membrane. Since there are no shear stresses on the boundary surfaces of the sample σ_x and σ_y are principal stresses. With the true biaxial shear tester the measurement of both stresses and strains is possible.

With the true biaxial shear tester experiments were carried out to investigate the influence of the stress history and different consolidation procedures on the unconfined yield strength (Schwedes and Schulze, 1990; Harder, 1986; Nowak, 1994). Only results of the second point will be mentioned here. To obtain a yield locus corresponding to Fig. 2.1.2 the minor principal stress σ_2 in the y-direction (Fig. 2.1.4) is kept constant during a test. The major principal stress σ_1 in the x-direction is increased continuously up to the point of steady-state flow with constant values of σ_1, σ_2 and ρ_b. Afterwards the state of stress is reduced, with smaller constant σ_2-values and smaller maximum σ_1-values. By setting $\sigma_2 = 0$ the unconfined yield strength σ_c can be measured directly. Additionally comparative measurements with Jenike's tester were performed. In Fig. 2.1.5 the flow function, a plot of σ_c versus the major consolidating stress σ_1 at steady-state

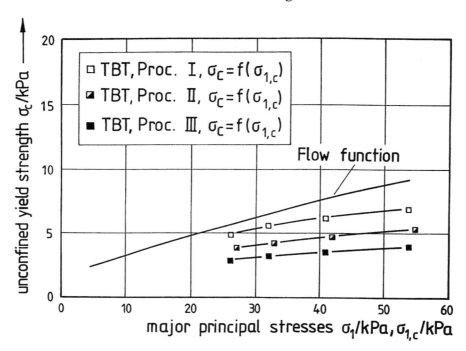

Fig. 2.1.5 Flow function of limestone. TBT = true biaxial test.

flow, is shown. Although two different kinds of shear testers were used, the measurements agree well (Schwedes and Schulze, 1990).

For investigation of the influence of different consolidating procedures – in analogy to the uniaxial test of Fig. 2.1.3 – samples were consolidated in the true biaxial shear tester from a low bulk density to a selected higher bulk density before the shear test started. The higher bulk density ρ_b could be obtained in different ways. Figure 2.1.6 demonstrates three different possibilities (I, II, III) to consolidate the sample to get the same sample volume and, hence, the same bulk density. In the case of procedure I the x-axis and in the case of procedure III the y-axis coincide with the direction of the major principal stress $\sigma_{1,c}$ at consolidation. In the case of procedure II in both directions the major principal stress $\sigma_{1,c}$ is acting. After consolidation the samples were sheared as described above. σ_2 in the y-direction was kept constant at $\sigma_2 = 0$ and σ_1 was increased up to the point of failure, leading to the unconfined yield strength σ_c. The results are plotted in Fig. 2.1.5 as σ_c versus $\sigma_{1,c}$, being the major principal stress at consolidation. The functions $\sigma_c = f(\sigma_{1,c})$ corresponding to procedures I, II and III are below the flow function $\sigma_c = f(\sigma_1)$. The distance between the function $\sigma_c = f(\sigma_{1,c})$ of procedure I and the flow function is quite small. Hence, the function $\sigma_c = f(\sigma_{1,c})$ of procedure I can be used as an estimation of the flow function. The

Flow property measurements

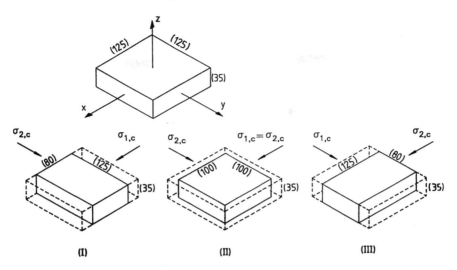

Fig. 2.1.6 Anisotropic consolidation.

functions of Fig. 2.1.5 are gained with a limestone sample ($x_{50} = 4.8\,\mu$m). The difference in the functions of Fig. 2.1.5 will be different for other bulk solids, i.e. a generalized estimate of the flow function by knowing only the function $\sigma_c = f(\sigma_{1,c})$ of procedure I is not possible.

Procedure I is identical to the procedure in Fig. 2.1.3 realized in uniaxial testers, e.g. the testers of Gerritsen (1986) and Maltby (Maltby and Enstad, 1993). The function $\sigma_c = f(\sigma_{1,c})$ of procedure II can be compared with experiments performed by Gerritsen after almost isotropic consolidation (triaxial test) (Gerritsen, 1982). Again a good qualitative agreement between Gerritsen's results and those with the true biaxial shear tester could be obtained (Schwedes and Schulze, 1990). More important with respect to the present section is the function $\sigma_c = f(\sigma_{1,c})$ of procedure III showing anisotropic behaviour of the measured limestone sample. A strong influence of the stress history on the strength of the sample exists, i.e. the strength is dependent on the direction of the applied stresses. There is one tester available in which procedure III of Fig. 2.1.6 is realized (Peschl, 1975). If this tester is used for bulk solids showing anisotropic behaviour it may be concluded that this tester leads to too small σ_c-values. It has to be mentioned that most bulk solids behave anisotropically.

The flow function as the dependence of the unconfined yield strength σ_c on the major consolidation stress σ_1 (at steady-state flow) can only be determined using testers where both stress states can be realized. Steady-state flow can be realized in Jenike's tester, in annular shear cells, in a torsional shear cell, in the true biaxial shear tester and in a very specialized triaxial cell (Schwedes and Schulze, 1990). The unconfined yield strength σ_c can be determined by running tests in Jenike's tester, in an annular shear cell

(Schulze, 1994), in uniaxial testers and in the true biaxial shear tester. Therefore only Jenike's tester, annular shear cells and the true biaxial shear tester can guarantee the measurement of flow functions $\sigma_c = f(\sigma_1)$ without further assumptions.

2.1.3 Application of measured flow properties

In the following it will be shown which flow properties have to be known for special applications and which testers are suitable for measuring these properties.

2.1.3.1 Design of silos for flow

The best known and the most applied method of designing silos for flow is that developed by Jenike (1964). He distinguishes two flow patterns, mass flow and funnel flow, the borderlines of which depend on the inclination θ of the hopper, the angle φ_e of the effective yield locus (Fig. 2.1.2) and the angle φ_w between the bulk solid and the hopper wall. For determining the angle φ_e steady-state flow has to be achieved in the tester. The wall friction angle φ_w can easily be tested with Jenike's tester, but also with other direct shear testers.

The most severe problems in the design of silos for flow are doming and piping. Jenike's procedure for avoiding doming starts from steady-state flow in the outlet area. After stopping the flow (aperture closed) and restarting it the flow criterion for doming can only be applied if the flow function is known. As stated before, the flow function can only be measured without further assumptions with the help of the Jenike tester, annular shear cells or the true biaxial shear tester. The latter is very complicated and cannot be proposed in its present form for application in the design of silos for flow.

Some bulk solids gain strength when stored under pressure without movement. Principally this time consolidation can be tested with all testers. Besides the fact that time consolidation can most easily be tested with Jenike's tester and a new version of an annular shear cell (Schulze, 1994) – easily with regard to time and equipment – only these testers yield time flow functions which have to be known for applying the doming and piping criteria.

Piping can occur directly after filling the silo or after a longer period of satisfactory flow, e.g. due to time consolidation. In the latter case the flow function and time flow functions have to be known to apply the flow–no-flow criteria. In the former case the pressures in the silo after filling have to be known, which are different from those during flow.

The anisotropic behaviour of bulk solids mentioned in connection with Fig. 2.1.5 (procedure III) is of no influence in the design of silos for flow. With help of Figs 2.1.5 and 2.1.6 it was explained that steady-state flow was achieved with σ_1 (at steady-state flow) acting in the x-direction. The unconfined yield strength was also measured with the major principal stress acting in the x-direction. During steady-state flow in a hopper the direction of the major principal stress is horizontal at the hopper axis. In a stable dome above the aperture the unconfined yield strength also acts horizontally in the hopper axis. Therefore the flow function reflects reality in the hopper area.

2.1.3.2 Design of silos for strength

To design silos for strength the stresses acting between the stored bulk solid and the silo walls have to be known. Since 1895 Janssen's equation has been used to calculate stresses in the bin section. His equation is still the basis for many national and international codes and recommendations (Martens, 1988). This equation contains besides geometrical terms and the acceleration due to gravity the bulk density ρ_b, the coefficient of wall friction $\mu = \tan\varphi_w$ and the horizontal stress ratio λ. For ρ_b the maximum possible density, a function of the largest σ_1-value in the silo, should be used. The coefficient of wall friction μ can be gained with the help of shear testers, if the tests are carried out at the appropriate stress level and if the results are correctly interpreted (Schwedes, 1985). It should be mentioned that the value of the angle used for the mass flow–funnel flow decision is generally not identical with the one needed in the design of silos for strength.

It is a lot more difficult to get reliable values for the parameter λ. In Janssen's equation and all following applications λ is defined as the ratio of the horizontal stress at the silo wall to the mean vertical stress. This means a locally acting stress is related to a stress that is the mean value of all stresses acting on a cross-section, i.e. two stresses acting on different areas are related. In research works and codes several different instructions for calculating λ are suggested. From the large numbers of different recommendations it can be seen that there is still uncertainty in calculating λ.

A step forward to a reliable determination of λ is the recommendation by codes (ISO CEN) to measure λ in a uniaxial compression test, using a modified oedometer. An oedometer is a standard tester in soil mechanics to measure the settlement behaviour of a soil under a vertical stress σ_v. Such a modified oedometer, called a lambdameter, was proposed by Kwade, Schulze and Schwedes (1994) (Fig. 2.1.7). The horizontal stress σ_h can be measured with the help of strain gauges, lined over the entire perimeter of the ring. For further details see Kwade, Schulze and Schwedes (1994). A large number of tests have been performed to investigate influences such as filling procedure, influences of side-wall friction, influence of friction at the lid and bottom, duration of the test, minimum stress level and others. Forty-one bulk solids having angles φ_e of the effective yield locus between 20° and 57° were tested in the lambdameter. The results are summarized in Fig. 2.1.8, where λ is plotted versus φ_e. For comparison the proposals by Koenen and Kézdi and the recommendation of the German code DIN 1055,

14 Bulk solids testing

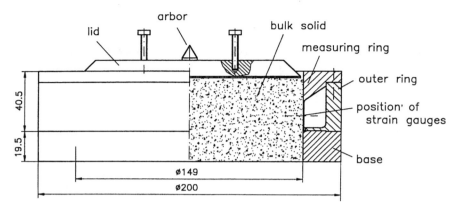

Fig. 2.1.7 Lambdameter.

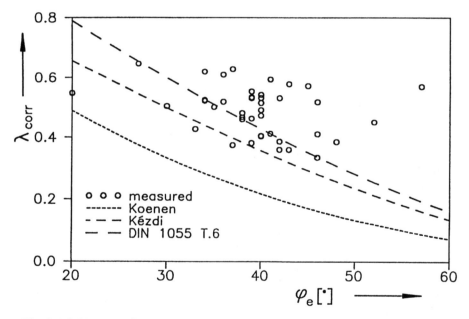

Fig. 2.1.8 Horizontal stress ratio λ.

part 6, are plotted in the graph. It can be concluded that none of the three is in line with the measured values and that especially with high values of φ_e great differences exist between the measured and the recommended λ-values.

The above problem of obtaining reliable λ-values for design results from the fact that no simple, theoretical model exists which combines known bulk solid properties like φ_e, φ_w or others with application in a satisfactory manner. As long as this relationship is not known, direct measurement in a specially designed tester like the lambdameter is the best solution.

2.1.3.3 Quality control, qualitative comparison

In section 2.1.3.1 it was shown that knowledge of the flow function, the time flow functions, the angle φ_e of the effective yield locus and the wall friction angle φ_w is necessary to design a silo properly. With estimates of the flow function only (Fig. 2.1.5) uncertainties remain and assumptions are necessary to obtain reliable flow. These assumptions are hard to check. Very often the testing of bulk solids is not done with respect to silo design. Other typical questions are:

- A special bulk solid has poor flow properties and these should be improved by adding small amounts of a flow aid. Which is the best kind and concentration of flow aid?
- A bulk solid having a low melting point has sufficient flow properties at room temperature. Up to which temperatures is satisfactory handling possible?
- The flow properties of a continuously produced bulk solid vary. Which deviations can be accepted?

To solve these problems it is sufficient to use estimates of the flow function, as long as the test procedure does not change from test to test. Testers which can be easily automated and give reproducible results are favourable. Annular shear cells, the torsional shear cell and uniaxial testers belong to this group. Other testers like the Johanson hang-up indicizer (Johanson, 1992; Bell et al., 1994) and the Jenike and Johanson quality control tester (Ploof and Carson, 1994) claim to be as good, but in these two testers and in others the states of stress are not homogeneous and therefore unknown. The results are dependent on wall friction and geometrical data (Schwedes, Schulze and Johanson, 1992). Thus no properties that are independent of the special tester used can be achieved. But for characterization of flow properties the main requirement is to obtain data not affected by the testing device. Therefore it is not advisable to use results from those tests as flow indices. Comparative tests with different bulk solids and different testers clearly show that the flow functions and their estimates differ (Bell et al., 1994; Ploof and Carson, 1994) and also that the ranking in flowability is not identical from tester to tester (Bell et al., 1994).

It is often mentioned as a disadvantage of the Jenike cell that it requires a high level of training and skill and much more time than other testers. This is only partly true. If a hopper is to be designed, then skill and time are needed to get the necessary information. If the need is only for quality control or product development, it is also possible to use the Jenike cell or annular shear cells with a simpler procedure. An estimate of a yield locus can be derived by running only one test (preshear and shear) and a repetition test, i.e. with four to six tests an estimate of the flow function can be determined being at least as good and reliable as results gained from the other testers. In particular, the use of an annular shear cell has advantages because sample preparation is significantly less expensive (Schulze, 1994).

With results of the testers mentioned, the flow function or estimates of the flow function can be derived. It is also possible to measure the effect of time, humidity, temperature and other influences on the flow function or the estimate of the flow function.

2.1.3.4 Calibration of constitutive models

Eibl and others have shown that the finite element method can be used with success to model pressures in silos (Häußler and Eibl, 1984). To apply this method a constitutive model has to be used. The models of Lade (1977) and Kolymbas (1991) are examples. Each constitutive model contains parameters which have to be identified from calibration tests. The most important demand for this calibration test is that the complete state of stress and the complete state of strain can be measured in the equivalent testers. From the testers mentioned, this requirement can only be fulfilled by the true biaxial shear tester and by very special triaxial cells (Schwedes and Schulze, 1990). Lade himself and also Eibl used results from triaxial tests for calibration. Feise (Feise, 1996) was able to show the advantages of using the true biaxial shear tester.

2.1.4 Conclusions

It can be concluded that no universal tester exists that is able to measure the required properties accurately within a reasonable time. Without naming the testers again the different applications will be mentioned with emphasis on the properties needed to solve the problems:

- Design of silo for flow: the flow function, the time flow functions, the angle φ_e of the effective yield locus and the angle of wall friction φ_w have to be known exactly.
- Quality control: an estimate of the flow function, which can be measured accurately and reproducibly, is sufficient.
- Calibration of constitutive models: the tester must allow homogeneous stressing and straining of the sample.
- Other applications: if no satisfactory and proven theoretical description exists between the measured bulk solid properties and the application, measuring the required parameter directly in an equivalent tester should be tried.

References

Bell, T.A., Ennis, B.J., Grygo, R.J., Scholten, W.J.F. and M.M. Schenkel, Practical evaluation of the Johanson hang-up indicizer, *Bulk Solids Handling* 14 (1994), 117

Feise, H., Modellierung des mechanischen Verhaltens von Schüttgütern, Ph.D. Dissertation, TU Braunschweig (1996)

Gerritsen, A.H., The mechanics of cohesive powders, Ph.D. Dissertation, Univ. Groningen (1982)

Gerritsen, A.H., *A Simple Method for Measuring Powder Flow Functions with a View to Hopper Design*, Preprints Partec Part III (Nuremberg) (1986), 257

Harder, J., Ermittlung der Fließeigenschaften kohäsiver Schüttgüter mit einer Zweiaxialbox, Ph.D. Dissertation, TU Braunschweig (1986)

Häußler, U. and J. Eibl, Numerical investigations on discharging silos, *J. Engng. Mechanics* 110 (1984), 957

ISO Working Group ISO/TC 98/SC3/WG5: *Eurocode for Actions on Structures.* Chapter 11: Loads in Silos and Tanks, Draft June 1990

Jenike, A.W., *Storage and Flow of Solids*, Bull. No. 123, Engng. Exp. Station, Univ. Utah (1964)

Johanson, J.R., The Johanson indicizer system vs. the Jenike shear tester, *Bulk Solids Handling* 12 (1992), 237

Kolymbas, D., An outline of hypoplasticity, *Archive of Applied Mechanics* 61 (1991), 143

Kwade, A., Schulze, D. and J. Schwedes, Determination of the stress ratio in uniaxial compression tests, *Beton- und Stahlbetonbau* 89 (1994), 58 and *Powder Handling and Processing* 6 (1994), 61

Lade, P.V., Elasto-plastic stress–strain theory for cohesionless soil with curved yield surfaces, *Int. J. Solids and Structure* 13 (1977), 1019

Maltby, L.P. and G.G. Enstad, Uniaxial tester, for quality control and flow property testing of powders, *Bulk Solids Handling* 13 (1993), 135

Martens, P., *Silohandbuch*, Verlag Ernst & Sohn, Berlin (1988)

Nowak, M., Spannungs-/Dehnungsverhalten von Kalkstein in der Zweiaxialbox, Ph.D. Dissertation, TU Braunschweig (1994)

Peschl, I.A.S.Z., Bulk Handling Seminar, Univ. Pittsburgh, Dec. 1975

Ploof, D.A. and J.W. Carson, Quality control tester to measure relative flowability of powders, *Bulk Solids Handling* 14 (1994), 127

Schulze, D., Development and application of a novel ring shear tester, *Aufbereitungstechnik* 35 (1994), 524

Schwedes, J., Influence of wall friction on silo design in process and structural engineering, *Ger. Chem. Eng.* 8 (1985), 131

Schwedes, J. and D. Schulze, Measurement of flow properties of bulk solids, *Powder Technol.* 61 (1990), 59

Schwedes, J., Schulze, D. and J.R. Johanson, Letters to the Editor in response to Johanson (1992) *Bulk Solids Handling* 12 (1992), 454

2.2 Measurement of the flowability of bulk solids

D. Schulze

Nomenclature

A	(m²)	area
F	(N)	force
ff_c		flowability; quotient of major consolidation stress σ_1 and unconfined yield strength σ_c
m	(kg)	mass
M	(N m)	torque
N	(N)	normal force
z	(m)	coordinate
α	(°)	angle
ρ_b	(kg/m³)	bulk density
σ	(Pa)	normal stress
σ_c	(Pa)	unconfined yield strength
σ_1	(Pa)	major principal stress, consolidation stress
τ	(Pa)	shear stress

Indices

if	incipient flow
sf	preshear, steady-state flow
M	measured value
v	vertical
V	consolidation, stiffening

2.2.1 Introduction

Knowledge of the flow properties of bulk solids is required for the design of silos and other bulk handling equipment in order to avoid flow problems (such as arching in hoppers and segregation, etc.). Further, a lot of information is required for the flowability evaluation of a product (such as comparative measurements, the need for flow-promoting devices or flow additives), production control and quality assurance.

For silo design, the Jenike shear cell equipment has become the standard measuring technique for bulk solids (Jenike, 1964; Schwedes, 1968, 1976; Martens, 1988, Molerus, 1985). Because the Jenike shear cell equipment is difficult to manipulate, other types of measuring equipment and procedures are considered for the evaluation of flowability, which may be based on different measuring principles and encompass different physical values.

2.2.2 Flowability

2.2.2.1 Principles and physical background

The meaning of 'good flowability' in general is defined as a gravity flow of granular bulk solids that does not require any assistance. Any product that is classified as of 'poor flowability' exhibits discharge problems or consolidates during storage or handling. A quantitative statement about flowability is only possible if one uses an objective characteristic value which encompasses those physical properties responsible for flow behaviour.

Figure 2.2.1 shows a hollow, split cylinder filled with fine grained bulk solid (cross-section shown inside wall of the cylinder to be considered frictionless). The bulk solids filling is compressed through the consolidation stress σ_1 in a vertical direction and consolidated. Subsequently, after removing the consolidation stress σ_1, the cylinder is taken away. If the consolidated cylindrical bulk solids specimen is now subjected to an increasing vertical compressive stress, then at a certain stress level, referred to as the

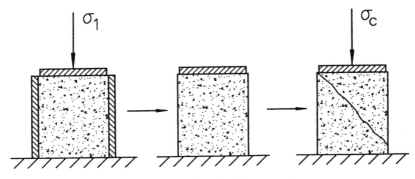

Fig. 2.2.1 Simplified model for unconfined yield strength.

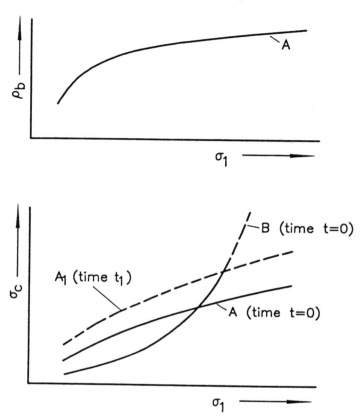

Fig. 2.2.2 Bulk density and unconfined yield strength as a function of consolidation stress.

unconfined yield strength (compressive strength) σ_c, the cylindrical specimen will collapse or flow. It will also exhibit a shear plane, specific for that bulk solid, in order to cause this cylindrical specimen to flow. The smaller this compressive strength (σ_c), the better the flowability.

The bulk solid strength is dependent on the level of consolidation obtained before: the larger the consolidation stress σ_1, the larger the bulk density ρ_b and the unconfined yield strength σ_c (compressive strength). The typical increase of the bulk density ρ_b and unconfined yield strength σ_c for product A is shown in Fig. 2.2.2. Very seldom can one observe a progressive increasing strength as indicated by curve B.

Many bulk solids have a tendency to increase their strength when they are subjected to a stationary stress in silo storage. This time-consolidated strength can also be measured using the method of Fig. 2.2.1, whereby the consolidation stress σ_1 is applied over a time period of t_1 and after that the strength σ_c is determined. In Fig. 2.2.2, this strength curve A_1 is shown as a

Measurement of the flowability of bulk solids

dotted line for product A, consolidated for a time t_1. It is not possible to establish such a time-consolidated strength without these measurements.

2.2.2.2 Specific value for characterizing the flowability

For the characteristic value of flowability the relationship of ff_c as being the quotient of σ_1 (consolidation stress) and σ_c (unconfined yield strength) will be used:

$$ff_c = \sigma_1/\sigma_c \qquad (2.2.1)$$

The larger ff_c, the smaller the bulk solids strength in relation to the consolidation stress, and therefore the more flowable the bulk solid. Jenike (1964) proposed the following classification:

$ff_c < 2$ very cohesive and non-flowing
$2 < ff_c < 4$ cohesive
$4 < ff_c < 10$ easy flowing
$10 < ff_c$ free flowing

As an extension to Jenike's listing, the indication for 'non-flowing' as $ff_c < 1$ and 'very cohesive' as $1 < ff_c < 2$ is introduced. In Fig. 2.2.3, curves A and B from Fig. 2.2.2 and the ranges of flowability are shown, as defined above. The relationship of ff_c and the resulting evaluation of flowability changes with the consolidation stress σ_1 (in most cases ff_c increases with σ_1 as shown for curve A). Consequently, the flowability of different bulk solids can only be compared using ff_c values if all measurements are taken at similar consolidation stresses. If for the characterization of a certain product

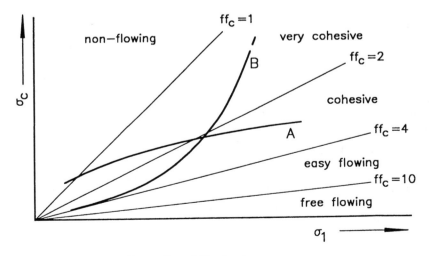

Fig. 2.2.3 Ranges of different flowability levels.

an ff_c value is given, the value of the consolidation stress σ_1 also has to be mentioned. Also the time-consolidated strength of different bulk solids must be compared with identical consolidation stresses and storage time. As shown in Fig. 2.2.3, the curves for bulk solid A and B indicate which bulk solid flows are more dependent on the consolidation stresses σ_1. Therefore, it is evident that for the solution of flow problems the consolidation stress and storage time should be measured as they occur (for instance, stresses and storage time occurring in a product stored in bags on pallets).

2.2.2.3 Measurement of flow properties with shear equipment

2.2.2.3.1 The Jenike shear tester

The performance of the uniaxial compression test (Fig. 2.2.1) for fine-grained solids is not without problems, as it is complicated to reduce the friction on the cylindrical walls and, due to the kind of consolidation, the unconfined yield strength values measured are too small (to be further explained in section 2.2.3.1) (Schwedes and Schulze, 1990; Harder, 1985; Gerritsen, 1982). Therefore, when a quantitative statement is required (e.g. silo design), shear cell equipment will be used. Figure 2.2.4 shows typical shear cell equipment developed by Jenike (Jenike, 1964; Schwedes, 1968, 1971, 1976; Molerus, 1985; Martens, 1988; The Inst. of Chem. Engnrs, 1989).

The bulk solid sample is to be poured into the shear cell for measurement. The shear cell consists of a bottom enclosed lower half, a ring-shaped upper half of equal diameter (upper ring) and a lid with a push bracket. The lid is loaded with a concentric normal force N. The bulk solid sample is subjected to a shear force, when the upper half of the shear cell moves with regard to the stationary bottom half. The shear force S is transmitted

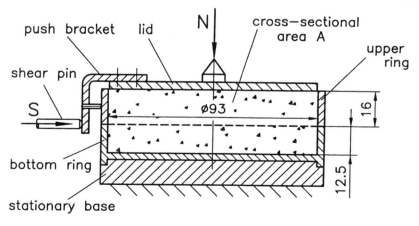

Fig. 2.2.4 Jenike shear cell (Jenike, 1964).

through the push bracket to the shear pin. The shear pin is connected to a force transducer so that the shear force can be measured and plotted using an amplifier and a chart recorder. From the normal load N and the shear force S one can calculate the normal stress σ and the shear stress τ acting in the assumed shear plane located between upper ring and bottom (dotted line, Fig. 2.2.4).

For testing, the bulk solid sample is first poured into the shear cell and preconsolidated manually. For the preconsolidation some additional equipment is used which is not shown in Fig. 2.2.4. The manual preconsolidation requires training and experience, because the sample is sensitive to the user's procedure.

Measurement following manual preconsolidation has to be carried out analogously to the uniaxial compression test in two steps: the sample is first consolidated ('preshear' or 'steady-state shear') and subsequently a point on the yield locus is measured ('shear' or 'shear to failure') (Jenike, 1964; The Inst. of Chem. Engnrs, 1989). For preshear, the bulk solid sample is placed under a predetermined normal stress σ_{sf}, obtained by a corresponding normal load N on the lid, and subsequently sheared whereby shear force S and shear stress τ, respectively, increase with time (Fig. 2.2.5). Together with the shear stress τ, the bulk density ρ_b and the strength of the sample also increase, until after some time a constant bulk density ρ_b and a constant shear stress (τ_{sf}) are reached. This condition can be called 'stationary flow'. The bulk density reached at the stationary flow as well as the steady-state shear stress τ_{sf} are characteristic of the applied normal stress σ_{sf}.

During the preshear period required to reach the 'stationary flow', the sample is conditioned to a specific state of consolidation. This condition can be followed on the chart recorder until the desired level is reached (recognized by a constant shear stress). After the 'steady-state shear' preparation, the sample load is brought back to zero (S = 0). The values of normal and shear stress at the 'stationary flow' point (σ_{sf}, τ_{sf}) will establish in the σ,τ-diagram the steady-state consolidation point (Fig. 2.2.5). After preshear, the

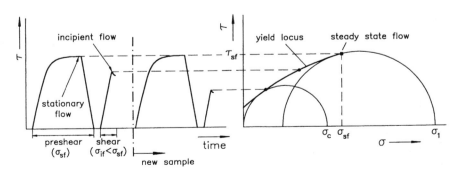

Fig. 2.2.5 Shear stress curves and yield locus.

test sample is now subjected to a smaller normal stress $\sigma_{if} < \sigma_{sf}$ and sheared to failure. At a specific shear stress level, the sample begins to yield, which corresponds to an expanding volume (lowering of bulk density) and a lowering of the shear stress (Fig. 2.2.5). The maximum value of the shear stress identifies the point where the yielding begins. The corresponding pair of σ- and τ-values (σ_{if}, τ_{if}) is a point of the flow boundary, the so-called yield locus. When more samples are presheared at identical normal stress σ_{sf}, but sheared to failure at different levels of normal stress $\sigma_{if} < \sigma_{sf}$, then the yield locus can be established.

From a yield locus valid for a specific bulk density ρ_b, one can develop the flow properties of the bulk solid. Mohr stress circles (Jenike, 1964; Schwedes, 1968; Molerus, 1985) are established in the σ,τ-diagram (Fig. 2.2.5). The larger half-circle in Fig. 2.2.5 runs through the steady-state consolidation point and is tangential to the yield locus. This circle represents the stresses in the sample specimen at the end of the consolidation procedure (stationary flow). As the determining value of the consolidation stress, the major principal stress σ_1 of the Mohr circle is used (the right intersection of the stress circle with the σ-axis). The unconfined yield strength σ_c is the major principal stress of a Mohr circle at a tangent to the yield locus and going through zero.

With σ_1 and σ_c one can obtain a pair of values for consolidation stress and unconfined yield strength that is equivalent to the uniaxial compression test in Fig. 2.2.1. For different values of the normal stress at preshear σ_{sf}, different yield loci can be developed with different values for σ_1 and σ_c. Thereby a relationship (flow function) can be established between σ_1 and σ_c, as shown in Fig. 2.2.2. For the time-consolidated strength, the sample specimen will, after the steady-state consolidation (preshear), be kept for a specific time period under a stress equal to σ_1. This sample will then subsequently be sheared to failure and a time yield locus developed. For this sample, a time-consolidated strength is displayed by showing larger shear stresses and subsequently larger σ_c-values.

Since the Jenike shear equipment can be considered the standard measuring device for the bulk solids technique, the flow properties, which one can obtain by proper operation and procedure, are to be designated as the 'correct' flow properties. The 'correctness' of test results from the Jenike shear equipment have also been corroborated by comparative measurements with more expensive shear testing equipment (Schwedes, 1971; Gerritsen, 1982; Haaker and Rademacher, 1983; Harder, 1985; Arthur, Dunstan and Enstad, 1985; Schwedes and Schulze, 1990; Haaker and Wiersma-van Schendel, 1993). New measuring techniques are also frequently compared in the literature with the results of the Jenike shear tester (e.g. Schwedes and Schulze, 1990; Maltby and Enstad, 1993), which enhances the position of the Jenike shear tester as a standard. Further, for the Jenike shear tester an internationally accepted standard measuring technique (The Inst. of Chem. Engnrs, 1989) as well as a certified reference

Measurement of the flowability of bulk solids

material for shear test measurements (Akers, 1990; BCR, 1994) have been established.

2.2.2.3.2 The ring shear tester

Although the Jenike shear tester is the standard measuring device for silo design, it can hardly be used for all types of bulk solids. This is due to the limited shear displacement which is at most twice the thickness of the upper ring. Some bulk solids (very elastic materials, some very moist materials) need a greater shear displacement to reach steady-state flow.

In principle, the translational tester can be used for quality control and comparative measurements (determination of ff_c), but it has the disadvantage that the bulk solid sample has to be preconsolidated manually where the degree of preconsolidation has to be adjusted by the operator. Therefore, operation of the translational shear tester is time-consuming and requires very well-trained personnel.

An alternative to the Jenike shear tester is the ring shear tester (annular shear tester). Ring shear testers have been used in bulk solids technology for more than 25 years (e.g. Carr and Walker, 1968; Münz, 1976; Gebhard, 1982; Höhne, 1985). In the following an improved ring shear tester called the RST-01.01 with an increased range of application is described (Schulze, 1994a, b).

The main part of the ring shear tester – the shear cell – is shown in Fig. 2.2.6. The (annular) ring shear cell contains the bulk solid sample. An

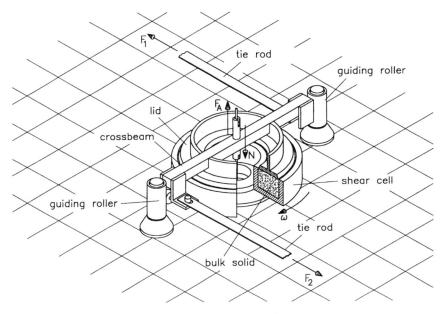

Fig. 2.2.6 Ring shear tester RST-01.01 (in principle).

annular lid attached to a crossbeam lies on top of the sample. The bottom of the shear cell and the lower side of the lid are provided with bars (height 4 mm) to avoid slipping of the bulk solid directly at the bottom or lid.

The shear cell is driven in the direction of the arrow ω. The lid is prevented from rotating by two tie rods which are connected to the crossbeam. Due to the relative displacement of the shear cell to the lid the bulk solid is sheared. The forces F_1 and F_2 acting in the tie rods are measured. From F_1 and F_2 the shear stress τ acting in the bulk solid is calculated (Carr and Walker, 1968; Münz, 1976; Gebhard, 1982). The tie rods fix the position of the lid in the direction of forces F_1 and F_2. To prevent the lid from moving horizontally in the direction perpendicular to the direction of the tie rods, two guiding rollers are installed. In combination with the rollers at the ends of the crossbeam the guiding rollers realize an almost frictionless guide for the lid. In contrast to ring shear testers known from the literature (e.g. Carr and Walker, 1968; Münz, 1976; Gebhard, 1982; Höhne, 1985) no additional guide bearing for the lid is necessary.

The normal force N is exerted on the sample by a weight hanger which is connected to the crossbeam in the axis of the shear cell. Furthermore, the crossbeam is connected to the counterweight system which exerts the upward directed force F_A to the crossbeam. F_A is equal to the weights of lid, crossbeam and hanger. Due to the counterweight system the normal stress σ acting on the surface of the bulk solid sample is only a function of the weights carried by the hanger (force N).

The mass of the counterweight is small in comparison to ring shear testers known from literature (e.g. Münz, 1976; Carr and Walker, 1968; Höhne, 1985). Thus frictional and inertia forces are reduced. In this way, more accurate measurements especially at low normal stresses are possible. Due to the guide mechanism of the lid, the shear cell together with the bulk solid sample and the lid can be removed from, and transferred back to, the tester without disturbing the sample (Schulze, 1994a, b). Therefore, time consolidation tests can be performed as with the Jenike shear tester (Jenike, 1964).

Due to the principle of construction, measurements at small consolidation stresses σ_1 down to approximately 400 Pa are possible. Compared with this, the lower limit of consolidation stresses for a standard Jenike tester is approx. 3–4 kPa.

The measurement procedure of the ring shear tester is similar to that used for the Jenike shear tester (Fig. 2.2.5) (Jenike, 1964; The Inst. of Chem. Engnrs, 1989). The bulk solid sample is sheared in two steps: the first is for the defined consolidation of the sample ('preshear'). The second is the measurement of a point of incipient flow of the consolidated sample ('shear'). When using a Jenike shear tester, for each measurement (preshear/shear) a new sample of bulk solid has to be prepared (Fig. 2.2.5). With the ring shear tester it is possible to measure a complete yield locus with only one sample of bulk solid whereby the same sample is presheared and sheared alternately.

Compared to the Jenike shear tester, the ring shear tester is easier to operate: there is no need for a manual preconsolidation of the sample which is essential for the Jenike shear tester due to its limited shear displacement (Jenike, 1964; The Inst. of Chem. Engnrs, 1989). Therefore, the ring shear tester is less sensitive to the operators' skill and leads to more objective results even with untrained personnel. Additionally, the time needed for the measurements decreases greatly. Due to the almost unlimited shear deformation of the ring shear tester, very elastic products and fine-grained, moist products like sewage sludge can also be tested.

To judge the performance of the new ring shear tester comparison measurements with a limestone powder have been carried out at consolidation stresses from approx. 400 Pa to 15 kPa (Schulze, 1994a, b). It was found that both testers yield similar results.

As with the Jenike shear tester, with the ring shear tester well-defined flow properties like the unconfined yield strength in dependence on the consolidation stress can also be obtained. Since the ring shear tester is easy to operate (no manual preconsolidation of the sample), it can be handled by relatively untrained personnel. Evaluation of the flow properties (e.g. flowability) from the measured data can be automated (computer program or diagrams). Furthermore, automation of the testing procedure is possible. Therefore, the ring shear tester is a significant alternative to so-called simple flowability testers. It combines the highlights of the Jenike shear tester (real flow properties are measured) with the advantages of flowability testers (easy to operate).

2.2.2.3.3 Simplified measurement procedure

If there is not enough time to measure a complete yield locus and if only a qualitative result is needed, with a shear tester a simplified measurement procedure can be used. It is possible to guess the yield locus on the basis of only one point of incipient flow and the point of stationary flow (Fig. 2.2.7(a)) by assuming the yield locus to be a straight line through both points (incipient flow and stationary flow). A less rough guess is possible using two points of incipient flow (Fig. 2.2.7(b)) where the yield locus is assumed to be a straight line through both points of incipient flow.

Comparative measurements (Bell *et al.*, 1995) have shown that with the one-point method acceptable results can be obtained which are better than those of a variety of simple flowability testers.

2.2.3 Influences on the measurements

2.2.3.1 Consolidation procedure

With preshear (consolidation) in the shear tester, the steady-state flow condition can be reached. The associated stress state is depicted by the largest stress (Mohr) circle in Fig. 2.2.5 and the stress circle SF in Fig. 2.2.8. With uniaxial compression (Fig. 2.2.1) and with identical major principal

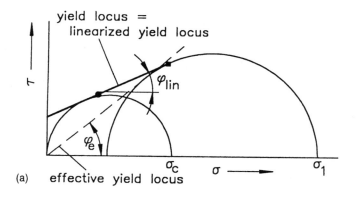

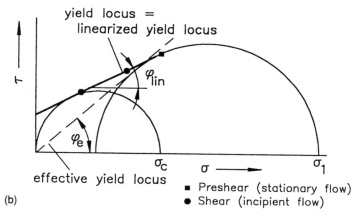

Fig. 2.2.7 1-point (a) and 2-point (b) yield locus.

stress σ_1 (consolidation stress), a smaller stress circle UC (with smaller shear stresses τ) is obtained (Harder, 1985; Lohnes and Bokhoven, 1985; Zachary and Lohnes, 1988; Schwedes and Schulze, 1990; Kwade, Schulze and Schwedes, 1994a, b). Also the bulk density ρ_b and the unconfined yield strength σ_c are smaller under uniaxial compression in comparison with the consolidation at steady-state shear under the same consolidation stress σ_1 (Koerner, 1977; Gerritsen, 1982; Haaker and Rademacher, 1983; Harder, 1985; Oshima and Hirota, 1985; Schwedes and Schulze, 1990; Nowak and Schwedes, 1993). Therefore it is apparent that the consolidation procedure influences the measurement results and that for similar values of the consolidation stress σ_1 but different consolidation procedures the measurement results are not the same.

An advantage of consolidation through shearing to reach the steady-state shear level versus uniaxial compression is the expected lesser spread of

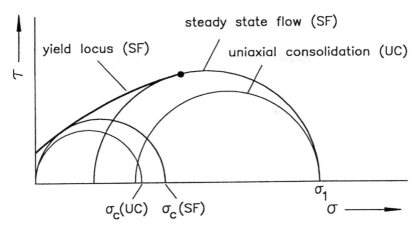

Fig. 2.2.8 Stress circles for steady-state flow (SF) and uniaxial compression (UC).

measurement values. Since the test specimen undergoes fairly long shear strain during preshear until the measured shear stress is constant, there is an indirect control of the actual degree of consolidation. Non-homogeneous sections (for instance: small cavities) in the test specimen, that could be formed during the filling cycle, will be eliminated through the deformation of the test specimen at preshear.

2.2.3.2 Anisotropy

A further important parameter is the direction of the major principal stress σ_1 during consolidation and during measurement of the bulk solids strength. In the uniaxial compression test of Fig. 2.2.1, the strength is measured in the same direction as the consolidation stress. For a shear cell as shown in Fig. 2.2.9 (Peschl, 1975; Peschl and Colijn, 1977), it is different, as the test specimen is compressed in a vertical direction (σ_1). The unconfined yield strength is then measured horizontally after the loaded top lid is removed. Measurements made according to Fig. 2.2.9 definitely result in smaller values for unconfined yield strength σ_c than the uniaxial test from Fig. 2.2.1. The reason for this is that bulk solids often behave anisotropically (Molerus, 1975, 1985; Harder, 1985; Gerritsen, 1985; Hirota and Oshima, 1987; Schwedes and Schulze, 1990; Saraber, Enstad and Haaker, 1991). The measured strength is smaller when the deviation between the directions of consolidation and the measurement of strength is larger.

2.2.3.3 Stresses in the working plane, stress distribution

For a quantitative statement it is necessary that the stresses in the working plane (shear plane, plane of failure) are known. The shear tester according

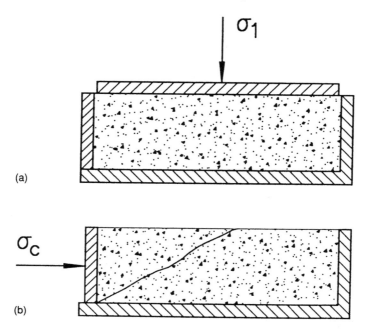

Fig. 2.2.9 Monoaxial shear tester (Peschl, 1975; Peschl and Colijn, 1977).

to Jenike, discussed in section 2.2.2.3, has the working plane located at the separation between the upper and bottom rings (Fig. 2.2.4). With a slight rise of the upper ring, any contact between these rings is avoided. Therefore, any measured shear force is not affected by possible friction forces between the rings. This also applies to the normal force (The Inst. of Chem. Engnrs, 1989). With this procedure, the average normal stress and average shear stress in the working plane are clearly known.

Further, the stresses anywhere in the working plane should be equal (homogeneous stress distribution). If this were not the case, then the bulk solid at the consolidation stage (preshear) would be consolidated differently at various locations and one would subsequently measure (at shear) the average strength of the variable range of consolidation among the bulk solids sample.

The problem with measuring equipment in not knowing the stresses exactly becomes evident in the recently proposed Johanson Hang-up Indicizer® (Johanson, 1992, 1993; Bell et al., 1994). The principle is shown in Fig. 2.2.10. A cylindrical test specimen of the bulk solid is compressed in the axial direction via a piston consisting of two concentric areas. Subsequently, the lower piston is removed and the inner part of the upper piston pushes on the test specimen, until failure occurs. From failure force a strength σ_c can be computed.

Because of the cylinder wall friction, the vertical stress σ_v (= consolidation stress σ_1) decreases downwards (Fig. 2.2.10), depending on the bulk

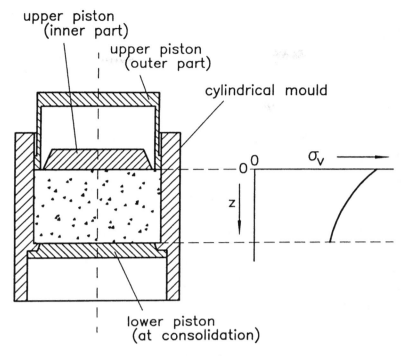

Fig. 2.2.10 Johanson Hang-up Indicizer® with vertical stress curve during consolidation.

solid properties (ratio of horizontal to vertical stress, wall friction angle). Neither the stress distribution nor the average stress values in the specimen are specifically known. During the measurement of the bulk solid's strength, the vertical stress decreases downwards towards zero (free surface), and the specimen is subjected along its height to a variable stress. Consequently, the bulk solid's strength, as measured with the Johanson Hang-up Indicizer®, is an 'average value', which results from various consolidation and stress levels that are not clearly defined. The measured 'average value' depends on the material properties, such as wall friction, and also on the height/diameter ratio of the test equipment (Schwedes and Schulze, 1992). The latter has been shown by experiments (van der Kraan and Scarlett, 1995). According to comparative measurements (Bell *et al.*, 1994, 1995), the test results for the bulk solid's strength are likely to be lower in comparison with the Jenike shear tester.

2.2.3.4 Requirements for test equipment to determine the flowability

To obtain a quantitative statement regarding the flowability of a bulk solid, as described in section 2.2.2.2, a defined measurement of the strength is required following the consolidation of the test specimen defined above. Any comparison of the measurement results is not possible without considering the test apparatus. If one does not want a quantitative statement, then all tests are in principle possible, whereby a test specimen is somehow consolidated and subsequently somehow the strength determined. As indicated in previous sections, the effects of wall friction, anisotropy, etc., may reduce the accuracy.

A test apparatus, which will provide quantitative information as described in section 2.2.2.2 for flowability, should conform to the following criteria:

1 Consolidation procedure with corresponding measurement of strength.
2 Consolidation of the bulk solid test specimen until the steady-state shear has been reached (preshear).
3 Equal direction of load application (major principal stresses) during consolidation and measurement of strength.
4 Reproducible loading application of the test specimen for consolidation (4a) and for measuring the strength (4b).
5 Known average stresses in the work plane with possibly the most uniform stress distribution for consolidation (5a) and for measuring the strength (5b).
6 Possibility for varying the consolidation stresses.
7 Possibility for measuring the increase of strength with time (time consolidation).

For comparative measurements concerning flowability according to section 2.2.2.2, criteria 1 and 4a/b and also 7 are important. However, for assurance of greater accuracy the other criteria should also be taken into account. In case many time-consolidated measurements are needed, it would be recommended to use one measuring device by which more test samples can be placed under load, apart from the basic shear tester (as with Jenike consolidation bench) (Jenike, 1964; The Inst. of Chem. Engnrs, 1989).

2.2.4 Review of known measuring techniques

In the following, some measuring techniques and equipment for the evaluation of the flowability of bulk solids are presented, which are simple, applicable and used in practice. Apparatus that will only be used in the framework of research (Schwedes, 1971; Arthur, Dunstan and Enstad, 1985; Gerritsen, 1982; Harder, 1984; Haaker and Wiersma-van Schendel, 1993; Nowak and Schwedes, 1993; Maltby, 1993; Nowak, 1994) is not included (for an overview see Schwedes, 1979; Schwedes and Schulze, 1990). The measuring techniques will be discussed in sequence of their application for the determination of the flowability as defined in section

Measurement of the flowability of bulk solids

2.2.2.2 and according to the criteria discussed in section 2.2.3.4. In order to be complete, techniques will also be included that do not cover a measurement of flowability according to section 2.2.2.2, but will assist in evaluating flow properties established by other means.

It must be accepted that any schematic listing of the many measurement techniques will not be precise in all aspects. An apparently poor evaluation does not necessarily exclude the application of the equipment for special purposes. When in doubt, before the procurement of any new equipment, one must review what must be measured and whether that piece of equipment can produce the required information, such as stress levels, condition of the bulk solids, storage time, etc. It is recommended to experiment in this respect with different types of equipment.

It may be helpful to make a choice from the selection of measuring techniques in Table 2.2.1. The explanation of the measuring technique is presented in a simplified schematic form for the most important measurement value. The index 'V' indicates a consolidation of the bulk solids for the measurement, the index 'M' indicates the measured value (such as m for mass, F for force, M for moment, α for angle and ρ_b for bulk density). N indicates a normal force which is constantly applied on the specimen of bulk solids during the test. After a short description of the measuring principles and some general comments, there follows a columnar listing according to compliance with the criteria 1 to 7 from section 2.2.3.4. If any criterion is not applicable, then a '–' sign is noted in the column.

The evaluation of the correctness of a measuring technique (comments in Table 2.2.1) establishes, in comparison with the Jenike shear tester, that the criteria (section 2.2.3.4) of a measurement technique are completely fulfilled and that these methods can be seen (section 2.2.2.3) as the 'correct' method. Use of the term 'quantitative statement' in Table 2.2.1 means that these measurements have the same values for strength as obtained from the Jenike shear tester. 'Limited quantitative statement' means that the measured values differ somewhat from the Jenike shear tester, while one of the criteria 1 to 7 from section 2.2.3.4 is not or not completely met. 'Qualitative statement' means that at least two of the criteria are not met, so that the results deviate more from the Jenike shear tester and therefore cannot be used for quantitative design such as silo design.

Concerning the fulfilment of the criteria listed in section 2.2.3.4, Table 2.2.1 indicates that the Jenike shear tester, the ring shear tester and the torsional shear tester are the most favourable. Since the operation of the Jenike shear tester requires quite a lot of training and experience, it would be reasonable to consider for comparative measurement the ring shear tester, whereby the torsional shear tester may show a larger deviation from the 'correct' measurements taken with the Jenike shear tester (Bell et al., 1994; Münz, 1976). The ring shear tester is more likely, if properly designed and applied, to match the 'correct' results of the Jenike shear tester (Arnold and Reed, 1987; Schulze, 1994a, b, 1995).

Table 2.2.1 Measuring techniques and equipment (part 1 of 16)

Measuring technique	Funnel
Short description	Bulk solids are fed through a funnel with varying outlet diameters. The measurement of the flowability is the minimum size of the outlet at which flow still occurs Alternative: measurement of the time required to discharge the solids for a given outlet. The shorter the time, the better the flowability
General comments	Simple comparison test without a quantitative statement concerning flowability and time consolidation. The filling method may affect the measurement (influence of the operator)

Criterion	1	2	3	4a/4b	5a/5b	6	7
Fulfilment	No	–	–	–	–	–	No

Table 2.2.1 Measuring techniques and equipment (part 2 of 16)

Measuring technique	Angle of repose 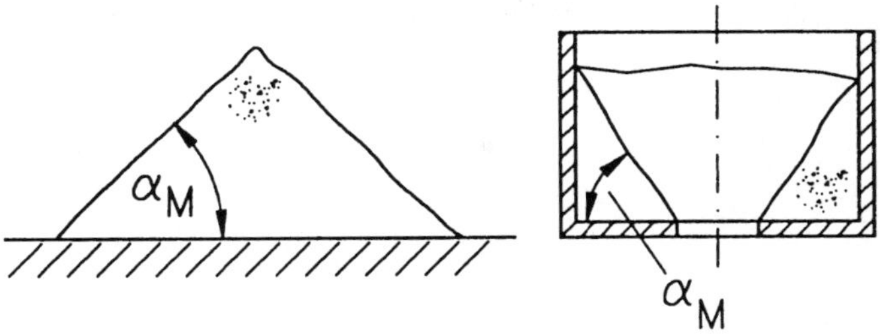
Short description	The angle of repose α_M of the loose bulk solids is measured, either of a cone or windrow. Other possibility: the slope angle α_M of the material remaining in a container with flat bottom and central outlet after discharge
General comments	The slope angle results from the material properties at very low compaction, which occurs at the surface of the cone. There is no statement possible about the behaviour of the materials under greater stresses (as in a silo) or about the time consolidation. The slope angle depends on the geometry of the heap: the slope angle of a cone is smaller than that of a windrow, and that of a windrow is smaller than that of the material remaining in a flat-bottomed container after discharge as shown in the figure above

Criterion	1	2	3	4a/4b	5a/5b	6	7
Fulfilment	No	–	–	–	–	–	No

Table 2.2.1 Measuring techniques and equipment (part 3 of 16)

Measuring technique	Imse test (Imse, 1972)
Short description	The bulk solids are put into a funnel located on top of a sieve: the funnel is then slowly raised. At the same time, the sieve is vibrated with the aid of a vibratory table. A measure of flowability is the mass m_M which is left on the sieve (Imse, 1972)
General comments	Simple comparison test (initially for cement) without a quantitative statement concerning flowability and time consolidation. Similar to the above funnel test, the results are dependent on the experimenter (process of filling) and on the degree of aeration There is no statement possible for the material under greater stresses as they occur, for example, in a silo

Criterion	1	2	3	4a/4b	5a/5b	6	7
Fulfilment	No	–	–	–	–	–	No

Measurement of the flowability of bulk solids 37

Table 2.2.1 Measuring techniques and equipment (part 4 of 16)

Measuring technique	Powder tester (Mayerhauser, 1989, Hosokawa, 1990) 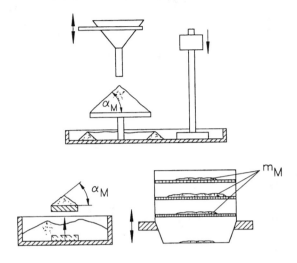
Short description	Combination of different tests; in order to determine the flowability the following measurements are made: 1. Upper part of illustration: the slope angle α_M of the material is measured as it falls from a vibrating funnel on to a round platen, and the slope angle – called the fall angle – after the platen has been hit five times by a falling weight 2. Spatula angle (bottom left picture): the slope angle α_M of the material on a spatula is measured, after the spatula has been lifted up with material outside the container 3. Screening of bulk solids with a defined oscillation over a predetermined time span on three sieves with different openings; and then determining the mass m_M of bulk solid left on each screen (bottom right picture) 4. Determination of loose and compacted bulk density; alternative (by larger solids): computation of a characteristic value describing the width of the particle size distribution Each one of the above tests provides a number between 0 and 25. The sum of the four tests becomes the flowability index
General comments	Qualitative comparison test for fine-grained bulk solids ('powder tester') without a quantitative statement concerning flowability and time consolidation as defined in section 2.2.2.2

Criterion	1	2	3	4a/4b	5a/5b	6	7
Fulfilment	No	–	–	–	–	–	No

Table 2.2.1 Measuring techniques and equipment (part 5 of 16)

Measuring technique	Stirrer

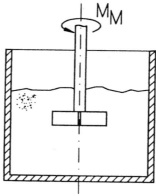

Short description	The bulk solids are filled in a container equipped with a stirrer. The flowability is determined by the measured torque M_M
General comments	The material is tested in a moving and aerated mode. Therefore, a quantitative statement cannot be made concerning the flowability and time consolidation

Criterion	1	2	3	4a/4b	5a/5b	6	7
Fulfilment	No	–	–	–	–	–	No

Table 2.2.1 Measuring techniques and equipment (part 6 of 16)

Measuring technique	Compressibility test (Kammler, 1985)

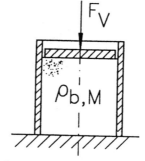

Short description	A bulk solid sample is compacted under increasing vertical stress or vertical force F_V, respectively. From the increase in bulk density ρ_b as a function of the vertical stress the flow behaviour is evaluated (poorer flow behaviour with increasing compressibility)
General comments	Qualitative comparison test for fine granular bulk solids without a quantitative statement concerning flowability and time consolidation, as defined in section 2.2.2.2

Criterion	1	2	3	4a/4b	5a/5b	6	7
Fulfilment	No	–	–	–	–	–	No

Measurement of the flowability of bulk solids

Table 2.2.1 Measuring techniques and equipment (part 7 of 16)

Measuring technique	Flowability test (Brabender, 1982) 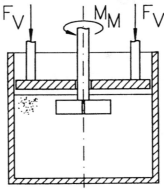
Short description	The bulk solid test specimen is being compacted by a plate in the vertical direction (force F_V). The plate is subsequently raised and the stirrer is slowly turned. The torque M_M is measured over the turning angle. The flowability is determined by the maximum value of the torque which corresponds to the start of flow
General comments	Qualitative comparison test concerning flowability. Measurement of time consolidation (qualitative) is possible. However, there is no quantitative statement concerning flowability and time consolidation. The stresses in the complex shear plane (plane of failure) are not known

Criterion	1	2	3	4a/4b	5a/5b	6	7
Fulfilment	Yes	No	No	Yes/yes	Yes*/no	Yes	Yes

*If the wall friction can be ignored (e.g. with a sufficiently small height/diameter ratio).

Table 2.2.1 Measuring techniques and equipment (part 8 of 16)

Measuring technique	Penetration test (Knight and Johnson, 1988)						
Short description	The bulk solid test specimen is being compacted vertically (force F_V). Subsequently, a pointed probe is pushed from the top into the material and the penetration force F_M is measured. With sufficient force a failure occurs along curved slip lines (see illustration). The bulk solid strength is determined from the force measured at the moment of failure (Knight and Johnson, 1988)						
General comments	Qualitative comparison test concerning flowability. Measurement of time consolidation (qualitative) is possible. However, there is no quantitative statement concerning flowability and time consolidation. The stresses in the shear plane (curved slip lines) are not known						
Criterion	1	2	3	4a/4b	5a/5b	6	7
Fulfilment	Yes	No	No	Yes/yes	Yes*/no	Yes	Yes

*If wall friction can be ignored (e.g. lubricated walls or sufficiently small height/diameter ratio).

Measurement of the flowability of bulk solids 41

Table 2.2.1 Measuring techniques and equipment (part 9 of 16)

Measuring technique	Uniaxial compression test
	F_V F_M
Short description	See the description of the simplified model of unconfined yield strength in section 2.2.2.1; applications refer to Gerritsen (1982), Maltby and Enstad (1993), Kozler and Novosad (1989), Williams, Birks and Bhattacharya (1970/71) and Beckhaus, Felgner and Runge (1992) In order to minimize the effect of friction between the solids and the cylinder wall, the wall must be 'friction-free'. This may be almost completely achieved if the wall is covered with a layer of rubber or plastic and a lubricant is put between the wall and the layer (Maltby and Enstad, 1993)
General comments	Limited quantitative statement concerning flowability and time consolidation for cohesive bulk solids with a tendency for smaller strength values because of the consolidation procedure 'uniaxial compaction' (section 2.2.3.1). Further, there is a danger of non-homogeneity (no steady-state flow, see section 2.2.3.1) The advantage is that it can be used for time consolidation measurements of coarse solids (e.g. fertilizers)

Criterion	1	2	3	4a/4b	5a/5b	6	7
Fulfilment	Yes	No	Yes	Yes/yes	Yes*/yes	Yes	Yes

*If wall friction can be ignored (lubricated walls).

Table 2.2.1 Measuring techniques and equipment (part 10 of 16)

Measuring technique	Monoaxial shear test (Peschl, 1975; Peschl and Colijn, 1977)

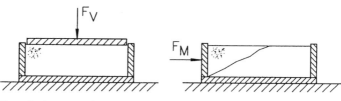

Short description	Description: see also section 2.2.3.3 The test is similar to the uniaxial compression test as described in section 2.2.2.1. The bulk solids are compressed in a vertical direction (F_V) and then, after removal of the vertical load, stressed in a horizontal direction by pushing a side wall into the material. From the force F_M measured at the moment of failure the unconfined yield strength is calculated (Peschl, 1975; Peschl and Colijn, 1977; Schwedes and Schulze, 1990)
General comments	Because of the uniaxial compression, the additional decrease of the measured strength through the anisotropic effects due to the difference in direction of 90° between consolidation and strength measurement, it is not possible to establish a quantitative statement concerning flowability and time consolidation. There is a danger of non-homogeneity of the bulk solids specimen, because it is compressed uniaxially without reaching the steady-state shear level (section 2.2.3.1). The stresses at consolidation will decrease slightly downwards due to the wall friction effect

Criterion	1	2	3	4a/4b	5a/5b	6	7
Fulfilment	Yes	No	No	Yes/yes	Yes*/yes*	Yes	Yes

*If wall friction can be ignored (e.g. sufficiently small height/diameter ratio or lubricated walls).

Table 2.2.1 Measuring techniques and equipment (part 11 of 16)

Measuring technique	Powder bed tester (Sankyo Dengyo)						
Short description	Combination of two measurements: 1. Determination of tensile strength (left-hand illustrations): the bulk solids are placed in a vertically split cell and compacted in a vertical direction (force F_V). Subsequently, the test specimen is, after removal of the load, horizontally pulled and the pull force at failure F_M is measured. From F_M the tensile strength is calculated 2. Right-hand illustrations: a sliding skid is placed on top of a 3 mm layer of solids. This layer is then consolidated by vertical force F_V, by placing weights on the skid. Subsequently, the skid is pulled horizontally over the test specimen at a lower vertical stress (normal force $N < F_V$) and the pull force at failure F_M is measured Evaluation: from the results of measurements 1 and 2 (sometimes several measurements are necessary) a yield locus is determined						
General comments	Qualitative statement regarding the flowability. The sample is consolidated uniaxially as for the uniaxial compression test (no steady-state shear), resulting in a lower measured strength. This effect is increased further through anisotropic effects due to the different directions of consolidation and measurement of strength (section 2.2.3.2) (Schwedes and Schulze, 1990; Oshima and Hirota, 1985; Hirota and Oshima, 1987). Furthermore, due to the wall friction in the split cell, the consolidation stress will decrease downwards						
Criterion	1	2	3	4a/4b	5a/5b	6	7
Fulfilment	Yes	No	No	Yes/yes	No*/yes	Yes	Yes

* Could be 'yes' if wall friction were reduced by lubricating the walls of the split cell.

Table 2.2.1 Measuring techniques and equipment (part 12 of 16)

Measuring technique	Johanson Hang-up Indicizer® (Johanson, 1992)

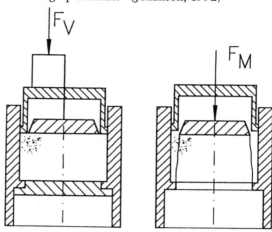

Short description	Description: see also section 2.2.3.3 A test specimen is vertically compacted (consolidated) within a cylindrical mould by a two-part piston (inner system and outer ring) with a force F_V. Subsequently, the compressive force is removed and also the bottom plate. The specimen is then pushed downwards by the inner piston until failure occurs. From the measured failure force F_M and the consolidation F_V a specific index is determined to evaluate the flowability in terms of an arching dimension and rathole diameter (Johanson, 1992, 1993; Bell et al., 1994)
General comments	Qualitative statement regarding flowability and time consolidation. The stresses at consolidation and during strength measurement are not fully known (e.g. wall friction effect) and are inhomogeneous; stress distribution can only be estimated. Further, there are influences of anisotropy (different directions of principal stresses during consolidation and strength measurement) and of the consolidation procedure 'uniaxial compression' (sections 2.2.3.1–2.2.3.3)

Criterion	1	2	3	4a/4b	5a/5b	6	7
Fulfilment	Yes	No	No	Yes/yes	No/no	Yes	Yes

Measurement of the flowability of bulk solids

Table 2.2.1 Measuring techniques and equipment (part 13 of 16)

Measuring technique	Quality control tester (Ploof and Carson, 1994) 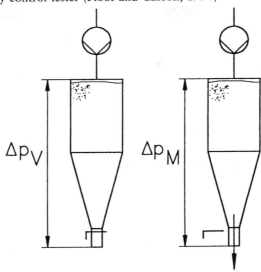
Short description	A model silo is filled with bulk solids. The outlet opening is closed off with a porous slide gate. The solids are compacted by an airstream flowing from top to bottom. The pressure differential across the bulk solid column Δp_V is measured and considered as consolidation pressure. In order to measure the strength of the bulk solids, the silo is again subjected to an air pressure after the slide gate is opened. The air pressure is gradually increased, until flow (of the bulk solid) is established. The maximum pressure differential Δp_M becomes a measure of the strength
General comments	Qualitative statement regarding flowability. Possible influences from the flowing air, such as transport of fine particles and change in moisture content. Stresses in the failure plane (near the outlet) are not known

Criterion	1	2	3	4a/4b	5a/5b	6	7
Fulfilment	Yes	No	Yes	Yes/yes	No/no	Yes	Yes

Table 2.2.1 Measuring techniques and equipment (part 14 of 16)

Measuring technique	Jenike shear tester (Jenike, 1964)

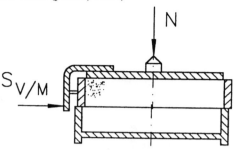

Short description	See description in section 2.2.2.3.1 If for comparisons a qualitative statement regarding flowability is sufficient, it is possible to conduct a simplified test by measuring only one shear point of the yield locus (section 2.2.2.3.3). The yield locus can then be approximated by a straight line through this point and the point representing the steady state shear (Schulze, 1994a,b; Schulze, 1995)
General comments	Quantitative statement for flowability and time consolidation is accepted when the complete test procedure is followed (see description in section 2.2.2.3.1). For a simplified procedure (section 2.2.2.3.3) only a qualitative statement applies. Operation of the Jenike shear tester requires training, which means that the results are operator sensitive (section 2.2.2.3.1)

Criterion	1	2	3	4a/4b	5a/5b	6	7
Fulfilment	Yes	Yes	Yes	Yes/yes	Yes/yes	Yes	Yes

Table 2.2.1 Measuring techniques and equipment (part 15 of 16)

Measuring technique	Torsional shear tester

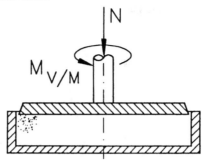

Short description	The test sample is contained in a shallow, cylindrical shear cell. Through a round, roughened lid on top of the sample a normal force N is applied. By rotation of the shear cell relative to the lid, a shear deformation is developed and the torque M_M is measured. The shear stress acting in the sample is calculated from the measured torque. As with the Jenike tester, the test sample is presheared and sheared to failure, so that a yield locus can be developed Simplified tests as described in section 2.2.2.3.3 are possible
General comments	Limited quantitative statement for flowability and time consolidation, because of the inhomogeneous deformation of the test sample (Schwedes, 1979; Münz, 1976). The deformation varies with the radius of the cell; at the perimeter it is maximum, in the centre it is zero, i.e. no shear deformation in the rotational axis. Therefore, the shear stress maximum (failure) does not develop simultaneously over the whole cross-section (Schwedes, 1979). From comparative measurements it follows that the results can differ from those of the Jenike tester (Bell et al., 1994; Münz, 1976)

Criterion	1	2	3	4a/4b	5a/5b	6	7
Fulfilment	Yes	Yes	Yes	Yes/yes	Yes/no	Yes	Yes

Table 2.2.1 Measuring techniques and equipment (part 16 of 16)

Measuring technique	Ring shear tester						
	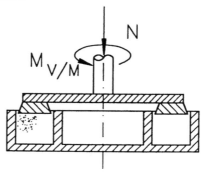						
Short description	See description in section 2.2.2.3.2 Similar to the torsional tester, but whereby the sample is contained in an annular trough. The normal force N is applied through a roughened annular lid. To shear the bulk solid sample, the shear cell rotates relative to the lid. The torque M_M necessary for shearing is measured. As with the Jenike tester, the test sample is presheared and sheared to failure, so that a yield locus can be developed Simplified tests as described in section 2.2.2.3.3 are possible						
General comments	Compared to the torsional tester, the inhomogeneity of the deformation, which results from the dependence of the shear stress on the radius, is less strong (Schwedes, 1979, Münz, 1976). With proper test procedure and correct design (sufficiently large ratio of inner to outer shear cell diameter; no stiff bearing for the lid) of the ring shear tester, test results as with the Jenike shear tester can be obtained (Münz, 1976; Schulze, 1944a,b, 1995). Thus with the ring shear tester a quantitative statement for flowability and time consolidation can be achieved						
Criterion	1	2	3	4a/4b	5a/5b	6	7
Fulfilment	Yes	Yes	Yes	Yes/yes	Yes/yes	Yes	Yes

2.2.5 Conclusions, future research

The flowability of bulk solids can be characterized by the relationship of the unconfined yield strength with the consolidation stress. Through experimental research, it has been established that this strength of the tested materials is best obtained by the Jenike shear tester and the ring shear tester. If there is no need for an accurate quantitative statement (comparative testing), then, in principle, other measuring techniques can also be used, which would mostly provide a qualitative statement or the results of which more or less deviate from the Jenike shear tester. It should be clearly understood that interpretation of the measurement values should not be affected by small external influences, such as the skill of filling or preparing the test specimen, wall friction and the dimensions of the shear testing equipment. Above all, the measuring technique should cover all the issues regarding important boundary conditions, such as stress levels, time consolidation and a study of the flowability as defined in section 2.2.2.2.

Future research is necessary in both areas mentioned above. Flowability testers have to be improved to yield the 'right' flowability like that measured in a Jenike tester or a ring shear tester, and at the same time the testers have to be easy to operate. The same is true for shear testers which are used for quantitative design of silos which have to be improved in respect of operation and time consumption.

References

Akers, R.J.: *The Certification of a Limestone Powder for Jenike Shear Testing – CRM 116*, Loughborough Univ. of Technology, UK, BCR/163/90 (Community Bureau of Reference, 1990)

Arnold, P.C.; Reed, A.R.: On the machine dependence of flow property measurements on bulk solids, *Bulk Solids Handling* 7 (1987) 3, pp. 397–400

Arthur, J.R.F.; Dunstan, T.; Enstad, G.G.: Determination of the flow function by means of a cubic plane strain tester, *Int. J. Bulk Solids Storage in Silos* 1 (1985) 2, pp. 7–10

BCR (Community Bureau of Reference) of the European Commission, Directorate for Science, Research and Development, Reference Materials (1994)

Beckhaus, R.; Felgner, W.; Runge, J.: Auslegung von Silos für verklebende grobkörnige Schüttgüter, *Chem.-Ing.-Tech.* 64 (1992) 3, pp. 292–293

Bell, T.A.; Ennis, B.J.; Grygo, R.J.; Scholten, W.J.F.; Schenkel, M.M.: Practical evaluation of the Johanson Hang-up Indicizer, *Bulk Solids Handling* 14 (1994) 1, pp. 117–125

Bell, T.A.; Grygo, R.J., Duffy, S.P., Puri, V.M.: Simplified methods of measuring powder cohesive strength, Preprints *PARTEC, 3rd Europ. Symp. Storage and Flow of Particulate Solids*, Nuremberg, March 1995, Germany, pp. 79–88

Brabender OHG, Duisburg: *Flowability test*, specification sheet No. 2124 (1982)

Carr, I.F.; Walker, D.M.: An annular shear cell for granular materials, *Powder Technology* 1 (1968), pp. 369–373

Gebhard, H.: Scherversuche an leicht verdichteten Schüttgütern unter besonderer Berücksichtigung des Verformungsverhaltens, Diss. Univ. Karlsruhe (1982)

Gerritsen, A.H.: The mechanics of cohesive powders, Diss. Rijksuniv. te Groningen, the Netherlands (1982)

Gerritsen, A.H.: The influence of the degree of stress anisotropy during consolidation on the strength of cohesive powder materials, *Powder Technol.* 43 (1985), pp. 61–70

Haaker, G.; Rademacher, F.J.C.: Direkte Messung der Fließeigenschaften von Schüttgütern durch Messung mit einem abgeänderten Triaxialgerät, *Aufbereitungs-Technik* 11 (1983), pp. 647–655

Haaker, G.; Wiersma-van Schendel, W.J.A.: A constant volume shear tester, *Bulk Solids Handling* 13 (1993) 1, pp. 129–133

Harder, J.: Ermittlung der Fließeigenschaften kohäsiver Schüttgüter mit einer Zweiaxialbox, Diss. TU Braunschweig (1985)

Hirota, M.; Oshima, T.: Shear properties of uniaxially pre-consolidated powder bed – non-uniformity of the shear stress acting on the shear plane, *Powder Technol.* 53 (1987), pp. 49–54

Höhne, D.: Die Vergleichbarkeit unterschiedlicher Methoden zur Ermittlung der Scherfestigkeit feinkörniger Schüttgüter, Diss. FIA Freiberg, GDR (1985)

Hosokawa Micron Corporation: Powder Characteristics Tester, Operating Instructions (1990)

Imse, W.: Messung der Fließfähigkeit von Zement, *Zement Kalk Gips* 25 (1972) 3, pp. 147–149

Jenike, A.W.: *Storage and Flow of Solids*, Bull. no. 123, Engng. Exp. Station, Univ. Utah, Salt Lake City (1964)

Johanson, J.R.: The Johanson Indicizer^{TM} system vs. the Jenike shear tester, *Bulk Solids Handling* 12 (1992) 2, pp. 237–240

Johanson, J.R.: Characterizing dry particulate solids for systems design, *Proc. Reliable Flow of Particulate Solids II*, Oslo, Norway, August 1993, EFChE Publ. Ser. No. 96, pp. 11–32

Kammler, R.R.: Verfahren zur Schnellbestimmung der Fließeigenschaften von Schüttgütern, *Aufbereitungs-Technik* 26 (1985) 3, pp. 136–141

Knight, P.C.; Johnson, S.H.: Measurement of powder cohesive strength with a penetration test, *Powder Technol.* 54 (1988), pp. 279–283

Koerner, R.M.: Compaction of powders using the triaxial method, *Journ. of Powder and Bulk Solids Technology* 1 (1977) 3, pp. 50–54

Kozler, J.; Novosad, J.: A method for testing the flowability of fertilizers, *Bulk Solids Handling* 9 (1989) 1, pp. 43–48

Kwade, A.; Schulze, D.; Schwedes, J.: Determination of the stress ratio in uniaxial compression tests, *Powder Handling and Processing* 6 (1994a) 1, pp. 61–65, and 2, pp. 199–203

Kwade, A.; Schulze, D.; Schwedes, J.: Die direkte Messung des Horizontallastverhältnisses, *Beton- und Stahlbetonbau* 89 (1994b) 3, pp. 58–63, and 4, pp. 117–119

Lohnes, R.A.; Bokhoven, W.H.: Experimental determination of K_0 stress ratios in grain, *Proc. 10th Annual Powder and Bulk Solids Conf.*, May 1985, Rosemont, IL, USA, pp. 231–237

Maltby, L.P.: Investigation of the behaviour of powders under and after consolidation, Diss. Norwegian Inst. of Technology (1993)

Maltby, L.P.; Enstad, G.G.: Uniaxial tester for quality control and flow property characterization of powders, *Bulk Solids Handling* 13 (1993) 1, pp. 135–139

Martens, P.: *Silohandbuch*, Verlag Ernst & Sohn, Berlin (1988)

Mayerhauser, D.: Pulver im Test, *Die Chemische Produktion*, Special issue Oct. 1989, pp. 24–31

Molerus, O.: Theory of yield of cohesive powders, *Powder Technol.* 12 (1975), pp. 259–275

Molerus, O.: *Schüttgutmechanik*, Springer-Verlag, Berlin, Heidelberg, New York, Tokyo (1985)

Münz, G.: Entwicklung eines Ringschergerätes zur Messung der Fließeigenschaften von Schüttgütern und Bestimmung des Einflusses der Teilchengrößenverteilung auf die Fließeigenschaften kohäsiver Kalksteinpulver, Diss., Univ. Karlsruhe, Germany (1976)

Nowak, M.: Spannungs-/Dehnungsverhalten von Kalkstein in der Zweiaxialbox, Diss. TU Braunschweig (1994)

Nowak, M.; Schwedes, J.: Measuring the fundamental material properties with true biaxial shear tester, *Proc. Reliable Flow of Particulate Solids II*, Oslo, Norway, August 1993, EFChE Publ. Ser. No. 96, pp. 285–305

Oshima, T.; Hirota, M.: Experimental examination on the shear process of powder bed, *KONA* 3 (1985), pp. 63–68

Peschl, I.A.S.Z.: Bulk Handling Seminar, University of Pittsburgh, December 1975

Peschl, I.A.S.Z.; Colijn, H.: New rotational shear testing technique, *Journal of Powder and Bulk Solids Technology* 1 (1977) 3, pp. 55–60

Ploof, D.A.; Carson, J.W.: Quality control tester to measure relative flowability of powders, *Bulk Solids Handling* 14 (1994) 1, pp. 127–132

Sankyo Dengyo Co., Ltd, Tokyo: *Powder Bed Tester*, Catalogue No. 111018903

Saraber, F.; Enstad, G.G.; Haaker, G.: Investigations on the anisotropic yield behaviour of a cohesive bulk solid, *Powder Technol.* 64 (1991), pp. 183–190

Schulze, D.: Entwicklung und Anwendung eines neuartigen Ringschergerätes, *Aufbereitungs-Technik* 35 (1994a) 10, pp. 524–535

Schulze, D.: A new ring shear tester for flowability and time consolidation measurements, *Proc. 1st International Particle Technology Forum*, August 1994 (1994b), Denver/Colorado, USA, pp. 11–16

Schulze, D.: Appropriate devices for the measurement of flow properties for silo design and quality control, Preprints *PARTEC, 3rd Europ. Symp. Storage and Flow of Particulate Solids*, Nuremberg March 1995, Germany, pp. 45–56

Schwedes, J.: *Fließverhalten von Schüttgütern in Bunkern*, Verlag Chemie, Weinheim, Germany (1968)

Schwedes, J.: Scherverhalten leicht verdichteter, kohäsiver Schüttgüter, Diss. Univ. Karlsruhe, Germany (1971)

Schwedes, J.: Fließverhalten von Schüttgütern in Bunkern, *Chem.-Ing.-Tech.* 48 (1976) 4, pp. 294–300

Schwedes, J.: Vergleichende Betrachtungen zum Einsatz von Schergeräten zur Messung von Schüttguteigenschaften, Preprints *PARTEC*, Nuremberg 1979, Germany, pp. 278–299

Schwedes, J.; Schulze, D.: Measurement of flow properties of bulk solids, *Powder Technol.* 61 (1990), pp. 59–68

Schwedes, J.; Schulze, D.: Letter to the editor, *Bulk Solids Handling* 12 (1992) 3, pp. 454–455

The Institution of Chemical Engineers (publisher): *Standard Shear Testing Technique for Particulate Solids Using the Jenike Shear Cell* Rugby, UK (1989)

Van der Kraan, M.; Scarlett, B.: Development of a tester for measuring caking behaviour of powders, Preprints *PARTEC, 3rd Europ. Symp. Storage and Flow of Particulate Solids*, Nuremberg March 1995, Germany, pp. 57–68

Williams, J.C.; Birks, A.H.; Bhattacharya, D.: The direct measurement of the failure function of a cohesive powder, *Powder Technol.* **4** (1970/71), pp. 328–337

Zachary, L.W.; Lohnes, R.A.: A confined compression test for bulk solids, *Proc. 13th Annual Powder and Bulk Solids Conf.*, May 1988, Rosemont, IL, USA, pp. 483–489

2.3 Flow property testing of particulate solids by uniaxial and biaxial testers

G.G. Enstad and H. Feise

2.3.1 Introduction

Although silos have been around for hundreds of years, and have been increasingly used by industry over the last century, they are still the type of construction giving most failures. At the same time they cause severe problems because they do not function in an optimal way. The reason for these problems is that the properties of powders are still very poorly understood. In order to fully understand the behaviour of powders in silos, the basic flow properties of powders or particulate solids have to be far better described than has been possible up to now.

So far, most of the investigations of flow properties of powders have been performed by means of direct shear testers. The Jenike shear tester, especially, is used world-wide to determine the flow properties necessary to design silos for flow according to the Jenike method. Other shear testers that are in common use are the ring shear tester and the Peschl torsional shear tester (section 2.1).

Shortcomings of direct shear testers are that they can only give indirect determinations of principal stresses, they do not give adequate information on deformations caused by the stresses, and they are not suited for studies of the consolidation of powders. In order to study basic flow properties, more sophisticated indirect shear testers need to be used, where principal stresses and deformations can be controlled or measured directly.

Axially symmetric triaxial testers have been adapted for powder testing, e.g. at the University of Twente (Haaker and Rademacher, 1983) and by Luong (1993). At the University of Braunschweig, a biaxial tester has been developed, which is essentially strain controlled with rigid boundaries

(Harder and Schwedes, 1985). A biaxial tester which is basically stress controlled, with flexible boundaries, has been developed at Tel-Tek, Dept. of Powder Science and Technology (POSTEC), and Telemark College in Norway (Maltby, 1993). It was originally developed in cooperation with University College London (Arthur, Dunstan and Enstad, 1985), which also has a similar unit. A fairly sophisticated uniaxial tester has also been developed by POSTEC (Maltby, 1993).

A more simplistic approach has been chosen by Johanson (1993), who recently developed a range of uniaxial devices for characterizing the flow properties of powders for the purpose of silo design and quality control. These testers, however, can only give qualitative results, and are not suited for basic research of flow properties of powders in general. On the other hand, by taking full advantage of indirect shear testers, it is possible to develop a far better knowledge of the basic behaviour of powders than that which is available at present.

A large number of constitutive models have been proposed and developed for powders. Most of these constitutive laws are so complicated that people not educated in the most advanced of mathematics, will have difficulty understanding what they mean. To use them, high-efficiency computers are needed. Still, very few of the existing constitutive laws can describe the anisotropic behaviour exhibited by most powders. This reflects the lack of proper experimental results upon which to base such laws.

The indirect shear testers used in bulk solids research can be grouped according to the dimension of the strain state: uniaxial, axisymmetric, biaxial, triaxial. Of these only uniaxial and biaxial testers will be considered in detail here.

2.3.2 Uniaxial tester

Uniaxial testers are used for two main purposes: determination of the uniaxial compressive strength and the measurement of the uniaxial consolidation behaviour. The well-known horizontal stress ratio λ is one of the uniaxial consolidation properties of a bulk solid.

The basic principles of the uniaxial tester developed at POSTEC are shown in Fig. 2.3.1. It is currently used to measure the uniaxial compressive strength. Figure 2.3.1(a) shows the consolidation stage. A powder sample has been poured into the cylindrical die, where it is compressed axially by the piston moving from the top downwards into the die. The axial movement of the piston as well as the axial force are measured, giving axial deformation and stress of the powder sample. It is therefore possible to determine stress as a function of deformation, or stress and strain as functions of time during an experiment.

In order to reduce the wall friction along the die walls to a minimum, the sample is wrapped with a rubber membrane and lubricating oil is applied between the membrane and the wall. To pour powder into the die,

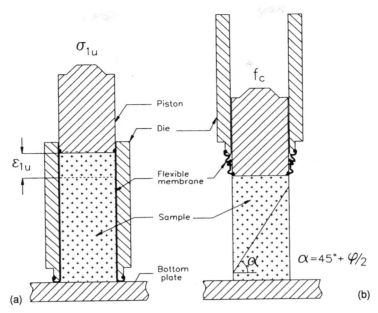

Fig. 2.3.1 Main principles of the uniaxial tester developed by POSTEC (Maltby, 1993): (a) uniaxial compaction; (b) compressive failure.

it is turned upside down, with the piston fixed in its upper position. With the powder in place, the die is covered with a bottom cup not shown in the figure, before it is turned back to its upright position, shown in Fig. 2.3.1(a).

Having consolidated the powder to the desired stress level, the stress is reduced by moving the piston upwards, and the die is pulled upwards, leaving the consolidated powder sample in an unconfined position, as shown in Fig. 2.3.1(b). To facilitate this movement of the die, it is slightly expanded downwards. With the die removed, the compressive strength of the sample is measured by moving the piston downwards until the sample fails. By consolidating several samples to different stress levels the compressive strength can be measured as a function of the uniaxial consolidation stress, similar to the flow function usually measured by means of the Jenike tester. However, as the consolidation is uniaxial and not a steady-state deformation, the compressive strengths measured with the uniaxial tester will usually be somewhat less than the unconfined failure strengths measured in the Jenike tester for the same maximum consolidation stress level σ_{1c}. Nevertheless, the measurement is well defined, and the results show very good reproducibility, giving clear indications of the flowability of the powder. At the same time the uniaxial tester also gives a lot of other information on the physical properties of the powder.

As the mass and volume of the sample are known during the whole procedure, the density is easily determined as a function of the uniaxial stress. During consolidation the stress increases exponentially with deformation. This observation is in agreement with what has been found with other testers.

If the deformation is stopped at a certain stress level, and the piston kept at the same position, the axial stress decays with time, first rapidly, then at a gradually decreasing rate. This relaxation goes on for a very long time.

If the piston is pulled back, there is an expansion, which cannot be fully described by linear elasticity (e.g. Hooke's law). The springback is also very small; for example for fine limestone it lies below 2% of the compressive deformation.

So far the uniaxial tester at POSTEC has not been equipped with transducers for the measurement of radial stress. However, this can be easily done. With that extra equipment in place, the tester will also give important information on the ratio between radial and axial stress at a silo wall, required for calculation of wall stresses based on the famous Janssen equation.

Uniaxial testers used to measure the consolidation properties of a bulk solid are called oedometers (Bauer, 1992) or lambdameters (Kwade, Schulze and Schwedes, 1994). They are equipped with axial and lateral stress sensors and also measure the axial deformation. In contrast to the slender sample of the POSTEC uniaxial tester they use a very low height to diameter ratio. Therefore wall friction is not as important as with the POSTEC tester and the rubber membrane and oil can be omitted. Kwade, Schulze and Schwedes (1994) investigated a large variety of bulk solids and showed that all of them do develop a constant lateral stress ratio. Measurements by Page (1995) show that this finding holds even for large stress ranges (0–300 MPa). In no case does the lateral stress ratio coincide with the coefficient of lateral pressure in the active Rankine state.

As the uniaxial tester is a fairly simple device, the information which can be obtained from it is naturally limited. To gain further insight into the behaviour of bulk solids, one has to use more complicated testers, e.g. the biaxial tester and the true triaxial tester.

2.3.3 Biaxial tester

The most sophisticated indirect shear tester currently used in bulk solids technology is the biaxial tester, also referred to as the true biaxial shear tester (Nowak and Schwedes, 1992). Three different types of biaxial testers are used: rigid-boundary, flexible-boundary and mixed-boundary testers.

The rigid-boundary biaxial tester is the one used most extensively for the measurement of the mechanical behaviour of particulate solids. Originally designed by Hambly (1969) it has until now been used for sand (Kuntsche, 1982), clay (Topolnicki, Gudehus and Mazurkiewicz, 1990) and fine limestone powder (Harder and Schwedes, 1985; Harder, 1986; Nowak and Schwedes, 1992, 1993; Feise and Schwedes, 1995).

Flow property testing of particulate solids

It basically consists of a brick-shaped sample covered by six steel plates (Fig. 2.3.2). Two of the plates, the top and bottom plates, are fixed and prohibit any vertical expansion of the sample. Hence all possible deformations are limited to the plane strain state and the tester is called 'biaxial'. Only the experiments with fine limestone are of relevance here, as all the others have been performed at stress levels far beyond what can be expected in silos. The loading system of the biaxial tester at the Technische Universität Braunschweig is shown in Fig. 2.3.2. It shows the four loading plates, which are supported in such a fashion that the distance between each pair of opposite plates (1–3 and 2–4) can be changed without changing the distance between the plates of the other pair. To reduce the friction between the loading plates and the sample, the sample is wrapped with thin rubber membranes and grease is applied to the plates' surfaces. The load cells, which measure the stress at the sample boundary, are mounted on the Nos 2 and 3 loading plates and the bottom plate. The set-up ensures that the sample will always retain a straight rectangular cross-section.

Figure 2.3.3 shows the flexible-boundary biaxial tester currently in use at TelTek in Norway (Maltby, Enstad and de Silva, 1995). In contrast to the rigid boundary biaxial tester its walls are made of rubber membranes. The membranes are parts of rubber bags that can be filled with air at varying pressures. The rubber bags are supported by internal frames, which are expandable in the horizontal direction, and fixed to external corner blocks. Starting from a straight position, the membrane will bulge inwards into the

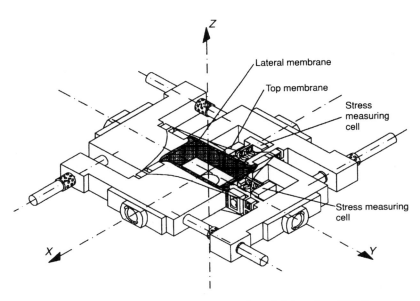

Fig. 2.3.2 Rigid-boundary biaxial tester (Nowak and Schwedes, 1993).

58   Bulk solids testing

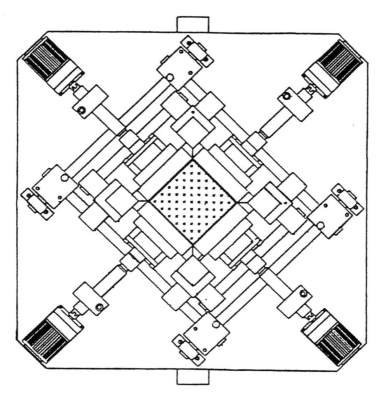

Fig. 2.3.3 Flexible-boundary biaxial tester (Maltby, 1993).

sample if the gas pressure is increased, and outwards if the gas pressure is decreased. This movement is detected by electric contacts. The corner blocks will then be moved to compensate for the deflation of the membrane until the contacts signal straight membranes again. The air pressure exerts only normal pressures on the faces of the sample. This type of biaxial tester has been used to determine flow functions directly (Arthur, Dunstan and Enstad, 1985), to investigate the anisotropic strength characteristics of limestone powder (Saraber, Enstad and Haaker, 1991), and the consolidation behaviour of the BCR-powder (Maltby, 1993; Maltby, Enstad and de Silva, 1995).

The mixed-boundary biaxial tester has been developed by Vardoulakis in Karlsruhe (Vardoulakis, Goldscheider and Gudehus, 1978). It has been used to investigate shear banding in sand. No experiments at low stress levels have been performed with a mixed-boundary biaxial tester.

Another variation of the biaxial tester is the so-called 'directional shear tester' of Dunstan, Jamebozogi and Akbarin-Miandouab (1994) and

Budiman, Sture and Ko (1992). It is meant to allow the application of any combination of normal and shear stresses on the sample's surfaces. It has been used to investigate the anisotropic effects in granular materials.

2.3.4 Experimental results from biaxial testers

2.3.4.1 Consolidation

The stresses and strains measured in a rigid-boundary or a flexible-boundary biaxial tester are experimental estimates of the principal stresses and strains experienced by the sample. The shear stresses and strains are small enough to be neglected. The series of stress and strain states applied to a sample during an experiment is called a 'stress path' or a 'strain path', respectively.

Strain paths which form a straight line through the origin in the principal strain space are called 'proportional strain paths'. According to experiments done by Nowak proportional strain paths lead to proportional stress paths (Nowak, 1993; Feise and Schwedes, 1995). The corresponding proportional stress and strain paths are called 'associated paths', their directions 'associated directions'. If the strain path is not proportional, but consists of two straight lines of which only the first is proportional, it will lead to a two-part stress path. The first part runs along the proportional stress path associated with the proportional part of the strain path. After the bend in the strain path the stress path approaches the proportional stress path associated to the direction of the second part of the strain path. It does not, however, reach it, but the two-part stress path will finally run parallel to the proportional path. This is called 'asymptotic behaviour' (Nowak and Schwedes, 1993; Nowak, 1993; Feise and Schwedes, 1995). The distance between the asymptotic and the respective proportional stress path depends on the deformation during the initial part of the strain path.

The proportional stress and strain paths are characterized by constant stress and strain ratios over the entire experiment. From this it appears reasonable to assume a constant horizontal stress ratio λ in the shaft of a silo. Here a uniaxial deformation prevails, which gives rise to a stress of the associated stress path. However, in the hopper section the deformation does not correspond to a proportional stress path. Therefore the K-value often used for the calculation of filling stresses in a hopper must depend on the position in the hopper (Schulze and Schwedes, 1992).

The consolidation experiments done in the biaxial testers confirm the finding mentioned in the section on the uniaxial tester: the hydrostatic stress corresponding to a certain bulk density increases logarithmically with increasing density (Nowak and Schwedes, 1993). Written in terms of the bulk porosity it reads:

$$n = n_i - C_c \ln \frac{\sigma_m}{\sigma_0} \qquad (2.3.1)$$

where σ_m is the hydrostatic stress, σ_0 the reference stress, C_c the compression index, n_i the reference porosity and n the porosity.

Nowak (Nowak and Schwedes, 1993; Nowak, 1993) also showed that the parameter C_c is equal for all proportional compression paths, while n_i depends on the direction of the proportional strain path. Maltby, Enstad and de Silva (1995) presented measurements from the flexible-boundary biaxial tester, which indicate that the above relationship also holds for compression paths where a slight extension in one direction is combined with a strong compression in the other.

2.3.4.2 Shearing

Of special importance in the field of silo technology is the constant volume shearing behaviour. For fine cohesive limestone Nowak (Nowak and Schwedes, 1992), Feise (Feise and Schwedes, 1995) and Maltby, Enstad and de Silva (1995) showed that the stress state becomes constant very quickly after the onset of constant volume deformation. It is therefore permissible to assume a 'steady-state flow' regime and a unique relationship between bulk density and steady-state stresses. Nowak also found that the steady-state flow behaviour of limestone follows the same rules as the critical state behaviour known from other materials (Nowak and Schwedes, 1993).

2.3.4.3 Anisotropy

The biaxial tester has been used extensively to investigate the anisotropic behaviour of bulk materials. The most recent work of Maltby (1993) looked at the compression behaviour of limestone after different types of consolidation. He found that the stresses needed to initiate plastic deformation depended strongly on the consolidation procedure. From his results he was able to estimate the shape of the yield locus and the consolidation locus for limestone (Maltby, Enstad and de Silva, 1995).

Figure 2.3.4 shows results from these experiments. The solid lines are estimates of the yield surface of BCR-limestone after different means of consolidation. All samples were consolidated to the same density. However, this density was reached via five different stress paths not shown in the figure. Starting at very low densities, all samples were initally consolidated biaxially with $\sigma_x = \sigma_y$. From the point $\sigma_x = \sigma_y = 7.5\,\text{kPa}$ five different consolidation paths were followed, ranging from equally biaxial (highest) to pure shear stress increase (lowest). Having reached the desired density, all samples were unloaded to the common point shown in Fig. 2.3.4. From here stresses were increased along the dashed lines and the onset of deformation was detected (circled dots). The yield surfaces become more slender and smaller the more anisotropic the consolidation procedure (Maltby, 1993; Maltby, Enstad and de Silva, 1995). Figure 2.3.4 clearly shows the depend-

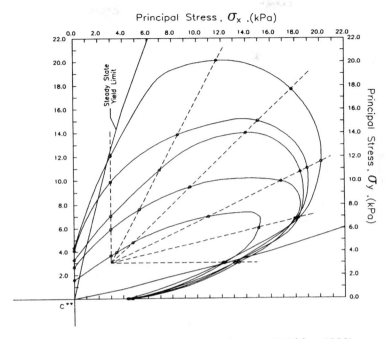

Fig. 2.3.4 Yield surface after anisotropic consolidation (Maltby, 1993).

ence of the yield surface on the loading history, which is far more complex than any of the current constitutive models provides for.

Harder (1986) investigated only the yield locus and the compressive strength after different types of consolidation. He found that the yield locus was larger if the direction of the major principal stress during consolidation and shearing coincided than it was if the major principal stresses during consolidation and shearing were perpendicular to each other. Schwedes and Schulze (1990) showed from measurements with several shear testers that the dependence of the unconfined yield strength on the major principal stress during steady-state flow does not show anisotropic effects, while the yield locus itself does.

The experiments of Harder (Harder and Schwedes, 1985; Schwedes and Schulze, 1990) as well as investigations by Saraber, Enstad and Haaker (1991) clearly show that several yield loci for the same bulk density exist. Even the steady-state stress at the same density depends on the consolidation. This is not so in the experiments of Nowak (1993).

2.3.4.4 Relaxation

A limited number of relaxation tests have been performed in the biaxial tester (Nowak, 1993). So far it is only possible to conclude that during relaxation all normal stresses decrease. It is not yet clear how different ways of deformation influence the relaxation behaviour. If the deformation prior to the relaxation phase is small, the stresses will not diminish to zero. Instead some stable stress level remains. The relaxation is divided into a very rapid decrease at the beginning and a much slower decrease later.

2.3.5 Future research goals

The results available so far indicate that the constitutive properties of powders are so complicated that any description will always remain a rough estimate. However, by investigating well-defined, simplified cases as in the uniaxial and biaxial testers, considerable improvements in our understanding of the basic flow properties of importance for the behaviour of powders in silos can be obtained.

2.3.5.1 Uniaxial tester

In the parallel part of the silo, the powder is approximately in a state of uniaxial deformation. The behaviour of the powder in this part of the silo is therefore analogous to that which can be studied in the uniaxial tester.

During filling of the silo, the powder is gradually consolidated as the stress increases with the increasing load of powder in the silo. This situation corresponds to the consolidation stage of a uniaxial test, and the bulk density of the powder as a function of the stress may be of special interest, as well as the ratio between axial and radial stress, which is required for the Janssen formula. These parameters should be investigated in the uniaxial tester.

During storage, the powder is in a state corresponding to the relaxation seen when the piston is locked in the same position after a certain level of stress has been reached in the uniaxial tester. In a silo the stress will be approximately constant and hence there will be a certain creep deformation of the powder which will give a slight increase in density during storage. This effect can be studied in the uniaxial tester.

The advantage of the uniaxial tester is that it represents the simplest possible case of deformation, where basic understanding of the behaviour of powders can be gained; at the same time important features of direct relevance for silos can be investigated. Other relations that can be studied are effects of consolidation rate and cyclic loading on compressive strength, density, elastic behaviour, effect of rate of loading during strength measurements, relationship between particle properties and flow properties.

2.3.5.2 Biaxial tester

The biaxial tester can be used for plane strain tests, which is approximately the type of deformation which exists in a wedge-shaped hopper, or plane flow hoppers. The biaxial tester is therefore of direct relevance for these types of hoppers, but the investigations which can be carried out will also give more general information on the flow behaviour of powders.

Using the biaxial tester, the effects of different stress and strain paths can be studied. Currently only sketchy information is available about the anisotropic behaviour of bulk solids, especially if induced cohesion is concerned. So far time or rate effects have also been neglected. It appears to be a well-suited task for the biaxial tester to investigate the rate dependence of multi-dimensional relaxation, creep and consolidation. Biaxial testers are limited as the stress in the third direction cannot be controlled, since the deformation in this direction is kept equal to zero. In order to control this stress also, true triaxial testers are required. With such testers, the effects of all possible stress and strain paths can be studied, offering the chance to study the constitutive behaviour of the powder in all situations where the principal stresses are confined to three given directions. This is not possible in normal triaxial testers, where axial symmetry means that two of the principal stresses are always equal.

Anisotropic behaviour can be studied in true biaxial and triaxial testers only by shifting the directions of the major principal stresses at angles of 90°. Investigations of anisotropic behaviour including angles other than 90° would require testers like those described by Dunstan, Jamebozogi and Akbarin-Miandouab (1994) and Budiman, Sture and Ko (1992). However, these testers are very complicated, and before investing in such demanding equipment, one should try to gain as much knowledge as possible from the simpler testers that are already available.

References

Arthur, J.R.F.; Dunstan, T.; Enstad, G.G.: Determination of the flow function by means of a cubic plane strain tester, *Int. J. Bulk Solids Storage in Silos*, 1 (1985) 2, 7–10.

Bauer, E.: *Zum mechanischen Verhalten granularer Stoffe unter vorwiegend oedometrischer Beanspruchung*, in Gutehus, G.; Natan, O. (eds.): Veröffentl. Inst. f. Bodenmechanik und Felsmechanik, Universität Karlsruhe, No. 130 (1992)

Budiman, J.S.; Sture, S.; Ko, H.-Y.: Constitutive behaviour of stress-induced anisotropic cohesive soil, *J. Geotechnical Engineering*, 118 (1992) 9, 1348–1359

Dunstan, T.; Jamebozogi, M.; Akbarin-Miandouab, S.: Powder strength after changes in the principal stress direction, *Powder Technology*, 81 (1994), 31–40

Feise, H.; Schwedes, J.: Investigation of the behaviour of a cohesive powder in the biaxial tester, *3rd European Symposium on Storage and Flow of Particulate Solids (Janssen Centennial), PARTEC 95*, 21–23 March 1995, Nuremberg, Germany, 119–128.

Haaker, G.; Rademacher, F.J.C.: Direkte Messung der Fließeigenschaften von Schüttgütern mit einem abgeänderten Triaxialgerät, *Aufbereitungstechnik*, 24 (1983) 11, 647–655

Hambly, E.C.: Plane strain behaviour of soft clay, Ph.D. thesis, University of Cambridge (1969)

Harder, J.: Ermittlung der Fließeigenschaften kohäsiver Schüttgüter mit einer Zweiaxialbox, Dissertation TU Braunschweig (1986)

Harder, J.; Schwedes, J.: The development of a true biaxial shear tester, *Part. Charact.* 2 (1985), 149–153

Johanson, J.R.: Characterizing dry particulate solids for systems design, *Proc. Intern. Symp. Reliable Flow of Particulate Solids II*, Oslo, Norway, Aug. 1993, EFCE Publ. Ser. No. 96, pp. 13–32

Kuntsche, K.: *Materialverhalten von wassergesättigtem Ton bei ebenen und zylindrischen Verformungen*, in A. Blinde, G. Gudehus, O. Natau (eds.): Veröffentl. Inst. f. Bodenmechanik und Felsmechanik, No. 91 (1982)

Kwade, A.; Schulze, D.; Schwedes, J.: Determination of the stress ratio in uniaxial compression tests, part 1: *Powder Handling and Processing*, 6 (1994) 1, 61–65, part 2: *Powder Handling and Processing*, 6 (1994) 2, 199–203

Luong, M.P.: Flow characteristics of granular bulk materials, *Part. Syst. Charact.*, 10 (1993), 79–85

Maltby, L.P.: Investigation of the behaviour of powders under and after consolidation, Dissertation 1993:56, Institute for Process Technology, Telemark College, (1993)

Maltby, L.P.; Enstad, G.G; de Silva, S.R.: Investigation of the behaviour of powders under and after consolidation, *Part. Syst. Charact.*, 12 (1995), 16–27

Nowak, M.: Spannungs-/Dehnungsverhalten von Kalkstein in der Zweiaxialbox, Dissertation TU Braunschweig (1993)

Nowak, M., Schwedes, J.: An investigation on the pure shearing of cohesive limestone with the true biaxial shear tester, *Chem. Eng. Technol.*, 15 (1992) 5, 295–299

Nowak, M.; Schwedes, J.: Measuring of fundamental material properties with the true biaxial shear tester, *Proc. Intern. Symp. Reliable Flow of Particulate Solids II*, Oslo, Norway, Aug. 1993, EFChE Publ. Ser. No. 96, 285–305

Page, N.: On stress states achieved during compression of granular materials, 5th *Intern. Conf. Bulk Materials Storage, Handling and Transportation*, Newcastle (NSW), 10–12 July 1995, *Proceedings*, Vol. 2 (1995), 409–414.

Saraber, F.; Enstad, G.G.; Haaker, G.: Investigations on the anisotropic yield behaviour of a cohesive bulk solid, *Powder Technology*, 64 (1991), 183–190.

Schwedes, J.; Schulze, D.: Measurement of flow properties of bulk solids, *Powder Technology* 61 (1990) 1, 59–68.

Schulze, D.; Schwedes, J.: Initial stresses – experimental data and calculations, *4th Int. Conf. on Bulk Materials Storage, Handling and Transportation*, Wollongong (Australia), July 1992, National Conference Publication No. 92/7, 453–458

Topolnicki, M.; Gudehus, G.; Mazurkiewicz, B.K.: Observed stress–strain behaviour of remoulded saturated clay under plane strain conditions, *Géotechnique*, 40 (1990) 2, 155–187

Vardoulakis, I.; Goldscheider, M.; Gudehus, G.: Formation of shear bands in sand bodies as a bifurcation problem, *International Journal for Numerical and Analytical Methods in Geomechanics*, 2 (1978), 99–128.

2.4 Reflections on triaxial testing, rheology and flowability

M.P. Luong

2.4.1 Introduction

Besides shear testing traditionally performed in chemical engineering, this section emphasizes an interest in the conventional cylindrical triaxial shear tester, widely used in soil mechanics, for a thorough understanding of both the mechanical behaviour (physical meaning of yield conditions and flow rules) and flow properties (indicator of arching effect) of granular bulk materials stored in silos.

The deformation behaviour of granular bulk materials under stress is highly complex and very difficult to obtain by testing. It is sometimes possible to describe very accurately by mathematical relationships the measured behaviour of a given material in a given test as shown in previous sections. However, it is not always possible to extend and/or make use of these relations for the purpose of predicting the behaviour of the same material under different loading conditions. A useful mathematical model or a material stress–strain–strength behaviour is one that can be employed to predict satisfactorily the material performance in all circumstances at hand.

To be satisfactory, a material model idealization should possess the following necessary properties:

- The model should be complete, i.e. able to make statements about the material behaviour for all stress and strain paths, and not merely restricted to a single class of paths.
- It should be possible to identify the model parameters by means of a small number of standard or simple tests.
- The model should be founded on some physical interpretation of the

ways in which the material is responding to changes in applied stress or strain (e.g. the material should not be modelled as elastic if permanent deformations are observed upon unloading).

2.4.2 Relevance of cylindrical triaxial shear testing

Flow problems are inherent in the storage of particulate solids in steel, reinforced concrete or composite silos, bunkers and hoppers. Any reduction or total blockage of material flow subsequently reduces storage capacity, leads to material degradation and loss of profitability through reduced efficiency, increased downtime, planned overcapacity and greater labour utilization (Shamlou, 1988). As a result of the high failure rate in silo structures, great effort has been spent in recent decades for better understanding of silo pressures and flowing phenomena. Nevertheless available methods for analysing silo pressures give results that vary over a wide range, even under static conditions, and are generally not on the safe side. Due to the underlying assumptions and their incompleteness, most approaches are restricted to the analysis of simple geometries and classical constitutive laws under static or at rest conditions, traditionally used in soil mechanics.

Under static conditions, granular materials behave like solids, yet they have a Coulomb yield criterion. Moreover they can transmit a lateral pressure caused by an overburden pressure, like Rankine passive or active stresses, similar in some ways to a statically equilibrated body of fluids with the associated hydrostatic pressure.

In designing a silo, at least two operational conditions must be considered, namely charging (filling) and discharging (emptying). When storing bulk solid materials in silos and especially during discharging, transport properties of disperse systems are involved in which the particles interact with each other. This interaction includes the manifold system conditions up to the disaggregated granular bed in which the particle motion is affected by their interaction with neighbouring particles and the inertial forces or mass forces generated by special equipment, applied to the particles.

2.4.3 Testing procedure

A cylindrical specimen is sealed in a rubber membrane and enclosed in a cell in which it can be subjected to fluid or air pressure p_0. A load, applied axially through a ram acting on the top cap, is used to control the deviator stress. Under these conditions the axial stress is the major principal stress σ_1, the intermediate and minor principal stresses (σ_2 and σ_3 respectively) are both equal to the cell pressure p_0 (Bishop and Henkel, 1962; Tatsuoka, 1988).

Alternatively an extension test may be carried out, by using a tension fitting between the ram and the top cap. In this case the axial stress is the minor principal stress σ_3 and the intermediate and major principal stresses

(σ_2 and σ_1 respectively) are equal to the cell pressure p_0. This procedure is less common.

If homogeneity of strain can be assumed in the case of an isotropic material, measurements of the axial force F, the confining pressure p_0, the specimen height H and its diameter D (or the cross-section S, or the volume V) allow the determination of the state of stress and strain (Fig. 2.4.1). H_0, D_0, S_0 and V_0 are the respective initial values.

$$\varepsilon_1 = \Delta H/H_0$$
$$\varepsilon_2 = \varepsilon_3 = \Delta D/D_0$$
$$\sigma_1 = F/S_0$$
$$\sigma_2 = \sigma_3 = p_0$$

The measurement of D is rather difficult. It may be obtained by using proximity transducers or by measuring the circumference of the specimen. Usually the volume change is measured and strain ε_3 may be deduced from

$$\varepsilon_v = \varepsilon_1 + 2\varepsilon_3 = -\Delta V/V_0 \qquad (2.4.1)$$

If the quantities H, D and V are known, this relationship may be used as a consistency condition for the three measurements. Diameter measurement is also needed to obtain the specimen cross-section in order to calculate the true stress σ_1.

$$\Delta\sigma_1/\sigma_1 = -\Delta S/S_0 = -2\Delta D/D_0 = \varepsilon_1 - \varepsilon_v \qquad (2.4.2)$$

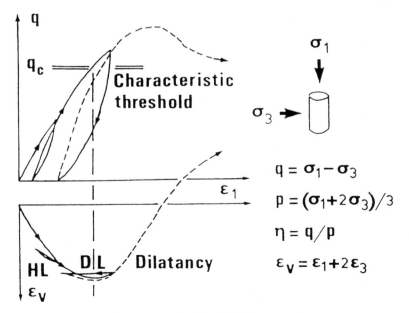

Fig. 2.4.1 Specimen under conventional triaxial shear testing.

The loading parameters of the conventional triaxial shear tests generally in use are

Mean stress $\quad p = (\sigma_1 + 2\sigma_3)/3$
Deviatoric stress $\quad q = \sigma_1 - \sigma_3$
Deviatoric level $\quad \eta = q/p$

The corresponding deformation parameters are defined by

Volumetric strain $\quad \varepsilon_v = \varepsilon_1 + 2\varepsilon_3$
Deviatoric strain $\quad \varepsilon_q = 2(\varepsilon_1 - \varepsilon_3)/3$
Dilatancy rate $\quad \delta = \varepsilon_v/\varepsilon_q$

The work increment $\dot{W}$ can be separated into a volumetric component $\dot{W}_v$ and a deviatoric component $\dot{W}_s$. Owing to some assumptions regarding the strain increment along the cylindrical triaxial stress path where elastic strain is relatively small, the dissipated irreversible work increment $\dot{W}^i$ is given by

$$\dot{W}^i = p\dot{\varepsilon}_v^i + q\dot{\varepsilon}_q^i \qquad (2.4.3)$$

With the notation $\sigma_1 \geq \sigma_2 \geq \sigma_3$ in compression used in soil mechanics, we note a jump of the principal stress axes between compression and extension states in the conventional triaxial test. In practice, these stress paths correspond, in the vicinity of the silo axis, to the loading paths applied to stored materials during filling (one major principal stress and two equal minor principal stresses) and emptying operations (two equal major principal stresses and one minor principal stress).

The Mohr–Coulomb criterion for a cohesionless material is given by

$$f(\sigma) = \max[\sigma_i(1 - \sin\varphi) - \sigma_j(1 + \sin\varphi)] \qquad (2.4.4)$$

where φ denotes the internal friction angle and the subscripts $i, j = 1$ to 3.

At failure the deviatoric levels in triaxial compression η_f^+ and extension η_f^- are respectively given by

$$\eta_f^+ = 6\sin\varphi_f^+ / (3 - \sin\varphi_f^+) \qquad (2.4.5)$$

$$\eta_f^- = 6\sin\varphi_f^- / (3 + \sin\varphi_f^-) \qquad (2.4.6)$$

2.4.4 Pressure evaluation on silo walls

Normal pressures acting on the walls of a silo storing a free-flowing material may vary with the method of filling, rate of filling, stiffness of the silo walls, variation in flow properties of the bulk solid, silo wall imperfections, segregation while filling, rate of deaeration, material temperature and temperature changes, and an increase in grain moisture causing swelling.

Conventional methods of pressure evaluation on silo walls are based on theories of arching, allowing the transfer of pressure from a yielding mass of stored material on to adjoining stationary parts. Most of the existing theories of arching deal with the pressure of dry material on a yielding horizontal strip:

1. Some workers consider the conditions for equilibrium of the rigid material which is located immediately above the loaded strip without attempting to investigate whether or not the results of the computations were compatible with the conditions for the equilibrium of the material at a greater distance from the strip (Janssen, 1895).
2. Other workers assumed without realistic justification that the entire mass of the stored material located above the yielding strip is in a rigid plastic equilibrium (Caquot, 1934).
3. A third group assumed that the vertical sections through the outer edges of the yielding strip represent surfaces of sliding and that the pressure on the yielding strip is equal to the difference between the weight of the material located above the strip and the full frictional resistance along the vertical sections. The real surfaces of sliding are curved and at the surface of the material their spacing is considerably greater than the width of the yielding strip. Hence the friction along the vertical sections cannot be fully active. The error due to ignoring this fact is on the unsafe side.

Hence the conventional methods for determining the stress field in silos are generally based on the limit equilibrium of a two-dimensional rigid plastic continuum, a failure criterion that does not take into account deformation characteristics, and a mass flow type of stored materials when emptying. Using classical notions of Rankine active and passive pressures, several workers have attempted to evaluate debatable stress distributions at the silo walls.

Experimentally a large number of studies, carried out in France (Brozzetti, 1989) and elsewhere, showed that the wall pressures varied with time and that outlet operations of a small quantity of material changed load values in a very significant manner.

This is also the case during the process of silo handling in filling and emptying. The applied loads on silo walls are a function of the shape, the bottom, the type of flow during emptying and the outlet location. The load distribution varies significantly with the nature of the stored materials: compressible types such as foodstuffs, abounding types such as pulverized coal cement, gypsum and limestone, or dilating types such as hard angular-grain mine products.

These experimental observations indicate the predominant influence of the rheological behaviour of bulk solid materials to be stored, on the determination of loads to be considered in silo design. Three types of constitutive models have been used to describe granular flow in various geometries:

1   Kinematic models.
2   Rate-independent or frictional models based on plasticity theory and soil mechanics.
3   Rate-dependent or collisional models based on the kinetic theory of gases.

It is noteworthy that none of them is wholly satisfactory or even superior to the others in all aspects.

Kinematic models are incomplete because they provide no information about stress field and density variation. Nevertheless, they have been reasonably successful in predicting velocity profiles in the converging flow zone of the flat-bottomed bins.

Frictional models have been in use for over two decades. The results of these studies show that the models can predict some, but not all, of the phenomena observed when granular materials flow through hoppers and bunkers.

Collisional models have been explored largely from the 1970s onwards. They have predicted some features of plane shear between parallel plates, and of flow down inclined planes.

Recently, hybrid frictional-collisional models have been developed and applied to these problems, with encouraging results. In this presentation, attention is confined to the frictional aspects of the behaviour of stored granular materials.

2.4.5 Characteristic state of a particulate material

2.4.5.1 Deformation mechanisms

In order to analyse and predict the macroscopic response of particulate solid behaviour, it is necessary to understand how the individual constituent elements interact at both the grain and aggregate levels due to the particular arrangement of the particles within the mass.

The principal grain properties are size, texture and shape. An elongated shape of elastic particles promotes bending mechanisms leading to a decrease of incidence angle of contact forces (Fig. 2.4.2). This induces a quasi-reversible compressibility that is especially large in the case of flocculent or honeycombed structures.

Qualitatively, aggregates may differ in texture with reference to the degree of fineness and uniformity, in structure with reference to the pattern in which the particles are arranged in the aggregate, and in consistency. Fine-grained materials may be stable even if the grains touch each other at very few points, provided the adhesion between the grains is of the same order of magnitude as the weight of grains.

Quantitatively, they may differ in porosity, relative density, water and gas content. A cohesionless granular material can be considered as a grain assembly where the discrete solid granules are in contact and free to move with respect to their neighbours. It is often assumed that the constituent

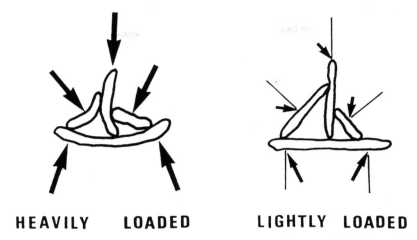

Fig. 2.4.2 Quasi-reversible deformation mechanism of elongated elastic particles.

grains are in direct, elastic contact with one another. The inherent nonlinearity of Hertz relationships between two elastic bodies indicates great difficulty in the application of contact theory to the study of granular media (Hardin, 1978).

Nevertheless, observed macroscopic deformations of the material are essentially derived from their structural modifications, that is, rearrangements of particles inducing irreversible contractive or dilative volume changes:

1 Compaction mechanism that corresponds to a closer packing of solid particles inducing a contractive behaviour due to the compressibility of both packing and particles.
2 Distortion mechanism caused by irreversible grain slidings, leading initially to a contractive behaviour, then interlocking disruption where the individual particles are plucked from their interlocking seats and made to slide over the adjacent particles with large distortion of particle arrangement, inducing significant dilative volume changes, a phenomenon known as dilatancy.
3 Attrition mechanism subsequent to asperity breakage and particle crushing that modifies the relative density: the resulting effect is a contractive behaviour.

2.4.5.2 Characteristic threshold

Extensive laboratory triaxial shear tests on diverse granular materials show that the lowest point on the volume change versus axial strain curve, that is, the point of minimum specimen volume, corresponds to a constant stress ratio (Kirkpatrick, 1961). The stress peak or maximum of shear resistance occurring at maximum dilatancy rate has been analysed and interpreted by the stress–dilatancy theory (Lee, 1966; Rowe, 1971). The asymptotic part of the stress–strain curve determines the ultimate strength of the well-known critical state concept (Schofield and Wroth, 1968). The cases of transient and repeated loadings require the analysis of the pre-peak part where the stress ratio η_c at zero dilatancy rate defines evidently the characteristic threshold of the granular material (Luong, 1980) associated with an angle of aggregate friction. The granular material is in a characteristic state having the following properties (Luong, 1978):

1. The volume change rate is zero.
2. The stress level, reached by the material, is an intrinsic parameter that defines a characteristic friction angle φ_c determining the interlocking capacity of the grain assembly. Its value is independent of initial material density.

2.4.6 Rheology of fly ash

Triaxial shear tests were conducted on cylindrical specimens of fly ash, 70 mm in diameter and 160 mm high. For each test, stress–strain curves recorded during loading give the volume change referred to the initial volume V_0 and the axial displacement ΔH with respect to the initial height H_0 as a function of the axial force ΔF referred to the initial section S_0 of the specimen.

Depending upon the confining pressure, two types of behaviour can be distinguished:

1. A volumetric contraction followed by a continuous dilation until material failure.
2. A continuous contraction until failure.

Analysis of experimental curves shows that, for a given material, the two types of behaviour do not occur randomly, but present a continuous evolution where the confining pressure (or overburden pressure representing the silo height) increases and prevents the breakdown of the granular structure interlocking.

When the material, subject to an imposed load level $p_0 \geq \gamma H_{\text{lim}}$, does not present a characteristic threshold, the granular interlocking breakdown does not occur for the corresponding silo height. Accordingly a practical result can be deduced: flowability is poor, even impossible, if this load level is exceeded. Some triaxial shear tests on fly ash (unit weight = 9.2 kN/m^3) have readily shown (Fig. 2.4.3) that for a silo height less than about 4.3 m corresponding to low values of confining pressures (<40 kPa), dilatancy occurs with a threshold of disaggregation of the particulate structure. Whereas with a greater confining pressure (σ_3 = 50 kPa), no dilatancy occurs and the arching effect is mobilized in the silo. A height limit H_{lim} without arching effect seems to be 5.4 m.

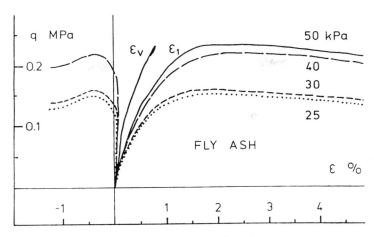

Fig. 2.4.3 Conventional triaxial shear tests on fly ash.

2.4.7 Flowability index

In pilot-plant as well as in plant design, the engineer often faces the problem of handling granular materials (Jenike, 1964; Shamlou, 1988), especially concerning their flow characteristics (Janssen, 1895; Caquot, 1934; Shield, 1955; Mandl and Fernandez-Luque, 1970; Goodman and Cowin, 1971) and their flow behaviour in bins, hoppers and feeders (Eibl and Rombach, 1987). Experience on silos in service (Carr, 1965; Brozzetti, 1989) suggests that diverse flow modes (Kühnemund, 1987) may occur depending on the nature of stored bulk materials. Problems with flow include erratic flow, loss of flow, flushing (or flooding), segregation, build-up of stagnant material, and degradation or caking. Lack of level control – with an unpredictable surface geometry in the bin, it is difficult to determine accurately the inventory of the bulk solid – may also take place.

Experimental observations suggest, as an indicator – when performing a conventional triaxial shear test – a flowability index I_f defined by the ratio of the distortional work W_{dc} prior to the characteristic threshold to the work W_{dm} mobilized up to the maximum strength at failure (Fig. 2.4.4): the lower this index, the easier the stored bulk material flows. For very soft and collapsible materials (for example fly ash or chemical powders), this index may be greater than one, even under very low confining pressures.

2.4.8 Concluding remarks

The experimental approach presented has shown some salient aspects of the rheological behaviour of particulate solids using the conventional triaxial shear tester.

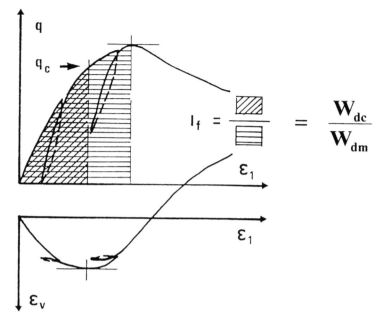

Fig. 2.4.4 Definition of the flowability index.

Experimental results provide the physical interpretation of parameters in use in constitutive models, such as yield conditions and flow rules, when describing granular flow in various silo geometries.

The flowability index I_f, taking into account stress and strain states, is a very useful and appropriate indicator when predicting the flow types of stored bulk materials in the course of the discharging process; arching effects may occur in cases where I_f is greater than one.

References

Bishop A.W. and Henkel D.J. (1962). *The Measurement of Soil Properties in the Triaxial Test*. Edward Arnold, London.

Brozzetti J. (1989). Description de la base expérimentale d'essais de cellules métalliques de stockage – présentation du programme d'essais. *Construction Métallique*, 2, 7–17.

Caquot A. (1934). *Equilibre des massifs à frottement interne*. Gauthiers-Villars, Paris.

Carr R.L. (1965). Evaluating flow properties of solids. *Chemical Engineering*, 18 Jan., 163–168.

Eibl J. and Rombach G. (1987). *Numerical Computation of Velocity- and Stress Fields in Silos. Theory and Applications*. SILOSY, Sklarska Poreba, Poland.

Goodman M.A. and Cowin S.C. (1971). Two problems in the gravity flow of granular materials. *J. Fluid Mechanics*, 45, 321–339.

Hardin B.O. (1978). The nature of stress–strain behavior of soils. *Proc. Conf. Earthquake Engineering and Soil Dynamics*, vol. 1, ASCE, Pasadena, USA, pp. 3–90.
Janssen H.A. (1895). Versuche über Gedreidedruck in Silozellen. *Z. Ver. Dt. Ing.*, **39-35**, 1045–1050.
Jenike A.W. (1964). Steady gravity flow of frictional-cohesive solids in converging channels. *ASME*, **86**, 5–11.
Kirkpatrick W.M. (1961). Discussion on soil properties and their measurement. *Proc. 6th ICSMFE*, Dunod, Paris, 131–133.
Kühnemund B. (1987). *Stockage en silos de produits en vrac*. Bühler-Miag, Nouvelles, **217**.
Lee I.K. (1966). Stress–dilatancy performance of feldspar. *ASCE*, **92, SM2**, 79–103.
Luong M.P. (1978). Etat caractéristique du sol. *C.R. Acad. Sci.*, **287 B**, 305–307.
Luong M.P. (1980). Stress–strain aspects of cohesionless soils under cyclic and transient loading. *Proc. ISSCTL*, Balkema, Rotterdam, 315–324.
Mandl G. and Fernandez-Luque R. (1970). Fully developed plastic flow of granular materials. *Géotechnique*, **20**, 277–307.
Rowe P.W. (1971). Theoretical meaning and observed values of deformations for soils. In *Stress–Strain Behaviour of Soils*, ed. by R.G.H Parry, Cambridge, 143–194.
Schofield A.N. and Wroth C.P. (1968). *Critical State Soil Mechanics*. McGraw-Hill, London.
Shamlou P.A. (1988). *Handling of Bulk Solids – Theory and Practice*. Butterworths, London.
Shield R.T. (1955). Stress and velocity fields in soil mechanics. *J. Math. Phys.*, **33**, 144–156.
Tatsuoka F. (1988). Some recent developments in triaxial testing systems for cohesionless soils. *ASTM*, **STP 977**, 7–67.

2.5 Wall friction and wear testing
G. Haaker

2.5.1 Introduction

Wall friction in the field of bulk solids handling has often been considered to be a rather simple phenomenon. It was believed that wall friction angles were in general constant values which could be established by simple tests, or could even be derived as a constant from the internal friction. In recent decades, however, it has been realized more and more that wall friction is a much more complex quantity, with a substantial impact on the reliability of industrial practice. In particular, the influence of wall friction on the flow behaviour, the mutual influence of wall friction on wear and attrition, the role of sliding velocity, stress levels and influence of time, have gained more consideration.

In spite of this growing interest, there still seems to be a lack of knowledge on this subject. The state of the art of this subject and needs for further research will be dealt with in this section.

2.5.2 The role of wall friction in storage and transport

Wall friction has a threefold influence on silos:

1. *Influence on the flow pattern* In silos generally two types of flow pattern can be distinguished, mass flow and funnel flow. Which type of pattern will occur depends on the cone angle α, the value of the effective internal friction angle ϕ_e, and the wall friction angle ϕ_w.

    The boundary lines between mass and funnel flow (as given in the original Jenike theory (Jenike, 1970)) are amply discussed in section 1.3. Although these boundaries are rather conservative, the possibility of wall friction changing with time should be kept in mind.

Wall friction and wear testing

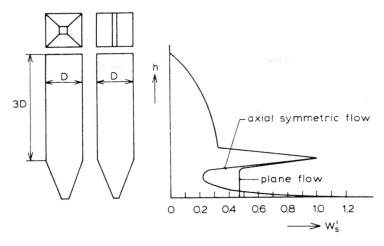

Fig. 2.5.1 Relative wear pattern for mass flow silos.

2 *Influence on wall and bottom loads* The normal and shear loads on the wall as well as the vertical load in the silo are strongly dependent on the value of the wall friction angle.

Expressions for the vertical load σ_v, wall load σ_w and wall shear load τ_w, based on Janssen's approach (Janssen, 1895) indicate that low wall frictions in general lead to higher loads. This implies that for structural reasons a fair estimate of wall friction values is needed.

Also in the case of vibrations, due to stick–slip effects, internal arch formation or flow patterns oscillating between mass and funnel flow, wall friction plays an important role.

3 *Influence on wear* Although the wear rate is dependent on the surface characteristics of both solid and wall material, it is the combination of sliding speed and wall friction that generates the friction power.

The relative wear pattern for two mass flow silos is given in Fig. 2.5.1, indicating the possibilities for zones of high wear.

2.5.3 Parameters with influence on wall friction

The wall friction is generally dependent on three groups of parameters:

1 *Bulk solid characteristics*: particle size and distribution, moisture content, shape and hardness, surface chemistry, surface morphology, temperature, etc.
2 *Wall surface characteristics*: roughness and hardness, adhesion behaviour, chemical composition, etc.
3 *Working conditions*: range of normal pressures, range of relative velocities, influence of time, segregation and attrition.

When measuring the wall friction groups 1 and 2 must be reflected in the right choice of relevant samples for bulk solid and wall materials. The conditions from group 3 must be taken into account by choosing the right tester, testing procedures and test conditions.

2.5.4 General views on wall friction

2.5.4.1 Definitions of wall friction angles

Wall friction plays a role in bulk solids handling whenever material may slip (or tend to slip) along a bounding surface such as a silo wall. The criterion for slip conditions can be expressed as the relation between normal and shear stresses on the wall, generally called the wall yield locus (WYL).

For an ideal Coulomb material without adhesion between bulk solid and wall, the WYL can be given as a straight line through the origin, as shown by line a in Fig. 2.5.2. In the case of adhesion, the WYL is a straight line with an offset C_w, as illustrated by line b. In many practical cases the combination of wall and bulk solid does not follow this ideal concept exactly, and a somewhat curved WYL is found, as given by line c.

From the wall yield loci as given, an angle of wall friction φ_w can be defined. In case of line a, a constant value can be derived from the angle between the WYL and the σ-axis. For materials as given by the lines b and c two possibilities exist. One can define a friction angle from the slope of the line, which can be constant or vary somewhat with the curvature. The problem with this definition is that in fact a kind of constant value for the friction is suggested, while in reality the ratio $\tau_w/\sigma_w = \tan\varphi_w$ is not a constant, but depends on the relevant normal stress level.

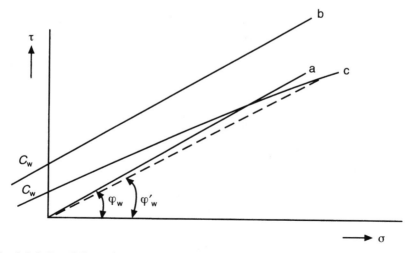

Fig. 2.5.2 Possibilities for wall yield loci and related friction angles.

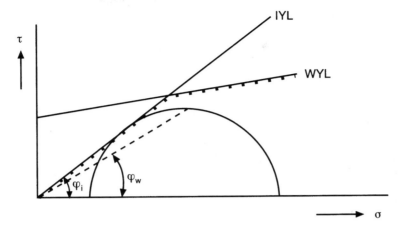

Fig. 2.5.3 Yield locus for rough wall.

For that reason it is more convenient to define the angle of wall friction as the inclination of the line from the origin to the point of interest on the WYL, indicated as φ'_w in the figure. This definition has the main advantage that in all cases the real ratio of shear to normal stress, leading to failure along the wall, is meant.

In some cases it might be possible, due to adhesion, that the wall friction angle is higher than the internal friction angle φ_i, given as the inclination of the internal yield locus (IYL) in Fig. 2.5.3. In these cases it is argued that a thin layer of material sticks to the wall, and failure takes place along this layer. This situation is called a rough surface. The complete WYL takes the shape of the dotted line in the figure.

For these cases Jenike (1970) suggests taking the wall friction angle somewhat smaller than the internal friction angle, due to smoothing of the static adhering layer. This leads to $\tan \varphi_w = \sin \varphi_i$, the stress situation as given for the top point of the drawn Mohr circle, which means a plane of maximum deformation.

2.5.4.2 Wall friction as treated in silo codes

In silo codes, dealing with loads on the bottom and walls, it is accepted nowadays that wall friction depends on the wall/bulk solid combination.

For instance in the German code DIN 1055, Part 6 (1987) three types of walls are distinguished: smooth, intermediate and rough. For the bulk solids in this code, a value for each of the three walls is given. These values, however, are only meant for load calculations, and have limited application to ascertain the type of flow. It is recommended in the commentary to the code to measure the wall friction with, for instance, a shear tester on the relevant wall/bulk solid combination in case more accurate values are needed.

Also in the commentary on the code of the American Concrete Institute (1977), values of the wall friction against concrete and steel are given for some materials, but it is stated there too that real values should be measured under the relevant conditions.

In the current version of Eurocode 1 (ENV 1991-4, 1995) values of the wall friction are given for 10 bulk solids, against steel and concrete. It is, however, recommended that those values are considered as mean values and only used as a simplified approach for calculating silo loads. They must be increased by a factor of 1.15, or decreased by 0.9, to produce the most unfavourable loading situations on a silo structure. It is also noted that the friction values are better measured on representative samples in appropriate conditions.

The same is true for the first edition of the International Standard ISO 11697 (1995) where the friction coefficients are given against a smooth wall (e.g. steel, aluminium) and may be increased by 0.1 in the case of a rough wall.

2.5.5 Measurement of wall friction

In this section only those testers which are or might be suitable for the field of bulk solids handling are discussed.

2.5.5.1 *The Jenike shear tester*

This tester (Jenike, 1970) is generally used to measure the flow properties and wall friction of bulk solids. The set-up for determination of wall friction is given in Fig. 2.5.4. In this tester a relevant sample of the bulk solid, enclosed by a stiff metal ring and vertically loaded by dead weight, is

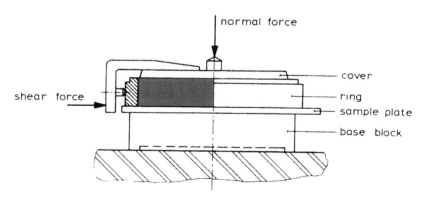

Fig. 2.5.4 Jenike shear tester for wall friction tests.

sheared over a steady sample plate. The general principle is to measure the shear load at a constant sliding speed as function of a series of increasing or decreasing loads. This leads to points of a wall yield locus (Fig. 2.5.3) from which the wall friction angle can be derived.

With the Jenike tester the wall friction at the start of sliding (quasi-static) and at continuous sliding (kinematic) can be measured. Also the influence of time on adhesion (caking effect) can be established. The measuring procedure for the tester is well described by Jenike (1970) and in a publication of the EFChE (1989).

Although the tester is easy to handle and gives reproducible results, there are some drawbacks that should be mentioned:

- A rather low and constant shearing velocity (1 or 2.5 mm/s), so the influence of the velocity cannot be measured.
- The dimensions of the test cell (100 mm diam.) restrict the maximum size of particles to 4 mm.
- A limited displacement of the bulk solid relative to the wall plate (<10 mm) and a limited range for vertical pressures from 0.5 to about 25 kPa.
- Rather poor means of letting the bulk material/wallplate run in. The procedure for running in for this tester is to rub the material firmly on to the surface of the wall sample. However, in normal storage situations large quantities of fresh material slide along the silo walls over time, thereby possibly changing the surface. The friction may be decreased due to a smoothing effect of the bulk solid, or increased by the deposition of a material layer on the surface of the plate. These effects cannot be measured by this tester.

It is worth noting that, although this tester is a commonly used apparatus for measuring wall friction, there does not exist a kind of reference bulk solid/wall sample combination with standard results for wall friction. Reference material does exist for internal flow properties (BCR 116, 1994).

2.5.5.2 Rotational shear testers

The main difference with this type of tester if compared with the Jenike tester is that the ring containing the bulk material rotates relative to the sample plate. The bulk solid particles slide along circular paths over the plate, which makes possible an unlimited strain. Various types of these testers exist, of which the one described by Peschl (1981) is the best known and is also commercially available. A possible drawback of this apparatus is the rather low and standard speed, but this can be improved, which should also permit a sufficient running-in procedure. With this type of tester the influence of time on frictional behaviour could be established, but serious drawbacks in this case are the variation of sliding speed along the radius and the fact that the bulk solid is not continuously refreshed.

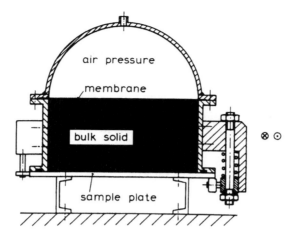

Fig. 2.5.5 Van den Berg and Scarlett tester.

2.5.5.3 Van den Bergh and Scarlett's wall friction tester

The basic idea of this tester is given in Fig. 2.5.5. The sample is enclosed in a steel housing and pressed against a sample baseplate by means of a rubber membrane activated by compressed air. The sample reciprocates over the baseplate at a stroke of 600 mm with constant, but variable, mean speed of 0.01–0.045 m/s, and vertical pressures ranging from zero up to 60 kPa.

The tester was developed to study the influence of attrition of particles on wall friction (van den Berg and Scarlett, 1986) but of course can be used for normal or time wall-friction tests. A drawback might be the reciprocal movement and the fact that the material is not refreshed. The tester can also be used in a vertical position or even upside down. In the last case the percolation away from the wall of particles arising from attrition will probably be of interest.

2.5.5.4 The Newcastle–Twente tester

These testers were developed through cooperation of the bulk solids groups of both universities. The idea of the Twente tester (Haaker, 1988; Haaker, Rozeboom and Verel, 1989) is given in Fig. 2.5.6; the Newcastle tester is somewhat different (Roberts, Ooms and Wiche, 1988; Roberts, Sollie and de Silva, 1992) but is built from the same principle.

A flat belt conveyor with a rough belt continuously withdraws bulk solid from a small silo. The thickness of the layer on the belt can be controlled by the adjustable front opening in the silo. On the moving material rests a horizontal holding plate under which the test specimen of

Wall friction and wear testing

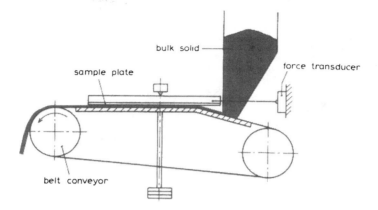

Fig. 2.5.6 Schematic drawing of Twente tester.

about 600 × 100 mm is attached. The holder with test plate is prevented from moving in a horizontal direction by two parallel steel wires, attached to a force transducer which measures the horizontal shear force.

The holder is vertically loaded by dead weight through a yoke and weight hanger. In order to ease the entrance of the bulk solid in the gap between conveyor belt and test plate, and to avoid collisions with the front of the holder, the first part of the belt is sloped. The range of vertical pressures feasible with the dead weight device is about 1–25 kPa, but can be extended if necessary by, for instance, a hydraulic device. The range of the sliding velocity is 0.003–0.023 m/s. With this tester the influence of sliding velocity, layer thickness, time, normal load and run-in procedures can be established. Some results have already been published.

2.5.5.5 The Newcastle large diameter wall friction tester

This tester was developed to measure wall friction of materials with a wide size distribution under normal stresses ranging from tensile to compressive stresses. The general construction is given in Fig. 2.5.7 (Scott and Keys, 1992).

The advantages over the Jenike shear tester are the wide cell diameter of 300 mm, allowing for particle sizes up to 25 mm, the speed ranging from 1 to 100 mm/min horizontal shear, and the range of normal stresses which allow measurement of shear under tensile loads up to compressive loads of 100 kPa.

Results with the tester have been published, indicating the influence of normal stresses, particle size, increasing or decreasing stresses. Comparison with measurements from a Jenike tester under the same conditions led to essentially the same results.

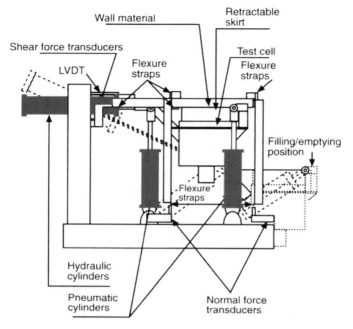

Fig. 2.5.7 The Newcastle large diameter tester.

2.5.6 Research into influencing parameters

The influence of several parameters on wall friction as mentioned in section 2.5.3 has been investigated and published, but not yet completely understood.

Roberts, Ooms and Wiche (1988) and Roberts, Sollie and de Silva (1992) report the influence on particle size, moisture content, surface roughness and the influence of vibrations on the frictional behaviour. From their results some qualitative conclusions can be drawn. Smooth surfaces generally produce low friction angles; increase of surface roughness produces higher wall friction for a bulk material with a range of particle sizes. For a fixed or limited size distribution the wall friction values depend on the relative roughness, particle size and surface roughness.

In the Australian code (AS 3774, 1990) wall roughness is taken into account. They distinguish four types of walls with increasing roughness, from polished through smooth and rough to corrugated. Friction angles with lower and upper bound are given for these walls for about 28 bulk solids, to be used for load calculations.

The moisture content of the bulk solids also has an effect on wall friction in most situations. It is generally assumed that wall friction increases with increasing moisture content, up to a certain level. From that point on, generally related to the point of saturation, the wall friction decreases, due to the lubricating effect of the liquid. Scott and Keys (1992) give examples of the influence of moisture. However, no general relation between (relative) moisture content and frictional behaviour is known.

2.5.7 Wear due to the solid wall contacts

The wear of walls of silos for bulk solids is amply discussed by among others Roberts (1986a, b) and Johanson (Johanson and Royal, 1980). The abrasive wear rate for a given bulk solid/wall combination is assumed to be a function of the normal pressure, the sliding velocity and the wall friction coefficient. Relative zones of possible high wear were presented in Fig. 2.5.1. The absolute wear is a function of the characteristics of both bulk solid and wall, like hardness, smoothness, etc. and the frictional power, related to normal pressure and velocity. In Fig. 2.5.8 a velocity versus pressure curve is given for two arbitrarily chosen mass flow silos.

It is clear from this figure that two distinct zones exist in the relation of velocity to pressure. The first represents the cylinder and upper part of the hopper in which the pressure ranges from zero to the peak values at the transition to the hopper, while the velocities are low and approximately constant. The second zone represents the situation towards the outlet where the pressures are much lower but the velocities increase to high values. Testers to predict the values of wear must by preference work in the velocity and pressure ranges as given in this figure.

A lot of wear testers are known; Roberts (1986a, b) and Haaker, Rozeboom and Verel (1989) give a more detailed discussion. The testers

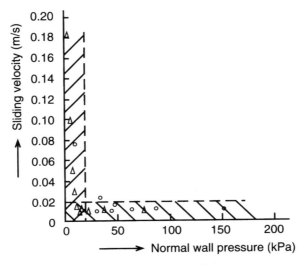

Fig. 2.5.8 Velocity/pressure curve for mass flow silos.

that reflect the actual silo conditions the best, with regard to pressures, velocities, refreshment of the bulk solid, etc., seem to be the belt testers according to the Newcastle/Twente principle (Fig. 2.5.6). However, the problem with this tester is possibly the time behaviour. When abrasive wear over longer periods, say a couple of weeks and longer, must be established, it seems not very efficient to let the testers run over these long periods. So it is required to accelerate the wear process in the tester without changing the actual wear mechanism that has to be simulated by the test. At this moment more experimental and theoretical work is needed into ways of decreasing the testing time.

It is worth noting that in 1994 a project on wall friction was started, in which 13 European and 2 Australian labs are involved. Measurements on nine combinations of wall sample plates and bulk solids (all from the same source) are performed on Jenike shear testers, following an exact prescribed procedure.

The aim of the project is to compare the results from the various laboratories and to validate this particular test method, with regard to reliability and applicability. In further phases of the project other test methods will be the subject of comparable measurements.

2.5.8 Conclusion

Although it is recognized nowadays that wall friction and related wear play an important role in the reliability of storage and transport processes, or in process engineering in general, there is still a lack of knowledge in this field. There is need for more research in order to understand the phenomena of wall friction and the role of the various parameters that are involved. Both theoretical and empirical work is needed to gain better insight in the reliability and applicability of the various testers and methods that are available in this field. Also new or enhanced kinds of testers or methods must be developed to cover the conditional areas where the present test methods fall short.

References

American Concrete Institute (1977) Code ACI-313-77, revised 1983 *Recommended Practice for Design and Construction of Bins, Silos etc.* . . . with commentary.
AS (Australian Standard) (1990) *Loads on Bulk Solid Containers.* AS 3774-1990, Published by Standards Australia, Sydney.
BCR (Community Bureau of Reference of the European Commission) (1994) *Reference Materials.* Report EUR 14022 EN, Luxembourg.
EFChE (1989) *Standard Shear Testing Technique SSTT,* Report from the EFChE, Working Party on the Mechanics of Particulate Solids, published by The Institution of Chemical Engineers.
ENV 1991-4 (1995) *Basis of Design and Actions on Structures,* Part 4: *Actions in Silos and Tanks,* draft, Sept. CEN, Brussels.

German Code DIN 1055 (1987) Part 6, *Loads in Silos*, May, with commentary. Berlin.
Haaker G. (1988) Measurement of wall friction and wear in bulk solids handling, *Proc. Symp. Silos Forschung und Praxis*, Karlsruhe, pp. 389–403.
Haaker G., Rozeboom J., Verel W. (1989) A study into wallfriction and wear in bulk solids handling, *Aufber. techn.* **30**(3), 122–129.
International Standard ISO 11697 (1995-E). *Basis for Design of Structures. Loads due to Bulk Materials*.
Janssen H.A. (1895) Getreidedruck in Silozellen, *Z. Ver. Dt. Ing.* **39**, 1045–1049.
Jenike A.W. (1970) *Storage and Flow of Solids*, Bulletin 123, Utah Engng Exp. Station, Univ. Utah, Salt Lake City, revised 1986.
Johanson J.R., Royal T.A. (1980) Measuring and use of wear properties for predicting life of materials handling equipment. *Wear* **60**, 111–121.
Peschl I.A.S.Z. (1981) New developments in the field of shear test equipment and their application in industry. *Proc. Int. Symp. Powd. Techn.*, Kyoto, pp. 150–164.
Roberts A.W. (1986a) *Surface Friction, Adhesion and Wear Characteristics in Bulk Solids Handling Equipment*. Research report, Univ. of Twente, Jan.
Roberts A.W. (1986b) *Abrasive Wear Testing Analysis in Bulk Solids Handling*. Research report, Univ. of Twente, Jan.
Roberts A.W., Ooms M., Wiche S.J. (1988) Concepts of boundary friction and wear in bulk solids handling operations. *Int. Jnl. of Bulk Solids Handling*, **10**(2), May, 189–198.
Roberts A.W., Sollie L.A., de Silva S.R. (1992) The interaction of bulk solid characteristics and surface parameters in friction measurements. *Proc. Symp. Attrition and Wear*, Utrecht, Oct., pp. 275–290.
Scott O.J., Keys S. (1992) The variation of boundary friction for granular products. *Proc. Int. Conf. on Bulk Materials*, Wollongong, Australia pp. 279–286.
Van den Berg W.J.B., Scarlett B. (1986) Experimental investigation of factors affecting the wall friction of brittle particulate solids. *Proc. First Int. Congr. Part. Techn.*, Nuremberg, Part 3, pp. 241–256.

2.6 The relevance of aeration and fluidization
D. Höhne and B. Scarlett

2.6.1 Introduction – the relevance for silo design

The material contained in a hopper is usually under a relatively high stress and is moving slowly. However, at the discharge outlet the bulk solid may be in an aerated or even fluidized state. The flow characteristics of the material can then be completely changed; some aerated powders flow like water, others never attain such a state. It is important to take into account such behaviour in the design of hoppers for three main reasons.

The most important is the phenomenon of 'flooding', which occurs when the material becomes excessively aerated and so the powder flow cannot be controlled. Sometimes a rapid flow of the material is itself sufficient to cause the dilation resulting in a counter-flow of air into the hopper. Otherwise, the problem may be intermittent. This arises due to a breakdown of arches or ratholes or due to segregation according to particle size in the hopper.

The second reason for taking aeration properties into consideration is the design of pneumatic discharge aids. One technique is to add air through 'fluidizing' pads mounted in the walls of the hopper. An even more drastic device blasts jets of air into the outlet in order to try to break an arch. Sometimes these devices are successful, sometimes they do more harm than good.

The third reason is the correct choice of discharge devices. If the flow is to be controlled by a discharging device such as a rotary feeder or a discharge screw, then the material must flow sufficiently smoothly.

Besides silo design, knowledge of aeration properties of powders is important in the design of other technological apparatuses like air-assisted

The relevance of aeration and fluidization

conveying systems, aerated or fluidized bed reactors or mills and air classifiers.

A differentiation should be made between the aerated and the fluidized state. In the literature a powder is said to be fluidized when the fluid flow exceeds the minimum fluidizing velocity. This is, however, an arbitrary definition and does not relate well to physical reality. In this section we shall define the state as aerated when the gas velocity is lower than the fully supported velocity and as fluidized when the velocity is larger than that value (Fig. 2.6.3). Because of this difference, some confusion may arise in relation to the literature, but the terminology is suggested because a subdivision which has direct physical meaning will ultimately be more useful.

2.6.2 Resistance laws for the permeation of packed beds

When packed beds are permeated by gas and are constrained to dilate, three different regimes can be distinguished. Dependent on gas velocity and thus on the Reynolds number they are the laminar, turbulent and transition areas.

In laminar flow the energy within the gas is consumed by the viscosity. In turbulent flow, however, the energy is used for the reorganization of the single vortex areas and is determined mostly by the fluid density.

The following parameters of the bulk solid influence the pressure drop over the height of the packed bed:

- the particle size and shape distributions
- the average porosity and the pore size distribution
- the particle roughness
- the adsorption state on the particle surface

Laminar flow conditions usually occur when a fine bulk material is permeated. In this case the pressure gradient is linearly dependent on the fluid velocity according to Darcy (1856):

$$v_f = \frac{k}{\eta_f} \frac{\Delta p}{H}$$

where v_f is the gas velocity, k the permeability, η_f the viscosity, Δp the pressure gradient and H the height of the bed.

If the porosity is homogeneous, however, it is possible with the Carman–Kozeny equation (Carman, 1937) to estimate the permeability of the bulk material from its specific surface area and porosity.

The models of Gupte (1970), based on dimensional analysis, as well as those of Molerus, Pahl and Rumpf (1971), which extended the investigations of Gupte, result in the same order of magnitude as predicted by the Carman–Kozeny equation. The model of Pärnt (1986), however, predicts higher pressure gradients since the particle shape is also considered. Pärnt's

90 Bulk solids testing

results correspond with the results of the models mentioned above for spherical particles.

The models postulated by Ergun (1952) and Molerus (1982a) are also valid for turbulent flow conditions. Whereas the theory of Ergun is based on experiments, the equation of Molerus is derived from theoretical considerations of the drag force and the interparticle forces.

2.6.3 Fluidization properties

Geldart (1973) has postulated that the fluidization behaviour of any powder–gas system falls into one of four groups. These groups are defined largely by the mean particle size of the powder and the difference between the particle density ρ_p and the fluid density ρ_f (Fig. 2.6.1).

Group A powders require only small amounts of air to become fluidized. They have small mean particle sizes and low particle densities (up to $1400\,kg/m^3$). These powders show considerable expansion between the minimum fluidizing velocity and the 'minimum bubbling velocity'. Bubbles rise more rapidly than the interstitial gas velocity. When the air supply is suddenly shut off, the bed collapses slowly.

Group B encompasses most materials with a mean particle size of 40–500 µm and a density range of about 1400–$4000\,kg/m^3$. The minimum fluidization velocities are appreciable (about 0.02–0.30 m/s) and bubbling occurs immediately after attaining fluidization. In this state the bed bubbles freely. Collapse of the bed is rapid when the fluid flow is shut off.

Group C powders are cohesive. The injected gas tends to form channels and thus such powders are difficult to fluidize. On the other hand, once they

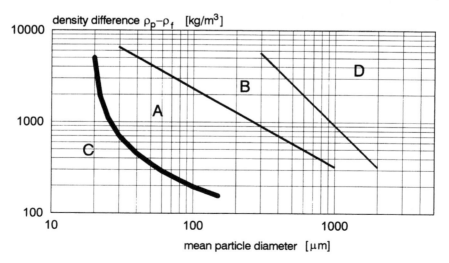

Fig. 2.6.1 Powder classification diagram for fluidization by air according to Geldart (1973).

become fluidized, the air is retained for long periods. Such powders will readily arch over a hopper outlet when deaerated. The difficulties in fluidizing group C powders arise because the interparticle forces are much greater than those which the fluid can exert on to the particles.

Group D powders are in general rather coarse, of high density and high permeability to the flow of gases. They can be used in spouted beds and, when dry, they give few problems in hoppers. They certainly do not flood.

In particular, in the transition from group C to group A or from group A to group B, no sharp boundaries are observed, though transitional regimes are obeyed.

Using Geldart's plot various researchers have investigated the criteria by which the various classes can be discriminated. The consensus of opinion is that the behaviour of powders can be explained in terms of the relative importance of their interparticle forces. This explains the clustering of the data: the density difference and the mean particle size are supposed to be reasonable indicators of fluid drag and interparticle forces.

Molerus (1982b) showed that a reasonable distinction can be made between classes C and A as well as between A and B by assuming that the criterion is a certain ratio of the interparticle forces and the fluid drag force.

Other investigators have concentrated on correlating the minimum fluidization and the minimum bubbling point with the mean particle size. Thonglimp, Hiquily and Laguerie (1984) have given an extensive review of all the published correlations.

The mean particle size can only give a rough indication of the forces involved in these correlations. Therefore, sometimes it is advantageous to use another weighting factor for the particle size in order to give a proper estimate of the effect of the distribution of the size on the interparticle forces. Alternatively, Piepers *et al.* (1984) defined a cohesion number using the angle of inclination which a bed can sustain at the minimum fluidizing velocity. Using this cohesion number and also a dimensionless number for the fluid drag he derived a new plot in which the boundaries between the classes are defined more clearly.

2.6.4 Characterization of the flow properties of bulk solids in the aerated state

Knowledge of the flow properties of aerated or fluidized powders is needed for the description or the control of the behaviour of bulk solids in technological equipment when air is introduced into the bulk material for a number of operations:

- discharge from storage hoppers or bins
- flow conditions in air-assisted gravity conveying systems
- transport behaviour in fluidized bed reactors, drum mills, air classifiers, etc.

The methods used for characterization of powder flow properties in the aerated state can be divided into three groups:

1. Empirical methods in simple test devices which simulate some important process condition to find a correlation between the test result and the behaviour of the bulk solid in this process.
2. Test methods adopted from fluid mechanics using the analogy in the flow behaviour of liquids and unconsolidated aerated powders.
3. Attempts to use measuring techniques of powder mechanics, such as shear cells, for the characterization of the flow properties of consolidated and aerated powders.

The variety in group 1 is very wide as it is also known for the characterization of unaerated powders (Schwedes, 1968). It is possible, for example, to determine the angle of repose in an aerated drum (Judd and Dixon, 1979; Donsi et al., 1984), to measure the discharge time of a powder from an aerated model hopper (Muschelknautz, 1979), or to estimate the length of a powder stream which is formed by the flow of a certain mass of this powder on to a fluidized chute (Fischer, 1967). The results of these test methods are valuable only when a correlation has been proved between the interesting process behaviour and the measuring values.

It has been confirmed in many studies that aerated powders behave in a liquid manner. This gives the possibility for the application of different types of viscometers to characterize the flow behaviour (group 2). Several authors used modified rotary viscometers equipped with a permeable bottom to aerate the powder during the test (Bagnold, 1954; Baylard and Inman, 1979; Savage et al., 1983).

Gottschalk (1984) modified a rotary viscometer taking into account the experience of Schügerl, Merz and Fetting (1961). He characterized the flow properties of quartz powders of different particle size distribution but could only achieve acceptable measurements in the completely fluidized state. A strong reduction of the shear stress with increasing air velocity was reported. This effect becomes more evident with decreasing particle size. The dependency on the shear rate showed a pseudoplastic behaviour in the range of small shear gradients, changing into a dilatant behaviour at higher gradients.

Lloyd and Webb (1987) used a viscometer of the Couette type making possible the measurement at air velocities smaller than the minimum fluidization velocity. It was found for alumina powder that small quantities of air greatly reduce the transmitted shear stress. The rate of this reduction with increased aeration is dependent on the fine particle content; the higher the proportion of fines the greater the reduction. Regarding the shear velocity, the powders exhibit two flow regimes. At low shear velocities, the shear stress is rate independent ('powder-like'). At higher velocities, the shear stress is a function of shear velocity ('liquid-like'). It was obvious that the addition of fine particles reduces the rate-independent region.

The relevance of aeration and fluidization

Hobbel and Scarlett (1985, 1987) also investigated the general consistency of aerated systems using Couette viscometer design; see also Scarlett and Hobbel (1985). The cylinders were made of gauze to eliminate slip and disturbance of the delicate structure. The consistency proved to be a function of the gas velocity and the speeds of both cylinders. In the low shear rate region the resistance diminished as the shear rate increased. This is called the mobilizing region, the decrease in resistance being due to the shearing of the bed and to vibrations introduced by the cylinders. As the shear rate is increased beyond the mobilizing region the resistance is relatively insensitive to the deformation rate, a situation comparable to the Coulomb behaviour of compressed powders. This interaction of the two state variables fluidizing air and particle shear rate is illustrated in Fig. 2.6.2.

Botterill and Abdul-Halim (1979) used a fluidized open channel for the determination of the 'viscosity' of powders by measuring the shear stresses

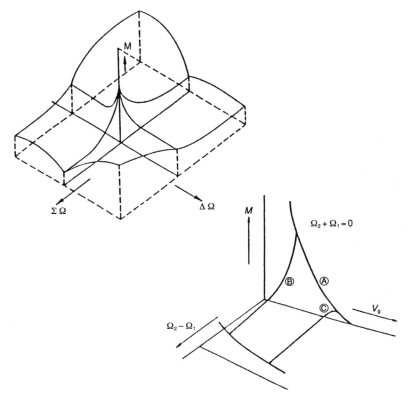

Fig. 2.6.2 The consistency of aerated powders as measured in a powder viscometer, according to Hobbel and Scarlett (1985). Ω_1 = speed inner cylinder, $\Delta\Omega = \Omega_2 - \Omega_1$, $\Sigma\Omega = \Omega_2 + \Omega_1$. Above: the torque as a function of the speed of both cylinders. Below: the consistency regions as a function of gas velocity. A = yield stress, B = mobilizing region, C = fluid region.

at the wall and at the bottom. They observed a strong reduction of the apparent viscosity with incipient aeration at gas velocities lower than the minimum fluidization velocity. After passing a minimum the viscosity increased with further growing gas velocity. Botterill determined both pseudoplastic and dilatant behaviour of the powders depending on the shear rate.

The rheological parameters make possible the description of the transport behaviour of unconsolidated freely flowing powders, e.g. in drum mills (Gottschalk and Husemann, 1989).

The relationship between aeration conditions and the flow properties of slightly consolidated powders is regarded as a precondition for the improvement of the design procedure of pneumatic discharge aids in silos. However, the measurement of the flow properties of consolidated powders undergoing aeration in a shear cell seems to be very complicated.

At present there is only one known successful attempt, by Runge *et al.* (1992), to measure the wall friction angle using a Jenike shear cell by aerating the powder sample through the wall material plate tested. A new research project is being prepared to measure the flow properties of consolidated powders in the aerated state by using a ring shear cell (Höhne, 1995) and simultaneously considering the influence of adsorbed layers. The aim is to relate the aeration properties to the interparticle forces of the fine-grained material.

2.6.5 Fluidizing curve

Aeratability of powders can be determined from a careful examination of the fluidizing curve of the material. Imagine an ideal powder in a bed subjected to gas flow from below. As the gas flow increases, starting from a packed bed, the pressure drop grows linearly until the entire weight of the bed is supported. At that point, the supporting point, the bed expands to release the stress due to the increasing flow. The pressure drop across the bed is constant and equal to the weight per unit area of the bed.

Decreasing the flow, the bed contracts until the minimum fluidizing point is reached and the powder returns to its original dense packing. The expansion and contraction curves coincide with no hysteresis. This is the feature of an ideal powder. The procedure is illustrated in Fig. 2.6.3 by the solid line.

A real powder does have interparticle attraction and friction forces. Any change in the relative position of the particles is counteracted by these forces. Due to this hindrance the bed resists any change and a marked hysteresis between expansion and contraction curves occurs. The contraction curve (dashed line in Fig. 2.6.3) lies below the expansion line because the interparticle forces create a residual structure in the bed. The more cohesive the powder and the larger the interparticle forces the greater the hysteresis and the larger the transition region between packed bed and fully supported fluidized bed.

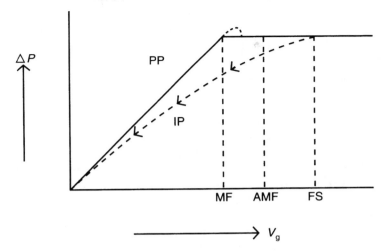

Fig. 2.6.3 Pressure drop vs. fluidizing gas velocity.

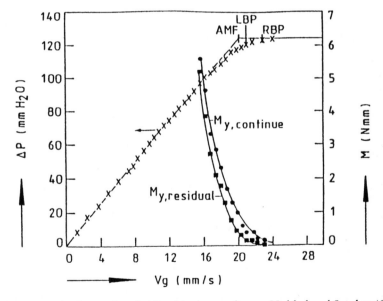

Fig. 2.6.4 Residual stress in a fluidized bed according to Hobbel and Scarlett (1985).

This is illustrated in Fig. 2.6.4 where the measurements of the residual stress in a bed are plotted on to the fluidizing curve. The residual stress only disappears completely when the bed is fully supported even though the fluidization and bubbling began earlier.

Distinguishing A and B powders or, more importantly, aeratable powders and very aeratable powders within class A, is a little more subtle. In most powders the bubbling point starts somewhat before the bed is fully fluidized but it tends to occur locally in established channels. This is the point marked LBP in the figure, meaning local bubbling point. Later the bubbles occur randomly throughout the bed, the point RBP. The nearer these two points occur, the more aeratable is the powder.

2.6.6 Conclusions

The flow properties of powders in the dilated state vary widely. In general very small particles lead to cohesive behaviour and very large particles flow more easily under gravity. Most powders lie in the region between these two and exhibit varying degrees of propensity to aerate. Powders which have a small particle size combined with low interparticle forces are clearly designated Geldart A powders and they tend to exhibit flooding behaviour at the outlet of hoppers. As the behaviour moves towards Geldart B class then the aeratability becomes less and eventually the powder is not suitable for some discharge devices.

Estimating the degree of aeratability is, at present, best achieved by carefully examining the fluidization curve. In the longer term, it should be possible to develop a much more scientific, quantitative measure and to relate it to the basic interparticle forces.

References

Bagnold, R.A. (1954), Experimental studies on a gravity free dispersion of large solids spheres in a Newtonian fluid under shear, *Proc. Royal Soc.*, 49–63

Baylard, J.A. and Inman, D.L. (1979), A reexamination of Bagnold's granular-fluid model and bed load transport equation, *J. Geophys. Res.*, 84, 7827–7833

Botterill, J.S.M. and Abdul-Halim, B.H. (1979), The open channel flow of fluidized solids, *Powder Technology*, 23, 67–78

Carman, P.C. (1937), Fluid flow through granular beds, *Trans. Am. Inst. Chem. Engrs.*, 15, 150–166

Darcy, H. (1856), *Les Fontaines de la Ville de Dijon*, Victor Dalmont, Paris

Donsi, G. et al. (1984), The measurement of characteristic angles of powders in the prediction of their behaviour in the gas fluidized state, *Powder Technology*, 37, 39–47

Ergun, S. (1952), Fluid flow through packed columns, *Chem. Engg. Progr.*, 48, 2, 89–94

Fischer, W. (1967), Fließverhalten von Zement, *Zement-Kalk-Gips*, 20, 4, 138–139

Geldart, D. (1973), Types of gas fluidization, *Powder Technology*, 7, 285

Gottschalk, J. (1984), Rheologische Untersuchungen an aufgelockerten Pulverschüttungen, *Freiberger Forschungshefte*, A 694, 63–81

Gottschalk, J. and Husemann, K. (1989), On characterization of conveying processes in ball mills by rheological parameters, *Powder Technology*, 58, 131–135

Gupte, A.R. (1970), Experimentelle Untersuchung der Einflüsse von Porosität und Korngrößenverteilung im Widerstandsgesetz der Porenströmung, Diss., Univ. Karlsruhe

Hobbel, E.F. and Scarlett, B. (1985), Measurement of the flow behaviour of aerated and fluidized powders using a rotating viscometer, *Particle Characterization*, 2, 154–159

Hobbel, E.F. and Scarlett, B. (1987), Experimental investigation of the effect of particle size distribution on the flow characteristics of a homogeneously fluidized bed, *Proc. 12th Annual Powder and Bulk Solids Conf.*, Rosemont, Ill., 93–101

Höhne, D. (1995), Influence of adsorbed layers on the flow properties of gas permeated fine powders, Project in *Special Research Area No. 285* of the Deutsche Forschungsgemeinschaft, TU Bergakademie Freiberg

Judd, M.R. and Dixon, P.D. (1979), The effect of aeration on the flowability of powders, *Transact. Inst. of Chem. Engineers*, London, 57, 1, 67–69

Lloyd, P.J. and Webb, P.J. (1987), The flooding of a powder – the importance of particle size distribution, *Powder Technology*, 51, 125–133

Molerus, O. (1982a), *Fluid-Feststoff-Strömungen*, Springer-Verlag, Berlin

Molerus, O. (1982b), Interpretation of Geldart's type A, B, C and D powders by taking into account interparticle cohesion forces, *Powder Technology*, 33, 81–87

Molerus, O., Pahl, M.H. and Rumpf, H. (1971), Die Porositätsfunktion in empirischen Gleichungen für den Durchströmungswiderstand im Bereich Re < 1, *Chemie-Ing.-Techn.*, 43, 6, 376–378

Muschelknautz, E. (1979), *Die Berechnung der pneumatischen Fließförderung*, Transmatic Vol. II, Krauskopf-Verlag, Mainz

Pärnt, A. (1986), Über den Einfluß von Verfahrensparametern auf das Durchströmungsverhalten von feinkörnigen Schüttgütern, Diss., Bergakademie Freiberg

Piepers, H.W., Cottaar, E.J.E., Verkooijen, A.H.H. and Rietema, K. (1984), Effects of pressure and type of gas on particle–particle interaction and the consequences for gas–solid fluidization, *Powder Technology*, 37, 55–70

Runge, J. et al. (1992), Vorrichtung zur Bestimmung der Wandreibung von Schüttgütern (Device for the determination of wall friction), *Patent DD 300 390*

Savage, S.B., Nedderman, R.M., Tüzün, U. and Houlsby, G.T. (1983), The flow of granular materials, part 3: Rapid shear flows, *Chem. Engg. Sci.*, 36, 189

Scarlett, B. and Hobbel, E.F. (1985), Stress–strain behaviour of aerated powders, *Proc. Symp. Reliable Flow of Particulate Solids*, Bergen, Norway, 46–61

Schügerl, K., Merz, M. and Fetting, F. (1961), Rheologische Eigenschaften von gasdurchströmten Fließbettsystemen, *Chem. Engg. Sci.*, 15, 1–38

Schwedes, J. (1968), *Fließverhalten von Schüttgütern in Bunkern*, Verlag Chemie, Weinheim

Thonglimp, V., Hiquily, N. and Laguerie, C. (1984), Vitesse minimale de fluidisation et expansion des couches fluidisées par un gaz, *Powder Technology*, 38, 233–253

2.7 The application of bulk solids testers in industry

E.J. Puik, J. Kater and P.J. Reuderink

2.7.1 Solids flow determination

The design of storage silos, solids containing reactors and their internals relates strongly to the failure behaviour of the bulk solid. In its turn, the failure behaviour is strongly dependent on the characteristics of the individual particles comprising the powder. Obviously, the surface characteristics of the particles (shape, size, friction and cohesiveness) as well as body characteristics (elasticity, density) are of importance. A scientific question of interest has always been which parameter or combinations of parameters determine(s) the failure behaviour of a powder. To find the answer is not only very difficult, but also very time consuming. Instead the scientific and industrial community focused on determination of the failure behaviour in terms of a few bulk powder parameters, in which the effects of the individual particles are lumped.

These bulk powder parameters, like internal angle of friction, wall friction and cohesiveness, can be measured with several types of shear testers, which have been (and still are being) developed, tested and used.

The main purpose of this section is not to make an elaborate comparison between the various types of testers, but to indicate limitations and needs for further improvement based on our industrial experience with Jenike and annular shear cell testers (see sections 2.7.3 to 2.7.5). Nevertheless, some remarks with respect to the comparison between Jenike and annular shear testers viewed from an industrial perspective should and will be made (section 2.7.2). For a detailed comparison of the testers the interested reader is referred to sections 2.1 and 2.2.

2.7.2 Jenike and annular shear testers in an industrial perspective

The main advantage of the annular (Carr and Walker, 1967) over the Jenike (1964) shear tester is the unlimited shear distance. In most of the cases the shear distance in the Jenike shear cell is insufficient. Nevertheless, in the industrial laboratory the annular shear cell does not seem to have ousted the Jenike shear cell. Two reasons for this can be given.

First of all, many years of experience have been gained with the Jenike shear tester. The limitations of this tester are familiar and a way to interpret its results has been found. In the many comparison studies (Wilms and Schwedes, 1988) the annular shear tester produces similar results to those of the Jenike tester. However, standardization of the annular shear tester is still hindered by questions concerning aspects like slip along the top lid and the distribution of the force field. Second, advice on flow behaviour is frequently based on comparison with earlier results obtained for powders with a well-known behaviour in plants. Earlier results in this context always refer to those measured with Jenike testers. Both points imply: if possible stick to Jenike.

For powders which cannot be tested with a Jenike tester the following dilemma arises: how can one be sure that the annular shear tester produces the same results as a Jenike tester, and as a result, can we be sure of the validity of silo design theories for these powders? Undoubtedly, the annular shear cell has tremendous potential, but it should be proven by means of actual silo tests that it can provide data leading to critical silo design.

The remarks made above refer to the use of the Jenike versus annular and vice versa. An additional remark can be made with respect to the industrial use of shear testers in general. Studies on the performance of testers tend to pay more attention to the measurement of friction angles than to compressive strength (flow function). However, from experience one can say that it is usually easier to arrive at a design guaranteeing mass flow than to guarantee that obstructions like arching will not occur. Moreover, since the latter may cause long plant shut-downs the associated costs may be tremendous. Therefore, it is most important to put emphasis on the accuracy of flow function measurement.

2.7.3 The ideal bulk solids tester

From an industrial point of view the best bulk solids testers are those which accurately and correctly measure the flow properties of a particulate material under actual process conditions with a minimum of costs. From this definition it becomes directly evident that the 'ideal' solids tester does not exist. For the following two aspects can be regarded as bottlenecks: accurate and correct measurement and actual conditions.

Before discussing these two 'bottlenecks' a third has to be identified which is indirectly coupled to the liability of the output of a shear tester: characterization must be performed on a 'realistic sample'. Obviously, even if the ideal shear tester did exist the investigator very often does not know whether the sample to be tested resembles exactly that in the actual industrial application. Knowledge is needed about the material in the shearing regions of a vessel. The 'nature' of the solid must be known, otherwise the 'wrong' material is characterized. A typical example is the case in which a bulk solid is used in highly polluting environments of some reactors; it may be extremely difficult to obtain this knowledge. Fortunately, in the case of storage vessels the exact characteristics of the solids are more easily measured or estimated.

2.7.4 Use of non-ideal bulk solids testers

Going back to the first two bottlenecks the following remarks can be made.

2.7.4.1 Accurate and correct measurement

The first bottleneck, i.e. measuring accurately and correctly, implies that:

1. Assuming that the exact nature of the solid is known, it must be assured that during the characterization measurement it is not changed. Segregation occurring during the test may result in a local deviation from the desired particle size distribution in case of powders with broad particle size distributions. To characterize this kind of powder requires advanced testers in which the nature of the powders can be controlled. Similarly, fines generation during testing influences the powder size distribution and thus may influence the outcome of the test. Another parameter to be controlled is the moisture content, or the amount of fluid in pasty-like or slurry-like powders.
2. It is very important that the operator knows exactly what the shear tester measures. In other words, mechanical limitations of the tester must be known and if possible eliminated. Typical mechanical limitations are:
   (a) *Effects of wall friction*. In any case the unwanted effects of wall friction must be eliminated. For small diameter particles this may not be a severe problem: in this case the width of the annulus in the annular shear tester or the width of the Jenike tester is many times the particle diameter. However, if the particle size is several millimetres or larger, wall friction effects will penetrate via particle contacts deep into the sample and influence the flow throughout the full sample volume of the tester. Typically, in industrial environments powders with average particle diameters ranging from a few μm to even more than a few mm have to be character-

ized. This may be overcome by designing a tester with variable width to be set by the type of powder to be characterized, or by installation of co-rotating walls (in case of the annular shear tester). The question remains: what is the most effective and reproducible route to reduce unwanted wall effects?

(b) *Slip effects.* To ensure good grip on the powder special attention has to be given to the design of the rings in an annular shear tester. Especially in the case of a powder with a broad particle size distribution (catalyst carriers) segregation can be induced by the grip of the rings on particles in a specific size window. In the case of a very fine and cohesive powder (soot and fly ashes) grip may be reduced to zero. The question remains: what are the design rules for these rings?

(c) *Annulus shape.* Clearly, due to the different curvature at the inner and outer diameters of the annular shear cell different local networks of contact forces will be generated. Its severity on the measured flow behaviour is probably linked to the particle diameter. The question is: what is the influence of the curvature in the annular shear tester given powder parameters like the average particle size?

(d) *Low loads.* In some cases the flow behaviour of highly compressible, low bulk density powders has to be measured at low pressures. This requires a mechanical construction that actually reduces the weight of the top lid of the cell confining the sample. In characterizations which aim at a precise determination of the cohesion as a function of, for example, the batch type of a powder, extremely low normal loads may be required. Though this can be solved by redesigning the shear tester, one can argue about the most effective way.

(e) *Highly fluctuating shear forces.* In many cases powders are being characterized which consist of rather hard, inelastic particles. The shear forces measured show fluctuations with large amplitudes. Very often, it is not possible to recognize a stabilized shear force.

3 Last, but certainly not least, accurate measurement implies the exclusion of operator dependencies. In other words, the effects of filling and operation procedures must be known and understood. A strict experimental procedure must be defined which guarantees repeatability of the experiments. For non-compressive powders this is usually not an issue. However, for low density highly compressible powders the filling method can become an inevitable problem that must be solved. Procedures to create homogeneously packed powders must be defined. These procedures should be able to handle cohesive and very fine powders which can be compressed by a factor of 10 or even more (fly ashes).

2.7.4.2 Actual conditions

Enormous differences may exist between the shear tester conditions and those of the powder handling technology. One of the most important process parameters is the temperature. Many powders behave differently at different temperatures (plastics, rubbers). How do you predict the flow behaviour of fly ash at several hundred degrees Celsius from experiments at room temperature? How do you predict the flow behaviour of an elastic rubber once it has been stored for one month in an environment where temperature varies between −10 and +60°C? How do you study the agglomeration behaviour of powders close to the melting temperature? Obviously there is a need for testers operating at high temperatures, allowing fast and labour-extensive characterization.

2.7.4.3 Costs

In principle, the costs of tester equipment are relatively low compared to the labour costs involved in operating the tester. In particular, in an industrial environment in which the handling of solids is core business and thus in which the characterization of the flow behaviour of powders is a frequent activity the wish exists to minimize the labour intensity. This can be done either by use of automation or by opening new, labour-extensive routes for flow characterization. This can be regarded as a challenge for scientific and industrial communities.

2.7.5 Non-consolidated, non-steady-state flow

A serious limitation of shear testers has to do with the fact that the failure behaviour of powders is being measured in a consolidated phase. In other words, the failure characteristics are being measured of powders which correspond to a sort of steady-state powder, which is presheared and in which the particles are distributed homogeneously. This implies that no information can be obtained from transient phase flow behaviour (start-up effects) as a function of for example the initial packing density. This limitation always leads to the need to do additional solids flow tests in (scaled down) copies of a silo. These tests are usually much more expensive than shear tests; however, they are regarded as of the utmost importance. The characterization of transient phases can be regarded as an insufficiently explored case in solids handling, for which dedicated table-top diagnostic tools are not available as standard.

2.7.6 Summary

The powders handled in industrial environments show characteristics with wide ranges: the average particle size can be as small as a few μm or as large as a few mm, the particles may be highly elastic or very hard, (non-) cohesive, (non-) compressible, (non-) wet, etc. Each extreme case or, even worse, each combination of cases, causes some kind of limitations in determination of the failure behaviour of a powder. In addition, failure behaviours should preferably be measured under process conditions. And finally, information is only obtained for consolidated powders, excluding 'transient' phase kind of failure behaviour.

References

J.F. Carr, D.M. Walker, An annular shear cell for granular material, *Powd. Technol.*, 1 (1967) 369.

A.W. Jenike, *Storage and Flow of Solids*, Bull. No. 123, Utah. Engng. Exp. Station, Univ. of Utah, Salt Lake City (1964).

J. Schwedes, H. Wilms, Comparative shear tests with ring shear tester and Jenike shear tester, *Aufberietungs Technik*, 2 (1988) 53.

2.8 Classification of bulk solids
H. Wilms and B. Kühnemund

Equipment design for bulk solids handling installations requires considerations concerning the individual bulk material and its respective properties. Previous sections have outlined various possibilities of how to measure the flow properties. Other process-relevant properties such as particle size distribution, moisture content, hardness, abrasiveness, chemical stability and many others have to be measured by methods other than shear tests. Some of these more general as well as some process-related property-testing techniques are outlined by the IMechE (1994). The most important properties regarding silo design are given in Svarovsky (1987).

However, prior to measuring process-related properties such as flow properties it is advantageous to describe, characterize and identify bulk solids. This is especially helpful whenever results from different research laboratories, different research projects or different industrial producers of a certain bulk solid have to be used by many researchers or institutions. Only if all relevant general data are specified and reveal agreement is a comparison on specific properties such as flow properties permissible and may be used to assess the quality of different measurements. Only with identification in addition to flow property measurements is it possible to compare results from different laboratories, publications, research institutions and test methods. Based on a respective identification of bulk solids, future research work can be accomplished in a more systematic manner with higher efficiency, less duplication and better coordination. Test data from different institutions can be used simultaneously, by other researchers.

2.8.1 Identification and symbolization of bulk solids

The Fédération Européene de la Manutention (FEM), i.e. the European Materials Handling Equipment Manufacturers' Association, has developed some general guidelines for characterization of bulk solids, i.e. document FEM 2581, as well as recommendations for specific properties and their use in equipment design, operation and manufacturing. The general bulk properties for identification are defined in document FEM 2582. This identification consists of eight groups of characteristics represented by abbreviations:

- name of bulk solid and its chemical formula (if available)
- particle size (distribution)
- particle shape
- angle of repose
- specific properties (26 properties are listed, e.g. cohesive, abrasive, corrosive, explosive, hygroscopic, toxic, radioactive, wet, etc.)
- moisture content
- bulk density
- additional information

With respect to silos, the more specific guidelines concerning specific flow properties are given in document FEM 2381 and the properties relevant for silo design are given in FEM 2321. Thus, the total set of documents is divided into three groups, i.e. general properties (FEM 2582), specific, process-related properties (FEM 2381) and equipment- or design-related properties (FEM 2321). Respective documents exist for mechanical and pneumatic conveying as well as for respective equipment design.

These FEM documents for general description of bulk materials properties are very helpful to define or identify certain bulk solids in our industrial world (Kühnemund, 1982). Measurement techniques, customary in the respective field or industry, are being used in standard procedures. In order to minimize expense of equipment and testing, the number of measurements has been reduced as far as possible. This, however, will result in a lower level of accuracy than may be required for design work. On the other hand, it may be sufficient for identification purposes to have at least some information on particle size, particle shape, moisture content and bulk density.

2.8.2 Data base considerations

For industrial applications, especially for project proposals and quotation purposes, all relevant properties must be known. In many industries, for example heat transfer equipment design, data bases serve as the standard method to derive the required properties. This procedure is established for equipment design for most fluids, including mixtures.

This method is easy to apply whenever the behaviour of a substance is uniquely and comprehensively described by its name and some process-related data like temperature, pressure and concentration. In this case the properties for other conditions and mixtures can be interpolated between measured points and can be derived for mixtures of pure substances. A well-known data base for fluid and heat transfer properties is, among others, the *VDI-Wärmeatlas* (1991). Such data bases can easily be transferred into computer networks.

Up to now, no such data base exists for bulk solids handling properties, because the number of influencing parameters is too large. A study in the cement industry revealed that more than 30 parameters are relevant for determining flow properties. This means that more than 30 parameters have to be measured in order to simplify the determination of flow properties. The flow properties could be taken from a data base, if shear tests have been performed with this individual material, and specified by these 30 parameters. Thus, it seems to be easier to measure the flow properties directly with a representative sample and then have more accurate knowledge than could be provided by any data base. Because of this background no data base for solids flow properties has so far been established.

Compilation of a data base using existing data from individual industrial or scientific sources will not be very helpful, because these data will always have been measured with regard to a specific application or problem using a non-standardized test procedure of unknown accuracy and reproducibility.

Respective data for structural design of silos include wall friction coefficients derived from evaluating pressure measurements in model or full-scale silos. These wall friction angles are suitable for structural design of silos, but may not be used for determining the required hopper wall inclination for mass flow in silos. This discrepancy is caused by applying different pressure levels and safety factors to the measured values before using them as suggested design values (Schwedes, 1984). Up to date, the largest number of properties are still listed in the international codes for structural design of silos (Wilms, 1991). However, the properties, such as bulk density, differ by as much as 40% when they are used for structural design of silos (Wilms, Rotter and Tomas, 1995). This demonstrates the questionability of using these data bases from existing data.

Building up a new and comprehensive data base will require a huge amount of testing by qualified and maybe even certified test laboratories using the same test equipment and following an identical test procedure, e.g. EFCE's *Standard Shear Testing Technique Using the Jenike Shear Cell* (IChemE, 1989). However, not only the flow properties derived from shear tests, but all other influencing parameters first have to be identified and then determined by approved procedures. Some of the most relevant properties besides those listed in FEM document 2582 are explained in the literature (Carson and Marinelli, 1979).

It seems to be possible to build up such a data base for a few well-known bulk solids, but it will certainly be impossible to do so for all industrially used bulk solids. However, even if such data bases were set up for a large variety of bulk solids, it would still be impossible to predict the properties of a mixture of two of these bulk solids. So far, no interpolation rules exist and only some limits for the properties of either the coarse or the fine fraction determining the flow properties in a mixture have been determined (Molerus and Nywlt, 1984; Husemann, Höhne and Schünemann, 1994). Besides all these technical problems the question of economic advantage and justification of such a test programme is still open.

Several companies, especially from the chemical industry, cement handling, equipment manufacturers, engineering contractors and consulting companies have proprietary data bases which are not published. Only very few results and respective evaluations from these data bases are known (Borg, 1986). An exchange of all these data and a summary with all these data would be a good starting point to build up a data base, but most probably these data will be inaccessible.

2.8.3 Classification

In order to minimize expenses for testing and test equipment it is industry's intention to describe bulk solids sufficiently by as few properties as possible. For industry it is already very helpful if the respective properties are known within certain ranges. This approach is followed by all institutions using a classification of bulk solids.

The first classification was defined by Jenike (1964), who classified bulk solids according to their flowability. He defined the ratio of consolidation stress σ_1 over compressive stress σ_c as a measure for the flowability, defined by

$$FF_c = \sigma_1/\sigma_c$$

With this classification, solids may be classified according to their FF_c-values. Tomas (Tomas and Schubert, 1982) has extended this system to sintered, hardened or time-consolidated bulk solids, then having FF_c-values smaller than 1. Jenike (1964) has defined the following classification:

$10 < FF_c$	cohesionless, free flowing
$4 < FF_c < 10$	easy flowing
$2 < FF_c < 4$	cohesive
$1 < FF_c < 2$	very cohesive, not flowing
$FF_c < 1$	hardened

Other approaches try to define a flowability number by adding points from various tests. This will, for example, lead to the Carr index (Carr, 1965a, b; Reisner and Eisenhart-Rothe, 1971; Schwedes, 1968). This index is based on four different tests to determine uniformity of the angle of repose, the compressibility, the angle of spatula and the cohesion, respectively. The Powder Characteristics Tester from Hosokawa (Mayerhauser, 1989) is based on this principle. The index includes data from 10 different measurements ranging from bulk density via the angle of repose to dispersibility. However, the same overall figure may result from completely different properties. Thus, this system is not at all accurate and may be misleading.

This Hosokawa Tester as well as the Quality Control Tester from Jenike and Johanson (Ploof and Carson, 1994) may be used for comparing powders with only slight deviations in properties from batch to batch, i.e. in quality assurance programmes, but not for measuring flow properties for equipment design or for comparing different bulk solids such as limestone and flour. Another tester especially suitable for comparative measurements in quality control is Peschl's (Peschl and Colijn, 1977) torsional shear tester. Other methods for classification are summarized by Schwedes (1968).

The Johanson Indicizer (1995) can be used to determine characteristic numbers indicating tendencies for arching and ratholing. Similar tests, each to be performed with an extra test apparatus, may reveal properties on flow rate, density, elasticity and wall friction.

Most of these testers can be used for quality control purposes, but it has to be kept in mind that most of the measured properties are dependent on geometry, material of construction or wall material and other parameters of the tester, i.e. not mechanical but machine-dependent properties are determined. Therefore, these data cannot usually be used for different applications other than quality control.

2.8.4 Conclusions

Identification and classification are important issues in bulk solids handling, both for optimization of research programmes with exchange of test results and for industry to specify and design equipment. Creation of data bases would be the best approach. However, most existing data are not publicly available because they have been compiled by companies or consulting groups. Even though it seems impracticable at this point in time, building of data bases should be encouraged.

These data bases should then go beyond flow property data and should include other mechanical properties required for complete identification of the specific bulk material as well. Such additional data relate to particle size, shape, hardness, structure, moisture content and others. This data base will then allow identification as well and may lead to improved methods of classification. Therefore, it is necessary to extend the scope of respective recommendations in order to have as much data available of as many bulk materials as possible for future inclusion into a data base. For the time being, all research programmes should therefore be obliged to use at least the FEM recommendations for identification of the bulk solids used in their tests.

References

Borg, L. ter Einfluß des Wandmaterials auf das Auslaufverhalten von Schüttgütern aus Silos. *Chemie-Ingenieur-Technik* 58(1986), 3, 262–263

Carr, R.L. Evaluating flow properties of bulk solids. *Chem. Engng.* 72(1965a), 2, 163–168

Carr, R.L. Classifying flow properties of bulk solids. *Chem. Engng.* 72(1965b), 3, 69–72.

Carson, J.W., Marinelli, J. Characterize bulk solids to ensure smooth flow. *Chem. Engng.* (1979), 4, 79–89

FEM-2381, *Specific Characteristics of Bulk Materials as Applicable to Storage in Silos*, Fédération Européenne de la Manutention, Paris, 1986

FEM-2321, *Influence of the Characteristics of Bulk Materials on the Design and Dimensioning of Silos*, Fédération Européenne de la Manutention, Paris, 1989

FEM-2581, *Properties of Bulk Materials*, Fédération Européenne de la Manutention, Paris, 1991a

FEM-2582, *General Properties of Bulk Materials and their Symbolization*, Fédération Européenne de la Manutention, Paris, 1991b

Husemann, K., Höhne, D., Schünemann, U. The influence of fine particle content on the flow properties of coarse bulk solids. *Aufbereitungs-Technik* 35(1994), 2, 61–70

IChemE *Standard Shear Testing Technique Using the Jenike Shear Cell*. The Institution of Chemical Engineers, Rugby (UK), 1989

IMechE *Guide to the Specification of Bulk Solids for Storage and Handling Applications*. The Institution of Mechanical Engineers, London, 1994

Jenike, A.W. *Storage and Flow of Solids*. Bull No 123, Utah Engng Exp. St., Univ. Utah, Salt Lake City, 1964

Johanson, J.R. Silos and discharge aids: analysing the options. *Bulk Handling International Directory*, Turret Group, Rickmansworth, 1995, 25–30

Kühnemund, B. Silolagerung von Schüttgütern. *Aufbereitungs-Technik* 23(1982), 2, 104–109

Mayerhauser, D. Der Hosokawa-Pulvertester. *Chemische Produktion* (1989), Special edition, 24–31

Molerus, O., Nywlt, M. The influence of fine particle content on the flow behaviour of bulk materials. *Powder Technology* 37(1984), 145–154

Peschl, I., Colijn, H. New rotational shear testing technique. *J. Powder and Bulk Solids Technology* 1(1977), 55–60

Ploof, D.A., Carson, J.W. Quality control tester to measure relative flowability of powders. *Bulk Solids Handling* 14(1994), 1, 127–132

Reisner, W., Eisenhart-Rothe, M.v. *Bins and Bunkers for Handling Bulk Materials*. Trans Tech Publications, Clausthal, 1971

Schwedes, J. *Fließverhalten von Schüttgütern in Bunkern*. Verlag Chemie, Weinheim, 1968

Schwedes, J. Einfluß der Wandreibung auf die Dimensionierung von Bunkern – Verfahrenstechnische und statische Gesichtspunkte. *Chemie-Ingenieur-Technik* 56(1984), 4, 291–298

Svarovsky, L. *Powder Testing Guide – Methods of Measuring the Physical Properties of Bulk Powders*. Elsevier, Barking (UK), 1987

Tomas, J., Schubert, H. Modeling of the strength and the flow properties of moist soluble bulk solids. *Aufbereitungs-Technik* 23(1982), 9, 507–515

VDI-Wärmeatlas: Berechnungsblätter für den Wärmeübergang. 6th edition, VDI-Verlag, Düsseldorf, 1991

Wilms, H. Criteria for evaluation of silo design codes. *Bulk Solids Handling* 11(1991), 1, 55–59

Wilms, H., Rotter, M., Tomas, J. Comparative pressure calculations using different codes. *Preprints Partec 95*, Nuremberg (1995), 251–260

3
Flow in silos

3.1 Flow patterns
J. Schwedes

Janssen published his work on wall pressures in 1895. It took more than 50 years before the first idea was published on the way the stored bulk solid moves into and out of the silo, when Brown and Hawksley (1947) reported on experiments with cohesionless bulk solids. During discharge five areas can be distinguished (Fig. 3.1.1): single particles roll freely along layer A, which itself is rapidly moving as a block over layer B, moving very slowly compared to layer A. Area E is not moving at all. The inclination of the dividing plane between B and E is greater than the angle of repose which can be observed on the free surface. As soon as particles or groups of particles reach zone C they are accelerated. Particles in area D lose contact with neighbours and fall freely. At incipient flow the areas D, C, A and B are formed one after the other. If the hopper walls are steep enough, so that all material is in motion, layers A and B can hardly be distinguished and the transition into zone C is fluent.

Figure 3.1.1 is derived by visual observation. No physical model exists which allows prediction of the observed regions. The same holds for the work of Kvapil, who investigated the flow of cohesionless bulk solids starting in the late 1950s (Kvapil, 1959, 1965). Whereas Brown and Hawksley restricted their work to silos with only small filling heights, there is no restriction in the work of Kvapil. According to Kvapil particles can perform two motions, primary and secondary. In primary motion particles move only in the direction of gravity, whereas in secondary motion they can also rotate and move with a horizontal component. The secondary motion is very important close to the aperture. The zones of motion have the shape of ellipsoids (Fig. 3.1.2). The ellipsoid of secondary motion can be found in

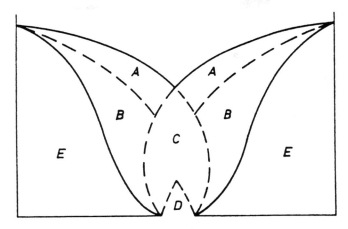

Fig. 3.1.1 Areas of flow due to Brown and Hawksley.

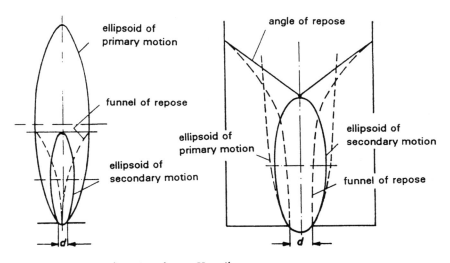

Fig. 3.1.2 Zones of motion due to Kvapil.

silos with limited and unlimited height, whereas the ellipsoid of primary motion exists only at unlimited height.

The state of unlimited height also appears at incipient flow. When the stored bulk solid starts to discharge both ellipsoids are growing. When the ellipsoid of primary motion has reached the upper surface of the filling, a funnel of repose is formed. The ellipsoid of secondary motion grows until it reaches the deepest point of the funnel of repose. Afterwards it decreases again. Later on a discharge funnel is formed which can be interpreted as a dividing plane between slow and fast moving areas.

Besides the flow patterns of Brown and Hawksley and of Kvapil a lot of other more speculative forms of flow pattern have been published (Hampe, 1987). None of them can be predicted quantitatively from properties of the stored bulk solid. The situation changed somewhat when Jenike published his theory (Jenike, 1964; Schwedes, 1968).

Jenike considered the force equilibrium at a small incremental volume and introduced the effective yield locus (EYL) as a yield criterion for steady-state flow (Fig. 3.1.3). With this he was able to derive a system of two partial, inhomogeneous differential equations describing the state of stress at steady-state flow.

Since the problems in the flow of bulk solids with regard to flow obstruction, stoppages, etc. arise in converging flow channels, especially close to the bottom opening, it is sufficient in this respect to know the stresses in this area only. These are independent of the boundary condition at the free surface up in the vertical part of the silo. They are mainly influenced by the conditions at the hopper walls. By transforming to polar coordinates (Fig. 3.1.4) Jenike introduced the following equation (Jenike, 1964; Schwedes, 1968):

$$\sigma = rg\rho_b(\theta', r)s(\theta', r) \qquad (3.1.1)$$

where σ is the mean stress of the Mohr stress circle (Fig. 3.1.3), r the radial coordinate (Fig. 3.1.4), θ' the angular coordinate (Fig. 3.1.4), ρ_b the bulk density and s a scalar function, derived from the numerical solution of the two partial differential equations.

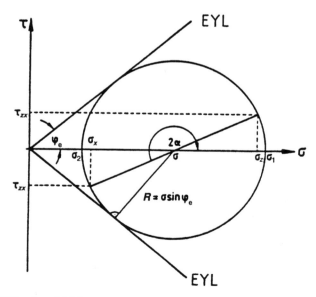

Fig. 3.1.3 Effective yield locus.

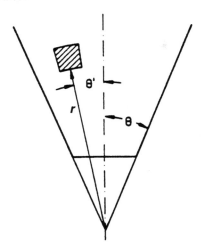

Fig. 3.1.4 Coordinates in the hopper.

As Johanson (Jenike and Johanson, 1962) could show, the stress field of equation (3.1.1) for steady-state flow approaches a special field close to the aperture, called the 'radial stress field'. For this the density is independent of r and θ' and the scalar function s only depends on the angular coordinate θ'. For the major principal stress σ_1 it follows from Fig. 3.1.3 that

$$\sigma_1 = rg\rho_b s(\theta')(1+\sin\varphi_e) \qquad (3.1.2)$$

In reality ρ_b has to be dependent on r. In practical applications this dependency can easily be incorporated by an iterative procedure.

The radial stress field only requires the solution of two ordinary differential equations. The scalar function $s(\theta')$ is also dependent on the angle θ, the inclination of the hopper wall against the vertical (Fig. 3.1.4), the angle φ_e of the effective yield locus (Fig. 3.1.3), being a bulk solids property, and the angle of wall friction φ_x, being dependent on the bulk solid and the wall material. A solution of the two differential equations only exists within a specific set of the three variables θ, φ_x and φ_e. Only within these limits is the angle of wall friction φ_x fully mobilized, i.e. the bulk solid is in motion along the hopper walls and therefore in the total hopper area. Jenike calls this flow pattern 'mass flow'. The border lines for mass flow are plotted in Fig. 3.1.5 for axisymmetric flow, prevailing in conical hoppers. Outside the border lines in Fig. 3.1.5, dependent on the angle φ_e, the set of differential equations cannot be solved, i.e. the bulk solid is not in motion along the hopper walls. Jenike calls this flow pattern 'funnel flow'. Figure 3.1.5 holds for axisymmetric flow. Similar graphs have been derived by Jenike for plain strain, prevailing in wedge-shaped hoppers, and for asymmetric plane strain, prevailing in a wedge with one wall vertical.

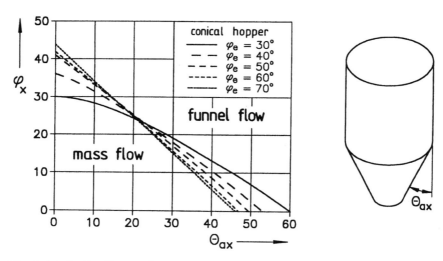

Fig. 3.1.5 Jenike diagram for axisymmetric flow.

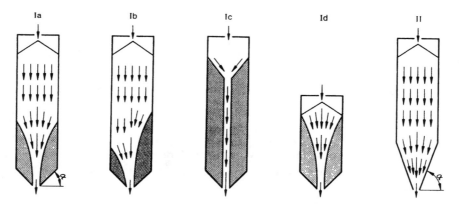

Fig. 3.1.6 Flow profiles according to German Standard DIN 1055, Part 6. Flow profiles: Ia–Id, funnel flow (also for flat bins); II, mass flow.

In funnel flow a convergent flow channel is formed within the stored bulk solid, the inclination of which still cannot be predicted. Further research is required especially in connection with the prediction of the point of intersection of the borderline to the dead zone with the silo walls. At this point high horizontal stresses have to be expected, since they are the reason for many silo failures. Figure 3.1.6 is taken from the German standard DIN 1055, part 6 (DIN 1055, 1987). It can be seen that many modes of funnel flow are possible, but only one mass flow pattern.

The actual flow patterns within funnel flow silos can be influenced in many ways, e.g. by the use of inserts, by the placement of several outlet openings, by increasing the outlet area, by using vibrated or aerated bottoms, by using other kinds of flow-promoting devices, but it should be borne in mind that a funnel flow silo can only be changed (transferred) into a mass flow silo if the inclinations of any converging silo part are steep enough for mass flow to occur and if the feeders at the outlet are able to withdraw bulk solid from the whole cross-section of the outlet area. As pointed out before, the borderline between moving and stationary material in funnel flow cannot be predicted independently of the way of influencing the flow pattern.

References

Brown, R.L. and Hawksley, P.W.G. *Fuel* 26 (1947), 159
DIN 1055, part 6 (1987)
Hampe, E. *Silos*, Vol. 1 (*Grundlagen*), VEB-Verlag für Bauwesen, Berlin (1987)
Jenike, A.W. *Storage and Flow of Solids*, Bull. 123, Utah Eng. Exp. Station, Univ. Utah, Salt Lake City (1964)
Jenike, A.W. and Johanson, J.R. Bull. 116, Utah Eng. Exp. Station, Univ. Utah, Salt Lake City (1962)
Kvapil, R. *Theorie der Schüttgüterbewegung*, VEB-Verlag Technik, Berlin (1959)
Kvapil, R. *Intern. J. Rock Mech. Min. Sci.* (1965), 35
Schwedes, J. *Fließverhalten von Schüttgütern in Bunkern*, Verlag Chemie, Weinheim (1968)

3.2 Wall stress distributions in silos with inserts, and loads on inserts

J. Strusch and J. Schwedes

3.2.1 Introduction

Inserts in silos are among a number of means used to influence the flow pattern and to relieve the feeder. Even inserts which are used to inject air into a silo or enhance the structural stability of the silo change the flow pattern. The change in the flow pattern changes the state of stress in a silo.

Vertically placed ropes, tie rods and discharge tubes are mainly subjected to shear stresses in the vertical direction. These loads can be estimated quite accurately using the theories developed for silos without inserts (Lyle, 1992).

Displacing inserts which lead to converging flow, e.g. cones and relieving bars, are subjected to normal stresses as well as to shear stresses. Up to now there are no experimentally proven equations for calculating the wall stress distributions in silos with displacing inserts and the loads on the inserts. Therefore a lot of failures occurred in silos with inserts in the past. The wall stress distributions in silos with displacing inserts and loads on those inserts will be discussed in the following.

3.2.2 Background

Measurements of wall normal stresses on silos with inserts have been carried out by Theimer (1974) and Nothdurft (1976). Their measurements show an increase in the wall normal stress at the level of the insert during filling and during discharging. Tüzün and Nedderman (1983) placed wedge-shaped inserts and square inserts in a tall silo of rectangular cross-section. The flow patterns were photographed through the float glass front wall of the silo. Wall normal and shear stresses along the side-walls of the silo were measured. Tüzün and Nedderman observed that the presence of an insert affected the wall stress distribution in different ways during filling and during discharging. During filling, the wall stresses at the level of the insert were generally larger than those observed without inserts. By contrast, during discharging, the wall stresses at the level of the insert were less than in the silo without an insert. Considering the flow pattern observations around inserts, Tüzün and Nedderman said that the observed disturbance of the flow field around an insert is coupled with peak values of the wall stresses measured at the level of the insert. Kroll (1975) measured no increase in the wall normal stress at the level of the insert. He only observed a reduction in the wall normal stress at the level of the insert and below it. Kahl (1976) measured the horizontal stress within the bulk solid with the help of a stress measuring cell, which was moving together with the bulk solid during discharging. He detected an increase in the horizontal stress at the level of the insert. Kahl concluded from his measurements that the bulk solid between insert and silo wall is deformed in a similar way to that in the hopper section of a silo. Scholz (1988) measured an increase in the wall normal stress at the level of the insert during filling and during discharging in the case of an insert positioned in the vertical section of the silo. Scholz (1988) observed no increase in the wall normal stress for an insert positioned in the hopper section.

Kroll (1975), Kahl (1976), Scholz (1988), Johanson and Kleysteuber (1966), Tsunakawa and Aoki (1975) and Polderman, Scott and Boom (1985) measured the vertical load exerted on inserts in silos. The measured vertical insert loads are significantly higher than the loads which result from Janssen's formula (1895) of the vertical stress in the vertical section of a silo.

Schlick (1994) carried out measurements of wall stresses on a silo with a central cone and a rotary plough feeder. He also analysed the flow pattern in such a silo.

Lyle (1992) used finite-element calculations to examine the influence of insert geometry and position in a silo on wall stress distributions and on insert loads.

All the investigations mentioned above have been carried out under symmetric conditions within the silos. Only Nothdurft (1976), Hoppe and Kahl (1977), Rolewicz (1982), Strusch, Lyle and Schwedes (1993) and Schlick (1994) showed that asymmetric conditions within the silo with an insert lead to an asymmetric flow pattern with completely asymmetric wall stress distributions and asymmetric insert loads.

At the Technical University Braunschweig, Germany, measurements of insert loads and wall stress distributions were carried out on a model silo, made of Perspex plates, such that the flow pattern can be observed and assigned to the measured insert loads and silo wall stresses (Strusch *et al.*, 1995). Furthermore, measurements of stresses on inserts and wall stress distributions were carried out on a steel silo which has a larger dimension

120   Flow in silos

than the model silo (Strusch et al., 1995). All the experimental results were analysed by means of finite-element calculations (Antes, Lehman and Strusch, 1995).

In the following the state of the art will be discussed by means of measurements carried out at the Technical University Braunschweig, Germany, on a model silo. The model silo is described in, for example, Strusch (1996) and measurements presented here have been carried out with a free-flowing plastic granulate.

3.2.3 Influence of symmetrically arranged inserts on the wall stress distribution

Figure 3.2.1 shows the wall stress distribution measured in the model silo with a wedge-shaped insert in the discharging state. The model silo has a rectangular base (400 × 800 mm) and a wedge-shaped hopper (hopper wall inclination angle relative to the vertical: 15°). The insert has a width of 100 mm and an inclination angle of 15° relative to the vertical. The insert is positioned in the vertical section. Discharging state means a state of stress shortly after the start of discharging, when the state of stress has become

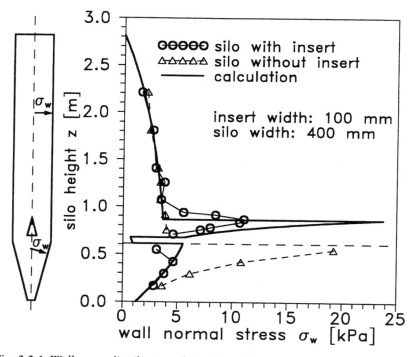

Fig. 3.2.1 Wall stress distribution of the silo with a symmetrically arranged insert, discharging state.

constant. With the granulate used this happens almost immediately after the start of discharging with a negligibly small drop in the bulk solid surface, compared to the filling state. The wall stress distribution of the silo without an insert in the discharging state is indicated as well. The measured wall normal stress σ_w of the vertical section and the hopper has been plotted as a function of silo height z.

The wall normal stress of the silo without an insert increases with increasing distance from the bulk solid surface until it has approached a limiting value. At the transition from the vertical section to the hopper a change in the wall normal direction occurs. Thus, at this point a discontinuity of the wall normal stress exists. A distinct stress peak – the so-called 'switch' – occurs at the transition (Jenike, Johanson and Carson, 1973). In the hopper a radial stress field can be clearly noticed: starting from the imaginary hopper apex the wall normal stress increases linearly with increasing distance. When the bulk solid has to converge in the flowing direction a radial stress field appears. During filling the direction of the major principal stress at the axis of symmetry is vertical, whereas the direction of the major principal stress becomes horizontal during discharging due to the converging flow of the bulk solid.

The wall stress distribution of the silo with insert shows an increase in the silo wall stress at the level of the insert top and a decrease below the insert. The reduction in the wall stress below the insert results from the fact that the insert takes up a part of the vertical load. On the other hand, the increase in the wall normal stress at the level of the insert top leads to an increase in that part of the bulk solid weight which is taken up by the silo walls by means of shear stresses. In the discharging state the insert in the vertical section does not influence the wall normal stress distribution near the hopper outlet. This experimental result is typical for the radial stress field. Stresses near the hopper outlet are in a wide range independent of the surcharge on the hopper.

Considering the wall stress distribution between insert and silo wall starting from the narrowest cross-section it can be seen that the wall normal stress increases proportionally with distance from this narrowest cross-section. It can be concluded from this proportionality that the bulk solid between insert and silo wall is deformed in a similar way to that in the hopper. While discharging, the radial stress field develops between insert and silo wall. Jenike (1961) gives a numerical solution for the radial stress field. Enstad (1981) has published an analytical solution for predicting stresses in wedge-shaped and conical mass flow hoppers. Walters (1973) also derived an analytical solution. For the results presented here the theory of Enstad (1981) for wedge-shaped hoppers is used to calculate the radial stress field between insert and silo wall (Strusch and Schwedes, 1994). Figure 3.2.1 shows the calculated wall stress distribution of the silo with insert. The wall normal stress in the vertical section is calculated by Janssen (1895). At the level of the insert and in the hopper the wall normal stress is calculated according to the theory of Enstad (1981). Figure 3.2.1 shows a good agreement between measured and calculated wall normal stresses. The calculated wall normal stress peak at the level of the insert top is higher than the measured stress peak. The measurement of such a distinct stress peak is very difficult, because the stress measuring plates of the cells integrate the stress gradient over the plate area and give only an average stress value.

The measured wall normal stresses of the filling state show that already in the filling state the bulk solid between insert and silo wall can be deformed in a similar way as in the discharging state leading to a slight increase in the wall normal stress at the level of the insert top (Strusch, Lyle and Schwedes, 1993).

For a symmetrically arranged insert in the hopper no increase in the wall normal stress at the level of the insert occurs (Strusch *et al.*, 1995). This can be explained by the converging flow of the bulk solid above the insert in the hopper. This also explains why no stress peak occurs at the level of the insert top.

3.2.4 Influence of asymmetrically arranged inserts on the wall stress distribution

Figure 3.2.2 shows the wall stress distribution in the discharging state when the insert is arranged asymmetrically. The wedge-shaped insert has been moved 100 mm from the axis of symmetry to the right silo side. Figure 3.2.2 also indicates the measured values in the discharging state for the silo without an insert. The measured wall stress values have been plotted separately for the left and right silo side to illustrate the influence of the asymmetric insert arrangement.

In the discharging state a stress peak at the upper level of the insert was measured. This stress peak only exists on the right silo side. On the left side a slight decrease in the silo wall stresses can be noted. Due to the proportions of the cross-sections between insert and silo the inverse result would also be conceivable, because the higher stress would be assigned to the greater cross-section. In order to understand the present wall stress distribution the flow pattern must be considered. Several experiments with various displacements of the insert have been carried out. The mean vertical velocity has been measured on both sides of the insert at the height of the insert top. It can be observed that on the side with the smaller cross-section the mean vertical velocity is a lot smaller than on the side with the greater cross-section. Due to the difference in velocity between both sides shear stresses are transferred from the region where the bulk solid is flowing faster to the region where it is flowing more slowly (Schulze, 1991). By means of these shear stresses the fast-flowing bulk solid can be supported by the slowly flowing bulk solid. Thus, the more significant silo wall stresses on the side with the smaller cross-section and the decrease in the wall stresses on the opposite side of the insert can be explained.

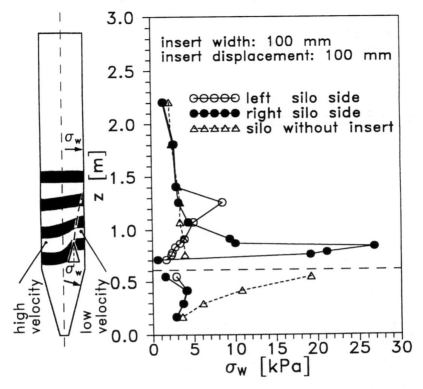

Fig. 3.2.2 Wall stress distribution of the silo with an asymmetrically arranged insert, discharging state.

At the level of the insert base the wall normal stress on the right silo side is lower than on the left. Also, in the upper part of the hopper the wall normal stress on the right side is lower than on the left. The fact that the wall normal stress at the level of the insert base is lower on the right side than on the left can be explained by the presence of the radial stress field. As shown in Fig. 3.2.1, the surcharge stress on the hopper has no significant influence on the stresses near the hopper outlet. The narrowest cross-section between insert and silo wall at the level of the insert base is equivalent to the hopper outlet. Corresponding to the conditions of the radial stress field the stresses here are mainly influenced by the width of the cross-section. Therefore the wall normal stress on the right side with the smaller cross-section is lower than on the left side with the greater cross-section. Further investigations of flow patterns in silos with asymmetrically arranged inserts show that these lower stresses on the side with the smaller cross-section are responsible for the lower velocity of the bulk solid on the side with the smaller cross-section.

Considering the wall stress distribution on the left side of the model silo starting from the narrowest cross-section between insert and silo wall, it can be seen that the wall normal stress increases proportionally to the distance from this narrowest cross-section. In the upper part of the vertical section a wall normal stress peak was measured, similar to the stress peak at the transition in a silo without an insert. It can be concluded from the proportionality between wall normal stress and distance to the narrowest cross-section that the bulk solid is deformed in a similar way to that in a hopper. The converging flow channel consists of the left silo wall and the bulk solid region with the low vertical velocity. The width of this region decreases with increasing distance from the insert top and reaches the right silo wall in the neighbourhood of the level where the stress peak of the left silo side was measured.

In the filling state – corresponding to the symmetrically arranged insert – no significant increase in the wall normal stresses exists (Strusch, Lyle and Schwedes, 1993).

The asymmetric arrangement of an insert in the hopper leads to an asymmetric flow pattern and an asymmetric wall stress distribution. As for an insert in the vertical section, the wall normal stress increases at the level of the insert on the silo side with the smaller cross-section. On the side with the greater cross-section the wall normal stress increases above the insert.

3.2.5 Vertical insert load during filling and discharging

Figure 3.2.3 shows the specific vertical insert load σ_i during filling and discharging on a wedge-shaped insert which has been installed above the transition between the vertical section and the hopper. The insert base is

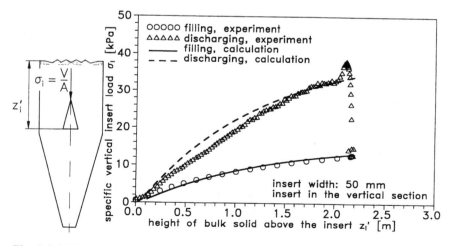

Fig. 3.2.3 Measured and calculated specific vertical insert loads σ_i.

situated 675 mm from the hopper outlet. The wedge-shaped insert has a width of 50 mm and an inclination angle of 15° relative to the vertical.

The specific insert load σ_i is plotted as a function of the height of the bulk solid above the insert z_i'. The specific insert load is defined as the measured vertical insert force V divided by the projectional area A in the vertical direction of the measuring section. During filling the specific insert load asymptotically approaches a maximum value. At the beginning of discharge load peaks were measured, being up to three times higher than the maximum filling load. The load peak at the beginning of discharging can be explained by dilation of the bulk solid during discharging. Dilation initiates at the hopper outlet and moves upwards in the vertical section with increasing bulk solid discharging. When dilation reaches the base of the insert, the bulk solid next to the insert cannot support itself so firmly on this dilated area. According to the force balance in the vertical direction, a larger part of the bulk solid above the insert supports itself on the insert. The load peak is effective for a very short time only. After the discharging of 7% of the silo content the insert load has levelled to 250% of the filling load. The load peak depends on the position of the insert in the silo, the insert width and the flow properties of the bulk solid. For inserts positioned in the vertical section the load peak is higher than for inserts positioned in the hopper. With smaller inserts the load peak increases.

Contrary to the behaviour shown in Fig. 3.2.3, where the specific vertical insert load during discharging is higher than during filling, the opposite was found for other bulk solids (Strusch, Lyle and Schwedes, 1993). The reason for this different behaviour cannot yet be explained.

The measurements of the wall normal stress show that a state of stress occurs between insert and silo wall corresponding to that in a hopper (Fig. 3.2.1). Therefore slice element methods, which have been developed for silo hoppers, were adopted to calculate insert loads (Strusch and Schwedes, 1994). The state of stress in a hopper during filling can be calculated well according to Motzkus (1974) and during discharging it can be calculated according to Enstad (1981) or Walters (1973). Figure 3.2.3 shows the calculated specific vertical load on the insert and the measured specific vertical load for filling and discharging. The dependence of the specific vertical insert load σ_i on the height of bulk solid above the insert z_i' is predicted correctly. The effect of higher specific vertical insert loads during discharging compared to those during filling is determined well and there is a good agreement between experiment and calculation regarding the ratio of filling to discharging loads.

3.2.6 Influence of insert position on the vertical insert load

In Fig. 3.2.4 measured and calculated values of specific vertical insert load σ_i are plotted for four different heights z_i of the insert base above the hopper outlet. The filling height of the silo has been kept constant for these experi-

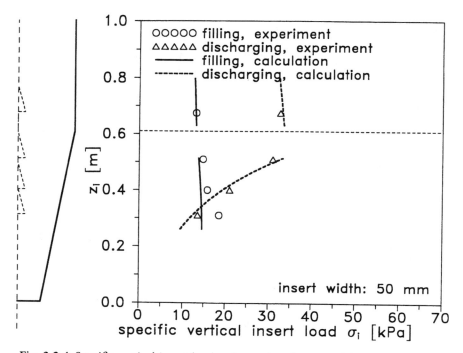

Fig. 3.2.4 Specific vertical insert load σ_i for various insert positions in the silo.

ments. For discharging the measured specific vertical insert loads decrease with decreasing distance from the hopper outlet. The calculated specific vertical insert loads correspond well to the measured values. The graph clearly reflects the influence of the radial stress field in the lower part of the hopper and the influence of the switch in the upper part. It can be deduced from the calculations that the maximum specific vertical insert load results for an insert positioned at the transition between vertical section and hopper.

3.2.7 Influence of insert geometry on the vertical insert load

Figure 3.2.5 shows the influence of the insert width on the specific vertical insert load for inserts positioned in the vertical section. The measured specific vertical insert loads σ_i for filling and discharging and the peak loads at the beginning of discharging are plotted as a function of the ratio of insert width b_i to silo width b.

For filling, the maximum specific vertical insert loads at the end of the filling process have been taken. For discharging, the maximum loads at steady-state flow are taken, when the peak loads due to the dilation process have levelled off. The measured specific vertical insert loads increase with

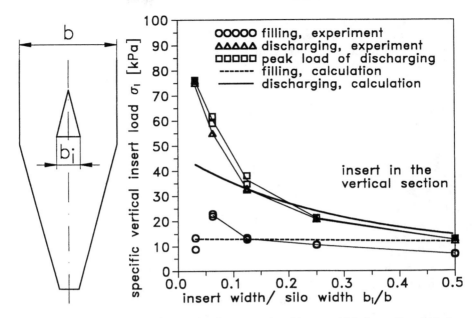

Fig. 3.2.5 Specific vertical insert load σ_i vs. ratio of insert width b_i to silo width b.

decreasing insert width, both for filling and discharging. This effect was obtained by a number of other authors (Kroll, 1975; Kahl, 1976; Scholz, 1988).

In Fig. 3.2.5 calculated insert loads are also plotted (Strusch and Schwedes, 1994). The calculated curves for discharging show the effect of increasing specific vertical insert load σ_i with decreasing insert width b_i, but the comparison of the measured and calculated specific vertical insert loads clearly shows that the calculation underestimated the measured values for small inserts. Furthermore, Fig. 3.2.5 shows that the effect of increasing specific vertical insert load with decreasing insert width cannot be predicted by the calculation for filling. The measured increase in specific vertical insert load with decreasing insert width can be explained by the deformation of the bulk solid flowing around the insert during filling. Its deformation is caused by the weight of the bulk solid above the insert. Due to the converging cross-section between insert and silo wall the bulk solid is compressed horizontally. Thus already during filling a converging flow of the bulk solid at the level of the insert begins and the specific vertical insert load approaches the higher values of discharging.

The different tendencies predicted for the specific vertical insert load during filling and discharging can be explained with help of the switch stresses prevailing at the transition from the active stress field into the passive stress field during discharging (Jenike, Johanson and Carson, 1973).

128   *Flow in silos*

In the vertical section the active stress field exists above the insert, whereas at the level of the insert the passive stress field prevails. Thus the stress field switches from active to passive at the top of the insert. Due to this discontinuity of the stress fields a stress peak, the so-called 'switch', appears at the top of the insert. The calculation of the wall stress distribution according to Enstad (1981) also shows a stress peak at the insert top (Fig. 3.2.1). In the filling state the active stress field also prevails at the level of the insert. Thus no stress peak occurs.

3.2.8 Influence of an asymmetric flow pattern on the resulting insert load

In this section the insert arrangement that has already been shown by means of the silo wall stresses in Figs. 3.2.1 and 3.2.2 will be examined. In Fig. 3.2.6 the angle δ of the resulting insert load against the vertical is plotted versus the height of the bulk solid above the insert z_i'. The angle of the resulting insert load is determined by the measured resulting horizontal load H and by the vertical load V, which have been measured at the insert in the model silo.

Figure 3.2.6 shows the angle δ of the resulting insert load for filling and discharging and for a symmetrical and an asymmetrical insert arrangement. For the symmetrical insert arrangement the angle δ does not significantly deviate from zero. Thus, the resulting horizontal insert load H can be neglected compared to the vertical insert load V.

If the insert has been displaced to the right-hand side the angle δ has a positive sign. This means that the resulting horizontal insert load H during filling acts from left to right. This corresponds to the fact that the side with the larger cross-section exerts a higher horizontal load on the insert. During

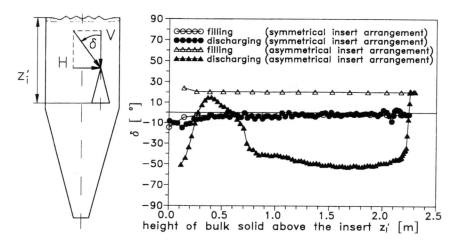

Fig. 3.2.6 Angle δ of the resulting insert load.

discharging the angle δ has a negative sign. Thus, the resulting horizontal insert load acts from right to left, in other words from the side with the smaller cross-section to the one with the larger cross-section. This behaviour corresponds to that of the wall stress distributions (Fig. 3.2.2). The angle δ is greater than 45° over a wide range of bulk solid height above the insert. Thus the resulting horizontal insert load is greater than the vertical insert load and cannot be neglected when an insert is dimensioned.

3.2.9 Conclusion and outlook

Measurements of wall stress distributions show that between insert and silo wall a stress state occurs which is similar to that in a hopper. Therefore theories which have been developed for silo hoppers can be adopted to calculate the stresses at the level of the insert. By means of these theories the peak of the wall normal stress at the level of the insert top can be explained. Also the influence of insert position on the vertical insert load can be explained. It appears that the theories for hoppers can be a useful instrument for a better understanding of how far inserts change the state of stress in silos. The comparison of measured and calculated values shows that specific vertical insert loads can be predicted well for large inserts.

With very small inserts the measured specific insert loads are higher than the calculated ones. This effect cannot be explained with the methods used. In further investigations the influence of small inserts on the specific vertical insert load has to be examined.

Experiments with an asymmetric arrangement of an insert in the vertical section or in the hopper show that an asymmetric arrangement of an insert results in an asymmetric flow pattern. An asymmetric flow pattern leads to asymmetric wall normal stresses and to asymmetric insert loads. However, an asymmetric flow pattern cannot only be caused by an asymmetric insert arrangement, but also by an irregular discharging of the bulk solid. In further experiments an upper bound of wall normal stresses and insert loads has to be found for silos with inserts and asymmetric flow pattern.

References

Antes, H.; Lehmann, L.; Strusch, J.: The effect of insert's characteristics on the stress distribution in silos, *Preprints 3rd Europ. Symp. Storage and Flow of Particulate Solids*, Nuremberg (1995), 173–182

Enstad, G.G.: A novel theory on the arching and doming in mass flow hoppers, Diss., Bergen, Norway (1981)

Hoppe, H.; Kahl, J.: Probleme bei Siloeinbauten, *Industrieanzeiger* **99** (1977) 80, 1554–1556

Janssen, H.A.: Getreidedruck in Silozellen, Z. Ver. Dt. Ing. **39** (1895), 1045–1049

Jenike, A.W.: *Gravity Flow of Bulk Solids*, Bulletin No. 108, Engng. Exp. Station, Univ. of Utah, Salt Lake City (1961)

Jenike, A.W.; Johanson, J.R.; Carson, J.W.: Bin loads – Part 2 and 3, *Journ. of Eng. for Industry, Trans. ASME*, Series B, **95** (1973) 1, 1–12

Johanson, J.R.; Kleysteuber, W.K.: Flow corrective inserts in bins, *Chem. Eng. Prog.*, **11** (1966) 62, 79–83

Kahl, J.: Grundlagenuntersuchungen über die Belastung von Siloeinbauten bei ruhenden und fließenden Schüttgütern, Diss., Techn. Univ. Clausthal, Federal Republic of Germany (1976)

Kroll, D.: Untersuchungen über die Belastung horizontaler Zuganker sowie vertikaler Hängependel und Gehänge durch Schüttgüter in Silozellen, Diss., Techn. Univ. Braunschweig, Federal Republic of Germany (1975)

Lyle, C.: Spannungsfelder in Silos mit starren, koaxialen Einbauten, Diss., Techn. Univ. Braunschweig, Federal Republic of Germany (1992)

Motzkus, U.: Belastung von Siloböden und Auslauftrichtern durch körnige Schüttgüter, Diss., Techn. Univ. Braunschweig, Federal Republic of Germany (1974)

Nothdurft, H.: Schüttgutlasten in Silozellen mit Querschnittsverengungen, Diss., Techn. Univ. Braunschweig, Federal Republic of Germany (1976)

Polderman, H.G.; Scott, A.M.; Boom, J.: Solids stresses in bunkers with inserts, *Int. Chem. Eng. Symp. Ser.* (1985) 91, 227–240

Rolewicz, J.M.: Belastung und Beanspruchung von räumlichen Siloeinbauten durch körnige Schüttgüter, Diss., Univ. Bochum, Federal Republic of Germany (1982)

Schlick, H.: Belastungs- und Fließverhältnisse in Silos mit zentralen Einbauten und Räumarmaustrag, Diss., Univ. Karlsruhe, Federal Republic of Germany (1994)

Scholz, V.: Untersuchungen zur Anordnung starrer koaxialer Einbauten in Schüttgutbehältern, Diss., Wilhelm-Pieck-Universität Rostock (1988)

Schulze, D.: Untersuchungen zur gegenseitigen Beeinflussung von Silo und Austragorgan, Diss., Techn. Univ. Braunschweig, Federal Republic of Germany (1991)

Strusch, J.: Wandnormalspannungen in einem Silo mit Einbau und Kräfte auf Einbauten, Diss., Techn. Univ. Braunschweig, Federal Republic of Germany (1996)

Strusch, J.; Lyle, C.; Schwedes, J.: The influence on the state of stress in silos by inserts, *Proceedings Int. Symposium 'Reliable Flow of Particulate Solids II'*, Oslo (1993), 727–738

Strusch, J.; Schwedes, J.: The use of slice element methods for calculating insert loads, *Bulk Solids Handling* **14** (1994) 3, 505–512

Strusch, J.; Schwedes, J.; Hardow, B., Kaldenhoff, M., Hering, K.: Insert loads and wall stress distributions in silos with inserts, *Preprints 3rd Europ. Symp. Storage and Flow of Particulate Solids*, Nuremberg (1995), 163–172

Theimer, F.: Japanische Druckversuche in Mehlsilozellen mit 'Nasenauslauf', *Die Mühle und Mischfuttertechnik* **111** (1974) 11, 153–159

Tsunakawa, H.; Aoki, R.: The vertical force of bulk solids on objects in bins, *Powder Technology* **11** (1975), 237–243

Tüzün, U.; Neddermann, R.M.: Flow of granular materials round obstacles, *Bulk Solids Handling* **3** (1983) 3, 507–517

Walters, J.K.: A theoretical analysis of stresses in axially symmetric hoppers and bunkers, *Chem. Eng. Sci.* **28** (1973), 779–789

3.3 Inserts in silos for blending
H. Wilms

In many industries large quantities of bulk solids have to be blended or homogenized. This process is required to minimize fluctuations in product quality or composition originating from batch processes and from varying raw material qualities. Blending requires either a relative motion of individual particles or a distinct alteration of the residence time distribution within the blending silos. Among other systems with fluidization or mechanical agitation, blending inserts are widely used to influence the velocity profile and/or the residence time distribution in blending silos. Most of these blenders operate by gravity only and thus are often referred to as gravity blenders.

Varying properties often homogenized in blending silos are the melt flow index of polymers, the calcium content in raw material for cement production, colour of cacao powder, or particle size distribution of any powder. A clear distinction between mixing and homogenizing is not possible because blending of pellets of different colours may be considered as mixing of components with different colours or as homogenizing of the colour as a property. Therefore, the term 'blending' is used to describe the process in blending silos (Wilms, 1986a, 1992).

3.3.1 Principle of gravity blending

The blending effect of gravity flow blenders is based on the fact that solids from at least two different zones in the blender are withdrawn simultaneously and mixed together. The blending effect can be intensified by recirculation of the material. It is obvious that the blending efficiency increases with the number of draw-off points. This basic idea as shown in

Fig. 3.3.1 can be put into practice in many different ways. Draw-off from different locations within the gravity blender, combination of the individual streams of material flow, and recirculation of the material can be performed in many different ways. Thus, there are many different designs outlined below.

Recirculation of the material can be performed either internally or externally. For a small number of draw-off points the number of recirculations to achieve a certain level of homogeneity has to be increased. One complete recirculation means conveying the complete nominal content of the blender once before it is emptied.

Since many gravity flow blenders are used as continuous blenders without any recirculation those blenders having a high number of draw-off points more and more become the industrial standard. Only when retrofitting a silo into a blender or when cleaning becomes a major concern, will minimization of internals be the objective.

A gravity flow blender can only achieve an optimum blending performance if the blending process extends over the complete content of the silo. This means that no stagnant zones may form. Gravity flow blenders, therefore, have to be designed for mass flow with consideration of the individual flow properties. In addition, these flow properties have to be used in order to avoid arching over the outlet or the draw-off points.

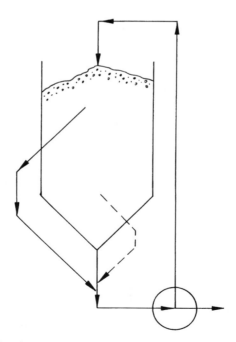

Fig. 3.3.1 Principle of gravity blending.

3.3.2 Blending internals in the hopper

The residence time distribution in the silo can be influenced by internals in the hopper (Johanson, 1982; Carson and Royal, 1992). The basic idea of a blending hopper near the outlet in the conical part of the silo is to vary the vertical flow velocities in the hopper. Such a blending hopper as shown in Fig. 3.3.2(a) will influence the vertical flow velocity in the hopper and the lower part of the cylinder. This principle was originally introduced by Jenike & Johanson, Inc. as a Binsert®.

The different velocities within the hopper and within the annulus will result in different residence times and, thus, lead to homogenization. The individual flow properties have to be considered for mass flow design of the respective hopper elements. Thus, formation of stagnant zones will be avoided by simultaneously achieving a maximum difference of the flow velocity in the centre and the annulus. The diameter and width of the respective hopper sections are chosen with respect to the flow properties in order to avoid arching across the annulus and across the outlet. This design principle enables design of the Binsert® blender for cohesive bulk solids. The Binsert®, therefore, may be an alternative for mechanical mixers of cohesive bulk solids. The non-uniform velocities in the hopper become more uniform in the cylindrical part of the silo. Thus, blending efficiency is reduced in

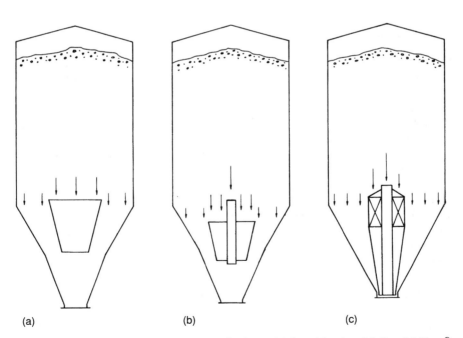

Fig. 3.3.2 Blending hoppers: (a) Binsert®; (b) multi-flow blender; (c) Combi-Flow® blender.

slender silos. To achieve a good homogenization with a single pass the aspect ratio H over D should be small and should not exceed $H:D = 1.75$ (Johanson, 1970).

Blending silos with a larger aspect ratio than 2 require more recirculation or will result in poorer blending behaviour if no additional solids are withdrawn from higher up in the cylindrical section. For this purpose the blending hopper can be equipped with a vertical pipe section (Fig. 3.3.2(b)) (Zeppelin, 1995). Thus, the blending effect can be improved for blenders with an aspect ratio in excess of that of the Binsert® blender. As with the Binsert®, this multi-flow blender features in the section below the insert a steeper hopper as is required to maintain the mass flow profile.

The Combi-Flow blender shown in Fig. 3.3.2(c) is also a combination of hopper- and pipe-shaped internals in the hopper (Wohnhas, 1995). Because of the different cross-sectional areas of the individual elements the flow velocities and mass flow rates from different regions around the circumference are varied. This will lead to draw-off from different levels of the lower cylindrical section and thus results in a homogenizing effect.

If the influence of such internals on the additional load on silos is being considered, then these internals in the hopper can be used for retrofitting existing storage silos into blenders. It is, however, essential that those silos were designed for mass flow because otherwise stagnant zones will form and will negatively influence the blending result and the structural design.

3.3.3 Blending silos with central pipes

An improvement in homogenizing, especially with slender silos, can be achieved by installing a central vertical pipe into which material can flow from various levels. The gravity blender shown in Fig. 3.3.3(a) has a central pipe composed of multiple hopper elements (Hoppe and Breucker, 1984). Bulk solids can flow via the annular slots into the central pipe at various levels. This material stream is combined with material flowing in the central pipe from the upper level. The combined material then flows into the next hopper element and a new stream of solids is added. This system enables flow from multiple layers in the silo into the central pipe. However, since the same absolute amount of material is always added at each level irrespective of the relative velocity, the composition of the material flow from the central pipe into the outlet is not composed of material with the same amount from all levels. The lower levels will usually contribute a higher percentage than the upper levels.

No arches may form across the annular slots and across the conical sections of the hopper segments. Therefore, only cohesionless or easy-flowing powders can be blended in this silo which has to be designed for mass flow in order to avoid stagnant zones. Since these internals are usually installed into standard silos only those bulk solids having sufficiently small wall friction angles can be homogenized in this type of silo.

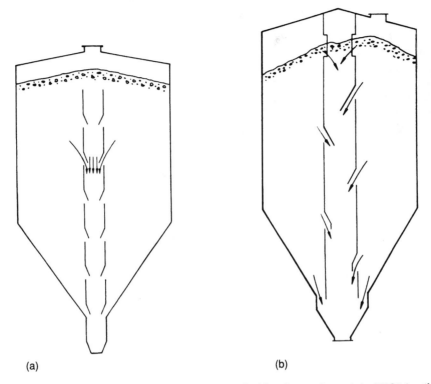

Fig. 3.3.3 Gravity blenders with central blending pipe: (a) WGM; (b) Centro-Blender®.

The Centro-Blender® (Fig. 3.3.3(b)) has a central pipe installed into a mass flow silo (Wilms and Kiesgen, 1991). The central pipe has intake openings at various levels. The intake openings and the central pipe diameter are designed in accordance with the flowability of the bulk solids. Though all of the openings are of identical size, different amounts of bulk solids flow into the central pipes at various levels. This is achieved by having baffles above each intake opening spanning different parts of the cross-section of the central pipe. By appropriate design of these baffles the same volumetric percentage can be drawn off from each individual level. Since equal amounts of bulk solid are withdrawn from various levels in the silo the Centro-Blender can achieve a sufficient homogenization with a single pass, i.e. without recirculation. An external pneumatic conveying system for recirculation can improve the blending efficiency. Standard Centro-Blenders are built in sizes of up to 300 m³ and are suitable for homogenization of powders, recycling and regrind materials as well as sticky plastic elastomers.

3.3.4 Blenders with internal recirculation

The pneumatic pellet blender (Fig. 3.3.4(a)) was developed for homogenization of plastic pellets. It features a vertical conveying pipe installed in the centre of the silo (Schwedes and Richter, 1976). The pellets are pneumatically conveyed through this pipe from the blending section at the lower end of the blender to the top level. Bulk solids are withdrawn mainly from two annular regions. The bulk solids in these two zones flow with different vertical velocities, v_A and v_B respectively. These vertical velocity differences

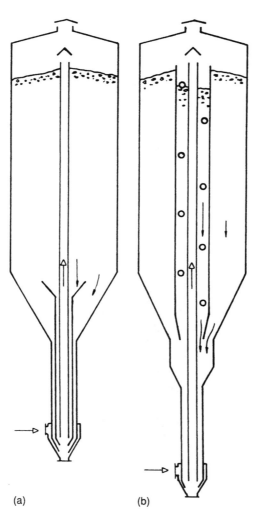

Fig. 3.3.4 Gravity blenders with internal recirculation: (a) pneumatic pellet blender PGM; (b) Circomix-Blender.

are caused by the difference in convergence of the blending cone with respect to the silo diameter and the width of the blending slots.

The long throttling section is required to reduce the leakage gas flow passing through the solids instead of being used for conveying the material. The throttling section needs to have very small cross-sections in order to cause a high pressure drop for the leakage air. This leakage gas flow can cause asymmetric flow in the annular slots of the throttling section thus creating a non-uniform pressure distribution around the central pipe.

The Circomix-Blender (Fig. 3.3.4(b)) (Krambrock, 1989) uses the same basic idea of the pneumatic pellet blender. However, the problems caused by uneven flow are avoided due to the larger cross-section in the blending area, since the material is already mixed in the blending chamber above and not below the throttling section. The slots are wider and do not cause trouble. The Circomix-Blender blends material from the top level with material coming from the lower hopper section. The basic idea is comparable to the pneumatic pellet blender, however, strict mass flow design leads to an improvement of this type of blender.

Both blenders withdraw solids from only two regions in the silo. This means that a relatively large number of recirculations is required for good blending. A sufficient homogenization is achieved after three to five recirculations. Since only a small pressure drop is required for recirculation using a vertical conveying pipe in the blender, it is sufficient to use radial fans for recirculation. A large number of recirculations requires a relatively long blending time compared to other gravity flow blenders. However, very large recirculation rates of up to 400 t/h can be achieved with the central recirculation system. In spite of the low power consumption of the radial fan the blending energy is still approximately 2 kWh/t because of the extended recirculation time.

3.3.5 Blenders with multiple blending pipes

The blenders with internal blending hopper (Fig. 3.3.2) or with internal recirculation (Fig. 3.3.4), withdraw bulk solids only from two different zones in the silo. An improvement in the blending efficiency can be achieved by withdrawing solids simultaneously from a larger number of regions in the silo. The larger the number of draw-off points in different levels in the silo, the better the blending efficiency with a single pass and the shorter the blending time. Especially when blending solids with an unknown and varying distribution of the relevant property over the height of the silo, then numerous draw-off points are necessary.

A blending system following this principle can be implemented into a silo by installing numerous vertical tubes with intake openings at different levels. The stream coming from the central outlet is then combined with those coming from these several tubes in a mixing chamber beneath the central outlet. If such a blending pipe has multiple intake openings then solids will only flow into that intake opening which is the uppermost one beneath the top level of solids. This often is referred to as the top hole concept.

The lower intake openings only become active with lower levels of fill and especially during discharge of the blender. By using such a system bulk solids can be withdrawn simultaneously and in defined quantities from numerous regions in the silo. All streams are blended together in a blending chamber underneath or inside the hopper into which all blending pipes lead. Simultaneous discharge of solids from various levels spreads the residence time distribution of the material in the silo.

The homogenization effect achieved with one pass depends on the number of tubes being installed in the silo and the placement of the intake openings. Since installation of a large number of tubes requires a considerable amount of structural support it is more advantageous to install multi-compartment tubes. These tubes usually have three independent compartments in the longitudinal direction, separated by vertical baffles. The larger overall tube diameter and these internal baffles provide a high stiffness which is advantageous from the structural point of view because these tubes will be subjected to lateral forces. Usually six blending pipes with three compartments each are installed in a silo resulting in 18 individual channels besides the central outlet. Thus, solids from 19 different locations are mixed in the mixing chamber. Flow in the hopper section and prevention of ratholing are controlled either by installing some sort of inverted cone or by designing the hopper for mass flow. The Flo-Tronics Blender (Stein, 1990) is equipped with a larger number of individual small diameter pipes (Fig. 3.3.5(a)) arranged in either one or two rings. The Phillips Blender in Fig. 3.3.5(b) uses an inverted cone to minimize the extent of stagnant zones whereas the Multi-Pipe Blender (Fig. 3.3.5(c)) uses the mass flow approach to prevent any formation of stagnant zones (Wilms, 1988). Both blenders use multi-compartment pipes.

The disadvantage of having many individual pipes with small diameters is that these blending pipes may be subject to lateral forces resulting from non-uniform flow conditions and funnel flow. It is because of this disadvantage that the Phillips and Multi-Pipe Blender use thicker multi-compartment pipes, either a bundle of individual pipes welded together or of an extruded aluminium profile. The geometry of the intake openings and the diameter of the blending pipe have to be chosen with respect to blender size and flowability of the bulk solids.

An alternative for avoiding lateral forces on the blending pipes is to position them directly at the silo wall. With this concept (Wilms, 1986b) all supports become unnecessary with unchanged blending performance for all non-segregating bulk solids, such as plastic pellets. The Fuller Gravi-Merge Blender (Anon, 1989) is a combination of the pneumatic pellet blender, optionally using an internal recirculation system, and the multiple pipe

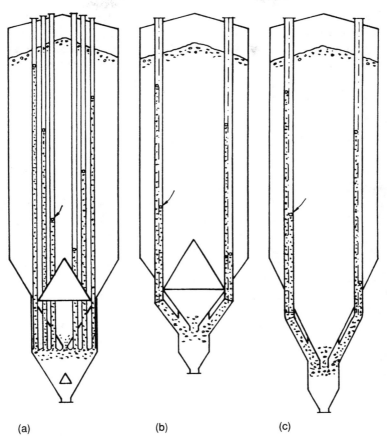

Fig. 3.3.5 Gravity blenders with blending pipes: (a) Flo-Tronics Blender; (b) Phillips Blender; (c) Multi-Pipe Blender.

blenders with blending pipes, i.e. extruded profiles, attached directly to the wall.

Different batches are usually poured into the blender successively, thereby forming individual layers. For homogenization of batches and layers it is advantageous to have an aspect ratio (height H : diameter D) of the cylindrical section of at least 2.5. For many applications it is then sufficient to have only one single pass through the blender. However, the material fed into the blender initially is within the blending chamber in the lower section of the tubes and hopper. Withdrawal of the first portion, therefore, does not lead to a sufficient homogenization, and recycling of at least a small portion of the whole content is necessary in batch operation. Data from blending tests supporting this approach have been published in the literature (Wilms, 1988).

The application of the mass flow approach to blender design leads to more uniform loading of the blending pipes. Therefore, only the Multi-Pipe Blender requires fewer support brackets than other designs. Besides the flexibility to incorporate these gravity blenders the low energy requirement for good blending has facilitated their application.

3.3.6 Operation of gravity blenders

Gravity blenders can easily be incorporated into any process, either batchwise or continuous. A very advantageous operation is to use two blenders in a row as single pass blenders without recirculation in continuous processes. This leads to better results than batchwise recirculation in two blenders working in parallel. With continuous operation, the final fluctuations are much smaller than with a batchwise operation. One very efficient approach is to build two blenders on top of each other, thus requiring only one vertical lift of the bulk solids.

However, most gravity blenders are used in batch operations with recirculation. In this case, a minimum recirculation is required to empty the lower section, blend chamber, blend hopper and blend pipes prior to discharge. This minimum amount depends on the blender design and is approximately 15% with multiple pipe blenders. More squat blenders with blending hoppers will require a higher degree of recirculation. With batch operation downstream continuous processes, multiple blenders (usually three) are operated in parallel with one being filled, one being recirculated and one being emptied.

3.3.7 Summary

Even though there is no single blender which has all advantages and can be used for all applications, there is a clearly increasing tendency to use the energy-efficient gravity flow blenders. All of these blenders influence the residence time distribution and/or velocity profile in the silo by means of internals. Of these, those designed for mass flow are the most suitable. A general survey on blending silos, including pneumatic, air-induced and mechanical blenders, volumes and possible applications is given in Fig. 3.3.6 (Wilms, 1992).

In addition, these internals influence the pressure distribution on the silo walls. The load distribution on the internals themselves is not completely known (Wilms, 1994) and some codes for structural design of silos explicitly exclude loads from internals.

References

Anon. Blending polymers in pellet and powder form *Powder Handling & Processing* 1 (1989), 2, 142

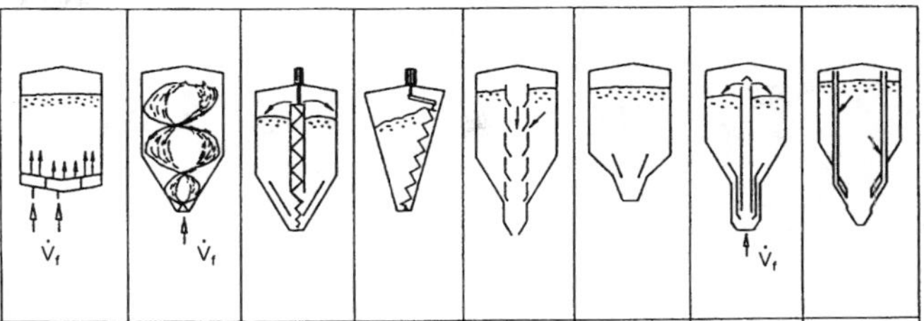

free flowing powder 50 μm < x < 500 μm	+	o	+	+	+	+	(+)	(+)
free flowing pellets 200 μm < x < 5000 μm	o	o	o	o	+	+	+	+
cohesive powders	–	+	+	+	(+)	+	–	–
vessel size up to [m³] (maximal)	1,000 (30,000)	200	100	30 (60)	200	200	600	1000
type of energy introduction	pneumatic		mechanical		gravity		pneumatic	gravity
specific energy requirement [kWh/t]	1-2	2-7	2-10		1-3		≈2	<1

Fig. 3.3.6 Survey on blending silos.

Carson, J.W.; Royal, T.A. In-bin blending improves process control *Powder Handling & Processing* 4 (1992), 3, 301–307
Hoppe, H.; Breucker, T. Pneumatische Mischer *Techn. Mitt.* 77 (1984), 12, 589–593
Johanson, J.R. In-bin blending *Chemical Engineering Progress* 66 (1970), 6
Johanson, J.R. Controlling flow patterns in bins by use of an insert *Bulk Solids Handling* 2 (1982), 3, 495–498
Krambrock, W. Schwerkraftmischer zum Kunststoffgranulat-Homogenisieren *Verfahrenstechnik* 23 (1989), 3, 30–38
Schwedes, J.; Richter, W. Der Pneumatische Granulatmischer *Aufbereitungs-Technik* 17 (1976), 3, 115–119
Stein, M.R. Gravity blenders: storage and blending in one step *Powder & Bulk Engng* (1990), 1, 32–36
Wilms, H. Homogenisieren von Schüttgütern in Silos *Chem.-Ing.-Techn.* 58 (1986a), 11, 867–875
Wilms, H. Homogenization of bulk solids in silos *Proc. 1st World Congress Powder Technol. Part III*, pp. 617–630, Nuremberg, 1986b
Wilms, H. Blending and homogenizing of bulk solids with the Zeppelin Multi-Pipe Gravity Blender *Bulk Solids Handling* 8 (1988), 6, 733–736
Wilms, H. Blending silos – an overview *Powder Handling & Processing* 44 (1992), 3, 293–299
Wilms, H. Silo design for flow and strength *Powder Handling & Processing* 6 (1994), 2, 193–197
Wilms, H.; Kiesgen, M. Zentralrohr-Mischsilo verbessert die Homogenität von Kunststoffen *Kunststoffe* 81 (1991), 12, 1100–1104
Wohnhas, N. Mischen und Homogenisieren von Schüttgütern *Schüttgut* 1 (1995), 2, 334–337
Zeppelin Multi-Flow Blender Zeppelin Schüttguttechnik GmbH, Weingarten, 1995

3.4 Simulation of blending silos
D. Schulze

Nomenclature

$a_{p,q}$	coefficient of the blending matrix
$b_{p,q}$	coefficient of matrix M_{ideal}
c	concentration
c_{ges}	concentration of the recirculated product
c_m	mean concentration in the blending silo
C	concentration vector
m	number of cells
M	blending matrix
M_{ideal}	matrix representing complete blending
n_i	number of layers of cell i
n_{theor}	theoretical number of layers of the entire silo
Q	volume flow rate (m³/s)
Q_i	volume flow rate through cell i (m³/s)
Q_{ges}	recirculated volume flow rate (m³/s)
t	time (s)
t_i	residence time of cell i (s)
t_m	mean residence time of the blending silo (s)
Δt	time period (s)
V	volume (m³)
ΔV	volume discharged per time period Δt (m³)
ΔV_i	volume discharged per time period Δt from cell i (m³)
V_i	volume of cell i (m³)
V_{ges}	silo volume (m³)
V_{tr}	volume of marked bulk solid (tracer volume) (m³)

Simulation of blending silos   143

z   number of cycles (recirculated volume divided by the silo volume)
γ   non-dimensional volume
η   non-dimensional residence time
φ   non-dimensional volume flow rate

Indices

i   numeration of the cells
j   numeration of the layers of a cell

3.4.1 Introduction

A blending silo is used for the blending and homogenizing ('homogenization silo') of bulk solids such as plastic pellets and aluminium powder. Examples of blending silos are shown in Fig. 3.4.1. The pneumatic pellet blender (Fig. 3.4.1(a)) (Schwedes and Richter, 1975, 1976; Krambrock, 1980, 1989) is a typical blending silo where the bulk solid is recirculated several times for blending. The bulk solid flowing out from the hopper is conveyed pneumatically upwards through the central tube and deposited again on the bulk

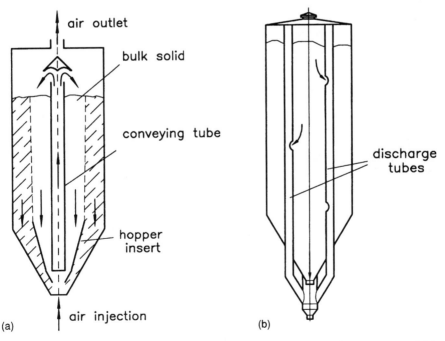

Fig. 3.4.1 (a) Pneumatic pellet blender (Schwedes and Richter, 1975, 1976; Krambrock, 1980, 1989); (b) Multiple pipe blender (Krambrock, 1980, 1989; Wilms, 1986, 1992).

solid surface after the separation of the conveying air. Through the differences of the flow velocities in the blending silo, which are influenced by the hopper-shaped insert, inside and outside the insert different residence times result. For example, the bulk solid in the hatched area in Fig. 3.4.1(a), which is flowing downwards outside the hopper-shaped insert, is slower than the bulk solid flowing inside the insert. Thereby a certain residence time distribution emerges and, hence, product from different areas of the blending silo becomes mixed. Through multiple recirculation of the silo contents blends can be achieved to any degree of uniformity required.

In the multiple pipe blender shown in Fig. 3.4.1(b) internal vertical tubes (so-called discharge tubes) are installed (Krambrock, 1980, 1989; Wilms, 1986, 1992). The bulk solid is discharged through the side openings of the tubes from different levels of the blending silo and brought together (mixed) at the silo outlet. Thereby a broad residence time distribution for the bulk solid flowing through the blending silo emerges. Because of its residence time distribution, which is clearly broader compared to that achievable with a pneumatic pellet blender (Fig. 3.4.1(a)), the multiple pipe blender is often used as a single pass blender, i.e. the bulk solid is not recirculated and runs through the blending silo only once.

The present section deals with the theoretical simulation of blending silos where the bulk solid is recirculated. The goal of such investigations is to optimize blending silos with respect to a smallest possible blending time and/or a small number of the necessary recirculations to achieve the desired degree of uniformity.

3.4.2 Blending silo simulation

The blending process in the blending silo is a more or less deterministic process because the residence time distribution is prescribed by the geometry of the blending silo and the flow properties of the bulk solid. As outlined above, the residence time distribution is the essential parameter for the blending effect.

In the past different approaches to the simulation of blending silos have been presented. The following approaches will be considered here:

- Layer model: The blending silo is regarded as a black box with a certain residence time distribution. By computer simulation the residence time distribution for optimal blending is sought after using a layer model (Schwedes and Richter, 1975, 1976; Krambrock, 1980, 1989; Schulze, 1995; Schulze and Lyle, 1995).
- Simulation on the basis of a measured residence time distribution (Carson and Royal, 1991, 1992).
- Simulation on the basis of a residence time distribution calculated from theoretically determined velocity profiles (Manjunath *et al.*, 1992; Craig *et al.*, 1994).

3.4.2.1 Layer model

3.4.2.1.1 Basic principle, introduction of non-dimensional numbers

A blending silo has a certain residence time distribution. One can represent a blending silo by a connection of several (m) silos i, which in the following are called cells. Each of these cells is characterized by a certain volume V_i and a volume flow rate Q_i (Fig. 3.4.2). Assuming, for example, for the blending silo shown in Fig. 3.4.1(a) that the bulk solid in the hatched area outside of the internal hopper has a different residence time from the bulk solid flowing through the internal hopper, one can represent the blender in a simplified way by two parallel cells of different residence time (Schwedes and Richter, 1975, 1976).

After volumes V_i and volume flow rates Q_i of each cell i have been chosen, the residence times t_i follow from

$$t_i = V_i / Q_i \tag{3.4.1}$$

The recirculation is realized by discharging the bulk solid at the bottom of each cell i and subsequently pouring it into the cells again at the top. The bulk solid discharged from a cell i has the time-dependent concentration $c_i(t)$. It is assumed that the bulk solid, which is simultaneously discharged from all cells i and recirculated, is mixed ideally during the recirculation.

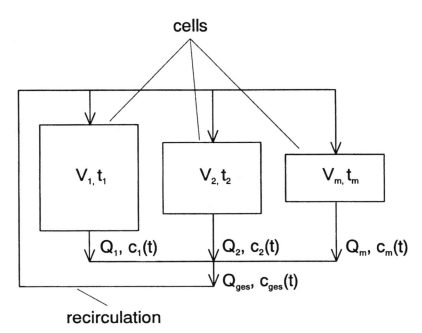

Fig. 3.4.2 Blending silo, represented by parallel cells.

The volume flow rate Q_{ges}, which is recirculated, results from the sum of the volume flow rates Q_i of all m cells.

$$Q_{ges} = \sum_{i=1}^{m} Q_i \qquad (3.4.2)$$

Accordingly, the concentration of the recirculated and thereby mixed product, $c_{ges}(t)$, is

$$c_{ges}(t) = \frac{1}{Q_{ges}} \sum_{i=1}^{m} \{c_i(t) Q_i\} \qquad (3.4.3)$$

For the non-dimensional representation of the blending silo at any amount of cells the following numbers are introduced (Schulze, 1995):

- Non-dimensional volume of cell i (ratio of the volume of cell i to the entire volume of the blending silo):

$$\gamma_i = \frac{V_i}{\sum V_i} = \frac{V_i}{V_{ges}} \qquad (3.4.4)$$

- Non-dimensional volume flow rate through cell i (ratio of the volume flow rate discharged from cell i to the volume flow rate discharged from the entire blending silo):

$$\varphi_i = \frac{Q_i}{\sum Q_i} = \frac{Q_i}{Q_{ges}} \qquad (3.4.5)$$

- Non-dimensional residence time of cell i (residence time of cell i divided by the mean residence time t_m of the blending silo, $t_m = V_{ges}/Q_{ges}$):

$$\eta_i = \frac{t_i}{t_m} = \frac{V_i/V_{ges}}{Q_i/Q_{ges}} = \frac{\gamma_i}{\varphi_i} \qquad (3.4.6)$$

For the simulation with the aid of a computer the recirculation process is subdivided in constant periods of time Δt. Each cell i is subdivided in n_i horizontal layers. The contents of each layer are characterized by a certain concentration $c_{i,j}$ (first index: cell number; second index: layer number). Figure 3.4.3 shows the principle of the layer model, which was used in Schwedes and Richter (1975, 1976), Krambrock (1980, 1989), Schulze (1995) and Schulze and Lyle (1995) for two parallel cells.

According to the layer model, the bulk solid is discharged stepwise. Per period Δt a volume ΔV is discharged, which consists of the volumes of the lowest layers of all cells. The discharged volume ΔV is mixed and – after the layers remaining in the cells move downwards one layer – again filled in above. Thereby in each cell the same volume is filled in which has previously been discharged from this cell.

The volume ΔV_i discharged per period Δt from a cell i is proportional to the volume flow rate Q_i:

$$\Delta V_i = Q_i \Delta t \qquad (3.4.7)$$

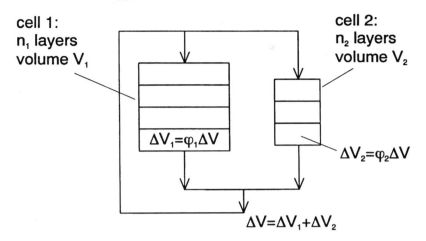

Fig. 3.4.3 Layer model of a blending silo with two cells ($m = 2$).

Hence, it follows

$$\frac{\Delta V_i}{\Delta V} = \frac{Q_i}{Q_{ges}} \quad (3.4.8)$$

and, using equation (3.4.5):

$$\Delta V_i = \varphi_i \Delta V \quad (3.4.9)$$

The layers in the individual cells are numbered from the top to the bottom (Fig. 3.4.4). The volume of each layer j in a cell i is equal to the partial volume ΔV_i, which is discharged per period Δt from cell i. The number of the layers in each individual cell, n_i, is to be calculated as

$$n_i = V_i/\Delta V_i \sim \gamma_i/\varphi_i \quad (3.4.10)$$

The number of layers, n_i, is equal to the number of time periods Δt which are necessary to recirculate the entire contents of cell i. The greater the number of layers, the longer the bulk solid remains in the corresponding cell, i.e. the values of n_i are proportional to the residence time t_i of cell i:

$$t_i = V_i/Q_i = V_i \, \Delta t/\Delta V_i = n_i \, \Delta t \quad (3.4.11)$$

Considering the whole blending silo as one unit, a theoretical number of layers n_{theor} can be assigned to it. n_{theor} is proportional to the mean residence time t_m of the blending silo:

$$n_{theor} = V_{ges}/\Delta V \quad (3.4.12)$$

$$t_m = V_{ges}/Q_{ges} = V_{ges} \, \Delta t/\Delta V = n_{theor} \Delta t \quad (3.4.13)$$

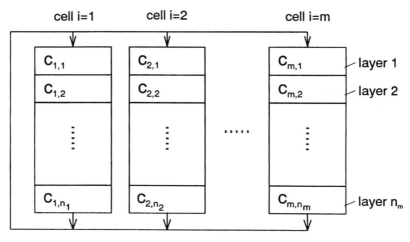

Fig. 3.4.4 Numeration of layers and cells.

n_{theor} indicates the number of periods Δt that are necessary to recirculate a volume of the size of the entire volume of the blending silo. If the blending silo consists only of one cell ($m = 1$), then $n_{theor} = n_1$, i.e. after the discharge of n_{theor} partial volumes of size $\Delta V = \Delta V_1$ the entire silo contents were recirculated and the content of each layer passed the outlet exactly once. Considering a blending silo with several parallel cells with different residence times t_i and/or numbers of layers n_i this is not the case: here at recirculation of n_{theor} partial volumes ΔV layers of cells with $n_i < n_{theor}$ will pass more than once, while in the cells with $n_i > n_{theor}$ the uppermost layer(s) will not arrive at the outlet after the recirculation of n_{theor} partial volumes ΔV.

The ratio of the number of layers n_i to the theoretical number of layers n_{theor} yields the non-dimensional residence time η_i:

$$\frac{n_i}{n_{theor}} = \frac{V_i/\Delta V_i}{V_{ges}/\Delta V} = \frac{\gamma_i}{\varphi_i} = \eta_i \qquad (3.4.14)$$

In equation (3.4.3) the concentration $c_{ges}(t)$ at the outlet of the blending silo is calculated from the time-dependent concentrations $c_i(t)$. In the layer model $c_i(t)$ is replaced by the concentration of the lowest layer of the corresponding cell:

$$c_{ges} = \sum_{i=1}^{m} \{c_{i,n_i} \varphi_i\} \qquad (3.4.15)$$

where n_i is the number of layers of cell i and m the number of cells.

With the derived non-dimensional numbers the simulation of the blending process in blending silos is possible without knowing the real dimensions of the examined system. Each blending silo can be characterized by an appropriate number of cells and the corresponding values of γ_i and φ_i (Schulze, 1995).

3.4.2.1.2 Simulation

For the simulation the number of cells, m, and the values of γ_i and φ_i first have to be defined. Therewith also the residence time distribution of the blending silo is determined. Then the number of layers, n_i, must be determined so that equation (3.4.14) is fulfilled. It may occur that for some numbers of layers (n_i) no integers will result if the given values of γ_i and φ_i are fulfilled exactly. In this case the n_i have to be rounded to obtain integers. From the new values of n_i the corresponding γ_i and φ_i have to be calculated, which will deviate somewhat from the values chosen first. Through the choice of sufficiently large numbers of layers, n_i, the deviation from the first chosen γ_i and φ_i can be limited.

When choosing the number of layers, certain minimum numbers are necessary to achieve sufficient precision in the calculations. At too few numbers of layers per period Δt too large a part of the silo contents is mixed, so that with decreasing numbers of layers the mixing results will appear more favourable. Preliminary examinations showed that the number of layers has no perceptible influence on the result of the simulation if the sum of the numbers of layers of all parallel cells is greater than 200.

At the recirculation of the contents of the blending silo, n_{theor} partial volumes ΔV have to be discharged to recirculate a volume of bulk solid which is equal to the silo volume, V_{ges} (equation (3.4.12)). The recirculation of a volume equal to V_{ges} is called a 'cycle' in the following. The number of cycles during the whole blending process is z. The recirculation of one layer according to one period Δt is called a 'recirculation step'.

Before starting the simulation the cells have to be 'filled', i.e. for each individual layer the initial concentration has to be chosen (e.g. for the simulation of a mixture of 10% black and 90% white particles, the concentration of 10% of the layers is '100% black' whereas the concentration of the remaining layers is '0% black'). Subsequently the contents of the blending silo are recirculated in periods Δt, until a given number of cycles z is reached.

Therewith each recirculation step (i.e. the recirculation of one partial volume ΔV) is carried out in the following order:

1. Discharge of layers $j = n_i$ (the lowest layers) from all m cells.
2. Calculation of the concentration c_{ges} of the mixture of the discharged layers (equation (3.4.15)).
3. Moving the contents of each layer remaining in the blending silo to the layer below (all cells): $c_{i,j} = c_{i,j-1}$.
4. Assigning the mixture concentration c_{ges}, which was calculated in step 2, to the top layers of all cells: $c_{i,1} = c_{ges}$.

150 Flow in silos

After having reached the given number of cycles, z, the contents of the individual cells are analysed with regard to the blending result, e.g. by calculating the variance of the concentrations found in the individual layers.

After completion of the blending process the blending silo has to be emptied. This non-stationary emptying process is not included in the calculations presented here. According to the construction of a blending silo, at emptying different phenomena can appear which cannot be described on the basis of a residence time distribution measured at the stationary conditions of the recirculation process (e.g. Fig. 3.4.1(b): as soon as the material level has dropped below a side opening of a discharge tube, no more bulk solid can flow through this opening).

Figure 3.4.5 shows a simple example for a simulation after the process described above. The blending silo is represented by two parallel cells, which have two and three, respectively, layers of identical volume ΔV_i. The corresponding values of γ_i and φ_i are shown in the figure. The volume flow rates through both cells are the same ($\varphi_1 = \varphi_2$). The ratio of the volumes of the cells is 3:2. For simplification the numbers of layers chosen is very small (see above: remarks on the choice of a sufficiently large number of layers).

The uppermost layer of cell 2 is filled with black bulk solid, the remaining layers contain white bulk solid (initial condition after filling, recirculation step 0). After the first recirculation step (from all cells the bottom layers are discharged, recirculated and mixed, and filled in on top again) the black material is found in the lowest layer of cell 2. At the next recirculation step the lowest (black) layer of cell 2 and the lowest (white) layer of cell 1 are discharged. From it a mixture '50% black' emerges, which is filled into the top layers of both cells. With increasing number of recirculation steps a more and more uniform distribution of the black bulk solid is achieved. After 10 recirculation steps (corresponding to the recirculation of a volume equal to four times the silo volume) an almost homogeneous mixture is achieved.

3.4.2.1.3 Blending matrix

For the simulation of blending silos following the layer model, in Schulze and Lyle (1995) it is proposed to use a so-called blending matrix. For the layer approach the blending silo is subdivided in parallel cells each with a certain residence time and a certain amount of layers (section 3.4.2.1.1). The contents of the individual layers are indicated by the concentrations $c_{i,j}$. This is shown is Fig. 3.4.6 by using a simplified model with two parallel cells (corresponding to the example given in Fig. 3.4.5).

The blending process described in section 3.4.2.1.1 emerges through the recirculation of the bulk solid. A recirculation step can be presented mathematically with the help of a transition matrix M, which moves the contents of the layers accordingly. For the example of Fig. 3.4.1 it follows:

Simulation of blending silos 151

2 cells with layers of equal volume
$\gamma_1 = 0.6; \gamma_2 = 0.4$
$\varphi_1 = \varphi_2 = 0.5$

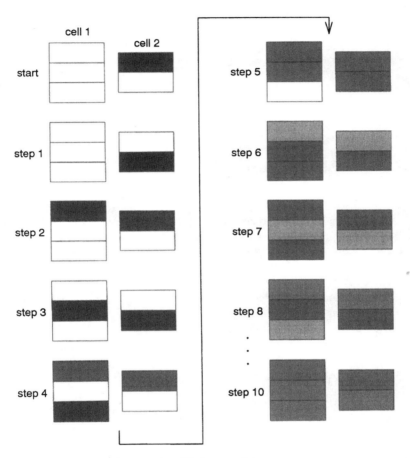

Fig. 3.4.5 Blending simulation (simplified example).

$$\begin{bmatrix} c_{1,1} \\ c_{1,2} \\ c_{1,3} \\ c_{2,1} \\ c_{2,2} \end{bmatrix}_{\text{step } k+1} = \begin{bmatrix} a_{11} & a_{12} & a_{13} & a_{14} & a_{15} \\ a_{21} & a_{22} & a_{23} & a_{24} & a_{25} \\ a_{31} & a_{32} & a_{33} & a_{34} & a_{35} \\ a_{41} & a_{42} & a_{43} & a_{44} & a_{45} \\ a_{51} & a_{52} & a_{53} & a_{54} & a_{55} \end{bmatrix} \cdot \begin{bmatrix} c_{1,1} \\ c_{1,2} \\ c_{1,3} \\ c_{2,1} \\ c_{2,2} \end{bmatrix}_{\text{step } k} \quad (3.4.16a)$$

$$C_{\text{step } k+1} = M \cdot C_{\text{step } k} \quad (3.4.16b)$$

Flow in silos

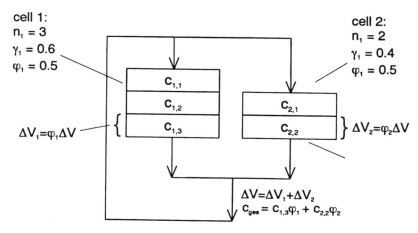

Fig. 3.4.6 Representation of a blending silo through cells and layers.

The contents of the layers of the cells are represented by the single-column 'concentration vector' C in equation (3.4.16) according to the example of Fig. 3.4.6. To perform a recirculation step (recirculation of a layer per cell, period Δt), the momentary concentration vector $C_{\text{step } k}$ is multiplied by the blending matrix M, so that a new concentration vector $C_{\text{step } k+1}$ is generated. Vector $C_{\text{step } k+1}$ contains the concentrations in the blending silo emerging after one recirculation step.

The number of rows of the concentration vector is equal to the sum of all layers of all cells which is equal to five for the example of Fig. 3.4.6. Just as large is the amount of columns and rows of the blending matrix M.

To simulate a blending process, which emerges through many (amount n) recirculation steps following one after another, the concentration vector $C_{\text{step } k+1}$ calculated from equation (3.4.16) is multiplied again with the blending matrix M, i.e. for each period Δt (n-times) the momentary concentration vector C is multiplied by the blending matrix as shown in equation (3.4.16). Mathematically equivalent to this procedure is the multiplication of the concentration vector C by the nth power of the blending matrix M:

$$\begin{bmatrix} c_{1,1} \\ c_{1,2} \\ c_{1,3} \\ c_{2,1} \\ c_{2,2} \end{bmatrix}_{\text{step } k+n} = \begin{bmatrix} a_{11} & a_{12} & a_{13} & a_{14} & a_{15} \\ a_{21} & a_{22} & a_{23} & a_{24} & a_{25} \\ a_{31} & a_{32} & a_{33} & a_{34} & a_{35} \\ a_{41} & a_{42} & a_{43} & a_{44} & a_{45} \\ a_{51} & a_{52} & a_{53} & a_{54} & a_{55} \end{bmatrix}^n \cdot \begin{bmatrix} c_{1,1} \\ c_{1,2} \\ c_{1,3} \\ c_{2,1} \\ c_{2,2} \end{bmatrix}_{\text{step } k} \qquad (3.4.17a)$$

$$C_{\text{step } k+n} = M^n \cdot C_{\text{step } k} \qquad (3.4.17b)$$

If n is chosen so that it corresponds to the entire blending process (e.g. corresponding to the recirculation of three times the silo volume), then the exponentiated blending matrix contains the information of the entire blending process through n recirculation steps, independent of the initial concentration or the initial distribution of the quantities to be mixed. The individual coefficients of the exponentiated blending matrix (M^n) indicate how the bulk solid from each individual layer is distributed to all layers of the blending silos through the whole blending process. If, for example, in equation (3.4.17) vector $C_{\text{step } k}$ represents the initial conditions ($k = 0$), then $C_{\text{step } k+n}$ will represent the concentrations after n recirculation steps, i.e. after the blending process. Then the coefficients of the exponentiated blending matrix indicate in which layers the initial contents of all individual layers can be found after the blending process.

For the representation of the entire blending process equation (3.4.17) can be written as follows:

$$C_{\text{step } n} = M^n \cdot C_{\text{start}} \qquad (3.4.18)$$

The exponentiated blending matrix (M^n) contains considerably more information than one can obtain from the simulations using the layer model (Schwedes and Richter, 1975, 1976; Krambrock, 1980, 1989). If one has calculated the exponentiated blending matrix, one can consider directly the result of the blending after n recirculation steps at different initial concentrations or different distributions of the quantities to be mixed in the blending silo (equation (3.4.18)).

The blending matrix M, which describes a single recirculation step, can be set up after the definition of the numbers of cells and layers (m and n_i, section 3.4.2.1.1). For the example shown in Figs 3.4.5 and 3.4.6, the blending matrix has the form shown in the following equation (note: first index: cell number, second index: layer number):

$$\begin{bmatrix} c_{1,1} \\ c_{1,2} \\ c_{1,3} \\ c_{2,1} \\ c_{2,2} \end{bmatrix}_{\text{step } k+1} = \begin{bmatrix} 0 & 0 & \varphi_1 & 0 & \varphi_2 \\ 1 & 0 & 0 & 0 & 0 \\ 0 & 1 & 0 & 0 & 0 \\ 0 & 0 & \varphi_1 & 0 & \varphi_2 \\ 0 & 0 & 0 & 1 & 0 \end{bmatrix} \cdot \begin{bmatrix} c_{1,1} \\ c_{1,2} \\ c_{1,3} \\ c_{2,1} \\ c_{2,2} \end{bmatrix}_{\text{step } k} \qquad (3.4.19)$$

At a recirculation step the contents of the lowest layers are taken from cells 1 and 2, respectively, recirculated and mixed. The mixture concentration c_{ges} follows from the concentrations of the lowest layers ($c_{1,3}$ and $c_{2,2}$) and the non-dimensional volume flow rates φ_1 and φ_2 of both cells according to equation (3.4.15):

$$c_{\text{ges}} = c_{1,3}\varphi_1 + c_{2,2}\varphi_2 \qquad (3.4.20)$$

The recirculated product of concentration c_{ges} is then poured into the top layers of both cells, i.e. after the recirculation step the concentrations in the top layers ($c_{1,1}$ and $c_{2,1}$) are equal to c_{ges}. This is considered in the blending matrix in equation (3.4.19) through the coefficients φ_1 and φ_2 in the first and fourth row. The remaining coefficients of the first and fourth row are equal to 0, because from the remaining 'non-lowest' layers no bulk solid is found in the top layers after this recirculation step. The contents of these layers move one layer downwards. That is to say, each layer – besides the top layers, in which the mixture is filled in – receives the complete contents of the layer above. This is realized in the blending matrix in equation (3.4.19) through the coefficients which are equal to 1 and which are ordered exactly one row underneath the main diagonal of the blending matrix.

A blending matrix can also be set up for more complex systems with more cells and layers. Because of the simple rules for the set-up of the blending matrix, this can be done automatically with the aid of a computer program.

3.4.2.1.4 Evaluation of the blending quality independent of the concentration

With the help of the blending matrix a blending silo can be optimized so that it yields the best mixing result which is possible for any concentration of the components to be mixed and their distribution in the beginning of the blending process. The aim of this approach is to find a blending silo yielding good blending results for as many different conditions as possible.

A valuation of a blending silo with regard to this possibility has to be carried out as follows: at first the coefficients of a matrix, which would lead from the initial condition directly to a complete mixture, have to be calculated (Schulze and Lyle, 1995). This matrix is called M_{ideal}. The less the coefficients of the exponentiated blending matrix (M^n) differ from the corresponding coefficients of the matrix M_{ideal}, the better the quality of the mixture. With the help of a kind of standard deviation which is calculated from these differences, a valuation of the blending silo independent of the concentration of the product to be mixed is possible. For more detailed information please refer to Schulze and Lyle (1995).

3.4.2.1.5 Application of the blending matrix on blending tests

The blending process is influenced essentially through the residence time distribution of the blending silo. Measurements of the residence time distribution in blending silos have already been carried out (e.g. Carson and Royal, 1991, 1992; Manjunath *et al.*, 1992; Craig *et al.*, 1994). In Dau and Ebert (1995a, b) a computer-controlled, optic on-line measuring technique is described where the concentration at the silo outlet can be measured continuously.

In order to measure the residence time distribution, the blending silo is to be filled so that finally a quantity of marked bulk solid (tracer) which is small with respect to the entire silo contents is given up. Then the bulk solid is discharged from the blending silo whereby unmarked bulk solid is refilled simultaneously at the same flow rate to keep the filling level constant (stationary conditions) (Schulze and Lyle, 1995; Carson and Royal, 1991, 1992).

At the outlet the marker concentration is measured over time. An example of a measured course of concentration is shown in the diagram in Fig. 3.4.7(a) where the starting point of the time axis indicates the beginning of discharge. Since with respect to the silo volume only a small quantity of

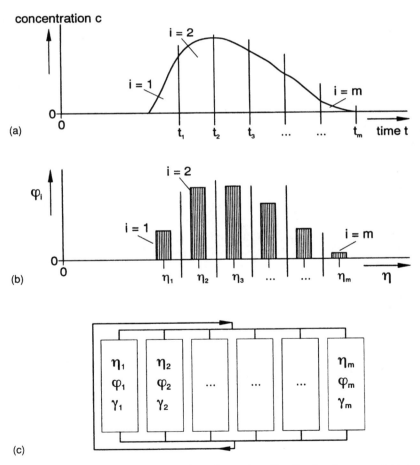

Fig. 3.4.7 (a) Example of a measured residence time distribution (concentration c vs. time t); (b) subdivision in samples; (c) representation by cells.

marked bulk solid is given up, the measured course of concentration is almost identical to the residence time distribution.

To obtain the parameters of the layer model and, hence, the blending matrix from the measured course of concentration $c(t)$, the course of concentration has to be subdivided (Fig. 3.4.7(a)). For each of the m intervals the medium non-dimensional residence time η_i, the non-dimensional volume flow rate φ_i, and the non-dimensional volume γ_i are to be calculated (Schulze and Lyle, 1995).

The non-dimensional residence time η_i of a certain interval i shown in Fig. 3.4.7(a) follows from its mean residence time which is to be divided by the mean residence time of the blending silo, $t_m = V_{ges}/Q_{ges}$:

$$\eta_i = \frac{t_{i-1} + t_i}{2t_m} \quad (3.4.21)$$

The non-dimensional volume flow rate φ_i follows from the volume of marked particles discharged during a time interval i divided by the entire volume of marked bulk solid, V_{tr}:

$$\varphi_i = \frac{\int_{t_{i-1}}^{t_i} Qc\,dt}{\int_0^\infty Qc\,dt} = \frac{\int_{t_{i-1}}^{t_i} Qc\,dt}{V_{tr}} \quad (3.4.22)$$

If η_i and φ_i are determined, γ_i follows according to equation (3.4.6):

$$\gamma_i = \eta_i \varphi_i \quad (3.4.23)$$

With the results of the equations presented above, the intervals chosen in Fig. 3.4.7(a) can be presented in a φ–η bar chart (Fig. 3.4.7(b)). Then, according to the layer model, a cell is assigned to each interval (Fig. 3.4.7(c)). The narrower the intervals chosen, the more cells are required and the more exactly will the blending matrix represent the actual conditions.

With the information given in Fig. 3.4.7(c) the numbers of layers (section 3.4.2.1.1) can be calculated and the blending matrix set up (section 3.4.2.1.3). If the blending matrix is known, the existing blending silo can be examined further through simulation using the computer, i.e. costly blending tests are not necessary. Possible tasks to be examined are:

- Blending of different concentrations.
- Determination of the required number of recirculations for a specific uniformity of the mixture.
- Comparison with other blending silos, whose residence time distributions and/or blending matrices are known.

3.4.2.1.6 Background of the 'black box approach'

Using the layer model, the blending silo is regarded as a 'black box'. The philosophy of the black box approach is as follows.

The optimization of a blending silo should be performed in two steps: in the first step the residence time distribution required for an optimal mixture is sought independently of the actual design of any blending silo (blending silo = 'black box'). After the optimal residence time distribution has been found, in the second step a blending silo can be constructed so that this optimal residence time distribution is achieved. Subsequently, attempts to describe the velocity distribution dependent on silo geometry and flow properties can be used (Manjunath *et al.*, 1992; Craig *et al.*, 1994), and/or model tests with varying silo geometries (hopper angles, inserts, etc.) can be carried out in order to find the geometry achieving the optimal residence time distribution (Carson and Royal, 1991, 1992; Manjunath *et al.*, 1992; Craig *et al.*, 1994).

3.4.2.2 Simulation on the basis of measured residence time distributions

In Carson and Royal (1991, 1992) the blending behaviour of a blending silo is simulated on the basis of a measured residence time distribution. The measurement of the residence time distribution is performed in a similar way to that described in section 3.4.2.1.5. A single layer of marked bulk solid is put on top of the silo contents. During discharge a constant level of bulk solid is maintained by adding unmarked bulk solid to the top surface. The concentration at the outlet is measured vs. the discharged volume or time, respectively.

The measured residence time distribution is then used for the simulation of blending, whereby single-pass blending as well as recirculating blending can be examined. For the simulation of recirculating blending, the same residence time distribution as measured in the single-layer test is applied to the recirculated bulk solid. To evaluate the blending result, the concentration at the silo outlet is examined.

In principle, the method described above is similar to that outlined in section 3.4.2.1.5: the residence time distribution of a blending silo is found to be the most important information about its behaviour. After having measured the residence time distribution, a blending silo can be simulated. Whereas in section 3.4.2.1.5 a blending matrix is determined on the basis of the residence time distribution, the calculations referred to in Carson and Royal are performed by directly using the residence time distribution for the simulation of the blending effect.

With the computer simulation due to Carson and Royal (1991, 1992) different conditions can be examined, e.g. fluctuating concentration of the input stream. The authors state that the results of model tests can be scaled up to full size blenders. More detailed information and examples are presented in their papers.

3.4.2.3 Simulation on the basis of calculated residence time distributions

In Manjunath *et al.* (1992) and Craig *et al.* (1994) the velocity profile in a silo is calculated on the basis of existing theories describing the stress and velocity fields in hoppers and cylinders. Therefore, depending on the silo geometry and the flow properties of the bulk solid to be blended, the residence time distribution is predicted. This allows the volume concentration of the bulk solid discharged from the outlet to be determined.

To evaluate the blending performance of a silo as the bulk solid is recirculated, linear systems theory is applied (Craig *et al.*, 1994) where the volume concentration at the silo outlet for continuous recirculation is given by the convolution integral principle.

Hence, on the basis of theoretically determined velocity distributions it is possible to simulate a blending silo. As an example (Craig *et al.*, 1994), the optimization of a silo with wedge-shaped hopper is demonstrated. Additionally, blending tests have been performed which show a good agreement with the theoretically determined results.

3.4.3 Summary and further research

In the present section different approaches for the simulation of blending silos are given. The layer model was derived first of all to find out the residence time distribution which will yield the optimal blending results. Since calculations according to the layer model were already performed in the 1970s, the basic principles of blending simulation have been outlined using this approach.

All the approaches presented here are valid only for stationary conditions, i.e. constant filling level in the silo and, hence, constant residence time distribution. For further research it seems to be of interest to examine also the non-stationary filling and discharging of blending silos. Especially for multi-pipe blenders a significant blending effect is achieved by only filling and then discharging the blender. A new measuring technique (Dau and Ebert, 1995a, b) makes it possible to perform a lot of blending tests in a reasonable time.

References

Carson, J.W.; Royal, T.A.: *Techniques of In-bin Blending*, IMechE (1991), paper no. C418/056

Carson, J.W.; Royal, T.A.: In-bin blending improves process control, *Powder Handling & Processing* 4 (1992) 3, pp. 301–307

Craig, D.A.; Roberts, A.W.; Manjunath, K.S.; De Silva, S.R.: Utilising the impulse response concept to predict blending capabilities of silos, *Powder Handling & Processing* 6 (1994) 4, pp. 373–378

Dau, G.; Ebert, F.: Die optoelektronische Konzentrationsmessung, *Schüttgut* 1 (1995a) 2, pp. 317–319

Dau, G.; Ebert, F.: On the mixing quality of a gravity mixer with different mixing elements, *Preprints PARTEC, 3rd Europ. Symp. Storage and Flow of Particulate Solids*, Nuremberg (1995b), pp. 293–302

Krambrock, W.: Möglichkeiten zum Mischen von Schüttgut, *Aufbereitungs-Technik* 2 (1980), pp. 45–56

Krambrock, W.: Schwerkraftmischer zum Kunststoffgranulat-Homogenisieren, *Verfahrenstechnik* **23** (1989) 3, pp. 30–38

Manjunath, K.S.; De Silva, S.R.; Roberts, A.W.: Homogenization of bulk powders in plane symmetric silos, *Powder Handling & Processing* **4** (1992) 3, pp. 283–292

Schulze, D.: Theoretische Betrachtungen von Mischsilos, 1: Grundlagen, *Schüttgut* **1** (1995) 3, pp. 483–486

Schulze, D.; Lyle C: Theoretische Betrachtungen von Mischsilos, 2: Mischmatrix und Beurteilungskriterien, *Schüttgut* **1** (1995) 4, pp. 615–618

Schwedes, J.; Richter, W.: Grundlagen zur Auslegung pneumatischer Granulatmischer, *VDI-Berichte* No. 232 (1975), pp. 295–301

Schwedes, J.; Richter, W.: Der pneumatische Granulatmischer, *Aufbereitungs-Technik* **3** (1976), pp. 115–119

Wilms, H.: Homogenisieren von Schüttgütern in Mischsilos, *Chem.-Ing.-Tech.* **58** (1986) 11, pp. 867–875

Wilms, H.: Blending silos, *Powder Handling & Processing* **4** (1992) 3, pp. 293–299

3.5 Segregation of particulate solids in silos
G.G. Enstad and J. Mosby

3.5.1 Introduction

Segregation is a general term for separation of entities with different characteristics. In the technical world segregation of particulate solids causes quality variations and instability in chemical reactions involving particulate solids. Segregation problems are common for mining companies handling thousands of tonnes of material, as well as for pharmaceutical companies with batches of a few kilograms.

In industry people have been aware of the problems caused by segregation of particulate solids for a considerable time. Most of the earliest publications are on segregation of coal (Holmes, 1934; Castaloni, 1935; Hebley, 1936; Sherman and Kaiser, 1937; Mitchell, 1938; Brown, 1939; Stock, 1944). Garve (1925) found that small particles were collected in the centre, and the coarser ones near the walls in a centrally filled coal silo. His interpretation of the cause was that coarser particles have greater momentum, and will therefore roll down and collect along the outer periphery of the cone. If the centre core in the silo is emptied first, the fine particles will come out first. This flow pattern was established by Wittich (1915). Garve studied the flow pattern of sand in semicircular model hoppers of different hopper half-angles; 45°, 37.5°, 30° and 13°. For all except the 13° angle, the flow was in a central core. For the hopper with the half-angle of 13°, the powder moved as a plug, but Garve concluded that such a steep hopper could not be used in practice, because there would be problems with bridging and hang-ups, and the storing capacity of the silo would be too small. Later workers, however, have come to other conclusions (Jenike, 1964).

Segregation of particulate solids in silos

Segregation of particulate solids occurs in most process stages, causing quality variations which are disturbing when mild, and disastrous when severe. The segregation problems may be especially severe in silos, where large quantities of particles are stored. Some demonstrations of such problems are provided by Fürll (1994).

3.5.2 Fundamental mechanisms and processes causing segregation

Based on an extensive study of the literature and the experience of the authors, segregation can be broadly classified into five processes and several mechanisms. The segregation processes are:

- heap segregation
- percolation
- displacement segregation
- fluid segregation
- impact segregation

3.5.2.1 Heap segregation

This is often referred to as a segregation mechanism, but here it is regarded as a segregation process, where as many as five segregation mechanisms can be active:

- Rolling (Matthée, 1967/68)
- Sieving (Shinohara, 1985)
- Push-away effects (Tanaka, 1971)
- Angle of repose effects (Johanson, 1988)
- Fluidization effects (Johanson, 1988)

Rolling and sieving are probably the most important mechanisms, while push-away, angle of repose and fluidization effects can be active in special cases. The rolling mechanism is active when single particles are moving down the heap slope, where big particles are rolling without being stopped by any obstacles before they come to the end of the slope, whereas small particles are stopped close to the top of the heap. The sieving mechanism is active when the powder slides in layers down the slope. In this case the small particles are sifting down through the openings between bigger particles, settling down on the static surface underneath the sliding layer. The push-away mechanism is active when there is a density difference, where the dense particles will push away the light particles, and settle down at the top of the heap. Generally it is found that particles of low mobility will settle down near the top of a heap. Low mobility particles are small, dense, angular or plastic particles.

Heap segregation will give results as shown in Fig. 3.5.1.

The angle of repose mechanism is active when one component at a time

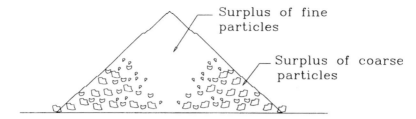

Fig. 3.5.1 Typical segregation heap.

is poured on to a heap. The components of the largest angles of repose are then collected in the centre of the heap.

The fluidizing mechanism is seen when a mixture containing a large amount of fine particles, is poured in a heap at a rather high filling rate. The powder may then be fluidized, and the fluidized layers will flow down the heap surface. The coarse particles will sediment through the fluidized layer and settle out near the centre of the heap, whereas the fine particles will proceed to the edge of the heap. This effect was seen in an investigation of the segregation of fine alumina and coarse sand, carried out in a student project at Telemark College (Augeli et al., 1994).

3.5.2.2 Percolation

This is caused by small particles moving through powder beds by falling into spaces between larger particles, particularly in high shear zones (Williams, 1976). Percolation is for instance encountered in many types of mixers (Stephens and Bridgwater, 1978), during filling and emptying of silos, especially funnel flow silos in which high shear zones are present, and during transport (e.g. in rail cars, trucks or on belts) during which powders are subjected to vibration.

3.5.2.3 Displacement segregation

This is also caused by vibration (Williams, 1976). Here large particles move upwards. The mechanism involved is a type of percolation, since when a large particle is displaced upwards, it is prevented from regaining its previous position due to the fact that small particles have occupied the empty space. The classical case is again transportation in rail cars, trucks or on belts, where the process of displacement segregation causes the large particles to end up on top of the rest of the mass.

3.5.2.4 Fluid segregation

This is caused by the influence of particle properties on the motion in a fluid (de Silva and Enstad, 1991). Three mechanisms may be involved:

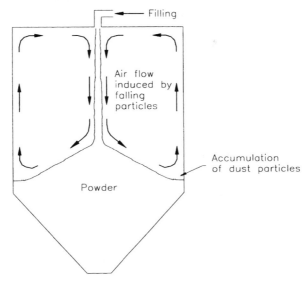

Fig. 3.5.2 Air current segregation in a silo.

- Trajectory segregation
- Air current segregation
- Fluidization segregation

The main reason for this type of segregation is the differences between drag forces and body forces caused by gravity or acceleration.

In a silo the falling particles fed into the silo will induce an air flow, which carries fine particles towards the walls, where they are collected, whereas coarse particles will settle out below the inlet point (Fig. 3.5.2).

3.5.2.5 Impact segregation

This causes particles with different characteristics to behave differently after impacts, either between themselves, or with walls of containing equipment (Enggrav *et al.*, 1989).

The segregation processes that are most important for silos are heap segregation, fluid segregation and percolation.

3.5.3 Influence of independent variables

Holmes (1934) was a pioneer in determining the influence of different variables. He determined the effect of size, density, feed rate, fall height, size of heap, content of fines and the presence of moisture on the surface of the particles.

164   Flow in silos

Particle properties that could affect the motion of a particle, will affect the segregation. These properties are:

- Size
- Density
- Shape
- Modulus of elasticity
- Friction coefficient
- Adhesion

Some of the properties could be influenced by process variables, such as adding water to the powder. In addition, it is generally found that segregation in silos increases with the size of the silo, and decreases with increasing feed rates (Shinohara, 1990).

3.5.4 Counteraction of segregation

Although modifications of the particles are often very difficult in practice, reduction of size by grinding (making materials more cohesive) or making the particles effectively monosized by some form of size enlargement, will generally reduce problems associated with segregation.

Many segregation problems in industry are related to the filling and discharging of silos, and the charging of other process equipment. Minimizing segregation during filling is one possibility, and counteraction during discharge is another.

To reduce segregation during filling it is possible to spread the feed as shown in Fig. 3.5.3. This concept is utilized by a number of other devices, spreading the feed into several feeding points.

Even when there is a considerable segregation taking place during the filling of a silo, as indicated in Fig. 3.5.4(a), the homogeneity of the material

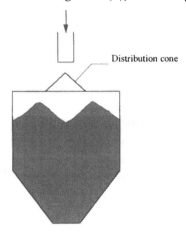

Fig. 3.5.3 Distributor at the top of the silo due to Garve (1925).

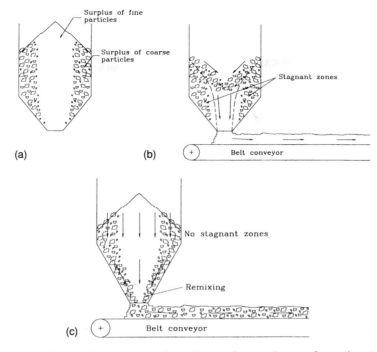

Fig. 3.5.4 Filling and discharging from funnel flow and mass flow silos: (a) after filling; (b) funnel flow; (c) mass flow.

discharged from the silo will depend on the mode of flow. In funnel flow, as shown in Fig. 3.5.4(b), the flow channel is first emptied, containing all the fines. Afterwards the material close to the wall is discharged, in this case containing the coarse particles. In mass flow both fine and coarse particles are discharged simultaneously, giving a fairly good remix as the powder is discharged from the silo (Fig. 3.5.4(c)).

3.5.5 Segregation testers

As explained above, segregation of particulate solids is caused by several mechanisms. The methods that can be used for counteraction may be different for the different mechanisms. Segregation testers might provide information about what are the most important segregation mechanisms in each case. This information may help to decide the best measures that can be taken to minimize segregation.

The testers available so far have been devoted to heap segregation (Shinohara, Shoji and Tanaka, 1972; Harris and Hildon, 1970; Drahun and Bridgwater, 1983; Bagster, 1983). The reproducibility of these testers has

166 Flow in silos

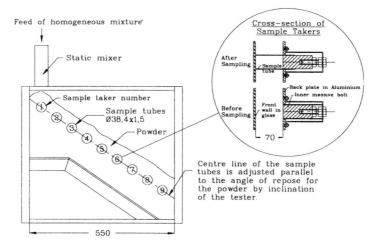

Fig. 3.5.5 The two-dimensional segregation tester at Tel-Tek, Dept. of POSTEC.

been poor, and a new tester has been developed at POSTEC, as shown in Fig. 3.5.5.

In order to reduce the quantity of powder used in the experiment, only one side of a two-dimensional heap is formed in the tester.

The tester is a box with a front wall in glass and a back wall in aluminium. The depth is 7 cm. The length of the surface measured along the sample takers is 63 cm. The tester is equipped with nine sample takers, and the tester is adjusted so that the sample takers are positioned on a line parallel to the angle of repose for the actual powder. The tester is shown together with a sample taker in Fig. 3.5.5.

The material to be tested is introduced in the upper left corner of the tester. The material will then flow down the inclined bottom plate, which has the function to reduce the amount of powder needed for an experiment.

In order to check the segregation during filling of a heap, it is extremely important to feed a homogeneous material into the tester. There are several possible ways of doing so. The first and the simplest is to homogenize, and pour the test material into a mass flow silo. The material could then be fed into the tester at a certain feed rate. The problem here is that you could have segregation during filling of the silo from the mixer, or, if the size difference within the material is large enough, there could be percolation in the mass flow silo. In order to ensure constant composition in the fed material, one has to check by taking samples of the feed.

The solution that has been chosen at POSTEC is to feed the two or more components separately. If the feeders are stable this feeding method will ensure a constant composition of the mixture over time. The components are fed into a static mixer to ensure a homogeneous feed over the cross-section of the tester.

Segregation of particulate solids in silos

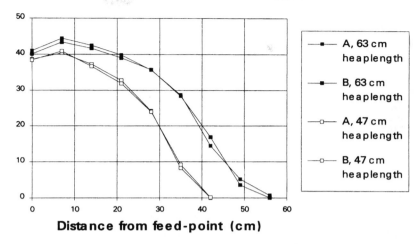

Fig. 3.5.6 Repeatability of the tests. Two typical examples.

In the two-dimensional tester the feeding from the static mixer is done through a slit so that the powder enters the heap as a sheet across the total depth of the tester.

To demonstrate the reproducibility, two different tests (heap length 47 and 63 cm) with two repetitions are shown in Fig. 3.5.6. The test powders are alumina (x_{50} = 90 μm) and Leighton Buzzard sand (x_{50} = 450 μm). The size distributions have no overlap.

Figure 3.5.6 shows typical test results of two parallels for two heap lengths. For the experiments with alumina and sand the standard deviation of each sample is always less than 1% of alumina. This proves that the reproducibility of the test is very good, and that segregation is not a random process, but predictable to a high degree. The tester can be used for basic studies of segregation, as well as testing the segregation properties of given powders.

3.5.6 Modelling of segregation

In order to reduce segregation it could be useful to have a computer-based model to predict the segregation likely to occur under given conditions. The model could also be used to predict the conditions which give as little segregation as possible.

In order to simulate a real segregation situation, a mathematical model for the actual segregation mechanisms that are likely to occur has to be defined. The greatest problem is that usually more than one segregation mechanism is responsible for the total segregation pattern in the bulk material. It is, therefore, a great challenge to develop a universal model for segregation. In spite of that, some have already tried to do so.

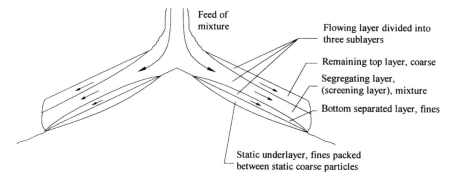

Fig. 3.5.7 Flow of particles in layers down a heap as assumed by Shinohara.

So far only the model due to Shinohara (1990) can be used to calculate the segregation pattern after forming a heap. The model covers only internal percolation in the flowing layers, the sieving mechanism.

Shinohara's model describes how a binary mixture of particles flows down a heap surface. This is supposed to be a layering process. The segregation is caused by differences in particle size, shape or density. The model is described by three general model parameters, the penetration rate Q, the packing rate P and the velocity ratio R. These parameters will depend on the physical parameters, such as the void fraction between particles, particle size, shape and density.

Every flowing layer is divided into three sublayers: the remaining top layer, the segregating layer and the bottom separated layer. Underneath the flowing layer is the static underlayer (Fig. 3.5.7).

The model gives four partial differential equations that can be solved numerically. A computer code which did this was used to compare with results from the POSTEC tester. However, only in special cases were satisfactory results obtained.

For the moment, therefore, this model has been abandoned, and a statistical approach has been chosen. The method is called 'multivariate analysis', and an example of which fits are obtained is shown in Fig. 3.5.8, which has been abstracted from a student report by Augeli et al. (1994). This model takes into account all variables of importance, like particle size, geometry of tester, particle density, mixing ratio, etc. A best fit to experimental data is found, and this fit can be used to predict segregation inside the region of the tests the fit is based on. This model will become better the more experimental data that are made available.

3.5.7 Further research

Basic investigations to study which parameters are the most important ones for segregation of particulate solids need to be continued. As many tests as

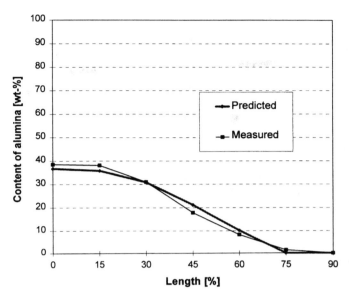

Fig. 3.5.8 Fitting a multivariate model to experimental data from the segregation tester at POSTEC (Augeli *et al.*, 1994).

possible should be carried out and used to further improve the statistical model. Further developments of the Shinohara model should also be carried out, as this might provide a simpler solution in special cases.

Similar work also has to be carried out on air-induced segregation.

More investigation is needed on percolations, to establish when and how important it is in comparison with the other segregation mechanisms.

A single test to characterize the segregation tendencies of a given powder is desirable, and should be established. The future goal would be to have a theory and a tester which would enable one to characterize the powder, and from that predict how severe the segregation problems in any given circumstances would be. That would enable one to choose solutions before any costly installations are put in place.

References

Augeli, J.; Dyrøy, A.; Huseby, G.; Kolstø, N.; Rafoss, A.K.: Modellering av segregering av particulære materialer. Student project at Telemark College, Institute of Technology. *Report Siv-6-94*, December 1994.

Bagster, D.F.: The influence of cohesion on segregation patterns in bins. *Intern. Conf. Bulk Materials Storage and Handling and Transportation*, Newcastle (1983), pp. 203–206.

Brown, R.L.: The fundamental principles of segregation. *The Institute of Fuel, Journal* 13 (1939).

Castanoli: *Amer. Min. Congress Yearbook* (1935) 270.
De Silva, S.; Enstad, G.G.: Bulk solids handling in Scandinavia, a case study in the aluminium industry. *Bulk Solids Handling*, 11 (1991) 1.
Drahun, J.A.; Bridgwater, J.: The mechanisms of free surface segregation. *Powder Technology*, 36 (1983), pp. 39–53.
Enggrav, S.; Halvorsen, K.; Holberg, J.K.; Wendelborg, K.: Segregering av partikulære materialer ved strømning gjennom skråstilte rør og påfølgende fylling i haug. Student project at Telemark College, Institute of Technology, Report 2-PT-6, December 1989.
Fürll, C.: Investigation of the segregation in big bins. *Powder Handling and Processing*, 6 (1994) 4.
Garve, T.W.: *Jnl. American Ceramic Soc.* (1925) 8, 668.
Harris, J.F.G.; Hildon, A.M.: Reducing segregation in binary powder mixtures with particular reference to oxygenated washing powders. *Ind. Eng. Chem. Process Des. Develop.*, 9 (1970) 3.
Hebley: Appalachian Coals, Inc., Fuel Engineers Meeting, July 1936.
Holmes, C.W.A.: The sampling of coal – II. *Colliery Engr.* (1934) 11.
Jenike, A.W.: *Storage and Flow of Solids*. University of Utah, Engineering Experiment Station, Salt Lake City, Bull. 123, November 1964.
Johanson, J.R.: Solids segregation – causes and solutions. *Powder and Bulk Eng.*, August 1988, 13–19.
Matthée, H.: Segregation phenomena relating to bunkering of bulk materials: theoretical consideration and experimental investigations. *Powder Technology* 1 (1967/68), 265–271.
Mitchell, D.R.: Segregation in the handling of coal. *American Institution of Mining, Metallurgical and Petroleum Engineers. Trans.* 130 (1938).
Sherman, R.A.; Kaiser, E.R.: Segregation of coal in an industrial steam plant bunker. *Combustion*, December 1937, 25–28.
Shinohara, K.: Some models on particle-segregation in filling hoppers. *Aufbereitungs-Technik*, 26 (1985) 3, 116–122.
Shinohara, K.: General segregation mechanism of binary solids mixtures filling two-dimensional hoppers. *Aufbereitungs-Technik*, 31 (1990) 9, 482–488.
Shinohara, K.; Idemitsu, Y.; Gotah, K.; Tanaka, T.: Mechanism of gravity flow of particles from a hopper. *Ind. Eng. Chem. Process Design and Development*, 9 (1968) 2.
Stephens, D.J.; Bridgwater, J.: The mixing and percolation of cohesionless particulate materials, Part II: Microscopic mechanisms for particles differing in size. *Powder Technology*, 21 (1978), 17–28.
Stock, A.J.: Coal segregation in boiler plants. *Mechanical Engineering* 66 (1944).
Tanaka, T.: Segregation models of solid mixtures composed of different densities and particle sizes. *Ind. Eng. Chem. Process Design and Development*, 10 (1971) 3, 332–340.
Williams, J.C.: The segregation of particulate materials. A review. *Powder Technology*, 15 (1976), 245–251.
Wittich: *Tonindustrie Zeitung*, July 1915.

3.6 Silo quaking
D. Schulze

3.6.1 Introduction

Silo quaking is the name of a phenomenon characterized by self-excited, pulsating flow in silos (Roberts and Wiche, 1991). The frequency of the vibrations can be greater than 1 Hz (sometimes audible as silo noise or 'silo music' with frequencies >20 Hz (Tejchman and Gudehus, 1993; Tejchman, 1996)), where commonly the amplitude is low (Purutyan *et al.*, 1993). On the other hand, very low frequencies can also occur (periods of minutes or hours) where significant shock loads on the silo structure arise.

Not every bulk solid will excite severe quaking. A significant quake or a thump is mostly a result of inertia forces which arise due to a rapid deceleration of the silo content or a part of it. Therefore, most bulk solids showing quaking effects are brittle and not too cohesive, thus making a rapid deceleration possible. Some bulk solids, from which quaking effects have been reported, are:

- Maize (Pieper, 1975)
- Corn (Pieper, 1975; Roberts and Wiche, 1991; Purutyan *et al.*, 1993; Tejchman, 1996)
- Cement clinker (Pieper, 1975; Jöhnk, 1985; Schwedes and Schulze, 1991; Tejchman, 1996)
- Coal (Wright and Rappen, 1984; Roberts and Wiche, 1991; Roberts, 1993; Purutyan *et al.*, 1993; Levison, 1994)
- Iron ore (Wei and Johanson, 1974; Purutyan *et al.*, 1993)
- Brittle, hard plastic pellets (Wei and Johanson, 1974; Tejchman, 1996)
- Rape seeds (Tejchman and Gudehus, 1993; Tejchman, 1996)
- Rye (Tejchman, 1996)
- Potato powder (Tejchman, 1996)

172 Flow in silos

Silo quaking can have different causes. Although several possible reasons for silo quaking are described in the literature and some of the silo quaking problems which occurred in the past have been solved, there is still a lack of knowledge. In the following the main effects will be outlined, mainly on a phenomenalistic basis. Since this section deals with the physical background of silo quaking it is not intended to present practical solutions for the redesign of quaking silos. For the latter reference should be made to the available literature (Wei and Johanson, 1974; Wright and Rappen, 1984; Jöhnk, 1985; Roberts and Wiche, 1991; Schwedes and Schulze, 1991; Purutyan et al., 1993; Roberts, 1993; Levison, 1994; Tejchman, 1996).

3.6.2 Changing flow profile (funnel flow)

In a silo either mass flow or funnel flow can take place (Fig. 3.6.1). In mass flow, the entire content of a silo is in motion when some bulk solid is discharged from the outlet. In funnel flow only part of the content is in motion while the rest of the bulk solid remains stagnant in so-called stagnant zones (dead zones). Typical causes of funnel flow are: too shallow or too rough hopper walls, maladjusted feeders, or protrusions into the flow channel from which stagnant zones may build up (Jenike, 1964).

If stagnant zones occur, it may happen that part (or all) of the stagnant bulk solid starts to flow suddenly. The reason for this is a change in the stresses acting on the stagnant bulk solid, e.g. an increase in the vertical

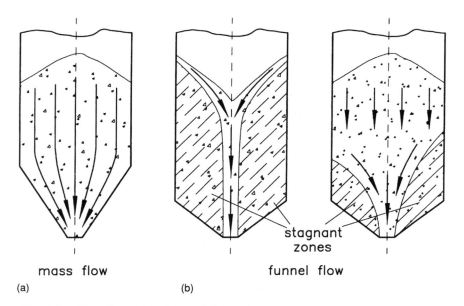

Fig. 3.6.1 Mass flow (a) and funnel flow (b).

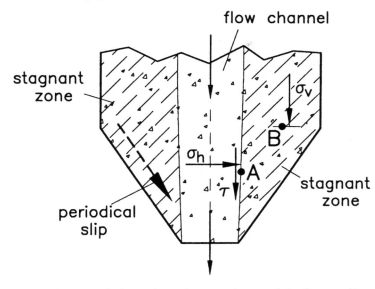

Fig. 3.6.2 Mechanism of silo quaking due to a change of the flow profile.

stresses acting from above, or a decrease in the stresses acting horizontally on the stagnant zone. The assumed mechanism is depicted in Fig. 3.6.2.

In Fig. 3.6.2 a funnel flow silo is shown where the hopper walls are not steep enough for mass flow. When, after filling, the bulk solid is initially discharged, at first a flow channel forms where the bulk solid flows downwards. Depending on the flow properties of the bulk solid, the shape of the flow channel will be more or less convergent. Here it is assumed that the flow channel is almost cylindrical. The bulk solid around the flow channel is at rest (stagnant zone, hatched area in Fig. 3.6.2).

After filling and before discharging, the stresses acting in the hopper and, hence, the bulk density, are relatively large. When the bulk solid inside the flow channel starts to flow, it dilates and the stresses and the bulk density decrease. Thereafter, the horizontal stress σ_h acting from the flow channel on the stagnant zone (e.g. at point A in Fig. 3.6.2) decreases. Due to the relative velocity between the flowing bulk solid and the stagnant zone, shear stresses τ develop (e.g. at point A in Fig. 3.6.2) acting downwards at the surface of the stagnant zone. Due to the downwards directed shear stresses, the vertical stresses σ_v inside the stagnant zones will increase (e.g. at point B, Fig. 3.6.2).

The changes in the stresses acting on the stagnant zone have the following effects:

- Less horizontal support of the bulk solid in the stagnant zone
- Increased vertical force acting on the bulk solid in the stagnant zone

Due to these modified stress conditions the bulk solid in the stagnant zone – and also the bulk solid above – will slip down the hopper wall. Within a short period of time the flow channel is filled with dense-packed bulk solid. Therefore, the bulk solid in the stagnant zone and above it cannot flow downwards any longer. Hence, it is decelerated more or less rapidly. The deceleration causes not only high stresses in the flow channel and a compression of the bulk solid inside (= high bulk density), but also a 'quake' or 'thump' (Roberts and Wiche, 1991; Purutyan et al., 1993). Afterwards, at further discharge, the cycle repeats: due to the high density of the bulk solid in the flow channel, the stagnant zones are supported by the bulk solid in the flow channel. With developing dilation of the bulk solid the horizontal support decreases etc., and finally, another thump will arise.

The mechanism outlined above can arise in a variety of circumstances. In the following some of them will be illustrated.

3.6.2.1 Hopper slope close to critical hopper slope for achieving mass flow

If the hopper slope is close to the critical hopper slope for achieving mass flow, the flow profile can change from mass flow to funnel flow and vice versa (Wei and Johanson, 1974; Carson and Johanson, 1977; Wright and Rappen, 1984; Roberts and Wiche, 1991; Purutyan et al., 1993), as shown in Fig. 3.6.2 and described in section 3.6.2. Thereby, the mass of the bulk solid in the stagnant zones begins to move and stops, begins to move and stops, and so on. If the bulk solid is very incompressible and inelastic, the inertia forces create excessive shock loads on the silo structure.

3.6.2.2 Unstable stagnant zones

Quaking due to a sudden change of the flow profile can also arise in a funnel flow silo where slipping on the hopper walls as shown in Fig. 3.6.2 is not possible, e.g. in a silo with very rough or flat hopper walls, or in a flat bottom silo. In a funnel flow silo, especially when storing free-flowing bulk solids, the stagnant zones are unstable. Due to the effects discussed in section 3.6.2 (decreasing horizontal support of the stagnant zones), stagnant material may enter the flow channel more or less periodically whereby the slip planes are within the bulk solid.

In principle, this quaking effect is the same as that described in section 3.6.2, but with the differences that here only a part of the stagnant bulk solid begins to move, and that the material does not slip directly on the hopper wall. Two examples are shown in Figs 3.6.3(a) and (b). In the case of Fig. 3.6.3(a) at first only the bulk solid inside the flow channel flows downwards. Due to the decreasing horizontal support and the increasing vertical stresses (section 3.6.2), almost the entire contents of the silo, namely the hatched part of the stagnant zone (Fig. 3.6.3(a)), begin moving by

Silo quaking

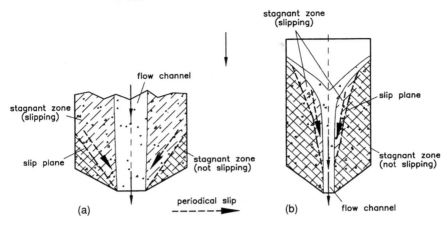

Fig. 3.6.3 Unstable stagnant zones.

sliding down a slip plane within the bulk solid (see dashed line), and decelerate suddenly thus creating a severe quake. The lower part of the stagnant zone (cross-hatched area in Fig. 3.6.3(a)) located below the slip plane still remains at rest. In the case of Fig. 3.6.3(b) only a small part of the stagnant zone (the hatched area above the slip plane) is unstable. The resulting vibrations or quakes will be the stronger the greater the mass of bulk solid that is accelerated and then decelerated periodically. Therefore, for the case of Fig. 3.6.3(a) more severe shocks are to be expected.

3.6.2.3 Excessive pressure concentration

Stagnant zones can be caused by too shallow hopper angles, but also by protrusions into the flow channel, mismatched flanges, only partially opened slide gates, or feeders which do not discharge the bulk solid across the whole outlet opening. In the latter four cases, following the principle outlined in section 3.6.2 and Fig. 3.6.2, in the stagnant zones arising high vertical stresses will occur, especially in the lower part of the stagnant zones (Fig. 3.6.4). This means that locally an 'excessive pressure concentration' (Wei and Johanson, 1974; Carson and Johanson, 1977; Purutyan *et al.*, 1993) takes place.

Due to the high vertical pressure in the stagnant zone – which is equivalent to high stored energy in this area – the stagnant zone can suddenly start to flow (slip) when the bulk solid in the flow channel adjacent to the stagnant zone becomes loose by dilation or by building up a void. As discussed above, a part of the stagnant zone (the hatched area in Fig. 3.6.4) will slip downwards on a slip plane within the bulk solid. The flowing bulk solid is then stopped after the flow channel is filled (the same effect as described in section 3.6.2). The resulting shock load acting on the silo structure is proportional to the mass of the bulk solid that slips (Purutyan

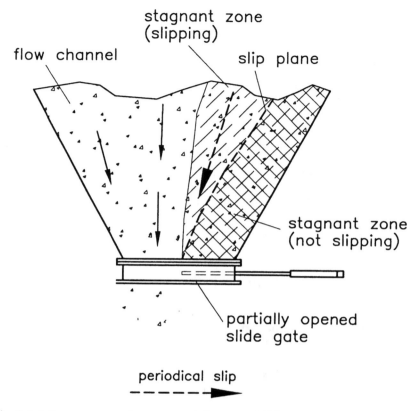

Fig. 3.6.4 Stagnant zone due to a partially opened slide gate.

et al., 1993). This sequence can be repeated periodically resulting in vibrations of the silo.

3.6.3 Large velocity gradient in flowing bulk solid

Even in mass flow, silos quakes and vibrations have been observed (Roberts and Wiche, 1991; Purutyan *et al.*, 1993; Roberts, 1993; Tejchman, 1996). In the vertical section of a mass flow hopper plug flow occurs if the filling height in the vertical section is greater than 0.75–1.0 times the diameter. In the hopper the bulk solid in the centre flows faster downwards than the material at the hopper walls, i.e. the velocity profile in the hopper is non-uniform. Typical velocity profiles are shown in Fig. 3.6.5. The higher the wall friction at the hopper walls, the more non-uniform the velocity profile.

Due to the different velocity profiles in the vertical section and in the hopper, in the region of the transition from the vertical section to the hopper the velocity profile must change. This change is assumed to be the source

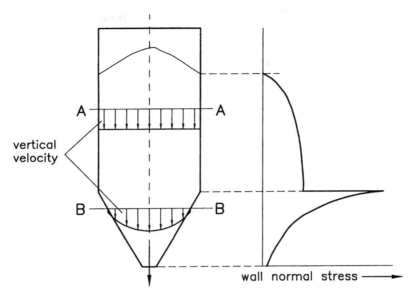

Fig. 3.6.5 Velocity profiles and stresses in a mass flow silo (Roberts and Wiche, 1991; Roberts, 1993).

of the quaking; however, different interpretations can be found in the literature.

In Roberts and Wiche (1991) and Roberts (1993) the following is assumed: when flowing downwards in the vertical section of a mass flow silo, the bulk density of the bulk solid increases due to the increasing stress (see wall normal stress distribution shown in Fig. 3.6.5). The maximum stress and density are reached at the transition from the vertical section to the hopper. In the hopper the bulk solid dilates (bulk density decreases) when flowing downwards because the stresses also decrease in the downwards direction. As a result of the dilation, it is assumed that the vertical support stresses decrease slightly, reducing the support given to the plug of bulk solid in the vertical section. This causes the plug to drop momentarily giving rise to a load pulse. The cycle is then repeated.

In Purutyan *et al.* (1993) it is assumed that quakes are caused by the fracture planes that form at the transition from the vertical section of the silo to the hopper section. These fracture planes are the result of the changing velocity profiles in the region of the transition. It is then postulated that these fracture planes cause periodic thumps.

Model tests (Purutyan *et al.*, 1993) have shown that for a given bulk solid discharged from a mass flow silo quaking will not occur in any case. The probability of quaking seems to become greater with increasing velocity gradients. For the case of a borderline mass flow condition (hopper angle close to the critical hopper angle for mass flow) quaking was detected in the

178   Flow in silos

model tests, whereas for a condition within the mass flow region (hopper clearly steeper than the critical angle for achieving mass flow) no quaking was observed.

Quaking due to the effect described in this section can also occur in a funnel flow silo. If the borderline between the stagnant zone and the flow channel intersects the silo wall in the lower region of the silo as shown in the right part of Fig. 3.6.1, a so-called effective transition is formed. The effective transition acts in a similar way to the transition between the vertical section of a mass flow silo and the hopper, and the funnel flow silo can be seen as a 'mass flow silo with a hopper made from bulk solid'. If the filling height above the effective transition is greater than 0.75–1.0 times the silo diameter, then the bulk solid above the effective transition flows downwards like a plug as shown in Fig. 3.6.5, and from the same causes outlined above quaking may occur.

In Levison (1994) it is reported that shocks occurred in a coal silo which was equipped with a kind of *en masse* feeder. The coal was discharged mainly from one end of the outlet slit (Fig. 3.6.6) thus creating a non-uniform velocity profile. Due to the great differences in the vertical velocity which has been measured at section A (Fig. 3.6.6), an inclined 'rupture' or 'failure' plane formed between the faster and the slower flowing coal. At this plane high shear forces are assumed to take place thus causing quakes (ruptures).

After improving the feeder to achieve a more uniform discharge, the shocks diminished. Obviously, the shocks resulted from the 'large velocity gradient' between the slower and faster flowing bulk solid.

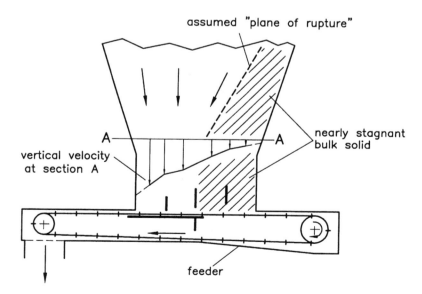

Fig. 3.6.6 Large velocity gradient due to non-uniform discharge (Levison, 1994).

3.6.4 Slip–stick wall friction

It is often observed when a bulk solid is sheared along a plate at a constant strain rate that the frictional force fluctuates with a well-defined frequency. The fluctuations may be due to the tendency of the bulk solid to adhere to the plate, or due to particles catching on and releasing from uneven surfaces on the plate. This starting and stopping of flow can propagate through the bulk solid on to a silo structure resulting in vibrations (Wei and Johanson, 1974; Carson and Johanson, 1977; Purutyan et al., 1993).

3.6.5 Flow from small outlets

The cohesive strength, permeability and compressibility of a bulk solid will affect the maximum rate of steady-state discharge through a given opening size. If discharge rates above this steady-state value are attempted, the flow becomes pulsating. The pulsations are due to formation and failure of arches above the outlet opening (Purutyan et al., 1993). The pulsations can be transmitted to the flowing bulk solid above, and hence to the silo structure.

3.6.6 Excitation by feeding

A feeder can exert a cyclic variation on the flow velocity of the bulk solid in a silo (Jenike, 1964). As an example, this can be the case when a free-flowing material is discharged by a star feeder (rotary valve) (Fig. 3.6.7). The chambers of the feeder will fill one after the other thus exciting a stepwise flow to the bulk solid. If the bulk solid is incompressible and inelastic, the latter can cause severe vibrations in the silo.

In Purutyan et al. (1993) feeder-excited vibrations of coal silos are described. The coal was discharged by belt feeders with picking idlers. Due to the sag between the idlers, a cyclic motion was initiated as the material moves over the idlers. The cyclic motion was transmitted to the flowing bulk solid above, and through it to the silo structure.

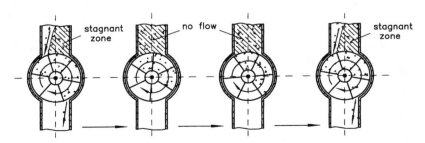

Fig. 3.6.7 Rotary feeder.

3.6.7 Collapsing arches and ratholes

If the outlet diameter is smaller than the critical arching or ratholing diameter, arches or ratholes can build up. A stable arch or rathole may collapse through external excitation, e.g. ambient vibrations or impact (Purutyan et al., 1993). The impact of the falling material causes a shock load on the silo structure. In contrast to periodic shocks described above, collapses of arches and ratholes are, as a rule, non-periodical and with varying magnitude.

3.6.8 Silo noise

Tejchman (1996) describes the occurrence of silo noise similar to a truck's horn in silos used for the storage of polymer granulates. The silos were made of aluminium and had a height/diameter ratio greater than 4 (Fig. 3.6.8). The noise arose when the silo was discharged at a mass flow rate above a certain level. Tejchman identifies the noise as a resonant effect of the silo cylinder which has a very small damping.

The reason for the noise is assumed in Tejchman (1996) to be self-induced pulsation of the bulk solid. Due to the smooth cylinder wall, a wall shear zone with a thickness of only 0.05–0.10 m developed. Furthermore, the shape of the top surface of the bulk solid on filling did not vary during discharge. The damping effect of this small shear zone is assumed to be small. Therefore, the pulsations were transferred to the cylinder wall. Due to this excitation, the cylinder wall started to vibrate thus creating the audible noise.

In order to prevent the silo noise, the cylinder wall roughness, and thereby the wall friction angle, was increased by installing aluminium waffle sheets to the cylinder's interior surface (Fig. 3.6.8). The result was that after the installation no audible dynamic effects were obtained during discharge. Furthermore, the thickness of the shear zone along the cylinder wall increased up to 0.20 m. Tejchman (1996) assumes that the dynamic effects were damped in this enlarged shear zone. The top surface of the bulk solid filling changed considerably during discharge, because due to the increased wall friction angle, the bulk solid near the silo axis moved downwards faster than that near the cylinder walls.

To model the self-induced pulsation, Tejchman (1996) presents a discrete mechanical model as well as FEM-based numerical calculations

Work on numerical modelling has also been carried out by Ruckenbrod (1995) in a Ph.D. study which combines existing knowledge and new experiments with finite element analysis based on continuum mechanics. This allowed an examination of the basis on which current hypotheses were founded. He demonstrated that wave-like pulses is silos were theoretically possible (Ruckenbrod and Eibl, 1993).

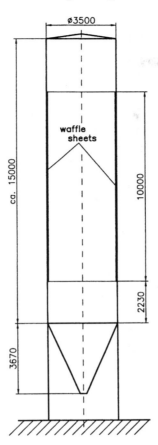

Fig. 3.6.8 Silo for the storage of polymer granulates (Tejchman, 1996).

3.6.9 Summary and future research

Due to the number of causes of silo quaking and vibration it is difficult to decide which of the effects mentioned is relevant for a given silo quaking problem. Whereas the causes described in sections 3.6.5–3.6.7 are relatively easy to identify, this is not the case for the other effects. Additionally, it is difficult to find solutions for the redesign of silos which are quaking or vibrating due to the effects described in sections 3.6.2–3.6.4 and 3.6.8 which are not too costly.

Further research is required to increase knowledge about the causes of quaking, and measurement techniques for the analysis of quaking or vibrating silos, and also ways of redesigning quaking or vibrating silos have to be further developed.

Up to now, little work has been done on the theoretical description of silo quaking (Kmita, 1992a, b; Ruckenbrod and Eibl, 1993; Tejchman and

Gudehus, 1993; Tejchman, 1996). At the present state, this valuable work cannot be used for the solution of all practical problems concerning silo quaking or vibrations, Therefore, further research work is also required in this field.

References

Carson, J.W.; Johanson, J.R.: Vibration caused by solids flow in storage bins, *Preprints International Powder and Bulk Solids Handling and Processing Conf.*, Rosemont, IL (1977), pp. 237–243

Jenike, A.W.: *Storage and Flow of Solids*, Bull. no. 123, Utah Eng. Exp. Station, Univ. of Utah, Salt Lake City (1964)

Jöhnk, H.: Reduzierung von Erschütterungen beim Abzug aus Klinkersilos, *Zement Kalk Gips* 38 (1985) 11, pp. 657–659

Kmita, J.: A study on the self-induced vibration in silos, *Bulk Solids Handling* 12 (1992a) 1, pp. 25–30

Kmita, J.: Measurement of dynamic pressures in silos during emptying, *Preprints International Conf. on Bulk Material Handling and Transportation*, Wollongong, Australia (1992b), pp. 425–427

Levison, B.; Munch-Andersen, J.: Shocks in coal silos, *Powder Handling & Processing* 6 (1994) 4, pp. 385–388

Pieper, K.: Über das 'Schlagen' in Silozellen, *Aufbereitungs-Technik* 16 (1975) 4, pp. 190–193

Purutyan, H.; Bengtson, K.E.; Carson, J.W.: Flow-induced silo vibrations, *Powder & Bulk Solids Conf./Exhib.*, Chicago (1993)

Roberts, A.W.: Mechanics of self excited dynamic loads in bins and silos, *Proc. Int. Symp. Reliable Flow of Particulate Solids II*, Oslo, Norway (1993), pp. 983–1004

Roberts, A.W.; Wiche, S.J.: *Silo-quaking – a Pulsating Load Problem during Discharge in Bins and Silos*, IMechE (1991), Paper no. C418/048

Ruckenbrod C.: Statische und dynamische Phänomene bei der Entleerung von Silozellen, Ph.D. Thesis, University of Karlsruhe, Heft 26, Massivbau Baustofftechnologie (1995)

Ruckenbrod, C.; Eibl, J.: Numerical results to discharge processes is silos. *Proc. Int. Symposium on Reliable Flow of Particulate Solids II.* EFChE Series No. 96, Oslo (1993), pp. 503–516

Schwedes, J.; Schulze, D.: Examples of modern silo design, *Bulk Solids Handling* 11 (1991) 1, pp. 47–52

Tejchman, J.: Modelling of shear localization and autogeneous dynamic effects in granular bodies, Habilitation, Univ. Karlsruhe (1996)

Tejchman, J.; Gudehus, G.: Silo-music and silo-quake experiments and a numerical Cosserat approach, *Powder Technology* 76 (1993), pp. 201–212

Wei, M.L.; Johanson, J.R.: Elimination of vibrations in an ore unloading bin, *Journ. of Eng. for Industry, Trans. of the ASME*, August 1974, pp. 761–765

Wright, H.; Rappen, A.: The phenomenon of silo-quaking – strategically placed air cannons solved shock load problems in 6 × 1000 t capacity borderline mass flow coal bunkers, *CHISA Conference*, Prague (1984)

3.7 Purge bin design requirements
H. Wilms

Some processes require conditioning of bulk solids by exposing the solids for a certain time to a gas flow having certain conditions. Respective requirements are drying, heating, cooling, degassing, chemical or physical reactions and polymer phase transition. In general, these operations are referred to as purging and respective vessels are named purge bins. Other terms used for the same purpose are fixed bed reactors, contact beds or degassers. The term 'purge bin' will be used in this section for all of the above operations.

3.7.1 Purge bin requirements

Generally, purging is intended to be a continuous operation. In this case, there are basically two requirements for any purge bin yielding homogeneous purging of the solids. These requirements are a uniform gas distribution and a constant exposure time of all solid particles to the gas flow. This latter requirement means residence times should vary as little as possible (sometimes expressed as a 'narrow' residence time distribution).

The simplest method for any purge bin would thus be to operate a fluidized bed batchwise. The aeration bottom of the fluidized bed would homogeneously distribute the gas flow across the whole cross-section. This concept would mean, because of its batch operation, a constant residence time for all particles and the fluidized bed would result in uniform and intense purging. However, in most cases a fluidized bed is not applicable as a purge bin because of the high gas velocities and thus large volumetric gas flow rates required and, mainly, because of the discontinuous operation. Continuous operation of a fluidized bed purge bin would result in a wide residence time distribution and thus is not acceptable.

3.7.2 Solids flow in purge bins

Therefore, another concept is needed for purge bin design. The requirement of a narrow residence time distribution of the solids can be achieved by designing the purge bin for mass flow (Jenike, 1970; Schwedes, 1970; Wilms, 1993). The flow properties, as determined with shear testers, have to be known to ensure mass flow design. In mass flow there will be a uniform vertical velocity of the particles within the cylinder. In the converging hopper section there will be a larger vertical velocity at the centre line than at the periphery because of the radial stress field in a mass flow hopper resulting in a radial velocity field. The mass flow bin with its downward solids velocity profile is shown in Fig. 3.7.1(a).

In order to minimize the effect of the different velocities in the hopper, purge bins should be built as slender as possible, i.e. having a large aspect ratio (cylindrical height H : diameter D). Thus, the volume of the hopper in relation to the total volume of the purge bin is minimized. In addition, the gas flow is usually introduced close to the transition. This means that the spreading of the residence time distribution in the hopper does not affect the purging operation any more as long as the purge bin is operated continuously. In this case, only the cylindrical part of the purge bin is used for purging and the mass flow hopper acts only as the feeder from the cylindrical vessel to a conveying system below having smaller dimensions. Thus, a

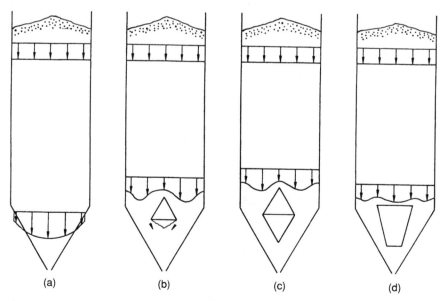

Fig. 3.7.1 Uniform solids flow in purge bins: (a) mass flow bin; (b) inverted cone; (c) frustoconical displacer; (d) Binsert®.

regular mass flow bin fulfils the requirement of creating a narrow residence time distribution.

Some applications, however, may require a large gas flow rate in combination with relatively small particle sizes. In order to prevent fluidization, a larger cross-section has to be chosen. In these cases, batchwise purging in a fluidized bed may be considered as an alternative.

Another option is to minimize the volume of the hopper by installing displacing internals in the hopper, such as inverted cones (Fig. 3.7.1(b)) or frustoconical displacers (Fig. 3.7.1(c)) to slow down the vertical solids' velocity in the centre of the bin. Another method is to use a Binsert® (Johanson, 1982) (Fig. 3.7.1(d)) designed to create a uniform velocity distribution across the cross-section of the hopper.

3.7.3 Purge bin aeration systems

The gas flow in a purge bin is usually introduced counter-current to the solids flow in order to achieve optimum purging by using maximum concentration or temperature differences. With the gravity flow of solids being downward in the vessel, the gas thus has to flow upwards.

The gas flow has to be distributed as uniformly as possible across the cross-section of the bin. However, only a very low height is required to equalize the gas flow if it is not uniformly distributed. This is because the total pressure drop from the injection point to the top surface is equal, no matter whether a longer or shorter streamline has to be overcome. In order to meet this equilibrium, the gas has to flow faster on a shorter streamline. However, the difference in streamline length and thus in velocity is only marginal in purge bins with large aspect ratios. There are several methods for introduction of the gas flow (Borho, Hilligardt and Rizk, 1985). They are shown in Fig. 3.7.2 and described as follows.

The most widely adopted method is to use an inverted cone in the centre of the bin near the transition (Fig. 3.7.2(a)). Gas is injected underneath this cone and is then distributed around the circumference of this cone into the bin. This inverted cone internal can be simultaneously used to equalize the velocity profile, as shown in Fig. 3.7.1(b). Another application comes from purging of gravity blenders which use inverted cones to improve the flow profile (Wilms, 1992).

The design depicted in Fig. 3.7.2(b) features an annulus just above the transition. This way only the cylindrical section is used as a purge bin and the converging section serves only as the feeder to a conveying or discharge system.

Such a system cannot be installed in the hopper, because the less steeply inclined conical baffle would transform mass flow into funnel flow or would require an uneconomically steep hopper. Therefore, the design given in Fig. 3.7.2(c) has to be used when installing the aeration ring below the transition. The mass flow hopper is followed by another mass flow hopper with

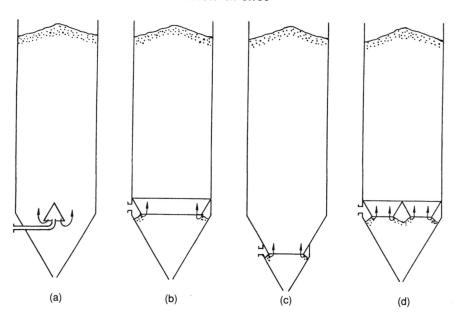

Fig. 3.7.2 Aeration systems in purge bins: (a) inverted cone; (b) peripheral aeration ring; (c) conical aeration ring; (d) aeration ring and cross-bars.

small vertical distance. This way a small annulus is formed between the two hoppers which serves as the aeration ring. The solids flowing out of the upper one into the lower one will lead to a free surface without any consolidation and thus it is ideal for introduction of the gas. Both designs according to Figs 3.7.2(b) and (c) avoid any internals in the centre of the bin and therefore are also favourable from the structural point of view.

The system shown in Fig. 3.7.2(d) utilizes in addition to the aeration ring shown in Fig. 3.7.2(b) two pyramid-shaped cross-bars open at the lower side (Carson, Royal and Pittinger, 1995). Thus, gas is introduced via the ring and also along the cross-bars. This way the gas is distributed more uniformly across the cross-section.

When the unpurged material in the hopper is to be minimized then the aeration system has to be effective all the way down to the outlet. This can be achieved by installing multiple aeration rings in the hopper according to those shown in Fig. 3.7.2(c). This system is shown in Fig. 3.7.3(a). One common purge gas supply is sufficient, if the width of the individual slots is sized in such a way that the higher pressure drop for the lowest aeration ring with the higher level of solids above this aeration ring is compensated by a larger slot width (Krambrock, Schwedes and Wilms, 1991) (Fig. 3.7.3(b)). An equivalent system uses pipes of different diameters inserted into the hopper at different levels. All the pipes are fed by one common purge gas supply line, as shown in Fig. 3.7.3(c). Again, the pressure drop for different

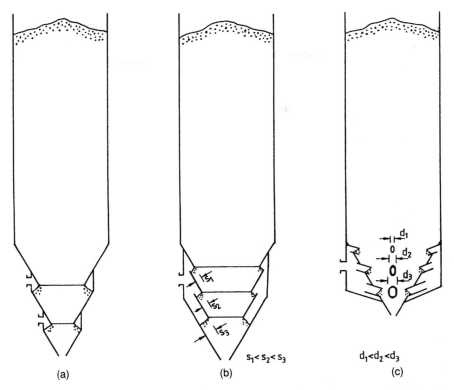

Fig. 3.7.3 Hopper aeration systems: (a) multiple conical aeration rings; (b) multiple slots with different width; (c) multiple pipe inserts with different diameter.

levels is kept constant by adjusting the pressure drop in the pipe insert by varying size and/or number at each level.

3.7.4 Aeration requirements and limitations

In order to maintain the required narrow residence time distribution in the cylindrical part of the purge bin, the fixed bed has to be maintained. Therefore, the solids may not be fluidized and consequently, the interstitial gas velocity has to be kept below the minimum fluidization velocity v_{mf} (Geldart, 1973). Within the aeration system, the cross-section of the flowing solids is smaller and thus the local interstitial gas velocity may reach the minimum fluidization velocity (Fig. 3.7.4(a)). Therefore, the fluidization properties have to be measured in laboratory equipment to evaluate the permissible gas velocities and gas flow rates respectively at a given geometry. If these properties are known, then the geometry of the purge bin and aeration system can be designed and optimized.

188 Flow in silos

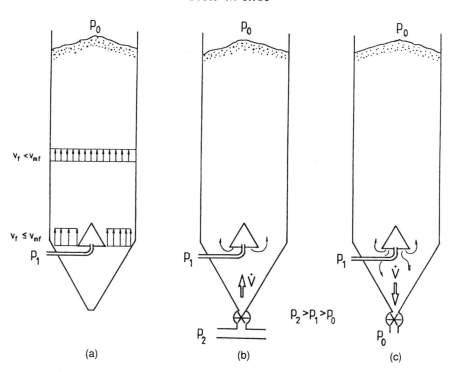

Fig. 3.7.4 Limitations on gas velocity and leakage flow: (a) limiting gas velocities; (b) leakage from a rotary feeder; (c) leakage to the outlet.

For fluidization of the solids it is required to have a velocity large enough for fluidization, i.e. at least v_{mf}, and the pressure has to be sufficiently large to lift the weight of the solids. If only the local velocity in the converging section exceeds the minimum fluidization velocity v_{mf}, and the pressure is smaller than necessary for lifting the weight, then the fixed bed structure will be maintained. Thus, local velocities higher than v_{mf} will not lead to fluidization. Only locally aerated spots of minor extent may form under these circumstances. If they are to be avoided, for example because of high friability of the product, then even the local velocities at the injection cross-section have to be kept below v_{mf} (Fig. 3.7.4(a)).

The counter-current gas flow reduces the effect of gravity on the flowing solids. This means that the tendency for arching increases for non-fluidized, cohesive bulk solids. Just below the point of fluidization, the weight of a slice element spanning the cross-section is almost completely carried by the pressure drop of the counter-current gas flow. Therefore, with cohesive bulk solids it is advisable to stay considerably below the minimum fluidization velocity. In addition it is advisable to size the cross-section at the gas injection zone larger than the minimum dimension for non-arching.

The pressure drop for the gas flow through the fixed bed of solids can best be calculated with Ergun's (1952) equation. The local gas velocities, gas properties and solids bulk density (porosity) have to be considered for this calculation.

It has to be kept in mind for all applications where solids from a purge bin are fed via a rotary feeder into a pneumatic conveying system or another reactor at higher pressure that the leakage air from the rotary feeder has to be added to the total gas flow through the powder bed. This situation is shown in Fig. 3.7.4(b). Especially for fine powders the permissible interstitial gas velocity may then exceed v_{mf}. When solids are discharged from a purge bin via a rotary feeder into ambient conditions (Fig. 3.7.4(c)), then the purge gas flow may tend to leak out downwards through the rotary feeder instead of passing through the fixed bed, because the downward pressure drop may then be smaller. This may have a negative influence on purging performance.

3.7.5 Structural design considerations

Structural design of purge bins is to be based on the solids and gas pressures prevailing in the bin. These two pressure profiles shown in Fig. 3.7.5, have to be added to derive the total design pressure of the purge bin. The solids pressure may be calculated according to the applicable national or inter-

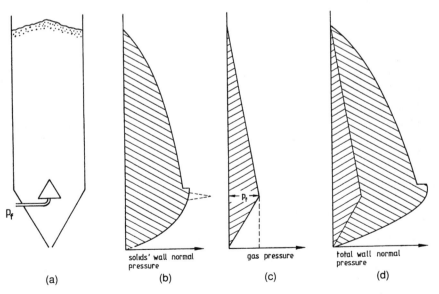

Fig. 3.7.5 Solids and gas pressure distribution in a purge bin: (a) purge bin system (example); (b) solids wall pressure profile; (c) gas pressure profile; (d) superposition of solids and gas pressure.

national standard. The respective German DIN 1055 Part 6 (1987) states that gas pressures from drying processes have to be fully taken into account in addition to the wall pressures at the level of injection. These gas pressures may be decreased linearly towards the pressure at the top surface. Respectively, this holds for a decrease towards the outlet and its respective pressure level. In case of a gas-tight closure of the purge bin outlet during purging, for example above another pressure system or in non-continuous operation, then the gas pressure may not be decreased for structural design purposes, but has to be kept constant (dashed line in Fig. 3.7.5).

Careful consideration has to be paid to the influence of any gas-distributing internals on the pressure profile and thus the wall loads. Internals may create some kind of local switch, resulting locally in higher loads on walls and internals (Strusch, Schwedes and Lyle, 1995; Hoppe, 1979). If the flow through or around these internals is not uniform, then extremely high load differences may act on the internals. Thus, minimizing the number and extent of internals will help in the design of structurally safe purge bins.

3.7.6 Summary

Purge bins can be successfully and reliably designed for most applications if the relevant flow properties for mass flow design and no arching as well as the limitations resulting from the minimum fluidization velocity v_{mf} are considered. The pressure drop across the height of the purge bin can be calculated according to known equations or measured with laboratory equipment.

More knowledge is desirable about the local gas distribution around the gas injection points, whether they are ring-shaped or nozzles (Wilms, 1994). Since the bulk solids are not homogeneous in density, it is so far only possible to obtain conservative results for arching under counter-current gas flow. The influence of internals on the wall pressure distribution is not yet fully understood and has to be improved by model experiments and development of calculation procedures. Because of this lack of knowledge, structural design of bins with internals is excluded from some codes (Wilms, 1991).

References

Borho, K.; Hilligardt, K.; Rizk, F. Zur Auslegung von Schachttrocknern *Chemie-Ingenieur-Technik* 61(1989), 3, 246–248

Carson, J.W.; Royal, T.A.; Pittinger, B.H. Bulk solids purge and conditioning vessels *Chemical Processing* 58(1995), 8, 77–80

DIN (1987) DIN 1055 *Design Loads for Buildings Part 6 Loads in Silo Bins* Ed. May 1987, Beuth Verlag, Berlin

Ergun, S. Fluid flow through packed columns *Chem. Eng. Prog.* 48(1952), 89–94

Geldart, D. Types of gas fluidization *Powder Technology* 7(1973), 285–292

Hoppe, H. Experimentelle Darstellung der Spannungsverteilung in Bunkern und Silos in Abhängigkeit vom Fließbild der Anlage. Diss., TU Clausthal, 1979

Jenike, A.W. *Storage and Flow of Solids*, Bull. No. 123, Utah Eng. Exp. St., Univ. Utah, Salt Lake City, 1970

Johanson, J.R. Controlling flow patterns in bins by use of an insert *Bulk Solids Handling* 2(1982), 3, 495–498

Krambrock, W.; Schwedes, J.; Wilms, H. Wanderbettreaktor, insbesondere zur Behandlung von Rauchgasen OS DE 40 40 246 A1, 1991

Schwedes, J. *Fließverhalten von Schüttgütern in Bunkern* Verlag Chemie, Weinheim, 1970

Strusch, J.; Schwedes, J.; Lyle, C. Wandspannungen in Silos mit Einbauten *Schüttgut* 1(1995), 1, 27–34

Wilms, H. Criteria for evaluation of silo design codes *Bulk Solids Handling* 11(1991), 1, 55–59

Wilms, H. Blending silos – an overview *Powder Handling & Processing* 4(1992), 3, 293–299

Wilms, H. Verfahrenstechnische und statische Aspekte der Siloauslegung *Chemie-Ingenieur-Technik* 65(1993), 3, 284–292

Wilms, H. Silo design for flow and strength *Powder Handling & Processing* 6 (1994), 2, 193–197

3.8 Flow patterns and velocity distributions in silos

E.J. Puik and P.J. Reuderink

3.8.1 Introduction

Depending on the hopper angle, the internal friction angle of the solids, and the wall friction of the solids, silos will flow either in mass flow or in core funnel flow. Each has its (dis-)advantages. With respect to flow patterns and velocity distributions a mass flow silo will be preferred in cases in which narrow residence time distributions or flat velocity profiles are required (reactors). Funnel flow silos typically have (very) broad residence time distributions. As such, a funnel flow silo will be chosen when storage capacity is needed. The design tools for mass and funnel flow silos are well known: most engineers use Jenike's original approach (proposed in 1961), although his modified theory (1987) is finding its way into engineering consultancies as well.

It is commonly known that the models used nowadays fail to predict flow patterns and velocity distributions correctly, even in rather simplified geometries (Cleaver, 1991). Nevertheless, in order to produce design codes applicable to a variety of geometries, Jenike's (1961) design theory, which applies to two-dimensional plane symmetrical and three-dimensional axisymmetrical silos only, has been modified based partly on empiricism. For geometries with internal structures, like inserts, pipes and flow promoters, hardly any theoretical support is available to predict flow patterns.

The aims of this section are to describe the need to have models and experiments, to briefly overview some of the models available to predict velocity profiles, and finally directions for further theoretical and experimental development which could lead to an enhanced confidence in the use of these models.

3.8.2 Theoretical and experimental research justification

Occasionally, it is not sufficient to know whether or not a reactor is in mass flow and more detailed information on the flow pattern is needed to calculate, for example, the residence time distribution of the bulk solid. Applications for which the residence time is of the utmost importance are silo blenders and bunkering reactor systems like purged bins (section 3.7) and trickle flow reactor systems. Usually, broad residence time distributions in silo blenders are closely linked with bad product quality, while the same for bunkering reactor systems indicate solids stagnancies and thus deactivation of catalyst in the stagnancies.

As mentioned in the introduction, published models perform poorly, especially when the geometry becomes complex. One could argue that this is not a serious problem since experiments can be performed with sophisticated diagnostic tools like radioactive tracer techniques, nuclear magnetic resonance (NMR) and dynamic tomography. Nevertheless, one must always be aware that the information obtained links with the specific geometry and the specific powder used in the experiment. As such, the experiments add information to a data bank of velocity profiles and residence time distributions for given combinations of powder and geometry. In other words, each time the geometry is changed or when the silo has to handle a different type of powder these experiments have to be repeated. In contrast to experiments, theories describe flow behaviour based on some kind of understanding. As such the predictive value of a theory is higher than 'just running a couple of experiments'. However, one cannot do without the other: experiments are needed to verify the theory.

3.8.3 Prediction of velocity profiles and residence times

Theoretical attempts to describe the flow in silos can be roughly divided into two categories: approaches that describe the material assuming it behaves like a continuum and approaches which consider the mechanical interaction between individual particles, usually referred to as discrete element methods. The continuum models can be roughly divided into analytical and finite element versions. The latter, in which sophisticated constitutive relationships are embedded in a finite element method, allow calculation of flow patterns in complex geometries and up- or downscaled versions of these geometries. However, numerical problems are encountered when large shears occur and physical problems are encountered due to the difficulty in describing the flow behaviour correctly in terms of constitutive relationships. Think for example of segregation effects, the description of (free) boundaries and shearing layers, stagnant zones, time effects (transient phase and time-fluctuating information) and local effects (like porosity).

The potential of the discrete element methods is in principle enormous. Almost anything that one would like to calculate is possible: (local) force fields, (local) velocity profiles, (local) porosities and stress states, fluctuating parameters in time and space and boundary effects. Unfortunately, here the limitations are set by computer power. Calculations are typically restricted to two-dimensional geometries and focused on:

1. how to reduce CPU-time by designing fast algorithms or application on massive parallel machines;
2. manipulation of the material parameters (mass, stiffness) or gravity to speed up the calculation time;
3. verification of assumptions used in simple analytical models like coaxiality of stress and strain tensors and of assumptions regarding the flow directions in converging sections;
4. the definition of the mechanics of contacting particles.

Nowadays, many groups are working on one (or more) of these topics. It is to be expected that the impact and influence of the distinct element methods increase rapidly.

In contrast to the finite element embedded continuum models, the residence time distributions and flow patterns can (in principle) be easily calculated using the distinct element methods: obviously, the flow behaviour results from direct particle–particle and particle–wall contacts. In other words, most important influences on flow patterns (geometry and shearing layers) are implicitly present due to the explicit contact fundamental to the model.

The complexity of both the routes mentioned above limits the application and further development of these models to universities and major industrial research centres only.

What is left are a number of largely analytical continuum models for the calculation of the flow patterns in two-dimensional plane symmetrical and three-dimensional axisymmetrical hoppers. An evaluation, supported by experimental verification, of these models is reported by Cleaver (1991). Cleaver distinguishes three categories of models (Table 3.8.1), absolute velocity distributions, kinematic models and plasticity models. Here it suf-

Table 3.8.1 Various approaches to predict velocity distributions in conical hoppers (collected from Cleaver, 1991)

Absolute velocity distribution	Example	Brown and Richards (1970)
Kinematic modelling		Litwiniszyn (1963)
		Mullins (1972)
		Nedderman and Tuzun (1979)
Plasticity theory		Jenike (1961)
		Jenike (1987)
		Polderman *et al.* (1987)
		Mroz and Szymansky (1971)

Flow patterns and velocity distributions in silos

fices to say that plasticity models based on a radial velocity field (e.g. Jenike) are to be preferred for most hopper flow cases, and predict velocity patterns with reasonable accuracy.

3.8.4 Simple analytical models

Apart from the disadvantages of the analytical continuum models (see also those of finite element embedded continuum models) some clear 'plusses' can be identified, which are also responsible for the broad applications of these models: one can easily calculate the velocity profiles and force distributions, the models are formulated in a rather straightforward way without too many mathematical and physical complications, they are cheap and fast, and some give reasonable agreement with experiments (when applied to simple converging sections only).

Although these models allow calculation of the velocity patterns in a hopper, the prediction of the residence time distribution of a material in a mass flow silo is not as straightforward as it might look. Problems occur when connecting the radial flow field in the hopper to the plug flow in the bin. In other words: how do we describe the transition area between hopper and bin? Another point of concern is the shear layer observed along walls of the bin and hopper: how to describe and which parameters govern the thickness of this layer and the delay of the particles in it? Bluntly, one could say that there is little use in refining models for hopper flow if these issues are not resolved. Obviously, using small-scale (2-D) discrete element methods focused on the calculation of the velocity profiles including the influences of walls on shear layers helps us to improve/correct the simple analytical models.

This brings us to a comparison of a few of these plasticity models: Jenike (1961), Jenike (1987) and Polderman et al. (1987). Given the context of this section it is beyond our intention to describe the theories in detail. The interested readers are referred to the articles given in the references. Basically, Jenike (1961) assumes incompressibility and axisymmetrical, steady-state flow directed towards the apex. Two equations for the velocity fields as a function of the distance to the apex and angle from the vertical in the conical section are derived based on continuity and coaxiality. Both equations are combined and solved using: (1) that the yield stresses in the material follow the Coulomb yield function (which is a 2-D concept), and (2) that the tangential stress (in 3-D) equals the major principal stress (also known as the Haar–von Karman hypothesis). Jenike (1987) is considered to predict the transition between mass and funnel flow better than the 1961 theory. It differs in two respects from his 1961 theory: first, the conical yields function is used, replacing the Coulomb yield function, and second, instead of using coaxiality Levy's flow rule is used. The latter imposes coaxiality, but it also inherently assigns a value to the tangential stress such that the Haar–von Karman hypothesis is not needed. Finally, Polderman *et al.* use the same basic assumptions as Jenike (1961), e.g. incompressibility, axisymmetric, steady-state, apex directed flow. The expression for the velocity field is derived by combining coaxiality and continuity, and subsequently solved by making use of the assumptions made in Walker's (1966) differential slice model. These assumptions imply that the horizontal stress is chosen to be constant and that the shear stress in the vertical plane varies linearly with the y coordinate.

An extensive data base of experimental data on velocity profiles in hoppers was generated by Cleaver (1991). Cleaver made use of different types of 'powders' (kale seed and polyprop granules) and different types of conical hoppers (20° and 30° hoppers, aluminium and sandpaper walls). Cleaver verified the assumptions of incompressible and radial flow (which turned out to hold), and compared the experimental results with predictions based on Jenike (1961) and Jenike (1987). He concluded that predictions based on the Jenike (1987) model coincide significantly better with the experimental outcome than predictions based on Jenike (1961), for 20° as well as 30° hoppers and for aluminium as well as sandpaper walls. To determine the performance of the Polderman model, we compared the experimental results of Cleaver with Polderman and found a close agreement for 20° hoppers, but a rather poor agreement in the case of 30° hoppers.

As mentioned earlier, the velocity profiles in a hopper, provided that these are predicted correctly, do not always result in correct residence time distributions: one must take into account the shear layers along the vertical walls in the cylindrical part of the silo, and a method to 'connect' the velocity profiles in this part to those in the conical part of the silo.

3.8.5 The future

The limitations of the approaches discussed in this section indicate that only a small tip of the iceberg has been 'visualized'. Only a few analytical continuum models predict velocity profiles and residence times to a reasonable degree of agreement with experiment. However, these models 'hold' only for simple geometries, steady-state flow and do not allow assessment of the influence of time and spatial dependencies or more complex geometries. The models that have the potential of extending their validity to a larger range of applications than those of the 'simple' analytical models are still at the beginning of the 'product life cycle' or 'S-curve'. A significant effort will have to be directed towards further development before the stage of maturity will be reached.

References

J.A.S. Cleaver, Velocity profiles in conical hoppers, Ph.D. thesis, Univ. of Cambridge (1991).

A.W. Jenike, *Gravity Flow of Bulk Solids*, Bull. 108, Univ. of Utah, Salt Lake City (1961).

A.W. Jenike, A theory of flow of particulate solids in converging and diverging channels based on a conical yield function, *Powd. Technol.*, 50 (1987) 229.

H.G. Polderman; J. Boom; E. de Hilster; A.M. Scott, Solids flow velocity profiles in mass flow hoppers, *Chem, Engin. Sci.*, 42 (1987) 737.

D.M. Walker, An approximate theory for pressure and arching in hoppers, *Chem. Engin. Sci.*, 21 (1966) 975.

4

Discharge, feeding and metering equipment

4.1 Feeders and flow-promoting devices

D. Schulze

4.1.1 Introduction

Feeders and flow-promoting devices influence the flow of bulk solids inside silos. Along with the silo geometry they are responsible for satisfactory or unsatisfactory silo operation. Hence, feeders and flow-promoting devices have to be chosen and designed for the specific bulk solid under consideration.

4.1.2 Task and function of feeders and flow-promoting devices

Feeders are used to discharge the bulk solid in a controlled way, whereas flow-promoting devices are used to initiate or support the flow of bulk solid inside the silo (e.g. in the case of arching or piping, Fig. 4.1.1) or to improve the flow (e.g. to change the flow profile from funnel flow to mass flow, Fig. 4.1.2).

Typical feeders are devices such as belt feeders, apron conveyors, en-masse conveyors, vibratory feeders, rotary valves and screw conveyors which are placed below the outlet of the silo. Cut-off devices such as slide or shell valves are also considered as feeders because they allow control of the discharge rate. Some feeders, for example the rotating discharge arm (rotating plough, Fig. 4.1.3(a)), are used as flow-promoting devices as well so that they can be included in both groups. The plough rotates around the silo axis above the flat silo bottom. The bulk solid is transported through the annular gap below the central cone to the outlet which is placed centrally beneath the cone. Another example is the vibrational hopper shown in Fig. 4.1.3(b). It stimulates the bulk solid to flow (flow-promoting device) as well as discharging in the same way (feeder).

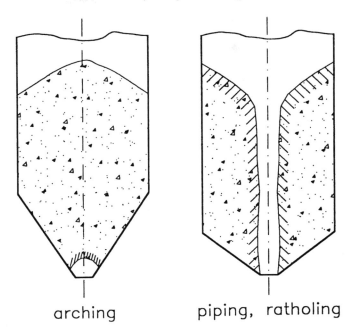

Fig. 4.1.1 Arching and piping (ratholing).

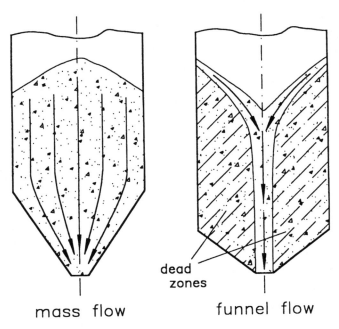

Fig. 4.1.2 Mass flow and funnel flow.

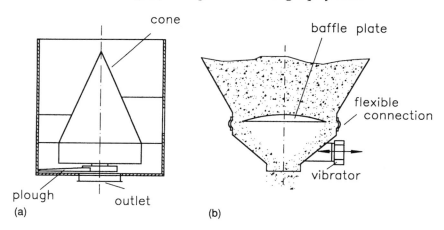

Fig. 4.1.3 Feeders acting as flow-promoting devices: (a) rotating plough; (b) vibrational hopper.

In short, flow-promoting devices are all devices and means to improve the flow of the bulk solid. They can be subdivided into the following groups:

- pneumatic flow-promoting devices (e.g. air injection)
- mechanical flow-promoting devices (e.g. stirrer)
- vibratory devices (vibration of the silo walls or installations inside of the silo)
- inserts
- alteration of the flow properties (addition of flow agents)

Pneumatic flow-promoting devices initiate the flow by air injection. Typical pneumatic flow-promoting devices are shown in Fig. 4.1.4. In the case of the systems in Fig. 4.1.4(a) to 4.1.4(c), the air is injected continuously with low velocities and low pressures. Devices used for this are, for example, hopper walls made of porous material (Fig. 4.1.4(a)), aeration pads (Fig. 4.1.4(b)), and aeration pipes (Fig. 4.1.4(c)). The injected air decreases the wall friction and loosens the bulk solid so that stable arches cannot be formed. Furthermore, the air flow supports the flow of the bulk solid towards the outlet. This kind of aeration is only useful in the case of fine-grained bulk solids (particle size smaller than ca. 300 μm) because the flow resistance of coarse materials is too small. Hence, in case of coarse bulk solids, high air speed and huge amounts of air would be necessary to achieve a satisfactory effect (Woodcock and Mason, 1987).

In addition to the continuous injection of small amounts of air, another possibility is the impulsive injection of compressed air by using air cannons (another name: shock blower, Fig. 4.1.4(d)). The air is stored in pressure vessels which are mounted on the silo wall at pressures of up to 10 bar and then injected into the bulk solid through nozzles. Due to the resulting

Feeders and flow-promoting devices

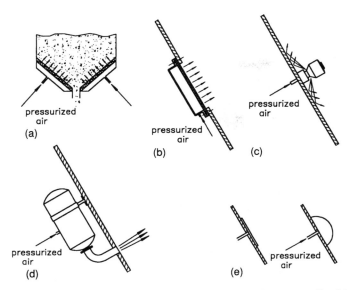

Fig. 4.1.4 Pneumatic flow-promoting devices: (a) porous hopper walls; (b) aeration pad; (c) aeration pipe; (d) air cannon; (e) inflatable pad.

pressure impulse ratholes and arches disintegrate and the bulk solid flows out of the silo. Air cannons have to be used only during the discharge of the silo. Otherwise they can cause a further consolidation of the bulk solid. It is important to consider the fact that the use of air cannons can cause problems as well (dust caused by large amounts of air; large local loads on the silo wall; loads on the hopper and feeders caused by huge amounts of falling bulk solid). Terziovski and Arnold (1990) report on a weighing container damaged by an oversized air cannon. Therefore, air cannons should only be used if there is no other alternative, such as a proper silo design or a modification of the silo. A typical application of air cannons is in the reconstruction of silos where flow problems occur and no other modification is possible. In the case of newly designed silos, air cannons are useful if the bulk solid shows a pronounced time consolidation effect.

In the case of inflatable pads, shown in Fig. 4.1.4(e), the air is not injected into the bulk solid, but is used to inflate the pads thus pressing against the bulk solid to initiate flow.

The simplest kind of mechanical flow-promoting devices are poke holes in the hopper wall where lances are pushed through to destroy arches and ratholes, or beating with a hammer against the silo wall. Further development of these basic methods lead to beaters and mechanical stirrers. As an example, Fig. 4.1.5 shows a mechanical stirrer placed above a rotary valve with a vertical axis. The mechanical stirrer ensures that the bulk solid is set

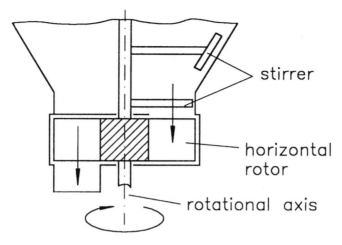

Fig. 4.1.5 Rotary valve with vertical axis and stirrer (Zeppelin, 1992).

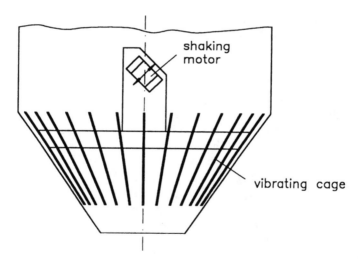

Fig. 4.1.6 Vibro-bi-plan (vibrated insert) (Woodcock and Mason, 1987).

in motion not only above the inlet of the rotary valve, but across the whole outlet cross-section.

Vibration devices are used for local vibration of the silo walls or special inserts, e.g. cage-shaped inserts as shown in Fig. 4.1.6. The vibration of the silo walls ensures a decrease in the wall friction angle so that mass flow can be achieved with larger hopper angles to the vertical. Furthermore, the vibrations decrease the strength of the bulk solid so that the probability that the arches and ratholes will disintegrate increases. The best effect is achieved with frequencies above 100 Hz (Roberts, 1984). It is important that vibrational devices are only used during the discharge of the silo. The vibration of a bulk solid which cannot flow out may lead to a further consolidation and, therefore, to an increase in flow problems.

Inserts are used to enhance the flow profile inside the silo. Figure 4.1.7 shows, for example, the so-called 'Binsert®' (Johanson, 1983) which is a hopper-shaped insert inside the silo hopper. To ensure mass flow the slope of the walls of the Binsert® must not exceed the maximum slope of the walls of a conical (axisymmetric) mass flow hopper (Θ_{ax}). The slope of the silo hopper walls with respect to the Binsert® walls must also not exceed Θ_{ax}. Therefore, by using the Binsert®, the height of a mass flow hopper can be clearly reduced compared to a hopper without a Binsert®, as shown in Figs 4.1.7(a) and (b). The Binsert® can be useful by presenting the opportunity to transform a funnel flow silo to a mass flow silo (reconstruction).

A further means of promoting the flow of a bulk solid is alteration of the flow properties by fluidization or by the addition of a flow agent (e.g. magnesium oxide, Aerosil®).

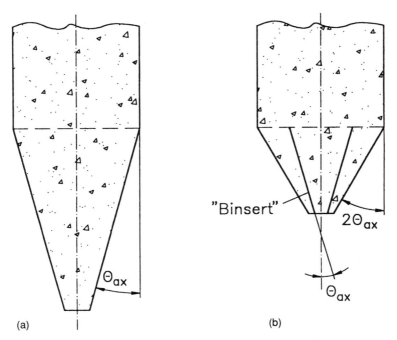

Fig. 4.1.7 Mass flow hopper (a) without and (b) with Binsert®.

4.1.3 Application of flow-promoting devices and feeders

A silo which is to operate without flow obstructions has to be designed with consideration of the flow properties of the bulk solid to be stored. The flow properties have to be measured for each particular case. This is the only way to make a quantitative statement about the appropriate silo geometry. Jenike's theory (Jenike, 1964; Schwedes, 1968, 1976; Molerus, 1985) used for silo design predicts the following geometrical figures (Fig. 4.1.8):

- Maximum angle of the hopper walls with respect to the vertical, Θ_{ax} (conical hopper) or Θ_{eb} (wedge-shaped hopper).
- Minimum diameter of the outlet d (conical hopper) or minimal width of the outlet slit b (wedge-shaped hopper) to avoid arching.
- Minimum size of the outlet to avoid piping (ratholing) in the case of funnel flow.
- In the case of bulk solids with time consolidation: dependence of the minimum outlet size on storage time t.

On the basis of these figures there are different possible concepts for the construction and operation of the silo and the choice of feeders and flow-promoting devices. Some of the different possibilities are shown for an

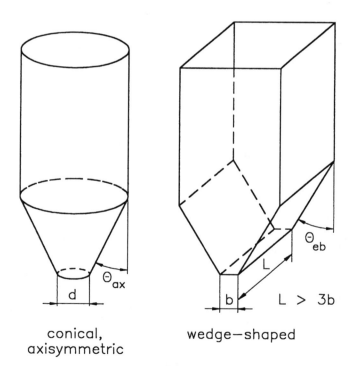

Fig. 4.1.8 Hopper geometries.

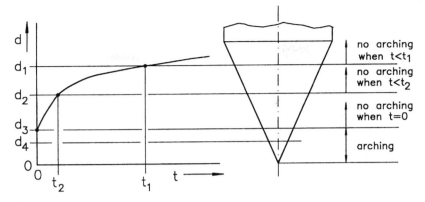

Fig. 4.1.9 Minimum outlet diameter dependence on the storage time at rest.

axisymmetric mass flow silo (conical hopper). The diagram in Fig. 4.1.9 shows the minimum outlet diameter to prevent arching, d, dependent on the storage time at rest, t (time between two consecutive discharge operations). Due to the strong time consolidation of the bulk solid the outlet diameter d increases strongly with time.

4.1.3.1 Concept 1: Design of the outlet diameter for the maximum storage time at rest

In this case, the outlet diameter d is large enough to prevent arching even after the maximum storage time at rest (e.g. after a weekend or holidays). In the example under consideration, the maximum storage time will be the time t_1 which requires the outlet diameter $d(t_1) = d_1$ (Fig. 4.1.9). The silo referring to this is shown in Fig. 4.1.10(a). A feeder of appropriate size (diameter d_1) has to be fitted to the outlet. The choice of feeder type depends on the outlet size, the bulk solid (fine-grained or coarse-grained, sticking, cohesive, moist, ...) and other requirements (e.g. accurate dosage). Since arching is not possible in the silo in Fig. 4.1.10(a), flow-promoting devices are not required.

In the Θ_{ax}–d-diagram of Fig. 4.1.11 silos of different shapes are represented. The shaft diameter of all the silos is 4000 mm. The silos are designed according to concept 1 for different bulk solids A, B, C and D. Points A, B, C and D represent the hopper geometries as a pair of values of maximum hopper slope angle (measured from the vertical) for mass flow (Θ_{ax}) and outlet diameter d for the maximum storage time at rest. Bulk solid A is a relatively good flowing material. It requires only a flat hopper slope angle for mass flow and a small outlet diameter d to prevent arching which can be fitted with a rotary valve as feeder and dosage device. Bulk solid B requires a more expensive technical solution: the hopper has to be designed steeper

208 Discharge, feeding and metering equipment

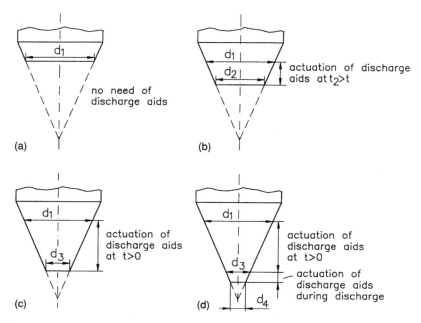

Fig. 4.1.10 Concepts of mass flow silos.

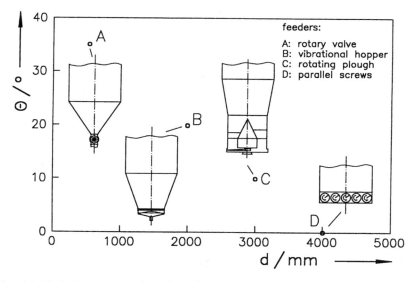

Fig. 4.1.11 Axisymmetric silos (shaft diameter 4000 mm).

to achieve mass flow. To prevent arching, an outlet diameter of 2000 mm is necessary which is realized with a vibrational hopper in this case.

For bulk solid C which has worse flow properties than bulk solid B, a hopper slope angle Θ_{ax} of 10° from the vertical is necessary to achieve mass flow. The feeder (here: rotating plough) has to operate across a diameter d of 3000 mm to avoid arching in the conical hopper. Bulk solid D has such a large wall friction angle that mass flow could not be achieved in any hopper (mass flow at $\Theta_{ax} = 0°$). Hence, the hopper has to be omitted and the silo shaft has to be fitted with a feeder which is able to feed across the whole cross-section of the silo (e.g. parallel screw feeders).

4.1.3.2 Concept 2: Choice of an outlet diameter $d_2 > d(t = 0)$, but $d_2 < d(t = t_1)$

If the outlet diameter d is chosen according to d_2 (Fig. 4.1.10(b)) then the outlet is large enough to prevent arching until a storage time at rest t_2 (Fig. 4.1.9). If a storage time $t_1 > t_2$ is necessary then stable arches can occur for storage times $t > t_2$. Hence, flow-promoting devices are required in the area where $d_2 < d < d_1$ to break the arches and to initiate flow after a storage time $t > t_2$ (Fig. 4.1.10(b)). The flow-promoting devices do not have to be used to stimulate the flow after storage time at rest $t < t_2$.

In the case of concept 2, the flow-promoting devices are only required to initiate flow after a certain storage time at rest. After the bulk solid is set in motion, the time consolidation is completely reduced, the bulk solid behaves in the same way as without time consolidation, and, therefore, the minimum outlet diameter $d_3 = d(t = 0)$ is valid which is smaller than the chosen outlet diameter d_2 (Fig. 4.1.9). Hence, the operation of flow-promoting devices is not required during further discharging. Only after another storage at rest for more than t_2 will the flow-promoting devices have to be used.

If more than one flow-promoting device (e.g. air cannons) is installed they should be switched on one after another, beginning with the one nearest the outlet opening and ending with the one at the highest position (Fig. 4.1.12).

This mode of operation has some advantages. The bulk solid, stressed by the flow-promoting devices, can easily fall into the void below the arch. Otherwise, if the distance between the void below the arch and the flow-promoting device is too great, the bulk solid may remain in its position and consolidate further. The second advantage is that the bulk solid falls down in small portions, thus limiting the additional load on the silo structure by the bulk solid collapsing and hence protecting the feeder from being destroyed.

The choice of the outlet diameter $d_3 = d(t = 0)$ (Fig. 4.1.10(c)) is the limiting case of concept 2. Here the flow-promoting devices must always be used if the bulk solid has been stored at rest for time intervals $t > 0$.

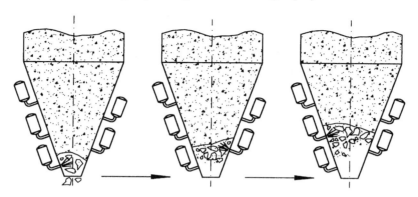

Fig. 4.1.12 Operation of flow-promoting devices.

4.1.3.3 Concept 3: Choice of the outlet diameter $d_4 < d(t = 0)$

For an outlet diameter $d_4 < d(t = 0)$ arching is possible even without time consolidation. Therefore, flow-promoting devices have to be used between the outlet and that position where the hopper diameter is equal to the minimum diameter to avoid arching after the maximum storage time at rest (d_1). During emptying, the flow-promoting devices which are located below diameter $d_3 = d(t = 0)$ have to be used constantly during discharging. The flow-promoting devices above that diameter have to be used only to initiate flow after a storage time $0 < t < t_1$ (as with concept 2).

The concepts described above are valid for mass flow silos. In the case of mass flow only the problem of arching exists (Fig. 4.1.1). Piping is only possible in funnel flow silos. In a mass flow silo the whole contents of the silo flows downwards during discharge (Fig. 4.1.2). Thus the time consolidation is reduced completely. In a funnel flow silo dead zones are formed in which the bulk solid remains at rest even during discharge. If the silo is not emptied completely at short time intervals, the bulk solid in the dead zones will remain at rest for long periods of time. Thus it can consolidate more and more so that it builds up stable ratholes and cannot be discharged. For this reason, funnel flow silos should be used only if the bulk solid has no or only limited time consolidation effect and if the other disadvantages of funnel flow silos like segregation, or wide residence time distribution (Jenike, 1964; Schwedes, 1968, 1976), are negligible.

It is impossible to make a general assessment of the concepts introduced for mass flow silos. Concept 1 is the simplest one from the point of view of performance and operation because flow-promoting devices are not necessary. The inexpert use of flow-promoting devices can cause problems, for example irregular flow of the bulk solid, caused by collapsed arches or ratholes, or flooding of the bulk solid (caused by pneumatic flow-promoting devices). Furthermore, there are no guidelines based on theory, meaning that the design of flow-promoting devices is based only on experience. There has been some work done on this topic (e.g. Terziovski and Arnold, 1990; Johanson, 1971; Kurz, 1974; Roberts, 1984), but there is still a lack of calculation methods which can be applied in practice. For this reason, one should strive at first to achieve concept 1.

In the case of bulk solids which hardly flow and show a pronounced time consolidation effect, a minimum outlet diameter of a few metres can occur even after a short duration of storage at rest (e.g. after a few hours or days). If the use of feeders with an appropriate cross-section (e.g. rotating plough, parallel screw feeder, points C and D in Fig. 4.1.11) is to be avoided then concept 2 might be a solution. The outlet diameter and the feeder size are chosen large enough to avoid arching without time consolidation. The flow-promoting devices ensure that the bulk solid is set in motion after a long storage time at rest. The disadvantages of flow-promoting devices (e.g. irregular flow of the bulk solid) of concept 2 occur only after a long storage time at rest. During continuous operation the flow-promoting devices do not have to be used. Hence, concept 2 is a possible alternative to concept 1.

In the case of concept 3, some of the flow-promoting devices (Fig. 4.1.10(d)) have to run continuously during discharge. Constantly operating flow-promoting devices (e.g. aeration hoppers and other aeration devices, shakers) are suitable for this application. Flow-promoting devices which work in a discontinuous way (e.g. air cannons) might result in an irregular outflow of the bulk solid. For this reason, concept 3 should only be used for the type of bulk solids which can be controlled safely using continuously operating flow-promoting devices. Concept 3 should not be used for bulk solids which hardly flow and have a pronounced time consolidation effect or tend to fluidize.

4.1.4 Feeder design

For the silo design concepts discussed in section 4.1.3 it was assumed that the bulk solid is discharged across the whole outlet cross-section. Even in a hopper designed for mass flow (mass flow means the entire contents of the silo are in motion during discharge, Fig. 4.1.2), mass flow can only occur if the latter condition is satisfied. The following design rules which will be explained later have to be considered when designing the feeder and the hopper/feeder interface:

1   To avoid dead zones, the gradient of all walls which are in contact with the bulk solid must be steep enough to achieve mass flow.
2   The feeder must be able to discharge the bulk solid across the whole outlet opening. Thus it is not necessary for the bulk solid to have the same velocity at every point on the outlet cross-section.

According to the definition of mass flow the entire contents of the silo have to be in motion during discharge. A constant velocity across the cross-

212 Discharge, feeding and metering equipment

section is not necessary. Measurements of stresses in silos (Schulze and Schwedes, 1990; Schwedes and Schulze, 1990) show that an irregular velocity distribution across the outlet cross-section can cause an asymmetric, irregular distribution of stresses acting in the bulk solid and on the silo walls. The stresses are lower in areas where the bulk solid flows faster downward than in areas where the bulk solid flows slower. The irregular stress distributions caused by eccentric discharge (Motzkus, 1974) result in an increased load on the silo structure and can result in damage to the silo.

4.1.4.1 Explanation of design rule no. 1

Two kinds of transition from the hopper to the feeder are shown in Fig. 4.1.13. In Fig. 4.1.13(a) the feeder is attached directly at the hopper outlet although the entrance cross-section of the feeder is smaller than the hopper outlet. Thus, a horizontal edge exists where dead zones are formed even if the hopper itself is designed for mass flow. Case (b) is the more expensive solution and makes use of a transition piece designed for mass flow.

Also inside a feeder all walls must be steep enough to avoid dead zones. In the double gate shown in Fig. 4.1.14(a) dead zones are formed on that side where the gate is closed. An alternative is the design shown in Fig. 4.1.14(b) where dead zones are prevented. If the cross-section is reduced inside a feeder as in the case of the rotary valve shown in Fig. 4.1.15 then the minimum cross-section has to be large enough to prevent arching. Furthermore, the inclined walls inside the feeder have to be steep enough to

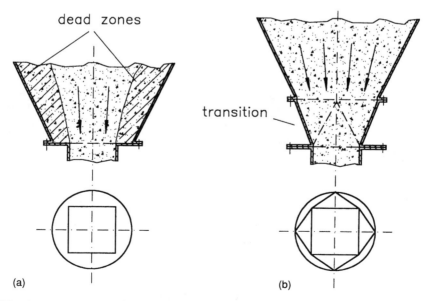

Fig. 4.1.13 Transition from the hopper to the feeder.

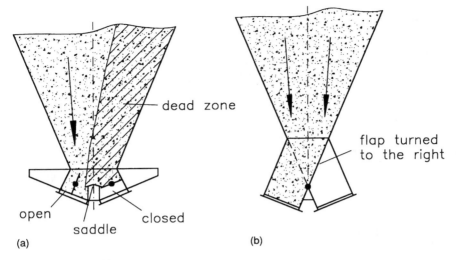

Fig. 4.1.14 Double gates.

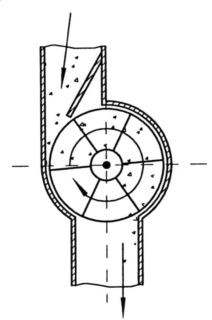

Fig. 4.1.15 Rotary valve.

avoid dead zones which can build up into the hopper, thus changing the flow profile of the silo from mass flow to funnel flow.

Another example of the formation of dead zones caused by feeder design is the slide gate shown in Fig. 4.1.16(a) which has two fixed triangular, horizontal metal sheets in its outlet area. Because of these sheets, dead

214 *Discharge, feeding and metering equipment*

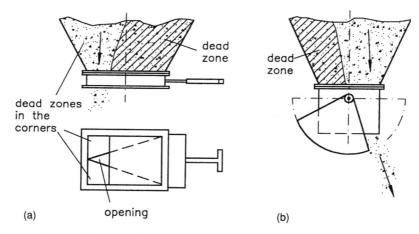

Fig. 4.1.16 (a) Slide gate; (b) shell valve.

zones are formed which result in funnel flow in the silo with all its disadvantages (flow problems, segregation, etc.). The same problems will occur with any configuration of valves and gates (e.g. shell valve, Fig. 4.1.16(b)) which are not opened completely during discharge. Hence, slide valves which are attached to a mass flow silo have to be designed and operated in such a way that the hopper outlet is opened completely during discharge.

4.1.4.2 Explanation of design rule no. 2

Many feeders tend to discharge the bulk solid only from a part of the outlet. Figure 4.1.17(a) shows a screw feeder that discharges only from the rear part of the outlet slit so that a dead zone is formed (= funnel flow) in the front part of the silo even though the hopper is designed for mass flow. The reason for this behaviour is that the screw is already filled with bulk solid in the rear part of the outlet slit so that no further bulk solid can enter the screw in the front part.

This behaviour can be changed by designing the screw so that the conveying capacity of the screw increases in the direction of conveying, for example by increasing the pitch of the screw in the direction of conveying (Fig. 4.1.17(b)). Using this method, the screw can discharge bulk solid across the whole length of the outlet slit. Other ways to realize increasing conveying capacity are increase in the outer diameter (Fig. 4.1.17(c)) or decrease in the shaft diameter in the direction of conveying. Combinations of these methods are also used (e.g. decreasing the core diameter with a constant screw pitch at the beginning and then increasing the screw pitch with constant shaft diameter) (Jenike, 1964; Schumacher, 1987).

The principle of increasing the capacity in the direction of conveying to achieve a discharge across the whole outlet cross-section can be applied to several types of feeders. En-masse conveyors (Fig. 4.1.18) should be

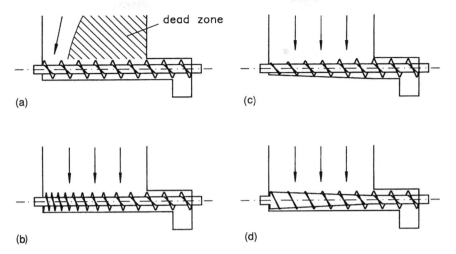

Fig. 4.1.17 Screw feeders.

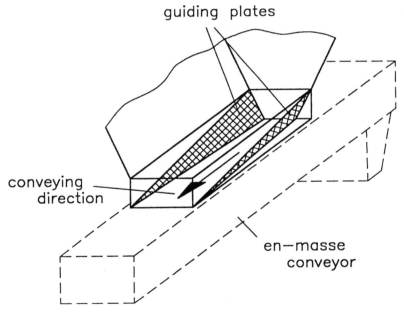

Fig. 4.1.18 En-masse conveyor with guiding plates (Meyer, 1989).

provided with so-called guiding plates in their inlet area. These sloped plates form an outlet of increasing width in the direction of conveying so that the volume transported, and therefore the capacity of the en-masse conveyor, increases in the direction of conveying. If the silo is designed without the guiding plates then the en-masse conveyor discharges the bulk solid in most cases from the rear part of the outlet slot (like the screw conveyor shown in Fig. 4.1.17(a)).

In addition, belt conveyors tend to produce an uneven discharge of the bulk solid from the outlet slit. A smooth belt conveyor and a widely opened slide gate at the front side of the silo result in a discharge of bulk solid from the front part of the outlet slit as shown in Fig. 4.1.19(a). The bulk solid is discharged more from the rear part if the conveyor belt is rough and the gate valve is opened less (Schulze and Schwedes, 1990, 1993a, b; Schwedes and Schulze 1990; Schulze, 1991). Other parameters which determine the discharge characteristic are the internal friction of the bulk solid (large internal friction promotes the discharge of bulk solid from the front part) and in some cases, the friction angle of the side skirts which are attached to the hopper outlet (large friction angle at the side skirts promotes the discharge of bulk solid from the front part of the outlet slit). Because of the large number of parameters, an exact prediction of where the bulk solid is discharged from is impossible, and only tendencies can be indicated. For this reason, it is advisable to use the principle of 'increasing capacities' for a belt conveyor to achieve a discharge of bulk solid across the whole outlet slot. This can be satisfied if the distance between the belt conveyor and the lower edge of the hopper increases (Fig. 4.1.19(b)). As a result more and more bulk solid can be transported by the belt in the direction of conveying.

Figure 4.1.19(c) shows another possible way to achieve a discharge of bulk solid across the whole outlet (Bridge and Carson, 1987). At the lower

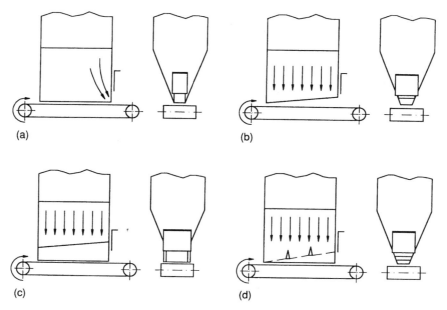

Fig. 4.1.19 Discharge characteristics of belt feeders.

edge of the bevelled hopper side skirts are attached. The distance between the side skirts increases in the direction of conveying. Because of this the width of the horizontally transported layer of bulk solid is increased. Additionally a slide gate is attached to the front wall of the hopper which allows the discharge behaviour to be adjusted. The gate valve has to be adjusted in such a way that the bulk solid flows out of the hopper as regularly as possible. Generally, the velocity of the belt has to be used to control the mass flow rate instead of the position of the slide gate.

Another possible way to produce a more regular discharge is by attaching inserts which achieve an increase in the height of the horizontally transported layer of bulk solid in the direction of conveying and therefore an increase in the capacity of the belt feeder (Fig. 4.1.19(d)). This method can also be applied to apron feeders or en-masse conveyors (Schulze and Schwedes, 1990; Schwedes and Schulze, 1990; Schulze, 1991). The inserts have to be designed so that neither arches nor dead zones can be formed on them.

The methods shown in Figs 4.1.19(b)–(d) only work if the friction angle between the conveyor belt and the bulk solid is sufficiently large to discharge the bulk solid from the rear part of the outlet slit.

Vibratory feeders tend to discharge the bulk solid from the front part of the outlet (Fig. 4.1.20(a)). A discharge of bulk solid also from the rear part is achieved by decreasing the ratio of the length of the outlet slit to the distance between feeder bottom and front end of the outlet slit to a value less than unity (Fig. 4.1.20(b)) (Reisner and Eisenhardt-Rothe, 1971; Bules, 1989); a reasonably regular discharge of bulk solid is achieved with a ratio of approximately 0.5 (Carroll, 1970).

When using a rotary valve for free-flowing bulk solids an irregular discharge of bulk solid can also occur if the chambers of the rotary valve are

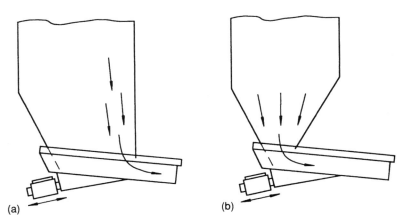

Fig. 4.1.20 Vibratory feeder.

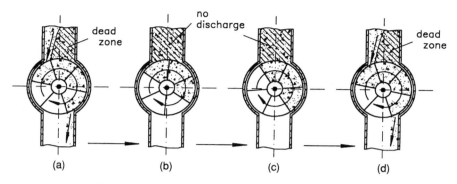

Fig. 4.1.21 Discharge of a free-flowing bulk solid with a rotary valve.

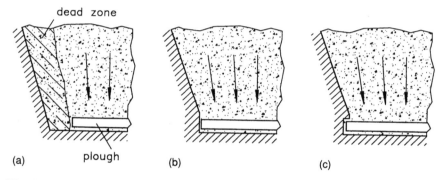

Fig. 4.1.22 Design of the hopper and the rotating plough.

filled with bulk solid as soon as they enter the area of the hopper outlet. The bulk solid is therefore discharged from the left part of the outlet as shown in Fig. 4.1.21. Furthermore, the bulk solid might flow downwards abruptly. The latter can lead to vibrations in the silo (silo quaking), especially with hard, brittle particles. A regular discharge of bulk solids across the outlet can be achieved through the following measures:

- Installation of a sloped sheet in the entrance area of the rotary valve (critical slope angles and minimum cross-sections have to be considered) (Fig. 4.1.15).
- Increasing the number of chambers
- Decreasing the volumes of the chambers
- Increasing the rotational velocity of the rotary valve

The formation of dead zones caused by the feeder can also occur if the feeder does not discharge bulk solid from the whole outlet area. An example of this is the rotating plough shown in Fig. 4.1.22(a). In this case, a dead zone is formed from the outer part of the outlet slit. To prevent dead zones, the wall and the plough have to be designed as shown in Fig. 4.1.22(b) or (c).

4.1.5 Summary and further research

A well-designed mass flow silo can only work well if the feeder and the hopper/feeder interface are also well designed. The subjects 'uniform withdrawal' and 'feeder load' are of interest in respect of the hopper/feeder interface.

To achieve the withdrawal of bulk solid across the whole outlet opening of a hopper – which is essential for achieving mass flow in a silo – the feeder and the area between hopper outlet and feeder – the hopper/feeder interface – have to be designed carefully. In particular, feeders below long outlet slits tend to discharge the bulk solid from only a part of the outlet opening. To avoid this, some feeders can be designed to have 'increasing capacity in the direction of conveying', i.e. the feeder can feed an increasing amount of bulk solid in the conveying direction.

Uniform withdrawal or at least withdrawal across the whole outlet opening has several advantages:

- Mass flow (if the hopper is designed for mass flow)
- Less flow problems due to the increased flow region
- Stresses acting on the silo structure become more uniform
- Less problems with segregation or silo quaking
- Smaller driving forces and torques

Up to now an exact prediction of the optimal geometry of the hopper/feeder interface is difficult to achieve, and only limited types of feeders (e.g. the belt feeder) have been examined. Therefore, knowledge of a wider range of feeders is required.

For flow-promoting devices, no design methods exist, for example, for air cannons or aeration devices. Therefore, further research is also required in this area.

References

Bridge, D.T.; Carson, J.W.: How to design efficient screw and belt feeders for bulk solids, *Powder and Bulk Solids 12th Annual Conf.*, Rosemont, IL (1987), pp. 1–23

Bules, W.S.: The care and feeding of a vibratory conveyor, *Bulk Solids Handling* 9 (1989) 2, pp. 209–210

Carroll, P.J.: Hopper design with vibratory feeders, *Chem. Engrg. Progr.* 66 (1970), pp. 44–49

Jenike, A.W.: *Storage and Flow of Solids*, Bull. No. 123, Utah Engng. Station, Univ. of Utah, Salt Lake City (1964)

Johanson, J.R.: The effect of the gaseous phase on pressures in a cylindrical silo, *Powder Technol.* 5 (1971/72), pp. 135–145

Johanson, J.R.: Controlling flow patterns in a bin by use of an insert, *Bulk Solids Handling* 2 (1983) 3, pp. 495-498

Kurz, H.P.: Fließverhalten von belüfteten Schüttgütern in Bunkern, Diss., University of Karlsruhe (1974)

Meyer, H.-J.: Experiences with coal bunkers and coal feeders, *Bulk Solids Handling* 9 (1989) 1, pp. 27-31

Molerus, O.: *Schüttgutmechanik*, Springer-Verlag, Berlin, Heidelberg, New York (1985)

Motzkus, U: Belastung von Silöböden und Auslauftrichtern durch körnige Schüttgüter, Diss. TU Braunschweig (1974)

Reisner, W.; v.Eisenhardt-Rothe, M.: *Silos und Bunker für die Schüttgutspeicherung*, Trans Tech Publications, Clausthal-Zellerfeld (1971)

Roberts, A.W.: Vibration of fine powders and its application, in: Fayed, M.E., Otten, L.: *Handbook of Powder Science and Technology*, Van Nostrand Reinhold Company Inc., New York (1984), pp. 181-229

Schulze, D.: Untersuchungen zur gegenseitigen Beeinflussung von Silo und Austragorgan, Diss. TU Braunschweig (1991)

Schulze, D.; Schwedes, J.: Experimental investigation of silo stresses under consideration of the influence of hopper/feeder interface, *Kona* 8 (1990), pp. 134-144

Schulze, D.; Schwedes, J.: Bulk solids flow in the hopper/feeder interface, Proceedings 'Reliable Flow of Particulate Solids II', Oslo, Norway, 23-25 August (1993a), EFChE Publ. Ser. No. 96, pp. 571-584

Schulze, D.; Schwedes, J.: Bulk solids flow in the hopper/feeder interface, *Powder Handling & Processing* 5 (1993b) 4, pp. 341-348

Schumacher, W.: Zum Förderverhalten von Bunkerabzugsschnecken mit Vollblattwendeln, Diss. RWTH Aachen (1987)

Schwedes, J.: *Fließverhalten von Schüttgütern in Bunkern*, Verlag Chemie, Weinheim (1968)

Schwedes, J.: Fließverhalten von Schüttgütern in Bunkern, *Chem.-Ing.-Techn.* 48 (1976) 4, pp. 294-300

Schwedes, J.; Schulze, D.: Influence of hopper/feeder interface on the stress field in a silo, Proc. 2nd World Congress Particle Technology, Kyoto, Japan, Sept. 1990, pp. 118-126

Terziovski, A.; Arnold, P.C.: On the effective sizing and placement of air blasters, *Bulk Solids Handling* 10 (1990) 2, pp. 181-185

Woodcock, C.R.; Mason, J.S.: *Bulk Solids Handling*, Leonard Hill, Glasgow and London (1987)

Zeppelin Schüttguttechnik GmbH, *Horizontal-Zellenradschleuse ROTOSTAR*, prospectus, Weingarten (1992)

4.2 Discharge of bulk solids from silos – description of discharge systems

H. Heinrici

4.2.1 Introduction

In order to permit a suitable discharge system to be selected, it is necessary to know the physical properties of the bulk solid, the silo geometry and the tasks which the discharge system is required to perform.

The physical properties of the bulk solid like particle size or bulk density influence the possible design of a discharge system. If these properties and the silo geometry are known it is possible to determine whether flow problems have to be anticipated when the silo is operated. If such problems cannot be avoided, a complex design of the discharge system will generally be required or additional facilities will be necessary.

The tasks which the discharge system is required to perform must be thoroughly investigated. When doing this, it is necessary to take into account the requirements related to silo filling and emptying, mode of silo operation and silo design.

4.2.2 Definitions

First various terms which are important in relation to discharge of bulk solids from silos will be explained.

- *Shut-off element.* A shut-off element completely stops the flow of bulk solid out of a silo.
- *Activation.* The flow properties of the bulk solid are changed by reducing internal friction and wall friction by additional energy. This improves discharge or makes discharge possible.
- *Discharging.* Discharging is the process of movement of the bulk solid

in the area of the discharge system. In general the bulk solid flows from a larger silo cross-section to a smaller one and then out of the silo.
- *Discharge aid.* Discharge aids are aids, devices and machines which serve to permit, improve and maintain bulk solid flow into and out of the silo if continuous flow under the force of gravity cannot be achieved.
- *Discharge element.* Discharge elements are devices and machines to which the bulk solid flows freely. This can be made possible under the force of gravity or with discharge aids. Shut-off and feeding may be sub-functions of a discharge element.
- *Discharge system.* The combination of discharge aids and discharge elements is termed the 'discharge system'.
- *Feeding.* Feeding means a reproducible and regulatory flow of bulk solid out of a silo. The flow of bulk solid is limited to the set feed rate by taking suitable measures. Depending upon the facilities used, feeding is carried out either volumetrically or gravimetrically. With volumetric feeding the volumetric discharge rate is influenced. Using additional facilities it is also possible to control a mass discharge rate with gravimetric feeding. These additional facilities consist of a gravimetric measuring instrument to determine the mass flow and an electronic control system for varying the volumetric discharge rate.

4.2.3 Selection of a discharge system

The procedure to select a suitable discharge system is illustrated by the assessment matrices shown in Figs 4.2.1–4.2.4. As a first step the properties of the bulk solid must be known. If they are not known, they must be determined since otherwise the subsequent questions cannot be answered with certainty. If possible data for the properties of the bulk solid are taken on the basis of experience this can lead to over- or underdimensioning of the discharge system.

The subsidiary conditions under which a discharge system must operate and the sub-functions it has to perform (e.g. wear, maintenance, safety functions) must be determined.

4.2.4 Assessment criteria for discharge aids and elements

4.2.4.1 Operating principles

Four different principles can be distinguished:

1. *Mechanically acting.* The bulk solid is conveyed by driven elements which can be rotating or translatory elements. The bulk solid may be moved positively or under friction or a combination of both.
2. *Oscillatory.* Oscillatory vibrations change the internal friction or the wall friction of the bulk solid.

Discharge of bulk solids from silos

3 *Pneumatically acting.* Depending upon the particular system, energy is supplied to the bulk solid by gas (generally air) which is admitted at different locations and at different times. The flow behaviour is improved by reducing the wall friction and/or the internal friction.

4 *Statically acting.* This means silo fixtures which cause a change in the flow profile of the bulk solid in the silo dependent upon their shape, arrangement and surface condition.

4.2.4.2 Bulk solid

Despite the great variety of properties which bulk solids show it is possible to classify between free-flowing and cohesive bulk solids.

Other important characteristics having an influence on the selection of discharge systems are:

- the risk of a dust explosion generated by the bulk solid
- the wear of the discharge system
- the risk of attrition of the bulk solid caused by the discharge system

4.2.4.3 Point of installation

It has to be distinguished whether the discharge system is fitted inside or outside the silo or which part of the silo (cone or vertical part).

4.2.4.4 Mode of operation of the discharge aids and elements

The devices may be operated continuously or intermittently. When operating intermittently the pause and/or operating intervals may be controlled as a function of time or as a function of a signal. Attachment and operation when necessary are other criteria relating to the mode of operation.

4.2.4.5 Installation and installation conditions

Installation during silo operation means that production does not have to be interrupted. It is also necessary to know whether the silo has to be designed for a given discharge system or whether mounting needs for the discharge system have to be adapted to the silo design.

4.2.4.6 Drive power

Electrical power, compressed air or hydraulic power may be used to drive the discharge system. Some discharge aids may also be actuated by the bulk solid itself.

Discharge, feeding and metering equipment

	Screw conveyor		Screw-floor	Turning beam floor	Slide frame	Scraper, single, fixed	Scraper, single, mobile	Scraper, multiple, mobile	Plough scraper
	Fixed	Turning							
Bulk solid									
Free-flowing	xxxx	xxx	xx	xxx	xx	xxx	xxx	xxx	xxx
Cohesive	xxx	xxxx	x	xxx	xxx	x xx	x xx	x xx	x xx
Dusty	xx	xx	x x	x x	x x	xx	xx	xx	xx
Abrasive	x	x	x	xx	xx	x	x	x	x
Breakable	x	x	x	xx	x	x	x	x	x
Function									
Feeding	xxx	xxxx	x	xxx	xxx	xxx	xxx	xxx	x
Shut-off									
Discharge									
Activating									
Point of installation									
Inside	xx	xx	x x	x x	x x	xx	xx	xx	xx
Outside									
Cone									
Vertical part of silo									
Mode of operation									
Continuous	x	x	x	xx	xx	x	x	x	x
Discontinuous									
Installation when necessary									
Installation									
During silo construction	x	x	x	x	x	x	x	x	x
With empty silo									
During operation									
Installation conditions									
Influences silo design	x	x	x	xx	x	x	x	x	x
Silo design influences discharge system									
Power									
Electrical	x	x	x	x	x	x	x	x	x
Hydraulic									

Discharge of bulk solids from silos

	Belt conveyor	Apron conveyor	'Redler'-conveyor
Bulk solid			
Free-flowing	x	x	x
Cohesive	x	x	x
Dusty	x	x	x
Abrasive	x		
Breakable	x		
Function			
Feeding	x	x	x
Shut-off	x	x	x
Discharge	x	x	x
Activating			
Point of installation			
Inside	x x	x x	x x
Outside			
Cone			
Vertical part of silo			
Mode of operation			
Continuous	x	x	x
Discontinuous			
Installation when necessary			
Installation			
During silo construction	x	x	x
With empty silo			
During operation			
Installation conditions			
Influences silo design	x	x	x
Silo design influences discharge system			
Power			
Electrical	x	x	x

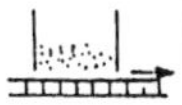

Fig. 4.2.1 Discharge system selection matrix: mechanically acting operating principle.

	Rubber cushion	Rotary feeder	Vibrating cone
Bulk solid			
Free-flowing	x	x	x
Cohesive	x	x	x
Dusty	x		x
Abrasive	x		
Breakable			
Function			
Feeding		x	x
Shut-off		x	x
Discharge	x	x	x
Activating			
Point of installation			
Inside	x	x	x
Outside	x	x	x
Cone			x
Vertical part of silo			
Mode of operation			
Continuous	x	x	x
Discontinuous	x	x	x
Installation when necessary			
Installation			
During silo construction	x	x	x
With empty silo			
During operation			
Installation conditions			
Influences silo design	x	x	x
Silo design influences discharge system		x	x
Power			
Electrical	x	x	x
Air			

Fig. 4.2.1 Continued

Discharge of bulk solids from silos

	Vibrator	Vibratory feeder	Vibrating cone	Vibrating frame	Vibrating blades
Bulk solid					
Free-flowing	xxxx	x	xxxx	xx	xxx
Cohesive		xxx	xxxx		
Dusty					
Abrasive					
Breakable					
Function					
Feeding		xxx			
Shut-off	x	xxx	xx	x	xxxx
Discharge					
Activating					
Point of installation					
Inside	xx	xx	xx	x	xx
Outside				x	
Cone					
Vertical part of silo					
Mode of operation					
Continuous	xxx	x	xx	x	x
Discontinuous					
Installation when necessary					
Installation					
During silo construction	xxx	xx	x	xx	xx
With empty silo	xx		xx	xx	
During operation					
Installation conditions					
Influences silo design	x	x	xx	xx	x
Silo design influences discharge system	x				
Power					
Electrical	xx	x	x	x	x
Air					

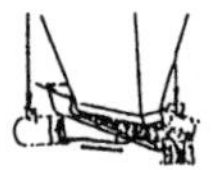

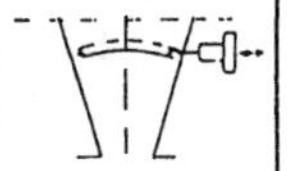

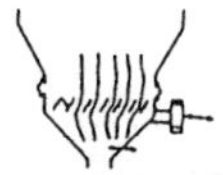

Fig. 4.2.2 Discharge system selection matrix: oscillatory operating system.

	Fluidized bottom	Fluidized trough	Air nozzle	Air cannon	Explosion (CARDOX)
Bulk solid					
Free-flowing	x	x			
Cohesive		xx	x	x	x
Dusty			x	x	x
Abrasive	x				
Breakable					
Function					
Feeding	xx	xxx			
Shut-off					
Discharge					x
Activating			x	x	
Point of installation					
Inside					
Outside					
Cone	x	xx	x	x	x
Vertical part of silo			xx	xx	xx
Mode of operation					
Continuous	xx	x	xxx		
Discontinuous				xx	xx
Installation when necessary					
Installation					
During silo construction	x	x	xx		
With empty silo				xx	x
During operation					
Installation conditions					
Influences silo design	x	x	x	xx	xx
Silo design influences discharge system			x		
Power					
Electrical					x
Air	x	x	x	x	

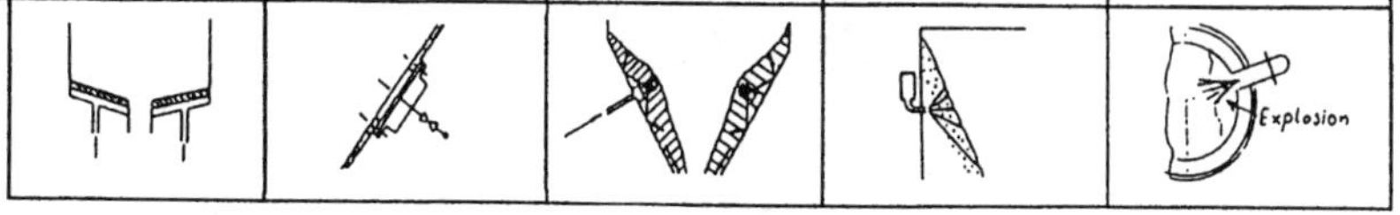

Fig. 4.2.3 Discharge system selection matrix: pneumatically acting operating system.

	Lining			Cone	Cone in cone (Binsert)®
	Stainless steel	Plastic	Paint		
Bulk solid					
Free-flowing	x	x	x	x	x
Cohesive	x	x	x	x	x
Dusty	x	x		x	x
Abrasive	x			x	x
Breakable	x	x	x		
Function					
Feeding					
Shut-off					
Discharge	x	x	x	x	x
Activating					
Point of installation					
Inside	x	x	x	x	x
Outside	x	x	x	x	x
Cone		x	x		
Vertical part of silo					
Mode of operation					
Continuous	x	x	x	x	x
Discontinuous					
Installation when necessary					
Installation					
During silo construction	x	x	x	x	x
With empty silo	x	x	x	x	x
During operation					
Installation conditions					
Influences silo design	x	x	x	x	x
Silo design influences discharge system					
Power					
Electrical					
Air					

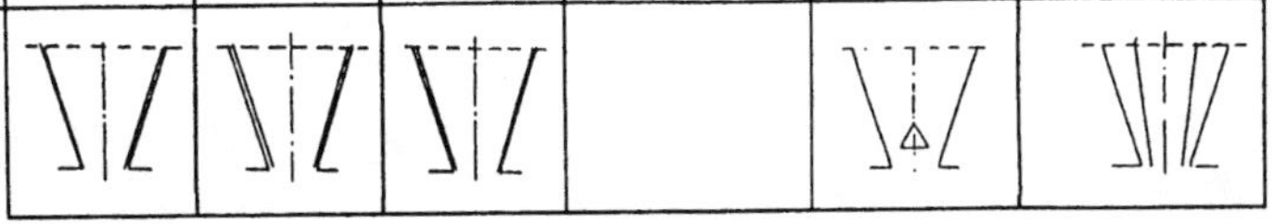

Fig. 4.2.4 Discharge system selection matrix: statically acting operating system.

4.2.5 Assessment matrix

The four principles of discharge systems are assessed in accordance with the above-described criteria in a matrix. The assessments are based upon conventional applications. Consequently situations in practice may differ substantially from the information in the matrix.

Research work is needed to verify and to enhance this matrix.

4.3 Continuous feeding of bulk solids
H. Heinrici

4.3.1 General

The feeding of bulk solids describes several operations within an industrial process in which the flow rate is controlled and measured.

Feeding can be done as a continuous or batch process. A typical example of a batch process is the filling of boxes, big bags, containers, etc. Here it is necessary to move, measure, control and stop the flow of a certain mass or volume often within given tolerances.

A continuous feeding (Fig. 4.3.1) is necessary when an even flow and a high accuracy during the feeding are demanded. Although continuous feeding systems usually run over a very long time there are also applications which require only a short running time.

Continuous feeding can be volumetric (constant volume flow, Fig. 4.3.2) or gravimetric (constant mass flow, Fig. 4.3.3). It should be noted, however, that accurate volumetric feeding does not necessarily entail accurate gravimetric feeding, because variations in bulk density result in an uneven mass flow. (Note: In this context, the term 'mass flow' describes the flow of mass, and not an internal flow pattern.)

Parameters to influence the bulk density are:

1. Flow profile in the bin.
2. Changes in the properties of the bulk material due to
    (a) segregation;
    (b) grain size;
    (c) surface shape;
    (d) moisture content.
3. 'Running' of the bin (filling, discharge).

232   *Discharge, feeding and metering equipment*

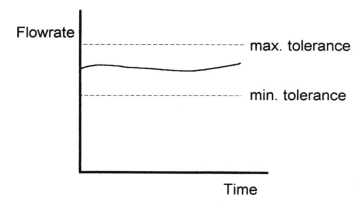

Fig. 4.3.1 Continuous feeding.

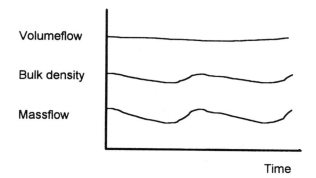

Fig. 4.3.2 Volumetric feeding.

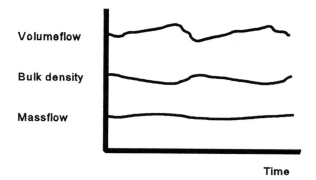

Fig. 4.3.3 Gravimetric feeding.

Gravimetric feeding is to be preferred in cases when the bulk density cannot be maintained constant within the required tolerances or when a signal acknowledgment of the actual feed rate is necessary. For this reason gravimetric feeding is generally preferred for applications requiring a higher degree of accuracy.

A gravimetric feeding system can be designed in such a manner that conveying of the bulk solid and measurement of the flow rate are done in a single unit. This principle is called an 'integrated feeding system' (Fig. 4.3.4). A typical example is a weigh feeder.

An alternative to this is to perform both operations (conveying and measurement) in separate units. In this case the feeding system consists of an adjustable feeder, like a screw feeder or rotary feeder, and a unit to measure the flow rate (Fig. 4.3.5).

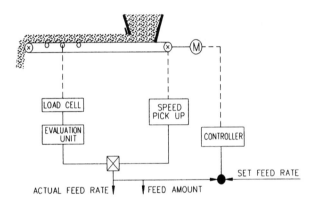

Fig. 4.3.4 Integrated feeding system.

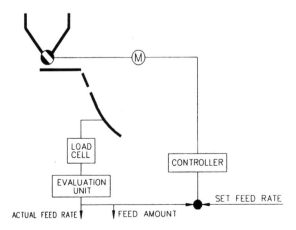

Fig. 4.3.5 Feeding system with prefeeder and flow meter.

234   *Discharge, feeding and metering equipment*

4.3.2 Continuous weighing of bulk solids

4.3.2.1 Belt weigher

The belt weigher is the most often used principle for the continuous weighing of bulk solids. It is incorporated in belt conveyors instead of at least one idler.

Belt weighers measure the belt load q (kg/m) which multiplied by the belt speed v_0 gives the mass flow. To get an acceptable accuracy the belt speed is determined by using a separate speed transducer (Fig. 4.3.6).

Most belt weighers use an electromechanical weighing principle. The weighing idler rests on at least one load cell. The load cell measures the force which is applied by the bulk solid on the belt between the two idlers adjacent to the weighing idler. By dividing this force by half of the distance between these two idlers one gets the belt load. The integration of the feed rate results in the amount of bulk solid conveyed.

4.3.2.2 Flow meter

Flow meters are distinguished by their physical measuring principles. It is common to them that they measure a reaction force caused by the bulk solid's flow.

4.3.2.2.1 Solids flow meter

Figure 4.3.5 shows a solids flow meter controlling a prefeeder. The solids flow meter consists of a transfer and a measuring chute. The bulk solid flows over the transfer chute to get an even flow. Then it enters the curved measuring chute and is deflected from a mainly vertical flow to a more horizontal one. The measuring chute is connected to a load cell. Caused by the deflection a centrifugal force is created which is proportional to the bulk solid's flow rate. The weighing unit shown in Fig. 4.3.5 measures the horizontal component of this reaction force. There is also a version available which measures the vertical component. The reaction force F can be described by:

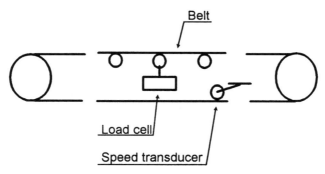

Fig. 4.3.6 Belt weigher and speed transducer.

$$F \approx m\varphi v$$

where F is the reaction force, m the mass flow rate, φ the deflection angle and v the velocity of bulk solid.

The deflection angle φ is a known figure, but the bulk solid's velocity v depends on the friction between bulk solid and transfer measuring chute respectively. To achieve a high accuracy with this flow meter it is necessary to have:

1 Constant bulk solid properties.
2 Constant friction between:
    (a) bulk solid/transfer chute;
    (b) bulk solid/measuring chute.
3 Constant bulk solid velocity.

4.3.2.2.2 Impact flow meter

Flow meters operating on the impact plate principle measure the reaction force F generated as the material stream hits an impact plate (Fig. 4.3.7). By the law of elastic impacts, this force depends on the impact and bounce-off velocities of the particles as well as on their elastic properties, as the impact force is dependent on the impact factor K:

$$F \approx m(1+K)w \sin\alpha \sin\gamma$$

where K is the impact factor, w the impact velocity, α the angle of impact plate and γ the angle between impact plate and falling line of bulk solid. Bulk solid parameters, such as particle size, moisture, fines proportion, aerated state and temperature enter heavily into the result of measurement. Therefore, satisfactory accuracies can be achieved with impact plate type

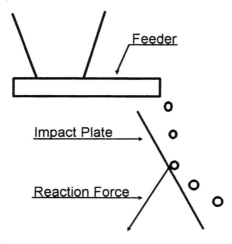

Fig. 4.3.7 Impact flow meter.

flow meters only if these parameters are constant and if, in addition, the material feed (height of fall, angle of impact) is reproducible.

As compared to the impact plate type, the accuracy to be achieved in a measuring chute type flow meter is bound to be better as a result of the principle employed, as the measuring chute, together with the preceding guide chute, assures a defined uniform guidance of the bulk solids flow. Thus, with this particular principle of measurement the impact factor is no longer of any effect. Due to the friction-dependent velocity of the solids particles in the measuring chute the characteristics of the bulk solid also here influence the result of the measurement.

4.3.2.3 Mass flow meter on Coriolis principle

The measuring effect due to the underlying measuring principle is essentially caused by Coriolis force, occurring as the particles flow over a measuring wheel. Measuring methods on the Coriolis principle are known from liquid flow measurements. They allow direct acquisition of the mass flow rate and enable very high accuracy requirements to be met, without the mechanical properties of the bulk solid having to the measured.

Realization of the measuring principle requires a measuring wheel rotating at a constant angular speed. The bulk solid flowing over this wheel requires an additional drive torque in order to maintain this speed at a constant level. This torque is strictly proportional to the mass flow rate (Fig. 4.3.8).

Application of the bulk solid flow to the measuring wheel is in the centre via a cone-shaped deflection device hit by the solids flow to be

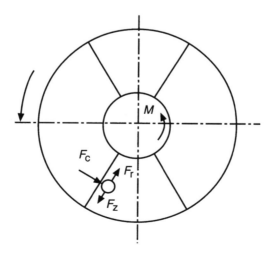

Fig. 4.3.8 Coriolis principle.

measured. After deflection, the solids particles are caught by the guide blades of the measuring wheels, accelerated and routed outside by centrifugal forces. The particles exit the measuring wheel at the guide blade discharge edge. Due to the rotation of the measuring wheel after a mass particle has entered the guide blade, centrifugal F_z, Coriolis F_c and frictional F_r forces become active. The mass particles are accelerated to the outside by the centrifugal force reduced by the frictional force. Frictional and centrifugal forces act in a radial direction, and only the Coriolis force F_c acts in a tangential direction, creating the reactive moment M to be compensated for by the drive, which is described by:

$$m = \frac{M}{\omega R^2}$$

where m is the mass flow rate, M the torque caused by Coriolis force, ω the angular speed and R the outer radius of measuring wheel.

By this relationship and with constant angular speed, the torque measured is directly proportional to the mass flow. Friction between particles and measuring wheel or among particles moving at different velocities is of no effect on the result of measurement. This measuring method is thus suitable for measuring bulk solids flow at a high accuracy, as, in contrast to impact plate and measuring chute type systems, physical quantities influenced by bulk solid's properties do not affect the sensitivity of the system.

4.3.3 Gravimetric feeding systems

4.3.3.1 Weigh feeder

The measuring principle of the belt weigher is used as the basis of the weigh feeder (Fig. 4.3.4).

A weigh feeder consists of:

- a belt feeder
- a drive unit with speed transducer to determine the belt speed
- a hopper with adjustable gate (speed-controlled weigh feeder)
- a belt weigher
- a controller

The controller multiplies the signal from the belt weigher (belt load, kg/m) with that from the speed transducer (belt speed, m/s) to get the instantaneous feed rate. The controller then changes either the belt speed or the belt load to get the set feed rate.

4.3.3.1.1 Speed-controlled weigh feeder

The speed-controlled weigh feeder is shown in Fig. 4.3.4. The belt load is roughly set by the adjustable gate at the front side of the hopper and is more or less constant. The belt speed is controlled.

4.3.3.1.2 Belt-load-controlled weigh feeder

The belt speed is constant and the belt load is controlled via a prefeeder. If a wide range of feed rates has to be fed the belt load can be small. Then errors caused by different belt thickness or tension will be more prominent.

4.3.3.2 Rotor scale

The rotor scale consists of a rotary feeder with a vertical axis and a weighing section. The bulk solid enters the rotor at the inlet and is conveyed by around 270° to the outlet. The vertical movement of the rotor around the axis between inlet and outlet is controlled by a weighing device. The torque generated by the bulk solid within the rotor multiplied by the rotor speed gives the actual feed rate. In the weighing electronics this actual feed rate is compared with the set feed rate and the rotor speed adjusted accordingly.

4.3.3.3 Loss-in-weight feeder

The loss-in-weight feeder (Fig. 4.3.9) operates on the principle of controlled loss-in-weight. Hopper and feeder with drive are mounted on at least one load cell. The loss-in-weight per time during discharge corresponds to the exact actual flow rate. A closed-loop control via speed change of the drive motor, for example that of a screw feeder, will enable a constant flow rate to be achieved. The bin is discharged by the feeder up to a certain minimum level. Then the bin will be refilled. A loss-in-weight feeder is a continuous feeding system because during refill of the hopper the feeder is still running although as a volumetric feeder. Because the refill time is short in comparison to the gravimetric discharge time the feed accuracy is not influenced by this refill period. To achieve this, however, the hopper has to be designed as a mass flow hopper to allow for a nearly constant bulk density.

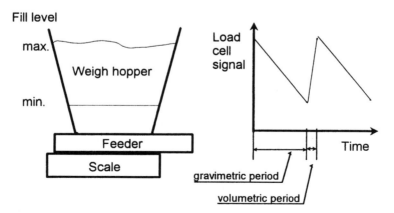

Fig. 4.3.9 Loss-in-weight feeder.

The loss-in-weight feeder is usually connected into the material flow via flexible unions at inlet and outlet, such that material flow is totally enclosed.

4.3.3.4 Feeding systems with prefeeder

A feeding system can also be built with a weighing system (belt weigher or flow meter) and a controllable prefeeder (Fig. 4.3.5). The signal from the weighing system controls the flow rate of the prefeeder which should be a screw feeder, vibratory feeder or star feeder.

4.4 Level control in silos
H. Wilms

Monitoring level control and ensuring adequate material supply for all downstream operations are the main activities for operators of silos. Control and measuring devices have to be designed or purchased with consideration of operating conditions including the flow properties of the bulk solids (Schwedes, 1970; Krambrock, 1979) and the flow profile in the silo (Martens, 1988).

4.4.1 Level control objectives

Level control in silos is performed to meet the three requirements outlined in Fig. 4.4.1 (Wilms, 1989):

1 Determination of the empty volume in the silo to derive the optimum point in time for the next material supply coming by truck or from upstream process units. This volume is characterized by the circled no. 1 in Fig. 4.4.1. This information is also important to allocate a certain silo for the next batch being produced. Piping in silos prevents the exact determination of the free space in silos by surface level detecting systems (see also Fig. 4.4.2(b)).
2 Inventory control requires the determination of the whole content in the silo, which is the dead plus the live volume. This information is necessary for financial or customs purposes, in-plant data processing, process balancing and cost control. This volume is given as volumes 2 and 3 in Fig. 4.4.1.
3 Control of the content in the silo to ensure continuous and undisturbed operation of downstream processes for a specified period of time, e.g. a

Level control in silos

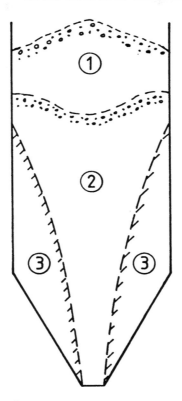

Fig. 4.4.1 Level control objectives.

night shift or weekend. Solids in stagnant zones in funnel flow silos influence the measurement because the extent of solids that can be discharged then is unknown. Only the total content can be determined and a level control system cannot differentiate between that portion that can be discharged and the material remaining in the stagnant zones. This is the volume 2 in Fig. 4.4.1. In mass flow silos, the volume of the stagnant zones 3 is equal to zero, facilitating level control measurement and interpretation of the results.

Level control in silos can be best automated with continuous level control systems, e.g. weighing systems (Wilms and Waggershauser, 1988). However, for economic reasons the application of weighing systems is limited, but receives increasing attention from computer-controlled process automation.

Level control in silos is strongly influenced by the flow profile (Martens, 1988; Wilms, 1989). This influence is shown in Fig. 4.4.2 for the two flow profiles mass flow and funnel flow. Three different types of level indicator

242 *Discharge, feeding and metering equipment*

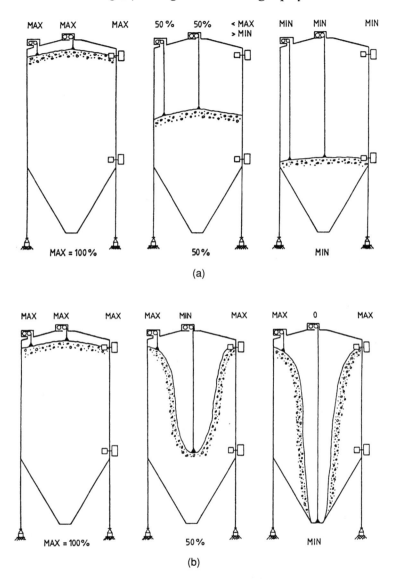

Fig. 4.4.2 Influence of the flow profile: (a) mass flow; (b) funnel flow.

(rotating paddle, plumbing weight, load cells) are shown to demonstrate the influence of the flow profile on limit switches, surface detecting instruments and gravimetric systems, respectively. In mass flow silos all systems yield correct readings at all levels of fill because the contour of the bulk solids' top surface does not change during discharge and because no stagnant zones influence the measurement. This statement holds for all level control systems, no matter whether it is a continuous weighing system, a surface detecting sensor like a 'yo-yo' (see below) or just a limit switch.

In funnel flow silos, however, the volume of, or the mass in, the stagnant zones cannot be determined, but only the total content, because the extent of the stagnant zones is unknown and changes with time and level of fill (section 3.1). Therefore, the live volume of the silo content cannot be determined. The information obtained from surface-detecting sensors depends on the position where the measurement device is placed. A silo which from the operator's point of view is empty due to piping will never provide sufficient space for refilling. Weighing the whole silo will only give information on the complete content but never on the portion that can be discharged.

These boundary conditions have to be kept in mind when selecting a level control system, because the inaccuracy resulting from funnel flow can be much larger than the error from a rather simple level control system and the most advanced system cannot compensate for design deficiencies of the silo.

4.4.2 Level control instruments

Not all systems known for level control in tanks for the storage of liquids can be used for silos (VDI, 1984). Because of the nonlinear pressure distribution in silos no pressure or differential pressure measurement – with the exception of a differential pressure limit switch – can be used in silos. Because of the completely different behaviour of solids and liquids it is not possible to use displacement or floating methods.

The best but most expensive method for continuous level and inventory control is gravimetric determination of the silo content by putting the whole silo on a weighing system (Fig. 4.4.3). Load cells (a) or strain gauges (b) are used for determination of the weight. The accuracy of a weighing system is influenced by external forces (platforms, connecting walkways, pipes), loads from wind, rain and snow and thus is not determined by the accuracy of the load cell alone. The influence of platforms and conveying lines can be minimized by using flexible connections (c) to all connecting structures. System accuracies of 1–2% are typical with consideration of time instabilities of the electronics. Therefore, short-term batching processes will have higher accuracies, especially if the electronics are calibrated to work in certain intervals. The accuracy is always defined with respect to the total system weight or the total mass of a certain interval.

Conventionally supporting silos by load cells (Fig. 4.4.3(a)) requires reinforcement of the skirts (d) in order to cope with the high local stresses resulting from only supporting the silo on three or four points around the circumference. Additionally, special securing devices (e) to prevent the silo from any horizontal movement, lift-off or tilting due to wind loads have to be installed.

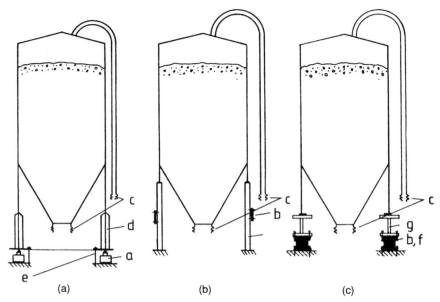

Fig. 4.4.3 Weighing systems.

Bolt-on strain gauge weighing systems (Fig. 4.4.3(b)) have the advantage that tensile forces resulting from wind loads can be compensated and that these systems can be retrofitted to silos on skirts or steel structures (Wilms and Waggershauser, 1988; Gallegas, 1985). No securing elements are needed. Since the strain gauges work on the elastic deformation of the structure or skirt, the accuracy decreases by additional safety factors for the steel structure or skirt. Additionally, the sensors may require insulation to avoid sudden temperature changes due to sunshine and resulting stress inhomogeneities.

Most of these disadvantages of bolt-on strain gauge systems are overcome, if these load measuring devices are used in calibrated load feet (f) being mounted like conventional load cells or with a load distributing support ring (g, Fig. 4.4.3(c)).

Conventional or mechanical level control systems are based to a large extent on the principle of dampening oscillations and motions (Fig. 4.4.4). The most frequently used instruments are rotating paddles (Fig. 4.4.4(a)), tuning forks (Fig. 4.4.4(b)) and vibrating rods (Fig. 4.4.4(c)) as limit switches as well as plumbing systems (Fig. 4.4.4(d)) for continuous level control. A rotating paddle (a) supported on the silo wall (b) is stopped when surcharged by bulk solids. The resulting torque from stopping the rotation then activates a limit switch to stop the motor (c) and to give a signal to the controls. In similar manner the frequency of a tuning fork (d) or a vibrating rod (e) is changed when the instrument is covered with bulk solids. A respective piezo-crystal sensor (f) detects these changes and transfers them

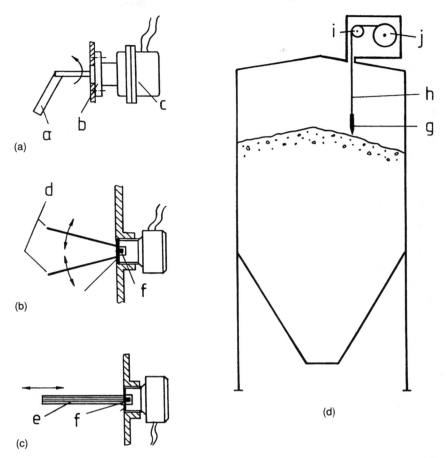

Fig. 4.4.4 Mechanical limit switches and level control systems: (a) rotating paddle; (b) tuning fork; (c) vibrating rod; (d) plumbing (yo-yo) system.

to the controls. These level control instruments are applicable only as limit switches and are widely used for low- and high-level alarms. Protective saddles have to be used to prevent failures for low-level alarms. This may cause voids in cohesive solids and thus malfunctions. Different plumbing weights like polymer cylinders, steel cages, light parachutes and similar are used, depending on application and bulk solids stored.

If information on a low- or high-level alarm from limit switches is not sufficient then continuous or so-called continuous methods have to be installed. The simplest method then is a plumbing or 'yo-yo' system (Fig. 4.4.4(d)). The yo-yo is operated by letting a plumbing weight (g) on a cable (h) down into the silo until the surface is hit. When the weight is supported by the bulk solids then the plumbing weight is pulled up again and the length of the cable is measured by means of the number of revolutions of a counting disc (i) next to the pulley (j). This is transformed directly into the height of fill in the silo. The yo-yo system may not be activated during filling because the cable with the weight cannot be pulled up again as soon as the plumbing weight is covered with bulk solids. Failure of the cable and loss of the plumbing weight may block the outlet or damage feeders. Therefore, it is dangerous to use yo-yo systems in funnel flow silos prone to piping.

Electronic level control instruments feature no moving parts within the silo. Ultrasonic level control systems (Fig. 4.4.5(a)) measure the time elapsed between emitting and receiving an ultrasonic signal. The system depends on the speed of sound and therefore is influenced by temperature and humidity. Fine dust can absorb and weaken the signal to undetectable levels and reflections from internals may give false information, especially since the signal is reflected at an inclined solids surface and therefore no strong direct reflection but only diffuse reflection can be used for the measurement. Ultrasonic level control systems require a minimum roughness of the surface (i.e. a minimum particle size) to achieve a sufficiently strong signal from diffuse reflection. This limits the particle size to at least in the millimetre range or very strong sound emitters are necessary. Short-range radar systems (Fig. 4.4.5(b)) operate in a similar way to ultrasonic systems and are mainly used in tall coal silos.

Level control systems based on the capacity of an electric field (capacitor) use the difference in dielectric constant between bulk solids and air. Humidity and temperature changes influence these systems when used for continuous level control, and not simply as limit switches. Small instruments with only the front plate being the sensors can be installed in the

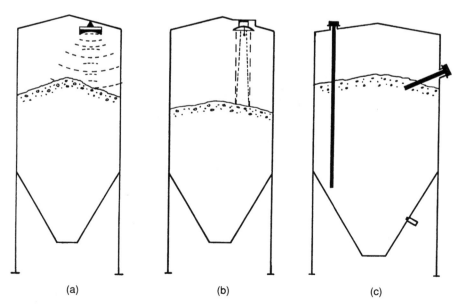

Fig. 4.4.5 Electronic level control instruments: (a) ultrasonic; (b) radar; (c) capacitance.

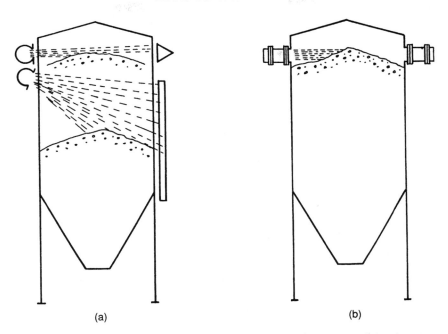

Fig. 4.4.6 Special level control systems: (a) X-ray absorption; (b) microwave barriers.

hopper as limit switches. Two cables have to pass through the full height of the silo in non-metallic silos or one cable is needed in metallic silos, using the silo wall as the second part of the capacitor (Fig. 4.4.5(c)).

Radio frequency signals passing through a two-conductor cable sensor will be reflected whenever there is distinct change in dielectric constant around the cable, i.e. at the solids level. The reflected signal received at the transmitter will have a different phase angle and this phase angle difference can be used to determine the solids level in a bin when scanning through a wide range of frequencies. This system, referred to as phase-tracking, does not need any calibration and is independent of temperature, dust, humidity and product variations (Cournane and Hawney, 1993).

Other level control systems are based on X-ray and microwave absorption (Fig. 4.4.6) or utilize the decay of radioactive isotopes for emitting and receiving signals, mainly as level switches for inaccessible vessels. X-ray systems can be used for continuous level control as well, but the range is rather limited.

4.4.3 Evaluation of level control instruments

The different level control instruments are evaluated (Fig. 4.4.7) on the basis of their applicability for either continuous level control or only as discontinuous limit switches, and also with respect to their suitability for different

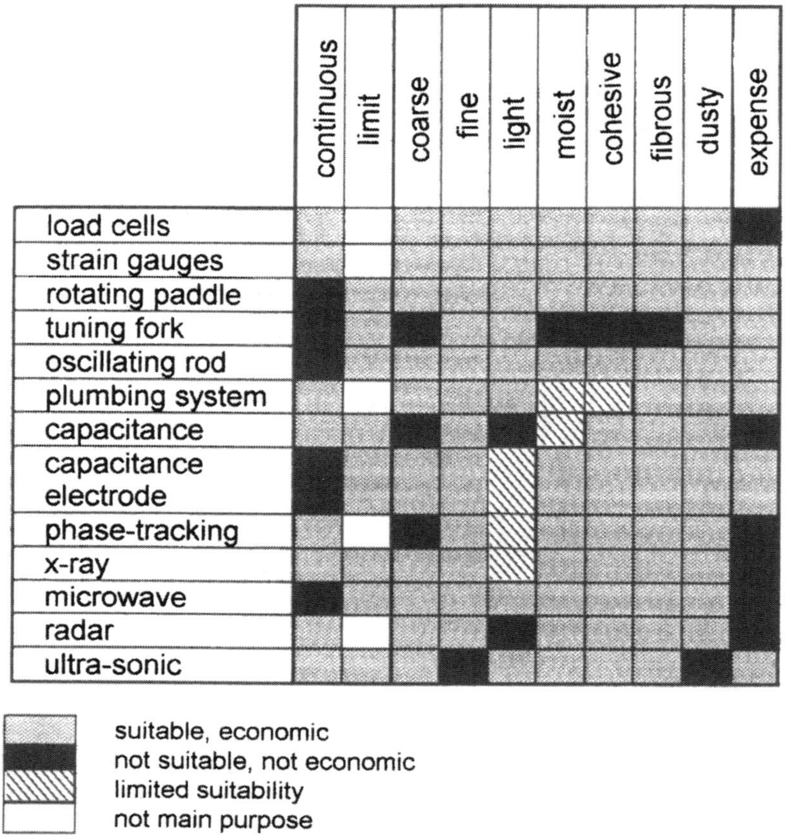

248   *Discharge, feeding and metering equipment*

	continuous	limit	coarse	fine	light	moist	cohesive	fibrous	dusty	expense
load cells	▨		▨	▨	▨	▨	▨	▨		■
strain gauges	▨		▨	▨	▨	▨	▨	▨		▨
rotating paddle	■	▨	▨	▨	▨	▨	▨	▨	▨	▨
tuning fork	■	▨	■	▨	■	▨	■	■	▨	▨
oscillating rod	■	▨	▨	▨	▨	▨	▨	▨	▨	▨
plumbing system		▨	▨	▨	▨	▥	▥	▨	▨	▨
capacitance	▨	▨	▨	▨	■	▥	▨	▨	▨	■
capacitance electrode	■	▨	▨	▥	▥	▥	▨	▨	▨	▨
phase-tracking	▨		■	▨	▥	▨	▨	▨	▨	▨
x-ray	▨	▨	▨	▨	▥	▨	▨	▨	▨	■
microwave	■	▨	▨	▨	▨	▨	▨	▨	▨	■
radar	▨		▨	▨	▨	▨	▨	▨	▨	■
ultra-sonic	▨	▨	▨	■	▨	▨	▨	▨	■	▨

suitable, economic
not suitable, not economic
limited suitability
not main purpose

Fig. 4.4.7 Comparison of level control instruments.

bulk solids (Wilms, 1989). The last column gives an indication whether the system has economic disadvantages.

4.4.4 Summary

Instrumentation of silos for level control has to be based on the requirements determined by the operator. Continuous level detectors and limit switches based on mechanical and electrical principles or on running time of reflected signals are currently state of the art. Weighing systems yield the highest system accuracies but are sensitive to external loads. Future developments will focus on computerized inventory control systems tied into overall machine, process or plant balancing procedures. Improvements have to be made regarding the sensitivity and reliability of ultrasonic equipment in dusty and humid environments as well as with respect to fine powders.

References

Cournane, T; and Hawney, H. Continuous level measurement using phase tracking. *Measurement & Control*, 27(1993), (June), 110–114

Gallegas, M. Bolt-on weighing system. *Bulk Solids Handling* 5(1985), 2, 391–393

Krambrock, W. Lagern und Umschlagen von Schüttgütern in der chemischen Industrie. *Chemie-Ingenieur-Technik* 51(1979), 2, 104–112

Martens, P. *Silohandbuch*. Verlag Ernst + Sohn, Berlin, 1988

Schwedes, J. *Fließverhalten von Schüttgütern in Bunkern*. Verlag Chemie, Weinheim, 1970

VDI, Füllstandmessung von Flüssigkeiten und Feststoffen (Schüttgütern). *VDI/VDE-Richtlinie* 3519, Blatt 1, Beuth Verlag, Berlin, 1984

Wilms, H. Füllstandmessung in Silos. *Chemie-Technik* 18(1989), 9, 70–76

Wilms, H.; and Waggershauser, K. Zeppelin weighing system for skirted silos. *Bulk Solids Handling* 8(1988), 1, 39–40

5

Silo fabricator's and system supplier's view
H. Wilms

5.1 INTRODUCTION

This evaluation has been compiled by one of the industrial participants who contributed to Part One on silo flow, as part of the CA-Silo project. An assessment of this CA-Silo project by any industrial participant can only reflect the opinion of the specific company, its structure and its market, but probably many of the following statements apply to other companies as well. A general statement valid for the whole bulk solids handling and silo fabricating industry could only come from a representative of an industrial association.

Thus, this project evaluation reflects only different viewpoints from a company which is a fabricator of aluminium and stainless steel storage and blending silos for powders, granules and pellets; of pressurized containers for bulk solid transport and purge bins and agitator vessels for solids, as well as a system supplier for design and supply of pneumatic conveying systems, components for automated bulk handling systems and turnkey bulk solids handling installations (Wilms, 1991, 1993).

Since all these activities focus on the handling of bulk solids, require knowledge of bulk solids behaviour and involve research and development activities, we, along with other companies representing a similar scope of supply and services, have joined the CA-Silo activities on silo flow and flow property testing. The main reasons for our industrial participation have been:

- to provide experience and expertise to the activities
- to help define the state of the art in industry
- to receive information from colleagues on current problems

- to help define research requirements for the future
- to exchange viewpoints with colleagues from research institutions, companies and agencies
- to offer cooperation for suitable development activities, and
- to look for partners for respective activities

Some areas of general interest to industry have been outlined at the beginning of the project. Research activities are necessary in these areas (Wilms, 1994). All of these items were defined from industrial needs to improve product performance and design reliability.

This list, which by no means can be complete, highlights the need for research. A lot of fundamental research into the behaviour of bulk solids flow is needed, but at least as much effort has to be put into application technology, equipment development and full-scale testing. No optimum results can be obtained by limiting research to universities and application to industry. Thus, a close cooperation between industrial and academic research is mandatory for the future. These problems have to be addressed by future research activities and then hopefully solved for the benefit of the reliability and safety of silo and bulk solids handling equipment.

Safety in silo design, fabrication and operation is not limited to technology, but also includes education, and making people aware of the risks associated with silo operation. Not even the best design of a silo can prevent an operator from climbing into the silo and drowning, or from using lances and discharge aids from underneath an open outlet. Consequent injury or even fatalities can only be avoided by better education of both design engineers and operators.

5.2 PROJECT EVALUATION

At the end of this CA-Silo project it makes sense to evaluate the results with respect to its objectives and the requirements faced in our industry. This view is totally a single company point of view, reflecting the nature of our business and the problems we face today. For a lot of questions we have found our own solutions, but as long as they are not confirmed by scientific evidence, they are not to be considered as state of the art or best available technology and thus leave industry with substantial risk. The following evaluation, therefore, has to be read as an incomplete list of questions, unsolved problems and suggestions for future research activities. It may be used for inspiring scientists in the research community to draw their attention to these questions and as examples of research results which will find direct implementation in industrial application and equipment development.

Because of the different nature of industry's business as fabricators, system suppliers and as contractors, the following evaluation has been split into these three different points of view.

5.2.1 Fabricator's view

Silo fabricators are nowadays not only responsible for their quality in fabrication and the structural stability, but also for the performance of the equipment and thus its design. Therefore, there is a special interest in results on flow and loads associated with certain flow profiles. However, flow profile and pressure distribution measurements have to be improved and verified. Especially, loads on internals such as blending and purging devices are not yet covered by codes as DIN 1055 Part 6 or similar. Much more work is required in these areas, since measurements have to be made in full-scale installations. In this respect, much more input and cooperation have to come from industry itself.

Full-scale measurements and tests can only be performed within operating plants. It is difficult to perform research in running plants, but only improved cooperation will finally lead to improved, safer or more economical designs. Therefore, it must be a goal for future research programmes to promote a better incorporation of the participation of industry, even if industry is not providing a major portion of the funds. This has always to be evaluated against know-how protection and intellectual property rights, because a lot of information will be available within companies, but will not be shared with others.

Some strange and severe vibration effects may happen in silos when discharging hard, monodisperse bulk solids such as cement clinker (Schwedes and Schulze, 1991), corn or some plastic pellets. In aluminium silos these vibrations are sometimes accompanied by noise emissions like those of a trumpet or signal horn. Feasible techniques for determination of any bulk solid's property responsible for these noise emissions, and concepts for easy retrofitting of existing silos have yet to be determined.

The performance of blending silos is influenced by the flow profile as well as the design of the blending internals and the blender operator. Results of respective tests are available in many companies, but do not make their way into general availability. Improvement of the blender internal design, however, can only result from a cooperation between a blender manufacturer and a user who is willing to share experience and to perform some tests or modifications.

For pressurized containers for bulk solid transport it is essential to maximize the useful volume of a vessel. Therefore, the inclination of walls has to be made as flat as possible while still retaining a full discharge ability. Discharge aids, such as vibratory or aeration devices, may serve for this purpose, but there is only limited information on optimum placement in the container. Additionally, bulk solids in containers are subject to varying temperatures and continuous vibration especially during transport on truck, rail and ship. The effect of vibration and shocks of up to several g in combination with time consolidation needs to be explored more deeply.

Project evaluation 253

A lot of fundamental research is required in the field of loads and power requirements for mechanical agitation of bulk solids in vessels in non-aerated states. This applies to agitator vessels and feeders like horizontal ploughs, rotating screws and rotating, bridge-breaking agitators.

5.2.2 System supplier's view

System suppliers need information not only for design improvement of individual equipment items, but at the same time require an additional in-depth view into the interaction between different equipment items, their interfacing and the required overall performance of the installation.

Some very important questions concern discharge aids, their selection, their optimum placement and their reach, to minimize the number of vibrators or aeration nozzles. The positive effects of both these discharge aids are known, but where are their limitations in view of optimum vibration frequency and intensity as well as formation of channels? Also their influence on structural integrity needs to be studied if there is concern about any impact.

Very poor flowing bulk solids may require mechanical extraction devices to discharge solids from a silo. The power requirement for these types of feeders and their structural interaction with the silo needs more attention.

Special test and design procedures need to be elaborated for elastic and fibrous bulk solids. Recycled plastic and other heterogeneous waste products receive a lot of attention for their use or disposal, but a lot of questions on their handling remain open.

5.2.3 Contractor's view

For contractors of turnkey bulk solids storage, blending and handling systems it is very important to know exactly what the latest and best available technology is. The state-of-the-art report in this respect is a very helpful tool. This state-of-the art report, unique of its kind, provides a sound survey on what is known today with this broad range of topics and the in-depth analysis of these topics by experts in the field. The many cross-links to the other topics besides silo flow and flow property testing help to define a problem in a wider scope. Thus, it may serve as a reference book for technical problems and solutions as well as a guide for defining research programmes and finding potential partners or experts.

Because the technology is constantly improved and adapted to new requirements, an update every couple of years is desirable. This then takes less effort to prepare than the first state-of-the-art report. Similar activities are needed in other fields as well, e.g. in pneumatic conveying technology, drying of bulk solids and heat transfer into stationary or moving bulk solids.

5.3 CONCLUDING REMARKS

After this project a lot of questions on bulk solids flow, handling and silo design still remain open. However, a lot of information has been shared between research organizations, industrial companies and, especially, across the borders in Europe. Every participant now is much more aware of where and from whom to get information, equipment or potential cooperation. In this respect, the project was successful.

Besides the open points listed in the previous paragraph and by Wilms (1991) which still need answers from future research activities, industrial participants have benefited from their participation in the CA-Silo project through discussions held with colleagues outside and following the project meetings.

For our company we can draw the conclusion that we did not learn much more than we knew before on solids' flow, flowability testing and the like. But, again, this was to be expected and is not at all disappointing. Our in-house expertise, experience and critical judgement of a project scope remain the cornerstones for successful design of reliable systems. Some cooperation was intensified and stimulated product development (Wilms, Krambrock and Heinrici, 1997) even when the respective project materialized outside the scope of CA-Silo.

Unfortunately, it was not possible to attract a larger number of industrial bodies and companies to this project. Therefore, a lot more could have been achieved. One possible reason for this may be the timing of this project, which coincided with a strong recession and a policy of getting lean in the companies. Therefore, not only was the money scarce, but even more important, time and people could not be allocated to this project. This, however, should not prevent the European Community from starting similar projects more regularly, maybe every 5–10 years, to redefine the state of the art and the research requirements.

REFERENCES

Schwedes, J.; Schulze, D. (1991) Examples of modern silo design, *Bulk Solids Handling* 11, 1, 47–52

Wilms, H. (1991) Zeppelin's extended activities in solids handling, *Bulk Solids Handling* 11 (1991), 1, 401–404

Wilms, H. (1993) Zeppelin Schüttguttechnik GmbH, *Bulk Solids Handling* 13, 1, 167

Wilms, H. (1994) Silo design for strength and flow, *Powder Handling & Processing* 6, 2, 193–197

Wilms, H.; Krambrock, W.; Heinrici, H. (1997) Discharge and feeding applications for horizontal rotary feeders, *Bulk Solids Handling* 17, 1, 27–32

6

Summary

J. Schwedes and H. Wilms

The work (Chapters 2–4) has been grouped in three categories: bulk solids testing; flow in silos; discharge, feeding and metering equipment.

6.1 BULK SOLIDS TESTING

Before designing a silo or any other apparatus or container in which bulk solids have to be handled, stored or transported, the flow properties of the bulk solid have to be measured and documented. This is done with the help of special testers, mainly shear testers. A lot of different shear testers are available. They are used for three different purposes:

- quality control, comparison of different bulk solids
- quantitative design of silos
- calibration of constitutive laws (especially relevant for numerical modelling)

Depending on the application, different requirements have to be fulfilled by the testers. It is mandatory to place a tester at the user's disposal which is not expensive with regard to time and investment – the latter is less important for application in industry. This tester has to deliver reproducible results which are not influenced by the technician running the tests. Such a tester, applicable for all three topics listed above, does not and will never exist. Therefore each application needs special testers. A lot of testers are available and used, not always with the necessary basic knowledge. Therefore, people using those testers have to be educated to enable them to understand what they are measuring. Only then can they evaluate the results and can judge the application. Comparative tests with different bulk solids, using different testers and performed by different laboratories, are required and strongly recommended.

In soil mechanics the triaxial tester is a very common tool to characterize flow properties. It seems that the potential of this method is not fully used in mechanical and process engineering. The same can be said with regard to the application of shear test results in soil mechanics.

Three of the many parameters influencing the flow properties of bulk solids will be mentioned in this summary. The first is the anisotropic behaviour of many, maybe all, particulate solids. The anisotropic behaviour is a result of the stress history and is terminated only if steady-state flow is reached. This strengthens the importance and necessity of achieving steady-state flow in any tester designed to characterize bulk solids flow behaviour. The anisotropic behaviour can be measured, for instance, with help of the true biaxial shear tester. There is a strong need for more research in order to learn how respective results can be transferred into application.

Fine-grained bulk solids have poor flow properties and due to their small particle sizes only a low permeability for gases. Bulk solids are dilatant media, i.e. during flow the bulk density or the porosity may increase or decrease. As a result, gas has to flow into or out of the particulate solid. A two-phase flow may be created by itself which can lead to flooding and other problems. Thus the flow of gases through packing of bulk solids is a very important aspect. It can be distinguished between aeration and fluidization. Both effects can be measured on a laboratory scale, but it is still difficult to use results of those tests for a quantitative design of, for instance, flow-promoting devices. Therefore, further research is strongly recommended to characterize two-phase flow and to apply the results to silo flow problems.

Wall friction seems to be a simple problem, but there are still a lot of unsolved problems. A few of them are listed here: dependence on stress level, velocity, time of application, wear, roughening, smoothing.

Data bases are very common for gases, liquids and solids. These substances are clearly defined by their names and chemical structures. Having bulk solids – a solid in a disperse phase – their properties depend on a lot of parameters such as particle size, particle size distribution, particle shape, bulk density. To measure the influences of these numerous parameters on the flow properties is a lot more difficult, time consuming, expensive and uncertain, than to measure the flow properties directly. There might be some reasons to use a data base for standards with regard to design of silos for strength but it is not very likely that a data base for flow properties will be set up. However, a standardized classification system would be helpful to gather data for a future data base system.

6.2 FLOW IN SILOS

Only qualitative statements, deduced from observations in model silos, were known before Jenike published his theory on mass flow and funnel flow in the 1960s. Knowing the angle of the effective yield locus, the angle of wall friction and the silo geometry (plane or axisymmetric geometry) the required inclination of the hopper wall for mass flow can be predicted. Many problems in silo flow do not exist in mass flow silos. In funnel flow a converging flow channel is formed within the stored particulate solid, the shape of which still cannot be predicted. Further research is strongly required, especially in connection with the prediction of the point of intersection of the borderline to the dead zone with the silo walls. At this point high horizontal stresses being the reason for many silo failures should be expected.

Flow patterns can be influenced by inserts, by vibration, by mechanical agitators or by blowing air into the silo. The effect of those methods can so far only be described qualitatively. There is a strong correlation between the placement of those inserts, the flow pattern and the stress distribution. Since this dependency is not known quantitatively, inserts are excluded from many standards for the design of silos for strength, e.g. the German DIN 1055, Part 6 and Eurocode (ENV1991-4).

Having funnel flow, predictions of the residence time distributions of the stored bulk solid are hardly possible and even in mass flow silos uncertainties exist at the transition from the bin-to-hopper section. This is of influence for processes taking place in silos, for mixing in silos, and is of major importance in segregation problems. Segregation mainly takes place during filling of a silo. Heap segregation, air-induced segregation and percolation can be distinguished, but it is difficult to predict the segregation behaviour of bulk solids in an industrial sized silo quantitatively. A mass flow silo can be a solution, but cannot always be manufactured. Further research is necessary.

'Silo quaking' describes a self-excited pulsating flow of bulk solids in silos, sometimes associated with noise emissions. A lot of factors can be mentioned, being of influence on silo quaking: changing of the flow profile, slip–stick behaviour, small outlets, collapsing arches and ratholes, excitation by the feeder and several others. Even in mass flow silos silo quaking has been observed. It is difficult to decide which of the effects mentioned is relevant for a given silo-quaking problem. There is a strong need to develop a measuring technique to analyse 'quaking' in model and in full-scale silos; first we have to understand the physics of quaking qualitatively and quantitatively. There is a strong correlation between flow patterns and stress distributions, being clearly shown in national standards for the design of silos for strength. As mentioned above, inserts and other methods to improve the flow behaviour influence the flow pattern and as a result also the stress distribution.

6.3 DISCHARGE, FEEDING AND METERING EQUIPMENT

Feeders are used to discharge bulk solids through the silo outlet and flow-promoting devices are methods to initiate and/or improve the flow of bulk solids into and out of silos. A feeder has to guarantee a uniform withdrawal of the bulk solid from the silo outlet. This is not easy to perform with slotted openings, which therefore have to have an increasing capacity in the direction of withdrawal. A lot of qualitative methods are known, but it is hardly possible to predict a uniform withdrawal quantitatively. Research in cooperation with industry is very important.

The same holds for flow-promoting devices. Using the method of Jenike to design silos for flow on the basis of measured flow properties, it can be predicted exactly where to install flow-promoting devices and how and when to use them. But it is hardly possible to design those devices quantitatively on the basis of flow properties. Four different methods, already mentioned in the paragraph on flow patterns, can be distinguished: mechanical devices, application of vibration, inducing air into the silo and installation of inserts. Research in these areas is under way, but has to be intensified.

Process control requires accurate information on silo content and bulk solids flow rates. Some feeders can be used in combination with weighing systems for loss-in-weight feeders. Other methods include mass and velocity measurements. The tendency to derive mass flow rates without calibrating feeders for a specific bulk solid will continue.

All in all, the state of the art in bulk solids storage in silos is well defined. Many problems can already be solved in regular applications, but special requirements like blending, purging, discharging and metering, including design of respective reliable equipment, still need further in-depth studies and research. In particular, design of improved equipment has to be based on bulk solids properties, thus requiring easy, standardized testing and a lot of relevant data. These data today are not publicly available. Thus the research and application communities, mainly universities and industry, have to move closer together to improve utilization of the available resources, i.e. manpower expertise, time and funds. A platform for establishing this research and application cooperation is needed.

Part Two

Concrete Structures

7

Introduction and scope
J. Eibl

This part deals with recommendations for the design of concrete silo structures. The key issues are actions, reinforcement and concreting.

Silo pressures relevant for concrete silos are substantially in international standards (DIN 1055, ENV 1991–4) whereas 'actions' such as temperature effects, differential settlements and dust explosions are only just being developed. These items are therefore dealt with in greater detail in this part.

8

Actions
J. Eibl

8.1 PRESSURE

The relevant pressures exerted by the bulk material may be taken from the draft European Standard, CEN/ENV 1991–4, *Actions on Silos and Tanks*. The rules given in this code are simplifications of far more extended investigations:

- In Landahl (1983), Häußler (1984) and Gladen (1985) filling as well as the higher discharging pressures have been calculated by FE-methods using rather complicated constitutive laws which realistically describe the material behaviour (Figs 8.1 and 8.2).

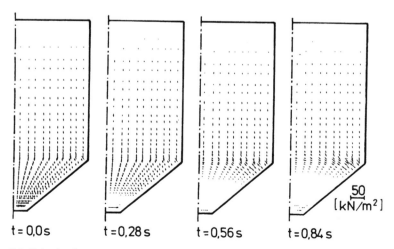

Fig. 8.1 Principal stresses at different time steps after hopper opening (Häußler, 1984).

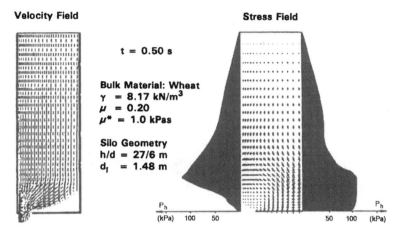

Fig. 8.2 Velocity and principal stress fields in a flat-bottomed silo with eccentric outlet (Rombach, 1991).

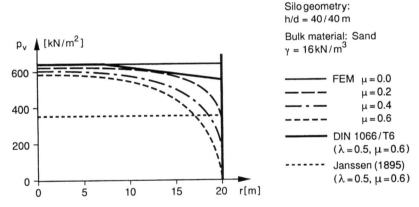

Fig. 8.3 Bottom pressures of a flat-bottomed silo.

- It could be shown that bottom pressures are by far not uniformly distributed (Fig. 8.3). This has to be taken into consideration especially in case of silo bins, for example supported by columns.
- In addition, realistic pressure distributions around eccentric outlets have been calculated for circular and rectangular silos (Fig. 8.4). The so-called switch as shown in Figs 8.5 and 8.6 can be explained by similar models.

One has to be aware that due to the state of the bulk material, for example its moisture content or grain size, a great scatter of pressures is inherent and should be considered while designing silos. This fact is also underlined by the widely varying pressures given by different design standards for the same reference model (Fig. 8.7).

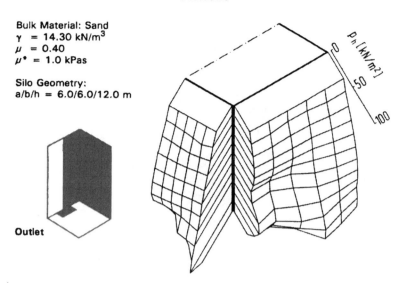

Fig. 8.4 Horizontal wall pressure distribution near eccentric outlet from three-dimensional calculations (Rombach, 1991).

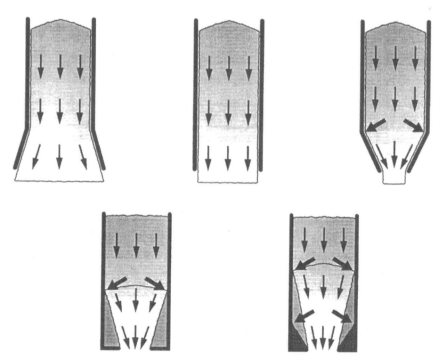

Fig. 8.5 A schematic model to switch pressure.

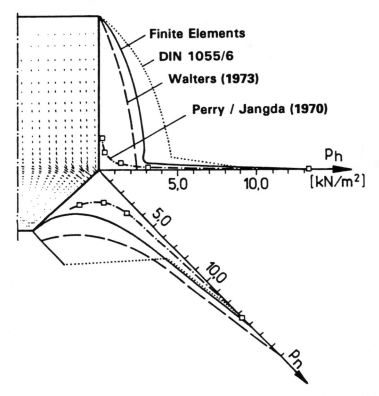

Fig. 8.6 Switch pressure from comparison calculation (Ruckenbrod and Eibl, 1992).

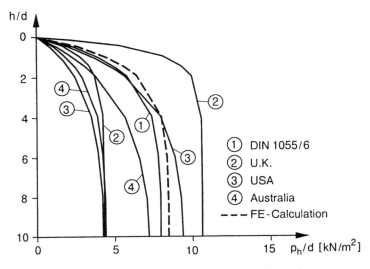

Fig. 8.7 Horizontal wall pressure according to several silo codes.

8.2 TEMPERATURE

The usual effects of temperature on an empty silo shell, such as caused by an environmental temperature change from about −15°C to +30°C are covered by the recommendation for reinforcement as given in Chapter 9. In such cases a special analytical or computational investigation is not necessary.

Significantly higher temperature gradients may occur in the case of storing materials that are either self-heating or already filled in with high temperature for example hot cement clinker. Then a thorough calculation of the resulting temperature distribution through the wall and the resulting internal forces and moments is necessary, and two essentially different situations have to be considered:

- high-temperature gradients in the walls above the bulk material due to hot air in the almost empty silo;
- reduced wall temperature gradients due to heat insulating effects of the bulk material in the almost filled silo.

An increase in tensile forces and relevant moments may also occur if due to a sudden temperature drop outside the silo wall, the latter shrinks on to the bulk material (Fig. 8.8).

The resulting forces may be calculated considering the different stiffnesses of the wall and the bulk material. The latter can be estimated proportional to the vertical stress σ_{zz} of the bulk material as follows:

$$E_s = (p_h/\varepsilon_h) = [C\sigma_{zz}]/(1-v_s) \qquad (8.2.1)$$

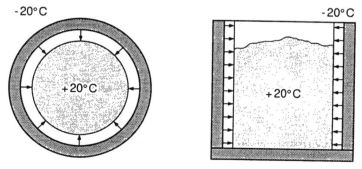

Fig. 8.8 Temperature shrinkage of silo walls due to global temperature change.

where C is a material parameter (dimensionless, e.g. for wheat $C = 104$), σ_{zz} the vertical pressure in the bulk material and v_s Poisson's ratio (e.g. for wheat $v_s = 0.3$). From the Australian Standard 6/1989 (Standard Association of Australia, 1989) C is roughly generalized to

$$C = 95(\gamma_b/\gamma_w)^{1.5} \qquad (8.2.2)$$

where γ_b is the specific weight of bulk material (kN/m³) and γ_w the specific weight of water (kN/m³).

If more accurate values are needed, experiments have to be done to determine the parameters of appropriate constitutive equations given, for example, by Kolymbas (1988) or Lade (1977). Using such material laws further information may be gained by means of nonlinear calculations according to Rombach (1991). Figure 8.9 shows results of more such refined investigations. Here the horizontal resistance of the bulk material due to inward and outward movements of the silo wall is depicted. These investigations clearly indicate that such a simple formula as given above can give only rough information to the designer, which nevertheless may be useful.

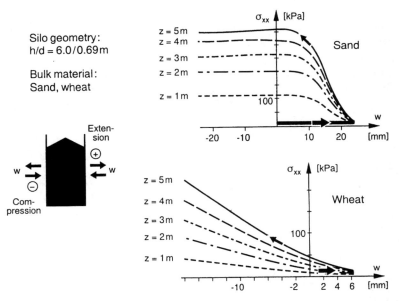

Fig. 8.9 Horizontal pressure versus displacement of a circular silo wall (Rombach, 1991).

8.3 DIFFERENTIAL SETTLEMENTS

The following observations should be noted when designing silo foundations:

- Unlike most buildings, the full live load occurs on silos.
- The silo load is an essentially higher percentage of the total load compared to other buildings.
- Large live loads change quickly as the silo is either filled or emptied. These events may be repeated frequently.
- For a silo group, the location of the resultant load may undergo extreme changes as some silos are filled and others emptied.

8.3.1 Assessment of differential settlements

The geotechnical engineer should also estimate settlements under service loads. Information should be provided on the forces resulting from dead and live loads, wind, earthquake and any other loads likely to affect the foundation.

For silo batteries, the settlement should be estimated with all silos filled and combinations with some silos filled and others empty. Attention must be paid to any vertical deformations of the foundation including warping. The complete settlement should be divided into its constituent parts (i.e. uniform, linear and local) because these components affect the structure in very different ways.

Below single silos and especially below voluminous silo batteries large soil pressures arise often accompanied by significant deformations. Especially in the case of silo batteries high membrane forces may result from such soil deformations. Appropriate investigations can be done easily using an elastic finite-element computer code. By means of these methods a single silo and silo battery according to Figs 8.10 and 8.11 have been investigated

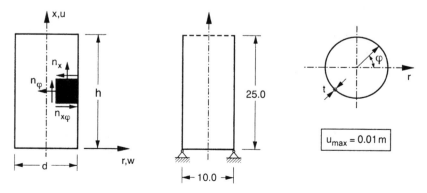

Fig. 8.10 Single silo with imposed settlement pattern $u = u_{max}(1 - |\cos\varphi|)$.

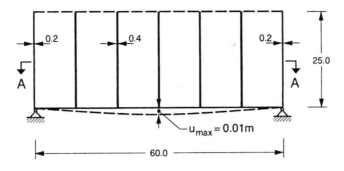

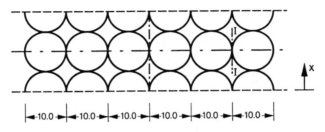

Fig. 8.11 Trough-shaped settlement of a silo battery.

with top covers which in the first case are rigidly fixed and in the second allow a relative deformation between cover and silo wall. Figure 8.12 shows an example of displacements of a silo battery. Figures 8.13 and 8.14 show that relative movements between both elements reduce the relevant membrane forces significantly (see also Ruckenbrod and Eibl, 1992).

However, if the roof slab is not fixed to the wall, all effects which result from the deformations of silo walls should be considered, such as ovalling, bending and relative displacement between the silo wall and the roof slab.

Silo foundation settlements will also influence further structures connected to silos and should therefore be considered thoroughly. Tilting may cause membrane and shear forces (Fig. 8.15, Resinger and Greiner, 1984). In any case the resulting forces should be examined for different deformation patterns according to the relevant loading pattern.

Depending on the stiffness configuration the soil beneath a silo group exerts non-uniform pressures on the structure (Fig. 8.16) and induces high shear forces and bending moments. Where large diameter circular bins are sited close together, independent foundations can be favourable.

Differential settlements of the foundation below supporting columns can cause large local forces in the silo structure (Fig. 8.15(b)). A small

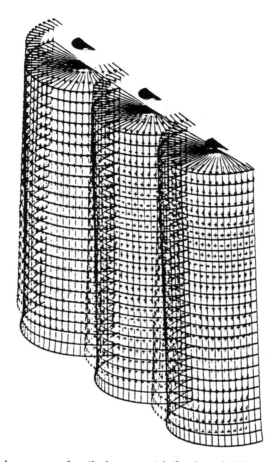

Fig. 8.12 Displacements of a silo battery with fixed roof slabs.

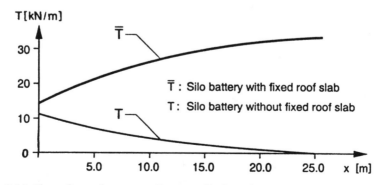

Fig. 8.13 Shear forces between adjacent cylinders along section I–I in Fig. 8.11.

Differential settlements

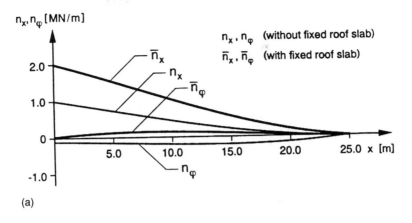

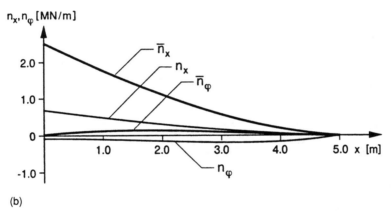

Fig. 8.14 Membrane forces of a single silo: (a) $h/d = 2.5$ ($\varphi = 0°$); (b) $h/d = 0.5$ ($\varphi = 0°$).

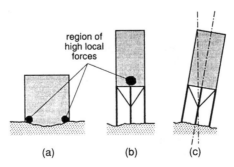

Fig. 8.15 Effects of differential settlement: (a) ground-supported silo; (b) column-supported silo; (c) tilting of a column-supported silo caused by ground rotation.

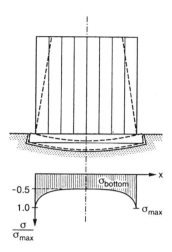

Fig. 8.16 Soil pressure below a silo battery (Eibl, 1986).

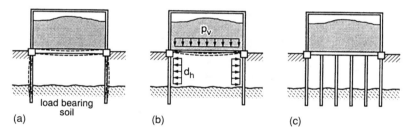

Fig. 8.17 Pile foundation problems.

differential settlement can change the axial forces in the columns considerably (Resinger and Greiner, 1984).

Using pile foundation additional loads induced by the stored bulk material have to be considered due to floor slab bending in the case of a strong connection with the pile caps (Fig. 8.17(a)) or due to additive lateral pressures acting on the piles in the case of soft soils (Fig. 8.17(b)). Arranging some more piles under the floor slab (Fig. 8.17(c)) may help to reduce these effects.

8.4 EARTHQUAKES

For the consideration of earthquake effects no finally agreed calculation procedures are available. Relevant studies are in progress at the author's institute. By a computer code it will be possible to consider the three-dimensional behaviour of the bulk material under cyclic loading due to a

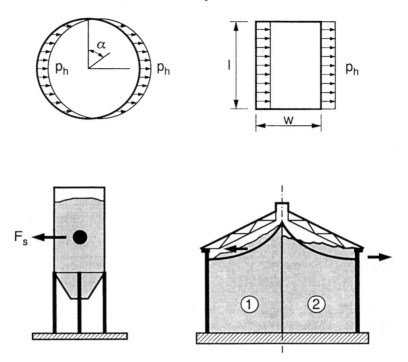

Fig. 8.18 Loads due to seismic actions.

given acceleration time history with regard to the interaction between the bulk material and the silo walls (Braun, 1996) (Chapter 29).

Vertical forces within columns or foundation walls may be calculated by approximating bulk material and structure as a single mass acting at its centre of gravity (Fig. 8.18).

Silo walls and the silo shell respectively, may be designed assuming a horizontal force resulting from pressures according to the following function. For cylindrical structures:

$$p_h = 0.5 d\gamma (a/g)(1 - \cos^2\alpha) \qquad (8.4.1)$$

where γ is the specific weight of material [kN/m³], d is the silo diameter, a the soil acceleration (e.g. 0.1–0.3 g) and α is $0 \leq \alpha \leq 2\pi$ (cylindrical structure). For quadratic or rectangular structures:

$$p_h = 0.5 w\gamma (a/g) \qquad (8.4.2)$$

where w is the side length and g, a the acceleration due to gravity and earthquake, respectively.

In the case of flat silos seismic actions may cause the stored material to form slip planes endangering roof structures and silo walls in the upper

8.5 DUST EXPLOSIONS

8.5.1 Preliminary remarks

Dust explosions in silos cause quite a number of fatalities every year all over the world and cause considerable damage to structures (Fig. 8.19). They can occur when bulk material particles, which are fine enough and evenly distributed in the air, react with oxygen in the air to produce an exothermic chain reaction.

Exploding dust of materials usually stored in silos will produce maximum pressures up to 800–1000 kPa in a closed space without any venting.

8.5.2 Explosive dusts and their characteristic values

Contrary to widely held belief, dusts from many bulk materials usually stored in silos can explode. The explosive behaviour of a dust is characterized by the value K_{ST}, the maximum rate of pressure dp/dt and by its maximum explosion pressure p_{max}.

Both K_{ST} and p_{max} are determined by standard procedures (see also VDI-Richtlinie 2263, 1995 and ISO-Standard 6184/1, 1991). The most important dust types and their respective design values are given in Table 8.1.

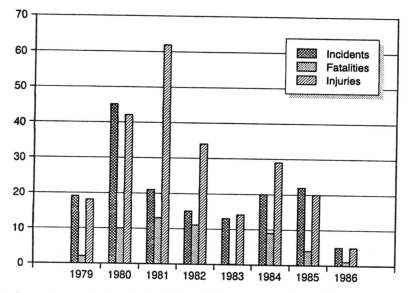

Fig. 8.19 Dust explosions in the USA (US Department of Agriculture).

Dust explosions

Table 8.1 Explosive dusts – design values

Material	K_{ST} (bar m/s)	p_{max} (bar)
Lignite	180	10.0
Cellulose	270	10.0
Pea flour	140	8.0
Rubber	140	9.0
Grain	130	9.0
Wood, wood dust	220	10.0
Coffee	90	9.0
Corn, ground corn	120	9.0
Maize starch	210	10.0
Malt, rye, wheat flour	100	9.0
Milk powder	160	9.0
Mixed food	40	8.0
Paper	60	9.0
Pigment	290	10.0
Soya flour	120	9.0
Coal	130	9.0
Cleaning products	270	9.0
Sugar	150	9.0

Lower values for K_{ST} and p_{max} are applicable for design, if they are proved for special production conditions, e.g. for a higher humidity or a more favourable particle size of the dust. Higher values can occur in the case of dust and gas mixtures – so-called hybrid mixtures.

8.5.3 Ignition sources

Dust explosions are usually ignited by a small energy source. Examples of typical ignition sources include:

- hot surfaces or sparks, e.g. generated by friction of a defective machine member or conveyer system;
- sparks from welding, grinding and cutting during repair work;
- glowing clusters, carried into the silo within the bulk material;
- sparks from foreign bodies;
- unsuitable or defective electrical products (e.g. lighting fixtures);
- heat development during drying.

8.5.4 Protective measures

A reduction of damage due to dust explosions can be achieved by localizing the effect of an explosion and reducing the maximal pressure p_{max}. To reach this aim, closed explosion sections have to be built, which are designed to be:

- pressure resistant against the maximum explosion pressure p_{max} according to Table 8.1 without venting, or
- resistant against a reduced design pressure p_{red}, attained by proper venting.

The flash of fire leaving a venting outlet should neither cause any impairment of the surrounding nor lead the explosion from one section to another. People should be endangered as little as possible by fragments of window panes or other structural elements. Hence, vent openings shall directly lead to the open through planned venting outlets, which reduce the explosion pressure. In the case of silo bins this may be done via the roof or in the case of other compartments via stairwells or windows high above ground level.

The venting system should be initiated at low pressure and show low inertia. However, it has to be considered that by a venting system with early release under small initial pressure a much larger amount of combustible dust–air mixture will be set free than by a slow-acting inert system.

As locking elements of the venting outlets the following devices can be recommended:

- reinforced and prestressed concrete slabs with a low mass
- pumice or aerated cement slabs
- steel lattice girder, if necessary covered with foil, wood or fibre boards
- metal sheets
- simple, light-weight glass security panes
- cardboard with appropriate insulation

8.5.5 Design pressure

The value of the design pressure p_{red}, the reduced maximum explosion pressure, depends on the type of dust, the dimensions of the space to be vented, the venting area, the initial release pressure p_a and the inertia of the venting system. This pressure may be calculated with the help of the design procedures listed in Appendix 8.A which also provides examples.

8.5.6 Design of structural elements

All load-bearing and encasing members of an explosion section have to be designed regarding the relevant explosion pressures. According to Eurocode 1, the explosion pressure may be treated as an 'accidental load'.

The maximum pressure occurs in empty silo bins. However, for the design partly filled states may also be relevant with corresponding pressures due to both explosion and acting bulk material.

When inertia forces arise due to a rapid gas discharge, followed by cooling of the hot smoke gas, a subatmospheric pressure may occur. This has to be taken into account when designing encasing structures.

All relevant members of venting devices have to be secured against flying-off due to the pressure wave. For example, explosion doors have to be fixed at joints, caps fastened by ropes or similar fixings. The velocities of moving elements can be calculated by means of the design methods given in Appendix 8.A.

At pressure relief due to venting, recoil forces occur, which have to be considered while designing the structural system, especially when light-weight venting outlets are chosen and are located horizontally and/or unsymmetrically. Also the recoil forces can be calculated by means of the given method.

The use of special expert knowledge is recommended for installations which are too complex for the use of the simple design methods mentioned, as well as for additional safety measures, for example when large plants are situated in densely populated areas.

APPENDIX 8.A
DRAFT OF A GUIDELINE FOR THE DESIGN OF SILO PLANTS AGAINST DUST EXPLOSIONS

8.A.1 General

The following methods to determine the relevant explosion pressures in vented silo plants and to design the necessary venting devices are suitable for:

1. Non-inert venting, for which the calculation methods for homogeneous dust distribution were taken from a draft of the VDI[1] guideline 3673, Jan. 1992. The latter was modified and expanded up to $H/D = 12$ for civil engineering purposes.
2. Venting by means of inert caps, which are accelerated vertically and have to be caught at a certain height.
3. Venting by inert explosion doors, which have to be stopped after a certain rotation angle.

The design method is applicable under the following conditions:

- $p_{max} \leq 10$ bar.
- A static strength of the venting system $p_a \leq$ equivalent to 0.1 bar, which may result from inertia forces and fixing devices including friction, spring forces, etc. The fixing forces can be neglected after beginning of the release process.
- The application methods are valid only for deflagration, but not for detonations, which do not usually occur in silo structures.
- No significant overpressure exists in the compartment before explosion.
- H/D ratio ≤ 12.

For other conditions special considerations and special advice is necessary.

[1] Richtline Verein Deutscher Ingenieure (VDI).

8.A.2 Formulae and symbols

The following abbreviations and expressions are used in this guideline:

8.A.2.1 Formulae

$$K_p = \frac{V^{0.767} K_{ST}}{A} \qquad (8.A.1)$$

$$K_m = \frac{\sqrt{m_p} K_{ST}^{5/4}}{n^{1/4} V^{0.041}} \qquad (8.A.2)$$

$$K_v = \frac{v A_E^V m_p}{V \sqrt{p_{red}}} \qquad (8.A.3)$$

$$K_\omega = \frac{\omega \left(A_E^V\right)^{3/2} m_p}{V \sqrt{p_{red}} \, n^{1/2}} \qquad (8.A.4)$$

$$m_p = \rho t \qquad (8.A.5)$$

$$A_E^T = f A_E \qquad (8.A.6)$$

$$F_R = 15 A_E^i p_{red} \qquad (8.A.7)$$

8.A.2.2 Symbols

Symbol	Unit	Meaning
H	m	Height of the silo cell to be vented or maximum dimension of the respective compartment
D	m	Diameter of cylindrical cells or diameter D^* of an equivalent circle equal in area
h	m	Free-flying height of the cap
d	m	Diameter of the cap or diameter d^* of an equivalent circle equal in area
D^*	m	Equivalent diameter $\sqrt{4A/\pi}$ with A equal to the area of the silo cell, or area calculated from the smallest dimension of a compartment with area $A = L_2 L_3$ (height $= L_3$ and $L_1 \geq L_2 \geq L_3$)
K_{ST}	bar m/s	Characteristic dust value
p_{red}	bar	Design explosion pressure (reduced explosion pressure due to venting)
V	m³	Volume of the silo bin or compartment
A	m²	Area equal to A_E^V, or equal to A_E when using Fig. 8.A.1
A_E	m²	Total area of vent openings without consideration of inertia effects

A_E^T	m²	Required total area of the vent opening with consideration of inertia effects
A_E^V	m²	Total area of existing vent openings
A_E^i	m²	Area of single vent opening
m_p	kg/m²	Area related mass of vent closure
ρ	kg/m³	Average density of vent closure
n		Number of vent openings (the distance of two vent openings must be greater than $d/2$, when regarded as separate)
f		Factor to increase the vent area in case of relevant inertia forces
v	m/s	Velocity of vent closures
ω	rad/s	Angular velocity of explosion doors
F_R	MN	Simplified assumption for a recoil force acting over a short time in the middle of the vent opening. In case of openings opposite to each other these forces may be compensated
t		Average thickness of closing elements

8.A.3 Application of the design method

By means of the formulae given in section 8.A.2.1 and the diagrams given in section 8.A.4 the following values can be determined:

- the necessary magnitude of the venting area for an intended design pressure p_{red} and a given characteristic dust value K_{ST} (section 8.A.3.1);
- the magnitude of the design pressure p_{red} for a given venting area A_E^V and a characteristic dust value K_{ST} (section 8.A.3.2);
- the permissible characteristic dust value K_{ST}^{max} depending on the endurable design pressure p_{red} and the given venting area A_E^V (section 8.A.3.3);
- the velocity v or angular velocity ω of the closing members as a basis to design the venting structure (section 8.A.3.4).

8.A.3.1 Magnitude of the venting area for a given design pressure p_{red} and characteristic dust value K_{ST}

With the H/D ratio of the silo cell or the compartment to be vented and the intended design pressure p_{red} the auxiliary value K_p can be obtained by means of the diagram for non-inert venting devices (Fig. 8.A.1). The required venting area A_E for non-inert venting is then calculated using equation (8.A.1).

For inert venting the equivalent mass m_p related to the area of the vent closure has to be determined by equation (8.A.5), while the auxiliary value K_m is derived using equation (8.A.2). The magnifier f to determine the

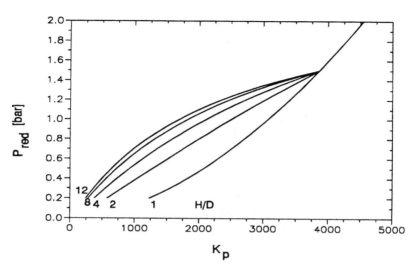

Fig. 8.A.1 Venting area for non-inert relief.

increased venting area due to inertia can then be obtained from the diagrams for inert relief (section 8.A.4) using K_m and p_{red}.

8.A.3.2 Design pressure p_{red} for a given venting area A_E^V and a characteristic dust value K_{ST}

By means of the H/D ratio and the auxiliary value K_p the design pressure p_{red} can be obtained directly from Fig. 8.A.1 in the case of non-inert venting.

For inert venting, p_{red} has to be determined by iterations according to the scheme given in Fig. 8.A.2.

8.A.3.3 Allowable characteristic dust value K_{ST}^{max} for a silo or silo compartment with given p_{red} and A_E^V

The H/D ratio and the design pressure p_{red} give the auxiliary value K_p according to Fig. 8.A.1. In a second step the maximum value for K_{ST} can then be calculated by equation (8.A.1) for non-inert venting.

For inert venting, K_{ST}^{max} must be determined by iterative calculation according to Fig. 8.A.3.

8.A.3.4 Velocity and angular velocity ω of the vent closures to design retaining structures

The velocity v of vent closures is determined for the ratios $h/d = 0.25$ and $h/d = 0.50$ using the corresponding diagrams in section 8.A.4.2. In case of $h/d = 0.25$ the open lateral area for venting is equal to the venting area of the closure which is used to find the pressure at non-inert relief.

Appendix 8.A

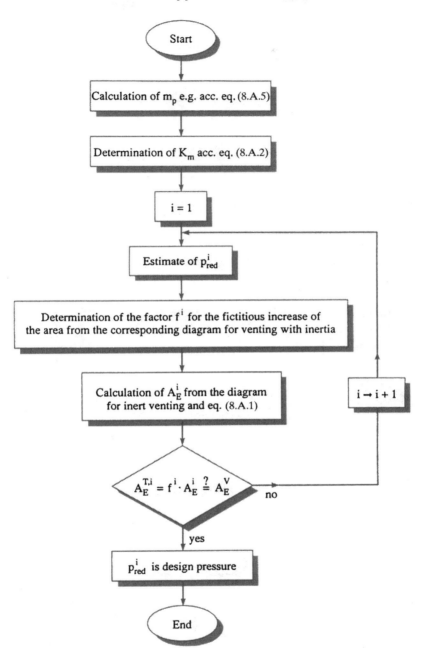

Fig. 8.A.2 Calculation of p_{red} for inert venting (see section 8.A.3.2).

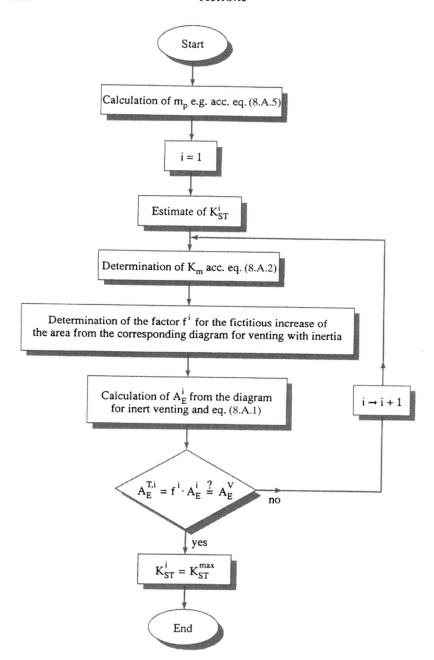

Fig. 8.A.3 Calculation of K_{ST}^{max} for inert venting (see section 8.A.3.3).

Appendix 8.A

By means of the auxiliary values K_p and K_m – see equations (8.A.1) and (8.A.2) – K_v can be found by use of the diagrams in section 8.A.4.2, to find finally the cap velocity v.

The angular velocity ω for explosion doors can be obtained from the diagrams in section 8.A.4.3 depending on the ratios H/D.

In a similar manner one finds by means of K_p and K_m – see equations (8.A.1) and (8.A.2) – the value K_ω from the diagrams in section 8.A.4.3, to determine the angular velocity ω of an explosion door.

With v and ω, respectively, the forces acting at the retaining structure and its connections are known.

8.A.4 Design charts

8.A.4.1 Non-inert venting

Alternatively to Fig. 8.A.1 the following equations may also be used, which are taken from VDI guideline 3673 for homogeneous distributed dust and slightly modified:

$$A_E = 3.264 \times 10^{-4} K_{ST} V^{0.767} p_{red}^{-0.569} K_{H/D}$$

$$K_{H/D} = 1 + \log_{10}\left(\frac{H}{D}\right)\left[0.758 - 4.305 \log_{10}(p_{red})\right]$$

$$0.2 \text{ bar} \leq p_{red} \leq 1.5 \text{ bar} \tag{8.A.8}$$

$$K_{H/D} = 1$$

$$1.5 \text{ bar} \leq p_{red} \leq 2.0 \text{ bar}$$

The auxiliary value K_p can be calculated from equation (8.A.1).

8.A.4.2 Cap structures

8.A.4.2.1 $H/D = 2$

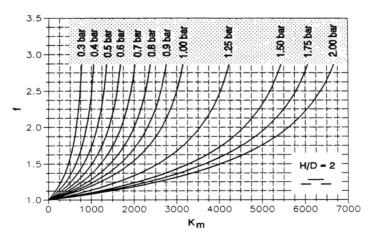

Fig. 8.A.4 Magnifier f for the venting area due to inertia effects for $H/D = 2$.

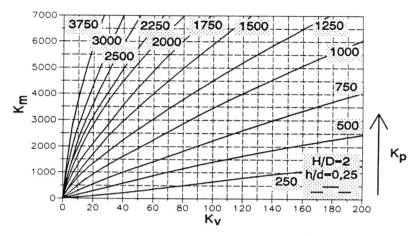

Fig. 8.A.5 Cap velocity v for $H/D = 2$ and $h/d = 0.25$.

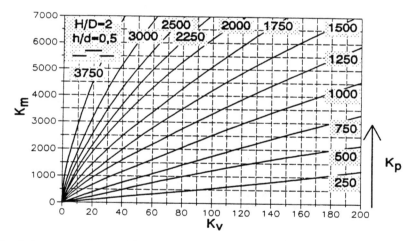

Fig. 8.A.6 Cap velocity v for $H/D = 2$ and $h/d = 0.50$.

8.A.4.2.2 $H/D = 4$

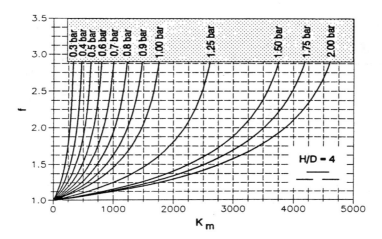

Fig. 8.A.7 Magnifier f for the venting area due to inertia effects for $H/D = 4$.

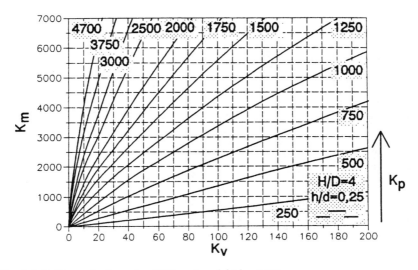

Fig. 8.A.8 Cap velocity v for $H/D = 4$ and $h/d = 0.25$.

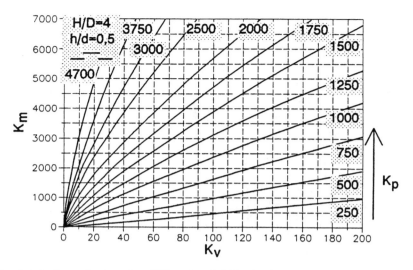

Fig. 8.A.9 Cap velocity v for $H/D = 4$ and $h/d = 0.50$.

8.A.4.2.3 $H/D = 8$

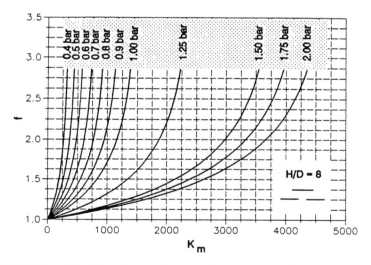

Fig. 8.A.10 Magnifier f for the venting area due to inertia effects for $H/D = 8$.

Appendix 8.A

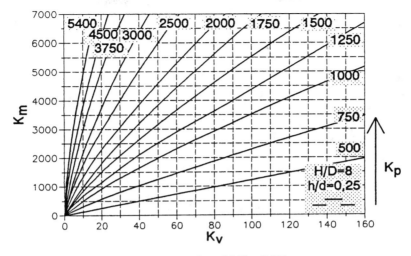

Fig. 8.A.11 Cap velocity v for $H/D = 8$ and $h/d = 0.25$.

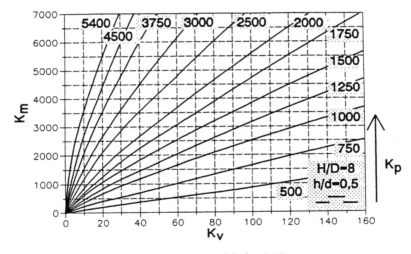

Fig. 8.A.12 Cap velocity v for $H/D = 8$ and $h/d = 0.50$.

8.A.4.2.4 H/D = 12

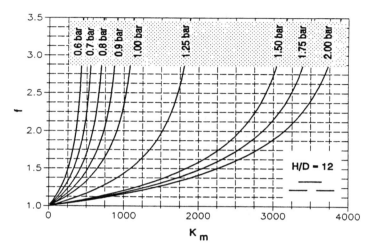

Fig. 8.A.13 Magnifier f for the venting area due to inertia effects for $H/D = 12$.

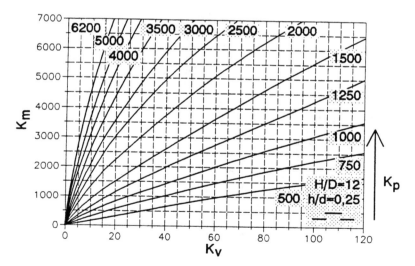

Fig. 8.A.14 Cap velocity v for $H/D = 12$ and $h/d = 0.25$.

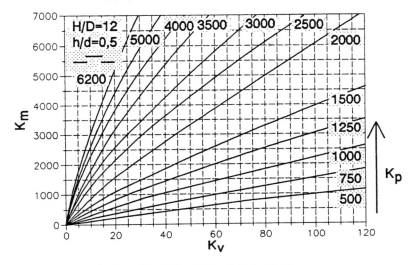

Fig. 8.A.15 Cap velocity v for $H/D = 12$ and $h/d = 0.50$.

8.A.4.3 Explosion door structures

8.A.4.3.1 $H/D = 2$

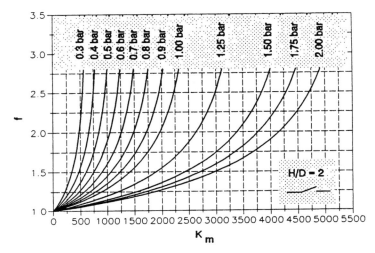

Fig. 8.A.16 Magnifier f for the venting area due to inertia effects for $H/D = 2$.

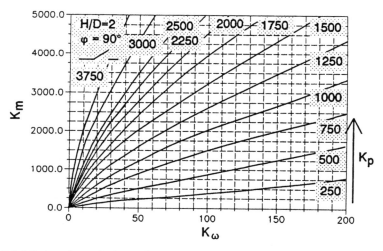

Fig. 8.A.17 Angular velocity ω for $H/D = 2$ and $\varphi = 90°$.

8.A.4.3.2 $H/D = 4$

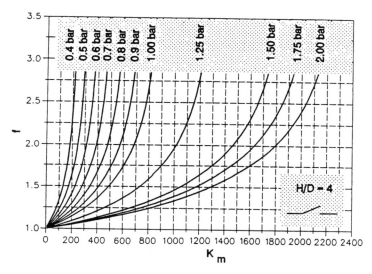

Fig. 8.A.18 Magnifier f for the venting area due to inertia effects for $H/D = 4$.

Appendix 8.A

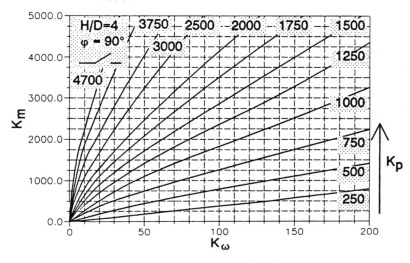

Fig. 8.A.19 Angular velocity ω for $H/D = 4$ and $\varphi = 90°$.

8.A.4.3.3 $H/D = 8$

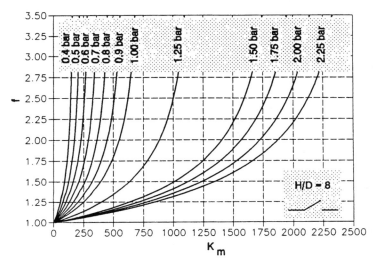

Fig. 8.A.20 Magnifier f for the venting area due to inertia effects for $H/D = 8$.

292 Actions

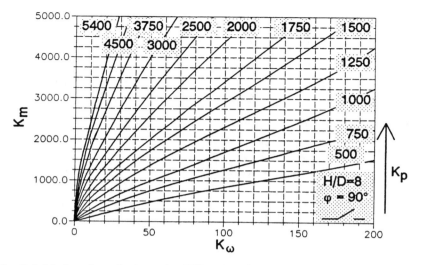

Fig. 8.A.21 Angular velocity ω for $H/D = 8$ and $\varphi = 90°$.

8.A.4.3.4 $H/D = 12$

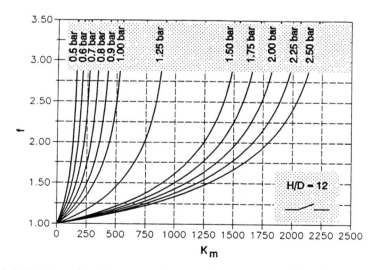

Fig. 8.A.22 Magnifier f for the venting area due to inertia effects for $H/D = 12$.

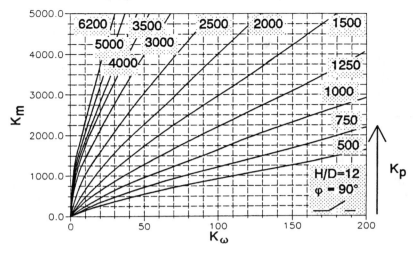

Fig. 8.A.23 Angular velocity ω for $H/D = 12$ and $\varphi = 90°$.

8.A.5 Examples

In the following, examples are given for the application of the 'Draft of a Guideline for the Design of Silo Plants Against Dust Explosions'. A grain silo plant and a storehouse for grain are treated to demonstrate how dust explosions can be prevented, and how their damaging effect can be minimized. The examples are described extensively to allow handling also for those engineers who are not acquainted with the design of structures against explosion.

8.A.5.1 General precautionary measures

In silo plants with integrated silo bins adjoining rooms may be endangered by secondary explosions, which occur when dust is squeezed out of vent openings and ignited. Explosions may be spread via transportation and ventilation systems. High flame velocities and high pressures can be found especially in long-stretched rooms. Such are for example filling floors above the silo bins or discharge floors below the silo, stairwells or elevator shafts. Damage to plants handling hazardous dusts can be significantly reduced either by physical separation in installing closed explosion compartments, or by providing venting devices in order to reduce the explosion pressure.

Connecting doors between closed explosion compartments should be built to withstand possible pressure.

The discharging floor should be separated from other rooms as well as from stairwells. A special protected entrance should be provided.

If explosion-proof elevators cannot be installed or if venting to the outer environment is not possible, a special closed elevator shaft with adequate pressure venting may be installed.

In most cases, pressure venting of silo bins can be realized by vent openings to the air on top of the bin. Of course, in this case the space above the silo cells has to be designed carefully with respect to such a pressure reduction device.

8.A.5.2 General advice for the design of vent openings

Venting openings represent the easiest way of reducing the pressure from dust explosions. Such systems have to meet at least the following requirements:

- Generally the locking elements have to be airtight, especially when food is stored. This is also required for silo cells which are charged pneumatically by using a slight overpressure.
- The surrounding should be endangered as little as possible by either detached fragments, or by the pressure wave or flashes of fire. Venting should be realized via elevated windows or on top of the bins directly upwards. The motion of massive locking elements has to be stopped by suitable supporting devices. Fragments of bursting diaphragms should not interfere with areas where people are used to staying.
- The locking elements should have a low mass. If the mass is too high, the required size of the venting area has to be enlarged as inertia effects influence the delay time until the whole vent opening is available for pressure reduction. Otherwise, the design pressure increases.
- The necessary force to initiate the venting process – fastening forces, weight of the venting closures, etc. – should be as low as possible, as it determines the initial pressure of the venting process. An increase in the release pressure p_a results in an enlargement of the required venting area or of the design pressure. The design rules which have been described are based on a release pressure of max 0.1 bar. Bigger release pressure calls for bigger venting areas than determined by these rules.
- The venting device must be appropriately maintained to avoid increased pressures, e.g. due to corrosion of joints.

For the design of relief vents there are two general possibilities shown in Fig. 8.A.24:

- Bursting diaphragms acting as vent closures fail in a non-inert manner under a certain release pressure p_a. Using this system, the design pressure can be lower than for inert closures. However, one has to take care that the surroundings are not endangered by detached fragments.

Appendix 8.A

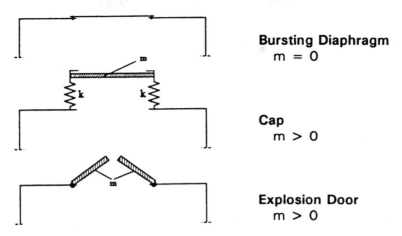

Bursting Diaphragm
m = 0

Cap
m > 0

Explosion Door
m > 0

Fig. 8.A.24 Possible venting systems.

- Caps and explosion doors represent inert vent closures. After a reasonable movement they have to be stopped, causing high forces to the retaining structure. The advantage of this solution is that this device can carry live loads of service conditions.

All forces resulting from such venting structures – e.g. as tensile forces – have to be considered.

8.A.5.3 First example – silo plant

8.A.5.3.1 Structural details

Figure 8.A.25 gives an overview of the silo plant. The following parameters are needed for design:

$$\text{Volume, } V = 4.5 \times 4.5 \times 48.06 = 973.2 \, \text{m}^3$$
$$\text{Top area and floor area, resp., } A = 4.5 \times 4.5 = 20.25 \, \text{m}^2$$
$$\text{Fictitious diameter, } D^* = \sqrt{4 \times 20.25/\pi} = 5.08 \, \text{m}$$
$$H/D^* = 48.06/5.08 = 9.46$$
$$\text{Grain, mixed dust, deposited}\dagger \; K_{ST} = 79 \, \text{bar m/s}$$
$$\text{Perimeter of the silo bin, } U = 4 \times 4.5 = 18.0 \, \text{m}$$
$$A/U = 20.25/18.0 = 1.125 \, \text{m}$$
$$\text{Bulk weight density of grain, } \gamma = 9.0 \, \text{kN/m}^3$$
$$\text{Horizontal/vertical pressure ratio, } \lambda = 0.60$$
$$\text{Wall friction coefficient}$$
$$\text{for concrete and grain, } \mu = 0.40$$

† From: Sicherheitstechnische Informations- und Arbeitsblätter 140 260–140 279, *BIA-Handbuch*, Verlag Erich Schmidt, Bielefeld.

296 Actions

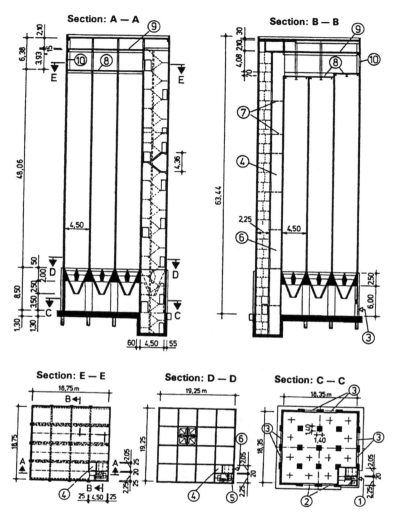

Fig. 8.A.25 Dust explosion precautions in a grain silo plant.

8.A.5.3.2 Design of the silo cells

It should be noted that at present almost no experience is available about vent closures. Hence, the following relevant design examples should be regarded as proposals, which have to be discussed and assessed further.

In the following example the venting of the silos is arranged upwards. The maximum venting area equals the silo area. As a cover wooden plates – *Tischlerplatten* – with a thickness of 3 cm will be used according to the German Standard DIN 68 705, having a nominal weight between 4.5 and

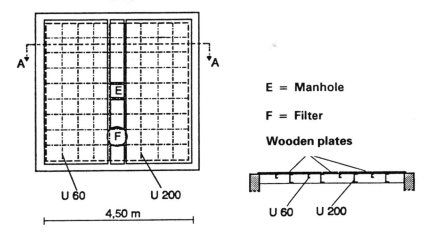

Fig. 8.A.26 Cover of silo cells.

8 kN/m^3. Therefore an estimated value of 650 kg/m^3 is assumed. This results in a mass of $m_p = 19.5$ kg/m^2.

The wooden plates are mounted on a steel grid and fixed by screws of low strength, e.g. of plastic (Fig. 8.A.26). The sum of the total resisting failure load of all connecting screws and the dead load of the wooden plates is below 10 kN/m^2 or below the intended initial pressure of 0.1 bar according to the design rule.

The closure is designed in such a manner, that in case of a dust explosion above the filling floor with a design pressure of $p_a = 0.4$ bar neither the girder grid nor the wooden plates will fail. Due to this measure, a secondary explosion inside the silo bins is prevented even if an explosion occurs outside the silo bin in the filling floor.

The available net venting area is about $A_E^V = 16.4$ m^2 after subtracting the steel grid area and the area of the filter.

8.A.5.3.3 Combination of load cases

In the following, three load cases will be examined:

- silo, filled
- silo, empty under dust explosion
- silo, partly filled under dust explosion

The required safety factors for the actions are chosen according to CEN/ENV 1992, Eurocode 2: *Description of Concrete Structures*. For details of the values for the partial safety factors refer to this and CEN/ENV 1993, Eurocode 3: *Design of Steel Structures*, respectively.

Generally, structural members have to be designed for combinations of several load cases. One distinguishes between the following:

298   *Actions*

- Fundamental combination with normal actions

$$S_d\left[\sum(\gamma_{G,i}G_{k,i}) + \gamma_Q Q_{k,1} + \sum_{i>1}(\gamma_Q \psi_{0,i} Q_{k,i}) + \gamma_P P_k\right]$$
$$\leq R_d\left[\frac{f_{ck}}{\gamma_c}; \frac{f_{yk}}{\gamma_s}; \frac{0.9 f_{Pk}}{\gamma_s}\right]$$
(8.A.9)

here for the relevant case 'filled silo' with

$$S_D = S_D\left[\gamma_Q Q_{\text{filling}}\right]$$

- Accidental design situations

$$S_{d,A} = S_d\left[\sum(\gamma_{GA,i}G_{k,i}) + A_d + \psi_{1,1}Q_{k,1} + \sum_{i>1}(\psi_{2,i}Q_{k,i}) + \gamma_P P_k\right]$$
$$\leq R_d\left[\frac{f_{ck}}{\gamma_c}; \frac{f_{yk}}{\gamma_s}; \frac{0.9 f_{Pk}}{\gamma_s}\right]$$
(8.A.10)

in the present case with

$$S_D = S_D\left[1.0 A_{\text{explosion}} + 1.0 Q_{\text{filling}}\right]$$

For the second case, Janssen's theory is modified by changing the upper boundary condition from $p = 0$ to p_{red} (refer to Fig. 8.A.27). Hence, the following solutions for vertical, horizontal and wall friction loading are obtained in the silo:

$$p_v(z) = \gamma z_0 s(z) \qquad z \geq 0$$
$$ = p_{\text{red}} \qquad z < 0$$
(8.A.11a)

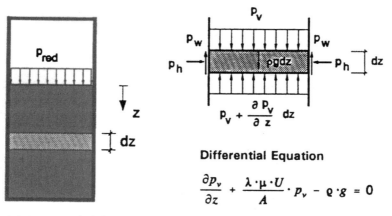

Fig. 8.A.27 Extended theory of Janssen.

$$p_h(z) = \gamma \lambda z_0 s(z) \quad z \geq 0$$
$$= p_{red} \quad z < 0 \tag{8.A.11b}$$

$$p_w(z) = \gamma \lambda \mu z_0 s(z) \quad z \geq 0$$
$$= 0 \quad z < 0 \tag{8.A.11c}$$

with

$$s(z) = 1 - \left(1 - \frac{p_{red}}{\gamma z_0}\right) e^{-z/z_0}$$
$$z_0 = \frac{A}{\lambda \mu U} \tag{8.A.12}$$

Neglecting wall friction along the silo height for simplified calculation the following expression is obtained for the resulting total load:

$$F_w(z) = \int p_w(z) dA = U \int p_w(z) dz$$
$$F_w(z_{max}) = U \gamma \lambda \mu z_0 \left[z + \left(z_0 - \frac{p_{red}}{\gamma}\right) e^{-z/z_0} \right]_0^{z_{max}} \tag{8.A.13}$$

When the resulting vertical load F_v has been calculated with the help of p_v, the total load can be determined from

$$\sum V = 0 = F_{expl} + F_{filling\ weight} - F_v - F_w$$
$$= p_{red} A + \gamma z_{max} A - p_v(z_{max}) A - F_w \tag{8.A.14}$$
$$F_w = A \left[p_{red} + \gamma A - p_v(z_{max}) \right]$$

8.A.5.3.4 Silo loading

Load case 'filled silo' The loads from bulk materials are determined according to the German Standard DIN 1055, Part 6 (ed. 5/1987). The calculation is performed according to Janssen's theory, which is also the basis of equations (8.A.11).

From equation (8.A.12) one finds for $z = H = 48.06$ m:

$$z_0 = \frac{20.25}{0.60 \times 0.40 \times 18.0} = 4.6875$$
$$s(48.06) = 1 - \left(1 - \frac{0}{9.0 \times 4.6875}\right) e^{-48.06/4.6875} = 1.0$$

and therefore:

$$p_v(48.06) = 9.0 \times 4.6875 \times 1.0 = 42.19 \, \text{kN/m}^2$$
$$p_h(48.06) = 0.60 \times 9.0 \times 4.6875 \times 1.0 = 25.31 \, \text{kN/m}^2$$
$$p_w(48.06) = 0.40 \times 0.60 \times 9.0 \times 4.6875 \times 1.0 = 10.13 \, \text{kN/m}^2$$
$$F_w(48.06) = 20.25(0 + 9.0 \times 48.06 - 42.19) = 7904.7 \, \text{kN}$$

This is the fundamental combination of EC 2 and therefore has to be multiplied by $\gamma_Q = 1.5$:

$$p_v(48.06) = 63.28 \, \text{kN/m}^2$$
$$p_h(48.06) = 37.97 \, \text{kN/m}^2$$
$$p_w(48.06) = 15.19 \, \text{kN/m}^2$$
$$F_w(48.06) = 11857 \, \text{kN}$$

Load case 'empty silo under dust explosion' The available venting area and the characteristic dust value K_{ST} are given in section 8.A.5.3.1. The design pressure p_{red} can be found only iteratively regarding the inert vent closure.

The calculation of the design load is carried out by analogy with section 8.A.3.2.

According to equation (8.A.2) the value of K_m is determined as

$$K_m = \frac{\sqrt{m_p} \, K_{ST}^{5/4}}{n^{1/4} V^{0.041}} = \frac{\sqrt{19.5} \times 79^{5/4}}{1^{1/4} \times 973.22^{0.041}} = 784.4$$

As for $H/D = 9.46$ no design diagram exists, p_{red} is determined for both values $H/D = 8$ and $H/D = 12$ from the given diagrams. Afterwards, the value is linearly interpolated for $H/D = 9.46$.

- $H/D = 8$: For the first iteration, $p_{red}^1 = 0.90$ is chosen. From Fig. 8.A.10 one obtains $f^1 = 1.62$ (Fig. 8.A.28). From Fig. 8.A.1 and equation (8.A.1) (Fig. 8.A.29) one finds

$$A_E^{T,1} = f^1 A_E^1 = 1.62 \times 9.99 \, \text{m}^2 = 16.18 \, \text{m}^2 \leq A_E^V = 16.40 \, \text{m}^2$$

- $H/D = 12$: The design pressure $p_{red}^1 = 1.0$ bar is chosen. From Fig. 8.A.13 it follows $f^1 = 1.71$. With the help of Fig. 8.A.1 and equations (8.A.1) and (8.A.8):

$$A_E^{T,1} = f^1 A_E^1 = 1.71 \times 9.18 \, \text{m}^2 = 15.70 \, \text{m}^2 < A_E^V = 16.40 \, \text{m}^2$$

At a second iteration with $p_{red}^2 = 0.99$ bar, one obtains $f^2 = 1.75$ from Fig. 8.A.13. Using Fig. 8.A.1 and equation (8.A.8):

Appendix 8.A

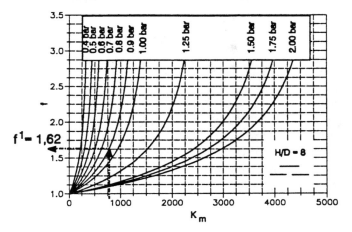

Fig. 8.A.28 Determination of magnifier f for the venting area.

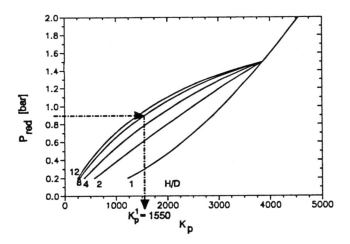

Fig. 8.A.29 Determination of the auxiliary value K_p.

$$A_E^{T,2} = f^2 A_E^2 = 1.75 \times 9.34 \, \text{m}^2 = 16.34 \, \text{m}^2 \le A_E^V = 16.40 \, \text{m}^2$$

With a linear interpolation between $H/D = 8$ and $H/D = 12$, the design pressure is obtained:

$$p_{\text{red}} = p_{\text{red}}^8 + \frac{9.46 - 8}{12 - 8}\left(p_{\text{red}}^{12} - p_{\text{red}}^8\right) = 0.90 + \frac{1.46}{4}(0.99 - 0.90) = 0.93 \, \text{bar}$$

Finally, the following loads are found for the load case 'empty silo under dust explosion':

$$p_v(48.06) = p_{red} = 93.0 \text{kN/m}^2$$
$$p_h(z) = p_{red} = 93.0 \text{kN/m}^2$$
$$p_w(z) = 0$$
$$F_w(z) = 0$$

Load case 'silo partly filled under dust explosion' At first the silo may be filled up to 25% (Fig. 8.A.30) thus making possible a dust explosion in the remaining volume. With respect to equations (8.A.11) the load case dust explosion has to be examined.

For the remaining volume the following values are valid:

$$H_{75\%} = 0.75 \times 48.06 = 36.05 \text{ m}$$
$$H_{75\%}/D = 7.10$$
$$V_{75\%} = 36.05 \times 20.25 = 730.01 \text{ m}^3$$

For further details, e.g. vent area, mass of the vent cover m_p, refer to the load case 'empty silo under dust explosion'.

From equation (8.A.2) the auxiliary value K_m can be found:

$$K_m = \frac{\sqrt{m_p}\, K_{ST}^{5/4}}{n^{1/4} V^{0.041}} = \frac{\sqrt{19.5} \times 79^{5/4}}{1^{1/4} \times 730.01^{0.041}} = 793.74$$

Again, there is no design diagram available for $H/D = 7.1$, but from $H/D = 4$ and $H/D = 8$, the relevant value may be calculated.

- $H/D = 4.0$: Estimated $p_{red}^1 = 0.60$ bar. From Fig. 8.A.10 it follows $f^1 = 2.71$. Equation (8.A.8) yields

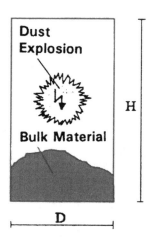

Fig. 8.A.30 Partly filled silo.

$$A_E^{T,1} = f^1 A_E^1 = 2.71 \times 11.0\,\text{m}^2 = 29.82\,\text{m}^2 > A_E^V = 16.40\,\text{m}^2$$

The iteration must be continued. Assume $p_{red}^2 = 0.71$ bar. Figure 8.A.7 leads to $f^2 = 1.80$. Hence, equation (8.A.8) gives

$$A_E^{T,2} = f^2 A_E^2 = 1.80 \times 9.07\,\text{m}^2 = 16.32\,\text{m}^2 \approx A_E^V = 16.40\,\text{m}^2$$

- $H/D = 8.0$: With the chosen value $p_{red}^1 = 0.90$ bar it follows from Fig. 8.A.10 $f^1 = 1.66$. From equation (8.A.8) then one obtains:

$$A_E^{T,1} = f^1 A_E^1 = 1.66 \times 8.01\,\text{m}^2 = 13.30\,\text{m}^2 < A_E^V = 16.40\,\text{m}^2$$

The iteration has to be repeated. With $p_{red}^2 = 0.85$ bar it follows $f^2 = 1.85$ and according to equation (8.A.8)

$$A_E^{T,2} = f^2 A_E^2 = 1.85 \times 8.70\,\text{m}^2 = 16.10\,\text{m}^2 \leq A_E^V = 16.40\,\text{m}^2$$

The linear interpolation between $H/D = 4$ and $H/D = 8$ gives

$$p_{red} = p_{red}^4 + \frac{7.10 - 4}{8 - 4}\left(p_{red}^8 - p_{red}^4\right) = 0.71 + \frac{3.10}{4}(0.85 - 0.71) = 0.82\,\text{bar}$$

This leads to a design pressure of $p_{red} = 82.0\,\text{kN/m}^2$.

For the load case 'silo partly filled' with 25% at $z_{max} = 12.02\,\text{m}$ on top of the bulk material the following boundary pressures result according to equations (8.A.11):

$$p_v(12.02) = 45.26\,\text{kN/m}^2$$
$$p_h(12.02) = 27.15\,\text{kN/m}^2$$
$$p_w(12.02) = 10.86\,\text{kN/m}^2$$
$$F_w(12.02) = 2933.8\,\text{kN}$$

The analysis of further load cases with partly filled silos up to 50 and 75%, respectively, are carried out by analogy. The results of five different filling ratios are summarized in Fig. 8.A.31. It is evident that vertical and horizontal loading of the load case 'empty silo' are relevant for the design. Nevertheless, the load case 'filled silo' is relevant for the wall friction.

8.A.5.3.5 Vent closures and retaining structural members

For the design of the vent closures the load case 'empty silo' is relevant.

As proposed in section 8.A.5.3.2 (Fig. 8.A.26) wooden plates are provided. In the case of a dust explosion they can move unrestrictedly after the connecting screws have failed, until they are stopped by the roof girders representing the retaining structure.

The impact force of the wooden plates exerted on the roof girders is determined from the velocity of the vent closure according to section 8.A.3.4. The existing height of the compartment is 3.93 m (Fig. 8.A.25).

304   *Actions*

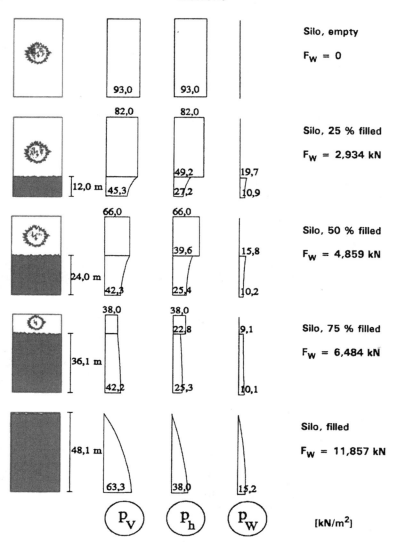

Fig. 8.A.31 Resulting loads for different filling states.

With $d^* = D^* = 5.08$ m it follows

$$\frac{h}{d} = \frac{3.93}{5.08} = 0.77 > 0.50$$

The velocity of the vent closure may be evaluated with the help of the diagrams for $h/d = 0.50$. This is possible, as the relevant values vary insignificantly in this range.

Appendix 8.A

The following starting values are obtained from an iteration between $H/D = 8$ and $H/D = 12$ in a manner similar to that used to investigate the load case 'empty silo under dust explosion':

$$K_m = 784.4 \quad p_{red} = 0.93 \text{ bar} \quad A_E^V = 16.40 \, \text{m}^2 \quad V = 973.22 \, \text{m}^3$$

$$K_p = \frac{V^{0.767} K_{ST}}{A_E^V} = \frac{973.22^{0.767} \times 79}{16.40} = 943.5$$

One obtains for:

- $H/D = 8$: from Fig. 8.A.12 $K_v = 24.1$ (Fig. 8.A.32)
- $H/D = 12$: from Fig. 8.A.15 $K_v = 30.4$

For a linear interpolation between $H/D = 8$ and $H/D = 12$ one finds

$$K_v^{9.46} = K_v^8 + \frac{9.46 - 8}{12 - 8}\left(K_v^{12} - K_v^8\right) = 24.1 + \frac{1.46}{4}(30.4 - 24.1) = 26.4$$

Subsequently, the velocity of the vent closures can be calculated from equation (8.A.3):

$$v = \frac{K_v V \sqrt{p_{red}}}{A_E^V m_p} = \frac{26.4 \times 973.22 \times \sqrt{0.93}}{16.40 \times 19.5} = 77.5 \, \text{m/s}$$

This velocity in connection with the mass of the vent closures determines the impact forces acting on the roof girder.

The roof cover is assumed to be made of trapezoidal-shaped sheet steel mounted on steel beams. These beams span in one direction and are fixed at

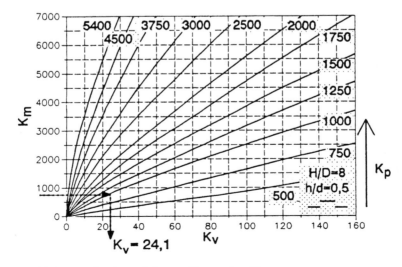

Fig. 8.A.32 Determination of the auxiliary value K_v.

306   Actions

the supports to the silo walls. At least two beams HEA 160 according to DIN 1052 made of St 37-2 are necessary.

For the following dynamic investigations, the wooden plates are idealized as single masses, presuming that smaller parts of the cover are connected (Fig. 8.A.26).

For energy dissipation, insulating panels are located below the steel beams. They have a thickness of 30 cm, a width of 16 cm – which is equal to that of the beams – and a density of 30 kg/m³, and are made of polystyrene or similar material. Figure 8.A.33 shows the idealized stress–strain relation for the deformation behaviour of the panel.

The real system is simplified in a mass–spring model as shown in Fig. 8.A.34.

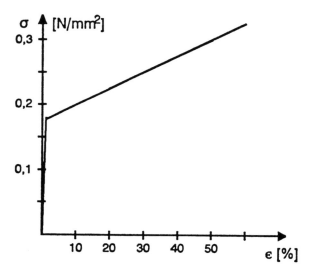

Fig. 8.A.33 Idealized stress–strain relation of polystyrene.

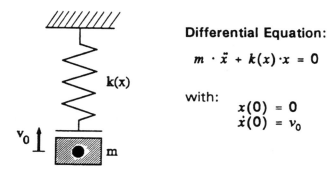

Fig. 8.A.34 Simple mass–spring model with nonlinear spring stiffness.

Appendix 8.A

The relevant differential equation becomes nonlinear due to the characteristic bilinear curve of the insulating panels. Its solution may be simplified regarding just the energy balance in order to evaluate the maximum values for forces and deformations.

$$E_{kin} = \frac{1}{2} mv^2 \tag{8.A.15}$$

$$E_{spring} = \int_0^x F ds = \frac{1}{2} k_1 x_1^2 + k_1(x - x_1)^2 + \frac{1}{2} k_2 (x - x_1)^2 \quad \text{for } x > x_1$$

where $k_i = E_i A / h$.

At maximal spring displacement the kinetic energy is transformed completely to potential energy, i.e. the energy is stored in the spring. Hence, the maximal displacement can be determined from

$$x_{max} = \sqrt{\frac{\frac{mhv^2}{2A} - \frac{E_1 x_1^2}{2}}{E_1 + \frac{1}{2} E_2}} + x_1 \tag{8.A.16}$$

as long as this value is greater than that of the elastic deformation.

Using the following parameters

m total mass of venting covers = $19.5 \times 20.25 = 394.88$ kg
v velocity of venting covers = 77.5 m/s
h height of polystyrene plates = 0.3 m
A total area of the polystyrene plates = $2 \times 0.16 \times 4.5 = 1.44$ m^2
x_1 upper limit for the elastic deformation = 0.006 m
E_1 elastic Young's modulus = 9.0 MN/m^2
E_2 Young's modulus when yielding = 0.25 MN/m^2

the maximal deformation is obtained:

$$x_{max} = \sqrt{\frac{\frac{394.88 \times 0.30 \times 77.5^2}{2 \times 1.44} - \frac{9.0 \times 10^6 \times 0.006^2}{2}}{9.0 \times 10^6 + \frac{1}{2} \times 0.25 \times 10^6}} + 0.006 = 0.1705 \text{ m}$$

and from there:

$$\varepsilon = \frac{x_{max}}{h} = 0.568$$

From Fig. 8.A.33 the respective stress for polystyrene can be determined:

$$\sigma = 0.317 \text{ MN/m}^2$$

The loading of one beam is calculated from the polystyrene stress and the beam width:

$$q = \sigma b = 0.3171 \times 0.16 \times 10^3 = 50.74\,\text{kN/m}$$

to find for a four-span beam with one span loaded:

$$\max|M| = 0.054 q l^2 = 0.054 \times 50.74 \times 4.75^2 = 61.82\,\text{kN m}$$

$$\max \sigma = \frac{\max|M|}{\text{exist } W} = \frac{61.82 \times 10^{-3}}{220.0 \times 10^{-6}} = 281\,\text{N/mm}^2 < \beta_\text{f} = 370\,\text{N/mm}^2$$

8.A.5.3.6 Discharging floor

The specific dimensions can be gathered from Fig. 8.A.25:

Volume, $V = (18.35 \times 18.35 - 5.0 \times 5.0) \times 6.0 = 1870.3\,\text{m}^3$
Fictitious height†, $H = 18.35\,\text{m}$
Fictitious floor area, $A = 6.0 \times 18.35 = 110.1\,\text{m}^2$
Fictitious diameter, $D^* = \sqrt{4 \times 110.1/\pi} = 11.84\,\text{m}$
$H/D^* = 1.55$
K_{ST} value‡ $= 79\,\text{bar m/s}$
p_{red} chosen $= 0.25\,\text{bar}$

Venting is realized via existing windows, which serve as bursting diaphragms. Again, the release pressure must be below 0.1 bar to meet the requirements of the design rule. Additionally, the window panes are assumed to fail almost without inertia. Hence, Fig. 8.A.1 and equation (8.A.8) are sufficient to determine the required venting area.

From Fig. 8.A.10 is obtained $K_p = 850$ and from equation (8.A.1) it follows $A_E = 30.0\,\text{m}^2$.

In the case of rather strong walls surrounding the bottom compartment the design pressure p_{red} may of course be raised to allow a much smaller vent area.

8.A.5.4 Second example – storehouse

In the following, precautionary measures will be investigated for a storehouse with respect to the damaging effects of dust explosions. Recommendations will be given for the design of the required vent areas. The example used is taken from NFPA-Code 68-1988.

8.A.5.4.1 Structural details

For an existing storehouse a change of use is planned. It has to be examined which types of dusts can be stored, i.e. the maximal value for $K_{ST}^{\max}$ has to be

---

† The greatest height has to be used to determine the value of H/D. For this reason, the height is called fictitious height.
‡ From: Sicherheitstechnische Informations- und Arbeitsblätter 140 260–140 279, *BIA-Handbuch*, Verlag Erich Schmidt, Bielefeld.

Appendix 8.A

determined. Because of a change of use, only rooflights and elevated windows in the walls were used for pressure venting. If necessary, further windows or the whole roof can be taken into account. The building is designed for $p_{red} = 0.25$ bar and for non-inert venting.

8.A.5.4.2 Building section 1

For details of the dimensions refer to Fig. 8.A.35.

$$\text{Volume, } V = 0.5 \times (6.0 + 9.0) \times 9.0 \times 52.0 = 3510 \, \text{m}^3$$
Fictitious height $H = 52.0$ m
Fictitious floor area, $A = 0.5 \times (6.0 + 9.0) \times 9.0 = 67.5 \, \text{m}^2$
Fictitious diameter, $D^* = \sqrt{4 \times 67.5/\pi} = 9.27$ m
$$H/D^* = 52.0/9.27 = 5.61$$
Design pressure, $p_{red} = 0.25$ bar

Windows and rooflights are used as vent areas with a total area of $156.0 \, \text{m}^2$. As the venting occurs non-inert, Fig. 8.A.1 can be used to determine

$$K_p = 396.0$$

From equation (8.A.1) it follows

$$K_{ST}^{max} = 118 \, \text{bar m/s}$$

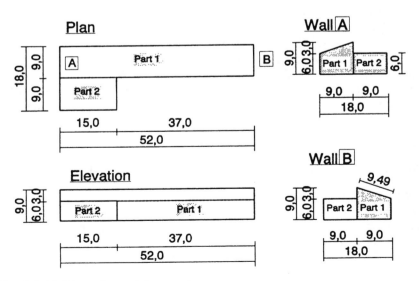

Fig. 8.A.35 Dimensions of the storehouse.

8.A.5.4.3 Building section 2

Again, the dimensions can be gathered from Fig. 8.A.35.

$$\text{Volume, } V = 6.0 \times 9.0 \times 15.0 = 810 \, \text{m}^3$$
$$\text{Fictitious height, } H = 15.0 \, \text{m}$$
$$\text{Fictitious floor area, } A = 6.0 \times 9.0 = 54.0 \, \text{m}^2$$
$$\text{Fictitious diameter, } D^* = \sqrt{4 \times 54.0/\pi} = 8.29 \, \text{m}$$
$$H/D^* = 15.0/8.29 = 1.81$$
$$\text{Design pressure, } p_{\text{red}} = 0.25 \, \text{bar}$$

Windows and rooflights are used as non-inert venting areas with a total area of $45.0 \, \text{m}^2$. Figure 8.A.1 for non-inert venting gives

$$K_p = 745.0$$

and from equation (8.A.1) it follows

$$K_{ST}^{max} = 197 \, \text{bar m/s}$$

8.A.5.4.4 Distribution of the venting areas

For both parts of the building the planned venting areas meet the requirements of stored materials with a maximum characteristic dust value up to $K_{ST}^{max} = 118 \, \text{bar m/s}$. If in addition the roof area of section 1 is used as venting area, even materials with significantly higher characteristic dust values may be accepted for storing.

For a further increase of the venting area, the remaining windows in the walls may be taken into account.

If venting areas are to be installed in the walls, care has to be taken that nobody is endangered in the environment.

The venting areas should only be arranged in the outer walls of the building. Otherwise a pressure venting into another explosion compartment could cause secondary explosions.

The total venting area might be too small to enable a sufficient pressure venting. In this case, the respective members of the building have to be strengthened in order to resist the explosion pressure without damage.

REFERENCES

Braun, A. (1996) Schüttgutbelastung auf Silozellen unter Erdbebeneinwirkung. Dissertation, University of Karlsruhe.

CEN/ENV 1991-4 *Actions on Silos and Tanks*. Brussels.

DIN 1055 (1987) Part 6, *Lasten in Silozellen*. Ausgabe.

Eibl, J. (1986) Konstruktive Hinweise zum Entwurf von Silobauten. *Der Bauingenieur*, 61, 353–361.

Gladen, W. (1985) *Numerische Untersuchungen der Lasten in Silozellen beim exzentrischen Entleeren*. Dissertation und Heft der Schriftenreihe des Instituts für Massivbau and Baustofftechnologie der Universität Karlsruhe.

Häussler, U. (1984) *Geschwindigkeits- und Spannungsfelder beim Entleeren von Silozellen.* Dissertation und Heft der Schriftenreihe des Instituts für Massivbau and Baustofftechnologie der Universität Karlsruhe.

ISO-Standard (1991) *ISO 6184/1: Explosion Protection Systems* – Part 1: Determination of Explosion Indices of Combustible Dusts in Air. Geneva.

Kolymbas, D. (1988) *Eine konsistente Theorie für Böden und andere körnige Stoffe.* Veröffentlichungen des Instituts für Boden- und Felsmechanik der Universität Karlsruhe, Heft 109, Karlsruhe.

Lade, P.V. (1977) Elasto-plastic stress–strain theory for cohesionless soils with curved yield surfaces. *Int. J. of Solids and Structures*, 19, 1019–1035.

Landahl, H. (1983) Berechnung der Druckverhältnisse in zylindrischen Silozellen mit nichtlinearem Stoffgesetz für den Füllzustand und beim Entleerungsbeginn. Dissertation, University of Dortmund.

Perry, M.C. and Jangda, H.A.C. (1970) Pressures in flowing and static sand model bunkers. *Powder Technology*, 4, 89–96.

Resinger, F. and Greiner, R. (1984) Verhalten stehender Behälter aus Stahl bei Baugrundsetzungen. *IKM-Kongress*, Weimar.

Rombach, G. (1991) *Schüttguteinwirkungen auf Silozellen – Exzentrische Entleerung.* Dissertation und Heft 14 der Schriftenreihe des Instituts für Massivbau und Baustofftechnologie der Universität Karlsruhe.

Ruckenbrod, C. and Eibl, J. (1992) Silo loading. In D. Behrens (ed.) *Strategies 2000, Proc. 4th World Congress Chemical Engineering*, Karlsruhe 1991, Brömers Druckerei Breidenstein GmbH, Frankfurt, pp. 902–920.

Standard Association of Australia (1989) *Loads on Bulk Solids Containers.* Draft Australian Standard, Sydney, Issue 6.

VDI Kommission (1995) *VDI-Richtlinie 2263, Staubbrände und Staubexplosionen.* Beuth Verlag, Berlin.

Walters, J.K. (1973) A theoretical analysis of stresses in silos with vertical walls. *Chemical Engineering Science*, 28, 13–21, 779–789.

9

Reinforcement

J. Eibl

9.1 MINIMUM REINFORCEMENT

Silo walls should have two layers of reinforcement, one layer near the inside face of the wall and the other near the outside face (Fig. 9.1).

Silo wall reinforcement in horizontal as well as vertical direction should not be less than 0.2% of the silo wall area on both inner and outer wall surface.

Embedded jackrods in case of slipform construction shall not be taken into account for vertical reinforcement.

9.2 CRACK CONTROL

If the temperature of bulk material is between −15°C and +30°C, it seems appropriate first to design the silo with regard to the bulk material pressure at ultimate limit state (ULS), neglecting temperature effects and determining the necessary reinforcement $A_{S,ULS}$.

In a second step the serviceability limit state (SLS) has to be checked. Under moment M_l and normal force N_l due to live load (l), neglecting temperature, tensile stresses occur:

$$\sigma_t = \frac{N_l}{A_c} + \frac{M_l}{W_c} \qquad W_c = \frac{bd^2}{6} \qquad (9.2.1)$$

If these tensile stresses are less than the tensile strength of concrete ($0 < \sigma_t < f_{ct}$), an additional investigation should then be done for $A_{S,SLS}$.

$$A_{S,SLS} = \frac{1}{z}\left[M + N_l(z - e_c)\right]\frac{1}{\sigma_s} \qquad (9.2.2)$$

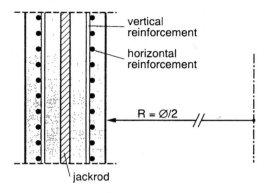

Fig. 9.1 Reinforcement of silo wall (vertical section).

where σ_s should be limited to

$$\sigma_s \leq 0.8 f_y \qquad (9.2.3a)$$

$$\sigma_s \leq 930 d_s^{-1/2} \quad (\text{N/mm}^2) \qquad (9.2.3b)$$

where N_l is the tensile force under service load ($N = 0$ if compression), M_l the bending moment under service load, $M_{cr} = f_{ct} b d^2/6$, M is the maximum bending moment $M = \max(M_{cr}, M_l)$, d_s the diameter of reinforcement (mm), f_y the yield strength of reinforcement, f_{ct} the tensile strength of concrete, e_c the reinforcement distance from cross-section centre and z the lever arm of internal forces.

Equation (9.2.3a) ensures that steel stress in the reinforcement remains under the yield limit regarding a safety factor of $\gamma = 1.25 = 1/0.8$. Equation (9.2.3b) is to ensure a reasonable crack width at SLS at the transition from the uncracked to the cracked state.

The larger of both $A_{S,SLS}$ and $A_{S,ULS}$ is then relevant.

9.3 PRESTRESSING

If the structure is prestressed, a reduced prestressing normal force $0.9 N_p$ may be used, provided the losses due to creep and shrinkage have been considered already.

If silos are to be post-tensioned, partial prestressing seems to be appropriate. A detailed crack width investigation may be omitted if mild reinforcement (section 9.2) is provided.

Concentrated cable forces normal to the silo wall due to sharp cable curvatures should be considered.

Special unbonded monostrand arrangements, as offered now (Fig. 9.2) may also be a very effective and economic prestressing tool, to avoid shear

Fig. 9.2 Prestressing with unbonded monostrands.

failures as discussed in section 9.4. Monostrands may also be used in connection with prefabricated concrete elements (Fig. 9.3).

9.4 INTERACTION OF SHEAR AND TENSILE FORCES

Near the corners of rectangular silo cells the bending moment is zero, while high tensile normal forces and shear forces act in the wall section (Fig. 9.4). In the case of only horizontal wall reinforcement without stirrups and oblique bars, shear failures under tensile normal force may occur. To avoid such damage a correct dimensioning of the wall sections including the effect of normal tensile force has to be carried out.

As latest investigations show (Emrich, 1993), no further measures need to be taken with respect to shear, as long as the ultimate shear stress is

Interaction of shear and tensile forces 315

Fig. 9.3 Prestressed prefabricated concrete elements.

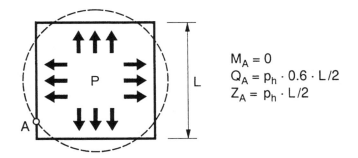

Fig. 9.4 Combined loading of the wall near corner (polygonal silo).

bounded to

$$\tau_u^{Q,N} \leq 0.04 A^3 \sqrt{\mu_L} \sqrt{\frac{\beta_{WN}}{A}} - 0.2 \frac{N_u}{d} \qquad (9.4.1)$$

where $\mu_L = \mu_{L,i} + \mu_{L,o}$, $\mu_{L,i}$, $\mu_{L,o}$ the percentage of horizontal reinforcement, inside and outside respectively, β_{WN} the nominal concrete compression strength, A the nominal concrete compression strength = $\beta_{WN,25} = 25 \text{ MN/m}^2$, d the cross-section width and N_u the ultimate horizontal normal force (kN/m), and as long as the percentage of the inner and outer horizontal reinforcement is greater than

Reinforcement

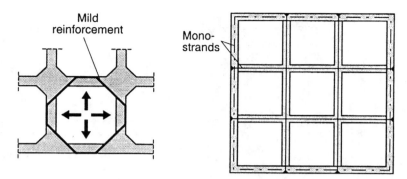

Fig. 9.5 Possible reinforcement arrangement at the cross-section corner.

$$\mu_{L,i}, \mu_{L,o} \geq \frac{1.5 N_u}{0.8 f_{s,y} d} \qquad (9.4.2)$$

Stirrups, difficult to place in the case of a sliding formwork, or oblique bars crossing the wall thickness may be of use (Fig. 9.5).

Probably the most favourable solution, as mentioned above, is the use of monostrands to prevent complete decompression from these local areas (Figs 9.2 and 9.3).

REFERENCE

Emrich, H. (1993) Zum Tragverhalten von Stahlbetonbauteilen unter Querkraft- und Längzugbeanspruchung. Research Report, IfMB, University of Karlsruhe

10

Concreting
J. Eibl

10.1 SLIPFORM PROBLEMS

Using sliding formwork (Fig. 10.1) special knowledge of the slipform technique should be evident in design, execution and control processes. A minimum wall thickness of 18 cm, special requirements due to concrete covering, concrete quality, reinforcement arrangement and control of the reinforcement arrangement and concrete quality should be observed. At all times, processes on the site have to be controlled by an engineer with sufficient sliding formwork experience.

The length and form of the reinforcing bars both have to be tuned to the narrowness of the working space on the sliding framework arrangement. Because of this, mesh reinforcement, long vertical bars and rods, closed stirrups and complicated forms of reinforcement bars should be avoided.

The author encountered silo failures where wind had induced bars with excessive length to vibrate, separating the concrete walls over its thickness into three layers. Insufficient bonding and premature extension of bars was the consequence. This effect caused the Deutscher Beton-Verein (German Concrete Association) to demand an increased anchorage length of all reinforcing bars in case of slipforms (Merkblatt Gleitbauverfahren, 2/1987).

Especially if mechanical devices circulating within the bin are to be installed, stiffness of the formwork has to be ensured to create a correct geometry of the structure.

For a good and tight surface the outside of the wall in particular should be subjected to a well-rounded after-treatment of the concrete surface.

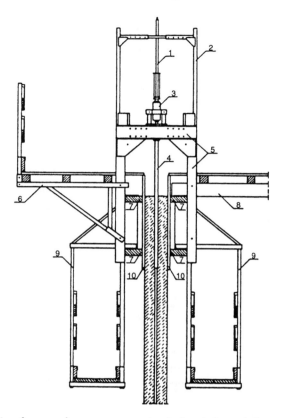

Fig. 10.1 Sliding formwork arrangement: 1 = jackrod; 2 = reinforcement deposit; 3 = jack; 4 = rod-cover; 5 = frame; 6 = cantilever stage; 7 = frame; 8 = rails; 9 = hanging stage; 10 = shuttering.

Using concrete with different added fly ash content the author has carried out tests with appropriate slipforms for concrete mix development. High-performance concrete gives a better corrosion protection of the reinforcement and may be necessary at great height above ground and under conditions with heavy acting winds.

10.2 CONCRETE SHIELDING

Abrasion on the inner side of the silo wall may cause contamination of the stored material and may disturb the reinforcement cover. It is necessary to differentiate between:

- mechanical attacks due to the filling and discharging process by hard and rough bulk materials;

- physical attacks due to erosion and corrosion with changing temperatures and moisture content;
- chemical attacks due to chemical reaction with acid, salty or organic products,

leading to different abrasional conditions:

- material deduction in extreme cases to a complete exposure of the reinforcement endangering the bearing capacity and safety of the silo construction;
- changing the concrete microstructure and influencing the flow behaviour, the wall friction coefficient and finally the silo pressure.

To study all relevant questions in this context, special experimental and theoretical investigations have been carried out (Fig. 10.2) (Kunterding, 1991).

Depending on the particular type of exposures, various types of failure mechanisms are responsible. In the case of exposure to bulk material, failure of the matrix, of the aggregates or of the matrix aggregate bond are possible. As a consequence of such an exposure even larger aggregate particles are gradually removed from the concrete due to debonding. Concrete for use under this condition should have a higher strength – high performance concrete. This can be reached by a water–cement ratio <0.35

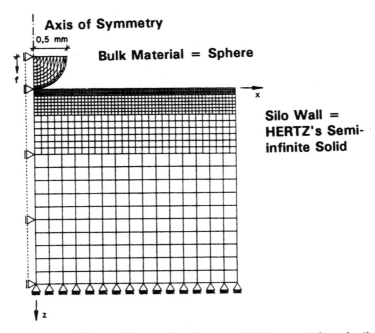

Fig. 10.2 FE modelling of interaction between bulk material and silo wall (Kunterding, 1991).

and by use of high-strength cements or by the use of additives like microsilica. To ensure that the surface of the concrete is not friable, the concrete should be cured for a sufficient period; then the resistance of the concrete surface will rise significantly.

A classification according to abrasion actions for some bulk materials is given in Table 10.1(a) and (b), while abrasion attack classes are given in Table 10.2. As the aggregate particles are directly exposed, the strength of the aggregate particles themselves also play a major role in the total behaviour of the concrete.

Fine aggregates should consist mainly of quartz or materials with a similar hardness. Coarse aggregates should consist of stone or artificial materials having a correspondingly high abrasion resistance. If the abrading action is extreme, the provision of a special wearing surface is recommended, replacing partially (up to 30%) the aggregates by microsilica or carborundum. By such means the abrasion resistance may be increased up to 1500% (Kunterding, 1991).

The resistance of concrete to chemical attacks depends primarily on its impermeability. Therefore the maximum water/cement ratios given in ENV 206, Table 3, 5a–5c should not be exceeded. In addition, particularly

Table 10.1(a) Abrasion classes for different bulk materials – mechanical attacks

Industrial products	Class	Refractory material	Class
Coal lignite	1	Bentonite, loose	1
Brown coal briquette (charged)	1	Expanded clay	1
Carbonized lignite	2	Lignite filter ash	2
Iron coal	2	Gypsum, ground	1
Coke	2	Blast furnace slag (granulated)	4
Mineral coal	2	Boilings	4
Lump briquette (charged)	2	Foam slag	1
Egg-shaped briquette and others	2	Natural pumice	1
Mid materials in mine works	2	Lime, burnt, in pieces	1
Washery rubbish in mine works	2	Limestone powder	1
Iron ore	4	Lime ash	1
Bog iron ore	4	Sand, gravel	
Brazil ore	4	fluorite, calcite,	
Carbide	1	dolomite, barite	2
Plastic granulates		magnetite, quartz	3
soft granulated	1	Broken, crushed stone < 5 mm	3
hard granulated	2	Broken, crushed stone > 5 mm	4
		Cement clinker	3
		Foamy lava, broken	2

Table 10.1(b) Abrasion classes for different bulk materials – physical/chemical attacks

Industrial and agricultural products	Class	Fertilizer	Class
Industrial products:		Carbamide	4
pyrite	2	Potash	3
soda	1	Potassium sulphate	3
halite, broken	1	Potassium chloride	1
Agricultural products:		N-single fertilizer	1
grains: barley, oat, wheat,		NK-fertilizer	2
rye, pulse, maize, rice, etc.:		NPK-fertilizer	3
storage, dry	1	P-fertilizer (without	
storage, moist	2	thomasphosphate)	2
oil-producing fruits, cattle	2	PK-fertilizer	2
concentrated foodstuff		Thomasphosphate*	2
whole meal, malt grist	1		
forage briquette and crops	1		
green flour and potato flakes	1		
oil pellets, soya beans	2		
sugar beet chips	1		

* Fertilizer consisting of waste (slag) from steel production.

Table 10.2 Abrasion attack classes

Abrasion attack class	Attack
1	Weak attack
2	Medium attack
3	Strong attack
4	Very strong attack

careful curing is necessary. In cases of exposure to highly aggressive chemicals, additional protective measures such as impermeable coatings are required. Further information can be found in Maliha and Hilsdorf (1994).

REFERENCES

Deutscher Beton-Verein (1987) *Merkblatt Gleitbauverfahren*. Fassung 2/1987.

Kunterding, R. (1991) *Beanspruchung der Oberfläche von Stahlbetonsilos durch Schüttgüter*. Dissertation und Heft 12 der Schriftenreihe des Instituts für Massivbau und Baustofftechnologie der Universität Karlsruihe.

Maliha, R. and Hilsdorf, H.K. (1994) Hochfester Beton in Gleitschalung. *Beton- und Stahlbetonbau*, 89(3), 80–82.

11

Concluding remarks
J. Eibl

The design of silo structures in reinforced concrete is now generally well understood. The problems identified are therefore usually related to either features associated with their high stiffness, or to quality control of the construction process. In particular in the case of inflexible structures, thermal actions and differential settlements arising from foundation problems will be more critical. Additionally, actions from earthquakes and dust explosions are still not understood sufficiently.

Quality control problems are often general to concrete structures (reinforced or prestressed) and designing for minimum reinforcement, crack control and suitable prestressing would be included. Slipform problems would be specific to silo structures.

Problems which have been identified and remain as key research objectives are:

- *Soil–structure interaction.* Soil–structure interaction for silos sensitive to differential settlements.
- *Earthquake effects.* Earthquake effects on silo walls directly enclosing the bulk material in the case of both slender high silos and shallow cylindrical bins with large diameter.
- *Multi-cell silos.* Temperature effects on wall stresses due to the interaction with the bulk material, and due to structural restraints.
- *Concrete performance in relation to wear.* The quality of the concrete mix and the treatment of the concrete until fully cured are key issues for better silo performance in relation to wear.

Part Three

Metal Structures

Foreword

J.M. Rotter

This Part presents a summary of the current state of knowledge of the behaviour of metal silo structures. The knowledge has been developed by both formal research and practical experience, and relates chiefly to the design of new silo structures and the assessment of existing silos in service.

Many research studies of different aspects of the structural behaviour and design of metal silos have been carried out in recent years. Summarizing reviews of recent research work may be found in other reports and papers (Trahair *et al.*, 1983; Gaylord and Gaylord, 1984; Safarian and Harris, 1985; Rotter *et al.*, 1986; Rotter, 1987, 1993, 1996; Martens, 1988; Hampe, 1991; Jarrett *et al.*, 1995; Teng and Rotter, 1993; Carson and Jenkyn, 1993).

This Part on the state of the art does not attempt to be comprehensive or to make value judgements on the merits of different studies. Instead, it aims to give a brief overview of many problems which are known to exist and of the current state of knowledge of them. Each chapter is divided into sections on established knowledge, areas of current research and problems known to be in need of future research.

For each of the topics discussed, sources of published literature are listed at the end of each chapter.

REFERENCES

Carson, J.W. and Jenkyn, R.T. (1993) Load development and structural considerations in silo design, *Proc., International Symposium: Reliable Flow of Particulate Solids II*, EFChE Publication Series No. 96, Oslo, 23–24 Aug., pp. 237–254.

Gaylord, E.H. and Gaylord, C.N. (1984) *Design of Steel Bins for Storage of Bulk Solids*, Prentice-Hall, New Jersey.

Hampe, E. (1991) *Silos*. Vol. 1 *Grundlagen*; Vol. 2 *Bauwerke*, Verlag für Bauwesen GmbH, Berlin. Vol. 1 256 pp., Vol. 2 252 pp.

Jarrett, N.D.; Brown, C.J. and Moore, D.B. (1995) Stress redistribution in rectangular planform silos, *Geotechnique*, 45 (1), 95–104.

Martens, P. (1988) (ed.) *Silo-Handbuch*, Ernst und Sohn, Berlin.

Rotter, J.M. (1987) The buckling and plastic collapse of ring stiffeners at cone/cylinder junctions, *Proc., Int. Colloq. on Stability of Plate and Shell Struct.*, Ghent, April, pp. 449–456.

Rotter, J.M. (1993) The design of circular metal silos for strength, *Proc., International Symposium: Reliable Flow of Particulate Solids II*, EFChE Publication Series No. 96, Oslo, 23–24 Aug., pp. 217–234.

Rotter, J.M. (1996) Shell structures: design standards, recent progress and unsolved problems, Invited plenary paper, *Proc., International Conference on Structural Steelwork*, Hong Kong, December 1996, pp. 621–636.

Rotter, J.M.; Ansourian, P. and Trahair, N.S. (1986) A survey of recent buckling research on metal silos, *Proc., 2nd Int. Conf. on Bulk Materials Storage, Handling and Transportation*, IEAust., Wollongong, July, pp. 82–88.

Safarian, S.S. and Harris, E.C. (1985) *Design and Construction of Silos and Bunkers*, Van Nostrand Reinhold, New York.

Teng, J.G. and Rotter, J.M. (1993) The strength of circular steel silos: new investigations, *Proc., Transactions of Civil Engineering*, Institution of Engineers, Australia, Vol. CE35, No. 1, March 1993, pp. 21–31.

Trahair, N.S.; Abel, A.; Ansourian, P.; Irvine, H.M. and Rotter, J.M. (1983) *Structural Design of Steel Bins for Bulk Solids*, Australian Institute of Steel Construction, Nov.

12
Overview of metal silos
J.M. Rotter

12.1 INTRODUCTION

Metal silos are currently produced in a great variety of forms: circular, square and rectangular in plan-form; squat bunkers and tall cylinders; silos with smooth isotropic walls, stiffened walls, built from horizontally or vertically corrugated sheets with orthogonal stiffeners, or patented special wall forms; silos supported on the ground and silos elevated on skirts or columns. This great variety, coupled with the complexity and variability arising from bulk solids loading, leads to a huge array of structural problems, which have in turn led to many structural failures. These failures continue unabated despite many disaster assessments and attempts at changes in governing rules to avoid them in the future. Jenkyn and Goodwill's (1987) review concluded that over 1000 structural failures occur in silos in North America alone every year: a majority of these failures are in metal silos. The failure record in Europe is less well documented, but there are few reasons for thinking that its record is any better.

Circular metal silos are complex thin branched shells of revolution subject to complicated loading and support conditions. A typical structure is shown in Fig. 12.1 with a cylindrical barrel section above a conical hopper, and with a conical roof. Each of these segments is susceptible to a variety of different failure modes, and additional modes arise for the joint elements between the segments. Failure modes, and thus design situations to be considered, are principally by buckling or by plastic collapse after extensive nonlinear deformations.

Rectangular metal silos have varied wall structural forms, and although the plate bending action may be easier to assess than the behaviour of a shell, these structures nevertheless present a complex interaction between

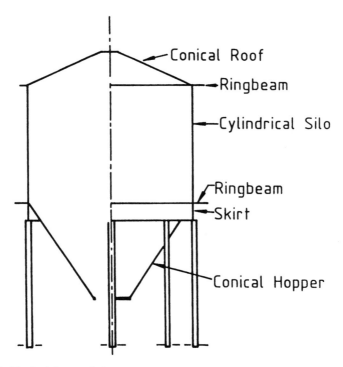

Fig. 12.1 Typical form of elevated granular solid storage silo.

bending and stretching behaviour. Economies can clearly be made by exploiting membrane effects in large deformations and the use of internal ties, but these two features have led to failures, and no research study has yet reached any complete understanding of the problem.

Despite the complex behaviour of both forms of structure, traditional design techniques for metal silos often use very simplified methods and rely heavily on the designer's experience. Such design techniques have become increasingly inadequate as the size of modern metal silos has risen.

Metal silos may be ground-supported or elevated (Fig. 12.2). A typical elevated circular silo consists of a cylindrical shell above a conical hopper. Elevated silos may be supported on a long skirt which is directly supported on the ground (Fig. 12.3(a)), or supported on columns (Fig. 12.3(b–d)). The columns may terminate below the transition junction (Fig. 12.3(b)), extend to the eaves (Fig. 12.3(c)), or terminate part way up the cylinder (Fig. 12.3(d)). A ground-supported silo, and an elevated silo on a deep skirt and/ or many columns may be deemed to be uniformly supported. For these silos, provided the filling and discharge processes exert symmetrical pressures on the wall, a fairly complete description of the structural strength requirements is now available. For metal silos on a small number of columns, and

Introduction 329

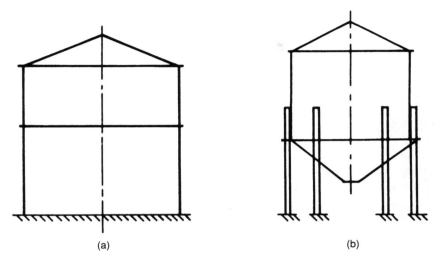

Fig. 12.2 Common circular metal silo forms: (a) ground-supported; (b) elevated.

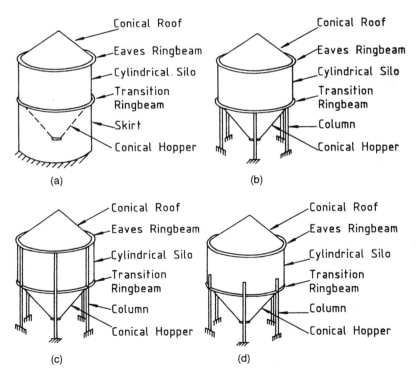

Fig. 12.3 Alternative support arrangements for elevated metal silos: (a) deep skirt bin; (b) column-supported bin with columns; (c) column-supported bin with columns extending to the eaves ring; (d) column-supported bin with engaged column.

for silos subject to eccentric filling, eccentric discharge and unsymmetrical pressures from other sources, our understanding is still very limited.

This chapter presents a summary of a large number of studies of the structural behaviour and design of metal silos.

12.2 THE BACKGROUND TO STRUCTURAL DESIGN

Silos are thin shell structures, and carry their loads chiefly by membrane tensile and compressive forces in the shell walls. Shells are extremely efficient structures, as is evidenced by their use in spacecraft, rockets, aircraft, automobiles, etc., but this very efficiency makes them susceptible to loading conditions which were not anticipated in the design. Silos have consequently had a relatively high rate of failure in the past, compared with other types of structure.

Civil and structural engineers have traditionally been thoroughly trained in the behaviour, analysis and design of beams and frames. Many are also taught the elements of plate bending, but few learn much about the analysis, behaviour and design of shells. Most civil engineers designing shell structures are substantially self-taught from design guides, tank design codes, and textbooks on the behaviour and analysis of shells, and from the experience of others working in the field.

Most steel silos are very thin shells, with a radius which may typically be between 300 and 3000 times the thickness of the wall ($300 < R/t < 3000$). This thinness must be borne in mind when studying steel silos as a class, as it leads to great differences between the silo and other civil engineered shells, such as offshore tubular structures.

12.3 TEXTS ON SHELL STRUCTURES

Unfortunately, most texts on shell structures are chiefly concerned with analysis. Many present large quantities of sophisticated mathematics with a few representative examples of idealized structures, so that it is not easy to extrapolate to different geometries, different loading cases and different support conditions in a quantitative way. In addition, the design details used as practical solutions to designers' problems are often extremely difficult to analyse with any rigour; such texts on shell analysis are of little help to the silo designer.

The shell is the most efficient of structural forms, carrying a wide range of different loadings by direct tension or compression (shells differ from arches in that many different load patterns can be carried without bending). For simple load cases, simple geometries and simple support conditions (such as axisymmetric filling of an on-ground silo), shells are easy to analyse. However, as soon as any one of these simplifying factors is missing, the determination of the stress distribution in a shell becomes very difficult using hand calculation methods.

12.4 STANDARDS AND CODES OF PRACTICE

The national and international standards and codes of practice for bin, silo and tank design present a very different picture from the shell analysis texts. The only codes of practice on bins and silos which give guidance on structural design are the ACI code (ACI 313-77, 1984) which relates only to concrete structures, the British code for the design of farm silage silos (BS 5061, 1974) and the Japanese code for small aluminium silos (JIS, 1987). Neither of these latter codes is helpful to the designers of large steel silos required at mines, railheads, power stations, port facilities and similar sites, for the storage of grain, coal, mineral ores and industrial chemicals.

There are a number of codes of practice for the design of tanks, of which the AWWA and API codes (AWWA D100-79, 1979; API-620, 1970) are the best known. These codes give the designer no more than an elementary understanding of the behaviour and stress distribution in the structure. It is not easy to use them in conjunction with a shell bending theory analysis, or a finite element analysis of the structure.

The tank design codes are relatively simple and appear to be quite satisfactory for simple fluid storage tanks. However, their provisions are less satisfactory for bulk solids storage structures, for which the loadings are much more complex, and the consequent structural behaviour and failure criteria more involved.

12.5 DESIGN GUIDES

A number of design guides for the structural design of steel silos are available (Trahair *et al.*, 1983; Ketchum, 1919; Lambert, 1968; Wozniak, 1979; Reimbert and Reimbert, 1976; Gaylord and Gaylord, 1984; Rotter, 1985e). The older of these contain provisions which have changed little over the past 20 years. Several research papers (Rotter, 1985a, b, c, d, 1986; Ansourian, 1985; Trahair, 1985) form the basis of more recent information (Rotter, 1985e). Much useful information of a different kind may be found in the excellent book by Gaylord and Gaylord (1984).

The only formal standards which address metal silo design at present are the Japanese aluminium silos standard (JIS, 1987), and a small appendix in the BMHB design guide (BMHB, 1985). A major development is, however, in progress, with the drafting of the first full metal silos standard as Eurocode 3 Part 4.1 on the design of steel silos (EC3 Part 4.1, 1997). It is expected that the first draft for public comment will be complete by the end of 1997.

12.6 ADVICE ON METAL SILO LOADS

There are a number of codes of practice dealing with the loads on silo walls (ACI 313-77, 1984; BS 5061, 1974; DIN 1055, 1986; ITBTP No. 189, 1975; BMHB, 1985; Gorenc *et al.*, 1986; JIS, 1987; ISO DIS 11697, 1992;

AFNOR P22-630, 1992; EC1 Part 4, 1993; AS 3774-96, 1996). Naturally these all address the question of design pressures under the most obvious granular solid loading conditions (concentric filling, concentric discharge in either funnel flow or mass flow mode). However, many of these avoid dealing with the more uncertain aspects of silo loadings, and consequently leave the structural engineer to make his/her own judgement. In addition, they often fail to advise the designer of some conditions which should be considered in the design, but which are less obvious.

12.7 CONCLUDING REMARKS

The following chapters of this Part are contributions from active researchers working on silo or shell buckling problems. While they may not always attempt to be complete, they do offer a starting point for both researchers and designers.

REFERENCES

ACI 313-77 (1984) American Concrete Institute, *Recommended Practice for Design and Construction of Concrete Bins, Silos and Bunkers for Storing Granular Materials*, ACI 313-77, Detroit, 1977 (revised 1984).

AFNOR P22-630 (1992) *Construction métallique Silos en acier: calculations des actions dans les cellules*, French national standards organization AFNOR, Jan. 1992, 34 pp.

Ansourian, P. (1985) Stability under wind loading, in *Design of Steel Bins for the Storage of Bulk Solids*, J.M. Rotter (ed.), Univ. Sydney, March, pp. 138–143.

API-620 (1970) *Recommended Rules for the Design and Construction of Large Welded Low-pressure Storage Tanks*, 4th edn, American Petroleum Institute, New York.

AS 3774-1996 (1996) *Loads on Bulk Solids Containers*, Australian Standard, Standards Association of Australia, Sydney, October.

AWWA D100-79 (1979) *Standard for Welded Steel Tanks for Water Storage*, American Water Works Association, Denver, Colorado.

BMHB (1985) *Draft Code of Practice for the Design of Silos, Bins, Bunkers and Hoppers*, 2nd edn, British Materials Handling Board, Ascot.

BS 5061 (1974) *Specifications for Cylindrical Forage Tower Silos and Recommendations for their Use*, BSI, London.

DIN (Deutsches Institut für Normung) (1986) *Design Loads for Buildings: Loads in Silo Bins*, DIN 1055 Part 6, Berlin, Sept.

EC1 Part 4 (1993) ENV 1991-4, Eurocode 1, *Basis of Design and Actions on Structures*, Part 4 – Silos and Tanks, Final Draft, 1993, Brussels.

Gaylord, E.H. and Gaylord, C.N. (1984) *Design of Steel Bins for Storage of Bulk Solids*, Prentice-Hall, New Jersey.

Gorenc, B.E.; Hogan, T.J. and Rotter, J.M. (eds) (1986) *Guidelines for the Assessment of Loads on Bulk Solids Containers*, Institution of Engineers, Australia.

ISO DIS 11697 (1992) *Basis for Design of Structures – Loads due to Bulk Materials*, ISO Draft international standard, ISO, Geneva, 23 pp.

References

ITBTP (Institut Technique du Bâtiment et des Travaux Publics) (1975) *Règles de Conception et de Calcul des Silos en Beton*, No. 189, Paris, December.

Jenkyn, R.T. and Goodwill, D.J. (1987) Silo failures: lessons to be learned, *Engineering Digest*, Sept, pp. 17–22.

JIS (1987) Japanese Industrial Standard B 8511 *Construction of Welded Aluminium and Aluminium Alloy Cylindrical Silos*, translated and published by Japanese Standards Association, Tokyo, Japan, Edition 1, 32 pp.

Ketchum, M.S. (1919) *Design of Walls, Bins and Grain Elevators*, 3rd edn, McGraw-Hill, New York.

Lambert, F.W. (1968) *The Theory and Practical Design of Bunkers*, Brit. Constr. Steelwk Assoc., London, Publ. 32.

Reimbert, M. and Reimbert, A. (1976) *Silos: Theory and Practice*, Trans Tech Publications.

Rotter, J.M. (1985a) Membrane theory of shells for bins and silos, in *Design of Steel Bins for the Storage of Bulk Solids*, edited by J.M. Rotter, University of Sydney, March, pp. 58–70.

Rotter, J.M. (1985b) Bending theory of shells for bins and silos, in *Design of Steel Bins for the Storage of Bulk Solids*, edited by J.M. Rotter, University of Sydney, March, pp. 71–81.

Rotter, J.M. (1985c) Buckling of ground-supported cylindrical steel bins under vertical compressive wall loads, *Proc. Metal Structures Conf.*, Instn Engrs Aust., Melbourne, May, pp. 112–127.

Rotter, J.M. (1985d) Analysis and design of ringbeams, in *Design of Steel Bins for the Storage of Bulk Solids*, edited by J.M. Rotter, Univ. Sydney, March, pp. 164–183.

Rotter, J.M., (ed.), (1985e) *Design of Steel Bins for the Storage of Bulk Solids*, University of Sydney, March.

Rotter, J.M. (1986) Recent studies of the stability of light gauge steel silo structures, *Proc. Eighth International Specialty Conference on Cold-Formed Steel Structures*, St Louis, Missouri, Nov, pp. 543–562.

Trahair, N.S. (1985) Design of roof structures, in *Design of Steel Bins for the Storage of Bulk Solids*, edited by J.M. Rotter, University of Sydney, March, pp. 189–197.

Trahair, N.S.; Abel, A.; Ansourian P.; Irvine, H.M. and Rotter, J.M. (1983) *Structural Design of Steel Bins for Bulk Solids*, Australian Institute of Steel Construction, Nov.

Wozniak, R.S. (1979) Steel tanks, *Structural Engineering Handbook*, 2nd edn, Section 23, Eds. E.H. and C.N. Gaylord, McGraw-Hill.

13

Structural forms of silos
M.J. Blackler

13.1 ROLLED STEEL PLATE CONSTRUCTION

Silos are most commonly constructed from uniform isotropic rolled steel plates. Most of the advice given in the present notes and references refers to this form of construction. Special remarks on this form are therefore not needed here.

Hoppers are almost always made from rolled plates, even when the cylindrical walls of the silo are built from corrugated sheets. Hoppers are usually very thin, and in biaxial tension. This arrangement is therefore quite appropriate.

13.2 STIFFENED PLATE CONSTRUCTION

Vertical and ring stiffeners are often used on silo walls. Vertical stiffeners are generally much more useful than ring stiffeners, so the latter are chiefly used for specific purposes at special points.

When vertical stiffeners are used to carry some of the vertical compressive load in the silo wall, careful attention should be given to compatibility in determining the vertical stress in the stiffener. In particular, the circumferential stress in the silo wall has a significant influence on the stress in the stiffener, through Poisson effects. This leads to a higher stress in the stiffener than might otherwise be expected. Some further discussion of this matter is given in section 5.1.7 of Trahair *et al.* (1983).

Ring stiffeners are often needed at the junctions between shell segments, and at the top of an open cylindrical wall. In addition, they can be used to enhance the wind buckling strength of a cylindrical wall considerably.

Determination of the buckling strength of a stiffened cylindrical wall is not particularly simple, and computational aids are desirable for the task. The eccentricity of the stiffeners from the shell wall also has a significant influence on the buckling strength. Advice on the determination of buckling strengths is available (Rotter, 1986; ECCS, 1988). Wind buckling calculations for concentrically stiffened walls are given by Trahair et al. (1983) and Ansourian (1985).

It is generally uneconomic to place both ring and vertical stiffeners on the same surface, because the stiffener intersections present fabrication difficulties. Ring stiffeners should not be placed on the inside surface of a silo, because of the interference with the flow of stored materials.

13.3 CORRUGATED SHEETING

Small and medium size silos are often built from corrugated sheets. The commonest application involves corrugations running circumferentially around the silo. Unstiffened construction of this form is often used up to about 6 m in height. A study of the axial load collapse strengths of unstiffened circumferentially corrugated steel cylindrical shells is presented elsewhere (Rotter, Zhang and Teng, 1987).

Once vertical stiffeners are adopted, they must be assumed to carry the entire vertical load in the wall, as the difference in stiffness between a compressible corrugation and a vertical stiffener is such that the stiffener will collapse before the wall carries a significant part of the total load.

Some large and very squat silos have been built in recent years from light corrugated sheets with the corrugations running vertically. External bands are required to support the internal pressures in the silo, but the required buckling strength in axial compression is easily achieved.

For both forms of corrugated silo, the buckling resistance under wind is often critical, and should be determined from a calculation of the cylinder as an orthotropic eccentrically stiffened shell (Trahair et al., 1983; Ansourian, 1985; Rotter, 1986; ECCS, 1988). Equations for the determination of the orthotropic properties of the sheeting are given in section 5.1.8 of Trahair et al. (1983).

13.4 SPIRALLY WOUND OR CLOSELY RING-STIFFENED SILOS

Some smaller silos are built with a spiral construction, or with closely spaced ring stiffeners at the joints between segments of the cylindrical wall. The rings or stiffened lips of the spiral do little to enhance the buckling strength unless they are placed at spacings no greater than about $\sqrt{Rt}$, in which R is the cylinder radius and t the wall thickness. The rings, and the local bending which they induce, represent a significant geometrical imperfection in the wall, and buckling strengths may be expected to be as low as those of silos constructed from rolled steel plate.

However, in addition, the axisymmetric buckling strength is often lowered below the classical elastic stress. This has an important consequence for the buckling strength gains due to internal pressure (Rotter, 1985). The buckling strength normally increases under internal pressure because the consequent circumferential tensions tend to iron out geometrical imperfection effects. However, these tensions do not affect the strength in the axisymmetric buckling mode, so that only small internal pressure strength gains can be expected in these silos. The internal pressure strength gains suggested by some references (e.g. ECCS, 1988) should not be used.

REFERENCES

Ansourian, P. (1985) Stability under wind loading, in *Design of Steel Bins for the Storage of Bulk Solids*, J.M. Rotter (ed.), Univ. Sydney, March, pp. 138–143.

ECCS (1988) *European Recommendations for Steel Construction: Buckling of Shells*, 4th edn, European Convention for Constructional Steelwork, Brussels.

Rotter, J.M. (1985) Buckling of ground-supported cylindrical steel bins under vertical compressive wall loads, *Proc. Metal Structures Conf.* Instn. Engrs Aust., Melbourne, May, pp. 112–127.

Rotter, J.M. (1986) The analysis of metal bins subject to eccentric discharge, *Proc Second International Conference on Bulk Materials Storage, Handling and Transportation*, Institution of Engineers, Australia, Wollongong, July, pp. 264–271.

Rotter, J.M.; Zhang, Q. and Teng, J.G. (1987) Corrugation collapse in circumferentially corrugated steel cylinders, *Proc. First National Structural Engineering Conference*, Institution of Engineers, Australia, Melbourne, 26–28 August, pp. 377–383.

Trahair, N.S.; Abel, A.; Ansourian, P.; Irvine, H.M. and Rotter, J.M. (1983) *Structural Design of Metal Bins for Bulk Solids*, Aust. Inst. of Steel Construction.

14

Effects of silo loads
J.M. Rotter

14.1 INTRODUCTION

The typical silo structure being considered here consists of a cylindrical silo body, which may or may not have a conical discharge hopper beneath it (Fig. 12.2). Under most loading conditions, the walls are subject to internal pressures and frictional tractions (distributed forces tangential to the shell surface) (Fig. 14.1). The patterns of these loads vary according to the type of loading to which the silo is subject, and the structural response varies accordingly.

14.2 SYMMETRICAL FILLING AND DISCHARGE

Under symmetrical filling and discharge, the normal pressure of solids against the wall of the silo (Fig. 14.2) induces circumferential (or hoop) tension in the cylindrical wall. This is the most easily understood, and generally the least important feature of steel silo loads. Advice on the pressures to be expected can be obtained from many sources, including national standards and texts on silo design.

The cylindrical wall may also be subject to frictional tractions due to the sliding of material down the wall (Fig. 14.1). The very slight settlements which occur in bulk solids as they are progressively loaded into the silo are almost always sufficient to mobilize the friction fully. These loads lead to axial (vertical) compressive loads in the wall, which increase progressively down the wall (Fig. 14.2). These forces must be resisted by axial stresses in

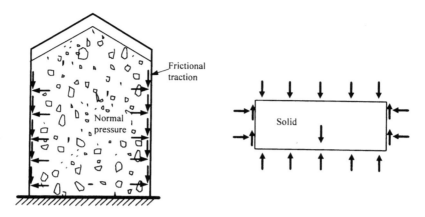

Fig. 14.1 Stored solids exert normal forces and frictional tractions on the silo wall.

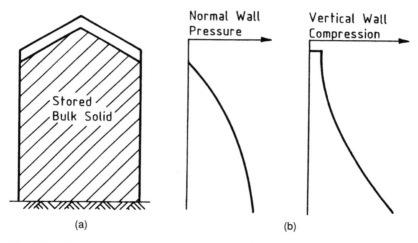

Fig. 14.2 Varying normal pressure and axial force in the silo wall: (a) on-ground silo; (b) typical pattern of wall forces.

the shell wall (which is very susceptible to buckling in this condition), or by the introduction of vertical stiffeners.

The stresses in the silo wall change during flow of the solid, whether in mass or funnel flow. Although the normal pressures may increase considerably, the axial compressive loads increase less so, but they do change. In particular, considerable changes towards unsymmetrical stresses and local high stresses may occur, leading to buckling failures of a more local, but none the less serious, character.

14.3 WIND LOADING WHEN EMPTY

When the silo is empty, external pressures induce small circumferential (or hoop) compressions in the cylindrical wall. These stresses are very small, but because the wall is only slightly curved (R/t is large where R = shell radius, t = shell thickness), the wall is susceptible to a buckling failure in this condition. Advice on the wind pressures to be expected in different regions and different terrain is best obtained from the local wind loading code. Further information is given in Chapter 17.

14.4 NON-SYMMETRICAL FILLING AND EARTHQUAKE

When a squat silo (height/diameter ratio less than 1) is non-symmetrically filled or unsymmetrically emptied (Fig. 14.3), the pressures on opposite walls can differ considerably. The variation of pressures around the silo wall is, however, slow. This results in an overall moment and an overall shear at the silo base. The moment is resisted by increased vertical forces in the silo walls (leading to the possibility of buckling under axial compression), whilst the shear is resisted by membrane shear stresses, which are at a maximum where the wall runs parallel to the direction of maximum filling (Rotter, 1983). Failures by buckling in membrane shear and under axial compression have been observed in experiments on squat eccentrically filled silos (Eccleston, 1987). The variation of pressures in a squat silo after eccentric filling were defined by Rotter (1983, 1985a).

Similar stress patterns are induced by other non-symmetrical loads, for example earthquake (Rotter and Hull, 1989), wind, conveyor tensions and other effects. Some of these are dealt with separately later (in particular, in Chapter 18).

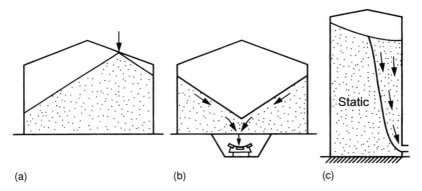

Fig. 14.3 Eccentric loading of the silo can arise from both filling and discharge: (a) eccentric filling; (b) unsymmetrical clean-out; (c) eccentric discharge.

14.5 NON-SYMMETRICAL OR ECCENTRIC DISCHARGE

Non-symmetrical or eccentric discharge is probably the most complex and least understood pattern of loading in silos. The pattern of material flow in the silo (Fig. 14.4) has a strong influence on the resulting pressures, and consequently on the resulting wall stress distributions.

Under some circumstances, an eccentric funnel flow zone develops in the stored material, adjacent to the wall (Fig. 14.5). The pressures in the flowing zone are usually small, whilst those in the adjacent static material are often much higher (Rotter, 1985c, 1986a; Rotter *et al.*, 1995; Chen, 1996). This non-uniformity of pressure distribution leads to a complex stress distribution, which may be characterized by the dominant effects: circumferential bending and axial compression. Both of these stresses vary quite rapidly around the circumference (Rotter, 1986a). A reasonable means of estimating the pressures in the static and flowing zones of the stored solid and applying them to metal silo design is given by Rotter (1986a). This method has been used for a number of successful designs with relatively low safety margins without mishap.

Much recent work has been undertaken to obtain better information on the pressures occurring under eccentric discharge, and their relationship to flow patterns in the solids. Some of this work, as applicable to circular silos, may be found in Rotter *et al.* (1995), Chen *et al.* (1995) and Chen (1996). Additional experimental findings on rectangular silos may be found in Lahlouh *et al.* (1995), with the first reports on this test series now appearing (Brown *et al.*, 1995).

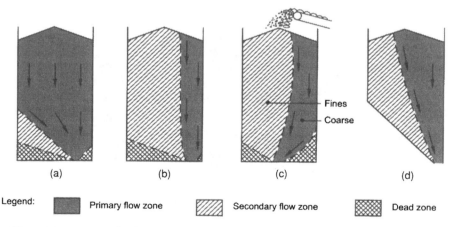

Fig. 14.4 Eccentric discharge can occur for a variety of reasons: (a) mixed or semi-mass flow; (b) pipe flow; (c) segregation; (d) unsymmetrical hopper.

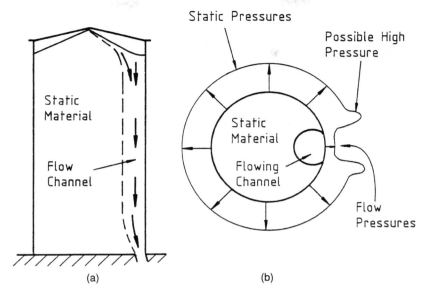

Fig. 14.5 Pipe flow eccentric discharge causes serious local unsymmetrical pressures: (a) elevation; (b) cross-section.

14.6 BULK SOLIDS LOADS ON HOPPERS

The conical hopper is generally supported from above, with a ring at the cylinder/cone transition (Figs 12.1 and 12.3). The pattern of forces exerted on the hopper varies between the initial filling condition and the discharge condition (Fig. 14.6). Under both conditions, the normal pressures induce both circumferential and meridional tensions, whilst the meridional frictional tractions induce only meridional tensions (Trahair et al., 1983; Rotter, 1986b; Teng and Rotter, 1991).

Near the hopper bottom, all stresses are low. A little higher up, the design is controlled by the circumferential tension, especially if meridional bolted joints (running down the hopper side) are used to join hopper sections together in the field.

The total vertical load on the hopper must pass through the hopper to the ring junction, and must be carried there by meridional tensile stresses. The upper part of the hopper is therefore dominated by meridional tensile considerations (Fig. 14.7(a)) (Rotter, 1986b).

It is useful to deal with the analysis of the supporting ring at the same time as that of the hopper. The meridional tension at the hopper top induces a circumferential compression in the transition ring (Fig. 14.7(c)) (Rotter, 1985d). In addition, the change from circumferential tensions in the hopper to high circumferential compression in the ring leads to a severe shell bending action near the top of the hopper and the cylinder walls. This

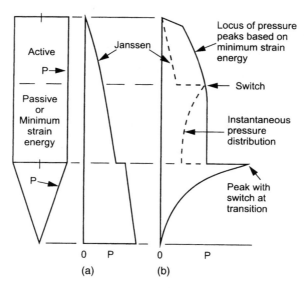

Fig. 14.6 The pressures on the hopper change dramatically between filling and discharge: (a) initial pressure; (b) flow pressure.

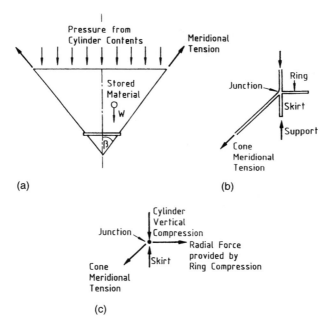

Fig. 14.7 The hopper load is transferred to the transition ring, where it induces circumferential compression: (a) vertical equilibrium of conical hopper; (b) junction local geometry; (c) static equilibrium at the junction.

bending is, however, very local, and the significance of the stresses requires some discussion (Rotter, 1990). Local bending is probably less important here than the potential asymmetry in membrane stresses arising from discrete supports (Rotter, 1990) and unsymmetrical pressure patterns.

14.7 LOCAL FORCES FROM BRACKETS AND COLUMN SUPPORTS

Where an elevated silo is supported on columns, or where brackets are used to introduce concentrated forces into the shell, the stress pattern involves a dispersion from very high stresses in a small zone to much smaller stresses over a wider region. Traditionally, a number of quite different simple rules of thumb have been used to cover this problem.

However, the patterns of stress depend significantly on the placement of ring stiffeners on the shell wall. The importance of ring stiffeners is recognized in the ring beam treatment of column supports, which dates back to Ketchum (1919), but the interaction of the shell wall with ring stiffeners has received very little attention until recent years. Hand methods of deducing stress distributions are still in their infancy, and appropriate criteria to determine when buckling may occur have only been recently developed (Teng and Rotter, 1990; Guggenberger, 1991; Rotter et al., 1993; Guggenberger, 1996).

14.8 DIFFERENTIAL TEMPERATURE CHANGES AND SWELLING OF STORED SOLID

A variety of different forces can be induced in the structure of a silo by differential changes of temperature between the silo and stored solid, or between the different structural components of the silo.

A sudden ambient temperature decrease can cause rapid cooling of the silo structure, leading to high circumferential tensions in the shell wall.

Swelling of a stored agricultural product has a very similar effect to that of a sudden decrease in ambient temperature.

Solar radiation on one side of a silo has been suspected of causing damage (Blight, 1985). Increased vertical stresses in the wall can result, if there is sufficient restraint against out-of-round displacements.

14.9 OUT-OF-PLUMB CONSTRUCTION

It is desirable that some allowance should be made for the possibility that a large silo may be constructed with its axis not quite vertical. A lateral force of 2.5% of the vertical force is often recommended for this purpose, but this load is rarely more significant than wind, earthquake or other horizontal forces. Moreover, most silos are built to better tolerances than this value implies.

14.10 DIFFERENTIAL SETTLEMENT OF FOUNDATIONS

Little is known about the magnitudes of differential settlements which may be expected to occur within a zone as small as the area of the base of a silo. Nevertheless, the consequential silo wall stresses can be large, because the silo structure is generally very stiff. Differential settlements which vary linearly under the silo are of little consequence, but settlements which vary more locally can be serious.

Studies of this problem have mainly addressed the problem of local settlement beneath a ground-supported squat structure (such as an oil tank), and the recent studies of Kemyab and Palmer (1989) and Lancaster et al. (1996) are relevant.

Other problems can be identified for elevated column-supported silos, for which Rotter devised a rule for the Australian Standard (AS 3774-1996). This simple procedure defines the change in individual column forces when small settlements occur beneath one support.

REFERENCES

AS 3774-1996 (1996) *Loads on Bulk Solids Containers*, Australian Standard, Standards Association of Australia, Sydney, October.

Blight, G.E. (1985) Temperature changes affect pressures in steel bins, *International Journal of Bulk Solids Storage in Silos*, 1(3), 1–7.

Brown, C.J. (1996) *Effect of Patch Loads on Rectangular Metal Silos* and Annex, Department of Mechanical Engineering, Brunel University, Uxbridge, UK, 300 pp.

Brown, C.J.; Lahlouh, E.H. and Rotter, J.M. (1995) Eccentric discharge in rectangular planform silos, *PARTEC95, 3rd European Symposium on Storage and Flow of Particulate Solids (Janssen Centennial)*, Nuremberg.

Chen, J.F. (1996) Granular solid – structure interaction in silos, PhD thesis, Department of Civil and Environmental Engineering, University of Edinburgh.

Chen, J.F.; Ooi, J.Y. and Rotter, J.M. (1995) A rigorous statistical technique for inferring circular silo wall pressures from wall strain measurements, *Engineering Structures*, 18(4), 321–331.

Eccleston, P.A. (1987) The buckling of squat silos after eccentric filling, BE thesis, University of Sydney.

Guggenberger, W. (1991) Nichtlineares Beulverhalten von Kreiszylinderschalen unter lokaler Axialbelastung. PhD thesis, TU Graz, Austria.

Guggenberger, W. (1996) Proposal for design rules of axially loaded steel cylinders on local supports, *Proc., International Conference on Structural Steelwork*, Hong Kong, December, pp. 1225–1230.

Guggenberger, W.; Wallner, S. and Greiner, R. (1996) *Influence of Stiffeners on Stresses and Strength of the Silo Shell Caused by Patch Loads*. Research report, Institut für Stahlbau, TU Graz, Austria.

Kemyab, H. and Palmer, S.C. (1989) Analysis of displacements and stresses in oil storage tanks caused by differential settlement, *Proc. Inst. Mech. Engrs, Part C, J. Mech. Engg. Sci.*, 203, 61–70.

Ketchum, M.S. (1919) *Design of Walls, Bins and Grain Elevators*, 3rd edn, McGraw-Hill, New York.

Lahlouh, E.H.; Brown, C.J. and Rotter, J.M. (1995) Loads in rectangular planform steel silos, Research report R95-027, Department of Civil and Environmental Engineering, University of Edinburgh, November.

Lancaster, E.R.; Calladine, C.R. and Palmer, S.C. (1996) Experimental observations on the buckling of a thin cylindrical shell subjected to axial compression, CUED/D-Struct/TR162, Department of Engineering, University of Cambridge, May.

Rotter, J.M. (1983) Structural effects of eccentric loading in shallow steel bins, *Proc. Second International Conference on the Design of Silos for Strength and Flow*, Stratford-upon-Avon, Nov., pp. 446–463.

Rotter, J.M. (1985a) Membrane theory of shells for bins and silos, in *Design of Steel Bins for the Storage of Bulk Solids*, edited by J.M. Rotter, University of Sydney, March, pp. 58–70.

Rotter, J.M. (1985b) Bending theory of shells for bins and silos, in *Design of Steel Bins for the Storage of Bulk Solids*, edited by J.M. Rotter, University of Sydney, March, pp. 71–81.

Rotter, J.M. (1985c) Buckling of ground-supported cylindrical steel bins under vertical compressive wall loads, *Proc. Metal Structures Conf.*, Instn Engrs Aust., Melbourne, May, pp. 112–127.

Rotter, J.M. (1985d) Analysis and design of ringbeams, in *Design of Steel Bins for the Storage of Bulk Solids*, edited by J.M. Rotter, University of Sydney, March, pp. 164–183.

Rotter, J.M. (1986a) The analysis of metal bins subject to eccentric discharge. *Proc. Second International Conference on Bulk Materials Storage Handling and Transportation*, Institution of Engineers, Australia, Wollongong, July, pp. 264–271.

Rotter, J.M. (1986b) On the significance of switch pressures at the transition in elevated steel bins, *Proc. Second International Conference on Bulk Materials Storage, Handling and Transportation*, Institution of Engineers, Australia, Wollongong, July, pp. 82–88.

Rotter, J.M. (1990) The structural design of light gauge silo hoppers, *J. Struct. Engrg, ASCE*, **116**(7), 1907–1922.

Rotter, J.M. and Hull, T.S. (1989) Wall loads in squat steel silos during earthquakes, *Engineering Structures*, **11**(3), 139–147.

Rotter, J.M.; Greiner, R.; Guggenberger, W.; Li, H.Y. and She, K.M. (1993) Proposed design rule for buckling strength assessment of cylindrical shells under local axial loads, submission to ECCS TWG8.4, Buckling of Shells, September.

Rotter, J.M.; Ooi, J.Y.; Chen, J.F.; Tiley, P.J.; Mackintosh, I. and Bennett, F.R. (1995) *Flow Pattern Measurement in Full Scale Silos*, British Materials Handling Board, 230 pp.

Teng, J.G. and Rotter, J.M. (1990) A study of buckling in column-supported cylinders, in *Contact Loading and Local Effects in Thin-Walled Plated and Shell Structures*, eds V. Krupka and M. Drdacky, *Proc., International Union for Theoretical and Applied Mechanics Symposium*, Prague, September, Academia Press, Prague, 1992, pp. 52–61.

Teng, J.G. and Rotter, J.M. (1991) The strength of welded steel silo hoppers under filling and flow pressures, *Journal of Structural Engineering, ASCE*, **117**(9), 2567–2583.

Trahair, N.S.; Abel, A.; Ansourian P.; Irvine, H.M. and Rotter, J.M. (1983) *Structural Design of Metal Bins for Bulk Solids*, Aust. Inst. of Steel Construction.

15

Cylindrical shells: symmetrical solids loadings
J.M. Rotter

15.1 BURSTING FAILURES IN CYLINDERS

The simplest mode of failure is that of bursting, or tensile rupture on a vertical section through the wall. This mode is quite uncommon, and is almost never the controlling design condition for isotropic silo walls. Failures are known where bolted joint connections of inadequate strength have been used, but this is such an elementary design error that it does not merit serious discussion. However, in squat silos with corrugated walls, this becomes a key design condition, and proper design for maximum pressure conditions is vital.

In this context, it should be noted that if the high 'overpressures' predicted by some authors are real, bursting failures should be relatively common, but there is little evidence of them in the field. One possible explanation is that most such silos with corrugated walls are used to store grain which displays pipe funnel flow and causes only minor overpressures.

15.2 BUCKLING OF UNIFORMLY LOADED AND UNIFORMLY SUPPORTED UNSTIFFENED CYLINDERS

15.2.1 General

The cylindrical shell in a symmetrically loaded metal silo is subject to axial compression from the downward frictional drag of the bulk solid on the

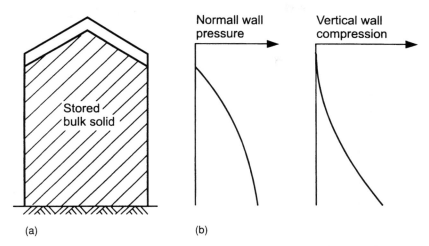

Fig. 15.1 Cylindrical silo with wall loads: (a) on-ground silo; (b) typical pattern of wall forces.

wall (Fig. 15.1). The buckling of unstiffened cylinders under this axial compression is the most common failure mode in metal silos and is generally the controlling design consideration for most parts of the cylinder. The classical elastic buckling stress of a perfect isotropic unstiffened cylinder is given by

$$\sigma_{cl} = \frac{E}{\sqrt{[3(1-v^2)]}} \frac{t}{R} \qquad (15.2.1)$$

in which E is the Young's modulus, v the Poisson's ratio, and R and t are the radius and thickness of the cylinder. The buckling strength of real cylinders in metal silos under axial compression depends on many other factors, including the form and amplitude of initial geometric imperfections, the type of joints, the boundary conditions, the level of internal pressurization and the stiffness of the stored bulk solid. The strengths found in tests on empty axially compressed cylinders are very highly scattered because of these factors (Fig. 15.2). Nevertheless, this classical buckling stress provides a simple reference value which may be used as a good starting point. In the following description, the term 'dimensionless buckling stress' is used to refer to the ratio of the actual buckling stress of a real cylinder to the classical stress given by equation (15.2.1).

348   *Cylindrical shells: symmetrical solids loadings*

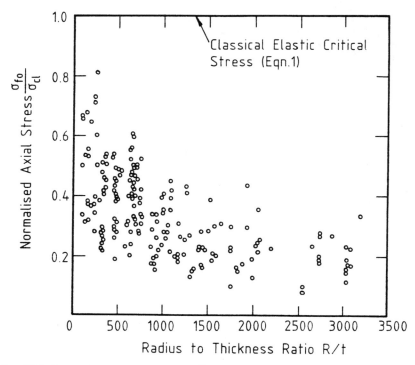

Fig. 15.2 Strength tests on empty axially compressed cylinders are very scattered.

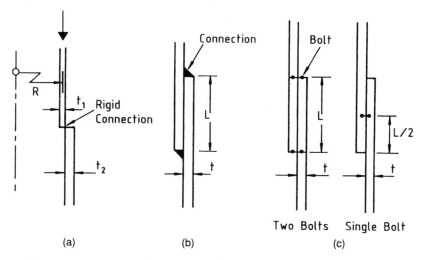

Fig. 15.3 Geometry and idealizations of a lap joint: (a) infinitesimally small; (b) welded; (c) bolted.

15.2.2 Buckling of lap-jointed cylinders

Circumferential lap joints are frequently used in light gauge circular silos. The lap joint causes a local eccentricity in the line of vertical thrust in the shell wall (Fig. 15.3), which induces local bending of the wall (Fig. 15.4) and consequent circumferential stresses as the shell moves inwards and outwards. The vertical and circumferential membrane stresses may combine to produce a buckling failure in the shell wall. Rotter and Teng (1989a) studied this buckling problem and concluded that a perfect long shell containing an infinitesimally short but rigid lap joint (Fig. 15.3(a)) buckles at 0.41 of the classical elastic critical stress of equation (15.2.1), regardless of the shell radius-to-thickness ratio. This is larger than the design strength specified in most design codes and texts (e.g. ECCS, 1988; Trahair *et al.*, 1983; Gaylord and Gaylord, 1984) for thin metal shells. An additional

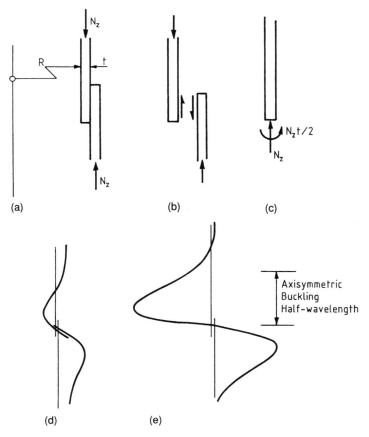

Fig. 15.4 Displacements and circumferential stresses caused by a lap joint: (a) lap joint; (b) load transfer; (c) simple model; (d) deflected shape; (e) circumferential membrane stresses.

350 *Cylindrical shells: symmetrical solids loadings*

axisymmetric dent type imperfection of one wall thickness just above the lap joint reduces the buckling strength only by a further 30%, so the perfect lap-jointed cylinder, allowing for its systematic laps, is not as imperfection-sensitive as a smooth-walled cylinder. Other parameters examined by Rotter and Teng (1989a) included the joint type (bolted or welded) (Figs 15.3(b) and (c)), the thickness of the lower strake, the lap length and the strength gains with internal pressurization. All these complications generally lead to an increase in strength over the idealized joint of Fig. 15.3(a). The message for the designer from this study is that a lap joint alone is not a detail which should cause special concern and that a 30% reduction in the design buckling strength of the cylinder below that of a smooth-walled cylinder is adequate to allow for its effect.

15.2.3 Buckling of cylinders with circumferential welded joints

Large circular metal silos are commonly constructed by joining pre-assembled circular strakes using circumferential welds (Fig. 15.5(a)). At each circumferential welded joint, a roughly axisymmetric depression is caused by plate rolling and weld shrinkage (Fig. 15.5(b)). Full-scale measurements of 10 000 tonne silos (Ding, Coleman and Rotter, 1996a, b) have revealed that these are indeed a common and serious form of practical imperfection. Ummenhofer and Knödel (1996) made similar but simpler measurements which indicated that, although the weld depression was a regular and common imperfection, it did not extend unchanged around the complete circumference. Thus, some allowance must be made for the fact that these imperfections are not completely axisymmetric.

The key feature of geometric imperfections (dents) is that the strength varies strongly with the amplitude of the imperfection (depth of the dent). A dent with an amplitude of a small part of the wall thickness causes a

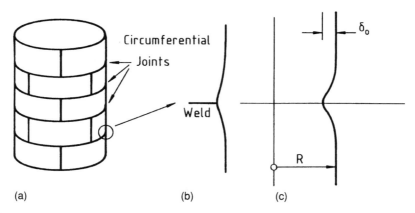

Fig. 15.5 Construction pattern of strakes and resulting circumferential welds with local imperfection: (a) welded silo; (b) detail near joint; (c) modelling.

Buckling of uniform unstiffened cylinders 351

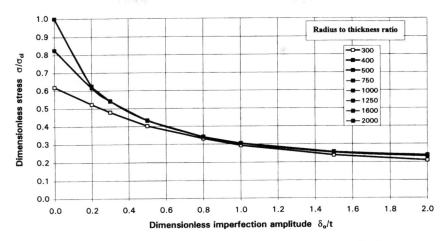

Fig. 15.6 Sensitivity of buckling strength to small geometric imperfections.

dramatic loss of strength, but the strength continues to fall as the dent becomes deeper (Fig. 15.6). When it is very deep, perhaps several times the thickness of the wall, increasing the depth generally no longer causes further strength losses, but this conclusion is sensitive to many aspects of the form of the dent.

In thin cylinders ($R/t > 500$), the buckling response is generally elastic, and the loss of strength depends only on the amplitude of the imperfection relative to the wall thickness t. However, in thicker cylinders where the classical elastic critical stress σ_{cl} is higher, yielding causes additional strength losses, especially for small imperfections (Fig. 15.6). However, most silos have walls thinner than this unless they are subject to unsymmetrical loading, so yielding affects their strength less under uniform unpressurized conditions.

Rotter and Teng (1989b) investigated the buckling of cylinders with idealized geometries for the welded joints, based on two alternative assumptions about the weld cooling process, and shell bending theory. They found the calculated buckling strengths to be comparable with the values given in design standards (based on tests alone) and lower than the strengths of most other imperfection forms which had been explored before with shapes that bear some relation to real structures. The key question here is the value of the 'knock-down factor' α or reduction below the classical elastic critical stress associated with elastic buckling. Different imperfections may be simply compared by examining the knock-down factor α for an imperfection amplitude of one wall thickness (quite common in practice). Amazigo and Budiansky's first study (1972) of a local imperfection had found this knock-down factor α at 0.32. Rotter and Teng (1989b) found values of 0.305 and 0.363 for their two imperfection forms. By changing the imperfection wavelength, this value dropped to 0.301. They extended the study later (Rotter and Teng, 1992) to compare cylinders with three different imperfection forms: an inward weld depression, an outward bulge of the same form and the continuous sinusoidal shape studied by Koiter (1963) and Hutchinson (1965) (Figs 15.7 and 15.8), which had minimum values of 0.30, 0.38 and 0.25 respectively. The latter is not a realistic imperfection form, but is useful as a reference value, since it is generally regarded as the worst shape that can be found. The imperfection sensitivity curves for these three imperfection geometries are shown in Fig. 15.9.

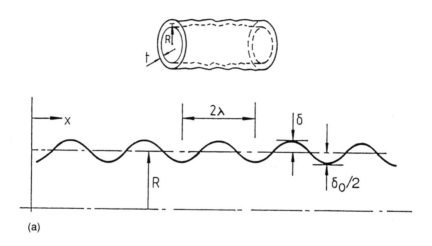

(a)

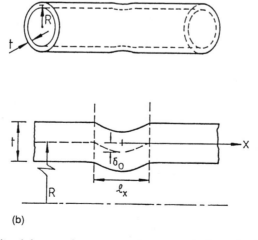

(b)

Fig. 15.7 Idealized forms of axisymmetric geometric imperfections: (a) sinusoidal imperfection on an infinite cylinder; (b) local axisymmetric imperfection.

Buckling of uniform unstiffened cylinders

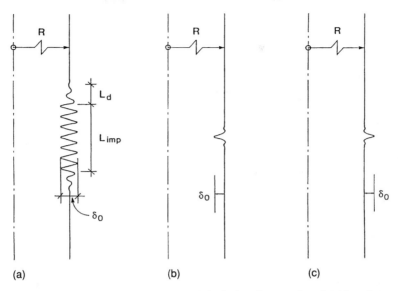

Fig. 15.8 Representations of (a) sinusoidal, (b) local inward and (c) local outward imperfections.

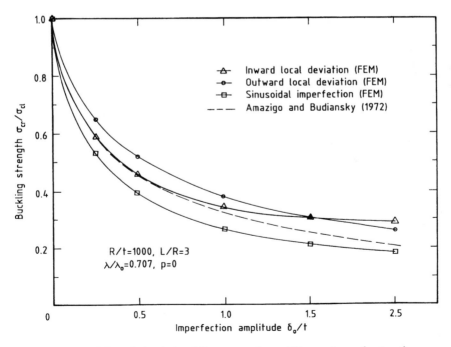

Fig. 15.9 Sensitivity of elastic buckling strength to different imperfection forms.

By examining the effects of imperfections at adjacent circumferential joints in a real structure, Rotter (1996) found that the knock-down factor for a local imperfection could fall further to values as low as $\alpha = 0.25$. Thus, these imperfections lead to calculated strengths which are quite comparable with lower bound design curves drawn from the experimental record.

Knödel, Ummenhofer and Schulz (1995) made similar calculations to the above with a wider variety of imperfection forms but without optimizing to find a weakest imperfection wavelength. Knödel and Ummenhofer (1996) considered the alternative assumptions available for practical numerical modelling of these imperfections and concluded that axisymmetric imperfections are generally to be preferred in design. Berry and Rotter (1996) extended this idea to show that it is not necessary for the imperfection to extend around the entire silo circumference to produce the effect of an axisymmetric imperfection. Instead, a relatively small zone of horizontal weld, with circumferentially invariant imperfection form, has the same effect as if it were completely axisymmetric (Fig. 15.10).

All the above relates to cylinders of uniform thickness. However, because the axial compression in a silo increases progressively with depth, the plate thickness is usually increased at lower levels. Thus, the critical point in a silo design is usually the lowest point in a thin plate where it reaches a joint and is increased in thickness. The first parametric studies of Rotter and

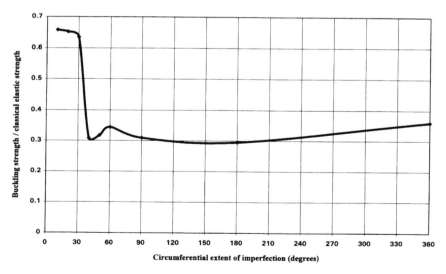

Fig. 15.10 Local inward axisymmetric imperfection with amplitude of one wall thickness: variation of buckling strength with the circumferential extent of the imperfection.

Teng (1989a, b), showed that the shell is much stronger where a plate thickness change occurs. When the strake thickness step change is large, the buckling strength of the thinner plate above the change is markedly increased. All current design rules ignore this strength enhancement.

15.2.4 Cylinders with circumferential welded joints and internal pressure

Internal pressure is almost always present in a silo cylinder wherever axial compression buckling is a problem, because the axial compression principally arises from the internal pressure. Internal pressure in a cylinder causes substantial increases in the buckling strength under axial compression (Weingarten et al., 1965a, b) (Fig. 15.11). Hutchinson (1965) developed an asymptotic theory to study the phenomenon, and found that the gain in strength depended on the form of the geometric imperfections which had led to the strength reduction in an unpressurized cylinder. Notably, the strength-reducing effect of non-symmetric imperfections in the cylinder was rapidly eliminated by internal pressure (Fig. 15.12), but an axisymmetric imperfection experienced much lower gains in strength. This fact is particularly important if laboratory experimental studies are used to define rules for standards: most laboratory models are manufactured in a manner which leads to unsymmetric imperfections, but real silos often have axisymmetric imperfections. Thus the laboratory test data base is a poor basis for rules in standards.

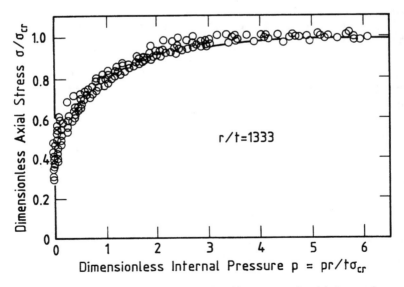

Fig. 15.11 Test results for the increase in buckling strength with internal pressure (after Weingarten et al., 1965b).

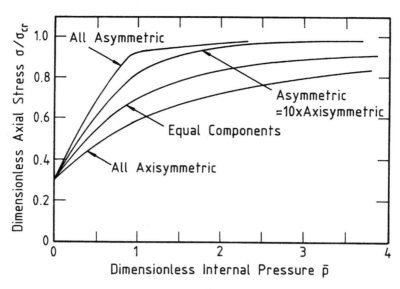

Fig. 15.12 Theoretically predicted strength gains with internal pressure for symmetric and non-symmetric imperfections (after Hutchinson, 1965).

Rotter and Teng (1989b, 1992) compared the theoretical strength gains due to internal pressure with the predictions of the ECCS code (1988), together with the approximate theory for sinusoidal imperfections developed by Hutchinson (1965). A sample is shown in Fig. 15.13, where the imperfection amplitude of each form has been adjusted to give the same strength under unpressurized conditions (i.e. a small sinusoidal imperfection, a moderate local inward deviation and a larger outward deviation). These comparisons suggest that the current ECCS rule may be slightly unsafe, but that sinusoidal and outward imperfections give much lower strength gains.

Thus this study confirmed Koiter's (1963) conclusion that the sinusoidal imperfection leads to the lowest buckling strength in an empty cylinder and that it also produces the lowest strength gains due to internal pressure (Fig. 15.13). However, as noted above, the sinusoidal imperfection is, however, not practically credible.

Even for the more practical local inward deviation, however, the strength gains predicted by the ECCS code (1988) rule are unconservative (Fig. 15.13). Furthermore, for cylinders with multiple close inward local deviations caused by adjacent circumferential welds between panels, the strength gains may be reduced further by interaction between the adjacent local inward deviations (Rotter, 1996). Thus the current ECCS rule should be applied with some caution.

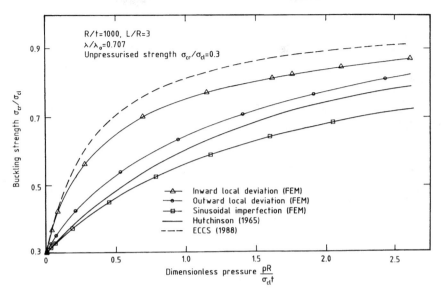

Fig. 15.13 Effect of axisymmetric imperfection form on internal pressure strength gains.

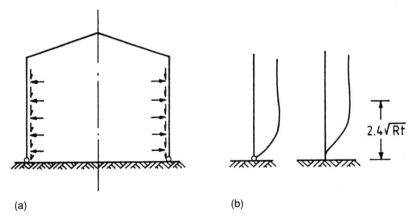

Fig. 15.14 'Elephant's foot' plastic instability near a boundary condition: (a) typical tank or silo; (b) deformed shapes very close to base.

When the internal pressure is very large, local plastic collapse can occur. This was first studied by Rotter (1990) as a collapse at a pinned or fixed base boundary condition (Fig. 15.14), known as 'elephant's foot' failure. He showed that the strengths of this elastic–plastic collapse mode were much lower than the von Mises envelope for the silo wall, and that formal account should be taken of them (Figs 15.15 and 15.16). In later studies (Rotter,

358   *Cylindrical shells: symmetrical solids loadings*

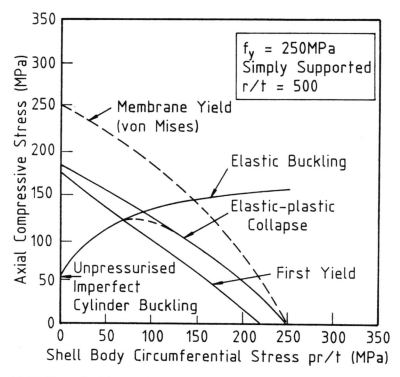

Fig. 15.15 Elastic buckling and plastic collapse strengths for compressed pressurized cylinders.

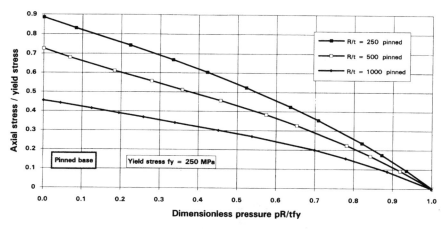

Fig. 15.16 Axisymmetric plastic collapse strengths (elephant's foot) for different shell thicknesses.

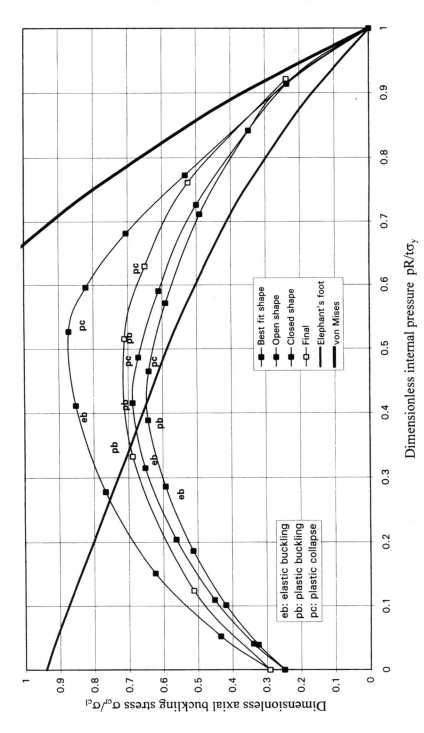

Fig. 15.17 Elastic buckling, plastic buckling and local plastic collapse strengths near an axisymmetric weld depression.

1988, 1996), the local plastic collapse strength at a local weld depression was also examined, using a variety of different imperfect geometries (Fig. 15.17). Provision for this local plastic buckling failure mode is missing from current standards.

15.2.5 Buckling of cylinders containing granular bulk solids

The finite stiffness of the stored bulk solid also increases the buckling strength. Its presence adjacent to an imperfection at which buckling may occur (Fig. 15.18) can evidently increase the cylinder's strength. This has long been recognized (Wozniak, 1979), but the first attempt to quantify it appears to have been that of Ansourian and Rotter (1981) based on the theoretical work of Seide (1962). However, no design recommendations could be drawn from these investigations.

A much more thorough and usable study was later performed by Rotter and Zhang (1990), who modelled the bulk solid as an elastic Winkler foundation in a shell buckling analysis. The bulk solid stiffness increases the buckling strength significantly, localizing the buckling deformations in a similar manner to that of internal pressure (Fig. 15.19). They also devised simple equations to relate the elastic foundation stiffness to the bulk solid properties, the critical buckling mode and the bulk solid stress level, which permit adoption into a design method (Fig. 15.20). Experiments (Rotter *et al.*, 1980; Bucklin, Ross and White, 1983; Knödel and Schulz, 1988; Zhang and Ansourian, 1991) have qualitatively confirmed the strengthening role of

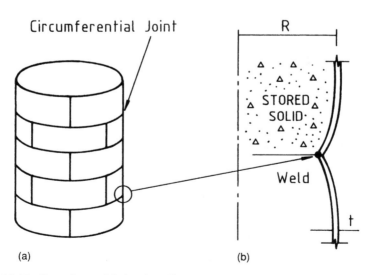

Fig. 15.18 Granular solid in the silo near an axisymmetric weld depression: (a) welded silo; (b) detail near joint.

Buckling of uniform unstiffened cylinders

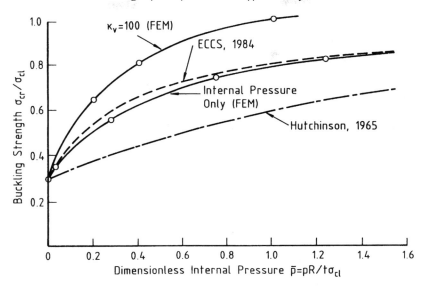

Fig. 15.19 Increases in buckling strength with internal pressure, and internal pressure in the presence of a stiff solid.

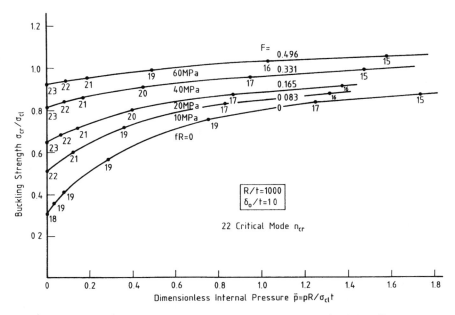

Fig. 15.20 Buckling strength predictions for a wide range of solid stiffnesses.

362 Cylindrical shells: symmetrical solids loadings

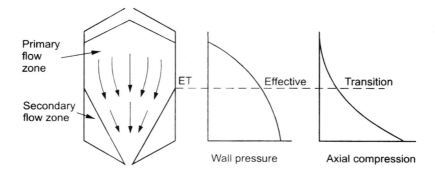

Fig. 15.21 Solids can be depended on to provide stiff restraint against buckling at points below the effective transition.

the stored bulk solid. Experiments on this phenomenon remain difficult because control of both the geometric imperfections and the stored solid stiffness is difficult at a laboratory scale.

However, quantification of the effect still depends on a good means of determining the effective modulus of a solid whose stiffness depends on the local stress state in it, and uncertainty remains on whether the stiffness can be relied on when the solid may move. However, design of a silo wall below the effective transition (Fig. 15.21) should be able to exploit this phenomenon, provided the location of the effective transition itself can be reliably predicted.

15.3 CIRCUMFERENTIALLY CORRUGATED CYLINDERS

15.3.1 Equivalent properties

Light gauge metal silos are often built from standard corrugated metal sheets with the corrugations running around the circumference. Elastic corrugated shells are often analysed as orthotropic shells with approximate equivalent orthotropic properties. The chief purpose of such analyses is to establish the buckling strength under wind loading, which depends on the bending, stretching, shearing and twisting stiffnesses, so many different properties must be defined. Several proposals for calculating these equivalent orthotropic properties are available, the best known being those of Abdel-Sayed (1970), Trahair *et al.* (1983) and Briassoulis (1986). The effect of the circumferential curvature of the cylinder was ignored in the development of all these relations, and their accuracy for use for corrugated cylinders was not established. Zhang and Rotter (1988) investigated the accuracy of these three proposals by modelling the corrugated cylinder rigorously as a doubly curved isotropic shell using finite element analysis. They found that the relations given by Abdel-Sayed appear to give the best predictions of the equivalent orthotropic properties for all terms except the axial meridional stiffness. For this term the relation of Trahair *et al.* (1983) is recommended. The circumferential curvature of the cylinder was found to affect some of the equivalent orthotropic properties significantly.

15.3.2 Plastic collapse

The corrugation under combined axial load and internal pressure may fail locally by plastic collapse of a single corrugation (Fig. 15.22). This failure mode is termed 'roll-down', 'recorrugation' or 'crushing'. In the analytical study by Rotter *et al.* (1987), two simple failure criteria were proposed, relating to meridional bending plastic collapse (Fig. 15.23) and biaxial membrane yielding failure. Each led to a simple equation for collapse strength. Comparisons with accurate finite element calculations showed that each of the two equations provides a close approximation to the rigorous axisymmetric collapse load for a particular range of corrugation geometries.

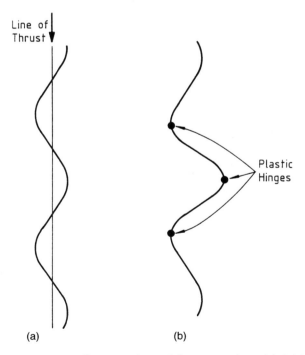

Fig. 15.22 Corrugation collapse under axial compression: (a) initial geometry; (b) collapse mechanism.

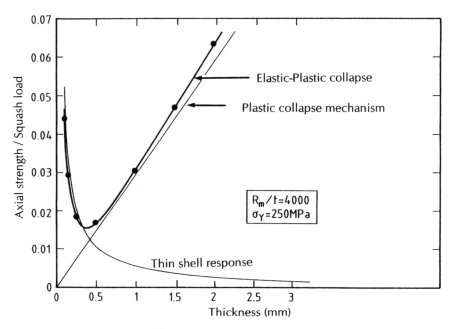

Fig. 15.23 Comparison of finite element calculations with simple plastic collapse and membrane yielding theories for corrugated walls.

REFERENCES

Abdel-Sayed, G. (1970) Critical shear loading of curved panels of corrugated sheets, *J. Engrg Mech. Div., ASCE*, **96**(EM6), Dec., 895–912.

Amazigo, J.C. and Budiansky, B. (1972) Asymptotic formulas for the buckling stresses of axially compressed cylinders with localised or random axisymmetric imperfections, *Journal Applied Mechanics, Transactions of the American Society of Mechanical Engineers*, E-39, 179–184.

Ansourian, P. and Rotter, J.M. (1981) Buckling: vertical load, in *Structural Aspects of Metal Silos and Tanks*, School of Civil and Mining Engineering, University of Sydney, Aug., pp. 10.1–10.24.

Berry, P.A. and Rotter, J.M. (1996) Partial axisymmetric imperfections and their effect on the buckling strength of axially compressed cylinders, *Proc. International Workshop on Imperfections in Metal Silos: Measurement, Characterisation and Strength Analysis*, CA-Silo, Lyon, France, 19 April, pp. 35–48.

Briassoulis, D. (1986) Equivalent orthotropic properties of corrugated sheets, *Computers and Structures*, **23**(2), 129–138.

Bucklin, R.A.; Ross, I.J. and White, G.M. (1983) The influence of grain pressure on the buckling loads of thin-walled bins, 1983 Summer Meeting, American Society of Agricultural Engineers, Paper No. 83-4005, Bozeman, Montana, June.

Ding, X.L.; Coleman, R.D. and Rotter, J.M. (1996a) Surface profiling system for measurement of engineering structures, *Journal of Surveying Engineering, ASCE*, **122**(1), Feb., 3–13.

Ding, X.L.; Coleman, R.D. and Rotter, J.M. (1996b) Technique for precise measurement of large-scale silos and tanks, *Journal of Surveying Engineering, ASCE*, **122**(1), Feb., 14–25.
ECCS (1988) *European Recommendations for Steel Construction: Buckling of Shells*, 4th edn, European Convention for Constructional Steelwork, Brussels.
Gaylord, E.H. and Gaylord, C.N. (1984) *Design of Steel Bins for Storage of Bulk Solids*, Prentice-Hall, New Jersey.
Hutchinson, J.W. (1965) Axial buckling of pressurised imperfect cylindrical shells, *AIAA J.*, **3**, 1461–1466.
Knödel, P. and Schulz, U. (1988) Buckling of silo bins by granular solids, *Proc. International Conference: 'Silos – Forschung und Praxis'*, University of Karlsruhe, October, pp. 287–302.
Knödel, P. and Ummenhofer, T. (1996) Substitute imperfections for the prediction of buckling loads in shell design, *Proc. Intl Workshop on Imperfections in Metal Silos: Measurement, Characterisation and Strength Analysis*, CA-Silo, Lyon, France, 19 April, pp. 87–102.
Knödel, P.; Ummenhofer, T. and Schulz, U. (1995) On the modelling of different types of imperfections in silo shells. *Thin-Walled Structures*, **23**, 283–293.
Koiter, W.T. (1963) *The Effect of Axisymmetric Imperfections on the Buckling of Cylindrical Shells under Axial Compression*, Koninklike Nederlandische Akademie van Wetenshappen, Proc. Ser. B66, pp. 265–279.
Rotter, J.M. (1987) The buckling and plastic collapse of ring stiffeners at cone/cylinder junctions, *Proc. Int. Colloq. on Stability of Plate and Shell Struct.*, Ghent, April, pp. 449–456.
Rotter, J.M. (1988) Calculated buckling strengths for the cylindrical wall of 10 000 tonne silos at Port Kembla, Investigation Report S663, School of Civil and Mining Engineering, University of Sydney, June.
Rotter, J.M. (1990) Local inelastic collapse of pressurised thin cylindrical steel shells under axial compression, *Journal of Structural Engineering, ASCE*, **116**(7), 1955–1970.
Rotter, J.M. (1996) Elastic plastic buckling and collapse in internally pressurised axially compressed silo cylinders with measured axisymmetric imperfections: interactions between imperfections, residual stresses and collapse, *Proc. International Workshop on Imperfections in Metal Silos: Measurement, Characterisation and Strength Analysis*, CA-Silo, Lyon, France, 19 April, pp. 119–140.
Rotter, J.M. and Teng, J.G. (1989a) Elastic stability of lap-jointed cylinders, *J. Struct. Engrg, ASCE*, **115**(3), 683–697.
Rotter, J.M. and Teng. J.G. (1989b) Elastic stability of cylindrical shells with weld depressions, *J. Struct. Engrg, ASCE*, **115**(5), 1244–1263.
Rotter, J.M. and Teng. J.-G. (1992) Buckling of pressurised axisymmetrically imperfect cylinders under axial loads, *Journal of Engineering Mechanics*, **118**(2), 229–247.
Rotter, J.M.; Trahair, N.S. and Ansourian, P. (1980) Stability of plate structures, *Proceedings, Symposium on Metal Bins for the Storage of Bulk Solids*, Australian Institute of Metal Construction/Australian Welding Research Association Joint Symposium, Sydney and Melbourne, Sept., pp. 36–40.
Rotter, J.M. and Zhang, Q. (1990) Elastic buckling of imperfect cylinders containing granular solids, *J. Struct. Engrg, ASCE*, **116**(8), 2253–2271.

Rotter, J.M., Zhang, Q. and Teng, J.G. (1987) Corrugation collapse in circumferentially corrugated steel cylinders, *First National Structural Engineering Conference*, Institution of Engineers, Melbourne, Australia, 26–28 August, 377 pp.

Seide, P. (1962) The stability under axial compression and lateral pressure of circular-cylindrical shells with a soft elastic core, *J. Aerospace Sci.*, **29**(7), 851–862.

Trahair, N.S.; Abel, A.; Ansourian, P.; Irvine, H.M. and Rotter, J.M. (1983) *Structural Design of Metal Bins for Bulk Solids*, Aust. Inst. of Steel Construction.

Ummenhofer, T. and Knödel, P. (1996) Typical imperfections of steel silo shells in civil engineering, *Proc. Intl Workshop on Imperfections in Metal Silos: Measurement, Characterisation and Strength Analysis*, CA-Silo, Lyon, France, 19 April, pp. 103–118.

Weingarten, V.I.; Morgan, E.J. and Seide, P. (1965a) Elastic stability of thin-walled cylindrical and conical shells under axial compression, *AIAA Jnl*, **3**(3), 500–505.

Weingarten, V.I.; Morgan, E.J. and Seide, P. (1965b) Elastic stability of thin-walled cylindrical and conical shells under combined internal pressure and axial compression, *AIAA Jnl*, **3**(6), 1118–1125.

Wozniak, R.S. (1979) Steel tanks, *Structural Engineering Handbook*, 2nd edn, Section 23, eds E.H. and C.N. Gaylord, McGraw-Hill.

Zhang, Q. and Ansourian, P. (1991) Stability of silo wall stiffened by particulate solids, *Civil Engrg Trans, IE Aust*, **CE33**(2), 137–141.

Zhang, Q. and Rotter, J.M. (1988) Equivalent orthotropic properties of cylindrical corrugated shells, *Proc., 11th Australasian Conf. on Mech. of Struct. and Matls*, Auckland, New Zealand, Aug., pp. 417–422.

16

Cylindrical shells: unsymmetrical solids loadings and supports
J.M. Rotter

16.1 LOCAL FORCES FROM BRACKETS AND COLUMN SUPPORTS

It has already been noted (section 14.7) that where an elevated silo is supported on columns or other methods are used which introduce concentrated forces into the shell, the stress pattern disperses from very high stresses in a small zone to much smaller stresses over a wider region. The patterns of stress depend significantly on the placement of ring stiffeners on the shell wall.

If the shell support is to be designed as a ring beam, an introductory treatment is given by Trahair et al. (1983). A considerable amount of further useful information is given by Rotter (1986). This treatment is rather more complicated, but is very useful to the serious designer. In particular, a test is given to check whether the traditional supporting ring beam model will be suitable for the planned structure. A similar model was earlier devised by Greiner (1984), and published in German.

Where a lighter form of construction is being undertaken, the traditional supporting ring beam is unnecessarily expensive. Small zones of the shell at the top and bottom of the shell wall will perform the role of rings, and the stresses in these may be estimated from information given elsewhere (Rotter, 1985b). The more serious concern is that of local buckling of the shell wall adjacent to the column.

The simplest means of support for a light silo is by the use of engaged columns (Fig. 12.3(d)). It is desirable that the middle surface of the shell should be directly above the centroid of the column cross-section, to minimize the bending effects arising from eccentricities of support. Transfer of forces from the column to the shell wall is by shear. The distribution of

368 *Cylindrical shells: unsymmetrical solids loadings*

shears is not uniform within the engagement length, so it is desirable to increase the capacity of the fillet welds by 50% above the requirements for uniform stress transfer.

In the shell wall above the column engagement length, an axial compression buckle may occur (failures of this type have been recorded). Studies leading towards a rational hand method of design are in progress at the present time, but a simple rule has been widely used in the past (Fig. 16.1). The total force in the column is assumed to disperse into the shell plating in a zone defined by a 30° slope to the vertical. Within this zone the support force is deemed to lead to a uniform stress.

The critical location is just above the column termination, and the calculated stress at this point is normally compared with the buckling strength under uniform axial compression. The dispersion is assumed to continue up the shell wall at the same angle, allowing a progressive reduction in shell thickness until the inclined lines from adjacent columns intersect. Current evidence suggests that the method may be a little conservative,

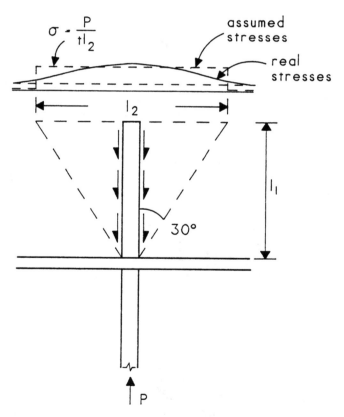

Fig. 16.1 Simple treatment of stresses from engaged columns in small silos.

Local buckling of cylinders above discrete supports

but the problem is probably too complicated for a quality rational method to be found quickly.

Where a finite element analysis is used to determine the stress distribution, care should be exercised to ensure that an adequate mesh refinement is chosen near the column, since very rapid stress gradients occur here. The axial stresses decline smoothly away from the support, and special techniques are required if the buckling strength is to be assessed using hand calculation and stresses taken from finite element calculations.

16.2 LOCAL BUCKLING OF CYLINDERS ABOVE DISCRETE SUPPORTS

Studies of the buckling behaviour of cylinders in column-supported metal silos and tanks are relatively recent. The first known studies (Teng and Rotter, 1990, 1991a,b, 1992; Guggenberger, 1991a,b) were of the linear bifurcation and nonlinear buckling behaviour of isolated perfect and imperfect cylinders directly supported on columns (Figs 12.3(b) and 16.2). This work forms a first step towards understanding the complicated buckling problem of practical column-supported metal silos. The buckling strength is

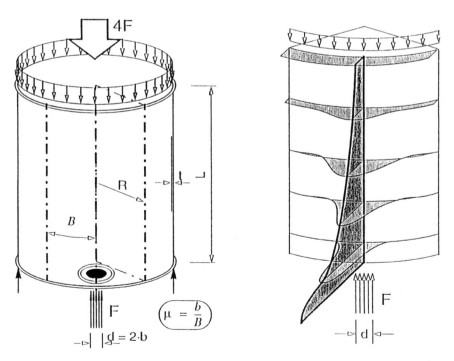

Fig. 16.2 Cylinder supported on several discrete supports: idealization. (After Greiner and Guggenberger, 1996)

370   *Cylindrical shells: unsymmetrical solids loadings*

most effectively described in terms of the dimensionless mean membrane stress above each column (the mean stress above the column divided by the classical elastic stress for a uniformly compressed cylinder (equation (15.2.1), section 15.2.1). This dimensionless stress at bifurcation takes values slightly above unity for perfect cylinders and of the order of 0.5 for imperfect cylinders, depending on many factors.

The linear bifurcation of perfect cylinders was studied by Teng and Rotter (1991a, 1992) and cylinders with an axisymmetric weld imperfection by Teng and Rotter (1990, 1991b, 1992). The studies of Guggenberger (1991a,b) used chiefly materially and geometrically nonlinear analysis to perform studies of a range of different geometrical arrangements. All these studies show that the dimensionless mean buckling stress is almost independent of the number of columns and the shell height, because the buckling deformations are quite localized above the column (Fig. 16.3). The reduction in strength caused by an imperfection of one wall thickness is found to be as great as 40% for a typical cylinder on a small number of columns. This demonstrates that a column-supported cylinder is very imperfection-sensitive, though less so than a uniformly compressed cylinder. A design rule proposal was made jointly by the two research groups (Rotter *et al.*, 1993) and a more complete one later (Guggenberger, 1996).

However, the studies described above differ in the assumed imperfections, the boundary condition above the support, the boundary condition at

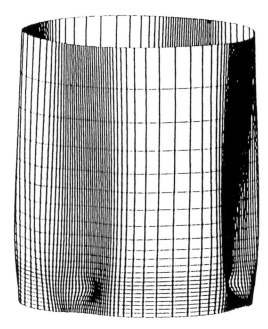

Fig. 16.3 Buckling mode in a discretely supported cylinder ($n = 4$, $R/t = 350$, $d/R = 0.20$, $R = 100$ mm, $H/R = 2$).

Local buckling of cylinders above discrete supports

the upper edge of the cylinder and a number of other features which lead to different strength determinations. One example of such a difference is the stress distribution above the support, which depends on whether the support is treated as flexible or rigid (Fig. 16.4). Since the buckle forms in a zone of rapidly changing stress and is influenced by both the stress distribution and restraint from the support, considerable differences can be found when quite small changes are made to the assumed conditions. Thus much further discussion is needed to decide on a final recommendation for a design rule.

Theoretical studies of the strengthening effect of internal pressure on buckling above a support were undertaken by Li (1994) and Greiner and Guggenberger (1996). These indicate that the same strengthening effects as are noted for uniformly compressed cylinders may also be expected, but naturally the gains are different and must be represented in a different manner.

Experiments were recently conducted on locally supported cylinders by Dhanens *et al.* (1993). Whilst a good match with these has been produced in finite element calculations (Greiner and Guggenberger, 1996), the steel used and the special conditions of the test make them unsuitable for immediate transfer into a design rule. Thus, development of design rules will probably come from more extensive finite element calculations. The dimensionless mean buckling stress above the support depends on many parameters, including the radius to thickness ratio, the support width, the height of the first strake of cylinder, the far end boundary conditions, and

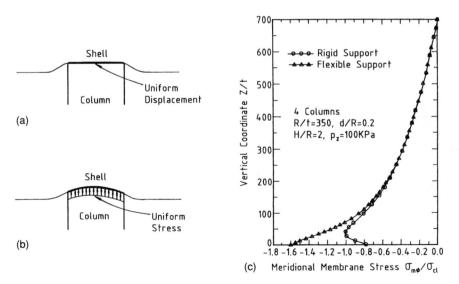

Fig. 16.4 Differences caused by treating the support as rigid or flexible: (a) rigid column support; (b) flexible column support; (c) meridional membrane stress above column centre line.

372 *Cylindrical shells: unsymmetrical solids loadings*

the boundary conditions at the support. This problem remains one which is being very actively researched.

16.3 BUCKLING OF UNSYMMETRICALLY LOADED CYLINDERS: PATCH LOADS

Silos subject to unsymmetrical pressures or patch loads can develop very high axial compressive stresses in limited parts of the wall. In particular, the high stresses do not extend around the silo circumference and may be

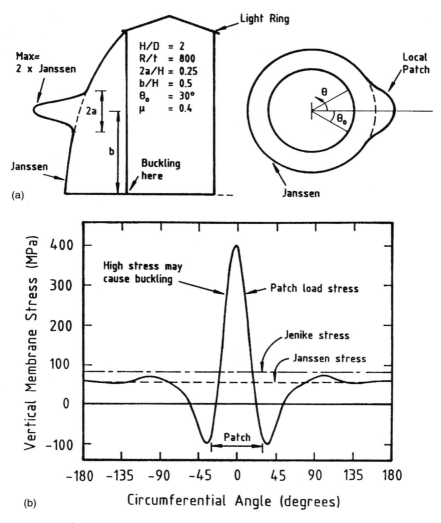

Fig. 16.5 A local patch load on a metal silo induces high axial stresses far from the load: (a) example silo; (b) vertical wall stresses near silo base.

limited to a small area (Fig. 16.5). If the design limits these stresses to values which are acceptable for uniform axial compression, very thick silo walls and uneconomic designs result.

Very little is known about buckling strengths in limited areas of axial compression, though the problem has been identified on several occasions (e.g. Öry and Reimerdes, 1987; Samuelson, 1987; Eggwertz and Samuelson, 1991). The best design advice currently available appears to be that of Rotter (1986). Much further work is needed on this topic, especially as the DIN and ISO codes for silo loads and the proposed draft Eurocode all specify a local patch load in all designs.

A research project into the effects of patch loads on metal silos was undertaken under the auspices of CA-Silo (Rotter, 1996b; Guggenberger et al., 1996; Brown, 1996), which explored the stress patterns in, and strength of, circular metal silos with unstiffened and stiffened walls, and of rectangular silos. A large body of new information was obtained, but the complexity of the problem and the wide variety of potential geometries mean that these studies are in their infancy.

16.4 BUCKLING OF UNSYMMETRICALLY LOADED CYLINDERS: ECCENTRIC DISCHARGE

Non-symmetrical or eccentric discharge is probably the most complex and least understood pattern of loading in silos. The pattern of material flow in the silo (Fig. 14.4) has a strong influence on the resulting pressures, and consequently on the resulting wall stress distributions.

Under some circumstances, an eccentric funnel flow zone develops in the stored material, adjacent to the wall (Fig. 16.6). The pressures in the flowing zone are usually small (Fig. 16.7), whilst those in the adjacent static material are often much higher (Jenike, 1967; Rotter, 1986; Chen et al., 1996). This non-uniformity of pressure distribution leads to a complex stress distribution, which may be characterized by the dominant effects: circumferential bending and axial compression (Fig. 16.8). Both of these stresses vary quite rapidly around the circumference (Rotter, 1986). A reasonable means of estimating the pressures in the static and flowing zones of the stored solid was given by Rotter (1986).

An experimental study of the problem was presented by Rotter et al. (1989), which showed that there is a critical height from which it is possible to eccentrically discharge a thin-walled silo without buckling failure, but as the initial filling level rose above this point, the failures become more and more dramatic and catastrophic.

An alternative pattern of speculated pressures due to eccentric discharge is given in the Australian Guidelines (Gorenc, Hogan and Rotter, 1986) and adopted with modifications into the Australian Standard (AS 3774, 1996). The latter is based on currently available (rather limited) experimental evidence rather than an attempt at rational analysis.

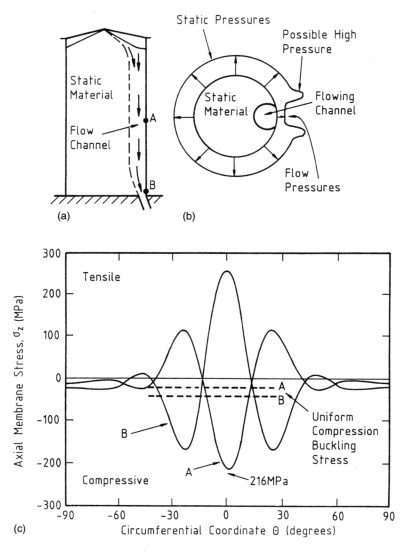

Fig. 16.6 Eccentric funnel flow in the stored material adjacent to the wall: (a) elevation; (b) cross-section; (c) variation of axial membrane stress.

Failures generally occur by buckling under axial compression, though circumferential snap-through buckling may also occur. It is therefore very desirable that a shell analysis should be performed on the structure to determine the stress distribution. Little work has been done to date on determining the buckling strengths of shells under localized elevated stresses, such as occur in this case, and the only suitable criterion of failure currently available appears to be that proposed by Rotter (1986).

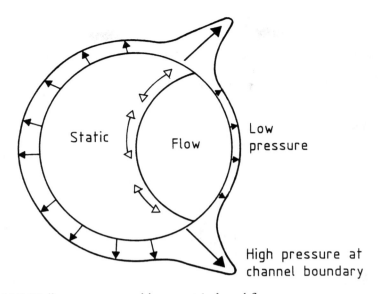

Fig. 16.7 Wall pressures caused by eccentric funnel flow.

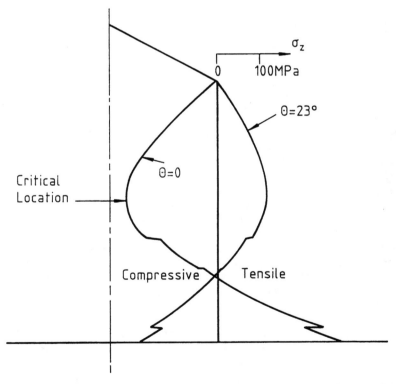

Fig. 16.8 Axial compression stress distributions in the silo wall caused by eccentric funnel flow.

An analysis of the problem which treats the silo shell as a simple ring is quite inadequate for predicting the failure modes (Jumikis et al., 1986; Rotter et al., 1989) or for predicting the buckling strengths of steel silos.

REFERENCES

AS 3774-1996 (1996) *Loads on Bulk Solids Containers*, Australian Standard, Standards Association of Australia, Sydney, October.

Brown, C.J. (1996) *Effect of Patch Loads on Rectangular Metal Silos* and Annex, Department of Mechanical Engineering, Brunel University, Uxbridge, UK, 300 pp.

Chen, J.F.; Tiley, P.J.; Ooi, J.Y. and Rotter, J.M. (1996) Flow patterns and pressures in an iron ore silo, *Proc., 12th International Congress of Chemical and Process Engineering, CHISA '96*, Prague, August, 12 pp.

Dhanens, F.; Lagae, G.; Rathe, J. and van Impe, R. (1993) Stresses in and buckling of unstiffened cylinders subjected to local axial loads. *J. Constr. Steel Res.*, 27, 89–106.

Eggwertz, S. and Samuelson, L.A. (1991) Buckling of shells with local reinforcements, in Jullien, J.F. (ed.), *Buckling of Shell Structures on Land, in the Sea and in the Air*. Elsevier, London, pp. 401–408.

Gorenc, B.E.; Hogan, T.J. and Rotter, J.M. (eds) (1986) *Guidelines for the Assessment of Loads on Bulk Solids Containers*, Institution of Engineers, Australia.

Greiner, R. (1984) Zur Laengskrafteinleitung in stehende zylindrische Behaelter aus Stahl, *Stahlbau*, 53(7), 210–215.

Greiner, R. and Guggenberger, W. (1996) Buckling behaviour of axially loaded cylinders on local supports – with and without internal pressure, *Proc., International Conference on Structural Steelwork*, Hong Kong, December, pp. 741–746.

Guggenberger, W. (1991a) Nichtlineares Beulverhalten von Kreiszylinderschalen unter lokaler Axialbelastung, PhD Thesis, TU Graz, Austria.

Guggenberger, W. (1991b) Buckling of cylindrical shells under local axial loads, *International Colloquium on Buckling of Shell Structures on Land, in the Sea and in the Air*, Villeurbanne, Lyon, France, 17–19 Sept., pp. 323–333.

Guggenberger, W. (1996) Proposal for design rules of axially loaded steel cylinders on local supports, *Proc., International Conference on Structural Steelwork*, Hong Kong, December, pp. 1225–1230.

Guggenberger, W.; Wallner, S. and Greiner, R. (1996) *Influence of Stiffeners on Stresses and Strength of the Silo Shell Caused by Patch Loads*, Research report, Institut für Stahlbau, TU Graz, Austria.

Jenike, A.W. (1967) Denting of circular bins with eccentric drawpoints, *Jnl Struct. Div., ASCE*, 93(ST1), 27–35.

Jumikis, P.T.; Rotter, J.M.; Fleming, S.P. and Porter, S.J. (1986) Experiments on the buckling of thin-walled model silo structures, *Proc. Second International Conference on Bulk Materials Storage Handling and Transportation*, Institution of Engineers, Australia, Wollongong, July, pp. 180–186.

Li, H.Y. (1994) Analysis of steel silo structures on discrete supports, PhD thesis, Department of Civil and Environmenral Engineering, University of Edinburgh, 233 pp.

Öry, H. and Reimerdes, H.G. (1987) Stresses in and stability of thin walled shells under non-ideal load distribution, *Proc. Int. Colloquium on the Stability of Plate and Shell Structures*, Gent, Belgium, 6–8 April, ECCS, pp. 555–561.

Rotter, J.M. (1985a) Membrane theory of shells for bins and silos, in *Design of Steel Bins for the Storage of Bulk Solids*, edited by J.M. Rotter, University of Sydney, March, pp. 58–70.

Rotter, J.M. (1985b) Analysis and design of ringbeams, in *Design of Steel Bins for the Storage of Bulk Solids*, edited by J.M. Rotter, Univ. Sydney, March, pp. 164–183.

Rotter, J.M. (1986) Recent studies on the stability of light gauge steel silo structures, *Proc., 8th International Specialty Conference on Cold-formed Steel Structures*, St Louis, Missouri, Nov., pp. 543–562.

Rotter, J.M. (1993) The design of circular metal silos for strength, *Proc., International Symposium: Reliable Flow of Particulate Solids II*, EFChE Publication Series No. 96, Oslo, 23–24 August, pp. 217–234.

Rotter, J.M. (1996a) Elastic plastic buckling and collapse in internally pressurised axially compressed silo cylinders with measured axisymmetric imperfections; interactions between imperfections, residual stresses and collapse, *Proc. International Workshop on Imperfections in Metal Silos: Measurement, Characterisation and Strength Analysis*, CA-Silo, Lyon, France, 19 April, pp. 119–140.

Rotter, J.M. (1996b) Patch load effects in unstiffened steel silos, *Proc CA-Silo Project on the Effect of Patch Loads on Metal Silos*, CA-Silo, Edinburgh, pp. 5–195.

Rotter, J.M.; Greiner, R.; Guggenberger, W.; Li, H.Y. and She, K.M. (1993) Proposed design rule for buckling strength assessment of cylindrical shells under local axial loads, submission to ECCS TWG8.4, Buckling of Shells, September.

Rotter, J.M.; Jumikis, P.T.; Fleming, S.P. and Porter, S.J. (1989) Experiments on the buckling of thin-walled model silo structures, *Journal of Constructional Steel Research*, 13(4), 271–299.

Samuelson, L.A. (1987) Design of cylindrical shells subjected to local loads in combination with axial or radial pressure, *Proc. Int. Colloquium on the Stability of Plate and Shell Structures*, Gent, Belgium, 6–8 April, ECCS, pp. 589–596.

Teng, J.G. and Rotter, J.M. (1990) A study of buckling in column-supported cylinders, *Contact Loading and Local Effects in Thin-Walled Plated and Shell Structures, Proc. of an IUTAM Symposium*, Springer.

Teng, J.G. and Rotter, J.M. (1991a) *Linear Bifurcation of Perfect Cylinders on Column Supports*, Res. Rept No. 91.01, Dept Civ. Engrg and Bldg Sci., Univ. of Edinburgh.

Teng, J.G. and Rotter, J.M. (1991b) *Linear Bifurcation of Column-Supported Imperfect Cylinders*, Res. Rept No. 91.03, Dept of Civ. Engrg and Bldg Sci., Univ. of Edinburgh.

Teng, J.G. and Rotter, J.M. (1992) Linear bifurcation of column-supported perfect cylinders: support modelling and boundary conditions, *Thin-Walled Struct.*, 14(3), 241–263.

Trahair, N.S.; Abel, A.; Ansourian, P. Irvine, H.M. and Rotter, J.M. (1983) *Structural Design of Steel Bins for Bulk Solids*, Australian Institute of Steel Construction, Nov.

17

Cylindrical shells: wind loading
R. Greiner

17.1 WIND LOADING PRESSURES WHEN THE SILO IS EMPTY

When the silo is empty, external pressures induce small circumferential (or hoop) compressions in the cylindrical wall. These stresses are very small, but because the wall may be only slightly curved (R/t is large), the wall is susceptible to a buckling failure in this condition. Advice on the wind pressures to be expected in different regions and different terrain is best obtained from the local (national) wind loading code.

The variation of pressure around the circumference may be of importance in design against wind. In particular, the vertical forces in the wall do not follow the pattern which is expected from engineering bending theory (linear variation across the diameter). Instead, the front half of the silo generally carries almost the whole of the horizontal force from the wind, and the maximum vertical compressive force in the wall develops at about 70° from the windward direction. Both the maximum compressive and the maximum tensile forces are affected by this load-carrying pattern. This is an important factor in the design of holding-down bolts and wind stiffening rings.

The wind pressure variation around an isolated silo depends on a number of parameters, which highly affect the ratio of pressure and suction components to the circumference:

- the Reynolds number of the wind flow
- the surface roughness of the wall
- the aspect ratio of the cylinder (height, diameter) (Refs A, B, C)
- the position of the cylinder relative to the ground level
- the approaching terrain conditions (Ref. D)

- the shape of the roof (flat, conical or spherical) (Refs A, B)
- the size of openings in the roof (vented or open-topped cylinders) (Refs D, E)

In the list above, Reference A is Maher (1966), B is Purdy, Maher and Frederick (1967), C is Gretler and Pflügel (1978), D is Ziolko (1978) and E is Esslinger et al. (1971).

A major influence results from the arrangement of nearby structures, including neighbouring bins of close spacing (Esslinger, Ahmed and Schroeder, 1971).

A considerable amount of experimental data has been accumulated on many of the above-mentioned effects. However, for design purposes simplified assumptions have to be made in many cases due to lack of specific information, especially for groups of silos.

Detailed advice on wind pressure distributions, their origins in experimental observations, may be found in Kwok (1985), and References A to E as described above. A summary on the relevant effects is given by Blackler (1986) and Derler (1993).

An overview on typical pressure distributions of isolated cylindrical models is given in Fig. 17.1 together with the distributions defined by two European codes (DIN, ÖNORM). Such distributions normally, for reasons of simplicity, are assumed to be constant over the height of the cylinder. The pressure coefficient at the windward generator usually is taken as 1.0, although due to friction effects of the ground surface this coefficient reaches not more than 0.80 in practical cases.

A good approximation of the pressure variation was given by Blackler (1986), taken from Gorenc et al. (1986):

$$C_S = -0.55 + 0.25\cos\phi + 0.75\cos 2\phi + 0.4\cos 3\phi - 0.05\cos 5\phi$$

in which ϕ is the circumferential angle from the windward direction and C_S is the external pressure coefficient. A similar formula has been derived by Greiner (1983a) from data as in Fig. 17.1:

$$C_S = -0.55 + 0.25\cos\phi + 1.0\cos 2\phi + 0.45\cos 3\phi - 0.15\cos 4\phi$$

The zone of the circumference under wind pressure (positive) may be defined by the angle of 30° and 45° to both sides of the windward generator.

In unroofed silos, silos under construction and silos with large self-opening vents an additional uniform, negative pressure is created due to internal suction through the air flow over the opening. Recommended pressure coefficients are:

$C_S = -0.8$ for slender cylinders ($h/d \geq 2$) and
$C_S = -0.5$ for square cylinders ($h/d \leq 1$), which may be used with interpolation. Even small openings lead to pressure coefficients of the magnitude given above.

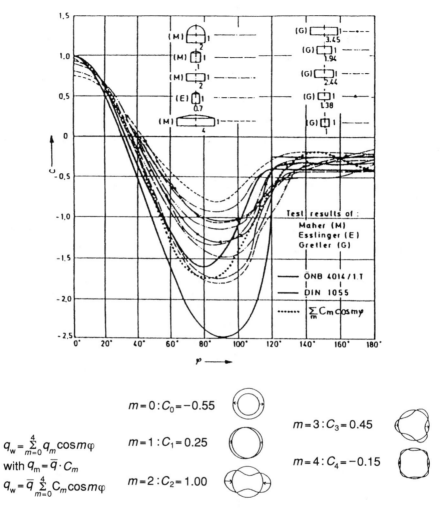

Fig. 17.1 Wind pressure distribution around circumference (with decomposition in Fourier series).

A view on the effect of two silos in close spacing under different wind direction, taken from the experimental measurements, is given in Fig. 17.2, which was presented by Esslinger, Ahmed and Schroeder (1971).

Roofs of cylindrical vessels, whether flat, conical or dome-shaped, show suction over the whole roof as long as the rise of the roof is low (Maher, 1966; Purdy, Maher and Frederick, 1967). For steep roofs like hemispherical domes the front area at the windward side is under pressure.

Wind loading pressures when the silo is empty 381

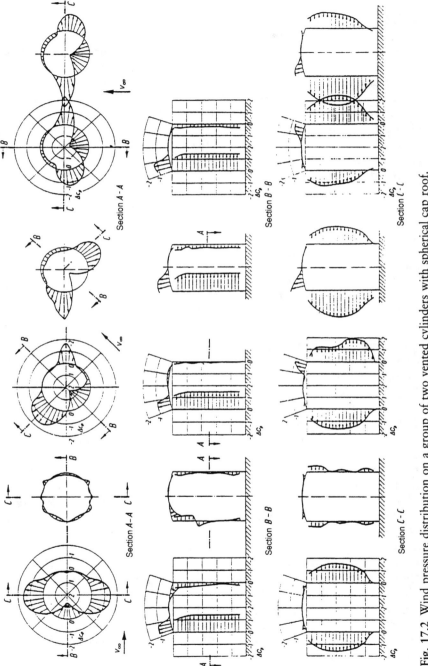

Fig. 17.2 Wind pressure distribution on a group of two vented cylinders with spherical cap roof.

17.2 INTERNAL FORCES IN CYLINDRICAL SHELLS UNDER WIND LOAD

The silos considered in this chapter are either empty or partially full. Wind pressure creates internal forces which are not normally decisive for the design of the wall. However, the highly non-axisymmetric variation of the pressure along the circumference affects the distribution of the internal forces so strongly that the resulting behaviour of the shell is sometimes not understood clearly enough. This is the reason for presenting the general shell behaviour under wind here. Below, there are also details like the holding-down bolts at the lower edge of the silo, the stiffening rings at the upper edge or the intermediate wind stiffeners in the wall, which are all to be designed in close connection with the wind-induced forces.

As already mentioned, the distribution of internal forces does not follow the typical pattern expected from the beam-bending theory when considering the silo as a thin-walled tubular beam with circular cross-section. This results from the behaviour of the empty silo as a shell which deforms considerably in its cross-section (ovalization). The exact solution requires the application of the full shell theory; however, almost the same results can be obtained by using the so-called semi-membrane theory (SMT), and in many cases even the membrane theory alone gives sufficient accuracy (Greiner 1983a).

The typical behaviour can be explained by using the analogy of beam-bending in the SMT. For this reason the wind pressure is decomposed in terms of a Fourier series. For each of the terms the shell behaves like a beam in longitudinal direction. Only the term $m = 1$ acts in the same way as a cantilever beam in the upright position with its upper edge free to deform and its lower end fixed (Fig. 17.3). The terms $m \geq 2$ are self-balancing groups of loadings which cause ovalization of the cross-section. Their boundary conditions at the upper edge depend on the stiffness of the ring or of the roof to the degree to which they prevent the ovalization of the shell. Their lower edge is either fixed, if the silo is anchored down, or simply supported, if only radial deflections are prevented (Fig. 17.3). It is, therefore, very important for the bearing behaviour of cylindrical shells whether their edges are axially restrained ($u = 0$) or not ($N_x = 0$), where u is the axial deformation and N_x the axial membrane force.

The bending stiffness of the wall in circumferential direction can be taken into account by an elastic bedding c (spring constant) of the beams.

The internal membrane forces N_x (meridional component) and $N_{x\phi}$ (shear component) follow the same axial distribution as the bending moment M_x and the shear force Q_x of the beam. The circumferential bending moment M_ϕ of the shell wall can be derived from the spring forces.

Figure 17.4, which is taken from Greiner (1983b), shows the results of a wind-loaded cylinder of $h/d = 0.5$ and $r/t = 800$ for three different boundary conditions at the upper edge (free during erection, ring-stiffened and closed). The bottom edge is anchored down. The wind pressure varia-

Internal forces in cylindrical shells under wind load

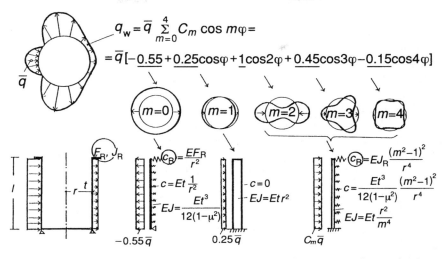

Fig. 17.3 Modelling of a wind-loaded cylinder using the semi-membrane theory.

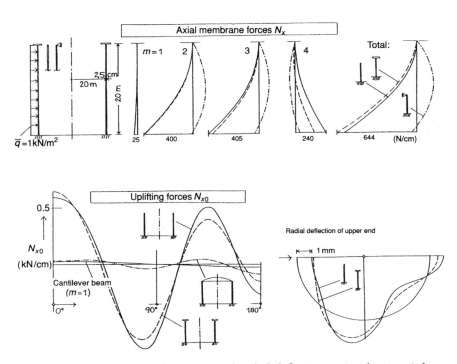

Fig. 17.4 Axial membrane forces N_x and radial deflection w (at the eaves) for a wind-loaded cylinder with three different types of stiffening at the eaves.

tion around the circumference was assumed to be as that in Fig. 17.3 for all three cases, although the open-topped cylinders would, in addition, have a uniformly distributed internal suction component, but this would not influence the internal forces discussed in this figure. The stiffness of the upper ring was taken five times higher than required by the API Standard (see section 17.5).

The meridional membrane forces were plotted along the windward generator for each of the Fourier terms $m = 1$ to 4 and also for the sum of them. A further presentation shows the variation of N_x at the bottom edge along the circumference as well as the radial deflections w at the upper edge.

Five effects can be recognized from the results:

- The overall cantilever action ($m = 1$) is very small compared to the self-balancing groups ($m \geq 2$).
- The effect of the ring is small compared to that of the roof.
- The distribution of N_x for the closed-topped cylinder does not show the usual magnitude of the end moment for the cases $m \geq 2$, which is due to the high shear deformation.
- The variation of the N_x forces at the bottom edge differs very much from the linear distribution of the cantilever beam ($m = 1$); (the similarity in the case of closed-topped cylinders is due to the low h/d ratio of the example and will vanish with longer shells).
- The closed-topped cylinder shows considerable axial compression forces N_x at mid-height of the windward zone.

Similar effects can also be shown for long cylinders (Greiner, 1983a). Figures 17.5 and 17.6 illustrate the behaviour of cylinders with closed top and $h/d = 2.5$. Boundary conditions and wind pressures variation are the same as used in Fig. 17.4.

Figure 17.5 demonstrates the decomposed terms $m = 1$ and $m \geq 2$ for N_x and $N_{x\phi}$ (the curves $c = 0$ indicate the results, when the circumferential bending stiffness is neglected).

Figure 17.6 gives the distributions for the total values N_x, $N_{x\phi}$ and w (radial deflection). The big differences of the N_x values compared to the linear beam-bending solution show that the cylinder cannot be considered as an overall cantilever beam. The axial tensile forces N_x cover a zone of about $2 \times 45°$ around the windward generator and have their maximum at the front bottom edge. However, there is also axial compression of about 50% of the magnitude of the tensile force at about mid-height of the shell. The shear forces $N_{x\phi}$ show similar differences from the sinusoidal shape of the beam-bending theory. Figure 17.7 illustrates the analogous results for a cylinder with open top.

The conclusion is that the distribution of internal forces of cylindrical shells can be very different from the simplified consideration of the shell as a cantilever beam due to the effect of ovalization. This affects mainly the holding-down forces at the bottom edge as well as the behaviour of upper

Internal forces in cylindrical shells under wind load   385

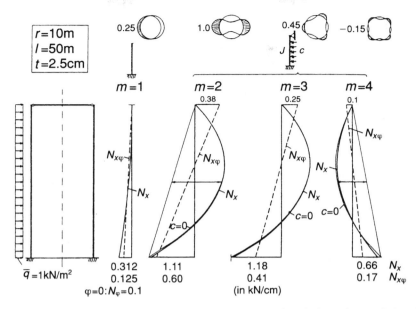

Fig. 17.5 Wind-loaded cylinder with closed roof: axial and shear forces down the windward generator for the individual terms of the Fourier series.

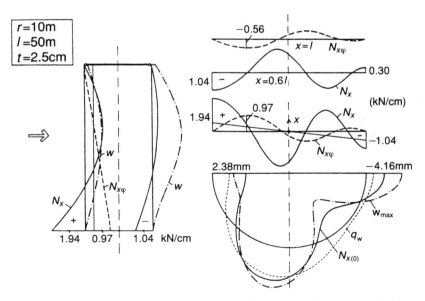

Fig. 17.6 Wind-loaded cylinder with closed roof: membrane forces N_x and $N_{x\phi}$ and radial deflection w for $\bar{q} = 1\,\text{kN/cm}^2$.

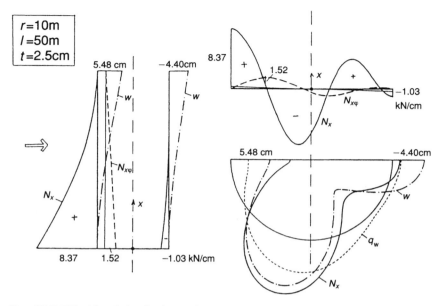

Fig. 17.7 Wind-loaded cylinder with open top: membrane forces N_x and $N_{x\phi}$ and radial deflection w for $\bar{q} = 1 \text{ kN/cm}^2$.

rings. Further, it could be shown that significant axial compression is created in the front area of closed-topped cylinders, which can affect the buckling resistance of the wall.

17.3 ANCHORING OF SILOS

The anchoring of silos is usually performed by holding-down bolts. These bolts are designed for the overturning moment due to wind when the silo is empty (the overturning due to an earthquake when the silo is full is not treated here). Although some standards allow the use of linear force distribution of an overall cantilever beam to determine the axial forces at the bottom edge of the silo, the examples above have shown that this can be far too unconservative in many cases. The longer and thinner the silo, the greater the difference from the linear distribution, showing axial tensile forces of 10 and more times the linear value.

A big effect on the magnitude of the axial tensile forces results from the degree of stiffening of the upper edge of the cylinder. Ring-stiffened silos create far higher forces than those with closed roofs. A study (Greiner, 1983b) on wind-loaded cylinders of different roof construction shows the problem in general, although the examples were rather short for typical silo structures (Fig. 17.8).

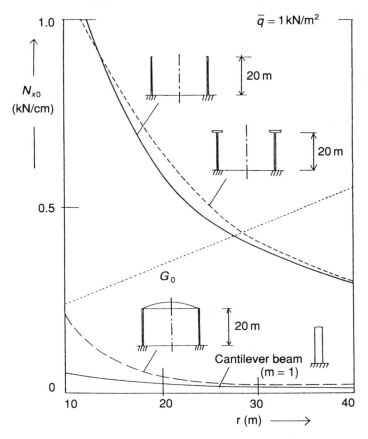

Fig. 17.8 Uplifting forces N_{x0} for wind-loaded cylinders with different types of stiffening at the upper edge.

Figure 17.8 presents the maximum tensile forces (uplifting forces) for three types of cylinders (see section 17.2) with varying radius. Further, the holding-down forces are given, which are due to the self-weight of the cylinders. Uplifting, although only of a local part of the circumference, is to be expected when the tensile force is higher than the force due to self-weight.

The comparison shows that cylinders of the h/d ratio used for silos are in general susceptible to uplifting; however, the results of the linear distribution calculated according to the beam theory would not predict that.

An important aspect for the anchoring of silos is the effect of foundation settlements. Such settlements, when of non-axisymmetric shape around the circumference, can cause high forces in anchor bolts of silos. For this reason – if foundation settlements have to be expected – the holding-down details should provide high ductility with respect to axial deformations. The lack of available data has been highlighted above (section 14.10)

Another consideration concerns the question of whether local uplifting could be allowed if the overall overturning safety of the silo is given. As mentioned above, the uplifting forces under wind are concentrated mainly in the front area of the silo, while large portions of the bottom edge are under compression and could contribute to the overall equilibrium. Such calculations have been carried out (Rammerstorfer, Auli and Fischer 1985; Ansourian, 1992), but they require a high amount of sophisticated analysis concerning the contact between silo and foundation. The local uplifting affects the distribution of internal forces very strongly and can cause buckling of the wall in the front zone or failure of the wind girder due to higher induced forces. However, if these forces are covered in the design of the wall and the wind girder accordingly and the overall overturning safety is given, there is nothing to be objected against local uplifting. In contrast, most of the large diameter tanks are not mechanically anchored.

However, one should bear in mind that uplifting is not allowed for silos under wind with a free upper end or an upper end insufficiently braced. In these cases uplifting would accompany large deformations of the cross-section and could result in disastrous failure.

17.4 BUCKLING OF THE SILO WALL UNDER WIND LOAD

Buckling of the silo wall under wind pressure is an important problem in the design of steel silos due to the slenderness of the steel plates, and it is even more significant when steels of higher strength are used. Buckling failure can occur with the silo in empty or partially full condition. In silos which have a roof or a sufficiently stiffened upper edge, the buckling deformations develop on the windward side in the shape of two or three buckles in the wall. The absence of the roof or of a bracing at the construction stage makes the silo most vulnerable to wind action and may cause an overall collapse of large parts of the wall.

Wind buckling is sometimes considered not to be a safety problem, because it occurs in the empty case and causes local wrinkles rather than a total collapse. However, the repair of wind-damaged silos is expensive and the reliable buckling design is therefore significant for economic reasons.

In general, there exist few data on the design of cylinders buckling under wind pressure, compared with those under uniform external pressure. Most studies focused on the aspect of the non-uniform pressure distribution and treated the problem for ideal shells of constant wall thickness, uniform boundary conditions and isolated position of the cylinder. The first studies were carried out analytically as well as experimentally in a wind tunnel in the period 1960–1980 (Rish, 1963; Wang and Billington, 1974; Kundurpi, Samevedam and Johns, 1975; Maderspach, Gaunt and Sword, 1973;

Greiner, 1975; Maderspach and Kamat, 1979). Further work between 1980 and 1985 was based mainly on wind tunnel testing (Resinger and Greiner, 1981, 1982; Johns, 1983; Uematsu and Uchiyama, 1985; Megson, Harrop and Miller, 1987) and on computational methods (Brendel *et al.*, 1981; Schweizerhof and Ramm, 1985; Blackler and Ansourian, 1984; Rammerstorfer, Auli and Fischer, 1985). The latest work in this field was carried out by Blackler (1986, 1988) and Ansourian (1992), both University of Sydney, by Esslinger and Poblotzki (1992), Braunschweig, and by Derler (1993), Technical University of Graz. So far, many complex aspects of wind buckling, e.g. the uplifting effect, the nonlinear behaviour and the imperfection sensitivity, have been treated numerically for certain parameters, but many questions on the quantitative effects for practical silo structures still remain. The following discussion gives an overview on the present state of research and design recommendations.

It is a traditional approach of most studies to relate the wind-buckling pressure, i.e. the stagnation q_w that causes buckling failure, to the buckling load q_u under uniform external pressure. The amount of deviation from unity expresses the effect of the non-uniformity of the pressure distribution. Figure 17.9 shows a diagram of test results in the wind tunnel plotted over a geometrical parameter ρ. This parameter ρ turned out to be quite useful and represents the theoretical circumferential wave number m_{th} under uniform external pressure according to the classical buckling theory.

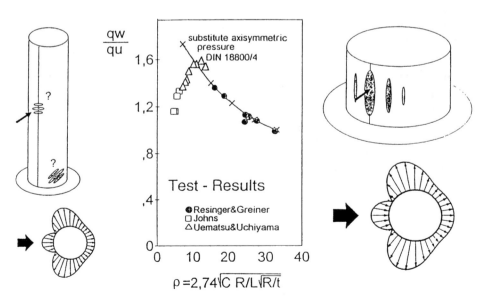

Fig. 17.9 Buckling loads of wind loaded cylinders with closed top: test results q_w versus buckling load under uniform external pressure q_u.

The coefficient C in the formula allows for the higher or lower restraint of boundary conditions different from simple supports at both ends of the silo:

for both ends simply supported (axially free): $C = 1$
for both ends clamped (axially restrained): $C = 1.5$
for one end clamped, the other end simply supported: $C = 1.25$
for one end free, other end clamped (axially restrained): $C = 0.6$

The diagram shows that the wind buckling pressures of cylinders with high p-values (i.e. buckling wave numbers) approach the buckling pressure under uniform external pressure ($q_w/q_u = 1$) with increasing wave numbers. For smaller p-values the wind buckling pressures increase to about $1.6 q_u$; however, for wave numbers smaller than 10 the ratios q_w/q_u drop down in a steep decrease.

This behaviour led to the design concept which transforms the variable wind pressure distribution into an 'equivalent uniform pressure'. This concept gives satisfying results for wave numbers $m_{th} \geq 10$ which means short (squat), thin-walled cylinders (Resinger and Greiner, 1981, 1982; Blackler, 1986). The wind buckling pressure can be calculated on the basis of the uniform buckling pressure q_u divided by κ:

$$q_w = q_u/\kappa \qquad \kappa = 0.46 + 0.017 m_{th} \leq 1.0$$

The reasoning for this concept is the following: If a large number of circumferential waves are formed within the zone of positive pressure under wind action, the response of the shell at the leading generator is similar to that under a uniform external pressure of magnitude equal to the stagnation pressure (Fig. 17.10).

If the number of waves is small, it is argued that the average wind pressure acting over one buckle is smaller and that the adjacent suction zone

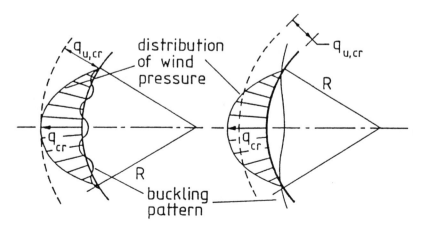

Fig. 17.10 Design concept of an 'equivalent uniform pressure': explanation of relationship to buckling wave number.

contributes a stabilizing effect. The equivalent uniform pressure therefore has a value below the stagnation pressure or in a different interpretation the wind buckling load is higher than the uniform buckling pressure. This concept has the advantage that it may be used only with standard buckling formulae (it has been adopted in the DIN code).

The mechanical explanation is that the buckling of short, thin-walled cylinders is dominated by the circumferential compression, while the axial and shear forces are small. The buckles show patterns very similar to those of the buckling case under uniform external pressure. However, only a few of them (two or three) occur in the pressurized windward area of the wall extending over the whole cylinder length. This has been shown by wind tunnel tests (Resinger and Greiner, 1981) as well as by numerical calculations (Derler, 1993).

The explanation of the steep drop of the wind buckling load, which occurs with decreasing m_{th} in the range lower than 10, has been found through a numerical study (Derler, 1993). The buckling modes show that the stability problem is no longer dominated by circumferential compression, but by the axial membrane force and the shear force. Since decreasing m_{th} mean longer shells, the axial membrane forces (like in a beam) increase accordingly and this effect becomes larger with decreasing m_{th}.

The result of a classical buckling analysis of closed-topped cylinders indicates that for long shells the buckling failure occurs at the bottom, while short shells show buckles over the whole length as if under circumferential pressure (Fig. 17.11). This is understandable since the axial and shear forces have their maximum at the bottom edge and grow higher with increasing cylinder length.

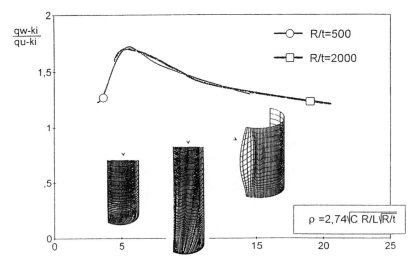

Fig. 17.11 Classical wind buckling loads $q_{w\text{-}ki}$ versus classical uniform external pressure $q_{u\text{-}ki}$.

However, using the nonlinear buckling theory (nonlinear buckling loads, GNL) leads to a different picture. While the range of short shells is practically unaffected, the buckling loads for long shells drop down significantly, in some cases to about 50% of the classical load (Fig. 17.12).

The buckling pattern of long shells also changes completely. For classical buckling, the buckles occur at the side of the lower edge. They move for longer shells to the front in the middle of the shell, where a significant flattening of the circular shape can be detected (Fig. 17.13). This flattening, a consequence of the ovalization due to the suction acting perpendicular to the wind direction, is the main reason that the buckling starts at mid-height, although the axial compression is lower there than at the bottom end.

Including imperfections leads to a further decrease of the buckling loads (buckling loads of imperfect shell, GNLI) (Fig. 17.14). In the range of short shells it is similar to the reduction with uniform external pressure, showing the well-known reduction coefficient of about 0.7.

In the range of long shells the imperfection-induced reduction is rather low bearing in mind that buckling is caused by the imperfection-sensitive axial compression. However, if the drop due to the nonlinearity is added, the total reduction is similar to those of axially compressed shells.

This study (Derler, 1993) indicates that the wind buckling design of 'short cylinders' ($m_{th} \geq \approx 8$) can relatively simply be covered by the concept of equivalent uniform pressure, but that 'long cylinders' ($m_{th} \leq \approx 8$) are governed mainly by axial compression (plus additional circumferential compression) at mid-height and can – up to now – not so easily be covered by simple rules.

In the short cylinder range design formulae can also be given for vented

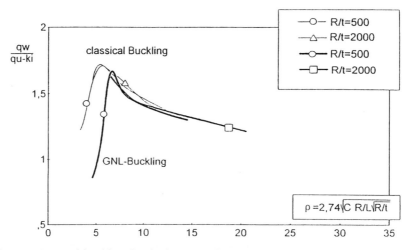

Fig. 17.12 Wind buckling loads determined using geometrically nonlinear buckling analysis (GNL).

Buckling of the silo wall under wind load

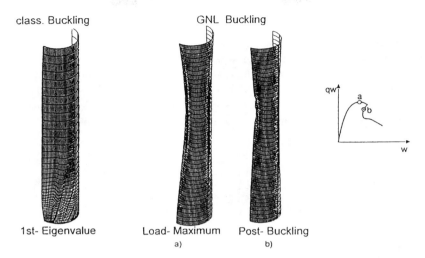

Fig. 17.13 Buckling modes of long wind-loaded cylinders: comparison of classical and geometrically nonlinear analysis.

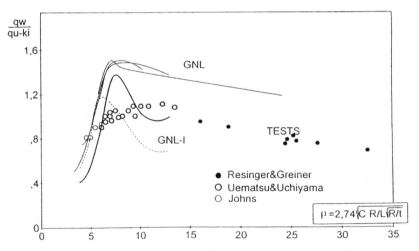

Fig. 17.14 Comparison of numerical predictions for wind-loaded cylinders with test data.

silos or those with open top. The κ factor is then increased by the internal suction coefficient ($C_S = 0.5$–0.8, section 17.1).

$$q_w = q_u / (\kappa + C_S)$$

Further design formulae can be derived for wind buckling of cylinders with stepped wall thickness in the 'short cylinder range' also using the concept of equivalent uniform pressure (Greiner, 1981).

17.5 RING STIFFENING OF SILOS FOR WIND LOADING

If silos are high, ring stiffeners may be applied in order to reduce the ovalization due to wind loads or sometimes in order to provide an easier construction. Such rings affect the distribution of internal forces as well as the buckling behaviour of the wall. Ring stiffeners may also be used to brace the upper end of silos. In general, such rings are very effective structural elements to significantly improve the bearing capacity of the shell.

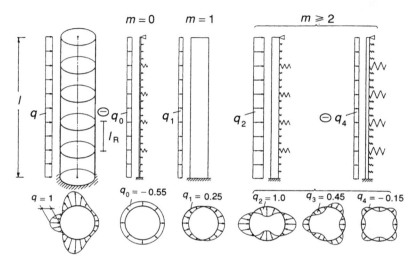

Fig. 17.15 Modelling of a ring-stiffened cylinder using the semi-membrane theory.

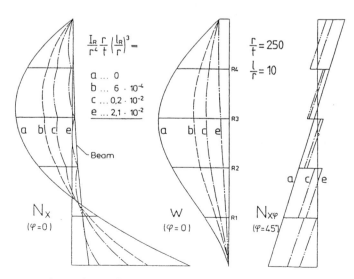

Fig. 17.16 Axial membrane forces N_x, shear forces $N_{x\phi}$ and radial deflection w for a ring-stiffened cylinder under wind with different ring stiffnesses.

17.5.1 Effects of ring stiffeners on internal forces

As discussed above (section 17.2) the semi-membrane theory (SMT) is a very useful means for calculating the forces in a wind-loaded cylinder. In addition to the model presented there, ring stiffeners now have to be introduced. This is done by elastic springs representing the in-plane stiffness of the rings for each specific wave number (Greiner, 1987).

Figure 17.15 shows such a modelling for a cylinder with four equally spaced rings and Fig. 17.16 the results of a parameter study for variable ring stiffness. The axial membrane forces N_x, the shear forces $N_{x\phi}$ and the radial deflections w (plotted along the windward generator $\phi = 0$ and at the generator $\phi = 45°$) illustrate the stiffening effect by the rings. The higher the ring stiffness, the more the shell results approach the linear distribution of the beam. Figure 17.17 presents the in-plane bending moments M_R of one

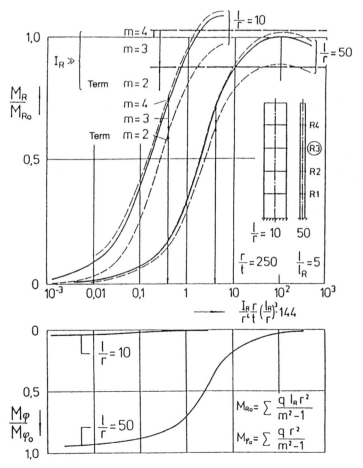

Fig. 17.17 Circumferential bending moments M_R in the ring and M_ϕ in the wall.

of the rings (R3) as well as the circumferential bending moment of the wall M_ϕ.

Two types of cylinders were considered: one with $l/r = 10$ and the other with $l/r = 50$, both with the same ratio $r/t = 250$. The ring moment M_R was related to the full moment M_{R0} in the ring, if the ring had to carry its full share of loading without assistance of the shell. M_ϕ was related to $M_{\phi 0}$ in the wall, if the wall had to carry its full loading without assistance of the ring. The strong effect of the Fourier term $m = 2$ (pure ovalization) is obvious. A considerable stiffness I_R of the ring is necessary to transfer the wind load to the ring.

The ring stiffening also has a considerable influence on the axial forces N_x at the bottom end of the cylinder. Figure 17.18 presents the circumferential distributions of N_x, related to N_{x1}, which is the maximum uplifting force due to the beam-bending theory. The higher the ring stiffness, the more the shell behaviour approaches that of the linear distribution of the beam.

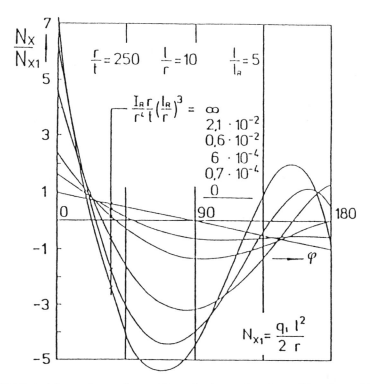

Fig. 17.18 Axial membrane forces N_x at the base of a ring-stiffened wind-loaded cylinder with different ring stiffnesses.

17.5.2 Effect of ring stiffeners on buckling behaviour

There is little published work available for the buckling design of ring-stiffened cylinders under wind loads. However, some investigations and design recommendations can be found.

17.5.2.1 Primary wind girder

For wind rings on the top of an open tank there exists a design formula, given originally in the API-Standard, but also taken over by the BS 2654 and DIN 4119 (previous version). The required minimum section modulus is

$$Z = 0.058 D^2 L$$

For the same type of ring a different requirement was formulated (Blackler, 1986; Ansourian, 1992). The minimum second moment of area of a ring-stiffener at the top on an open cylinder, required to prevent the buckling mode in which the top cross-section deforms, is

$$I_{R,Cr} = 0.048 t^3 L$$

This value follows from a numerical study carried out for the *Mindeststeifigkeit* (limiting stiffness) under uniform external pressure. It is recommended also for wind buckling by the authors. The resulting ring section of this second formula is very much smaller than that of the API-rule.

From the viewpoint of proper design requirements the formulae given above are not fully satisfactory. The background of the API-formula could not be found and the basis of the second formula is a cylinder clamped at the bottom end under uniform external pressure. Further research is necessary in order to solve the problem of unanchored bottom edges of cylinders, to investigate the effect of the variable wind pressure around the circumference and to look into the behaviour of long, silo-type cylinders.

17.5.2.2 Secondary wind stiffeners

Design data exist in BS 2654 in the form of standard angle sections specified as a function of the tank diameter.

A formula for the stiffness of intermediate rings, required to cause the inter-ring buckling mode, is presented by Blackler (1986):

$$I_{R,Cr} = 0.077 t^3 L N^{0.45}$$

in which N is the number of intermediate rings. The formula was derived from numerical studies for the *Mindeststeifigkeit* on simply supported cylinders under uniform external pressure. A similar study was presented (Resinger and Greiner, 1982) giving very similar results for the 'limiting' stiffness of intermediate rings under uniform external pressure. Also in this case calculations under wind pressure distribution, different boundary conditions and different parameters L/D are missing.

REFERENCES

Ansourian, P. (1992) On the buckling analysis and design of silos and tanks, *J. Constructional Steel Research*, 23, 273–284.

Blackler, M.J. (1986) Stability of silos and tanks under internal and external pressure. PhD thesis, University of Sydney, Oct.

Blackler, M.J. (1988) Buckling of steel silos and wind action, *Proc. of Silo-Conference*, University Karlsruhe, pp. 318–330.

Blackler, M.J. and Ansourian, P. (1984) Stability of stiffened cylindrical bins, *Proc. 9th Australasian Conf. on Mech. of Struct. and Mater.*, Univ. of Sydney.

Brendel, B.; Ramm, E.; Fischer, D.F. and Rammerstorfer, F.G. (1981) Linear and non-linear stability analysis of thin cylindrical shells under wind loads. *J. Struct. Mech.*, 9(1), 91–113.

Derler, P. (1993) Load-carrying behaviour of cylindrical shells under wind load (in German), PhD thesis, Technical University of Graz, August.

Esslinger, M. and Poblotzki, G. (1992) Buckling under wind pressure (in German), *Der Stahlbau*, 61(1), 21–26.

Esslinger, M.; Ahmed, S. and Schroeder, H. (1971) Stationary wind loads of opentopped and roof-topped cylindrical silos (in German) *Der Stahlbau*, pp. 1–8.

Gorenc, B.E.; Hogan, T.J. and Rotter, J.M. (eds) (1986) *Guidelines for the Assessment of Loads on Bulk Solid Containers*, Institution of Engineers, Australia.

Greiner, R. (1975) Comments on the paper of Maderspach and Kamat, 1975 (in German), *Der Stahlbau*, 1975, pp. 31–32.

Greiner, R. (1981) Buckling of cylindrical shells with stepped wall-thickness under windload (in German), *Der Stahlbau*, 50(6), 176–179.

Greiner, R. (1983a) Analysis and construction of cylindrical steel cylinders under non-axisymmetric loading (in German), *Proc. Wissenschaft und Praxis*, Vol. 31, FHS Biberach/Riss.

Greiner, R. (1983b) Structural problems of silos and tanks (in German), *Austrian Conference of Constructional Steelwork*.

Greiner, R. (1987) Tanks and silos as stiffened structures (in German), *Proc Wissenschaft und Praxis*, Vol. 46, FHS Biberach/Riss.

Gretler, W. and Pflügel, M. (1978) Wind tunnel tests of cylindrical shells at the TU Graz, unpublished.

Johns, D.J. (1983) Wind induced static instability of cylindrical shells. *J. Wind Eng. and Ind. Aerodynamics*, 13, 261–270.

Kundurpi, P.S.; Samevedam, G. and Johns, D.J. (1975) Stability of cantilever shells under wind loads. *Proc. ASCE*, 101, EM5, Oct. 517–530.

Kwok, K.C.S. (1985) Wind loads on circular storage bins, in *Design of Steel Bins for the Storage of Bulk Solids*, edited by J.M. Rotter, Univ. Sydney, March, pp. 49–54.

Maderspach, V.; Gaunt, J.T. and Sword, J.H. (1973) Buckling of cylindrical shells due to wind loading (in German), *Der Stahlbau*, 9, 269–277.

Maderspach, V. and Kamat, M. (1979) Buckling of open cylindrical tank due to wind loading (in German), *Der Stahlbau*, **2**, 53–56.

Maher, F. (1966) Wind loads on dome-cylinder and dome-cone shapes. *ASCE J. Struct. Div.*, pp. 79–96.

Megson, T.; Harrop, J. and Miller, M. (1987) The stability of large diameter and thin-walled steel tanks subjected to wind loading. *Proc. of International Colloquium*, University Ghent, April 6–8, pp. 529–538.

Purdy, D.; Maher, F. and Frederick, D. (1967) Model studies of wind loads on flat-top cylinders. *ASCE J. Struct. Div.*, 379–395.

Rammerstorfer, F.G.; Auli, W. and Fischer, F. (1985) Uplifting and stability of wind-loaded vertical cylindrical shells. *Engineering Computations*, **2**, 170–180.

Resinger, F. and Greiner, R. (1981) Circular cylindrical shell under wind pressure – Application of the calculations to above ground tanks (in German), *Der Stahlbau*, **3**, 65–72.

Resinger, F. and Greiner, R. (1982) Buckling of wind loaded cylindrical shells – Application to unstiffened and ring-stiffened tanks. *Proc. State of the art colloquium*, University of Stuttgart, Germany, 6–7 May.

Rish, R.F. (1963) Collapse of cylindrical elastic shells under wind loading. *The Engineer*, **216**, 669–672.

Schweizerhof, K. and Ramm, E. (1985) Stability of cylindrical shells under wind loading with particular reference to follower load effect. *Proc. Joint US–Australian Workshop on Loading, Analysis and Stability of Thin-Shell Bins, Tanks and Silos*, University of Sydney, March.

Uematsu, Y. and Uchiyama, K. (1985) Deflection and buckling behaviour of thin, circular cylindrical shells under wind loads. *J. Wind Eng. and Ind. Aerodynamics*, **18**(3), 2451–262.

Wang, Y. and Billington, D.P. (1974) Buckling of cylindrical shells by wind pressure. *Proc. ASCE*, **100**, EM5, Oct., pp. 1005–1023.

Ziolko, J. (1978) Model studies of wind pressure on steel tanks with floating roof (in German). *Der Stahlbau*, 1978, 321–329.

18
Cylindrical shells: other actions
D. Briassoulis

18.1 INTRODUCTION

Determination of static and dynamic pressures exerted by stored granular or powder materials in silos and the analysis of the corresponding structural behaviour of silos has been the subject of extensive research as is apparent from the relevant international literature. There are specific loading conditions, however, concerning silo structures which are not very well covered in the technical literature. Among them are loading due to earthquake, temperature changes, differential settlements and pressures induced by stored silage material.

18.2 EARTHQUAKE

Very few national or international standards include explicit requirements concerning the design of silos against earthquakes. Most standards for silos do not cover the subject at all, or they refer to general building codes, or as happens with the recently introduced Eurocode for actions in silos and tanks, they are simply referred to the earthquake loading issue as another loading case to be considered, offering only general suggestions. As a result, in practice silos are designed against earthquakes according to the corresponding codes for buildings and equipment.

The Uniform Building Code (UBC, 1994) which is in effect in the USA suggests that flat-bottom tanks or other tanks with supported bottoms, founded at or below grade, shall be designed using the procedures for rigid structures (those with period T less than 0.06 s), for the equivalent lateral seismic force V which is obtained by

$$V = 0.5ZIW$$

where:

Z = seismic-zone coefficient (given as 0.075, 0.15, 0.20, 0.30 and 0.40 for the US seismic zones 1, 2A, 2B, 3, and 4, respectively);
I = structure importance factor which is taken as 1.25 for essential and hazardous facilities and 1 for others;
W = total weight of tank plus contents.

Alternatively such tanks may be designed using a response spectrum analysis.

Tanks which are not covered by the above procedures (e.g. non-rigid structures) shall be designed to resist an equivalent lateral seismic force V:

$$V = \frac{ZIC}{R_w}W$$

where:

C = coefficient given by the UBC in terms of the fundamental period of vibration of the structure T, in seconds, in the direction of the seismic load (horizontal acceleration):

$$C = \frac{1.25S}{T^{2/3}} \leq 2.75$$

S = site coefficient given in the UBC for various soil profiles (S = 1.0, 1.2, 1.5 and 2.0 for soil profiles S1 to S4 respectively); in the case of unknown soil conditions, it is suggested that a value of S = 1.2 is used (Gaylord and Gaylord, 1984);
R_w = numerical coefficient given as follows: R_w = 4 for bins and hoppers on braced or unbraced legs and R_w = 5 for storage tanks.

The calculated lateral force V is assumed to be distributed in proportion to the vertical distribution of W.

According to ANSI ASCE 7-95 (1996), flat-bottom storage tanks mounted at grade shall be designed to meet the force provisions of API (STD 650, 1993) or AWWA (D100, 1984). Alternatively, the equivalent seismic force may be calculated with ANSI procedures analogous to the UBC procedures (with different definitions and values for the various coefficients, a coefficient representing the effective peak velocity-related acceleration, in place of the seismic zone coefficient, etc.). Thus, for flat-bottom storage tanks at grade, the seismic design force (F_p) centred at centre of gravity is given by:

$$F_p = 4.0 C_a I_p W_p$$

where:

W_p = component operating weight;
C_a = seismic coefficient (given as a function of soil profile type A to E and shaking intensity A_v; from $A_v < 0.05g$ to $A_v > 0.5g$);
I_p = component importance factor that varies between 1.0 and 1.5.

Special provisions for cases of tanks with an I_p of 1.5 or tanks greater than 6.2 m in diameter and tanks with height-to-diameter ratio greater than 1.0 are required by ANSI (sloshing effects should be considered, etc.).

Tanks not covered by the above procedures shall be designed to resist an equivalent lateral seismic force V which should be at least equal to

$$V = C_s W$$

where:

C_s = seismic response coefficient determined in terms of the fundamental period of vibration of the structure T, in seconds, in the direction under consideration:

$$C_s = \frac{1.2 C_v}{RT^{2/3}}$$

C_v = seismic coefficient based upon the soil profile type (A–E) and the value of shaking intensity A_v (from $A_v < 0.05\,g$ to $A_v > 0.5\,g$);
R = response modification factor given as $R = 3$ for bins and hoppers on braced or unbraced legs.

According to the American Concrete Institute code for the design of concrete silos storing granular materials (ACI-313R-91, 1991), silos shall be designed and constructed to withstand lateral seismic forces calculated using the UBC. Since a portion of the seismic energy is absorbed through intergranular movement and friction, the dynamic effect of the stored material is considered to be reduced. Accordingly. ACI-313R-91 allows for the total weight W to be calculated as the sum of the tank's weight plus 80% of the weight of the stored material (effective live load).

From a general point of view, two conditions should be distinguished for silos under earthquake action (Rotter, 1991). The first is that of the squat silo, which responds in a quasi-static manner, with differential pressures across opposite faces. The pressure variation results in a moment resultant and a shear resultant at the silo base (a situation analogous to that arising from non-symmetrical filling). The moment is resisted through the development of axial stress resultants (Briassoulis, 1992) which may lead to buckling problems. The shear resultant at the base is resisted through the development of membrane shear stresses, which, in turn, may lead to a failure by buckling in membrane shear. The second condition concerns the elevated silo, which responds in a manner similar to an elevated water tank, and where the solid can be assumed to respond integrally with the wall: the key aspects are the stiffness of the supports and foundation, and the mass of the elevated solid.

The above-mentioned general design approach has already been adopted by Eurocode 1, *Basis of Design and Actions on Structures, Part 4 – Silos and Tanks*. Eurocode 1 offers some general suggestions but no specific guidance. The earthquake acceleration is to be calculated according to Eurocode 8 (the design rules offered in Eurocode 1 for the design of silos for seismic actions supplement general rules for the calculation of seismic actions on structures given in ENV 1998 and may be incorporated into ENV 1998 at a later stage). Eurocode 1 suggests that the silo and the stored particulate material may be regarded as a single rigid mass. Horizontal

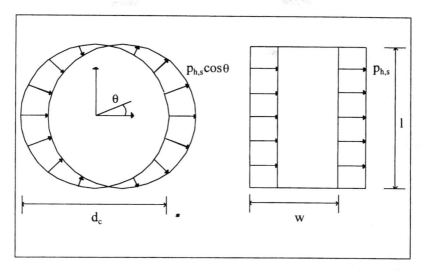

Fig. 18.1 Plan views of earthquake pressure distributions on vertical walled sections of silos with circular and rectangular cross-sections.

accelerations result in vertical loads on the silo supporting system and foundation. In calculating these vertical loads, the seismic actions due to the weight of the silo and the particulate material are regarded as one force acting at the centre of gravity of the silo structure and the stored particulate material system. In addition, the horizontal load to be applied to the silo walls is considered to be equivalent to the mass of the particulate material multiplied by the value of the earthquake acceleration. The horizontal distribution of the earthquake pressure for circular silos is given by the Eurocode as $p_{h,s}\cos\theta$, with $p_{h,s}$ (unit of pressure on the silo wall) given by (Fig. 18.1)

$$p_{h,s} = \frac{d_c}{2}\gamma\frac{a}{g}$$

while the total horizontal load per unit of height $P_{h,s}$ (horizontal force/unit length of meridional) due to seismic actions is given by integrating the above equation:

$$P_{h,s} = \frac{\pi}{4}d_c^2\gamma\frac{a}{g}$$

where a is the horizontal acceleration due to an earthquake, g the acceleration of gravity, d_c the silo diameter and γ the bulk weight density of stored material. The horizontal pressure is considered to be constant over the height of the silo except near the top where the resultant of the seismic pressure and the filling or discharge pressure shall not be less than zero (note: there is a mistake in the current version of the Eurocode where the total load $P_{h,s}$ is denoted by the same notation as the earthquake pressure: $p_{h,s}$).

The corresponding earthquake pressure for silos of rectangular cross-section is given by the Eurocode as $p_{h,s}$ (unit of pressure on the silo wall):

$$p_{h,s} = \frac{w}{2}\gamma\frac{a}{g}$$

(Note: there is a mistake in the current version of the Eurocode where this equation is missing.) The total horizontal load per unit of height $P_{h,s}$ due to seismic actions for silos of rectangular cross-section is given by the Eurocode by integrating the above equation:

$$P_{h,s} = wl\gamma\frac{a}{g}$$

where w and l are the dimensions of the square cross-section along the seismic actions and perpendicular to it, respectively. The horizontal pressure is again considered to be constant over the height of the silo except near the top where the resultant of the seismic pressure and the filling or discharge pressure shall not be less than zero (note: there is a mistake in the current version of the Eurocode where the total load $P_{h,s}$ is given by a wrong expression).

Historically, the alternative approaches introduced and utilized by earthquake engineering for the design of earthquake-resisting structures have followed the sequential development of three different concepts. The first concept was simply focusing on the protection of structures against earthquakes through the enhancement of the structure's strength. Then, the concept of the structure's ductility was introduced, placing emphasis on energy dissipation rather than on strength resistance. The most recently developed concept is known as the flexibility concept. The solutions proposed by the flexibility concept may be described as base isolation systems. The idea is to lower the forces transmitted to the structure by decreasing the stiffness of the soil–structure interface (Kitazawa, Ikeda and Kawamura, 1984). Base isolation systems are already in use in New Zealand, France and Japan while their acceptance is growing elsewhere (Tarics, 1987).

A specific case of earthquake-loaded silos is discussed by van Wijk (1991). This work presents the analysis of a Euro-type mammoth silo, based on the flexibility concept (this type of silo has two interconnected walls: an inner wall which is designed to carry the lateral pressures and an outer wall with columns, which is designed to carry the vertical loads exerted by the stored material). In general, the shear stress developed in the bulk solid of a conventional silo remains low as the wall assumes most of the energy needed to accelerate the bulk solid. This results in high wall loads. For the Euro-type silo, however, the shearing resistance of the inner wall is low allowing for the stored material to develop shear stresses. Thus, in this type of silo, the acceleration forces are mainly transmitted through the bulk solid itself. Therefore, as the (inner) wall flexibility is increased the wall loads are decreased and the lateral displacement is increased. This requires calculation of the clearance between inner wall and external columns. In general, the examples presented by van Wijk (1991) reveal the limits of ideal plasticity. In problems where low strains are involved, and especially those with some periodic character (like temperature- or earthquake-induced strains), elasticity is expected to play an important role. Consequently, low strain constitutive behaviour of bulk solids represents an important factor in the analysis and design of silos for earthquakes.

Earthquake-proof design of silos in Japan follows the general guidelines given by the *Japanese Building Standards Law* (1981), the *Design Recommendation for Storage Tanks and Their Supports* (AIJ, 1984), the *Recommendation for Earthquake-Proof Design of Thermal Power Stations* (JEA, 1983) and other codes of practice. As most coal silos in Japan are located in coastal zones, particularly on reclaimed land, and grouped piles are often used as supporting systems, the Japanese engineers recommend that aseismic design should take into consideration the interaction among the grouped pile foundation, the silo body and the coal during earthquakes (Sakai et al., 1985). The limited number of data based on model tests, the complicated dynamic behaviour of granular materials and the unclear elasto-plastic behaviour of structures have forced the Japanese engineers to carry out aseismic design over recent decades in accordance with conventional static–dynamic analysis and design procedures (e.g. assume a section, calculate earthquake loads, carry out static analysis, check assumed section: if inadequate go back; if OK, then carry out dynamic analysis: if OK, end of the procedure, otherwise alter the section (Sakai et al., 1985)).

Most earthquake regulations and standards offer the possibility of making dynamic analysis based on calculating the lower eigenvalues/modes of the silo. The response of the structure in each mode is obtained for a design earthquake spectrum compatible with the seismic zone of the region. The design spectra are usually prescribed by authorities. The expected response of the structure is determined from the superimposition of the corresponding modal responses.

Whereas the dynamic behaviour of grain silos with large aspect ratios can be analysed satisfactorily, this is not so in the case of large-diameter coal silos with significant interaction between silo and coal (Kitazawa, Ikeda and Kawamura, 1984). Vibration tests on silo models were employed to investigate: (a) the dynamic interaction between the cylindrical silo wall and the coal and determine the coal pressure on the silo wall; (b) the effect of the nonlinear mechanical properties of coal on the dynamic behaviour of coal silos and (c) verify earthquake response analysis programs.

A Japanese concrete type coal silo is analysed in Kitazawa, Ikeda and Kawamura (1984). The influence factors between different parts of the silo during an earthquake are analysed by means of a 1/30 model of a 15 000 t capacity silo. The dynamic behaviour such as the interaction between the cylindrical silo and the coal was experimentally examined using a shaking table. According to this analysis, 75–80% of the base shear generated by the coal is exerted on to the cylindrical wall. The higher the input acceleration, the smaller the base shear per unit acceleration shared by the cylindrical wall. Although the share ratio of base shear varies depending on the difference in the mechanical properties of the granular materials, the degree of its change is small as compared to the difference in the mechanical properties. The effect of the roof stiffness characteristics is insignificant if the silo is filled with granular material. The resonance frequency becomes high for a high input acceleration as the responses of the coal in the central part and near the cylindrical wall, respectively, do not synchronize. Furthermore, the damping effect of the coal was shown to be so large that 40% can be considered as equivalent viscous damping (note that the damping ratio for an empty silo is 3% whereas it becomes about 20% in the case of a silo filled with coal (Kitazawa, Ikeda and Kawamura, 1984)).

18.3 DIFFERENTIAL TEMPERATURE EFFECTS

Thermally induced stresses in cylindrical silos may become critical in some cases. Most codes and standards require that silos shall be designed to resist (among others) thermal stresses due to temperature differences between stored material and outside air. One of the first analytical approaches to this subject was introduced by Andersen (1966). The expression derived by Andersen is based on the membrane theory for thin shells, assuming that behaviour of grain is linearly elastic for the incremental strain associated with thermal contraction. The horizontal pressure developed on the wall of a cylindrical shell p_t as a result of a differential change of the temperature ΔT is given by Andersen (1966) as follows:

$$p_t = \frac{\alpha E \Delta T}{\dfrac{r}{t} + (1-v)\dfrac{E}{E_l}}$$

where r is the radius of the silo, t the thickness of cylinder wall, α the coefficient of thermal expansion of wall, v Poisson's ratio of granular material, ΔT the decrease in temperature of wall, E the modulus of elasticity of wall material and E_l the modulus of elasticity of stored granular material in horizontal direction. Note that the hoop stress in the wall is calculated by $\sigma = p_t r/t$.

In an experimental study, Manbeck and Nelson (1975) conducted triaxial tests on bulk wheat and determined that strain depends nonlinearly on the horizontal stress and on the ratio of horizontal to vertical stresses in the grain mass. A formulation for calculating the incremental grain pressure and silo wall forces and moments caused by a drop in outside temperature was presented in Bartali and Hatfield (1990). The effects of uniformly decreased temperature across the wall thickness and of temperature gradient are considered in this work. As expected, it was confirmed that grain pressure increases when the silo wall contracts in response to a uniform decrease in wall temperature, except near the restrained edge. The pressure increase was shown to be greater for smaller silo radii. The pressure increase was also shown to vary with the assumed initial value of pressure ratio k. The uniform decrease in wall temperature caused incremental circumferential normal force throughout the height of the silo and moment near the restrained edge. The temperature gradient resulted in the development of moments along most of the silo, except near the unrestrained edge, where circumferential normal tension develops.

Thermally induced loads were also measured experimentally in Li, Puri and Manbeck (1990) by using a model bin. The model bin was filled with wheat and was subjected to three temperature cycles with an amplitude of 10°C (rate 10°C/h). A linear regression relationship was used for thermal overpressure p_t as a function of temperature drop (ΔT):

$$p_t = C_p (\Delta T)$$

where C_p is the thermal pressure coefficient (kPa/°C).

The correlation between thermal lateral pressure on the bin wall and ambient temperature change was found to be linear with the coefficient of determination r^2 being greater than 88%. The mean thermal pressure coefficient was 22 kPa/°C with a range of variation 0.36–0.41 kPa/°C. Comparisons with the preceding cycle indicated that the thermal pressure coefficient increased with cycle number by 63.6% (second cycle) and 5.5% (third cycle) during the temperature decreasing mode and by 5.2 and 2.5% during the temperature increasing mode. Comparisons within the same cycle indicated that C_t for the temperature increasing mode was 72.7, 11.1 and 7.8% higher than the values for temperature decreasing mode (first, second and third cycles). Thermal overpressure approached an equilibrium profile after three complete cycles.

Experimental results with steel bins used to store wheat suggested that temperature stresses are not particularly large and they can ordinarily be covered by the usual factors of safety (Gaylord and Gaylord, 1984). What is more important though, are the conditions (i.e. temperature) under which the temperature drop occurs. Thus, if the specific temperature drop of the above-mentioned experiments was to occur at low temperatures (e.g. from 20 to −30°C), a brittle fracture crack might be initiated. This implies that if the steel does not have adequate notch toughness at these temperatures, a failure of a vertical joint might occur, especially if the vertical joints are not free of flaws (Gaylord and Gaylord, 1984). Therefore, the key factor in designing steel silos against temperature stresses appears to be the protection against brittle failure by choosing steel with adequate notch toughness and strength and by a thorough inspection of the welds, rather than trying to keep the stress resultant due to the superimposed stored material and thermal induced stresses below a critical allowable level (Gaylord and Gaylord, 1984).

As far as load combinations are concerned, the ACI code suggests that the combined ultimate loading for consideration of thermal stresses due to stored hot material should be

$$U = 1.4D + 1.7L$$

where U is the required ultimate strength to resist internal force or moment, L the force or moment due to live load and D the force or moment due to combined dead and thermal loads. The method adapted by the ACI code for the determination of additional reinforcement to resist thermal stresses ignores temperature differences up to 44.5°C.

18.4 DIFFERENTIAL SETTLEMENT EFFECTS

Literature concerning loading in silos induced by differential settlement is scarce. A specific case of settlement of three heavy silo structures at two cement plants located along the south arm of the Fraser River delta in Canada is discussed in McCammon and Butler (1990). The analysis of this case indicates that rather large structures can be founded directly on sediments like those of the Fraser River type if some settlement is acceptable. It is shown that site treatments such as preloading, vibro-compaction, and the use of piles are effective ways of reducing post-construction settlement of upper loose soils. Vibro-compaction of upper loose soils is also considered to provide resistance to liquefaction during earthquakes.

18.5 LOADING DUE TO EXPLOSIONS

Air–dust mixtures in silos may become explosive in certain concentrations with disastrous consequences. According to some records, there have been over 4000 explosions of such mixtures in the past 12 years in Europe (note that this number is not limited to silos). One of the most common design approaches to cope with this problem concerns pressure relief techniques by venting.

Dust from grain products may ignite under certain conditions and explode. Thus, a dust cloud may become ignited for a minimum concentration at $0.02 \, \text{kg/m}^3$ of grain dust (or flour dust) (Gurfinkel, 1979). If the concentration exceeds $2 \, \text{kg/m}^3$ possible ignition results in an incomplete combustion which prevents the occurrence of explosion. Dry dust accumulated on floors, walls, etc. is highly oxygenated and quite dangerous.

In the case of a dust explosion, great amounts of energy are released, creating rapid pressures of the order of $21\,500 \, \text{t/m}^2$ per second (Gurfinkel, 1979). Ignition temperatures are in the range 390–490°C for a relative humidity between 30 and 90% (Gurfinkel, 1979).

18.6 LOADING DUE TO STORED SILAGE

A rather significant proportion of silos is used for storing silage for agricultural purposes. The determination of pressures induced by silage on silo walls is much more complicated as compared to that concerning granular materials. Available methods for estimating lateral pressure, average vertical pressure, and capacity in farm silos give results which vary within a wide range. In most countries there is no standard available concerning calculation of wall loads in tower silos due to storage of silage. Among the few standards dealing with this subject, one may cite the German DIN 1055 (1984), the Canadian Farm Building Code (CFBC) (1990) and the recommended practice by the ISA (1981). The research work which has been devoted to silage-induced pressures is rather limited. Recent developments in the technology of production, handling and feeding of ensiled farm products in farms have led to the construction of large farm silos. This, in turn, imposes an urgent need for the development of a rational method for determining (or evaluating) silage-induced lateral and vertical pressures in farm silos as well as their capacities.

Cylindrical farm silos used to store relatively dry silage (moisture less than 65%) or high moisture granular material which is characterized as non-flowable, can be designed based on Janssen's theory (such silos are classified in CFBC as class I silos; (CFBC, 1990; Jofriet and Negi, 1992)). However, the variation in density of the highly compressible silage material has to be taken into consideration. To this end, the CFBC specifies that the lateral pressure at the silo mid-height shall be calculated based on the average density whereas at the bottom, calculations shall be based on a density 20% higher than the average (average densities are provided in the code). Then, the lateral pressure is considered to vary linearly between the pressure value at the top (where the pressure is assumed to be 4 kPa), the mid-height and the bottom values. In cases of silos unloaded from the bottom, a uniform lateral overpressure equal to 2.5–3.0 times the normal silage pressure at the floor level, is considered to be applied over a height equal to 1/6 of the silo diameter (CFBC, 1990). In addition, an impact factor varying from 1 (at mid-height) to 1.25 (at the bottom) shall be applied to account for the dynamic effect of moving silage in cases of bottom unloading silos.

In cases of silos used to store wet materials, liquid pressure builds up in the bottom (CFBC, 1990; Jofriet and Negi, 1992). The total lateral pressure is then calculated as the superimposition of the liquid pressure and the effective wall pressure due to solid material (i.e. pressures calculated conventionally for solid material). In any case, liquid pressures should not be ignored as they may be as high as three times the effective pressures. The CFBC classifies top-unloading silos used to store wet silage as class II silos. In class II silos, saturation is expected when the moisture content M (on a wet basis, %) is greater than

$$M > 80 - 0.5(H+D)$$

where H and D are the silo height and diameter in metres, respectively. The depth to the level of saturation z_s (m) is estimated according to the CFBC by the empirical equation

$$z_s = 160 - 2M - D$$

Then, the total pressure $P(z)$ below the saturation level z_s is given by (i.e. liquid plus effective pressure due to stored solid material at depth $z > z_s$, in kPa):

$$P(z) = P_s + (z - z_s)\left(11 - \frac{4\mu k P_s}{D}\right)$$

where P_s is the lateral wall pressure at depth z_s in kPa, μ is the friction coefficient between silage and wall and k is the pressure ratio, as they appear in Janssen's formula, respectively.

According to the British Standard BS 5061 (1974) the lateral pressure P_t (kPa) at depth z (m) in drained cylindrical silage silos is given by

$$P_t = 9.8 + 0.75\left(9.8 - \frac{29.5}{D}\right)(z-3) \qquad z > 3 \text{ m}$$

In cases of crops ensiled in watertight silos, the factor 0.75 in the above equation is changed to 1.0.

The German Standard DIN 1055 gives the lateral pressure P_t (kPa) developed in silos up to 20 m high as a function of the depth z (m) through the relationship

$$P_t = 4.0z$$

The above equation is only applicable to silos used to store silage with moisture ranging from 60 to 77% (wet basis).

Research work has been carried out recently aiming at examining the above-mentioned provisions of the CFBC. Based on a parametric study of farm silos filled with alfalfa silage, Jofriet and Negi (1992) suggested further modifications in the CFBC. Thus, as the CFBC values for the saturation height were found to be smaller than the corresponding values obtained analytically, the saturation height $H_s = H - z_s$ in cases of drained silos is proposed to be calculated (estimated) by the following equation:

$$H - z_s = 1.1H + 1.2M - 95 \qquad 65\% < M < 75\% \qquad 2.5 < \frac{H}{D} < 4$$

Also, the following equation is proposed for predicting (estimating) the saturation height $H_s = H - z_s$ in cases of undrained silos (note that the saturation height of undrained silos is greater than the corresponding height obtained for drained silos – Jofriet and Negi (1992)):

$$H - z_s = H + 0.9M - 70 \qquad 65\% < M < 75\% \qquad 2.5 < \frac{H}{D} < 4$$

The equation used in the CFBC for the calculation of lateral pressures in cases of undrained silos was found to be fairly good. However, the analytical results suggested that for a drained silo, no increase in liquid pressure occurs below a point halfway between saturation level and the silo bottom. Based on this, it is recommended that the equation of the CFBC for $P(z)$ is used to calculate lateral pressures in drained silos for z below saturation level and down to halfway between saturation level and silo bottom (Jofriet and Negi, 1992):

$$P(z) = P_s + (z - z_s)\left(11 - \frac{4\mu k P_s}{D}\right) \qquad z_s < z < \frac{H - z_s}{2}$$

Below this level, it is recommended that the total pressure is kept constant:

$$P(z) = P_s + \frac{H - z_s}{2}\left(11 - \frac{4\mu k P_s}{D}\right) \qquad \frac{H - z_s}{2} < z < H$$

A method which takes into account the complex nature of ensiled farm products, loading history and boundary conditions has been developed by Bishara, El-Azazy and Huang (1982). The complex nature of ensiled material is characterized as nonlinear visco-elastic whereas nonlinear finite element analysis is used to analyse the silo wall–fill material interaction. The finite element procedure takes into consideration that ensiled farm products are nonlinear visco-elastic materials and that the effects of loading history, friction between the silo wall and the ensiled material as well as other boundary conditions must be considered in a comprehensive manner. The analysis of Bishara, El-Azazy and Huang (1982) yields simple expressions for the evaluation of lateral and vertical pressures in circular silos due to corn silage. The expressions were obtained by using nonlinear regression analysis of a large number of finite element solutions. Based on this analysis, the average vertical pressure and the lateral pressure at any depth (y) is shown to develop immediately after filling. A rapid relaxation takes place after half a day reducing lateral pressure by about 15% and the average vertical pressure by about 10%. For a certain silage height, the average vertical pressure and lateral pressure at any depth increase as the internal diameter increases. The average vertical pressure and lateral pressure at any elevation from the base increase as the silage height increases. However, as a result of the friction between the silo wall and silage, the resulting average vertical pressure becomes only a fraction of the weight of the silage above that level. Both lateral pressure and average vertical pressure increase almost linearly from 0 at the top of the settled silage to a maximum value at about 85% of the silage height. The average vertical pressure within the lower 15% of the silo height remains almost constant, while the lateral pressure decreases from its maximum value to almost a zero value at the base.

In addition to analytical approaches, experiments have been carried out to investigate the pressures exerted by silage on silo walls. Thus, results from a two-year experiment to obtain wall pressures in a large bunker silo are presented in Zhao and Jofriet (1991). The maximum values of silage pressure measured were found to exceed the 1983 CFBC by a factor of 3.8 and 4.5 while they exceeded the new (1990) code by a factor of about 1.3.

In another work (Zhao and Jofriet, 1992) a finite element method (FEM) of analysis was used to investigate wall pressure exerted by silage on bunker silo walls. A good agreement was obtained between the finite element analysis results and experimental values obtained in a field experiment. The results obtained indicate that silage-induced pressures increase linearly with depth. An equivalent liquid pressure formula can be used for the prediction of these pressures. The density of the equivalent liquid is given as the product of the silage bulk density by the pressure ratio. The pressure ratio in the case of bunker silos depends on wall slope, silage surcharge angle and friction angle between wall and silage material (Zhao and Jofriet, 1992). The ratio increases with the angle of the wall and also with the surcharge angle. If the wall slope decreases from 90 to 75° the wall pressure increases by as much as 45%, suggesting that the silo wall should be kept as vertical as possible.

The work of Negi et al. (1989) presents the results of a two-year measurement of haylage pressures in a bottom-unloading monolithic silo. The results are in agreement with the predictions of the Canadian Standard for bottom-unloading silos. Accordingly, it is confirmed that the lower and upper limits for the pressure ratio of alfalfa haylage in concrete silos may be considered to vary between 0.5 and 0.6, whereas the values for wall friction may be estimated to be 0.4, 0.5 and 0.6 corresponding to moisture contents of 60, 50 and 40% (wet basis), for this material and silo type. In another experiment (Negi et al., 1992), the pressure ratio was measured for silage and grain. For whole-plant corn silage the k ratio was found to be influenced by the orientation of fibres.

One of the most complicated problems in calculating pressures due to silage concerns the characteristics of these materials. Thus, it has been observed that some materials like soy shreds behave as cohesive bulk solids when stored in silos (Hoeckman and Meulewaeter, 1988). The work of Hoeckman and Meulewaeter (1988) presents some important characteristics for soy shreds as they were investigated in the laboratory. Concerning corn silage, the National Silo Association recommends an equivalent fluid density (EFD) of 320kg/m^3 for designing silos containing corn silage with moisture content in the range 68–72%. Lateral pressures may be calculated by using Rankine's equation with a maximum density of 1040kg/m^3 and a minimum angle of internal friction of 32° (in order to obtain EFD = 320kg/m^3).

As far as potatoes are concerned, they are considered to exert pressures similar to semi-fluids. Thus, stored potatoes exert horizontal wall pressures, vertical friction loads on the walls and vertical floor loads. However, loads induced by stored potatoes are erratic. Relevant design data are based on an 80% confidence interval.

REFERENCES

ACI-313R-91 (1991) ACI Committee 313R *Standard Practice for Design and Construction of Concrete Silos and Stacking Tubes for Storing Granular Materials, and Commentary: ACI 313R-91*, American Concrete Institute, Detroit, 40 pp.

AIJ (1984) *Design Recommendation for Storage Tanks and Their Supports*, Architectural Institute of Japan.

Andersen, P. (1966) Temperature stresses in steel grain storage tanks, *Civil Engineering, ASCE*, 36(1), 74.

ANSI ASCE 7-95 (1996) *Minimum Design Loads for Buildings and Other Structures*, American National Standards Institute, Inc., New York.

Bartali, F.J. and Hatfield, (1990) Forces in cylindrical grain silos caused by decreasing ambient temperature, *ACI Structural Journal*, 87, 10–116.

Bishara, S.; El-Azazy, S.; Huang, T. (1982) Practical analysis of cylindrical farm silos based on finite element solutions, *ACI Structural Journal*, 78–80, 456–462.

Briassoulis, D. (1992) An integrated physical model for cylindrical shells, *Journal of Structural Engineering, ASCE*, 118(8), 2168–2185.

BS 5061 (1974) *Specifications for Cylindrical Forage Tower Silos and Recommendations for Their Use*, British Standards Institution, London.

CFBC (1990) Canadian Farm Buiding Code, NRCC No. 30627, Ottawa.

Gaylord, E.H. and Gaylord, C.N. (1984) *Design of Steel Bins for Storage of Bulk Solids*, Prentice-Hall, New Jersey.

Gurfinkel, G. (1979) *Reinforced Concrete Bunkers and Silos. Structural Engineering Handbook*, McGraw-Hill Book Co., New York, p. 22.

Hoeckman and L. Meulewaeter (1988) Experimental investigation of some important soy shreds characteristics, *Bulk Solids Handling*, 8(2), 155–168.

ISA (1981) Standards Committee, International Silo Association Inc., Des Moines, Iowa.

Japanese Building Standard Law, May 1981, Japanese Building Standard Cabinet Order, July 1981.

JEA (1983) *Recommendation for Earthquake-Proof Design of Thermal Power Stations*, JEAG 3605–1983, Japanese Electrical Association.

Jofriet, J.C. and Negi, S.C. (1992) Structural design loads for bins and silos, an overview, *International Conference on Agricultural Engineering*, AGENG 1992, Paper no. 9202–1.

Kitazawa, A. Ikeda and Kawamura, S. (1984) Study on a base isolation system, *Proceedings of the 8th World Conf. on Earthquake Engineering*.

Li, V.M. Puri and H.B. Manbeck (1990) Loads in a scaled, model bin subjected to cyclic ambient temperature, *Transactions of ASAE*, 33(2), 651–656.

McCammon, R.C. and Butler (1990) 'Deep-seated consolidation settlements in the Fraser River delta', *Canadian Geotechnique J.*, 28, 298–303.

Manbeck, H.B. and Nelson, G.L. (1975) Three dimensional constitutive equations for wheat en masse, *Transactions of ASAE*, **18**(6), 1122–1127.

Negi, S.C.; Jofriet, J.C.; Zhao, Q. and Law, G.J. (1992) Measurements of the at-rest pressure ratio of silage and grains, *J. Agric. Engng. Res.*, **51**, 274–283.

Negi, S.; Quah, Jofriet, J.C. and Bellman, H.E. (1989) On the storage pressures and properties of alfalfa in a bottom-unloading silo, *Transactions of ASAE*, **32**(6), 2159–2164.

Rotter, J.M. (1991) *Strength Criteria for Steel Silo Structures*, I. Mech. Eng., C418/035.

Sakai, H. Matsumura, Sasaki, M.; Nakamura, N.; Kobayashi, M. and Kitagawa, Y. (1985) Study on the dynamic behaviour of coal silos against earthquakes, *Bulk Solids Handling*, **5**(5), 1021–1026.

Tarics, A.G. (1987) The acceptance of the base isolation for earthquake protection of buildings, *Proceedings of the Eighth World Conference on Soil Dynamics and Earthquake Engineering*.

UBC (1994) *Uniform Building Code*, International Conference of Building Officials, Whittier, California.

van Wijk, L.A. (1991) Dutch developments of earthquake resistant Euro-type mammoth silos, *Bulk Solids Handling*, **11**(2), 441–445.

Zhao, Q. and Jofriet, J.C. (1991) Structural loads on bunker silo walls: experimental study, *J. Agric. Engng. Res.*, **50**, 273–290.

Zhao, Q. and Jofriet, J.C. (1992) Structural loads on bunker silo walls: numerical study, *J. Agric. Engng. Res.*, **51**, 1–13.

19

Conical hopper shells
J.M. Rotter

19.1 GENERAL

The hopper in a silo supports the majority of the material stored within the silo (Fig. 19.1), and the force derived from this load must generally pass up the hopper, through the transition junction and into the supports (Fig. 19.2). The top of the hopper, its connection to the transition ring, and its support at this key point are thus absolutely vital to the integrity of the silo. The discussion presented here therefore begins with the hopper itself, but very quickly becomes concerned with transition rings and the relationships between the hopper and ring. A summary of design criteria with the relevant equations was presented by Rotter (1990).

The hopper sustains pressures normal to the wall (Fig. 19.3), and frictional tractions down the wall, which induce biaxial tension in the shell wall (Fig. 19.4). Current hopper design techniques (Trahair *et al.*, 1983; Gaylord and Gaylord, 1984; Rotter, 1985, 1990) generally assume that the membrane theory of shells can be applied to the hopper, and that the predicted first yield load under biaxial membrane stresses constitutes a limit to the hopper strength. This is the simplest realistic design approach and is termed the 'membrane theory yield failure criterion'.

The hopper is subjected to pressure patterns which are generally seen to be very different according to whether the hopper has just been filled, possibly with a period of stationary storage (filling pressures) or is being or has been discharged (discharge pressures). The differences between the two patterns are shown in Fig. 19.5, where the very high 'switch' pressure at the

416 Conical hopper shells

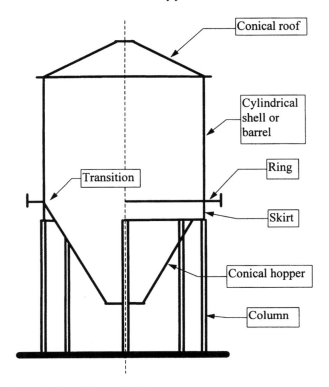

Fig. 19.1 Elevated silo with conical hopper.

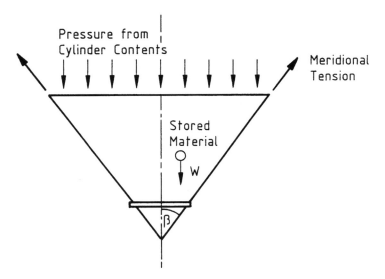

Fig. 19.2 Global equilibrium of the hopper (irrespective of pressure distributions).

General

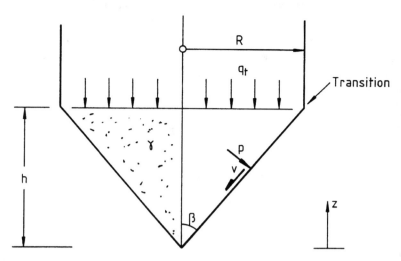

Fig. 19.3 Pressures and tractions on hopper wall.

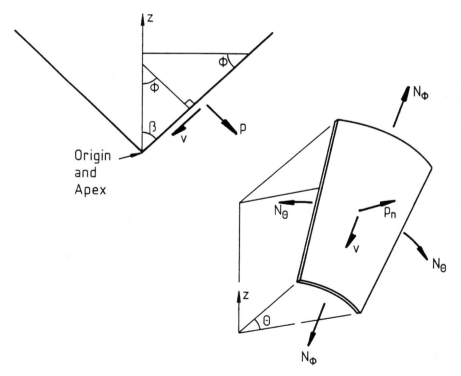

Fig. 19.4 Membrane stress resultants in the hopper wall.

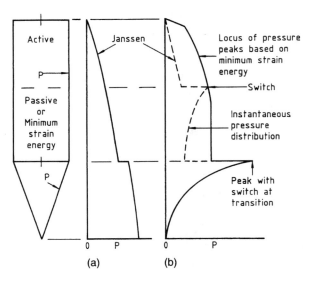

Fig. 19.5 Typical pressure distributions for which the hopper must be designed: (a) initial pressures; (b) flow pressures.

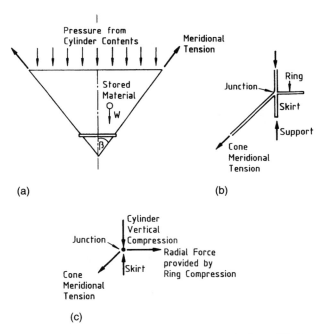

Fig. 19.6 Equilibrium of the transition junction: (a) vertical equilibrium of conical hopper; (b) junction local geometry; (c) static equilibrium at the junction.

transition is very evident. These differences naturally need consideration in studies of hopper strength.

At the top of the hopper, the meridional tension which has developed (Fig. 19.2) is transferred to the transition junction. Equilibrium dictates (Fig. 19.6) that this tension induces a circumferential compression in the junction, so design of the junction is dominated by considerations of compressive failure, at least when the loading and support are symmetrical. Where conditions are not symmetrical, the problem becomes much more complicated.

19.2 PLASTIC COLLAPSE LOADS OF HOPPERS

Teng and Rotter (1988a, 1989a, b) carried out studies to determine the formal plastic limit loads of hoppers using a small deflection elastic–plastic finite element analysis. The plastic collapse mechanism is similar to that shown in Fig. 19.7(a), though this image strictly includes the effect of large deformations. They performed a parametric study on multi-strake hoppers under linearly varying pressures and proposed simple equations for the assessment of limit loads. They showed that the plastic limit loads are generally slightly higher than the membrane theory yield load. These studies by Teng and Rotter did not explore the effect of transition switch pressures (Fig. 19.5) on hopper strength. Later, Teng and Rotter (1990, 1991a, 1992) investigated the failure behaviour of welded hoppers of uniform thickness under Walker's (1966) pressure distributions for both filling and discharge as noted below.

19.3 MEMBRANE YIELDING OF HOPPERS

Teng and Rotter's later studies (Teng and Rotter, 1990, 1991a) showed that first yield in the hopper of a skirt-supported silo generally occurs at the hopper top at a low load, but this yielding does not bear any direct relation to the strength of the hopper unless a fatigue failure is possible. However, when membrane yielding is reached in the body of the hopper, an abrupt loss of stiffness occurs at a load very close to the membrane theory yield load. The membrane theory yield load (Trahair *et al.*, 1983; Gaylord and Gaylord, 1984) is thus a safe but close lower bound for use in design if large deformations in the hopper are to be prevented.

A steep hopper with a short cylinder under filling pressures can sustain little additional load once this stiffness reduction occurs. Such hoppers fail by membrane yielding and the membrane theory yield load is a close approximation of the failure strength.

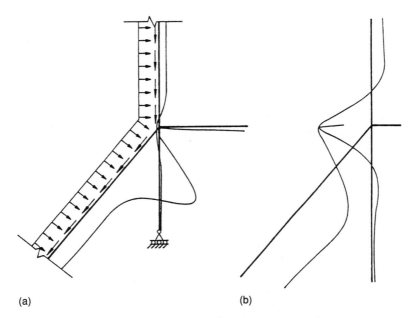

Fig. 19.7 Plastic collapse failure modes for the hopper and transition junction: (a) collapse at top of hopper; (b) collapse mode of junction.

19.4 MERIDIONAL RUPTURE OF HOPPERS

Most hoppers can sustain an increasing load with increasing deformations after the stiffness reduction at membrane yielding in the hopper body. Teng and Rotter (1990, 1991a) showed that these hoppers eventually fail by rupture when, as originally suggested by Rotter (1985), the meridional membrane stress at the top of the hopper reaches the maximum value on the von Mises yield locus, which is $1.155\sigma_y$. Simple design equations were given in Rotter (1990) and Teng and Rotter (1990, 1991a) for the design of hoppers against rupture failure. Design of a welded hopper only for rupture failure has two advantages: first, the strength of the hopper depends only on the total weight on the hopper and not on the pressure distribution on the wall. This greatly simplifies the design process. Second, lighter structures are produced, and the design emphasis is placed on the most critical joint in the structure (Rotter, 1990).

19.5 TRANSITION JUNCTIONS UNDER CIRCUMFERENTIALLY UNIFORM LOADS

19.5.1 Introduction

If the transition junction is not very strong, failure of the ring at the transition junction may precede hopper failure. The strength of the junction may be limited by plastic collapse of the junction (Fig. 19.7(b)) or by elastic

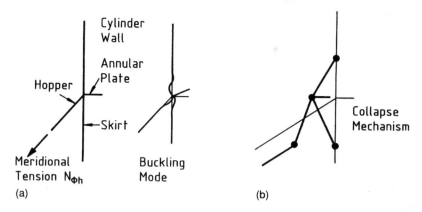

Fig. 19.8 Simplified images of transition junction failure modes: (a) geometry and buckling mode of ring; (b) plastic collapse mechanism.

or elastic–plastic buckling of the ring. The collapse mechanism and buckling mode are shown in Fig. 19.8.

19.5.2 Elastic buckling of annular section rings

The elastic out-of-plane buckling of annular plate rings at the transition was studied by Jumikis and Rotter (1983). They developed simple equations for the buckling strength taking into account the flexural restraint of the adjacent shells. This was extended by Sharma et al. (1987).

19.5.3 Elastic buckling of rings of general section attached to the junction

Rotter and Jumikis (1985) undertook an extensive numerical study of the elastic buckling of T-section rings at the transition junction, ignoring the elastic restraint from the adjacent shell walls. They proposed a complicated empirical relation to predict the buckling strength. Later, Teng and Rotter (1988b) presented a closed form solution for out-of-plane buckling of restrained monosymmetric rings, and derived a simplified equation for the buckling of T-section rings at silo transition junctions ignoring the flexural restraint from the adjacent silo walls.

19.5.4 Plastic collapse of transition junctions

The first description of transition junction plastic collapse is due to Rotter (1985, 1987), who also devised a simple rationally based equation to predict the collapse strength. The collapse mechanism involves two plastic hinge circles in each shell segment: one at the transition and the other within the shell segment (Fig. 19.8). Teng and Rotter (1991b, c) conducted a comprehensive study of this problem and showed that the simple equation of Rotter (1985, 1987) becomes slightly unconservative if the shell segments meeting at the junction have very different thicknesses. A more complicated version of Rotter's (1985) original equation was proposed (Teng and Rotter, 1991b, c), which was found to match many finite element analyses well over a wide range of geometries. Further work to generalize the results to complex junctions was performed by Teng (1996), who proposed a more complete design method.

19.5.5 Plastic buckling of transition rings

For rings in which the plastic collapse and elastic buckling strengths are comparable, plastic buckling may be the critical strength consideration. The first brief study of plastic buckling in annular plate rings was that of Rotter (1987), followed soon after by the more comprehensive work of Teng and Rotter (1991d) in which both annular plate and T-section rings were investigated. The simple proposals of Rotter (1987), which suggested that the buckling strength was closely modelled by the plastic collapse load and the elastic buckling load of a ring which is simply supported on its inner edge, were generally confirmed, so these two simple criteria remain as good design equations.

19.6 HOPPERS AND TRANSITION JUNCTIONS IN COLUMN-SUPPORTED SILOS

19.6.1 General

The above discussion was concerned only with silos which are uniformly supported all around the circumference on a deep skirt, stiff ring, or many columns (Fig. 12.3(a)). The conditions which govern failures in column-supported silos are much less well understood. Most of the known critical design considerations for column-supported hoppers were reviewed by Rotter (1990). The stresses in the hopper of a column-supported silo can be quite non-uniform, with much higher meridional tensions near the columns than at the midspan position. An example is shown in Fig. 19.9, where the variation of the all-important meridional tension in the hopper is shown for a line down the hopper below the support, and a line midway between supports. The stresses near the hopper bottom are unaffected by the support, but towards the top, where stresses are high anyway, much higher values occur. The variation of these stresses around the circumference of the hopper top is shown in Fig. 19.10, where the huge local stress near the column is evident. Failure by rupture of the hopper top under meridional stresses is not ductile, so the highest stress can easily induce a tearing failure which will progress rapidly around the circumference. The hopper then falls from the silo and the stored contents fall out.

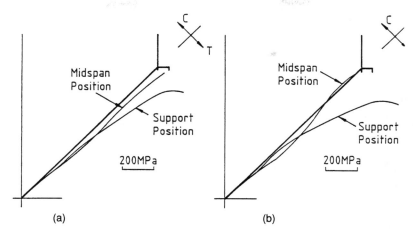

Fig. 19.9 Silo on discrete column supports: effect on meridional tension in the hopper beneath the support and midway between supports: (a) design A; (b) design B.

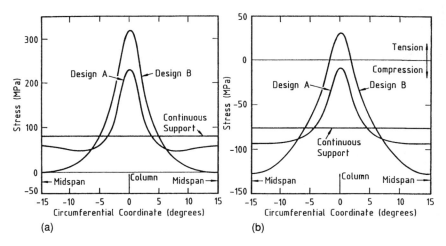

Fig. 19.10 Silo on discrete column supports: variation around the circumference of meridional tension at the top of the hopper: (a) meridional membrane stress; (b) circumferential membrane stress.

The magnitude of the local meridional stress at the hopper top depends on many geometrical factors. The problem is especially severe in light gauge construction with small numbers of columns. The non-uniformity is much larger when the transition ring is small and/or the cylinder wall is flexible (e.g. corrugated) (Rotter, 1990).

In addition to the above catastrophic failure, the column-supported transition junction may also fail by plastic collapse of the junction, or elastic buckling of the ring, with the possibility of plastic buckling of the ring between these two cases. One study (Teng and Rotter, 1989c) has examined the conditions under which elastic buckling may be expected, but the criteria for plastic failure remain unclear at present. These failure modes, although seen in practice and unsightly, are not catastrophic in the manner of hopper failures, so they have drawn less attention to date.

19.6.2 Buckling of rings in column-supported silos

In column-supported silos with only a few columns, the circumferential stresses in the ring vary both around the circumference and over the cross-section (Teng and Rotter, 1989c). Teng and Rotter (1989c) presented simple equations based on a closed-form solution to predict the strength of rings simply supported at the inner edge. Two simple conclusions are useful. First, the maximum compressive stress in the ring at buckling is always larger (possibly much larger) than the buckling stress of the same ring under uniform compression. Thus if the maximum compressive stress is kept below the buckling stress of a uniformly compressed ring, as suggested by Rotter (1985), the design will be conservative, though sometimes very conservative. Second, the critical point for buckling failure is at the column support position, so only this area need be examined if the ring is uniform.

REFERENCES

Gaylord, E.H. and Gaylord, C.N. (1984) *Design of Steel Bins for Storage of Bulk Solids*, Prentice-Hall, New Jersey.

Jumikis, P.T. and Rotter, J.M. (1983) Buckling of simple ringbeams for bins and tanks, *Proc., Int. Conf. Bulk Matls Storage, Handling and Transpn*, IEAust, Newcastle, Aug., pp. 323–328.

Rotter, J.M. (1985) Analysis and design of ringbeams, in *Design of Steel Bins for the Storage of Bulk Solids*, edited by J.M. Rotter, Univ. Sydney, March, pp. 164–183.

Rotter, J.M. (1987) The buckling and plastic collapse of ring stiffeners at cone/cylinder junctions, *Proc. Int. Colloq. on Stability of Plate and Shell Struct.*, Ghent, April, pp. 449–456.

Rotter, J.M. (1990) The structural design of light gauge silo hoppers, *J. Struct. Engrg, ASCE*, **116**(7), 1907–1922.

Rotter, J.M. and Jumikis, P.T. (1985) Elastic buckling of stiffened ringbeams for large elevated bins, *Proc., Metal Struct. Conf.*, IEAust, Melbourne, pp. 104–111.

Sharma, U.C.; Rotter, J.M. and Jumikis, P.T. (1987) Shell restraint to ringbeam buckling in elevated steel silos, *First National Structural Engineering Conference*, Melbourne, Institution of Engineers, Australia, pp. 604–609.

Teng, J.G. (1996) The effective area method for collapse strength prediction of complex metal shell intersections, *Proc., International Conference on Structural Steelwork*, Hong Kong, December, pp. 767–774.

Teng, J.G. and Rotter, J.M. (1988a) *Plastic Collapse of Restrained Metal Silo Hoppers*, Res. Rept R. 580, Sch. of Civ. and Min. Engrg, Univ. of Sydney, Australia.

Teng, J.G. and Rotter, J.M. (1988b) Buckling of restrained monosymmetric rings, *J. Engrg Mech., ASCE*, **114**(10), 1651–1671.

Teng, J.G. and Rotter, J.M. (1989a) Plastic collapse of restrained metal silo hoppers, *J. Constr. Metal Res.*, **14**(2), 135–158.

Teng, J.G. and Rotter, J.M. (1989b) The strength of silo transition rings and hoppers, *Mechanical Engrg Trans, IEAust*, **ME14**(4), 170–177.

Teng, J.G. and Rotter, J.M. (1989c) Buckling of rings in column-supported bins and tanks, *Thin Walled Structs*, 7(3 & 4), 251–280.

Teng, J.G. and Rotter, J.M. (1990) *Hopper Failure: Pressures, Failure Modes and Strengths*, Res. Rept 90.08, Dept of Civ. Engrg and Bldg Sci., Univ. of Edinburgh.

Teng, J.G. and Rotter, J.M. (1991a) The strength of welded metal silo hoppers under filling and flow pressures, *J. Struct. Engrg, ASCE*, **117**(9), 2567–2583.

Teng, J.G. and Rotter, J.M. (1991b) The collapse behaviour and strength of metal silo junctions – Part I: Collapse mechanics, *J. Struct. Engrg, ASCE*, **117**(12), Dec. 1991, 3587–3604.

Teng, J.G. and Rotter, J.M. (1991c) The collapse behaviour and strength of metal silo junctions – Part II: Parametric study, *J. Struct. Engrg, ASCE*, **117**(12), Dec. 1991, 3605–3622.

Teng, J.G. and Rotter, J.M. (1991d) Plastic buckling of rings at metal silo transition junctions, *J. Constr. Metal Res.*, **19**, 1–18.

Teng, J.G. and Rotter, J.M. (1992) Recent research on the behaviour and design of steel silo hoppers and transition junctions, Special Edition on Australian Research, *Journal of Constructional Steel Research*, **23**, 313–343.

Trahair, N.S.; Abel, A.; Ansourian, P.; Irvine, H.M. and Rotter, J.M. (1983) *Structural Design of Steel Bins for Bulk Solids*, Australian Institute of Steel Construction, Nov.

Walker, D.M. (1966) An approximate theory for pressures and arching in hoppers, *Chem. Engrg Sci.*, **21**, 975–977.

20
Rectangular silo structures
C.J. Brown

20.1 GENERAL

The design and performance of metal rectangular planform silos are very different from those of circular silos. Pressure/displacement relationships, their interaction and their importance in the performance of rectangular planform silos are often poorly understood. Features which may be significant in order to achieve optimal designs are often overlooked in favour of conservative designs.

This chapter focuses on the special features specific to the design and performance of rectangular silos. Many of the more general factors relating to the design of steel silos are covered elsewhere (e.g. Chapters 12 and 13) with reference to circular planform silos. Some of the same comments will apply to rectangular planform structures but are not repeated here (e.g. the effect of temperature on the stored bulk solid, earthquake action).

20.2 DEFINITION

A definition of the terms and dimensions relating to rectangular planform storage structures is given in the Eurocode *Actions in Silos and Tanks* (ENV 1991-4). In particular, the hydraulic radius – the ratio of cross-section area of the vertical section to the perimeter of the vertical section – is defined. The 'width' of the silo is defined as w, while d_c is the diameter of the largest inscribed circle, and may be relevant for calculation of patch loads.

20.3 BACKGROUND

Trahair (1985) has given a definitive outline of silos and their structural form. The rectangular planform is not intrinsically the most efficient structural form because circular silos use membrane action effectively while rectangular silos use less efficient bending of the silo walls as the primary load-supporting action. This is a significant feature in determining the size of rectangular planform steel silos, because while small unstiffened silos may always be economically viable, and values of d_c up to 4 or 5 m may be feasible with stiffened designs, silos with larger plan dimensions are likely to be circular planform.

Figure 20.1 shows different schematic configurations for rectangular planform silos. Figure 20.1(a) shows a small silo, typical of use in the process industry, where mass flow is essential, and internal corners are radiused for ease of cleaning. Figure 20.1(b) shows a slender silo in which stiffeners are used (shown schematically) to give plates which are of approximately square aspect ratio, while Fig. 20.1(c) shows a squatter silo, in which both vertical and horizontal stiffeners are required (columns are not shown for clarity).

For a given wall thickness, rectangular planform silos do not have the same strength reserves (yield stresses may be reached earlier), and they are not as naturally stiff as circular planform silos. They will therefore generally require more material (thickness) in construction because of this fundamental feature. Fabrication and transport costs can be reduced however, because rectangular planform silos are constructed from readily available plate material which will require a minimum of further working before it is ready for use. This contrasts with the plate preparation (e.g. possibly rolling) that may be required for circular planform silos.

Despite the inherent disadvantages, there are many instances where rectangular storage structures are common, and their use is essential. Coal-fired power stations frequently use rectangular planform storage structures for the steady delivery of boiler fuel, and there are offshore applications as well. One of the key reasons for using rectangular silos is to give maximum use of the limited plan area available.

Rectangular silos are often stiffened, and have large reserves of strength; this underlines the lack of knowledge about the real potential for the use of thin-walled plate structures. In this respect, the materials handling industry has shown the need for lightweight structures and the use of highly flexible fabric-like containers in the construction and materials handling industries demonstrates the large reserves of strength in thin-walled rectangular structures with stiffened corners. The French silo industry has led the way with regulations for designs which enhance the corner stiffness by the use of ties (*Silos en acier*, P22-630, 1992).

One of the obvious features of rectangular planform structures is the presence of corners. Locally increased wall friction may exist. If the stored material has a moderately high moisture content, or if the roof is in any way imperfect and does not completely prevent moisture ingress, the possibility of corrosion at the corners of the silo is high, and this should be an important design criterion for unlined silos.

Consideration of other polygonal planforms is omitted here; these are very specialized. Multi-cell silos are also used, and in this case they may

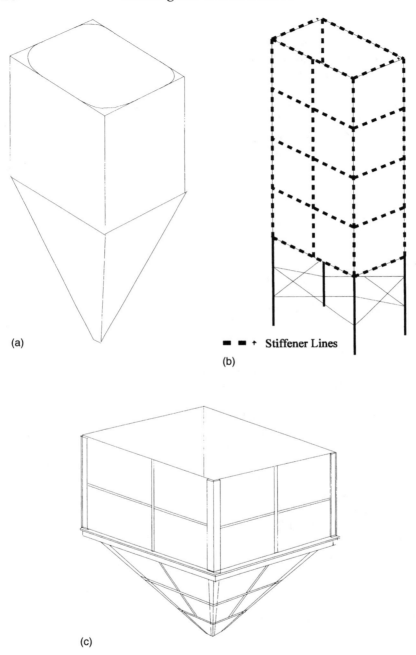

Fig. 20.1 Schematic configurations for rectangular planform silos: (a) a small silo with radiused internal corners; (b) a slender silo incorporating stiffeners to give a roughly square aspect ratio; (c) a squat silo requiring both horizontal and vertical stiffeners.

often be rectangular planform. Interactions between cells (e.g. full/empty condition in adjacent cells) must be considered most carefully, but again generalization is difficult.

20.4 FUNCTIONAL DESIGN

The functional design of a rectangular planform structure is based on the same criteria described elsewhere for circular planform silos. Once the hydraulic radius is defined for a rectangular planform silo, the recommended design procedures for both the flow and pressure (and hence structural design) relate to this. Mass flow or internal flow patterns are possible, and may determine the proportions of the final structure – e.g. squat or slender. The same design precautions should be taken against other problems identified for circular silos, such as ratholing in flow, or special loading (e.g. from thermal expansion) of the stored material.

Funnel flow can be achieved without the need to use a hopper; an outlet opening of sufficient dimension in the base of a flat-bottomed silo will be adequate to allow material flow, but will lead to incomplete emptying of the stored material. Nevertheless, this can provide an effective solution in some cases. Funnel (or internal) flow with a hopper can lead to complete clear-out of the stored material. Mass flow, by definition, leads to complete clear-out, and is attractive because of its first-in first-out working condition. The clear-out condition may be important for corrosion prevention in corners; alternatively corners may be radiused (Fig. 20.1(a)).

Figure 20.2 shows the common outlet configurations for single silo discharging centrally, while Fig. 20.3 shows a possible configuration for eccentric discharge. Eccentricity of either inlet or outlet generally has a significant disadvantageous effect on the flow pattern in both the bin and hopper, and on the wall pressures in the entire system, but may be necessary because of the geometric layout of the process.

20.5 WALL PRESSURES

Wall pressures to be used for design are defined by different national (e.g. DIN 1055, BMHB Code, Australian Code) and European Standards (ENV 1991–4 *Actions in Silos and Tanks*, 1994). Nevertheless, these standards can lead to differences and discrepancies for design pressures used by different individuals in different member states. This is well discussed and documented by Wilms, Rotter and Tomas (1995). Some of the code design criteria are based on experience with concrete silos or circular planform silos; neither may be appropriate for rectangular steel silos.

Significant research undertaken by Pieper (1969) involved experimental work to determine wall pressures. The tests were carried out on a model constructed from a series of plates, and the load on each plate was measured to determine the variation of wall pressure with height. The model was

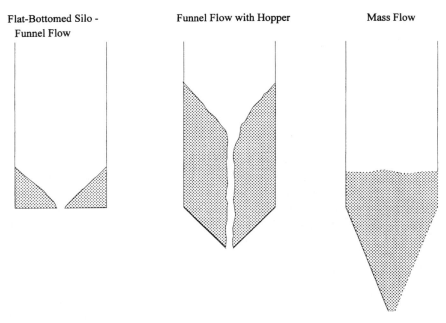

Fig. 20.2 Common outlet configurations for single silo discharging centrally.

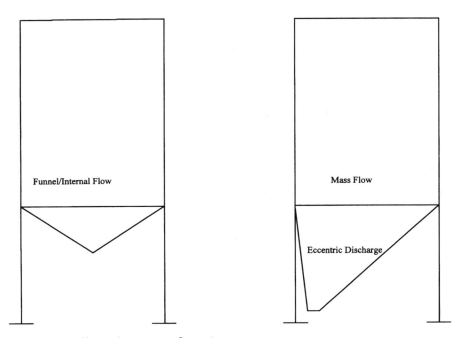

Fig. 20.3 Different hopper configurations.

effectively rigid walled, and variation across the wall at any given height was not measured. Pieper showed that the pressures determined by using the theories of Janssen (1895) were appropriate for rectangular silos and that results could be transferred to larger silos by using the ratio of area to perimeter – the hydraulic radius. There was note of some variations that occurred, but for many years this was considered to be an acceptable basis for design.

Work by Jarrett, Brown and Moore (1995), Brown, Lahlouh and Rotter (1995) and by Lahlouh, Brown and Rotter (1995) on two different pilot-scale relatively flexible steel silos has shown that even in relatively stiff silos where the deflections were significantly less than the wall thickness, the flexibility of the wall allows a large redistribution of the wall pressures on a horizontal plane to take place. Some form of arching across the silo wall has been postulated as an explanation. While the Janssen distribution showed a reasonable approximation to the variation in average wall pressure with height, the distribution of horizontal pressure at any level was far from uniform. While Janssen's original work suggested that in rectangular silos a slightly larger pressure may be expected at midspan, the variations in horizontal wall pressure that were observed showed the lower pressures being coincident with the positions of largest wall deformation, and the larger pressures occurring near the stiffer corners. The ratio of these horizontal pressures was often up to 6:1.

Furthermore, the later studies have been limited to only two materials (Leighton Buzzard sand and pea gravel) which have similar properties apart from the grain size; changing this one parameter seems to have a significant effect in the resulting pressures.

The studies determined the effect of different structural support and filling and discharge conditions. The use of eccentric filling and discharge procedures is common, and the effect on flow and pressure of using eccentric discharge is little understood. The studies by Lahlouh, Brown and Rotter have shown the effect of modifying discharge position, but the redistribution of wall pressures is often a dominant feature in determining design pressures.

Research publications specifically aimed at the investigation of the performance of rectangular silos are quite limited. One of the more useful was produced by Michael (Lightfoot and Michael, 1966) whose thesis investigated the performance of coal bunkers. The investigation looked at a 'live' steel coal bunker, an aluminium model, and a conventional design theory to try and take some account of the composite action taking place between the vertical stiffeners in the bunker and the plate, and hence to lead to greater economies of design in the longer term.

Work carried out at Chartres (e.g. described by Khelil, Sokol and Roth, 1989) on full-scale square and rectangular planform silos did not attempt to determine distributions on a horizontal plane.

It is difficult to recommend a less conservative approach to current design when evidence is based on so few tests and rigorous mathematical models are not generally available. Further work is needed, as such an approach might lead to both a better understanding of silo structural behaviour and significant savings in design.

The Eurocode (ENV 1991-4 *Actions in Silos and Tanks*, 1994) suggests the use of a patch load to represent peak local bending loads imposed from the stored bulk solid which may result from variation in loading, but the relevance of this for rectangular planform silos is not clear. The objective of the patch load is to ensure that the shell will not fail if systematic high local loads occur; it also requires a 'rigorous' analysis to be completed, i.e. for designers to go further than a simple membrane and bending analysis (Rotter, 1985a, b). The need for either is less obvious with simple plate structures, although greater efficiency might be gained if the full effect of membrane action is allowed (see below). For slender silos, typical stress increases can be up to 30%, while some squatter structures may have higher increases. The patch load is used to augment the calculated uniform pressures. Partial factors of safety on the loads are explicit and reduced from values in alternative codes (e.g. DIN 1055). There are thus potential savings in many cases (for example in centrally discharging slender unstiffened silos) when total loads are less. It should also be noted that the largest stress increases are obtained when the patch load is placed at midspan, while research has shown that pressure peaks in unstiffened structures occur near the ends of the horizontal span.

Wind loading is the other main form of loading that should be considered, and a body of information (Chapter 17) is now available to enable the designer to calculate appropriate loads. The data for rectangular silos are well documented because the loading coefficients have been extensively computed for domestic dwellings of different aspect ratios, whose planform is also rectangular. Particular care should be taken with rectangular silos in the empty condition, as there is no lateral support from the ensiled material.

20.6 STRUCTURAL DESIGN

The primary objective of the structural design is to transmit the loads to the foundations within specified limits for safety and serviceability. The mechanisms for such load transfer are various, and will depend on the particular location and support system used (for instance, some structures may be 'top hung' to ensure no obstruction below the hopper – as in power station applications). However, many silos are supported on columns and ring beams, and so some general observations about the special nature of design of rectangular planform structures can be made.

20.6.1 Structural actions

As bulk solid is charged into the silo, material already in the silo will tend to be compressed towards the outlet. Wall friction is generated, and will increase to a maximum as further bulk solid is added. This is the basis of the expression derived by Janssen (1895) which leads to asymptotic maxima for the vertical stress in the stored bulk solid, and for the lateral wall pressure, provided the silo is of sufficient height.

$$P_v = P_\infty \left(1 - e^{-\mu k Z/R}\right)$$

$$P_\infty = \frac{\gamma R}{\mu}$$

$$P_h = k P_v$$

where P_v is the vertical pressure in the bulk solid, P_h the horizontal pressure against the wall, μ the wall friction coefficient, γ the bulk density of the stored solid, k a factor relating horizontal to vertical pressure, which is highly dependent on ϕ, the angle of internal friction, R is the hydraulic radius (area/perimeter) and z the depth from the top of the fill.

For tall silos with high wall friction, or small hydraulic radii, the wall pressure rapidly approaches P_∞ and the distribution of normal and frictional forces may be considered close to uniform, while for squat silos storing bulk solids a geostatic approximation to the wall pressures may be more appropriate.

The structural actions taking place in a simple rectangular planform structure are shown in Fig. 20.4. The wall is in primary bending from the lateral load generated by the stored bulk solid, in tension from the primary membrane action, and in compression from wall friction.

A simple mathematical model, assuming bending in a horizontal strip and fixity against rotation at the corners, shows the relative magnitudes of stress due to elastic bending and membrane actions. If w is the width of the silo, and t is the wall thickness, then the ratio of horizontal membrane tension to bending stress is 1 to (w/t), and it can be seen that the membrane action is potentially very small in slender structures.

The tensile bending stress and the tensile membrane stress are additive. More importantly, the compressive element of bending and the compressive load in the plate from wall friction are also cumulative effects, but the ratio is less easily determined, particularly as the load path of the (compressive) friction force may be difficult to ascertain (Fig 20.5).

The analysis described above assumes that lateral wall deflections are small. If larger displacements are allowed to occur then the membrane capacity of the plate would be used more efficiently, but this potential for economy has not been investigated.

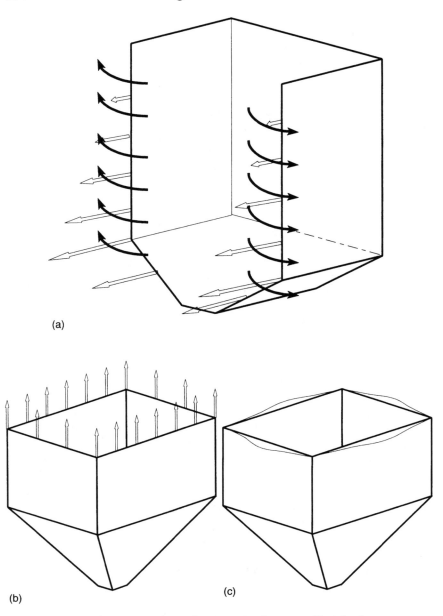

Fig. 20.4 Structural actions taking place in a simple rectangular planform structure.

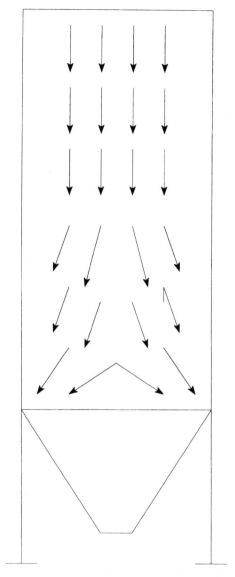

Fig. 20.5 Schematic representation of load path for friction forces.

20.6.2 Vertical walls

The criteria determining the required thickness of plate depend on the design concept; as usual a significant factor to consider is the most effective way of transferring the imposed loads to the ground (foundations). Because of the common use of stiffeners in plated structures, the plate elements are sometimes considered as little more than one-way spanning strips, transferring load to the stiffener(s) which is then seen as part of a grillage of members distributing load to the corner supporting columns and transition ring beams. Depending on plate proportions and spans, this approach can lead to a very stiff, heavy and potentially inefficient design, but also one with a high reserve of strength. Although some membrane action provides the reactive force for the lateral loads, as shown in Fig. 20.4(b), this approach is not attempting to make full use of the available membrane capacity of the plate. Gaylord and Gaylord (1984) give a good review of the design process, while the appropriate expressions for continuous structures (i.e. those where there is continuity of the structural action in the wall plates at their intersection) are given by Safarian and Harris (1985) and by Troitsky (1980). (It should be noted that these two references contain much design material.)

Whichever form of construction is used for the wall, the wall friction will generate membrane compressions at the corners in silos which are column supported (with or without ring beam), and quite large compressions occur towards the lower regions of the plates. This is shown schematically in Fig. 20.5. The phenomenon may be exaggerated if large displacements are occurring and secondary membrane features become more significant. As the corners are also the region where flexural bending stresses predominate they are one of the key regions for strength design.

An unstiffened structure, in which larger deflections of the wall are allowed to take place, and hence where both bending and membrane action in the steel plate occur, may be economic. In some of the pilot-scale silos (Jarrett, Brown and Moore, 1995; Lahlouh, Brown and Rotter, 1995) significant reserves of steel strength were available with unstiffened walls, and w/t ratios of 200:1 and 250:1. The allowable deflections may have to be of the order of the wall thickness, however, for the membrane effect to become significant, and this may mean that serviceability criteria cannot be satisfied. An appropriate numerical (e.g. finite element) model using large displacement theory will be necessary to ensure that both strength and serviceability criteria are met, and wall buckling (section 20.7) must be checked.

The use of corrugated sheeting, or ribbed sheeting spanning horizontally, is becoming more widespread, particularly in France where it is being used without vertical stiffening. To prevent spreading of the corners of the structure, ties have been used to provide restraint and stiffness (Fig. 20.6). Much of the information on ties is retained by industry, and as little openly published work exists, the limits for which this form may be safe are not well determined. It may be that, restricted to use in funnel flow silos, savings are possible; using ties in mass flow silos may lead to unexpected difficulties.

Where tall box-like silos are built, the possibility of shear lag should be examined, as this could lead to problems particularly with light ring-beam

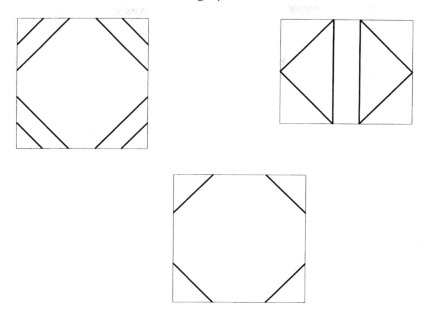

Fig. 20.6 Typical layout of corner ties in rectangular planform silos.

connections, and column-supported bins. Shear lag describes the action in which the relative flexural stiffnesses of different components will play a significant part, and is demonstrated in the simple example shown in Fig. 20.7. If the upper beam is loaded, and is connected to a lower, more flexible beam which is supported at its ends, then the load will not be uniform in the lower beam; there will be a compressive action at the junction of the beams near the supports, and a tensile action at midspan.

In silos, if the ring beam is end supported, and obtains little stiffness from the hopper (if a hopper exists), then tensile forces may exist between ring beam and hopper.

In a conventional hopper/bin construction, the hopper is likely to be connected to the bin by means of a ring beam, and the resulting construction will tend to be stiff against lateral loads from the stored bulk solid. The same may not be true at the top of the bin, and a ring stiffener at this level can be extremely effective in limiting large transverse deformations that might otherwise occur in the wall plates.

20.7 BUCKLING OF SILO WALLS

Buckling of plated structures is well understood (Rotter, Ansourian and Trahair, 1986; Murray, 1985; Bulson, 1970) and it has been shown (e.g. Chapter 14) that both loading and unloading cycles of silos may generate tractive forces on the silo wall. The elastic critical condition should be

438 *Rectangular silo structures*

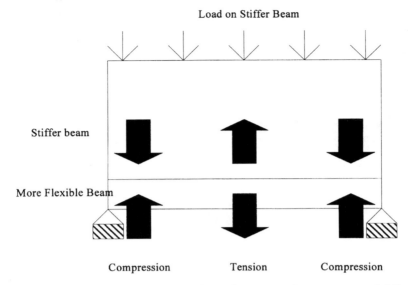

Fig. 20.7 Under loads, compressive and tensile actions of components of differing flexural stiffness result in shear lag.

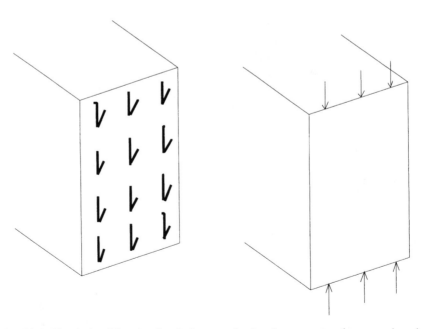

Fig. 20.8 Elastic buckling loads of plates under in-plane tractive forces and under equivalent end loads.

considered as governing silo design; while post-elastic strength may exist, it would not be appropriate to consider this for silo design. Brown (1991) has shown that the elastic buckling loads of plates subjected to in-plane tractive forces are considerably greater than those given by an analysis assuming equivalent end-loads. This is shown in Fig. 20.8.

It is often stated that the stiffening effect of the stored material increases the buckling load of plated structures. For shell structures there may be some evidence of this, but for plate structures it may be that in the worst case the buckled form would not utilize any stiffening from the stored medium. Figure 20.9 shows two possible buckled forms for a plate under the action of uniform tractive forces. In the first case the stiffening effect of the stored solid would increase the buckling load, while in the second this stiffening effect would not be mobilized. The ratio of the total force is 1:1.34. The lateral shortening effect which would be introduced by plate buckling may or may not be mobilized, depending on the form of construction (e.g. welded joints may provide sufficient restraints while simple connections might not).

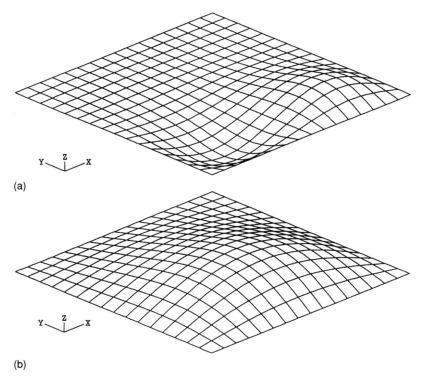

Fig. 20.9 Buckled forms for a plate under uniform tractive loads: (a) the stiffening effect of the stored solid would increase the buckling load; (b) a stiffening effect of the stored solid would not come into play.

The behaviour of silos whose side lengths lie approximately in the ratio $0.8 < a/b < 1.25$ may be considered as bidirectional, where a and b are side widths but for lower and greater ratios, the silo may take on the characteristics of a bunker; the design of walls in bunkers may be based on a one-way spanning slab, and true plate (biaxial) action is not occurring.

20.8 PYRAMIDAL HOPPERS

Like the vertical walls, plates forming trapezoidal hoppers are statically indeterminate structures, and the determination of the load path may be complex. The plates of a hopper may be subject to quite significant transverse loads, depending on the eccentricity of the outlet and the properties of the ensiled material. Hence designing hoppers as laterally loaded plates with in-plane loads may be appropriate.

There may be little need to add stiffeners to small hopper structures, but the already stiff hopper structure may require some stiffening when larger (5 m or similar) hopper dimensions are used. It is quite common to find the same level of stiffening (or even greater) in the hopper as has been used in the bin. Conversely, the hopper may be supported from a ring beam, and the walls will try to pull in on the ensiled material as more material is charged into the hopper.

20.9 RESEARCH FOCUS

There is much work to be carried out in the study of the structural behaviour of rectangular planform silos.

The most obvious requirement occurs because the designer appears to have no knowledge of the real factors of safety on the design of the structure, and real behaviour in the post-elastic region is little known. The behavioural feature that the applied loads change as a result of the structural deformations means that great caution is currently exercised by designers. More research effort has the potential to lead to significant savings. In particular, designs utilizing the membrane stiffness of the wall plates can lead to greater economy of design. There have been many advances in numerical modelling in the past decade, and this expertise should be applied to rectangular planform silos to enhance their design possibilities.

The problems associated with eccentric discharge have been identified \and are common to the different silo planforms. For eccentric discharge in rectangular hoppers, the lateral loads may be the governing design condition.

The French silo construction industry has started to use corner ties extensively in square planform silos, and the benefits and problems ensuing from such a practice are not well understood, particularly outside France. There are no available research data on the use of ties.

Patch loads should be applied to silo structures under the loading requirements of the ENV, yet it is not known what increases of stress are generated, and whether the values are appropriate in all cases. This aspect deserves further study for rectangular planform silos.

Finally, eccentricity of inlet and outlet are known to have significant effects on the pressures in any silo form. Limiting the eccentricity of outlet to $0.25d$ (ENV, 1994) is a tacit acceptance of our limits of knowledge.

REFERENCES

Australian Code *Loads on bulk solids containers*, AS 3774-1990, Standards Australia, Sydney.

BMHB Code, British Materials Handling Board, *Draft Code of Practice for the Design of Silos*, Ascot, UK, 1987.

Brown, C.J., 'Elastic buckling of plates subjected to distributed tangential loads', *Computers and Structures*, 41(1), pp. 151–155, 1991.

Brown, C.J.; Lahlouh, E.H. and Rotter, J.M., 'Eccentric discharge in rectangular planform silos', *PARTEC 95, 3rd European Symposium on Storage and Flow of Particulate Solids* (Janssen Centennial), Nuremberg, 1995, pp. 241–250.

Bulson, P.S. *The Stability of Flat Plates*, Chatto and Windus, London, 1970.

DIN 1055 Part 6, *Lasten in Silozellen*, Berlin.

ENV 1991-4 *Actions in Silos and Tanks*, Brussels.

Gaylord, E.H. and Gaylord, C.N., *Design of Steel Bins for Storage of Bulk Solids*, Prentice-Hall International, New Jersey, 1984.

Janssen, H.A., 'Versuche über Getreidedruck in Silozellen', *Zeitschrift VDI*, 39(35), pp. 1045–1049, 1895.

Jarrett, N.D.; Brown, C.J. and Moore, D.B. 'Stress redistribution in rectangular planform silos', *Géotechnique*, 45(1), pp. 95–104, March 1995.

Khelil, A.; Sokol, L. and Roth, J.C. 'Comparaison des résultats des essais in situ avec différents modèles globaux d'évaluation des pressions sur les parois', *Construction Métallique*, No. 2, pp. 51–64, June 1989.

Lahlouh, E.H.; Brown, C.J. and Rotter, J.M. '*Loads on Rectangular Planform Steel Silos*', Report No. R95-027, University of Edinburgh, 1995.

Lightfoot, E. and Michael, D. 'Prismatic coal bunkers in structural steelwork', *The Structural Engineer*, 44, pp. 55–62, 1966.

Murray, N.W., 'Design aspects of thin-walled steel silos', in *Design of Steel Bins for the Storage of Bulk Solids*, J.M. Rotter (ed.), University of Sydney, March 1985, pp. 158–163.

Pieper, K., 'Investigation of silo loads in measuring models', *Trans. A.S.M.E. J. Engineering for Industry*, pp. 365–372, 1969.

Rotter, J.M., 'Membrane theory of shells for bins and silos', in *Design of Steel Bins for the Storage of Bulk Solids*, J.M. Rotter (ed.), University of Sydney, March 1985a, pp. 58–70.

Rotter, J.M. 'Bending theory of shells for bins and silos', in *Design of Steel Bins for the Storage of Bulk Solids*, J.M. Rotter (ed.), University of Sydney, March 1985b, pp. 71–81.

Rotter, J.M.; Ansourian, P. and Trahair, N.S. 'A survey of recent buckling research on steel silos' in *Steel Structures – Recent Research Advances and Their Applications to Design*, M. Pavlovic (ed.) Elsevier, London, 1986, pp. 359–377.

Safarian, S.S. and Harris, E.C., *Design and Construction of Silos and Bunkers*, Van Nostrand Reinhold, New York, 1985.

Silos en acier, P22-630, January 1992, France.

Trahair, N.S., 'Characteristics of structural form' in *Design of Steel Bins for the Storage of Bulk Solids*, J.M. Rotter (ed.), University of Sydney, School of Civil and Mining Engineering, 1985, pp. 55–57.

Troitsky, M.S., 'On the structural analysis of rectangular steel bins', *J. Powder and Bulk Solids Technology*, 4(4), pp. 19–25, 1980.

Wilms, H.; Rotter, J.M. and Tomas, J. 'Comparative pressure calculations using different codes', *PARTEC 95, 3rd European Symposium on Storage and Flow of Particulate Solids* (Janssen Centennial), Nuremberg, 1995.

21

Internal structures (ties and internals)
A. Khelil

21.1 INTRODUCTION

Internal equipment (ties, screws, emptying tubes, etc.) is often used for different main functions:

- ties for global stability of squares or rectangular cross-sections, with thin walls;
- screws for moving material and to facilitate discharge of the material;
- emptying tube to regulate the flow of the material;
- other equipment (flow inducers essentially).

21.2 INTERNAL TIES

21.2.1 Introduction

Internal ties are used in square or rectangular silos with thin walls to bound the out-of-deformations of the panels. In France, Germany and other agricultural countries, this concept of associated ties and panels is widely applied. One of the advantages of this structure is the ease of building and repairing the silo, and the structural effects are easier to calculate. Rectangular bins tend to have large reserves of strength. This is not generally the case with circular silos for which care is needed in design to prevent overstress or buckling of the silo wall. Material loads in the silo are applied directly to the wall plate, and transferred via the plate to the ties and to the stiffeners. Frictional forces result in vertical compression of the wall and, of the column supports, cause in-plane bending of the wall. The main disadvantage is the geometrical arrangement of the ties which disturbs the flow during discharge, hence provoking the change of the ties' behaviour (compression of the ties).

21.2.2 Structural design

A typical rectangular silo with ties (Cell A of Chartres experimental base) is shown in Fig. 21.1 (Brozzetti, 1989). Different geometries should be considered (Fig. 21.2). The structural design consists of:

- designing the column
- designing the ties
- designing the wall plates

The columns are subjected to frictional forces resulting in the vertical compression of the wall and to the actions exerted by the ties (vertical and horizontal components).

The French draft code (AFNOR P22-630, 1992) formula for actions exerted by the ensiled material on the tie (Fig. 21.3) is

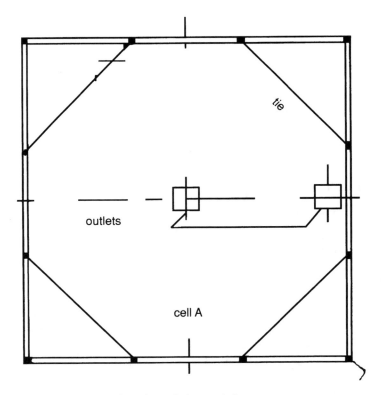

Fig. 21.1 Typical rectangular silo with internal ties.

k = 4 for the filling state
k = 2 for the emptying state

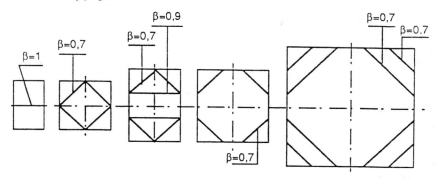

Fig. 21.2 Different arrangements for the ties.

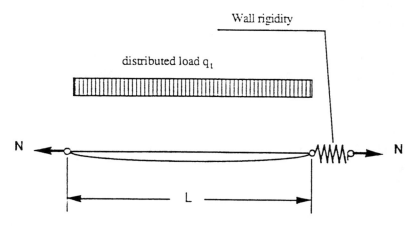

Fig. 21.3 Modelling of the loading and wall–tie interaction.

$$q_t = C_t v b$$

where v is the vertical pressure through the material at position of the tie (kN/m²) and b the tie width (in a horizontal projection) (m),

$$C_t = \frac{C_f b}{k\sqrt{b}}$$

C_t is the friction coefficient of the material on the tie and C_f the coefficient which depends on the rugosity: $C_f = 1$ for circular smooth section, $C_f = 1.2$ for square section; β is the coefficient which depends on the tie position in the silo, $k = 4$ for the filling state and $k = 2$ for the emptying state.

446 *Internal structures*

The design of the wall should be made taking into account the tie–wall interaction and the frictional force exerted by the ensiled material during filling and discharging processes.

21.2.3 Review of research work

For this type of structure, there is very little new information appearing in the literature. We simply note the works of Pieper and Kroll (Kroll, 1974), Sokol (1988) and the French standards drafting group. The Pieper and Kroll experimental work concerns the influence of the ties' dispositions on the pressure. Particular points have been studied, such as:

- the flowing time according to the number of the ties;
- the vertical load on the tie during filling and emptying processes;
- the part (percentage) of the vertical load exerted by the material on the tie;
- the vertical load on the tie in the form of a cross;
- the vertical distribution of the load on the ties at different levels of the silo.

The full results of analysis at the Chartres site have not yet been published. The first results obtained from a square cell show that the flow pattern can modify the functions of the ties.

21.2.4 Future work

- The global behaviour of the ties–wall structure during filling and discharging processes.
- The influence of the geometrical arrangement of the ties on the flow pattern.
- The effect on the vertical loads applied to ties of:
  influence of the filling and discharging processes;
  geometrical arrangements.

The investigation of the measurements of the stress, pressure and strain on the full-scale silos equipped with internal ties is necessary for verification of the theoretical formula of the vertical distribution load on the ties and for the correct structural design.

21.3 MECHANICAL EMPTYING WITH SCREWS

21.3.1 Introduction

Rotary helicoidal screws are used to remove the material towards the outlet. This technique of mechanical discharge concerns silos with a flat bottom. Experimental wall pressure during mechanical discharge (Cells D and C at

Chartres experimental base) was conducted in France using wheat as ensiled material (Fig. 21.4).

The results obtained show that the pressures vary both around the periphery of the silo in a given horizontal plane and at every level of the silo. The wall is then subjected to ovalization moments (Fig. 21.5).

The screw which turns around the axis and around itself allows the ensiled material to be put through towards the orifice and provokes a partial activation of the material in the level of walls.

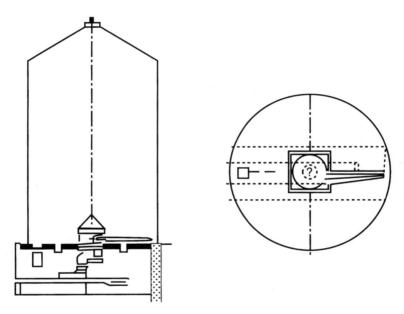

Fig. 21.4 Typical silo equipped with a screw discharge system.

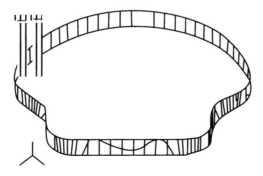

Fig. 21.5 Ovalization moments at depth 7.5 m for a cylindrical silo (6 m diameter × 8 m high).

448 *Internal structures*

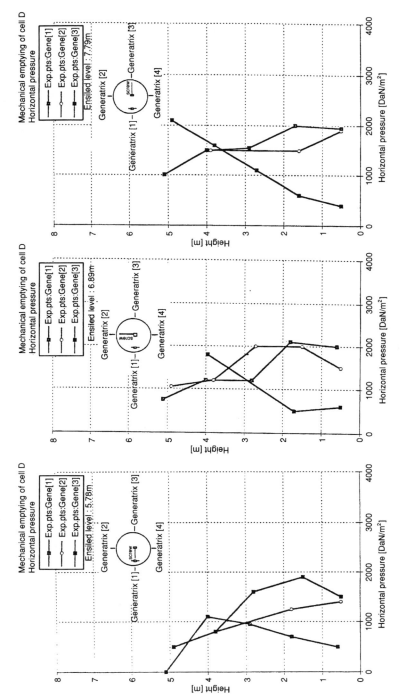

Fig. 21.6 Horizontal pressure versus depth, for different positions on the wall and different screw positions.

The horizontal stress versus the average height of the ensiled material measured from the walls by means of transducers during the mechanical discharge shows many dispersion values. This irregularity is a consequence of the periodic passage of the screw on the right of the generatrix where the measurement is done (Khelil, 1989). The screw in its rotation movement provokes a sort of pipe flow. This pipe flow can be assimilated to the flow pattern which arises during eccentric discharge.

Figure 21.6 gives the variations of horizontal stress on three generatrices of the cell D, when the screw is on the right of generatrices 3, 2 and 1. It appears the equivalent behaviour to eccentric discharge by simulating an orifice of discharge turning respectively around generatrices 3, 2 and 1.

21.3.2 Comparison between mechanically centred and eccentric emptying

The variation of two curves of pressure versus depth (Fig. 21.7) on the generatrices on the side of the orifice of eccentric discharge and on the right of the screw respectively is equivalent. As the screw turns around the axis, the rotary movement of the pipe flow generates maximum efforts on the upper part of the cell. These maximum forces can be approximated by the same formula used in the eccentric discharge case. For the eccentric discharge, maximum forces are applied on the upper part and are limited around the generatrix near the orifice. In the mechanical discharge case, they are alternatively applied on all perimeters of the upper part by following the screw movement.

21.4 EMPTYING TUBES

The emptying tubes or 'anti-dynamic tubes' are used essentially to regulate the flow and to neutralize the overpressure forces. A number of techniques have been developed by diverse authors and are patented. Reimbert and Reimbert (1976) presented a means of preventing increases of pressures during withdrawal of wheat. The tube enforces a funnel flow pattern so that most of the dynamic flow pressures will not extend to the silo walls. To prove the effectiveness of the tube in eliminating dynamic forces during emptying, some tests are carried out on the silos (Cooperative Agricole de Masnières, France) equipped with emptying tubes. The results obtained show that there was no increase in the pressures on the walls during emptying. The emptying pressures are then considered similar to those during the filling process.

21.5 OTHER INTERNAL EQUIPMENT

Other internal equipment is essentially the flow inducers which are used to promote flow in industrial silos. All these techniques are described by Gaylord and Gaylord (1984) and by Reimbert and Reimbert (1976).

450   *Internal structures*

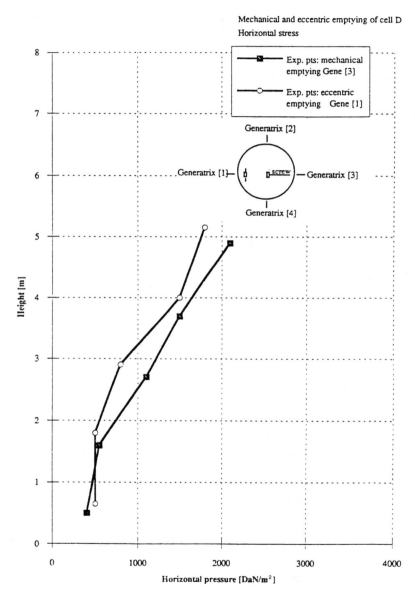

Fig. 21.7 Horizontal pressure versus depth: mechanical emptying and eccentric discharge.

REFERENCES

AFNOR P22-630 (1992) *Construction métallique Silos en acier: calcul des actions dans les cellules*, French National Standards Organization AFNOR, Jan., 34 pp.

Brozzetti, J. (1989) Description de la base expérimentale d'essais de cellules métalliques de stockage, *CTICN* No. 2.

Gaylord, E.H. and Gaylord, C.N (1984) *Design of Steel Bins for Storage of Bulk Solids*, Prentice-Hall, New Jersey.

Khelil, A. (1989) Etude du champ de vitesses et de contraintes dans les silos métalliques, Thèse doctoral, INPL.

Kroll, D. (1974) Untersuchung über die Belastung horizontaler Zuganker sowie vertikaler Hängependeln und Gehänge durch Schüttguter in Silozellen. Dissertation, TU Braunschweig.

Reimbert, M. and Reimbert A. (1976) *Silos: Theory and Practice*, Trans. Tech. Publications.

Sokol, L. (1988) Calcul des tirants dans les silos tenant compte de l'effet de chainette, *CTICN* No. 1.

22

Finite element analysis of the stress state and stability of metal silo structures
T. Ummenhofer

22.1 INTRODUCTION

The objective of this chapter is to inform the reader briefly about work done on silo problems by the use of finite element calculations and to make the reader aware of the existing problems concerning the application of numerical codes. The author cannot claim for the completeness of the representation of all the work that has been done in this field. But from the point of view of the author the important contributions are listed and the interested reader is referred to the references.

Due to the increasing capacities of computational resources during the last 20 years the finite element method is used increasingly. Nowadays finite element analysis is a necessary and helpful tool to treat stress and stability problems of shell structures. Although the new generation of general purpose programs is easy to handle, application of the finite element codes requires a deep understanding of shell behaviour and experience in the modelling and the interpretation of the results.

The calculations concerning structural systems can be divided into two main parts:

- determination of the stress state in the structure;
- determination of critical loads and investigation of the buckling behaviour.

22.2 STRESS STATE IN SILO STRUCTURES

Knowledge of stress state in silo structures is important in aspects of stability (local buckling, overall buckling) and material utilization (yielding, fatigue). Local reinforcements, cut-outs and column supports cause stress concentrations which can strongly affect the load-carrying behaviour of the structure. If stiffeners and the shell structure are modelled simultaneously, the use of appropriate shell elements is required. In these cases it is useful to use degenerated shell elements which allow the modelling of thin and moderately thick parts of the structure simultaneously (Ramm, 1976; Ramm and Matzenmiller, 1986). Otherwise special stiffener elements can be used (Weimar, 1988). The mesh in the vicinity of the stress concentrations has to be fine enough because of the high gradients of the stress functions in these regions. If material nonlinearities have to be introduced, the nonlinear behaviour can be described by bilinear or multilinear functions. The choice of an appropriate yield criterion is important.

The stress state in column-supported shells was investigated by Knoedel, Ummenhofer and Brenner (1994), Guggenberger (1991), Rotter *et al.* (1991), Rotter and Teng (1992) and Dhanens *et al.* (1993). Stress concentrations at the end of local stiffeners were calculated by Eggwertz and Samuelson (1991). To determine the anchorage forces, the stress state in the bottom area of an empty wind-loaded silo was evaluated by Briassoulis and Pecknold (1986). Esslinger and Melzer (1980) investigated the influence of the unevenness of the foundation area of a ground-supported silo on the stress state in the shell.

22.3 STABILITY OF SILO SHELLS

A much more difficult task than the determination of the stress state in the silo shell is the determination of the critical loads of the silo structure (bin, hopper). Two different types of analysis are used and often combined:

- the tracing of the nonlinear load deflection path by a fully nonlinear analysis;
- the determination of critical states and eigenvectors by an eigenvalue analysis.

For perfect systems mainly under membrane action the use of classical eigenvalue analyses is recommended because of the only slight nonlinearities in the load deflection relation. For imperfect systems the change of the tangent stiffness matrix due to nonlinearities has to be recognized, hence a fully nonlinear analysis or a combination of a nonlinear analysis and eigenvalue determination is appropriate (Riks, 1972). A comparison of the results of the different procedures for the determination of the buckling load of a column-supported silo can be found in Guggenberger (1991). It has to be noted that all the analyses mentioned are based on the assumption of a quasi-static problem, but when the limit point is reached a change to a dynamic problem occurs. The determination of post-buckling paths should be carried out based on dynamic analysis or quasi-viscous analysis (Kröplin,

1982). Comprehensive discussions about the various ways of determining critical states can be found in Brendel and Ramm (1982) and Wagner (1991).

To test the FE code used and to determine the minimum mesh density, results can be compared to published benchmark tests on shell stability codes (Stein, 1989), where calculations using various FE codes are listed. The numerical examples include a geometrically imperfect shell with nonlinear material properties.

The analysis of perfect cylindrical shells and hoppers and also of axisymmetric imperfect systems can be carried out by the use of axisymmetric shell elements. The advantage of this type of element is the decreased computational effort. The disadvantage is that non-uniform loading in the circumferential direction has to be expanded in Fourier series which is time consuming. If general imperfections are introduced into the numerical model, it is usually necessary to use 3-D shell elements. Combescure (1986, 1994) provides one formulation where this is not necessary.

Stability analyses of perfect bins under axial loading containing granular solids were described by Rotter and Zhang (1990) and Zhang and Ansourian (1991). Rotter and Zhang (1990) and Knoedel (1994) each undertook studies of imperfect silos with axisymmetric imperfections. Knebel and Schweizerhof (1995) investigated the effect of sinusoidal dimple imperfections. Real imperfection distributions were introduced by Knoedel, Ummenhofer and Schulz (1995). Teng and Rotter (1990), Rotter et al. (1991), Ramm and Buechter (1991), Guggenberger (1991) and Rotter and Teng (1992) used 3-D elements to investigate the stability of column-supported shells. Imperfections were accounted for in the numerical models and the strengthening effect of the bulk solid was neglected. Derler (1993) investigated the stability of empty, wind-loaded shells. The buckling behaviour of unstiffened and stiffened cylinder–cone junctions has been investigated by Greiner and Ofner (1991). Knoedel and Maierhoefer (1989) calculated the buckling loads of empty cylindrical shells under axial compression with simultaneous edge moments.

22.4 STABILITY OF PLATES

During recent years most emphasis has been put on circular silos because the utilization of the material is even higher compared to rectangular silos. The stability of plates subjected to distributed tangential loads was investigated by Brown (1991). Usually the deflection criterion, e.g. buckling load of the plates, governs the design. But if the deflections grow larger the deformed plate activates membrane effects. Plastic stresses develop in the edge areas and therefore the fatigue behaviour of the material has to be taken into account if cyclic loading effects occur.

22.5 IMPERFECTION MODELS

The assessment of imperfections is most important for determining the load-bearing capacity of a thin-walled shell structure. Some remarks on the modelling of imperfections can be found in Knoedel, Ummenhofer and Schulz (1995). Substitute imperfections in the form of axisymmetric imperfections are widely used because they are known to cause the strongest reduction of buckling loads compared to non-symmetric single-mode imperfections. Various shapes of axisymmetric imperfections have been used to determine the buckling strength of thin-walled cylinders. Knoedel and Maierhofer (1989), Knoedel (1994) and Knoedel, Ummenhofer and Brenner (1994) used a so-called procedural imperfection which corresponds to the lowest axisymmetric buckling mode of the perfect shell. Rotter and Teng (1989) and Rotter and Zhang (1990) used an axisymmetric local inward imperfection to represent a circumferential weld, the shape of which was based on shell-bending responses. Teng and Rotter (1992) compared the influence of different imperfection shapes on the buckling load of a cylindrical shell like local inward and outward deviations and also imperfection shapes which are extended sinusoidally in a longitudinal direction. Haefner (1982) used two different axisymmetric imperfection shapes to model the imperfection shape of a circumferential weld; he also considered the effect of additional residual stresses in the vicinity of the weld on the buckling load. Hillmann (1985) confirmed the results of Haefner by an independent numerical study. Juercke *et al.* (1983) investigated the effect of axisymmetric bulge imperfections on the buckling load of cylindrical shells.

Another kind of substitute imperfections are asymmetric shapes in the form of the eigenvectors corresponding to the lower eigenvalues of the system. This kind of imperfection is used by Guggenberger (1991) and Ramm and Buechter (1991).

While a lower bound is still sought by the use of most detrimental substitute imperfections, first attempts to separate the various imperfections and their influence on the buckling load are in progress. Knebel *et al.* (1992, 1993) produced special test specimens and simulated all measured imperfections in the FEM model (see also Knoedel, Ummenhofer and Schulz, 1995). The unevenness of the load distribution around the shell circumference is accounted for. The comparison between the experimental and numerical buckling loads gives reasonable results.

A completely different imperfection model is introduced by Wagenhuber (1989), who describes all shell imperfections by a so-called disturbance energy. He determines the buckling load of the shell, based on the level of the disturbance energy.

22.6 THE MODELLING OF BULK SOLIDS

The presence of bulk solids can increase the buckling strength of silo shells significantly. The internal pressure due to the lateral strain of the bulk solid straightens imperfections and increases the buckling strength of the shell, provided that the shell is thin and material plasticity effects do not affect the buckling behaviour. A second positive effect on the buckling strength of the shell results from the resistance the bulk solid is offering when the shell wall is moving inwards. The strengthening effect of the bulk solid is dependent on a number of parameters and depends strongly on the flow mechanism of the bulk solid (Rotter and Zhang, 1990; Knoedel, 1994). When the bulk solid is in motion like in mass flow silos the resistance against wall inward displacements decreases significantly; this has to be accounted for. The positive effect of the internal pressure and the presence of bulk solids cannot be found with rectangular planform silos, because the plates are able to buckle under the same conditions in the outward direction where no stiffening effect occurs.

At the moment the calculation of buckling loads of 3-D modelled shells is nearly not possible by describing the bulk solid by volume elements because of the huge demand of computational time. Therefore approximate models have to be introduced which describe the resistance the bulk solid exerts onto the deforming shell. The simplest of them is the Winkler foundation model (Winkler, 1876) which describes the bulk solid foundation by simple linear springs. This model is used by Rotter and Zhang (1990) to calculate the buckling loads of perfect and imperfect shells containing granular solids and later by Zhang and Ansourian (1991) for additional perfect shells. Knoedel (1994) extended the Winkler model into a trilinear law which prevents the existence of tension stresses between the shell wall and the bulk solid. A discussion about various possibilities of Winkler-type models can be found in Knebel and Schweizerhof (1995).

A disadvantage of Winkler-type foundation models is that they are not able to account for the increasing stiffness due to the shear resistance in the bulk solid, when the wall displacement is not constant. An analytic determination of the foundation modulus for a perfect linear elastic continuum and harmonically varying waves in the circumferential and longitudinal directions can be found in Seide (1962). Rotter and Zhang (1990) modelled the bulk solid using axisymmetric volume elements and determined the foundation modulus dependence on the harmonic wave number and the length of the zone experiencing displacement. The rise of the foundation modulus with buckling wave number was easily described by a factor which is used to amplify the foundation modulus for axisymmetric displacement. The results are naturally very similar to those of Seide.

In the following, the ordinary Winkler model is used. Because the buckling deformation of the shell cannot be determined in advance, this procedure is only applicable by a conservative approximation of the number of buckles to be expected. A more satisfactory approach could be achieved by the implementation of a Pasternak foundation model (1954), which has not yet been done.

By modelling the bulk solid by an elastic continuum strong simplifications of the real behaviour of a bulk solid are made. First results of calculations with a sinusoidal shaped 2-D model and the implementation of a specific material law for sand and wheat indicate that the real foundation behaviour can be quite different and that the foundation modulus can be reduced significantly compared with that of an elastic continuum (Tejchmann, 1995).

22.7 COMBINING CODES AND NUMERICAL STABILITY CALCULATIONS

The shell stability codes DIN 18 800 T4 (1990) and ECCS (1988) do not provide rules for a numerical determination of the buckling load. If a general shell of revolution has to be designed the numerical buckling analysis has to be verified by buckling experiments (Schmidt and Krysik, 1988; Schmidt, 1991). For this reason, the German Committee for Steel Construction (DASt-Ri 017, 1994) offered within the new DASt recommendation the opportunity to include numerical stability calculations directly in the design process and to avoid experimental investigations if desired.

22.8 CURRENT RESEARCH FOCUS

Useful topics for future research activities on buckling in the presence of granular solids include:

- numerical simulation of the welding procedure and the determination of residual stresses and welding deformations and their influence on the stability of the shell;
- the inclusion of a Pasternak model in the numerical codes to model the reaction of granular bulk solids on the wall deformation of the shell.

REFERENCES

Brendel, B. and Ramm, E. (1982) Nichtlineare Stabilitaetsuntersuchungen mit der Methode der Finiten Elemente. *Ingenieur Archiv*, 51, 337–362.

Briassoulis, D. and Pecknold, D.A. (1986) Anchorage requirements for wind-loaded empty silos. *J. Struc. Eng.*, 112, 308–325.

Brown, C.J. (1991) Elastic buckling of plates subjected to distributed tangential loads, *Computers and Structures*, 41(1), 151–155.

Combescure, A. (1986) Static and dynamic buckling of large thin shells, *Nuclear Engineering and Design*, 92, 339–354.

Combescure, A. (1994) Etude de la stabilité nonlinéaire géométrique et nonlinéaire matériau des coques minces, Habilitation, INSA de Lyon, 122 pp., Habilitation HDR 940–12.

DASt-Ri 017 (1994) *Beulsicherheitsnachweis für Schalen – spezielle Fälle*. Deutscher Ausschuss für Stahlbau.

Derler, P. (1993) Load-carrying behaviour of cylindrical shells under wind loading. PhD thesis, Technical University of Graz, August (in German).

Dhanens, F., Lagae, G., Rathe, J. and van Impe, R. (1993) Stresses in and buckling of unstiffened cylinders subjected to local axial loads. *J. Constr. Steel Res.*, 27, 89–106.

DIN 18 800 Part 4 (1990) *Steel Structures, Stability, Buckling of Shells*. Normenausschuss Bauwesen, Deutsches Institut für Normung e.V., Beuth Verlag GmbH, Berlin, November.

ECCS (1988), *European Recommendations for Steel Construction: Buckling of Shells*, 4th edn, European Convention for Constructional Steelwork, Brussels.

Eggwertz, S. and Samuelson, L.A. (1991) Buckling of shells with local reinforcements, *International Colloquium on Buckling of Shell Structures on Land, in the Sea and in the Air*, Villeurbanne, Lyon, France, 17–19 Sept., pp. 401–408.

Esslinger, M. and Melzer, H.W. (1980) Über den Einfluß von Bodensenkungen auf den Spannungs- und Deformationszustand von Silos. *Stahlbau*, 49, 129–134.

Greiner, R. and Ofner, R. (1991) Elastic plastic buckling at cone cylinder junctions of silos. in Jullien, J.F. (ed.): *Buckling of Shell Structures on Land, in the Sea and in the Air*. Elsevier, London, pp. 304–312.

Guggenberger, W. (1991) Nichtlineares Beulverhalten von Kreiszylinderschalen unter lokaler Axialbelastung, PhD thesis, TU Graz, Austria.

Haefner, L. (1982) Effect of a circumferential weld on the stability and ultimate load of a circular cylinder under axial. PhD Thesis, University of Stuttgart (in German).

Hillmann, J. (1985) Grenzlasten und Tragverhalten axial gestauchter Kreiszylinderschalen im Vor- und Nachbeulbereich. PhD thesis, University of Braunschweig.

Juercke, R.K.; Kraetzig, W.B. and Wittek, U. (1983) Circular cylindrical shells with bulge imperfections. *Stahlbau* 52(8), 241–244 (in German).

Knebel, K. and Schweizerhof, K. (1995) Buckling of cylindrical shells containing granular solids. *Thin-Walled Structures*, 23, 295–312.

Knebel, K.; Schweizerhof, K.; Peil, U.; Schulz, U. and Ummenhofer, T. (1992) Stabilitaet duennwandiger Stahlsilos unter Schuettgutbelastung. G. Gudehus, ed., *3rd Int. Conf. Silos – Research and Practice*, 8–9 October, Sonderforschungbereich 219 University of Karlsruhe, pp. 65–74.

Knebel, K.; Schweizerhof, K.; Peil, U.; Schulz, U. and Ummenhofer, T. (1993) Sonderforschungsbereich 219: Silobauwerke und ihre spezifischen Beanspruchungen. *Arbeits- und Ergebnisbericht für die Jahre 1990–1992*. University of Karlsruhe, April, pp. 135–170.

Knoedel, P. (1994) Stability analyses of cylindrical steel bins. PhD thesis, University of Karlsruhe (in German).

Knoedel, P. and Maierhoefer, D. (1989) Zur Stabilitaet von Zylindern unter Axiallast und Randstoermomenten. *Stahlbau* 58, 81–86.

Knoedel, P.; Ummenhofer, T. and Brenner, J. (1994) On the stability of thin-walled cylindrical shells under longitudinal local loads. in: Saal, H. and Bucak, O. (eds.): *Neue Entwicklungen im Konstruktiven Ingenieurbau*. (Festschrift Mang/Steinhardt), Versuchsanstalt für Stahl, Holz und Steine, University of Karlsruhe, 1994 (in German).

Knoedel, P.; Ummenhofer, T. and Schulz, U. (1995) On the modelling of different types of imperfections in silo shells. *Thin-Walled Structures*, 23, 283–293.

Kröplin, B.-H. (1982) *Quasi viskose Berechnung von nichtlinearen Stabilitaetsproblemen*. Bericht No. 82-37, TU Braunschweig, Institut für Statik.

Pasternak, P.L. (1954) *On a New Method of Analysis of an Elastic Foundation by Means of Two Foundation Constants* (in Russian). Gosudarstvennoe Itsdatelsvo Literaturi po Stroitelstvu i Arkhitekture, Moscow, USSR.

Ramm, E. (1976) Geometrisch nichtlineare Elastostatik und finite Elemente. Habilitationsschrift, University of Stuttgart.

Ramm, E. and Buechter, N. (1991) Buckling of cylindrical and conical shells under concentrated loading. in Jullien, J.F. (ed.): *Buckling of Shell Structures on Land, in the Sea and in the Air*. Elsevier, London, pp. 313–322.

Ramm, E. and Matzenmiller, A. (1986) *Large Deformation Shell Analyses Based on the Degeneration Concept*. State-of-the-art-texts on 'Finite Element Methods for Plate and Shell Structures', Pineridge Press, Swansea, UK.

Riks, E. (1972) The application of Newton's method to the problem of elastic stability. *Journal of Applied Mechanics*, December, 1060–1065.

Rotter, J.M. and Teng, J.-G. (1989) Elastic stability of lap-jointed cylinders. *J. Struct. Engrg, ASCE*, 115(3), 683–697.

Rotter, J.M. and Teng, J.-G. (1992) Linear bifurcation of perfect column-supported cylinders: support modelling and boundary conditions. *Thin-Walled Structures*, 13, 241–263.

Rotter, J.M.; Teng, J.-G. and Hong-Yu, Li (1991) Buckling of thin elastic cylinders on column supports. in Jullien, J.F. (ed.): *Buckling of Shell Structures on Land, in the Sea and in the Air*. Elsevier, London, pp. 334–343.

Rotter, J.M. and Zhang, Q. (1990) Elastic buckling of imperfect cylinders containing granular solids, *Journal of Structural Engineering*, 116(8), August, 2253–2271.

Schmidt, H. (1991) Stabilitaet von Kreiszylinderschalen – Imperfektionsempfindlichkeit und Bemessung. *DVS-Berichte*, Vol. 133, pp. 120–123.

Schmidt, H. and Krysik, R. (1988) Beulsicherheitsnachweis fuer baupraktische staehlerne Rotationsschalen mit beliebiger Meridiangeometrie – mit oder ohne Versuche? In: *Festschrift Heinz Duddeck*, TU Braunschweig, pp. 271–288.

Seide, P. (1962) The stability under axial compression and lateral pressure of circular-cylindrical shells with a soft elastic core, *J. Aerospace Sciences*, 29(7), July, 851–862.

Stein, E. (1989) (ed.) *Nichtlineare Berechnungen im konstruktiven Ingenieurbau*, Springer-Verlag, Berlin, pp. 679–684.

Tejchmann, J. (1995) Private communication with T. Ummenhofer.

Teng, J.G. and Rotter, J.M. (1990) *A Study of Buckling in Column-Supported Cylinders. Contact Loading and Local Effects in Thin-Walled Plate and Shell Structures*, Preliminary Report of an IUTAM Symposium, Prague, Sept.

Teng, J.G. and Rotter, J.M. (1992) On the buckling of imperfect pressurised cylinders under axial compression, *J. Engrg Mech., ASCE*, 118(2).

Wagenhuber, W. (1989) *Imperfektionssensitivitaet und rechnerischer Nachweis der Beulsicherheit duenner Schalen*. Bericht Nr. 89/59, Institut für Statik, TU Braunschweig.

Wagner, W. (1991) Zur Behandlung von Stabilitätsproblemen der Elastostatik mit der Methode der Finiten Elemente. Habilitationsschrift, University of Hannover, April.

Weimar, K. (1988) Ein nichtlineares Balkenelement mit Anwendung als Laengssteifen axialbelasteter Zylinder. PhD Thesis, Institut für Baustatik, University of Stuttgart.

Winkler, E. (1876) *Die Lehre von der Elasticitaet und Festigkeit*. Prague Dominicus.

Zhang, J.Q. and Ansourian, P. (1991) Stability of silo walls stiffened by particulate solids, *Civil Engineering Transactions, Institution of Engineers in Australia*, CE33(2), April, 137–141.

23

Challenges for the future and concluding comments
J.M. Rotter

Metal silo structures continue to present many challenges of understanding and design for the researcher and practitioner alike. It will be long before the quality of understanding of the interaction of stored solids and structural performance is adequate for the needs of quality modern design.

A short description of the problems which are probably most pressing is given below.

23.1 DEVELOPMENT OF EUROCODE 3 (SILOS, TANKS AND PIPELINES)

The European standard on the structural design of metal silos, tanks and pipelines is under development at the time of writing. The draft standard currently consists of three separate parts, termed 'application standards', which are:

- Eurocode 3 Part 4.1 *Silos*
- Eurocode 3 Part 4.2 *Tanks*
- Eurocode 3 Part 4.3 *Pipelines*

together with two generic standards to which they refer for the higher-order, more general, rules

- Eurocode 3 Part 1.6 *Strength and Stability of Shell Structures*
- Eurocode 3 Part 1.7 *Strength and Stability of Transversely Loaded Plated Structures*

The generic standard on the strength and stability of shells contains several different methods of tackling shell calculations, with different failure criteria for each, thus allowing the designer to use simple or sophisticated rules, hand calculations or computer calculations, and permitting the researcher to undertake complicated design-relevant calculations which satisfy the criteria of the standard.

However, there remain very many outstanding practical problems for which the standard can give no answers, but which occur regularly in normal design. In particular, four areas are particularly in need of further research work.

The first is the strength of the silo wall under non-trivial stress states. Patch loads, eccentric discharge, combined wind and solids loading, loads from feeders, local supports and holes and doors in the shell all lead to complex local stress conditions, for which very little research has been done in the past. These need urgent attention.

The second is the strength of the silo wall when common but unresearched structural geometries are used. These include the interaction between discrete supports, ring beams and shell walls, the strength of rectangular silos with ties, the strength of repaired damaged silo walls, multi-segment hopper structures, and the strength of corrugated walls with vertical corrugations.

The third area is that of hopper design. Although a few studies, described in Chapter 19, have attempted to define the strength of hoppers theoretically, no studies are yet known in which hoppers have been tested to destruction to investigate their strength. The first such study is currently in progress at Edinburgh University, but this is limited in scope. In addition, though unsymmetrical hoppers are quite commonly designed for small agricultural silos and have some clear advantages, no theoretical or experimental study appears to have studied strength criteria or design processes for them.

The fourth area needing urgent attention relates to section 23.2 below. The quality of construction varies enormously between factory and on-site construction, and varies between fabricators and according to the fabrication technology used. It is most desirable that the quality should be assessable, identified by key tolerance measures, and the developed strength be related to these tolerance measures. The draft standard currently includes three quality levels, and it is most desirable that research be undertaken to ensure that these are appropriately specified for all current design situations, and that the tolerance measures adopted are the best which can be devised to associate with strength variations.

23.2 IMPERFECTIONS IN REAL SILOS AND EFFECT ON STRENGTH

The geometric imperfections in the walls of a silo have a marked effect on its buckling strength. Different forms of imperfection are important for different stress conditions, which means that different loading cases (filling, discharge, wind, earthquake, eccentric discharge, etc.) may well need different imperfections to be controlled with tolerance measurements.

The current state of knowledge identifies that some forms of imperfections cause large losses of strength whilst others are relatively insignificant. A deep dent may thus be of no consequence because it happens to be in a beneficial form, whilst a shallow depression may be extremely damaging to strength even though it looks relatively minor. Not only does the form of the imperfection matter greatly, but the strength reductions are highly nonlinear in the amplitude of the imperfection, so that an imperfection of doubled depth does not necessarily cause a doubling of the loss of strength.

Much work is still needed on several questions.

- The forms and amplitudes of imperfections which occur in real silos, how these are related to the method of fabrication, and whether they can be estimated with any confidence in advance.
- The relationship between the measured imperfections and strength assessments: which parts of the realistic imperfections are serious and which can be ignored.
- How should tolerance measures to control the amplitudes be arranged to address the imperfection forms which cause greatest strength loss?
- What form and magnitude of imperfections should be assumed in research calculations to underpin design rules?
- Where do the imperfections occur, and how are they related to the stress distributions developing in the silo wall, and the changes of plate thickness used in most silos?
- How do the geometric imperfections affect the pressures which granular solids apply to the wall, and if these are beneficial (as seems often to be the case) are they reliable?

Some of these questions have been partly addressed in a collaborative project undertaken under the auspices of CA-Silo (Rotter, 1996a). That project has illustrated the very large scale of the task before the research community to try to answer these questions, but it has also illustrated that quite modest advances can bring very valuable benefits in improved design rules. This topic will continue to be a strong focus for research studies in shell stability.

23.3 NON-SYMMETRIC PRESSURE DISTRIBUTIONS AND THEIR EFFECTS ON METAL SILOS

The classic picture of silo pressures derives from Janssen's original work and indicates that the pressure on a silo wall is essentially a fixed value at any defined level in the silo, though this value may change from filling to discharge. This picture is inaccurate for many silos, with serious structural consequences.

Non-symmetric pressures arise from a number of sources. The most quickly identifiable are:

- uncontrolled asymmetry of flow patterns
- uncontrolled asymmetry of geometric imperfections
- planned or unplanned asymmetry of eccentric discharge

The effects of non-symmetric pressure patterns depend strongly on the structural geometry. Squat structures respond quite differently from tall slender structures, and the roof boundary condition can influence the stress pattern markedly. Ring stiffeners change the stress distribution most forcefully by restraining out-of-round displacements at specific locations.

Depending on the geometry, non-symmetric normal pressures can lead to failure modes involving buckling under axial compression, snap-through circumferential buckling, or local plastic collapse. These different failures occur at different positions in the structure and are not necessarily close to the position of the strong non-symmetric applied pressure.

One of the major challenges for code drafters is to ensure that all designs are arranged to develop adequate strength to resist these rather unpredictable unsymmetrical pressure components. In general, reinforced concrete silo shells need two layers of reinforcement to ensure that some circumferential bending strength is available in the wall: no such simple ideas appear to be available for metal silo structures. Thus, the representation of unsymmetrical pressures for metal silo design purposes requires more work. This representation must be undertaken with an understanding in mind of the effects which real unsymmetrical pressures have on the structure so that a simplified design 'substitute' loading can be used which has a comparable effect. In addition, some awareness of the failure modes being addressed is critically important in the development of these potential rules for standards.

If the idea of a 'patch load' can be developed further for use in metal silo design, then much work is needed to decide the appropriate size, shape, pressure distribution and magnitude of the peak patch pressure, as well as its placement on the silo wall. These are not simple questions to answer, as the collaborative research project undertaken under the auspices of CA-Silo in 1996 (Rotter, 1996b; Guggenberger *et al.*, 1996; Brown, 1996) showed that most of the simple ideas which one might imagine to be applicable are in serious error.

Such a patch of pressure loading must also be calibrated against experimental pressure measurements to ensure that the experimentally observed pressures and the 'substitute' pressures have a similar effect on the structure's strength, and are calibrated with a defined probability of occurrence.

23.4 LOCAL LOADS, SUPPORTS, BRACKETS, HOLES, ATTACHMENTS, INTERNALS, ETC.

Many loads are applied to silo structures which are not directly related to the granular solid. The silo is often a rather complex structure, susceptible to complex failure modes, so the strength of the silo under these loads remains a serious problem of prediction.

The principal conditions which need much further investigation are:

- local supports beneath the silo wall;
- local supports attached to the sides of silo;
- stringer ribs as a load-introduction system (e.g. supporting overhead conveyor);
- access holes in silo walls, and stiffeners associated with them;
- internal structures within the silo, and consequent loading on wall.

Each of the above has been the subject of some very limited investigations in the past, but there is insufficient information available on any of them to devise a general design rule for a standard. Current design is largely based on empirical extrapolation from existing structures, and whilst this may be adequate when the scale is very similar, it has been the cause of many failures when the extrapolation has been too great and the mechanics have not been understood. Much research remains to be done on these matters.

23.5 COST-EFFECTIVE LIGHT RECTANGULAR SILOS

For many conditions, rectangular silos present an economic form. While these silos are less efficient in their use of material, reduced fabrication costs, or the complete exploitation of available space, makes them highly effective. The structural system for carrying loads is quite different from that of shell structures, and considerable work is needed to develop both design models and failure criteria for drafting into standards.

Good design models are needed which capture the alternative performances of light and heavy construction. In heavy construction, thick stiffened walls are used, and the dominant action is bending. In light construction, larger displacements are allowed to develop, and the dominant load-support mechanism is non-uniform membrane action. The former is simple but expensive: the latter is more difficult to implement in design but can be very cost-effective. Research is needed into good design techniques to exploit large deformation effects in rectangular silos.

A second feature of rectangular silos which needs investigation is the effect of non-uniform wall pressures on the design. These occur as a result of wall flexibility, but also as a consequence of unsymmetrical or eccentric flow patterns. Methods of design for non-uniform pressures, together with a clear definition of the limitations and reliability of such designs, are needed to exploit this form of construction properly.

In large rectangular silo structures, the bending moments in the walls can be greatly reduced by the use of internal ties across the diameter or across the corners of the silo. Reductions in bending moments permit much reduced material costs, together with reduced fabrication costs. However, the interaction of the ties with the flowing solid, the optimum hanging

466 *Challenges for the future and concluding comments*

profile for the ties, and the conditions under which walls are pulled inwards by excessive tie forces, all need further investigation.

The patch load, defined originally for circular concrete silos, is currently codified for rectangular silos as well. It is not clear whether it is needed for or appropriate to rectangular structures. Further studies should explore the role of patch loads in rectangular silos.

23.6 NUMERICAL MODELLING IN THE DESIGN PROCESS

The power of modern computers and the development of versatile software means that numerical modelling is becoming more and more a part of normal design as each year passes. Because of the complexity of the response, metal silos are a natural prime area in which numerical modelling can assist the designer greatly. Unfortunately most standards do not address the question of the use of computer analysis in design very clearly or effectively.

In the development of the draft Eurocode 3 Part 1.6, the generic standard on the 'Strength and stability of shells', a major effort has been made to codify the requirements for the use of different numerical analyses as part of the design, with a hierarchy of different analyses and their associated criteria of failure. This should provide a framework for future development which will assist in design, diagnostic investigation, forensic analysis and research (Rotter, 1996c).

Five levels of structural modelling are permitted in the current draft:

- membrane theory;
- linear bending analysis;
- materially nonlinear analysis;
- materially and geometrically nonlinear analysis;
- materially and geometrically nonlinear analysis including modelling of imperfections.

For each level of modelling, it is necessary to define:

- the criteria of failure (which differ depending on the modelling);
- the strength reduction factors to be applied to the numerical output.

These criteria and strength reduction factors are currently based on very limited information, and a major research effort is needed to develop a knowledge base which can be used to develop safe economic rules.

It is important to recognise that even the very best and most thorough analysis cannot be sure to identify the weakest condition directly, and that current design is based on empirical lower bounds to experimental results. These lower bounds are so low that it is difficult to perform a credible realistic analysis which leads to strength predictions as low as the rules in standards. Much work is needed to resolve this issue and to understand the reasons for the discrepancies.

A further important issue in the application of numerical modelling to silo design relates to realistic loading cases. Most designers using a numerical analysis will seek to use linear analysis, involving the bending theory of shells. Where this is done using load cases which arise from patch loads or measured silo pressure distributions, it is extremely difficult to determine appropriate failure criteria. A vigorous debate is currently in progress (Rotter, 1996c) concerning the combination of different stress components (axial membrane stress, circumferential membrane stress and membrane shear stress) into a single failure criterion. Some would argue that the highest value of each of the three stresses should be combined, irrespective of how far apart the peak values occur. Others would prefer a rule relating to stress combinations at any single point in the structure, but it remains to be demonstrated that this procedure is always conservative.

23.7 CONCLUSIONS

Metal silo structures remain structures with complex structural responses to granular solids loadings. The interaction between the structure and the stored solid is strong, and many phenomena are present in these structures which are not seen in either concrete silo structures or metal building structures.

The incidence of failures in metal silos continues to be unacceptably high, but there are many different reasons and causes of failures. A continuing major research effort into structural behaviour and the definition of metal silo strength will be needed for at least the next decade. One benefit of such a research effort is that it has extensive close relationships with other areas in need of continuing research: aerospace vehicles, pressure vessels and nuclear containments.

REFERENCES

Brown, C.J. (1996) *Effect of Patch Loads on Rectangular Metal Silos* and Annex, Department of Mechanical Engineering, Brunel University, Uxbridge, UK, 300 pp.

Guggenberger, W.; Wallner, S. and Greiner, R. (1996) *Influence of Stiffeners on Stresses and Strength of the Silo Shell Caused by Patch Loads*, Research report, Institut für Stahlbau, Technical University of Graz, Austria.

Rotter, J.M. (1996a) Elastic plastic buckling and collapse in internally pressurised axially compressed silo cylinders with measured axisymmetric imperfections: interactions between imperfections, residual stresses and collapse, *Proc. International Workshop on Imperfections in Metal Silos: Measurement, Characterisation and Strength Analysis*, CA-Silo, Lyon, France, 19 April, pp. 119–140.

Rotter, J.M. (1996b) Patch load effects in unstiffened steel silos, *Proc. CA-Silo Project on the Effect of Patch Loads on Metal Silos*, CA-Silo, Edinburgh, pp. 5–195.

Rotter, J.M. (1996c) Shell structures: design standards, recent progress and unsolved problems, Invited plenary paper, *Proc., International Conference on Structural Steelwork*, Hong Kong, December, pp. 621–636.

Part Four

Numerical Simulation of Particulate Solids

24

Introduction and scope

G. Rombach and J. Martinez

24.1 NUMERICAL SIMULATION AND SILO PROBLEMS

As a result of the high failure rate in silo structures, great effort has been made in recent decades to gain a better understanding of silo pressures and flow phenomena. Nevertheless considerable uncertainty still exists concerning the pressures to which the silo structure is subjected. Up to now, in most countries the wall pressures in silos are calculated by means of the same analytical solution which was established by Janssen nearly 100 years ago. Due to its basic assumption and also its incompleteness, this simple model as well as most other analytical models published in the past are sufficient for the analysis of simple geometrical shapes and the bulk material at rest conditions. However, silo designers have to face up to more difficult situations due to silo geometry, complex behaviour of the bulk material and its interaction with the silo walls, the filling and discharging process or external actions.

24.1.1 Silo geometry

Silo geometry is not always a simple axisymmetric cylinder; it often exhibits a prismatic shape with a square or rectangular cross-section which needs three-dimensional numerical modelling. Moreover, local singularities such as eccentric outlets, inserts, internal ties or wall imperfections give rise to complicated boundary problems impossible to solve by simple analytical models.

Introduction and scope

24.1.2 Bulk solids behaviour

Bulk solids exhibit complex mechanical behaviour such as anisotropy, stress or strain dependency, plasticity, dilatancy and so on. Some of these characteristics are present as soon as the filling process starts, for instance the anisotropy induced by gravity. Most of the above mechanical properties are essentially mobilised during the discharge because of the large strains and displacements developed within the bulk material at this stage. Any of these features needs sophisticated mathematical modelling and in parallel, a rigorous measurement and determination of the mechanical parameters of the bulk material.

24.1.3 Interactions between the bulk solid and the silo walls

Modelling the mechanical interaction between the cell walls and the stored material is a great challenge, as the interface between these two very different materials can be quite complex. For smooth walls along which a slip surface can be developed, the definition of a constant friction coefficient between the walls and the bulk material can be satisfactory and allow simple analytical modelling such as Janssen's solution. In the case of rough walls, the discharge process can give rise to finite thickness shear bands which localize large shear strains and dilatancy. This phenomenon can increase the normal stresses and requires sophisticated modelling.

In other respects, the cell deformability under the action of the stored material, particularly in the case of plane walls subjected to transversal bending, can drastically affect the wall pressures. We have to face a strong interaction problem here with a coupling between the bulk pressure and the wall deformability. In the case of silos, the solution to this problem needs numerical techniques.

24.1.4 Filling and emptying

Filling and emptying are two fundamentally different mechanical processes. During filling, the material is densified and exhibits small strains, while during emptying the material dilates and exhibits large strains which mobilizes complex mechanical properties of the bulk material. Moreover, the change from filling to emptying gives rise to non-stationary phenomena, such as sudden modifications of the stress field. In other respects, the filling and emptying processes produce heterogeneous compacity fields which give unsymmetrical wall pressures and extreme overall equilibrium conditions for the structure.

24.1.5 External forces

Most often, simple calculation methods only take into consideration the vertical static effect of gravity. Silos are often directly exposed to climatic actions, e.g. wind and temperature, or loaded with hot bulk material producing horizontal non-symmetric repeated loading of the structure. These kinds of loading give rise to highly heterogeneous internal force fields which need accurate modelling, especially coupled effects such as differential dilatation of the wall and the bulk material have to be considered.

Another extreme case of loading is related to earthquakes. The particularities of silos, and especially of large squat ones, is a high flexibility of the structure itself and a great overall mass, when filled with the stored material the presence of which modifies the system rigidity. Therefore, direct use of practical methods from other kinds of structures can be dangerous. Hence, fundamental numerical simulations are required.

24.2 NUMERICAL SIMULATION AND EXPERIMENTAL TESTING

The evidence that numerical simulation is a useful tool to investigate silo structures under different working conditions does not mean that experimental testing is no longer a necessity. Direct observation and measurement of reality remain essential at different levels. First, at the scale of the material sample, the correct modelling of the mechanical behaviour of bulk materials requires an accurate determination of the constitutive material parameters. This may lead to sophisticated tests such as compression and extension triaxial tests which are more representative of the stress paths followed by the material during the stages of filling and emptying than the usual simple shear test. Second, at the scale of the structure, full-scale tests are required not only for the observation of the overall and local behaviour of the structure and the measurement of wall pressure but also for the assessment and calibration of predictive models used for numerical simulations. Nevertheless, accurate measurements of the wall pressures and the flow velocities in full-scale silos imply rather heavy and time-consuming experiments, expensive equipment and sophisticated techniques. In this case, the interest of numerical simulation used as a predictive model, is to reduce the amount of experimental testing by allowing extrapolations from a reduced set of experiments. Numerical simulation then allows the generalizing of experimental results thus enhancing their value. In the same way, it also allows us to make parametric studies of the influence of a single parameter independently of the others, which is a difficult and often an impossible task to do experimentally. Moreover, numerical simulation is useful for back-calculation techniques in order to identify the mechanical parameters the direct measurement of which is difficult.

24.3 NUMERICAL SIMULATION AND PRACTICAL DESIGN

It has been demonstrated above how numerical methods have been developed to overcome difficulties impossible to solve by traditional analytical tools. The use of these new methods is facilitated by increasing computational power which permits improved accuracy and more sophisticated models. Because of the complexity of the models used, most of these numerical methods are still research tools. As a research tool, numerical simulation produces a better understanding and a more accurate description of the physical phenomena occurring in silos and it consequently contributes to the enhancement of silo design. In addition, sophisticated models and analysis can be helpful for the evaluation of simple and accurate models for the practical design of silos.

The direct utilization of numerical models such as nonlinear finite element codes, requires good experience in material mechanics as well as in numerical techniques. It is important to control the input parameters used in complex constitutive models as their physical significance is not always evident. Moreover the results can depend on purely numerical parameters such as spatial and time discretization and load increment magnitude. Consequently, in order that practical design takes improved benefit from research results, great effort must be made to produce simplified methods, such as explicit analytical formulae or graphical charts, directly usable in current practical design.

24.4 PRESENTATION OF THE CONTENTS OF THIS PART

This Part was originally written to form a basis for the collaborative activities of the CA-Silo project working on numerical simulation and constitutive laws. Professor G. Rombach, the first chairman of the working group, assembled the data for the comparison of existing programs and the original contributions to the initial report of the working group. Professor Rombach had to resign his chairmanship for business reasons at the end of 1994. The second chairman, Professor J. Martinez, has appended contributions from other workers on FEM.

The scope of this Part is to show what benefits numerical simulation provides for the improvement of silo design and safety, and to illustrate how the work done in different European institutions contributes to this. In spite of a large panel composed of the contributors to this Part, the following reports do not pretend to present an exhaustive view in the area of numerical simulation and constitutive laws, but to give several approaches to solve a large set of silo specific problems. This Part mainly emphasizes bulk material models and loads due to bulk materials. The different contributions can be grouped into three main areas:

- finite element models
- constitutive material laws
- discrete element models

First, a general finite element model is presented by Rombach and Eibl based on a static Lagrangian and a dynamic Eulerian formulation with different constitutive laws for the bulk material: hypo-elasticity, elastoplasticity, viscosity as well as linear and nonlinear wall friction. Simplified models are then described for quasi-static (Ragneau and Ooi) or purely kinematic (Ooi and Rotter) conditions. Specific effects on wall pressures had been investigated by Eibl and his co-workers: an interesting stochastic calculation of stresses taking into account the scatter of the input material parameters (Dahlhaus and Eibl) and a complete dynamic calculation of wall pressures under earthquake loading using a time history method (Braun and Eibl).

An overview of the different classes of constitutive laws for bulk materials, from simple linear elastic to elasto-plastic polar models using the Cosserat medium concept and creep models, is given by Feise and Schwedes. A discussion on the use of these different constitutive models in relation to practical conditions in silos is presented by Weidner and Nielsen. The interest and the general characteristics of discrete particle models as a more fundamental microscopic approach for the description of granular media, are described by Tüzün, while Martinez and Masson present a simplified concept, the lattice grain models, which has been developed to be able to manage large sets of particles. The advantages and disadvantages of discrete particle models compared with finite element models are discussed by Reuderink from the point of view of practical design. While Rotter presents a wide set of challenges for the future research on numerical simulation including priorities for research programmes, some concluding comments are given by the second chairman of the working group.

25

Comparison of existing programs
G. Rombach

25.1 INTRODUCTION

For coordinated research activities detailed knowledge about the available software for numerical simulation of granular solid behaviour in silos is needed. To obtain this information a questionnaire was sent to researchers in Europe working in that field. Responses were received from those listed in Table 25.1.

The main results are given in the following sections.

25.2 TYPE OF MODEL

As can be seen from Table 25.2, two different numerical models are widely used:

- models based on the finite element method (FEM)
- discrete particle models

25.3 COMPUTER LANGUAGE

For collaboration in the field of numerical programs the same computer language is helpful. As can be seen from Table 25.3, three different computer languages are used:

- FORTRAN is used in most finite element programs and some discrete particle models.
- PASCAL and C are used for some discrete particle models.

Table 25.1 Computer programs

	Author/user	Name of program
1.	Aubry (Ecole Central Paris)	GEFDYN
2.	Eibl (Karlsruhe University, Germany)	SILO
3.	Eibl (Karlsruhe University, Germany)	–
4.	Eibl (Karlsruhe University, Germany)	(ABAQUS)
5.	Klisinski (Luleå University, Sweden)	SILO
6.	Klisinski (Luleå University, Sweden)	BULKFEM
7.	Martinez (INSA, Rennes, France)	AMG/PLAXIS
8.	Ragneau (INSA, Rennes, France)	MODACSIL
9.	Schwedes (Braunschweig University, Germany)	(ABAQUS)
10.	Schwedes (Braunschweig University, Germany)	HAUFWERK
11.	Tüzün (University of Surrey, UK)	HOPFLO
12.	Ooi and Carter (Edinburgh University, Scotland)	AFENA
13.	Ooi (Edinburgh University, Scotland)	(ABAQUS)
14.	Rong (Edinburgh University, Scotland)	DEM.F
15.	Thompson (Edinburgh University, Scotland)	SIMULEX
16.	Cundall (INSA, Rennes, France)	TRUBALL, PFC

Table 25.2 Type of model

Type of model	1	2	3	4	5	6	7	8	9	10	11	12	13	14	15	16
Finite element method	×	×	×	×	×	×		×	×	×		×	×			
Discrete particle model						×							×		×	×	×

Table 25.3 Computer language

Computer language	1	2	3	4	5	6	7	8	9	10	11	12	13	14	15	16
FORTRAN	×	×	×	×	×	×		×	×	×		×	×	×		×
C															×	
Pascal							×				×					

25.4 FEATURES

The programs have been improved substantially in recent years. With most programs, not only static (filling processes) but dynamic (discharging silos) phenomena can be studied (Table 25.4). There are no limitations with regard to the geometry; two-dimensional, axisymmetric and three-dimensional calculations can be done (Table 25.5).

Rupture zones in the form of shear bands can be simulated with all discrete particle models but only with two finite element programs (Table 25.7).

It is known that the density of the granular bulk material changes considerably from a dense state under at-rest conditions to a loose state

Table 25.4 Static/dynamic code

Static/dynamic	1	2	3	4	5	6	7	8	9	10	11	12	13	14	15	16
Static	×	×	×	×	×	×	×	×	×	×	×	×	×	×	×	×
Dynamic	×	×	×	×	×	×	×		×		×		×	×	×	×

Table 25.5 Spatial discretization

Spatial discretization	1	2	3	4	5	6	7	8	9	10	11	12	13	14	15	16
2-D (axisymmetric)	×	×	×	×	×	×	×	×	×	×	×	×	×	×	×	×
3-D	×	×	×	×				×	×		×		×			×

Table 25.6 Finite elements

Finite elements	1	2	3	4	5	6	7	8	9	10	11	12	13	14	15	16
Triangular					×	×		×	×	×		×	×			
Isoparametric	×	×	×	×				×	×			×	×			
Quadrilateral		×	×	×				×	×			×	×			

Table 25.7 Shear bands

Shear bands	1	2	3	4	5	6	7	8	9	10	11	12	13	14	15	16
Possible	×	×				×				×				×	×	×
Not included				×	×		×	×	×			×	×			

Table 25.8 Density variations

Density	1	2	3	4	5	6	7	8	9	10	11	12	13	14	15	16
Constant							×									
Not constant	×	×			×	×	×		×	×	×	×	×	×	×	×

Material models

during discharge. This effect is implemented in nearly all programs (Table 25.8).

Some programs are used to study special phenomena:

- sedimentation or removal of material (Aubry)
- stochastic phenomena (Eibl)
- earthquake loads (Eibl)
- anisotropic solids
- wall structure–solid interactions (wall imperfections and stiffness)

25.5 MATERIAL MODELS

The results of many numerical simulations depend strongly on the underlying assumptions, especially on the material model used. Discrete particle models are based on interaction mechanisms between single particles.

In finite element calculations a stress–strain relation for the continuum is required. Besides the well-known elastic–plastic models and yield criteria

Table 25.9 Material parameters

Material parameters	1	2	3	4	5	6	7	8	9	10	11	12	13	14	15	16
From experiment	×				×	×		×	×	×	×	×	×			×
From the literature		×	×	×	×	×	×		×	×	×	×	×	×	×	

Table 25.10 Cohesive/non-cohesive material

Model used for:	1	2	3	4	5	6	7	8	9	10	11	12	13	14	15	16
Cohesive materials	×	×	×	×			×	×			×	×				
Non-cohesive materials	×	×	×	×	×	×	×	×	×	×	×	×	×	×	×	×

Table 25.11 Static/dynamic calculations

Model used for:	1	2	3	4	5	6	7	8	9	10	11	12	13	14	15	16
Solids	×	×	×	×	×	×		×	×	×	×	×	×			×
Flowing granular material			×	×	×	×	×	×			×			×	×	×

such as Mohr–Coulomb, Tresca, Drucker–Prager, etc., the following material laws are used in FE programs:

- Lade
- Kolymbas
- Boyce
- Wilde
- critical state

The material laws have been modified for cohesive bulk solids and for dynamic calculations.

26

A dynamic finite element model for silo pressures and solids flow
G. Rombach and J. Eibl

26.1 INTRODUCTION

The finite element method has become well established in silo research. Due to its versatility a great variety of silo problems can be studied. Calculations starting with the bulk material at rest up to flowing material are possible. In principle there are no restrictions with regard to the silo geometry and to the bulk material. The behaviour of granular materials in silos is rather complex. Therefore the assumptions and simplifications in any numerical simulation must be checked carefully.

The following demonstrates the versatility of finite element simulations in silos. First, the mechanical and numerical models are described. Then some results of practical interest are discussed.

The numerical method presented in this chapter takes into consideration all relevant parameters like the interaction between the structure and the filling material, the stiffness of the structure and the decreasing density of the granular media during flow. For the granular bulk material a constitutive highly nonlinear material model is used which covers the solid-like behaviour of the material during small deformation rates as well as the fluid-like behaviour during flow conditions. The numerical model is based on a consistent continuum mechanics approach formulated in a Eulerian frame of reference. It provides transient velocity and stress fields within the granular bulk material during flow as well as the resulting wall loads.

It should be emphasized that the intention of these numerical simulations is not to provide a computer code for the design of silos, but to explain the principal phenomena not well understood until now.

The results of the numerical simulations may be of interest for the design of silos.

26.2 THE MECHANICAL AND NUMERICAL MODEL

The behaviour of the granular bulk material is described in a fixed Eulerian frame of reference, using the well-established theory of continuum mechanics. As the simulation of flowing material is of main interest, a dynamic equilibrium condition including inertia effects is used:

$$\nabla T + \rho(b_v - \dot{v}) = 0 \qquad (26.2.1)$$

Here T is the Cauchy stress tensor, ρ the bulk density of the material and b_v the bodyforce per unit volume. For the local derivative of the velocity vector v, the acceleration is given:

$$\dot{v} = \frac{\partial v}{\partial t} = \nabla v \cdot v \qquad (26.2.2)$$

This Eulerian formulation encounters difficulties especially when nonlinear material models are used since the history of motion for every material point must be traced. But it is the only model well suited to describe the behaviour of the material from static conditions up to steady-state flowing conditions. This is important as the greatest wall pressures often do not occur at flow initiation but some time after the bulk material has started to flow.

It is known from many experiments that the density of the bulk material ρ changes within a wide range from a dense state after filling to a very loose state during discharge, which has to be taken into account. This is done separately for each finite element by integration of the conservation of mass equation (26.2.3).

$$\frac{\partial \rho}{\partial t} + \text{tr}(\nabla \rho v) = 0 \quad \Rightarrow \quad V \frac{\partial \rho}{\partial t} + \rho \oint_s |v \cdot n| dS = 0 \qquad (26.2.3)$$

Here V is the volume of the finite element which as well as n and S are constant due to the Eulerian frame.

For the constitutive formulation the following kinematic relations are also needed:

$$d = 0.5(\nabla v + \nabla v) \qquad d_{ij} = 0.5(v_{i,j} + v_{j,i}) \qquad (26.2.4)$$

$$w = 0.5(\nabla v + \nabla v) \qquad w_{ij} = 0.5(v_{i,j} - v_{j,i}) \qquad (26.2.5)$$

The main problem, however, is the formulation of a realistic constitutive relation (Kolymbas, 1988; Lade, 1977; Weidner, 1990). The difficulties arise from large deformations during discharge and the complex behaviour of bulk material. During storage or at-rest conditions the bulk material may be regarded as a solid, whereas during discharge it behaves like a fluid.

Simplifications like the commonly used Mohr–Coulomb yield criterion or similar approaches do not lead to satisfactory results.

The material model must be valid for a range from high stresses and low strains to describe storage behaviour, to low stresses and high strains at flow.

As there was no such formulation available regarding static as well as dynamic conditions, according to Häußler and Eibl (1984) the corotational stress rate due to Jauman $\overset{\circ}{T}$ (equation 26.2.7) was divided into a rate-independent static part $\overset{\circ}{T}_s$ and a rate-dependent viscous part $\overset{\circ}{T}_v$.

$$\overset{\circ}{T} = \frac{\partial T}{\partial t} + Tw - wT \qquad (26.2.6)$$

$$\overset{\circ}{T} = \overset{\circ}{T}_s + \overset{\circ}{T}_v = Hd + G\overset{\circ}{d} \qquad (26.2.7)$$

Here the physical properties of the bulk material are represented by two fourth-order tensors H and G. For the static material tensor H, two different rate-independent formulations are used. The first one is an elastic–plastic model developed by Lade (1977). Within this formulation the strain increment Δe is divided into three different parts:

$$\Delta e = \Delta e_e + \Delta e_p + \Delta e_c \qquad (26.2.8)$$

The elastic strain increment Δe_e is calculated by means of a hypoelastic law with Young's modulus depending on the minimum principal stress. The two plastic components are determined by an associated (Δe_c) and a non-associated (Δe_p) flow rule.

The second one is a rate type formulation developed by Kolymbas (1988). Here the Jaumann stress rate is calculated by means of the following equation:

$$\overset{\circ}{T} = C_1(TD + DT)/2 + C_2 \text{tr}(TD)1 + C_3 T \sqrt{\text{tr}D^2} + C_4 \frac{T^2}{\text{tr}T}\sqrt{\text{tr}D^2} \qquad (26.2.9)$$

C_1, C_2, C_3 and C_4 being material parameters.

Several comparison calculations have been carried out with both material models (Rombach, 1991; Weidner, 1990) and testing the materials with regard to silo relevant pressure paths. Significant differences have only been obtained for silos with inclined walls or hoppers (Rombach, 1991).

For the rate-dependent material tensor G several rather complex models for fast-flowing materials have been proposed (e.g. Bagnold, 1954; Haff, 1963; Savage, 1979; Shahinpoor, 1981). These formulations are based on the conditions of energy and impulse conservation in mechanical models with slip-collision of single idealized particles. Underlying assumptions include:

- spherical particles
- steady-state conditions

- no material constants for practical relevant grains
- two-dimensional flow

So the authors did not use these models. Instead of such complex models, the investigations started with the generally accepted belief that, in the case under consideration, shear stresses in rapid flowing granular materials are proportional to the shear rate similar to the deviatoric part of a Newtonian fluid, where the viscosity parameter v depends on the trace of the strain rate:

$$\overset{\circ}{T}_v = G : \overset{\circ}{d} \qquad G_{ijrs} = 2v^* \sqrt{\mathrm{tr} d'^2} \left(\delta_{ij} \delta_{js} \right) \qquad (26.2.10)$$

where d' is the deviator of strain rate and v^* the viscosity parameter. This formulation is in agreement with experimental and theoretical studies carried out by Stadler and Buggisch (1985). The time integration of the material model (equations 26.2.6 and 26.2.7), and the calculation of Cauchy stresses are given in Häußler (1985).

The differential equations (26.2.1–26.2.6) and the constitutive relations (26.2.7–26.2.10) form a consistent set of equations to determine the 16 unknowns: v, d, w, T, ρ. The finite element method was used in space, the finite difference method in time, with v being the primary unknown, to solve this system of equations. The bulk material is discretized by standard two- and three-dimensional isoparametric elements. In the case of axisymmetric geometries for the silo walls two-node ring elements are used. In agreement with experimental results the numerical studies have shown (Rombach, 1991) that the material pressure in silos is very sensitive to wall deformations. The two element groups mentioned before are coupled by a special thin layer interface element which has been developed to allow for the interaction between the bulk material and the silo wall. Linear as well as nonlinear friction behaviour can be dealt with. Comparison calculations have shown that in most cases the linear Coulomb friction model describes the material behaviour at the silo walls with sufficient accuracy. More details are given in Häußler (1985) and Rombach (1991).

26.3 RESULTS

On the basis of this consistent model and the developed finite element program a great variety of silo problems like the influence of silo geometry, the location of the openings, pressures in hoppers, the interaction between the filling material and the walls have been studied systematically (Gladen, 1985; Häußler, 1985; Landahl, 1983; Rombach, 1991). Calculations have been carried out with different bulk materials like sand, wheat and sugar and different silo geometries. The numerical results were compared with experimental data showing a good overall agreement (Eibl and Rombach, 1987a,b; Rombach and Eibl, 1988, 1989; Rombach, 1991). Computations can be done over a long period starting from static conditions up to material velocities of more than 10 m/s, limited only by computer capacity.

Results

The following results have been chosen to give an overview of the principal phenomena which were the main object of these studies.

26.3.1 Material flow in hoppers

An initial application covers velocity, stress, and density fields in a mass flow hopper at the beginning of the discharging process. In a two-dimensional computation an example of dry sand was treated, the geometry of which is given in Fig. 26.1, where for reasons of symmetry only one-half of the bin was discretized.

The calculations had to start at $t = 0.00$ s. The first figure in Fig. 26.2 ($t = 0.00$ s) shows the results found by a numerical simulation of the filling process, which, as has been proved, also has a great influence on the discharging phase and the pressure distribution afterwards. Due to the small velocities viscous and mass terms can be omitted during this phase. All the bottom nodes were fixed in the vertical direction.

The opening phase starts when all nodes at the outlet are allowed to move freely in a vertical direction, so that the bulk material is accelerated. As one can see (Fig. 26.2), soon after the start of flow ($t = 0.2$ s), the vertical pressure directly above the outlet decreases to nearly zero. The orientation of the larger principal stresses changes from a vertical to a horizontal direction, resulting in significant wall pressure redistribution. In this phase the velocity field in Fig. 26.3 indicates that only the bottom parts are moving, while the material at top of the hopper is still at rest.

As a consequence the density of the bulk material ρ changes over a wide range as can be seen in Fig. 26.4. Starting with $\rho = 1480 \text{ kg/m}^3$ after filling, the density decreases to $\rho = 460 \text{ kg/m}^3$ after $t = 1.85$ s.

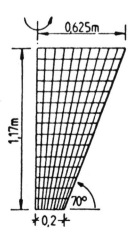

Discretization:
150 8-noded isoparametric elements
15 6-noded interface elements
Time step Δt=0.001 sec

Bulk Material:
Karlsruhe sand, loose γ=14.5 kN/m³
Coefficient of wall friction: μ = 0.4

Fig. 26.1 Geometry and discretization.

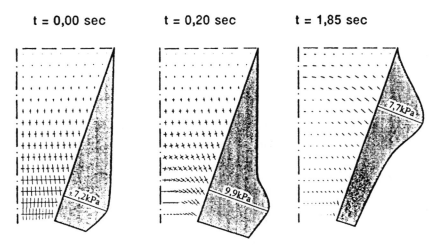

Fig. 26.2 Principal stress field for different time steps.

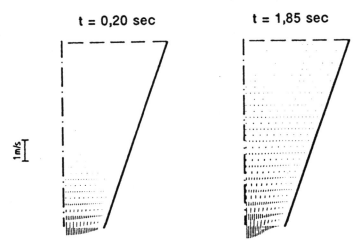

Fig. 26.3 Velocity for different time steps.

26.3.2 Interaction between silo wall and bulk material

The buckling resistance of metal silo walls is usually treated in a simplified manner, regarding the structure–material interaction as an elastic support for the wall structure. In doing so the horizontal resistance of the bulk material, as activated by in- and outgoing deformations of the silo wall, is of interest. The same problem is relevant if one tries to study the tensile forces raised by a fast temperature drop outside the silo, when the wall shrinks on to the filling material (Fig. 26.5).

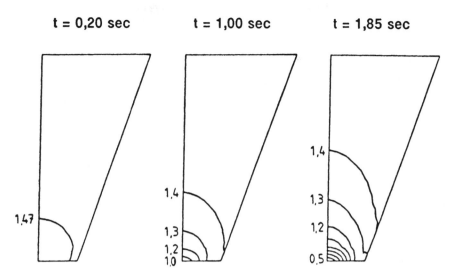

Fig. 26.4 Bulk density contours at discharge ($\times 10^3$ kg/m^3).

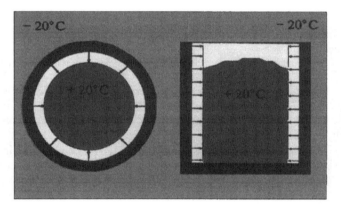

Fig. 26.5 Temperature shrinkage of silo wall due to global temperature change.

In Fig. 26.6, therefore, the results of the following computer simulation are given. The whole silo wall shown in Fig. 26.5 was first moved outwards and then inwards as a rigid body, and the horizontal pressures – given here for sand and wheat – were calculated at different heights. It is obvious that simulation of this complex behaviour by means of an elastic support is very problematic.

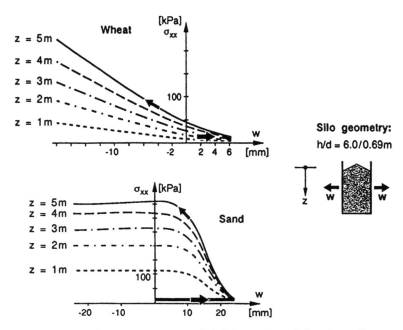

Fig. 26.6 Horizontal pressure versus radial deformation of the silo wall.

26.3.3 Eccentric discharging silo

In spite of the fact that many silos have eccentric outlets, only very rough formulae for pressure calculations of eccentrically discharged bins are available at present. Therefore, numerical studies with different bulk materials have been carried out. In the following only two examples are presented (Rombach, 1991).

First, an eccentrically discharging rectangular wheat bin (Fig. 26.7) with a height of 27 m and a width of 6 m under plane strain condition is shown. After filling ($t = 0.0$ s) an active pressure field develops. The maximum principal stresses are orientated in a vertical direction. A typical exponential wall pressure curve is obtained. During discharging a significant stress redistribution occurs. At the outlet region the wall pressure is reduced to a very low level, surrounded by a region of high stresses, caused by stress arching, which leads to wall pressure peaks on both wall sides. In the upper part of the bin the stresses remain nearly constant. In contrast to the assumptions in many analytical attempts to study discharging behaviour, the material in this region is not in a limit state condition.

A comparison of the design pressures in accordance with the design standards from several countries (Fig. 26.7) shows that only the Australian code tries to model these unsymmetrical pressure distributions in a partly satisfactory manner.

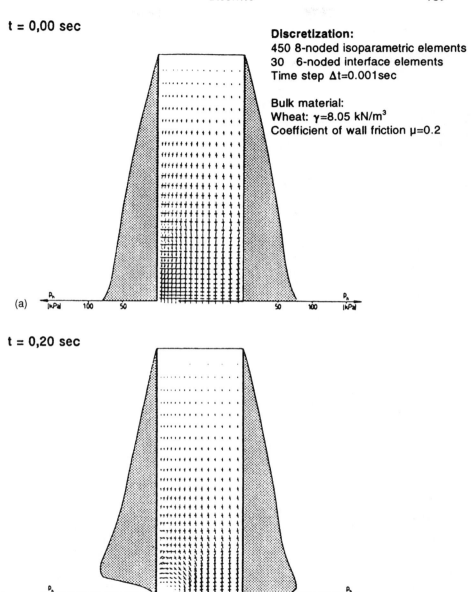

Fig. 26.7 (a) and (b) Principal stress field and wall pressures on an eccentrically discharged slot type silo at different time steps. (*contd on next page*)

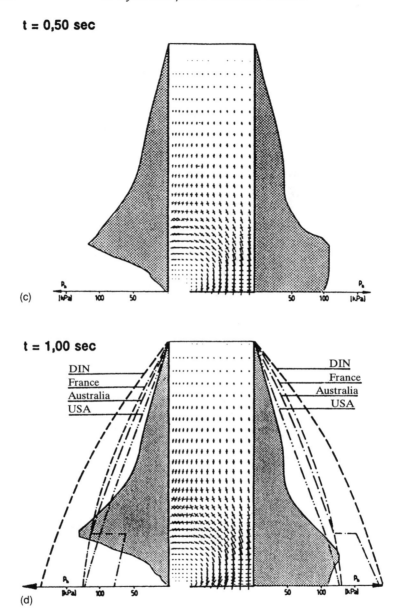

Fig. 26.7 (c) and (d) Principal stress field and wall pressures on an eccentrically discharged slot type silo at different time steps in comparison to several international standards.

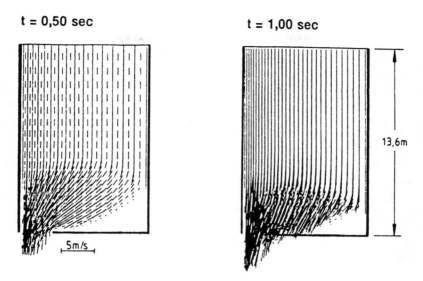

Fig. 26.8 Velocity field in an eccentrically discharged silo.

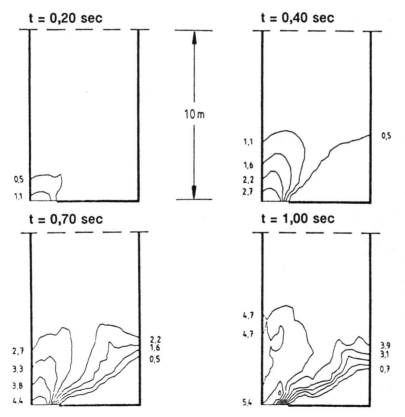

Fig. 26.9 Velocity field at different time steps in an eccentrically discharged silo (m/s).

The relevant velocity fields are given in Fig. 26.8 as a vector plot and by means of contour lines (Fig. 26.9). The velocity field in Fig. 26.8 shows typical funnel flow areas, where in some parts the material is completely at rest. While in the upper part of the bin the bulk material moves like a rigid mass, above the bottom an 'internal hopper' of curved shape can be seen. At the narrow transition zone between the material at rest and the flowing range a steep velocity gradient can be observed.

Since in many cases silos have a rectangular cross-section, rectangular or unsymmetrical silo geometries were also analysed in three-dimensional investigations. Due to the highly nonlinear material behaviour these dynamic three-dimensional computations were restricted by the available computer capacity. Therefore the results in the following example were gained by discretizing only 12 m above the flat bottom and the rest of the full height of 15 m was approximated by a constant vertical pressure p_v (Fig. 26.10).

In Fig. 26.11 the wall pressure on side 1 and 2 is given after filling ($t = 0$ s) and after $t = 1.0$ s. As in the plane strain example, great pressure redistributions can be seen within a very short time of opening. Around the outlet region the wall pressure is reduced to a very low level, while a three-dimensional stress arch produces pressure peaks on the surrounding wall areas. No such behaviour is covered by the pressure design patterns in the relevant standards.

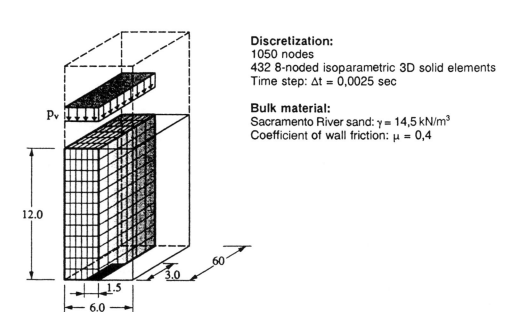

Discretization:
1050 nodes
432 8-noded isoparametric 3D solid elements
Time step: Δt = 0,0025 sec

Bulk material:
Sacramento River sand: γ = 14,5 kN/m³
Coefficient of wall friction: μ = 0,4

Fig. 26.10 Geometry and discretization.

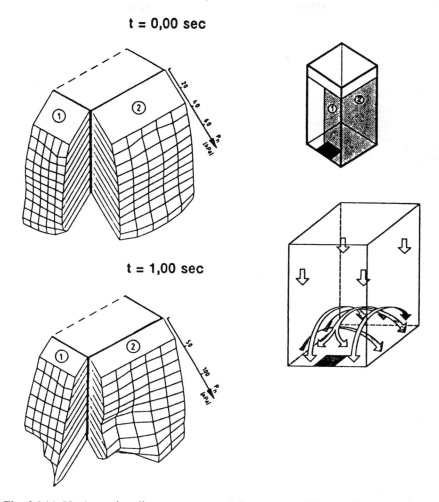

Fig. 26.11 Horizontal wall pressure at $t = 0.0$ s (rest condition) and at $t = 1.0$ s on wall side 1 and 2.

REFERENCES

Bagnold, R.A. (1954) Experiments on gravity-free dispersion of large solid spheres in a Newtonian fluid under shear. *Proc. of Royal Society of London*, Series A, **225**, pp. 49–63.
CEN TC 250/SC1/PT8 (March 1992) *Basis of Design and Actions of Structures, Part 4; Actions in Silos and Tanks*, Brussels.
DIN 1055 Part 6 (May 1987) *Lastannahmen für Bauten; Lasten in Silozellen*.
Eibl, J. and Rombach, G. (1987a) Numerical investigations on discharging silos. *Proc. ICOMNIG*, Innsbruck, April, pp. 317–320.
Eibl, J. and Rombach, G. (1987b) Stress and velocity fields at discharging of silos. *Proc. NUMETA*, Swansea, July, pp. D28/1–9.

FIP (Fédération Intérnationale de la Précontrainte) (March 1987) Report: *Comparative Silo Design*, Karlsruhe.

FIP-Working Group 'Silo Design' (July 1990) *Recommendation for Concrete Silo Design* (Draft), Karlsruhe.

Geniev, G.A. (1958) Questions of the dynamics of granular mass (Voprosi Dinamiki Siputchei Sredi). *Scientific Information*, Second issue, Government Publication of Literature on Construction and Architecture, Moscow.

Gladen, W. (1985) Numerische Untersuchung der Lasten in Silozellen beim exzentrischen Entleeren. Thesis, Karlsruhe University.

Häußler, U. (1985) Geschwindigkeits- und Spannungsfelder beim Entleeren von Silozellen. Thesis, Karlsruhe University.

Häußler, U. and Eibl, J. (1984) Numerical investigations on discharging silos. *Journal of Engineering Mechanics*, 110, pp. 957–971.

Haff, F. (1963) Grain flow as a fluid-mechanical phenomenon. *J. Fluid Mechanics*, 134, pp. 403–430.

ISO/TC98/SC3 Working Group 5 (August 1991) *Loads on Structures from Bulk Materials* (ISO-CD 11697).

Janssen, H.A. (1895) Versuche über Getreidedruck in Silozellen. *VDI Zeitschrift* No. 39, pp. 1045–1049.

Jenike, A.W. and Johanson, J.R. (1979) Bin loads. *Journal of the Structural Division*, ASCE, 93, No. ST4, pp. 319–329.

Kolymbas, D. (1988) *Ein konstitutive Theorie für Böden und andere körnige Stoffe.* Publication No. 109 of Institute for Soil Mechanics, Karlsruhe University.

Lade, P.V. (1977) Elasto-plastic stress–strain theory for cohesionless soils with curved yield surfaces. *Int. J. of Solids and Structures*, 19, pp. 1019–1035.

Landahl, H. (1983) Berechnung der Druckverhältnisse in zylindrischen Silozellen mit nichtlinearen Stoffgesetz für den Füllzustand und beim Entleerungsbeginn. Thesis, Dortmund University.

Reimbert, M. and Reimbert, A. (1976) *Silos – theory and practice.* Editions Trans. Tech. Publications, Rockport, USA.

Rombach, G. (1991) Schüttguteinwirkungen auf Silozellen – Exzentrische Entleerung. Thesis, Karlsruhe University.

Rombach, G. and Eibl, J. (October 1988) Consistent modelling of filling and discharging processes in silos. *Proc. Silos – Forschung und Praxis*, Karlsruhe University, pp. 1–16.

Rombach, G. and Eibl, J. (June 1989) Numerical simulation of filling and discharging processes in silos. *Proc. 3rd Int. Conf. on Bulk Materials*, Newcastle, pp. 48–52.

Savage, S.B. (1979) Gravity flow of cohesionless granular materials in chutes and channels. *J. Fluid Mechanics*, 92, pp. 53–96.

Shahinpoor, M. (1981) On rapid flow of bulk solids. *Bulk Solids Handling*, 1, pp. 487–500.

Stadler, R. and Buggisch, H. (August 1985) Influence of the deformation rate on shear stresses in bulk solids – theoretical aspects and experimental results. EFCE Publication Series No. 49, *Proc. Reliable Flow of Particulate Solids*, Bergen.

Walters, J.K. (1973) A theoretical analysis of stresses in axially symmetric hoppers and bunkers. *Chemical Engineering Science*, 28, pp. 779–789.

Weidner, J. (1990) Vergleich von Stoffgesetzen granularer Schüttgüter zur Silodruckermittlung. Thesis, Karlsruhe University.

27

Finite element models for specific applications
E. Ragneau, J.Y. Ooi and J.M. Rotter

27.1 MODACSIL – CODE FOR STRESS CALCULATION IN SILOS AND HOPPERS

The development of the finite element code, MODACSIL, at INSA (Rennes, France) is part of a national research programme on cereal materials stored in steel silos carried out to support the draft of the recent French Norm P22-630 (NF, 1992). In this research programme, three main topics have been investigated: full-scale experiments on silos to measure pressures along the wall, laboratory tests on cereal products to characterize the bulk material law, and numerical investigations.

The main purpose of these numerical investigations has been to develop a code which is not too sophisticated, but takes into account the most important bulk properties of cereal materials. The granular medium considered as a material continuum is discretized normally by plane triangular elements (axisymmetric silos) or hexahedron elements with eight nodes (three-dimensional silos); for regions close to the wall, special isoparametric contact elements are developed to take into account the friction condition efficiently.

During the filling stage, the meshes defined automatically by means of an appropriate subroutine are set in action progressively by adding up horizontal layers. For each loading increment, due to the added weight of a horizontal finite element layer, the general equilibrium equations have to be satisfied according to the nonlinear constitutive law of ensiled material. A nonlinear hyper-elastic law, the Boyce model (Boyce, 1980; Fig. 27.1(a)), has been adopted with an application domain bounded by a yield criterion

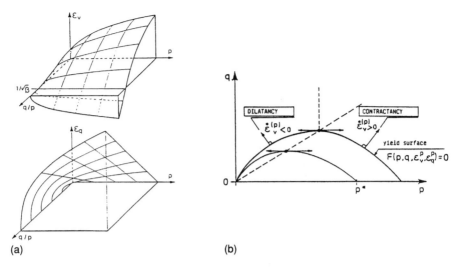

Fig. 27.1 (a) Elastic Boyce law; (b) Wilde criterion.

(Wilde model, 1979; Fig. 27.1(b)). The choice of such an elastoplastic modelling allows for the inclusion of some important bulk properties:

- The ensiled material can show a higher rigidity when the spheric stress increases.
- The dilatancy effect can be checked by acting upon the deviatoric part of the stress tensor.
- The concept of a characteristic threshold beyond which the volumetric strain rate changes its sign can easily be taken into account.
- The internal friction angle which is usually a basic datum for engineers can be introduced in the above modelling to define the failure limit state of the material.

For numerical resolution, three different types of nonlinearity have to be solved: two of them are related to the material behaviour, the third is due to the numerical formulation adopted to simulate the boundary conditions (contact element – Fig. 27.2). To succeed in solving these nonlinearities, an iterative process based on the Newton–Raphson algorithm has been adopted with the use of tangential stiffness matrices of elements at every iteration.

Considering now the discharging stage, some simplified assumptions have been set up in order to obtain an efficient finite element approach. The region taken by the flow is schematized in Fig. 27.3 which assumes a radial flow in the lower part of the silo. The generating line of the flow cone is approximately the line of maximum shear of the ensiled material at the limit state. Also, a theoretical investigation (Ragneau and Aribert, 1995a) to

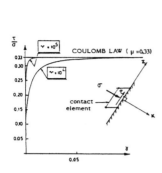
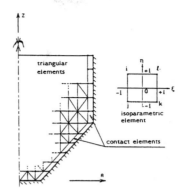

Fig. 27.2 Contact element.

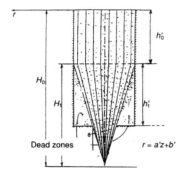
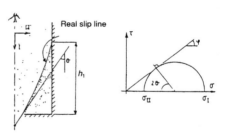

Fig. 27.3 Schematization of the flow.

solve the general dynamic equations in the flow zone has proved that inertia terms can be neglected entirely for usual flow rates. So in the upper part of the silo where the flow trajectories are parallel, the modelling established for the filling stage is valid, again provided that the friction condition is based on a friction angle less than that for the filling stage (effect of lubrication). In the lower part of the flow where trajectories are radial, the stress distribution along the interface between the flow zone and the dead zone can be related to those which occur in an equivalent hopper whose friction angle is very close to the internal friction angle of the bulk material. So the previous finite element program can be used again: after the cell filling, the stress distribution along the defined interface is known; then the simulation of the cell emptying consists of applying the stress increase due to the hopper flow effect by means of equivalent external forces located at the nodal points of the interface.

Some illustrations of numerical results compared to experimental re-

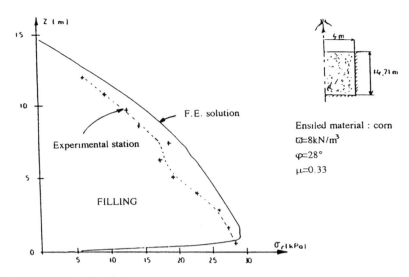

Fig. 27.4 Filling of cell C.

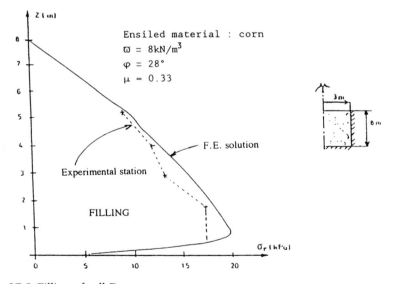

Fig. 27.5 Filling of cell D.

sults are given in Figs 27.4–27.7: they show a satisfying agreement between the model and full-scale measurements (Brozzetti, 1989). This model has been used to investigate different kinds of silo geometries (slender silos, squat silos, hoppers, etc.) and is now used to study unsymmetrical effects due to the eccentricity of the outlet in a three-dimensional silo (square or

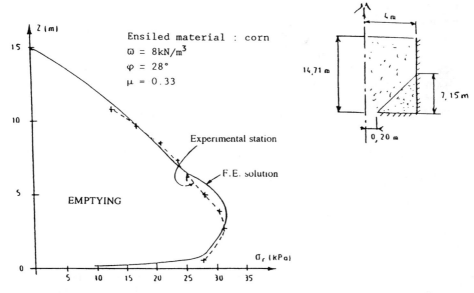

Fig. 27.6 Emptying of cell C.

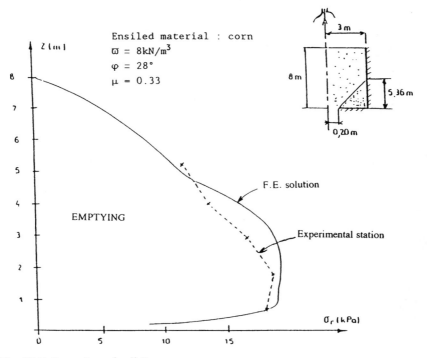

Fig. 27.7 Emptying of cell D.

500 Finite element models for specific applications

rectangular cross-section). The simplified assumptions adopted at different levels of the program increase its efficiency to produce realistic solutions at any time during the filling and discharging stages. But one main difficulty which has to be emphasized about the use of such a finite element program deals with the required discretization to obtain significant results, in particular, in three-dimensional problems: it needs big computer facilities and leads to very large algebraic systems of linear equations, and these must be used to obtain useful results not affected by numerical scattering.

27.2 AFENA AND KAFOPS CODES FROM EDINBURGH

27.2.1 Pressure predictions

At Edinburgh University, the finite element method has been used extensively to study various silo phenomena including wall pressures, solids flow, arching and the effects of wall imperfections. The main purpose is not to develop an all-embracing model of the very complex phenomena occurring during solids flow in a silo, but rather to account for the most important features, to explore phenomena commonly ignored in other studies and to produce sensible predictions of silo problems pertinent to industrial applications.

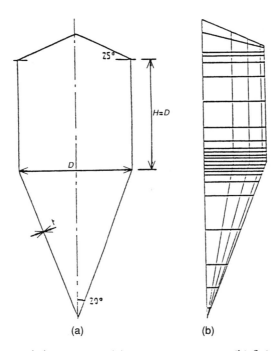

Fig. 27.8 Characteristic geometry: (a) structure geometry; (b) finite element mesh.

The AFENA program was initially developed at Sydney University, Australia (Carter, Booker and Davis, 1977) and has been further developed at Edinburgh University specifically for studying silo problems. The silo and its contents are modelled as axisymmetric or planar solids using 8- and 12-node isoparametric elements (Fig. 27.8). The stored material can be modelled using several elastic–plastic models including Mohr–Coulomb, Drücker–Prager, Lade–Duncan (1975), Matsuoka (1974) and modified critical state (Roscoe and Burland, 1968) (Fig. 27.9), with associated and non-associated flow. The elastic phase can be represented by a variety of anisotropic and alternative stress-dependent relations.

The solid–wall contact is modelled using a zero thickness curvilinear interface element (Fig. 27.10) (Ooi and Rotter, 1990). The elastic–plastic interface can model slip–stick and opening–closing phenomena. In finite element analysis, slip against the wall must be directed parallel to the wall. The abrupt transition from the vertical section of a silo to the conical hopper presents a serious numerical problem because material just above it must slide vertically, while that below it must slide in an inclined direction. Investigations were conducted to explore avoiding this singularity problem by using a small curved transition (Fig. 27.11). It has been found that cubic elements with slope and curvature compatibility throughout the whole

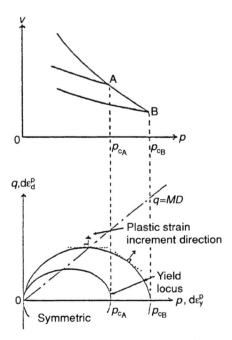

Fig. 27.9 Yield loci for the modified critical state model.

502 *Finite element models for specific applications*

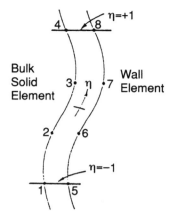

Fig. 27.10 Cubic contact element.

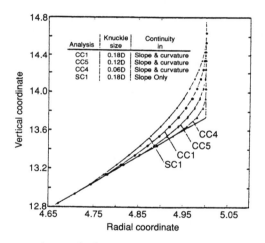

Fig. 27.11 Geometry of smoothed transition.

smoothed transition produce more acceptable local stress variations, without the need to smooth the output artificially.

Many silo configurations have been studied (Ooi and Rotter, 1989, 1990a, b). An example of an elastic–plastic storing pressure prediction for a cylinder–hopper configuration is shown in Fig. 27.12. Finite element studies have also been undertaken on silo arching over the outlet, with particular application to coal silos. Many solids display markedly anisotropic effects when they are poured into a silo (Nielsen, 1983), principally because the particles themselves are far from spherical. This phenomenon is almost universally ignored in numerical studies of silo pressures and flow. These effects of anisotropic behaviour on silo storing pressures are of

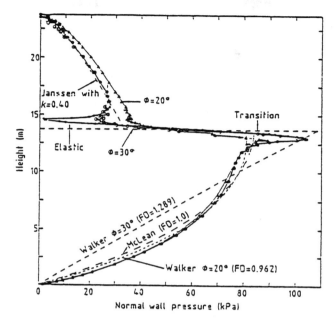

Fig. 27.12 Pressure during storing.

major interest to this group. Further studies have attempted to determine the role of geometric imperfections in the wall in changing pressures from the accepted Janssen distribution to patterns commonly associated with flow phenomena (Ooi and She, 1994).

27.2.2 Flow predictions

Another finite element program developed at Edinburgh University, KAFOPS, is based on the kinematic theory of solids flow (Tüzün and Nedderman, 1979a, b), extended to permit more variable material descriptions and formulated in a finite element format in axisymmetric and planar forms. The program has produced some satisfactory predictions of simple flow situations (Watson and Rotter, 1994). An example of the predicted velocity distribution is shown in Fig. 27.13. The flow channel boundary in funnel flow can also be approximately determined. This kinematic theory has now been extended further into a time domain analysis, incorporating the different particle trajectories observed in the different flow zones in a core-flow situation. It permits prediction of the complete discharge process, including the sloughing of initially dead material into the developing flow channel. The first predictions using this extended kinematic method are in very good agreement with the experimental observations in a full-scale experiment, and the technique holds considerable promise for the future.

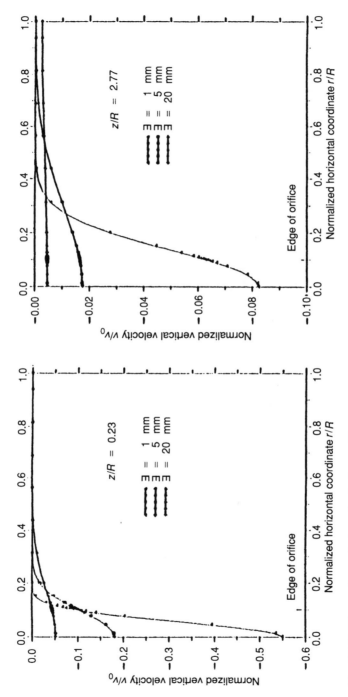

Fig. 27.13 Kinematic prediction of velocity profiles.

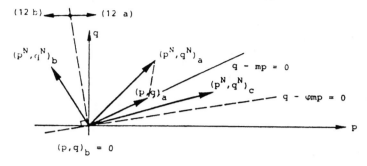

Fig. 27.14 Stress projection for different Newtonian stress states resulting in a stress which is (a) plastic, (b) zero or (c) Newtonian (identity projection).

27.3 FINITE ELEMENT METHOD FOR GRAVITATIONAL FLOW OF A GRANULAR MATERIAL

The model briefly described below has been developed in Sweden (Runesson and Nilsson, 1986). It has been built in order to investigate the emptying of a silo (axisymmetric and plane strain problems) during the transient and permanent stages. The motion of the granular material subjected to gravitational forces is modelled as the motion of a viscous plastic fluid. The rate of deformation tensor is thus decomposed into one Newtonian part and another plastic part obeying a non-associated flow rule (Fig. 27.14).

The yield criterion is defined by the Drücker–Prager straight line (without any cohesion):

$q - mp = 0$ (Fig. 27.15), with $m = f(\varphi)\sin\varphi$ (φ being the internal friction angle).

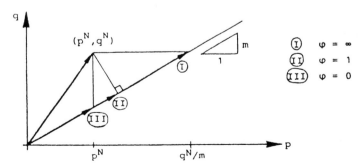

Fig. 27.15 Stress solution for certain φ-values.

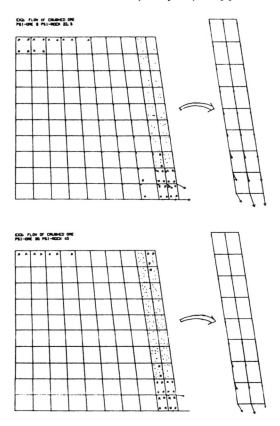

Fig. 27.16 Velocity fields and zones of plastic yielding.

The discretization of the silo is based on rectangular elements (four- and eight-node elements); on each node, the unknown quantities are the components of the flow rate which have to satisfy the Navier–Stokes equations. The stress tensor is found as a function of the Newtonian stress, which is the true stress in the creeping part of the bulk mass. When the plastic yielding occurs, there are plastic corrections affecting the stress field as follows:

$$p = k_m p^N \quad \text{with } k_m = \frac{1}{1+\varphi m^2}\left(1 + \frac{1}{k}\varphi m^2\right) \quad k = m\frac{p^N}{q^N} \quad (27.3.1)$$

$$q = k_d q^N \quad \text{with } k_d = \frac{1}{1+\varphi m^2}\left(k + \varphi m^2\right) \quad \varphi = \frac{K}{3G(1+\beta)} \quad (27.3.2)$$

where K and G mean the dynamic bulk and shear viscosity.

These relations define the stress as the projection in 'adjusted complementary viscous rate of dissipation' of the Newtonian stress on to the yield surface at each spatial point. The plastic strains are computed with respect to a plastic potential g characterized by a dilatancy angle ψ:

$$g(p,q) = q - np \quad \text{with} \quad n = f(\psi) \sin\psi$$

The finite element method developed for transient flow includes the convective acceleration terms. A time-stepping algorithm is devised which adopts modified Newton iterations for the solution of the nonlinear equations in each time step arising from the backward Euler differencing scheme.

REFERENCES

Aribert, J.M. and Ragneau, E. (1990) Stress calculations in silos by finite element method using different behaviour laws for ensiled material. *Proc. 2nd European Symposium 'Chisa '90'*, Prague.

Boyce, H.R. (1980) A non linear model for the elastic behaviour of granular material under repeated loading. *International Symposium on Soils under Cyclic and Transient Loading*. Swansea, UK.

Brozzetti, J. (1989) Description de la base expérimentale d'essais de cellules métalliques de stockage; présentation du programme d'essais. *Revue de Construction Métallique* No. 2.

Carter, J.P.; Booker, J.R. and Davis, E.H. (1977) Finite deformation of an elastic-plastic soil. *Int. J. Numerical and Analytical Methods in Geomechanics*, 1, 245–253.

Lade, P.V. and Duncan, J.M. (1975) Elastoplastic stress–strain theory for cohesionless soil. *Proc. ASCE*, **101**, GT10, 1037–1053.

Luong, M.P. (1989) Rhéologie des grains agroalimentaires ensilés. *Revue de Construction Métallique* No. 2.

Matsuoka, H. (1974) Stress–strain relationships of sands based on the mobilized plane. *Soils and Foundations*, **14**(2), 47–61.

NF P22-630 (1992) Norme expérimentale Française, AFNOR.

Nielsen, J. (1983) Load distribution in silos influenced by anisotropic grain behaviour. *Proc., Int. Conf. on Bulk Materials Storage, Handling and Transptn*, I.E. Aust., Newcastle, August, 226–230.

Ooi, J.Y. and Rotter, J.M. (1990a) Wall pressures in squat steel silos from finite element analysis. *Computers and Structures*, **37**(4), 361–374.

Ooi, J.Y. and Rotter, J.M. (1990b) Elastic predictions of pressures in conical silo hoppers. *Engineering Structures*, **13**(2), 2–12.

Ooi, J.Y. and Rotter, J.M. (1989) Elastic and plastic predictions of the storing pressures in conical hoppers. *Transactions of Mechanical Engineering*, I. E. Australia, ME14, No. 3, 165–169.

Ooi, J.Y. and She, K.M. (1994) Non-linear analysis of wall pressure in imperfect silos. submitted to *Int. J. Solids and Structures*.

Ragneau, E. (1993) Modélisation numérique et nouvelles méthodes analytiques pour le calcul des actions dans les silos cylindro-coniques (remplissage et vidange). Thèse de Doctorat, INSA de Rennes.

Ragneau, E. and Aribert, J.M. (1993) Prediction of loads in silos during filling and emptying stages by a finite element method. *International Conference FEM-CAD*, Paris, I.I.T.T. Editor.

Ragneau, E. and Aribert, J.M. (1995a) Silo pressure calculation: from a finite element method to simplified analytical solutions. *International Journal of Bulk Solids Handling* No. 1.

Ragneau, E. and Aribert, J.M. (1995b) F.E.M. applied to the determination of grain action exerted in a silo by a pulverulent material. *European Journal of Finite Element Method* No. 2, Hermès Editor, France.

Ragneau, E.; Aribert, J.M. and Sanad, A.M. (1994) Modèle tri-dimensionnel aux Eléments Finis pour le calcul des actions sur les parois d'un silo (remplissage et vidange). *Revue de Construction Métallique* No. 2.

Roscoe, K.H. and Burland, J.B. (1968) On the generalised stress–strain behaviour of 'Wet' clay. *Engineering Plasticity* (J. Heyman and F.A. Leckie, eds), Cambridge University Press, 535–609.

Runesson, K. and Nilsson, L. (1986) Finite element modelling of the gravitational flow of a granular material. *International Journal of Bulk Solids Handling*, 6(5).

Tüzün, U. and Nedderman, R.M. (1979a) A kinematic model for the flow of granular materials. *Powder Technology*, 22(2), 243–253.

Tüzün, U. and Nedderman, R.M. (1979b) Experimental evidence supporting kinematic modelling of the flow of granular media in the absence of air drag. *Powder Technology*, 24(2), 257–266.

Watson, G.R. and Rotter, J.M. (1994) A finite element analysis of planar granular solids flow. to appear in *Chemical Engineering Science*.

Wilde, (1979) *Principes mathématiques et physiques des modèles élastoplastiques des sols pulvérulents*. Compte rendu du colloque Franco-Polonais de Paris. LCPC, France.

28

Stochastic finite element analysis of filling pressures
F. Dahlhaus and J. Eibl

28.1 INTRODUCTION

Nowadays the design of silo structures is usually based on the deterministic values of the bulk material. As can be seen from a lot of experimental results these characteristic values show an inherently big scatter, due to the fact that in the case of many organic materials these parameters depend on moisture. It is well known for example that Canadian wheat behaves differently from German wheat and so on. This is also confirmed by the experience that sometimes silo structures behave well over several years and suddenly fail without having changed the type of stored material. Therefore the definition of characteristic values of these parameters within the frame of a modern safety philosophy is of special interest to the final design.

To get a better insight into the scatter of the maximum pressures that are caused by such uncertainties in the material behaviour the authors have installed a data bank where more than 300 silo experiments with all material data and the resulting pressures are stored. They form the basis of a better interpretation of experimentally measured pressures and also of further pressure investigations using the theory of stochastic finite elements. The method proposed herein allows for Taylor series expansion of the response about arbitrary reference values of the basic random variables. A computer code has been developed for the application of this method to bulk materials exhibiting nonlinear behaviour. The main idea is to get more information on local pressure peaks currently covered empirically by patch loads within several standards.

As the authors have been engaged in writing the Standards DIN 1055/6 (1987), an ISO code (1991), a recommendation for the design of silos on

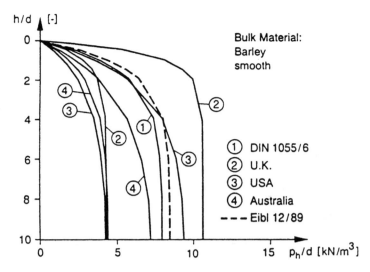

Fig. 28.1 Horizontal wall pressure according to several silo codes.

behalf of FIP (1990) and now a Eurocode (CEN TC 250, 1990), a lot of comparisons between the different existing standards were made. Figure 28.1 shows a typical example which demonstrates how much the various recommended design values deviate from each other. In the authors' opinion this is a consequence of lacking knowledge of the inherent scatter of the bulk material parameters.

28.2 THE NUMERICAL MODEL

The behaviour of the granular bulk material is described in a Lagrangian frame of reference using the well-established theory of continuum mechanics. As the simulation of stochastic effects in the bulk material is of main interest here, the stochastic finite element method (SFEM) has been applied. In contrast to the deterministic formulation (FEM) that is often used for structural analysis, the perturbation method proposed herein involves first- or second-order Taylor series expansion around the mean values of the basic random variables.

The governing equation of the virtual work principle for nonlinear problems including random functions of the material tensor C of the form

$$C_{ijkl} \approx C^0_{ijkl} + \xi C'_{ijkl} + \xi^2 C''_{ijkl} \qquad (28.2.1)$$

is expressed by

$$\int_{^tV} {^t}C_{ijkl} e_{kl} \delta e_{ij} d^t V + \int_{^tV} {^t}\tau_{ij} \delta \eta_{ij} d^t V = {^{t+\Delta t}}R \delta u - \int_{^tV} {^t}\tau_{ij} \delta e_{ij} d^t V \qquad (28.2.2)$$

By equating equal-order terms the following zeroth- and first-order equations corresponding to equation (28.2.2) are

$$\int_V C^0_{ijkl} e^0_{kl} \delta e_{ij} dV - \int_{'V} {}^t\tau_{ij} \delta\eta_{ij} d'V = \int_V f_i^{B0} \delta u_i^B dV + \int_S f_i^{S0} \delta u_i^S dS - \int_{'V} {}^t\tau_{ij} \delta e_{ij} d'V \quad (28.2.3)$$

$$\int_V C^0_{ijkl} e'_{kl} \delta e_{ij} dV = \int_V f_i^{B'} \delta u_i^B dV + \int_S f_i^{S'} \delta u_i^S dS - \int_V C'_{ijkl} \frac{1}{2}\left(u^0_{k,l} + u^0_{l,k}\right) \delta e_{ij} d'V \quad (28.2.4)$$

If only a first-order Taylor series expansion is employed, the mean response is found directly as the solution of the zeroth-order equations, which is just the solution of an ordinary deterministic structural problem. The inclusion of the second-order terms has an effect only on the mean values of the response and is usually believed to be of minor importance compared to the zeroth-order terms.

The nonlinear finite element matrix equations derived from equation (28.2.2) are

$$\left[{}^{(t+\Delta t)}K_L^{(i-1)} + {}^{(t+\Delta t)}K_{NL}^{(i-1)}\right]\Delta U^{(i)} = {}^{(t+\Delta t)}R - {}^{(t+\Delta t)}F^{(i)} \quad (28.2.5)$$

The random function $b(x)$ is defined by its expectation $b(x)$, its coefficient of variation α and its autocorrelation $R(b(x_i), b(x_j))$, where b_i are the nodal values of $b(x)$, that is the values of b at x_i, $i = 1, \ldots, q$. The matrices K, U and R are expanded about b via Taylor series:

$$K = K + \sum_{i=1}^{q} K_{b_i} db_i + \frac{1}{2} \sum_{i,j=1}^{q} K_{b_i b_j} db_i db_j \quad (28.2.6)$$

$$U = U + \sum_{i=1}^{q} U_{b_i} db_i + \frac{1}{2} \sum_{i,j=1}^{q} U_{b_i b_j} db_i db_j \quad (28.2.7)$$

$$R = R + \sum_{i=1}^{q} K_{b_i} db_i + \frac{1}{2} \sum_{i,j=1}^{q} R_{b_i b_j} db_i db_j \quad (28.2.8)$$

Substituting equations (28.2.6)–(28.2.8) into equation (28.2.5) and equating equal-order terms the means and covariances of the response can be found in terms of the means and covariances of the basic random variables and the response gradients with respect to the same variables. The covariance matrix of the displacements can be shown to be

$$\text{Cov}(\Delta U^i, \Delta U^j) = \sum_{r,s=1}^{q} [K]^{-1} K_{br}(\Delta U) \text{Cov}(b_r, b_s)(\Delta U)^T K_{bs}^T [K]^{-T} \quad (28.2.9)$$

Similarly, the covariances of the strains and the stresses can be found.

The physical quantities of the bulk material are represented by a fourth-order tensor H for which a rate-type formulation developed by Kolymbas (1988) is used. Herein the Jaumann stress rate is calculated by means of the following equation:

$$\overset{\circ}{T} = \frac{C_1}{2}(TD + DT) + C_2 \text{tr}(TD)I + C_3 \sqrt{\text{tr}D^2}\, T + C_4 \frac{\sqrt{\text{tr}D^2}}{\text{tr}T} T^2 \quad (28.2.10)$$

with

$$C_1 = C_1(E_0, \beta_0) \qquad C_3 = C_3(E_0, \beta_0, \beta_1, \phi)$$
$$C_2 = C_2(E_0, \beta_0, \beta_1, \phi) \qquad C_4 = C_4(E_0, \beta_0, \beta_1, \phi)$$

The material constants C_1, C_2, C_3, C_4 are functions of the modulus of elasticity E_0, the angles of dilatancy β_0, β_1 and of the angle of internal friction ϕ. In the following these parameters are introduced as random variables.

28.3 RESULTS

Based on the SFEM formulation developed previously, the variations of static pressures during the filling phase were calculated. For all material parameters the expectation, the coefficient of variation of the random field $b(x)$ and the spatial autocorrelation function that is shown together with the chosen finite element model in Fig. 28.2 are assumed as follows:

$$E[b(x_i)] = b_0 \quad (28.3.1)$$

$$R[b(x_i), b(x_j)] = \exp(-|x_i - x_j|/\theta) \quad (28.3.2)$$

$$\alpha = 0.05 \quad (28.3.3)$$

where x_i, θ and $b(x_i)$ denote the location, the correlation length and the random function at x_i, respectively. It should be noted that the autocorrelation between any two points depends only on the interval between these points and not on their locations.

The variances of horizontal and vertical pressures after filling were computed for different cases of spatial correlation. In Fig. 28.3 the coefficients of variation are shown as a function of the correlation length θ in case of a variation of the modulus E_0. The maximum values of about 0.02 are obtained if the random field is assumed to have an uncorrelated structure ($\theta \geq 0$). These values clearly remain under the coefficients of the input parameter $\alpha = 0.05$. With an increase of the correlation length θ the sensitivity of the stresses decreases. From this it can be concluded that the wall pressure is not decisively influenced by stochastic variations of this material parameter. The spatial distribution of the pressure variations are shown in Fig. 28.4 as a function of the silo diameter and the silo height.

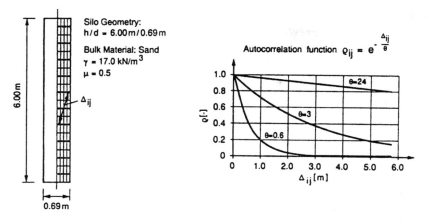

Fig. 28.2 Stochastic finite element model and autocorrelation function characterizing homogeneous random fields.

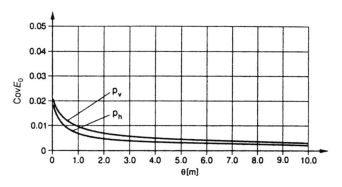

Fig. 28.3 Coefficient of horizontal and vertical pressure variations – 5% variation of E_0.

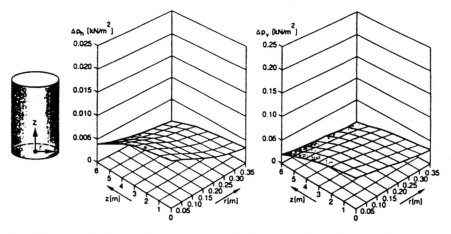

Fig. 28.4 Spatial distribution of standard deviations – 5% variation of E_0.

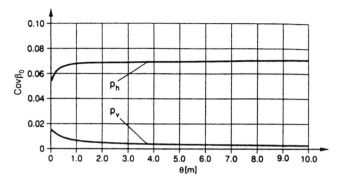

Fig. 28.5 Coefficient of horizontal and vertical pressure variations – 5% variation of β_0.

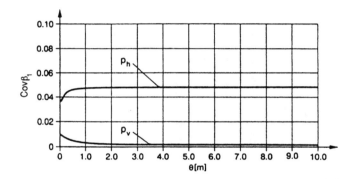

Fig. 28.6 Coefficient of horizontal and vertical pressure variations – 5% variation of β_1.

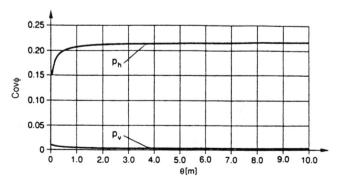

Fig. 28.7 Coefficient of horizontal and vertical pressure variations – 5% variation of ϕ.

The variances of the stresses due to variations of the angle of dilatancy β_0, β_1 are shown in Figs 28.5 and 28.6. In contrast to the modulus E_0 these parameters have a large influence on the horizontal wall pressure, while the vertical pressure variations are small. The maximum coefficient of variation in case of β_1 is found to be nearly 0.05. This value is even exceeded due to

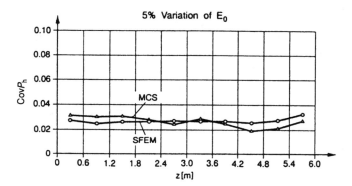

Fig. 28.8 Comparison of coefficients of horizontal wall pressure variations calculated by SFEM and MCS.

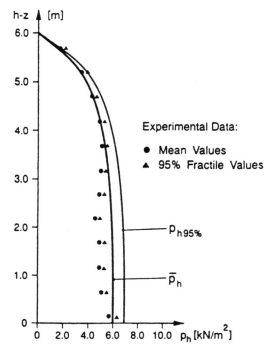

Fig. 28.9 Comparison of the SFEM solutions and experimentally measured horizontal wall pressure variations.

a variation of the parameter β_0. The greatest influence on the wall pressure is observed as a result of a variation of the angle of internal friction ϕ. The coefficients of stress variations are plotted in Fig. 28.7. Again the vertical pressure is hardly influenced, while the maximum coefficient of variation of the wall pressure is 0.22.

To verify the results of SFEM mentioned above, a Monte Carlo simulation (MCS) of 300 realizations has been carried out. The coefficients of variation of the wall pressure calculated by both methods are shown as a function of the silo height in Fig. 28.8. As can be seen, the SFEM solutions compare well in accuracy with the MCS solutions.

Based on experimentally measured scatters of the bulk material parameters, 95% fractile values of the wall pressure were determined. These values are shown together with the experimentally measured data by Schütz and Pieper (1980) in Fig. 28.9. Partially the SFEM variances are in fairly good agreement with those obtained from a statistical analysis of the experimental results.

28.4 SUMMARY AND CONCLUSIONS

The stochastic behaviour of granular materials within circular silo bins at rest is modelled by means of probabilistic numerical methods based on the continuum theory. The aim of these studies that are still under way, is to explore the pressure variations and the resulting fluctuations of the wall stresses to develop improved and simplified design recommendations. The basic theory is presented, together with the initial principal results.

REFERENCES

CEN TC 250/SC1/PT8 (March 1990) *Basis of Design and Actions of Structures, Part 4; Actions in Silos and Tanks*, Brussels.

DIN 1055 Teil 6 (1987) *Lastannahmen für Bauten; Lasten in Silozellen*. Ausgabe 5, Berlin.

FIP-Working Group 'Silo Design' (July 1990) *Recommendation for Concrete Silo Design* (Draft), Karlsruhe.

ISO/TC98/SC3 Working Group 5 (August 1991) *Loads on Structures from Bulk Material* (ISO-CD 11697), Geneva.

Kolymbas, D. (1988) *Eine konstitutive Theorie für Böden und andere körnige Stoffe*. Veröffentlichung des Institutes für Boden und Felsmechanik der Universität Karlsruhe, No. 109, Karlsruhe.

Schütz, M. and Pieper, K. (1980) *Norm-Meßsilo für Schüttguteigenschaften*. University of Braunschweig.

FURTHER READING

Belytschko, T. and Liu, W.K. (1986) Random field finite elements. *International Journal for Numerical Methods in Engineering*, **23**, 1831–1845.

Eibl, J. and Kobler, G. (1977) Ableitung von Sicherheitsfaktoren. *Beitrag zum Sicherheitsseminar des Instituts für Bautechnik*, Berlin, pp. 85–104.
Eibl, J. and Stempniewski, L. (1987) *Zur Anwendung finiter Elemente bei der stochastischen Berechnung von Plattentragwerken*. Institut für Massivbau und Baustofftechnologie, University of Karlsruhe.
Eibl, J. and Stempniewski, L. (1989) Fragen zum Nachweis der Tragsicherheit bei Berücksichtigung nichtlinearer Stoffgesetze, Sicherheit von Bauwerken – Safety of Structures – *Günter Breitschaft Symposium*, IfBt, Berlin, pp. 30–37.
Schuëller, G.I. (1981) *Einführung in die Tragsicherheit und Zuverlässigkeit von Tragwerken*, Berlin.
Vanmarcke, E. (1983) *Random Fields: Analysis and Synthesis*. The MIT Press, Cambridge, Massachusetts.
Vanmarcke, E. (1983) Stochastic finite element analysis of simple beams. *Journal of Engineering Mechanics*, **109**(5), 1203–1214.

29

Pressures under earthquake loading
A. Braun and J. Eibl

29.1 INTRODUCTION – PROBLEM

Silos used for coal, grain and other products also need to be designed in earthquake-endangered areas. During such loadings, the silo walls experience additional stresses resulting from unsymmetrical pressure distributions in the silo. These pressure arrangements can lead to ovalization of the silo wall, especially for silos with a diameter to height ratio equal to or less than one. Later, the dynamic loads lead to compactions of the bulk material as well as changes of material parameters such as the angle of internal friction. In standard silo design, wall pressures from such effects are not usually taken into account. Instead, the system is reduced to a cantilever beam with several point masses being situated on top of each other to calculate appropriate additional static horizontal loads (ACI 313-77, 1983; DIN 4149, 1981; Hampe, 1991; Martens, 1988; Safarian and Harris, 1985). This procedure is in accordance with the codes of practice, where earthquake loads are covered only in a general way. Certainly one cannot be satisfied with the current situation. The following contribution deals with the bulk material–structure interaction in a silo under earthquake excitation and may in this way help to solve the problem.

29.2 STATE OF KNOWLEDGE

In dynamic analysis, the following numerical methods are commonly applied:

- the pseudostatic method
- the time-history method

- the response-spectra method
- the probabilistic method

A number of tests have been performed in recent years, in which silo models were exposed to dynamic, earthquake-typical loads (Harris and von Nad, 1985; Sasaki and Yoshimura, 1988; Yokota, Sugita and Mita, 1983). On the whole these tests were used only to analyse the influence of the effective bulk material mass on the dynamic response of the whole system (Jiang and Zhao, 1988). In addition, little can be found in the international standards about loads on the wall resulting from seismic acceleration of the bulk material. For computational purposes, the silo is generally approximated by a cantilever beam with different point masses. Due to this simplification, only rough estimates of the loads on the whole system and their effect on the foundation and the supporting construction can be expected from the calculation (Gorenc, Hogan and Rotter, 1986).

In Germany, earthquake loads are taken into consideration by the proximity method of DIN 4149 (1981) which includes the following assumptions:

- The silo is formed as a cantilever beam with different point masses.
- These masses are excited by additional static loads.
- The dynamic soil behaviour is modelled by a dynamic soil stiffness.

The proximity method may be applied provided the following conditions are met:

- The silo walls must extend down to the foundation.
- The filling level of the bulk material has to be at least three-quarters of the total height of the silo.

The dynamic behaviour of the structure as a whole and its effects on the foundation can be analysed by this method. On the other hand, no information is obtained about the pressure distribution in the silo.

Boswell (1983) gave a summary of the current international knowledge on the topic at the Second International Silo Conference. The following assumptions are included in the American Code of Practice ACI 313-77 (1983):

- 80% of the maximum live load can be used as the effective load W_{eff}. The minimum horizontal ground force due to an earthquake is thus determined from the formula:

$$H_e = ZC_p\left[W_G + W_{eff}\right] \qquad (29.2.1)$$

where W_G is the weight of the structure, Z the earthquake zone factor and C_p the factor which depends upon the support conditions.

- The lateral mass is less than the total solid mass to allow for the frictional and energy dissipation properties of granular material.
- The horizontal force should be distributed vertically throughout a

structure in direct proportion to the lateral stiffness of the main structural components.
- The horizontal ground movement of an earthquake is the destructive motion.

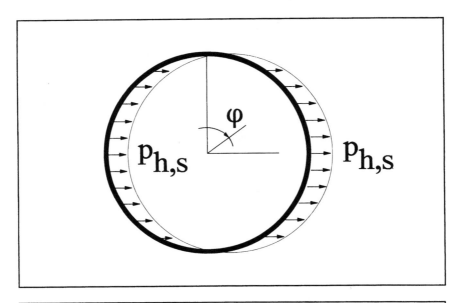

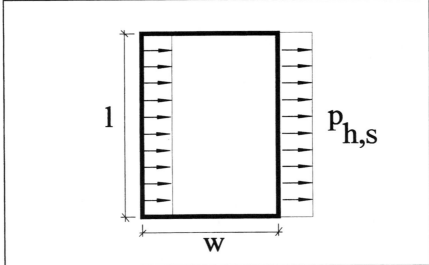

Fig. 29.1 Additional stress distribution.

Additional horizontal pressures resulting from earthquake effects are taken into account in the Australian Code and in the draft of Eurocode 1, Part 4 *Actions in Silos and Tanks* (CEN TC 250, 1992) by simple proximity indications. The prediction of a supplementary horizontal pressure component $p_{h,s}$, given separately for cylindrical and rectangular silo geometries in the draft of Eurocode 1, are shown in Fig. 29.1.

$$p_{h,s} = \frac{1}{2} d(\cos\varphi)\gamma \frac{a}{g} \quad 0 \leq \varphi \leq \pi \quad (29.2.2)$$

$$p_{h,s} = \frac{1}{2} w \gamma \frac{a}{g} \quad (29.2.3)$$

The goal of the current investigation is to gain information about the distribution and magnitude of pressures in the silo during seismic loading. Besides this, the influence of the silo structure should be analysed. The silo walls and the bulk material are modelled by a three-dimensional FEM system taking into account geometrical and material nonlinearities. In particular for the bulk material, a realistic description of the material behaviour by a highly nonlinear model is used. The following questions should be answered in the project:

- How large are the maximum horizontal and vertical pressures in the silo?
- Does the density of the bulk material have an essential influence?
- What is the influence of the filling height of the bulk material and the stiffness of the wall?
- What accelerations occur in the bulk material?
- What deformations and stresses are generated in the wall?

29.3 MECHANICAL AND NUMERICAL MODEL

The behaviour of the bulk material is described in a Lagrangian frame of reference, using the well-established theory of continuum mechanics (Bathe, 1986; Zienkiewicz, 1984) and the finite element program ABAQUS (1993). Systematic investigations with respect to appropriate material laws were carried out by Weidner (1990) at the University of Karlsruhe. On the part of numerical simulations we can rely on the experiences of Eibl and Stempniewski (1987), Rombach (1991) and Stempniewski (1990).

The FEM simulation of silo response to earthquakes in this work is divided into two parts. First of all, static filling pressures are calculated. These pressures from the initial state are used for the dynamic analysis of the filled silo in a second step. To compute the time evolution, the time-history method is used. The model is based on the following equation:

$$[M]\frac{d^2}{dt^2}(\vec{u}) + [R(\vec{u})]\vec{u} = -[M]\vec{g}\ddot{u}_E \quad (29.3.1)$$

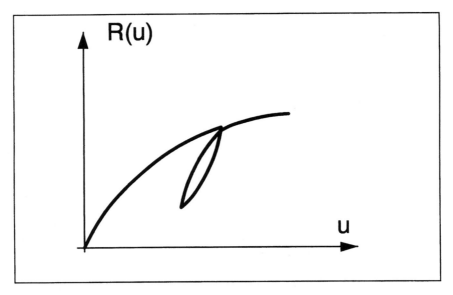

Fig. 29.2 Nonlinear material behaviour of the bulk material.

with an $R(u)$ behaviour as sketched in Fig. 29.2.

The equilibrium can be described as

$$\int_V C_{ijrs} e_{rs} \delta e_{ij} dV + \int_V {}^t S_{ij} \delta \eta_{ij} dV = {}^{t+\Delta t} R \delta u - \int_V {}^t S_{ij} \delta e_{ij} dV \\ - \int_V \rho^{t+\Delta t} \ddot{u}_i \delta u_i dV \quad (29.3.2)$$

with the assumptions

$$S_{ij} = C_{ijrs} \varepsilon_{rs} \qquad \delta \varepsilon_{ij} = \delta e_{ij} \quad (29.3.3)$$

Then we can write

$$\left({}^t [K_{NL}] \right) \{u\} = {}^{t+\Delta t}\{R\} - {}^t\{F\} - \{M\}^{t+\Delta t}\{\ddot{u}\} \quad (29.3.4)$$

where $[M]$ is the mass matrix, $[K_{NL}]$ is the nonlinear stiffness matrix and $\{u\}$ is the vector of nodal displacements. $\{R\}$ is an external load vector, which may include body forces and external pressure loads. Vector $\{F\}$ represents the nodal forces corresponding to the element stresses. Equation (29.3.5) shows the material law used.

$$\overset{\circ}{T} = H(T, D) : D \quad (29.3.5)$$

While the equilibrium equations (29.3.1)–(29.3.4) may be found in any textbook on continuum theory, the symbolically written equation (29.3.5) incorporates the main difficulty, namely the realistic description of the material behaviour within the frame of constitutive equations. This rate-type formulation was developed by Kolymbas (1988) and has been modified by Wu (1992) and Bauer (1992). Equation (29.3.1) is generally valid for the

Initial results

time-history method as well as for a nonlinear material law as it is used for the bulk material. Energy dissipation effects are taken into consideration via the nonlinear behaviour. The stress rate in the Kolymbas model is calculated by means of the following equation:

$$\overset{\circ}{T} = C_1(TD + DT)/2 + C_2 \text{tr}(TD)I + C_3 T \sqrt{\text{tr}D^2} + C_4 \frac{T^2}{\text{tr}T} \sqrt{\text{tr}D^2} \quad (29.3.6)$$

where $C_1 \ldots C_4$ are material parameters, $\overset{\circ}{T}$ the Jaumann stress rate, T the Cauchy stress tensor and D the deformation rate tensor. The constitutive parameters C_1–C_4 have to be determined from experimental triaxial test data for different bulk materials. The extended version by Bauer reads:

$$\overset{\circ}{T} = \left[C_1 \text{tr}(T)D + C_2 \frac{(\text{tr}TD)T}{\text{tr}T} + \left(C_3 \frac{T^2}{\text{tr}T} \|D\| + C_4 \frac{T^{*2}}{\text{tr}T} \|D\| \right) I_e \right] \\ \times [1 + f_t][1 + f_m] \quad (29.3.7)$$

where I_e is the density index, f_t the compaction function and f_m the function for dissipation influence.

In the FEM analysis, the bulk material is discretized by standard three-dimensional isoparametric elements. Shell elements are used to represent the silo wall. The two element groups are coupled by slide line elements, which allow interaction between the bulk material and the silo wall. Linear friction behaviour is assumed. Comparative calculations (Rombach, 1991) have shown that in most cases the linear Coulomb friction model describes the material behaviour at the silo walls with sufficient accuracy.

29.4 INITIAL RESULTS

The silo model under consideration has a height of 10.50 m and a diameter of 10.00 m. The container is filled with dense sand up to a level of 10.00 m. For reasons of symmetry, only half of the silo was modelled as shown in Fig. 29.3. The roof is ignored in the present study. Geometric imperfections like deviations from the circular form of the cross-section of the silo or local imperfections of the foundation are neglected. The foundation is assumed to be rigid, but bottom friction is taken into consideration.

The stress distribution in the silo after filling is shown in Fig. 29.4. Starting from this initial state, the response to earthquake excitation was studied for the arbitrary chosen example of the N–S component of the Friaul earthquake (15 September 1976) where a maximum horizontal ground acceleration of 2.18 m/s^2 was observed. In the future we will use artificially generated acceleration histories which were generated using the program SIMQKE (1976). Figure 29.5 shows the applied earthquake acceleration history. A plot of the computed horizontal acceleration at node 941 is shown in Fig. 29.6 and the computed pressures at elements 1, 6 and 10 are given in Figs 29.7–29.9.

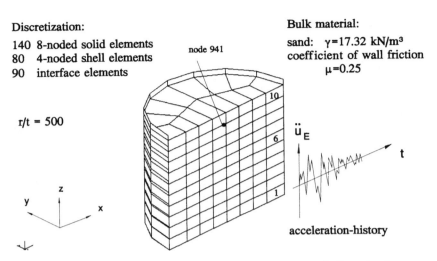

Fig. 29.3 Three-dimensional calculation of silo geometry and discretization.

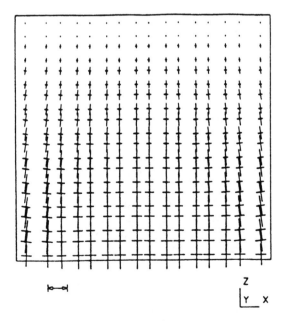

Fig. 29.4 Principal stresses in the silo after filling.

Initial results

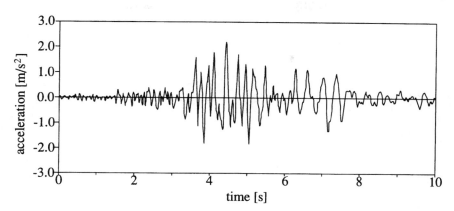

Fig. 29.5 Input acceleration at the silo bottom.

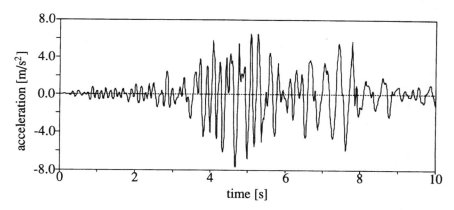

Fig. 29.6 Computed horizontal acceleration at node 941.

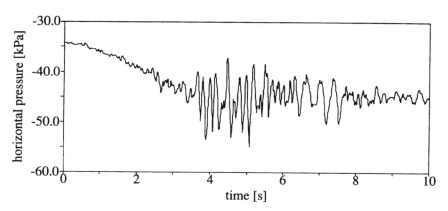

Fig. 29.7 Horizontal pressure at element 1.

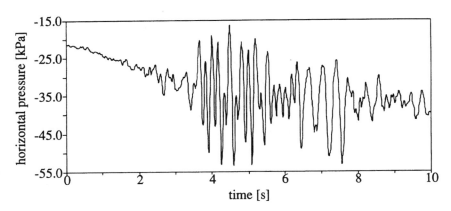

Fig. 29.8 Horizontal pressure at element 6.

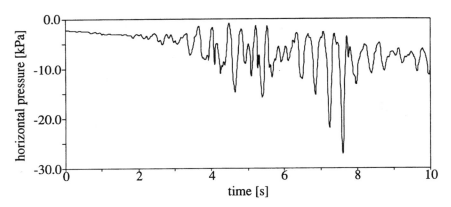

Fig. 29.9 Horizontal pressure at element 10.

29.5 SUMMARY AND CONCLUSIONS

A numerical analysis of an earthquake-loaded silo based on the finite element method has been presented in this chapter. The model takes into consideration the bulk material–structure interaction and the nonlinear material behaviour of the bulk material. In the near future we will study the influence of mesh refinement, filling height, different acceleration histories and wall stiffness. Here the basic theory is presented, together with the first principal results.

REFERENCES

ABAQUS Manual (1993) Version 5.2/5.3. Hibbit, Karlson & Sorensen, Inc., Pawtucket, RI, USA.
ACI 313-77 (1983) *Recommended Practice for Design and Construction of Concrete Bins, Silos and Bunkers for Storing Granular Materials*; Revision, Detroit.

References

Bathe, K.J. (1986) *Finite-Element-Methoden*; Springer-Verlag, Berlin.

Bauer, E. (1992) Zum mechanischen Verhalten granularer Stoffe unter vorwiegend ödome trischer Beanspruchung; Veröffentlichungen des Instituts für Felsmechanik der Universität Karlsruhe, Dissertation.

Boswell, L.T. (Nov. 1983) Current practice in the analysis and design of bulk storage silos subjected to earthquake motion; *Proceedings Second International Conference on Design of Silos for Strength and Flow*, Stratford, pp. 95–106.

CEN TC 250/SC1/PT8 (September 1992) *Basis of Design and Actions on Structures, Part 4, Action in Silos and Tanks*; Draft, Brussels.

DIN 4149 (April 1981) *Bauten in deutschen Erdbebengebieten – Lastannahmen, Bemessung und Ausführung üblicher Hochbauten*; Ausgabe, Berlin.

Eibl, J. and Stempniewski, L. (1987) Dynamic analysis of liquid-filled tanks including plasticity and fluid interaction – earthquake effects. G. de Roeck *et al.* (eds) *Proceedings of Shell and Spatial Structures – Computational Aspects*, Springer-Verlag, Heidelberg, pp. 261–269.

Gorenc, B.E.; Hogan, T.J. and Rotter, J.M. (1986) *Guidelines for the Assessment of Loads on Bulk Solids Containers*; The Institution of Engineers, Sydney.

Hampe, E. (1991) *Silos Band 2 – Bauwerke*; Berlin, Verlag für Bauwesen GmbH.

Harris, E.C. and von Nad, J.D. (1985) Experimental determination of effective weight of stored material for use in seismic design of silos; *ACI Journal*, 82, 828–833.

Jiang, J. and Zhao, Y. (1988) Study on seismic behaviour of silo structure; *Ninth World Conference on Earthquake Engineering*, Tokyo-Kyoto 1988, Abstracts Vol.1, Paper No. F10-06.

Kolymbas, D. (1988) *Eine konstitutive Theorie für Böden und andere körnige Stoffe*; Veröffentlichungen des Institutes für Boden- und Felsmechanik der Universität Karlsruhe No. 109.

Martens, P. (ed.) (1988) *Silo Handbuch*; Berlin, Verlag Wilhelm Ernst & Sohn.

Rombach, G.A. (1991) Schüttguteinwirkungen auf Silozellen – Exzentrische Entleerung. Dissertation, University of Karlsruhe.

Safarian, S.S. and Harris, E.C. (1985) *Design and Construction of Silos and Bunkers*; New York, Van Nostrand Reinhold.

Sasaki, Y. and Yoshimura, J. (1988) Seismic response of concrete stave silos with structural discontinuity; *Ninth World Conference on Earthquake Engineering*, Tokyo-Kyoto, Abstracts Vol.1, Paper No. F10-08.

SIMQKE (November 1976) *A Program for Artificial Motion Generation, User Manual and Documentation*; Department of Civil Engineering, Massachusetts Institute of Technology.

Stempniewski, L. (1990) Flüssigkeitsgefüllte Stahlbetonbehälter unter Erdbebeneinwirkung; Dissertation, University of Karlsruhe.

Weidner, J. (1990) Vergleich von Stoffgesetzen granularer Schüttgüter zur Silodruckermittlung; Dissertation, University of Karlsruhe.

Wu, W. (1992) Hypoplastizität als mathematisches Modell zum mechanischen Verhalten granularer Stoffe; Veröffentlichungen des Institutes für Boden- und Felsmechanik der Universität Karlsruhe, Dissertation.

Yokota, H.; Sugita, M. and Mita, A. (Nov. 1983) Vibration tests and analysis of coal-silo model; *Proceedings Second International Conference on Design of Silos for Strength and Flow*, Stratford, pp. 107–117.

Zienkiewicz, O.C. (1984) *Methode der Finiten Elemente*; Vienna, Hanser.

30
Constitutive laws for granular materials
H. Feise and J. Schwedes

30.1 SCOPE

The variety of materials stored in silos is enormous. While larger silos are used for grain or cement, smaller silos store anything from hay silage on the farm to ultrafine powders in the processing industry. Most materials stored in silos are considered 'granular' – whatever that means. In the following we will use the relatively unbiased term 'bulk solid' for the material stored in silos.

The number of different constitutive models for bulk solid materials is extensive, so only a few can be considered here. Most of them have been developed by civil engineers trying to describe the behaviour of sand, clay or rock. As the conditions concerning loading, density and flow are quite different from those experienced by bulk solids, only a limited number are suitable for modelling silo problems. Therefore only such models will be mentioned which have already been used in conjunction with silos. All these models consider the bulk solid as a continuum. Even the micromechanical models mentioned in section 30.8 are continuum models as they formulate equations which can be generalized for the entire volume of the bulk solid and can be used without reference to the individual particle. In contrast, discrete element models consider a bulk solid as an array of individual bodies and model their contact behaviour. They are not the subject of this chapter.

Any constitutive model is an abstraction from real behaviour. To be useful the abstract – generally mathematical – formulation must represent in some manner certain effects exhibited by bulk solids. While the relative importance of many effects is controversial, some undisputed – basic – ones can be used to judge the proposed models against:

- *Plasticity:* Bulk solids, when deformed, dissipate energy. This leads to irreversible deformations, hence we call this behaviour plasticity.
- *Dilatancy:* When shearing bulk solids one recognizes that the material changes its density even if the hydrostatic stress does not change.
- *Critical state:* Continuous shear deformation of a bulk solid eventually leads to a state where unlimited deformation at a constant stress becomes possible.
- *Barotropy:* The material behaviour depends on the stress level.
- *Pyknotropy:* The behaviour of the bulk material depends on the bulk density, even if the density of the solid particles remains the same.
- *Argotropy:* The material exhibits time dependence. In our case this means the material is sensitive to changes in the deformation rate. This includes all kinds of viscosity.
- *Cohesion:* Most bulk solids cannot sustain any significant tensile stress. As soon as they are loaded in tension they disintegrate. Such materials are termed 'cohesionless'. Bulk solids which can support a (small) tensile load and exhibit cohesion, are 'cohesive'.

30.2 ELASTIC MODELS

The most simplified models of bulk solid behaviour can be summarized as 'elastic models'. Ooi and Rotter (1989, 1990) used a linear elastic model similar to the one developed by Hooke for metal elasticity. The well-known equations read:

$$T = \lambda \operatorname{tr} E 1 + 2\mu E$$

where T is the stress tensor, E the strain tensor, 1 the unit tensor and λ, μ Lamé's constants.

This model has limited applicability for bulk solids, as it cannot describe any of the effects mentioned above. Ooi and Rotter use it, since it is simple and time-saving in numerical computations. The same argument has led other researchers (e.g. Dickinson and Jofried, 1987) to use linear isotropic elasticity.

Bishara, Ayoub and Mahdy (1983) used a nonlinear elastic model. In their equations the 'elastic constants' depend on the actual density, the angle of internal friction and the stress level. By this measure they try to accommodate barotropy and pyknotropy. However, their model cannot as yet describe irreversible deformation or dilation.

The hypoelastic theory is the first that can be used successfully for bulk solids. It is able to describe a limiting state (hypoelastic yielding). The material model is still isotropic and rate-independent (Weidner, 1990).

30.3 NON-ELASTIC MODELS

All models which can describe irreversible deformations are considered 'plastic'. However, all models which derive their irreversibility solely from time effects (creep models) will be excluded. In other words, the model must include static equilibrium.

Most constitutive models which comply with the definition above have been derived from models for metal plasticity (von Mises, Tresca). They divide the strain rate into a reversible and an irreversible part:

$$D = D^e + D^p$$

where D is the strain rate, D^e the reversible (elastic) strain rate and D^p the irreversible (plastic) strain rate.

A yield surface is used to distinguish between elastic and plastic deformation. The yield surface is a bounding surface in stress space, which limits the permissible stress states. Whenever the stress remains inside the yield surface the deformation is completely reversible. Any plastic deformation always leads to a stress on the yield surface. Ideal-plastic models keep the yield surface fixed, while hardening models transform it depending on some hardening parameter. The general equation reads:

$$f(T) - \psi = 0$$

where $f(T)$ is the function of the yield surface and ψ the hardening parameter (ideal-plastic: ψ = constant).

The second group of non-elastic constitutive models comprises rate-type models. These models are mostly formulated as a generalization of hypoelastic models. They define the change in stress over time as a function of actual stress, strain rate and some internal variables (e.g. bulk density). Their general equation reads:

$$\dot{T} = h(T, D, \rho_b \cdots)$$

It is formulated without the notion of a yield surface.

30.4 ELASTIC–PLASTIC MODELS

The first model used to describe inelastic behaviour of bulk solids is named after Mohr–Coulomb. It has been utilized in several silo theories and by some workers for finite element calculations (Ooi and Rotter, 1989; Smith and Lohnes, 1982). The basic idea is that in a plane loaded by a certain normal stress the material can only sustain some maximum shear stress. If the shear loading becomes bigger, the material starts to flow. The sustainable shear stress depends on the angle of internal friction (φ) and the cohesion (c). The cohesion c is defined as the sustainable shear stress in a plane with zero normal stress. To be usable as a general constitutive law, this idea has to be extended. One can write:

$$(\sigma_1 - \sigma_3)_{max} = m(\sigma_1 + \sigma_3) + n$$

where σ_1, σ_3 are the maximum and minimum principal stress, $m = m(\varphi)$ a material parameter and $n = n(c, \varphi)$ a material parameter.

In Fig. 30.1 the Mohr–Coulomb yield surface and the corresponding Tresca yield surface of metal plasticity are drawn in principal stress space. The Mohr–Coulomb model is rate-independent and isotropic. However, it does describe plasticity, dilatancy, barotopy and cohesion.

While the Mohr–Coulomb model can be viewed as a generalization of the Tresca model, the Drucker–Prager model can be considered derived from the von Mises model. It generalizes the Mohr–Coulomb yield surface to

$$q_{max} - a - p - b = 0$$

where p is the hydrostatic stress ($\frac{1}{3}\text{tr}T$), q_{max} the maximum sustainable deviatoric stress (generalized shear stress), $a = a(\varphi)$ a material parameter and $b = b(\varphi, c)$ a material parameter.

The Drucker–Prager yield surface is shown in Fig. 30.2. It can be seen that this surface does not have the edges of the Mohr–Coulomb yield surface. It is therefore numerically easier to handle and has been used more extensively by researchers (e.g. Link and Elwi, 1990; Ragneau and Aribert, 1993; Runesson and Nilsson, 1986). Like the Mohr–Coulomb model it can describe plasticity, dilatancy, barotropy and cohesion. It is, however, still rate-independent and isotropic.

All elastic–plastic constitutive models have to define two things besides the yield surface: the elastic behaviour and the plastic flow rule. The elastic

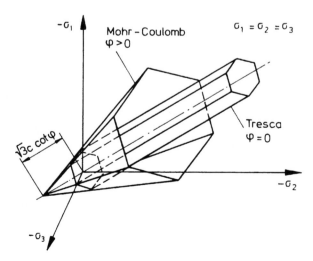

Fig. 30.1 Tresca and Mohr–Coulomb yield surfaces (Weidner, 1990).

532 *Constitutive laws for granular materials*

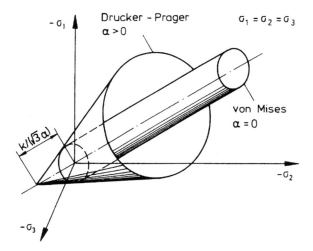

Fig. 30.2 Drucker–Prager and von Mises yield surfaces in principal stress space (Weidner, 1990).

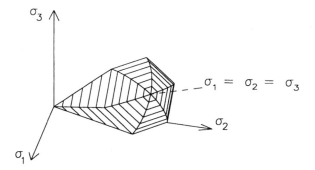

Fig. 30.3 Closed yield surface.

behaviour determines the material response inside the yield surface when no yielding takes place. For this, all types of linear and nonlinear elastic models can be and have been used (e.g. Ragneau and Aribert, 1993; Häussler and Eibl, 1984; Smith and Lohnes, 1982). In the case of the flow rule two basic types exist. The associated flow rule uses the shape of the yield surface to determine the flow direction, while the non-associated flow rules use an additional surface, called flow potential, for the same purpose.

The two classical models of Mohr–Coulomb and Drucker–Prager have a serious disadvantage when confronted with isotropic loading (Schwedes, 1971). As can be seen from Figs 30.1 and 30.2 the region of the isotropic – or purely hydrostatic – stress always lies within the yield surface, therefore no irreversible deformations can be predicted from such loading. However, experiments show plastic deformation from isotropic loading. This shortcoming can be overcome by constitutive models employing a 'closed yield surface' (Schwedes, 1971). These surfaces have a 'drop-like' shape in the principal stress space. Often they are made up of two or more yield surfaces – one 'yield-cone' resembling Fig. 30.2 and one 'yield cap' limiting the elastic region in the direction of hydrostatic loading (Fig. 30.3).

Ragneau and Aribert (1993) used a closed cap model developed by Wilde which employs only one closed yield surface. A model developed by Lade (e.g. Häussler and Eibl, 1984; Wu and Schmidt, 1992) and derivatives from it (e.g. Runesson, Enstad and Macari-Pasqualino, 1989; Höhl and Schwedes, 1992) has been more popular in silo research. The Lade model comprises two yield surfaces. The yield cone is curved and called a plastic expansive yield surface. The plastic expansive flow rule is non-associated in contrast to the second flow rule called the plastic collapse flow rule. The plastic collapse yield surface is a spherical yield cap. The total strain rate is divided into three parts

$$D = D^e + D^c + D^p$$

where the elastic strain rate D^e is reversible while the plastic collapse strain rate D^c and the plastic expansive strain rate D^p are irreversible. Both plastic deformations are defined with isotropic hardening rules, which means the yield surfaces become larger during loading but do not change shape or direction. The size of the plastic expansive yield surface is limited by a failure surface. This model can describe plasticity, dilatancy, critical state and barotropy. However, it does not include cohesion.

Höhl has introduced stress-induced cohesion into the constitutive model of Arslan (Höhl and Schwedes, 1992). The Arslan model closely resembles the Lade model. However, the yield cone (plastic expansive yield surface) is not curved but straight. In his generalized Arslan model, Höhl shifts the tip of the yield cone and the centre of the yield cap along the hydrostatic axis into the tensile regime (Fig. 30.4), to the isotropic tensile strength $T_t = \sigma_t \cdot 1$. The tensile strength σ_t itself depends on the plastic collapse hardening via a saturation function. This dependency gives rise to a minimum tensile strength even in the zero stress state and a maximum tensile strength which cannot be exceeded.

All elastic–plastic models mentioned so far have not included time dependence (argotropy). However, several researchers have found it necessary to include viscosity in their constitutive model. Often purely numerical reasons are given for this measure; the viscosity is used to condition the resulting differential equation (e.g. Häussler and Eibl, 1984; Lyle, 1991; Weidner, 1990; Wu and Schmidt, 1992; Lehmann and Antes, 1993), while Runesson and Nilsson (1986) or Gudehus, Kolymbas and Tejchman (1986) consider it part of their physical modelling.

Most popular has been a viscosity model in analogy to a Newtonian fluid

534 Constitutive laws for granular materials

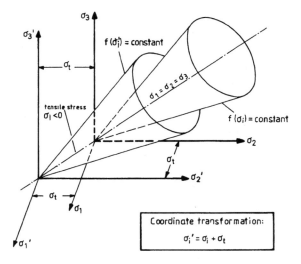

Fig. 30.4 Shifted yield cone in principal stress space (Höhl and Schwedes, 1992).

$$T_v = 2v\left(D - \frac{1}{3}(\text{tr}D)1\right)$$

where T_v is the viscous stress tensor and v the viscosity number. This gives some rate-dependent shear stress; however, it does not give any volumetric viscosity. Modifications have been proposed by Runesson and Nilsson (1986). Stadler and Buggisch (1985) have introduced a viscous equation for rapid flow of bulk solid materials reading

$$T_v = 2v\sqrt{\text{tr}(D')^2}\, D$$

with $D' = D - \frac{1}{3}\text{tr}(D)$ the strain rate deviator. This gives a nonlinear dependence of stress on strain rate and the desired volumetric viscosity.

Gudehus, Kolymbas and Tejchman (1986) proposed a Prandtl–Eyring type viscosity for bulk solid materials, where the stress rate also has a nonlinear dependence on strain rate:

$$\dot{T}_v = \frac{A \cdot D_2}{\sqrt{B^2 + \text{tr}(D^2)}}$$

where A, B are materials parameters and D_2 the second stretching tensor.

30.5 RATE-TYPE MODELS

In soil mechanics a number of other ideas of constitutive modelling have been used besides elastic–plastic models, e.g. endochronic theories, rate-type

Ooi, J.Y. and Rotter, J.M. (1990) Wall pressures in squat steel silos from simple finite element analysis, *Computers + Structures*, 37(4), 361–174.

Ragneau, E. and Aribert, J.M. (1993) Predictions of loads in silos during filling and emptying stages by a finite element method, *International Conference FEM-CAD 93*, Paris, June.

Ruckenbrod, C. and Eibl, J. (1993) Numerical results to discharge processes in silos, *Proc. Int. Symp. Reliable Flow of Particulate Solids II*, EFChE Pub. Series, No. 96, Oslo (Norway), 23–25 August, 503–516.

Runesson, K.; Enstad, G. and Macari-Pasqualino, E.J. (1989) Analysis and Calibration of a Plasticity Model for Powder Materials, 1–33.

Runesson, K. and Nilsson, L. (1986) Finite element modelling of the gravitational flow of a granular material, *Bulk Solids Handling*, 6(5), 877–884.

Schwedes, J. (1971) Scherverhalten leicht verdichteter kohäsiver Schüttgüter, Dissertation, University of Karlsruhe.

Sikora, Z. (1992) *Hypoplastic Flow of Granular Materials – a Numerical Approach*, Institut für Bodenmechanik und Felsmechanik, University of Karlsruhe.

Smith, D.L. and Lohnes, R.A. (1982) Frictional properties and stress–strain relationships for use in the finite element analysis of grain silos, *Journal of Powder + Bulk Solids Technology* 6, 4–10.

Stadler, R. and Buggisch, H.W. (1985) Influence of the deformation rate on shear stresses in bulk solids, *Proc. Reliable Flow of Particulate Solids*, EFCE Pub. Series, No. 49, Bergen (Norway).

Tejchman, J. and Gudehus, G. (1993) Silo-music and silo-quake experiments and a numerical Cosserat approach, *Powder Technology* 76, 201–212.

Weidner, J. (1990) Vergleich von Stoffgesetzen granularer Schüttgüter zur Silodruckermittlung, Dissertation, University of Karlsruhe.

Wu, Y.H. and Schmidt, L.C. (1992) Comparison of calculated and observed filling and flow pressures in silos and hoppers, *Int. Conf. on Bulk Materials Handling and Transportation*, Wollongong, 6–8 July, Vol. 2.

sion, e the porosity and H_0 the cohesive force without consolidation. Molerus' theory is based on Jenike's (1964) ideas and has not been extended to a model suitable to be used as a general constitutive model in finite element calculations. Both models appear to be able to describe plasticity, cohesion and dilation.

While micromechanical approaches have not yet found extensive application in silo technology, they are currently being worked on quite strenuously, mostly in the area of civil engineering. One of the most radical models was designed by Brough (1993). With his 'single particle equivalent concept' he found that the absence of inter-particle shear forces does not coincide with isotropic loading, as is generally believed. His model has not yet been elaborated upon far enough to allow classification by the above-mentioned six criteria or the application to silo problems.

REFERENCES

Bishara, A.G.; Ayoub, S.F. and Mahdy, A.S. (1983) Static pressures in concrete circular silos storing granular materials, *ACI Journal*, 210–216.

Brough, W.A. (1993) *Introduction to Particulate Mechanics on the Basis of the Single Particle Equivalent Concept*, Presses de l'Ecole Nationale des Ponts et Chaussées, Paris.

Chandrangsu, K. and Bishara, A.G. (July 1978) Nonlinear finite element analysis of farm silos, *Journal of the Structural Division, ASCE*, 1045–1059.

Dickinson, R.R. and Jofried, J.C. (1987) The functional design of silos storing highly cohesive bulk solids, *Bulk Solids Handling*, 7(2), 187–192.

Gudehus, G.; Kolymbas, D. and Tejchman, J. (1986) Behaviour of granular materials in cylindrical silos, *Powder Technology*, 48, 81–90.

Häussler, U. and Eibl, J. (1984) Numerical investigations on discharging silos, *Journal of Engineering Mechanics*, 110(6), 957–971.

Höhl, H.W. and Schwedes, J. (1992) Extension of elastoplastic constitutive models with respect to cohesive bulk solids, *Powder Technology*, 70, 31–42.

Jenike, A.W. (1964) *Storage and Flow of Solids*, Bulletin No. 123, Salt Lake City, Utah, 1–198.

Lehmann, L. and Antes, H. (1993) On the effect of inserts on the silo discharge process, *Proc. Int. Symp. Reliable Flow of Particulate Solids II*, EFChE Pub. Series, No. 96, (23–25 August 1993), Oslo, 715–726.

Link, R.A. and Elwi, A.E. (1990) Incipient flow in silo–hopper configurations, *Journal of Engineering Mechanics* 116(1), 172–188.

Lyle, C. (1991) Spannungsfelder in Silos mit starren, koaxialen Einbauten, TU Braunschweig, Dissertation.

Molerus, O. (1978) Effect of interparticle cohesive forces on the flow behaviour of powders, *Powder Technology* 20, 161–175.

Nagao, T. (1990) Evaluation of intergrain interactions in the constitutive equations of mechanics of granular materials, *Second World Congress on Particle Technology*, Kyoto (Japan).

Ooi, J.Y. and Rotter, J.M. (1989) Elastic and plastic predictions of the storing pressures in conical hoppers, *Transactions of Mechanical Engineering*, 14(3), 165–169.

bulk solids are scarce. They have, however, been published by Tejchman and Gudehus (1993) in an elasto-plastic framework and by Sikora (1992) for a hypoplastic model. Both models introduce the median grain size d_{50} as an internal length scale.

30.7 CREEP MODELS

The major part of silo research is concerned with granular media. However, some research, especially in the area of farm silos, has been looking at quite different materials. Changdrangsu and Bishara (1978) have published results from a study on silage. The material showed a very substantial time dependence which was tackled by a nonlinear creep model. They used an exponential decay function, reading in its general form

$$\varepsilon = \int_0^t J(t-t^*)f(\sigma)\frac{d\sigma}{dt^*}dt^*$$

where ε is the strain, t, t^* the time and σ the stress.

30.8 MICROSCOPIC MODELS

Microscopic models for bulk solid behaviour are much rarer than macroscopic models. They have not yet been used for any finite element calculations. While macroscopic models start out from the notions of continua, stress and strain, microscopic models look at the individual particle and the forces acting on it and derive overall equations from it.

Nagao (1990) has published a model considering a particle under general interaction. The total force acting on the particle comprises five parts:

$$P = P_a + P_s + P_m + P_w + P_e$$

where P_a is the elastic-plastic contact force, P_e the electrostatic force, P_w the van der Waals' force, P_m the magnetic force, P_s the liquid surface tension and P the total particle force. He then derived macroscopic equations incorporating these effects for a randomly distributed granular assembly. The equations are too large to be presented here.

Another model has been used by Molerus (1978), who tried to incorporate the microscopic parameters connected with the interparticle cohesion into a macroscopic model of the Mohr–Coulomb type. He defines the flow criterion at stationary flow as

$$\tau_{max} = \left(\sigma_M + \frac{\tan \varphi_i}{\tan \varphi_e}\sigma_0(e, H_0)\right)\sin \varphi_e$$

where τ_{max} is the maximum shear stress of an 'end Mohr circle', σ_M the centre of an 'end Mohr circle', φ_e the angle of effective friction, φ_i the angle of internal friction, σ_0 the isotropic tensile stress without previous compres-

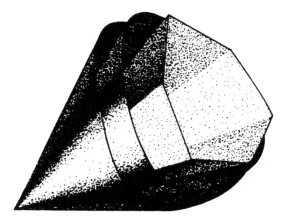

Fig. 30.5 Limiting surfaces in hypoplasticity (Sikora, 1992).

models. Only one model of the rate type has made its way into bulk solid mechanics so far. This model has been developed by Kolymbas (see e.g. Gudehus, Kolymbas and Tejchman, 1986) and enhanced by other researches (e.g. Sikora, 1992). Its general equation reads:

$$\dot{T} = h(T, D) + N(T) \cdot \sqrt{\mathrm{tr}(D^2)}$$

where $\dot{T}$ is the objective stress rate, $h(\ )$ the linear tensorial function in D, first order in T, $N(\ )$ the first-order tensorial function in T and $\sqrt{[\mathrm{tr}(D^2)]}$ the Euclidean norm of D.

Several proposals for h and N have been published (Sikora, 1992). This model is considered hypoplastic, as it does not use any potential – in contrast to the elastic–plastic models mentioned so far – but does describe irreversible deformation – in contrast to hypoelastic models. Depending on the special form of this model used, it can describe plasticity, dilatancy, critical state, barotropy and pyknotropy (Ruckenbrod and Eibl, 1993). The model does not distinguish between reversible and irreversible strains and does not employ a yield surface. However, it does have a set of limiting surfaces quite similar in shape to the elasto-plastic yield cones shown above (Fig. 30.5).

30.6 POLAR MODELS

All theories mentioned so far have viewed bulk solids as a homogeneous non-polar continuum. This means that the stress tensor has the well-known symmetrical form. However, bulk solids are not homogeneous and continuous. They consist of a variety of granules well able to introduce a mode of local rotation quite different from the overall one. Micropolar models (Cosserat theory) attempt to capture this effect. But micropolar models for

31

The choice of constitutive laws for silo media

J. Nielsen and J. Weidner

NOMENCLATURE

β	angle of dilatancy
ε_1	vertical strain
$\varepsilon_{2,3}$	horizontal strain
ε_v	volumetric strain
λ	relation between horizontal and vertical stress
μ	coefficient of wall friction
σ_1	vertical stress
$\sigma_{2,3}$	horizontal stress
φ	angle of internal friction
$(\ )_a$	active state
$(\ )_p$	passive state

31.1 INTRODUCTION

The pressure distribution at the walls of a silo depends very much on the physical behaviour of the stored media. Therefore theories for the determination of such loads are based on certain assumptions about this behaviour – the constitutive laws.

Janssen's equations (1895) are based on two such assumptions: firstly, that the coefficient of wall friction μ, that is the relation between the shear stress along the wall and the normal pressure against the wall, is a constant. Secondly, that the relation λ between the horizontal and the vertical pressure is constant in a silo. The theory based on these assumptions has proven to be realistic for the pressure distribution in silos during filling and in the at rest condition, but the discharge pressures are in many cases far from well described. Looking at the assumptions this might not be very surprising because Janssen did not take into account the rupture or flow of the stored medium.

In order to obtain an improved description of the flow pressure Janssen's assumptions have been supplemented with a failure criterion of an ideal plastic material – the Mohr–Coulomb criterion for instance. In this way the angle of internal friction φ has been introduced as an additional strength parameter. Such theories, of which a general view is given by Hampe (1987), lead to so-called active and passive states of stress and have been able to produce more realistic results, especially for the regions at rupture.

However, between the active and the passive state of stress there is a wide pressure range in which the stresses are determined by the actual strains. A considerable part of the medium in the vertical section of a silo is probably in this state which an ideal plastic material model cannot describe correctly. More realistic calculations using the finite element method have been carried out at the University of Karlsruhe (Eibl and Rombach, 1987) among others. The calculations are based on the constitutive laws of Lade (1977) and Kolymbas (1988), but these laws are not primarily developed for silo applications.

The considerations described below are concerned with the questions of how to verify a law with respect to silo applications and how to choose an appropriate one. This latter question is not trivial because the more realistic constitutive law is often very complicated. However, in the end one should not use a law that is more complicated than necessary for a special purpose. For instance for steel and concrete, for which realistic material laws may be given, the pure elastic and ideal elastic–plastic theories are successfully applied in many cases.

31.2 SILO-RELEVANT STRESS–STRAIN HISTORIES

31.2.1 Preliminaries

As already argued, constitutive laws for materials stored in a silo should be selected with respect to their ability to describe silo-relevant stress–strain histories, and several such histories may exist. Two principal ones are presented. For constitutive laws which are able to describe these special histories well it is assumed that they also yield reasonable results in a finite element application on silos.

Stresses and strains are positive for tension and extension respectively.

31.2.2 Filling

The following two stress–strain histories are proposed for filling (Fig. 31.1). Both paths can be divided into three steps respectively:

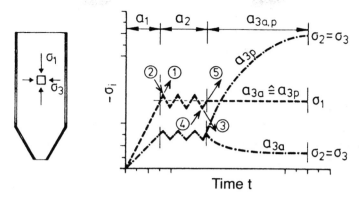

Fig. 31.1 Stress–strain history relevant for filling (numbers in circles refer to section 31.3.3).

- a_1: consolidation with the horizontal strains $\varepsilon_2 = \varepsilon_3 = 0$ until a specified vertical pressure σ_1;
- a_2: change in the vertical stress level $\Delta\sigma_1 = \pm 0.1\sigma_1$ with the horizontal strains $\varepsilon_2 = \varepsilon_3 = $ constant (equal to zero);
- a_{3a}: decrease of the horizontal stress level $\sigma_2 = \sigma_3$ until rupture with $\sigma_1 = $ constant, or
- a_{3p}: increase of the horizontal stress level $\sigma_2 = \sigma_3$ until rupture with $\sigma_1 = $ constant.

The filling into perfect silos with stiff walls corresponds to step a_1. The design pressure in top unloaded bins and the stresses in most dead zones during flow are covered by this case.

Step a_2 describes several kinds of stress redistributions. They may be caused by consolidation movements in combination with wall imperfections and by the interaction with silo wall movements. An example of the latter case is the elastic support of steel walls exposed to buckling.

When the redistributions of step a_2 become very big the steps a_{3a} and a_{3p} are supposed to be relevant. The indices a and p are the abbreviations for active and passive respectively.

31.2.3 Discharge

In mass flow silos the stress history for a distinct volume element may be divided into the following steps (Fig. 31.2):

- b_1: consolidation with the horizontal strains $\varepsilon_2 = \varepsilon_3 = 0$ until a specified vertical pressure σ_1 (see step a_1);
- b_2: change of the horizontal stress $\sigma_2 = \sigma_3$ to σ_1 linearly with time combined with a simultaneous change of the vertical stress σ_1 to $0.5\sigma_1$;
- b_3: decrease of the vertical stress σ_1 until rupture with the horizontal stresses $\sigma_2 = \sigma_3 = $ constant.

During discharge the stress condition in the upper part of the silo is similar to the condition for filling (step b_1).

Passing the so-called transition zone, the vertical stresses are decreasing while the horizontal stresses are increasing; this means that the principal stress axes are rotated from an active to a passive stress state as described in loading step b_2.

Finally flowing through the rupture zone just above the outlet the volume element experiences very small vertical stresses and big strains.

Dynamic phenomena during discharge involve considerable stress oscillations. They may originate from energy releases in overconsolidated media. Relevant stress–strain histories for such cases are much more complex than those proposed in this chapter.

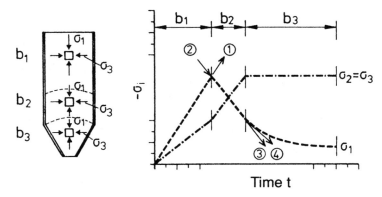

Fig. 31.2 Stress–strain history relevant for discharge (numbers in circles refer to section 31.3.4).

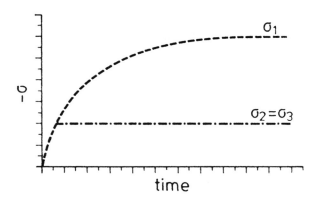

Fig. 31.3 Standard triaxial compression test.

31.3 SIMULATIONS WITH THE LAWS OF LADE AND KOLYMBAS

31.3.1 Preliminaries

For the calibration of both laws the result of at least one standard triaxial compression test is needed (Fig. 31.3). The material parameters have been determined with the data base of a cohesionless Karlsruhe sand (Hettler

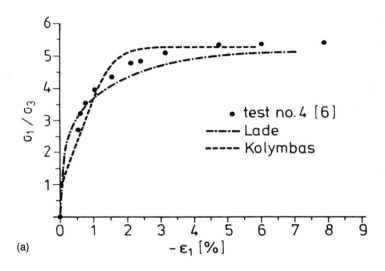

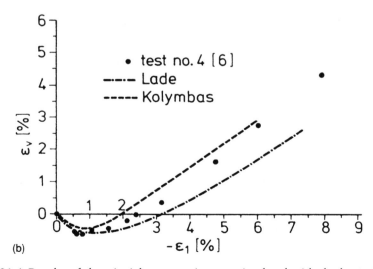

Fig. 31.4 Results of the triaxial compression test simulated with the laws of Lade and Kolymbas: (a) (σ_1/σ_3)–ε_1 graph; (b) ε_v–ε_1 graph.

et al., 1984). All the calculations reported in this paper are based on these parameters. The stress–strain histories presented have been simulated with a computer program using the finite element method.

The chosen pressure level is considerably higher than in a silo. A level of about 30–40 kPa is more realistic. But no test results were available to determine the parameters of the Kolymbas law at that stress level.

31.3.2 Standard triaxial compression test

The results of the calculations for the standard triaxial compression test with a confining pressure of $\sigma_3 = 300$ kPa are shown in Fig. 31.4. They are in good agreement with the observations of the test. ε_v is the volumetric strain.

The important figures of this calibration test are seen in Table 31.1. Especially the pressure coefficient $\lambda_a = (\sigma_3/\sigma_1)_a$ and the angle of dilatancy β_a at the limit condition are of interest. There are only slight differences.

It is remarkable that the Kolymbas law arrives at an almost horizontal asymptote (Fig. 31.4), i.e. the limit condition when the magnitude of the strains is still very small. Thus the material initially behaves in a stiffer manner than it would according to Lade's law for this special stress path.

Table 31.1 Pressure coefficient λ_a and angle of dilatancy β_a of the standard triaxial compression test with a confining pressure of $\sigma_3 = 300$ kPa

	λ_a	β_a (°)
Test no. 4 (Hettler et al., 1984)	0.189	−36.8
Lade	0.195	−35.0
Kolymbas	0.189	−36.1

31.3.3 Stress–strain history for filling

Figure 31.5 shows the results of the proposed stress paths for filling. The prescribed history of the axial stress σ_1 during the three steps, described in section 31.2.2, is the following:

- a_1: $-\sigma_1 = 0$–400 kPa;
- a_2: $-\sigma_1 = 400$–440–360–400 kPa;
- $a_{3a,p}$: $-\sigma_1 = 400$ kPa.

The graphs in Fig. 31.5 show that the results qualitatively look similar with both constitutive laws. However, the quantitative differences are in some cases big and are summarized in Tables 31.2–31.4.

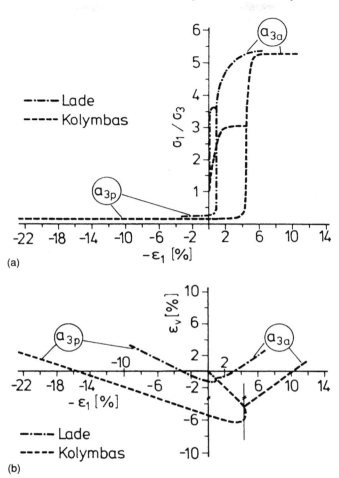

Fig. 31.5 Results from a computer simulation of the filling history: (a) (σ_1/σ_3)–ε_1 graph; (b) ε_v–ε_1 graph.

Table 31.2 Comparison of the pressure coefficients λ

	λ_0	λ_a	λ_p
Lade	0.280	0.187	6.935
Kolymbas	0.329	0.189	7.210

Table 31.2 shows three pressure coefficients λ:

- λ_0 for the material at rest (step a_1),
- λ_a for an active stress state (step a_{3a}),
- λ_p for a passive stress state (step a_{3p}).

The pressure coefficients determined with the two material models are reasonably close to each other. It should be noticed that the values determined with Lade's law are dependent on the first stress invariant.

In Table 31.3 the stiffnesses $E_i = d\sigma_1/d\varepsilon_1$ for different loadings and unloadings during step a_2 are summarized. The five compared values are labelled according to the numbers shown in Fig. 31.1. The smaller values with the Kolymbas law especially for E_1, E_4 and E_5 are predicting greater strains than with Lade's law during loading step a_2. This softer behaviour is

Table 31.3 Stiffnesses E_i (MPa) for different loadings and unloadings during step a_2 of the filling history (labels on E correspond to the numbers shown in Fig. 31.1)

	E_1	E_2	E_3	E_4	E_5
Lade	185	265	240	200	200
Kolymbas	60	160	130	50	55

Table 31.4 Comparison of the strains of the filling history

	a_1	a_2	a_{3a} and a_{3p}	
	$\varepsilon_1 = \varepsilon_v$ (%)	$\varepsilon_1 = \varepsilon_v$ (%)	ε_1 (%)	ε_v (%)
Lade	−0.9187	−0.9068	−6.1303	2.0659
			9.3154	3.2437
Kolymbas	−4.4198	−4.4387	−11.7470	1.0815
			29.6323	4.8394

Table 31.5 Pressure coefficient $\lambda_{a,p}$ and angle of dilatancy $\beta_{a,p}$ for the loading steps a_{3a} and a_{3p} of the filling history

		λ	β (°)
Lade	Active	0.187	−36.5
	Passive	6.935	29.1
Kolymbas	Active	0.189	−36.1
	Passive	7.210	19.1

maintained in the following steps a_{3a} and a_{3p}. Thus the total strains for the whole filling history of both laws differ considerably in size. The strains at the end of the single loading steps are shown in Table 31.4.

Table 31.5 compares the same values as shown in Table 31.1, section 31.3.2, but here for the limit conditions of the loading steps a_{3a} and a_{3p}. The angle of dilatancy β only differs seriously for the passive path.

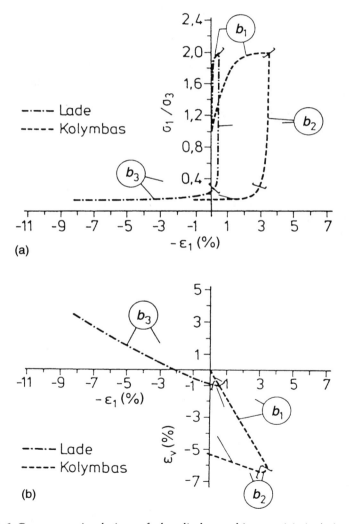

Fig. 31.6 Computer simulation of the discharge history: (a) (σ_1/σ_3)–ε_1 graph; (b) ε_v–ε_1 graph.

31.3.4 Stress–strain history for discharge

Figure 31.6 contains results of the computer simulation for the proposed stress path for discharge. The prescribed history of the axial stress σ_1 for the loading steps, described in section 31.2.3, is the following:

- b_1: $-\sigma_1 = 0-400\,\text{kPa}$;
- b_2: $-\sigma_1 = 400-200\,\text{kPa}$;
- b_3: $-\sigma_1 = 200-0\,\text{kPa}$.

In Table 31.6 the stiffnesses $E_i = d\sigma_1/d\varepsilon_1$ for loading and unloading at the beginning and at the end of loading step b_2 are seen (see also Fig. 31.2). Table 31.7 compares the resulting total strains at the end of the three loading steps b_i respectively. Kolymbas' law predicts, compared to Lade's law, greater strains for the first step b_1. Thus the development of the strains during the proposed discharge history is also very different.

Table 31.8 contains the pressure coefficients $\lambda_p = (\sigma_3/\sigma_1)_p$ and the corresponding angle of dilatancy β_p at the end of loading step b_3. The difference of the passive angles of dilatancy β_p is again big (see also Table 31.5).

31.3.5 Summary

The different pressure coefficients λ and the angles of dilatancy β determined with Kolymbas' and Lade's material model are altogether in fairly good agreement with each other except for the passive angle of dilatancy β_p.

Table 31.6 Stiffnesses E_i (MPa) for loading and un- and reloading during step b_2 of the discharge history (labels on E correspond to the numbers shown in Fig. 31.2)

	E_1	E_2	E_3	E_4
Lade	295	235	175	145
Kolymbas	65	250	30	40

Table 31.7 Comparison of the strains of the discharge history

	b_1		b_2		b_3	
	ε_1 (%)	ε_v (%)	ε_1 (%)	ε_v (%)	ε_1 (%)	ε_v (%)
Lade	−0.4749	−0.8767	−0.4005	−0.9239	8.2502	3.3870
Kolymbas	−3.4986	−5.9610	−3.1797	−6.4120	0.6537	−5.0762

Table 31.8 Pressure coefficient λ_p and angle of dilatancy β_p for the loading step b_3 of the discharge history

	λ_p	β_p (°)
Lade	7.538	30.2
Kolymbas	7.209	19.0

This result is not very surprising because Lade's failure criterion and Kolymbas' singularity condition are almost identical (Weidner, 1990). With Lade's law the pressure coefficient λ as well as the angle of dilatancy β are slightly dependent on the first stress invariant.

Greater differences are observed for the strains during the filling and discharge histories. The strain paths predicted by Lade's law still seem to be reasonable, but problems arise with Kolymbas' law. The stiffnesses and strains are apparently physically not sound in the cases of the proposed loading steps. Especially looking at the first part of loading step a_{3p} the material experiences a noticeable negative strain in all principal directions although the horizontal stresses $\sigma_2 = \sigma_3$ are increased and the vertical stress σ_1 is held constant. This shortcoming is marked in Fig. 31.5(b). Nevertheless it should be emphazised that both laws were composed for monotonic loading explicitly.

31.4 CONCLUSION

Two constitutive laws for granular materials, which both simulate satisfactorily the results from a standard triaxial test, have led to very different and in some cases physically unsound results for stress–strain histories which are likely to occur in silos during filling and discharge. This calls for improved constitutive laws for silo applications.

It must be underlined that constitutive laws have to be verified and selected with respect to their current application. A big need for laboratory test results for silo-relevant stress–strain histories has been revealed. Such tests would make it possible to check the material models not only qualitatively but also quantitatively. The proposed stress–strain histories are to be seen as a first proposal for such tests.

ACKNOWLEDGEMENTS

The Sonderforschungsbereich 219 of the University of Karlsruhe is acknowledged for its support to one of the authors, Nielsen, as a guest researcher, which made the cooperation in this work possible. All the computer calculations referred to in this chapter were done by Weidner.

REFERENCES

Eibl, J. and Rombach, G. *Silosy*, Sklarska Poreba (Poland), 1987, p. 43.
Hampe, E. *Silos, Grundlagen*, Vol. 1, VEB Verlag, Berlin, 1987.
Hettler, A.; Gudehus, G. et al., *Constitutive Relations for Soils*, Balkema, Rotterdam, 1984, p. 55.
Janssen, H.A. *VDI-Zeitschrift* **39** (1895) p. 1045.
Kolymbas, D. *Veröffentl. Inst. Bodenmech. Felsmech. Univ. Karlsruhe*, Heft 109 (1988).
Lade, P.V. *Int. J. Solids Struc.* **13** (1977) p. 1019.
Weidner, J. *Schriftenreihe des Instituts für Massivbau und Baustofftechnologie, Univ. Karlsruhe*, Heft 10 (1990).

32

Numerical simulations based on discrete particle models

U. Tüzün

32.1 INTRODUCTION

In contrast to finite element simulations discrete particle models are based on a mechanical model of individual idealized particles and not on a continuum model. They are mainly used to study phenomena associated with flowing material. Works published in the field of hard sphere analyses and collision dynamics include works by Walton and Braun (1986a, b), Campbell and Zhang (1992), Campbell (1993) and Herrmann (1993). Tsuji *et al.* (1987; 1992) and Cundall and Strack (1979) have written on Hooke's law interactions, while Tüzün and Heyes (1996), Heyes and Melrose (1993), Thornton and Randall (1988) and Thornton and Yin (1991) have studied continuous force interactions and micro-contact interactions respectively.

32.2 SPECIFIC APPLICATIONS

The methods mentioned above have been used by researchers in the following applications: in lean phase flows (e.g. pneumatic conveying) by Tsuji *et al.* (1987; 1992) and Herrmann (1993); in high shear flows (e.g. chute flows) by Walton and Braun (1986a, b), Campbell and Zhang (1992) and Herrmann (1993); in slow shearing flows (e.g. hopper flow) by Campbell (1993), Tüzün and Heyes (1996), Langston *et al.* (1995a, b) and Thornton and Yin (1991); and in compaction and deformation (e.g. agglomeration, attrition) by Thornton and Randall (1988) and Thornton and Yin (1991).

32.3 MODELLING HOPPER FLOWS BY DISCRETE PARTICLE SIMULATIONS

32.3.1 Simultaneous quantification of macroscopic and microstructural phenomena

Macroscopic phenomena can be divided into two categories, that is, the prediction of discharge rates and the prediction of wall stresses during filling and discharge. On the other hand, microstructural phenomena include internal stress distributions, relative particle velocities and voidage distributions.

The aim is to develop a comprehensive simulation technique to account simultaneously for both macroscopic and microstructural phenomena. Previous work has used either very simple (spring constants, hard spheres) or very detailed (Hertzian contact mechanics) representations of the granular interactions. Very little quantitative comparison between the models and the experimental data is available in the current literature. The literature is confined to comparing simulations visually with experimental flow fields (e.g. comparing particle trajectories) which does not demonstrate the adequacy of a chosen technique in predicting quantitatively the stress, voidage and velocity fields. In order to bring credibility to the discrete particle simulation approach, there must be a substantial quantitative agreement between the model and real systems. Further refinement of the models should be reflected in the enhanced predictive capacity for both macroscopic as well as microstructural phenomena.

Current approximate analytical and more rigorous numerical (i.e. finite element) flow models based on continuum mechanics include very limited and idealized descriptions of the microstructure (e.g. constant voidage) and macroscopic constitutive stress–strain relationships with no reference to single particle properties. If the discrete particle simulation results can be shown to be rigorously quantitative, then the method offers a much wider scope for investigating the effects of specific material properties (e.g. particle size, shape, roughness) which cannot at present be incorporated into the continuum models. Nevertheless, the quantitatively accurate discrete particle simulations should pave the way for improved continuum models with a sound microstructural foundation.

32.3.2 Quantitative basis for model discrimination

There are three quite distinct levels of description of the mechanics of granular flow.

- *Macroscopic bulk stress–strain relationships*: These do not recognize variability with assembly microstructure and, therefore, cannot be used to study the effects of particle polydispersity which is often the most important subject of interest in materials handling.

Furthermore, the continuum mechanical approach can only predict limiting states of behaviour (e.g. active and passive stress states in the hopper flow, elastic and plastic limits of bulk volumetric deformations) which are not sensitive to many of the key single particle properties and their distributions within the bulk assembly.

- *Micro-contact mechanical stress–particle deformation relationships*: In this case, the flow events are described within a single contact region which does not itself lead to an explicit description of the assembly mechanics in the absence of specific assumptions about the distributions of contact geometries at the scale of the single particle. Moreover, to effect a description of the assembly behaviour it becomes necessary to assume either (i) that all individual contacts are uniformly loaded (known to be unrealistic) or (ii) a specific form for the spatial distribution of 'active' contacts at any given time, for example Thornton and Randall (1988) and Thornton and Yin (1991).

- *Effective microstructural stress–relative particle displacement relationships*: These provide a functional description of the assembly behaviour by considering interactions on the scale of the nominal particle size. Although not based on rigorous contact mechanics, these relationships can nevertheless provide a faithful description of the system at the assembly level by incorporating variations in particle size and shape. Essentially, all particle interactions within the assembly are assumed to obey a load-displacement criterion which incorporates the effect of the relative geometric dislocations of individual particles within the flow field. Hence all forces are scaled by the particle size scale rather than by surface roughness distance scale (Langston, Tüzün and Heyes, 1995a).

32.3.3 Model verification by experiment

Most of the model verifications of discrete simulations have so far been carried out in essentially two-dimensional, 'plane-strain' vessels where the particles are represented by 'hard' or 'soft' discs depending on the frictional algorithm adopted. The simulation results are compared with model chute flows in two dimensions (Walton, 1986a, b; Campbell, 1993), and model flat bottom and wedge-shaped hoppers (Langston, Tüzün and Heyes, 1995b). Tsuji *et al.* (1987, 1992) have also reported two-dimensional pneumatic flow and fluidized flow simulations by also incorporating the gas–solid interactions in their models.

Verification of the three-dimensional simulations using spherical particles has proved more difficult due to the relative inaccessibility of the internal flow and stress fields. Measurements of the wall stresses using contact stress transducers provide a basis for verifying the simulation results at the wall boundary; however, direct comparison is yet to be reported between internal stress measurements and simulation results. The same applies to particle trajectories and velocity fields in three-dimensional flow where non-intrusive measurement requires the use of remote imaging techniques such as gamma-ray tomography (Broadbent, Bridgwater and Parker, 1993), nuclear magnetic resonance (Nakagawa et al., 1993) and electrical impedance (Williams et al., 1993).

32.4 FUTURE DIRECTIONS IN DISCRETE PARTICLE HOPPER FLOW SIMULATIONS

The present simulations are limited to systems from 1000 to 100 000 particles depending upon the complexity of the force interaction algorithms used. With continuing advances in computer power, it is expected that studies with systems incorporating particle numbers of the order of 10^6 particles will become routine. It is believed that all the essential physics should in principle be captured in simulations of this scale and an exact match between the size of the real industrial installation and the size of the simulation should not be necessary. Quite clearly, to prove this point, many more quantitative measurements of the internal stress and velocity fields in three-dimensional geometries are necessary to complement the enhancement in computer power.

Immediate attention is currently focused on the interactions between the particles and the interstitial or the carrier fluid. The work to date makes only semi-empirical correlations of the packed-bed pressure drop – particle size – and voidage such as due to Carman-Kozeny or Ergun, for example, Tsuji et al. (1992). Direct micro-scale coupling of the interfacial and interparticle interactions in dense phase granular flows is yet to be demonstrated with discrete particle simulations and future work should therefore concentrate on this further development.

The inclusion of short-range surface active forces such as due to van der Waals', electrostatic or liquid bridge effects in the current force interaction models will allow realistic simulations of the flow of fine powder systems where such forces are known to affect the dynamic frictional processes accompanying bulk flow.

The effect of particle size and shape polydispersity on the bulk flow is another area of current investigation which can be readily modelled using the discrete particle simulation approach. Processes such as segregation and agglomeration accompanying polydisperse flow fields is an area of significant interest to powder-processing industries such as chemical, pharmaceutical, food, ceramics, etc. In a series of simulations involving different particle size distributions, non-spherical particle shapes and different hopper geometries, it is possible to demonstrate a large range of effects contributing to the non-uniform and transient flows observed in practice.

REFERENCES

Broadbent, C., Bridgwater, J. and Parker, D. (1993), *Powder Technology*, **76**, 317.
Campbell, C.S. (1993), *Powders and Grains 1993* (ed. Thornton C.), Balkema, Rotterdam, pp. 289–294.
Campbell, C.S. and Zhang, Y. (1992) *Advances in Micromechanics of Granular Materials* (eds Shen H.H. et al.), Elsevier, Amsterdam, pp. 261–270.
Cundall, P.A. and Strack, O. (1979), *Géotechnique*, **29**, 47.
Herrmann, H.J. (1993), *Proceedings of Neptis-I, Discrete Particle Simulations in Powder Technology*, Nishing Eng. Co., Osaka, Japan (January 18–20).
Heyes, D.M. and Melrose, J.R. (1993), *J. Chem Phys.*, **98**, 5873.
Langston, P.A.; Tüzün, U. and Heyes, D.M. (1995a), *Chem. Eng. Sci.*, **50**, 967.
Langston, P.A.; Tüzün, U. and Heyes, D.M. (1995b), *Powder Technology*, **85**, 153.
Nakagawa, M. et al. (1993), *Powders and Grains 93*, (ed. Thornton C.), Balkema, Rotterdam, pp. 383–387.
Thornton, C. and Randall, C.W. (1988), *Micromechanics of Granular Materials*, (eds Satake M., Jenkins J.T.), Elsevier, p. 133.
Thornton, C. and Yin, K.K. (1991), *Powder Technology*, **65**, 153.
Tsuji, Y.; Tanaka, T. and Ishida, T. (1992), *Powder Technology*, **71**, 239.
Tsuji, Y. et al. (1987), *Int. Journ. Mult. Flow*, **13**(5), 71.
Tüzün, U. and Heyes, D.M. (1996) Distinct element simulations and dynamic microstructural imaging of slow granular flows, *Mechanics of Granular and Porous Materials* (eds Fleck N.A. and Cocks A.C.F.), Kluwer Academic, London, pp. 263–275.
Walton, O.R. and Braun, R.L. (1986a), *J. Rheology*, **30**(5), 949.
Walton, O.R. and Braun, R.L. (1986b), *Acta Mechanica*, **63**, 73.
Williams, R.A. et al. (1993), *Tomographic Techniques for Process Design and Operation*, Comp. Mech. Publ., Boston, USA, pp. 251–264.

33

Lattice grain models

J. Martinez and S. Masson

33.1 DEFINITION AND GENERAL FEATURES

A lattice grain model (LGrM) is based upon the use of a cellular automaton (CA). A CA is a logical device, formed by a large set of elements lying on a regular lattice, which processes local interactions between elements according to a very simple and repetitive rule. Mechanical applications of CAs were first used in the hydrodynamics field with the lattice gas models. For a few years, some two-dimensional applications to granular flow have been developed by Baxter and Behringer (1990, 1991), Gutt and Haff (1990), Fitt and Wilmott (1992), Savage (1993), Peng and Herrmann (1994), Deserable, Martinez and Masson (1994), Martinez, Masson and Deserable (1995) and Masson (1996).

LGrMs are discrete both with space and time. Grains are placed on the lattice nodes and move along the links. The system evolution is processed by a succession of elementary steps. The state change between two successive steps is governed by the transition rule. This rule, either deterministic or partly probabilistic, is fully locally defined and often purely kinematic. Grains are fictitious or very simply characterized. In this way, LGrMs can be considered as very simplified discrete models. Compared to more physically sophisticated discrete models, such as the distinct element method, LGrM simulation is markedly less time-consuming and permits the study of large-scale problems (more than 10^6 particles). LGrMs sacrifice interaction complexity between individual particles in exchange for consideration of large numbers of particles.

33.2 CHARACTERISTICS OF LGrMs FOR THE SIMULATION OF SILO FLOWS

A list of LGrMs for the simulation of granular flows in silos is given in Table 33.1. The models are compared in terms of their mechanical principles, the corresponding mechanical parameters, the lattice topology used, the type of transition rule – deterministic or probabilistic – and the calculation processing mode – synchronous or sequential. The space filling under gravity is the simplest mechanical principle used: a void (vacant site) located at a particular lattice node is filled with a grain falling from the above layer. Thus, the granular flow is associated with the upward propagation and diffusion of voids. This principle of kinematical modelling of flow is related to the analytical works of Litwiniszyn (1964), Müllins (1972) and Nedderman and Tüzün (1979) and to the simulation works of Caram and Hong (1992) and Osinov (1994).

The principles of the models of Baxter and Behringer, Gutt and Haff and Masson et al. rely on more mechanical concepts. In the Baxter and Behringer model, the direction of displacement of a grain corresponds to the direction in which the mechanical energy needed is minimal. The energy function introduced by the authors is the sum of two terms: the action of gravity and the interactions between neighbouring grains, including friction, dilatancy and relative orientation of stick-like grains.

The model of Gutt and Haff is inspired by the lattice gas models of hydrodynamics. It is based on inelastic collisions between grains. The authors take into account grain velocity of any value by setting the time duration of a transition step so that the fastest grain travels one lattice spacing during this step. Each grain velocity is incremented due to the acceleration of gravity and is changed when a collision occurs. Collisions are calculated assuming that the grains are smooth hard discs with a given coefficient of restitution.

The model of Masson et al. is based on the transmission of the weight of the grain inside the granular material. Locally, only normal forces are considered and weight is transmitted from the top to the bottom by satisfying force equilibrium for each grain. In the case of a hyperstatic grain, that is a grain with three supports, equilibrium is written introducing a lateral/vertical force distribution factor. This factor, inspired by the λ coefficient of the Janssen theory, sets the vertical load distribution between the vertical and the lateral directions. On the other hand, when a grain is unstable, unbalanced forces become inertia forces.

Two-dimensional lattice topology used in LGrMs is either triangular (Baxter and Behringer, 1990, 1991; Gutt and Haff, 1990; Masson, 1996) or rectangular (Savage, 1993). The triangular lattice forms a regular, hexavalent network of links associated with a honeycomb tessellation of cells and provides the highest symmetries we can obtain for a two-dimensional regular tiling. Savage's model runs on a rectangular lattice but

Table 33.1 Characteristics of lattice grain models for the simulation of silo flows

Authors	Baxter and Behringer (1990, 1991)	Gutt and Haff (1990)	Savage (1993)	Deserable, Martinez and Masson (1994), Martinez, Masson and Deserable (1995)	Masson (1996)
Mechanical principles	Minimization of an energy function	Inelastic collisions (binary) Conservation of momentum	Space filling under gravity (Void diffusion)	Space filling under gravity (Void diffusion)	Force transmission Static equilibrium of grain
Mechanical parameters	Gravity Orientation of grain Friction Dilatancy	Gravity Restitution Actual velocity	Gravity Angle of repose	Gravity Dissipation level Inertial effects	Gravity Lateral/vertical force distribution factor Wall friction
Lattice topology	Triangular lattice One grain per cell	Triangular lattice One grain per cell	Rectangular lattice but hexavalent One grain per cell	Triangular lattice One grain per cell	Triangular lattice One grain per cell
Transition rule	Deterministic	Deterministic	Probabilistic	Essentially probabilistic	Deterministic
Transition mode	Synchronous: mechanism of propagation –interaction	Sequential: but no coupling between the order in which the cells are treated and the grain motions	Sequential: treatment of cells from the bottom to the top	Synchronous: mechanism of request-exchange	Synchronous: mechanism of request-exchange

Main results on the simulation of silo flow 559

the grains can move along the diagonal directions, so the network is actually hexavalent (displacements along horizontal links are not allowed). This lattice is not regular but provides a means to effectively vary the internal friction angle by varying the aspect ratio of the cell.

All the models presented in Table 33.1 obey the exclusion principle that no node contains more than one grain. It can be noticed that Fitt and Wilmott (1992) have developed an LGrM, simulating segregation in free surface flow, in which cells are filled by a volume of material composed of grains of two size species and by a vacant part. A grain can fall into a cell in the layer below if there is a sufficient vacant volume to receive it.

Two transition modes can be used in LGrMs for the simulation of silo flows, even though, strictly speaking, a CA must be synchronous to ensure no coupling between the order of computational treatment of the cells and the simulation process. However, in the case of silo flow, it seems quite sensible to perform gravity-induced displacements in a sequential order starting from the bottom and moving upwards. This is the case of the model of Savage. A synchronous mode provides a more universal model and the technical advantage to be implemented on a multi-processor computer in a straightforward manner. Synchronous transition uses a two-step mechanism: the first step consists of determining the direction of potential displacement independently for each grain and the second consists of determining collectively (with the nearest neighbours) the effective displacement of each grain.

33.3 MAIN RESULTS ON THE SIMULATION OF SILO FLOW

The simulations of silo flows carried out by LGrMs have given quite interesting results in spite of the simplicity of the models. The well-known flow modes found in silos, i.e. mass flow and funnel flow, can be obtained (Martinez et al., 1995). Savage (1993) shows (Fig. 33.1) that LGrM simulation qualitatively reproduces actual flow characteristics such as free surface shape and boundary flow position at various stages of the emptying. On the other hand, due to the coarse discreteness of displacement in LGrMs, more diffusion of the coloured bands is observed in the simulation than is evident in the photos from the experiments.

The simulations of hopper emptying carried out by Baxter and Behringer show a funnel flow in the case of spherical grains: grain motion occurs within a central core in which the density is uniformly lowered. The flow is relatively structureless and the free surface develops a shape characteristic of physical flows. In the case of elongated grains, there is alignment of the grain orientations over large regions. The simulation correctly captures the qualitative large-scale features seen in real flows. Another interesting result presented by Baxter and Behringer and also by Martinez, Masson and Deserable (1995) is that there is no monotonic variation in the flow rate during emptying (Fig. 33.2). This fact, i.e. a mean flow rate independent of

560 *Lattice grain models*

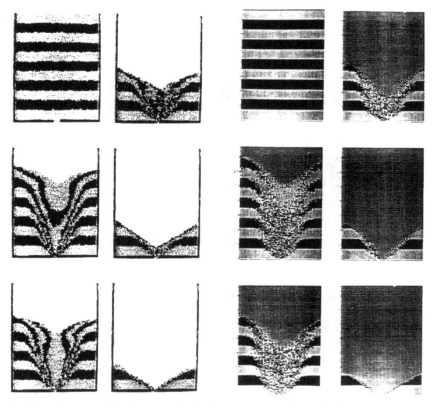

Fig. 33.1 Photographs showing flow characteristics obtained during experiment (left) and LGrM simulation (right) (from Savage, 1993).

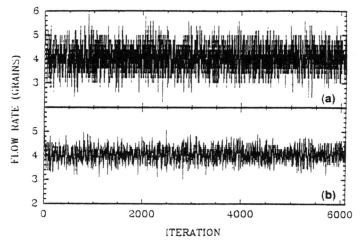

Fig. 33.2 Variation in flowrate during simulations of hopper emptying (from Baxter and Behringer, 1991).

Main results on the simulation of silo flow 561

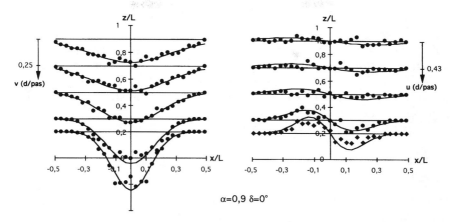

Fig. 33.3 Velocity profiles (v = vertical, u = horizontal) in the flow converging zone during hopper emptying (from Masson, 1996).

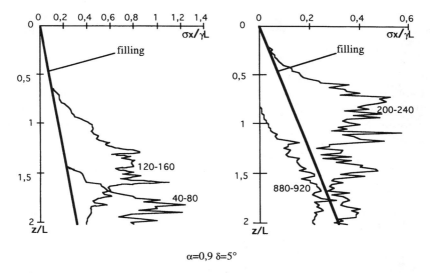

Fig. 33.4 Variation in wall pressures during models of hopper emptying (from Masson, 1996). Numbers correspond to simulation steps.

the height of material in the silo, is consistent with experimental results. Moreover, the velocity profiles in the flow converging zone computed by Masson (Fig. 33.3) are in good agreement with the predictions of Nedderman and Tüzün. Several experimental works have confirmed the relevance of these predictions, as for instance Khelil (1989).

LGrMs not only give realistic flow patterns but they can also provide interesting results in terms of wall pressure. The model of Masson *et al.*

which takes into account the grain weight transmission gives wall pressure profiles at filling similar to Janssen's solution. During the initiation of flow, voids propagate upwards and break some supports of grains, leading to a change in the force distribution. The effect of this can be an overpressure at the wall which travels upwards as voids propagate up to the top surface (Fig. 33.4). This result is related to the switch effect sometimes observed in real silos at the beginning of emptying.

33.4 CONCLUSIONS AND SUGGESTIONS FOR FUTURE RESEARCH

From the point of view of computational efficiency, LGrMs are powerful tools for the simulation of systems with a large number of grains as in silos. Despite their extreme simplicity, the degree of agreement with actual flows is very satisfactory. The results obtained by the various models show realistic silo flow patterns including flow mode, flow rate and velocity profiles. Moreover, force transmission can be introduced in models and gives wall pressure profiles comparable to classical solutions used in silos. Due to all these observations further investigations of this modelling approach appear to be worth pursuing.

Future research should stress the mechanical aspects of the transition rule by introducing more significant material properties such as size, shape, friction, etc. The establishment of a simple model of force transmission which would take these properties into account appears to be a very interesting challenge. Furthermore, the development of three-dimensional simulations should be considered.

REFERENCES

Baxter, G.W. and Behringer, R.P. (1990) Cellular automata models of granular flow. *Phys. Rev. A*, **42**(2), 1017.

Baxter, G.W. and Behringer, R.P. (1991) Cellular automata models for the flow of granular materials. *Physica D*, **51**, 465.

Caram, H.S. and Hong, D.C. (1992) Diffusing void model for granular flow. *Modern Physics Letters B*, **6**(13), 761.

Deserable, D.; Martinez, J. and Masson, S. (1994) Hopper flows observed with a cellular automaton for granular media, in *1st Int. Particle Tech. Forum*, Denver, USA.

Fitt, A.D. and Wilmott, P. (1992) Cellular-automaton model for segregation of two-species granular flow. *Phys. Rev. A*, **45**(4), 2383.

Gutt, G.M. and Haff, P.K. (1990) An automata model of granular materials, in *Proc. 5th Distributed Memory Computing Conference*, Vol. 1, IEEE Computer Society Press, p. 522.

Khelil, A. (1989) Etude du champ de vitesse et de contraintes dans les silos métalliques. Thèse de Doctorat, INPL, Nancy, France.

Litwiniszyn, J. (1964) An application of the random walk argument to the mechanics of granular media, in *International Union of Theoretical and Applied Mechanics Symposium*, Grenoble, France.

Martinez, J.; Masson, S. and Deserable, D. (1995) Simulation of silo flows with a cellular automaton for granular media, in *3rd Eur. Symp. on Storage and Flow of Particulate Solids*, Nuremberg, Germany.

Masson, S. (1996) *Simulations numériques discrètes de l'écoulement de matériaux granulaires dans les silos – utilisation de la méthode des élements distincts et elaboration de modèles de grains sur réseau*. Thèse de Doctorat, INSA Rennes, France: to be published.

Müllins, W.W. (1972) Stochastic theory of particle flow under gravity. *J. Appl. Phys.*, **43**, 665.

Nedderman, R.M. and Tüzün, U. (1979) A kinematic model for the flow of granular materials. *Powder Technol.*, **22**, 243.

Osinov, V.A. (1994) A model of a discrete stochastic medium for the problems of loose material flow. *Continuum Mech. Thermodyn.*, **6**, 51.

Peng, G. and Herrmann, H.J. (1994) Density waves of granular flow in a pipe using lattice-gas automata. *Phys. Rev. E*, **49**(3), 1796.

Savage, S.B. (1993) Disorder, diffusion and structure formation in granular flows. *Disorder and Granular Media*, Bideau, D. and Hansen, A. (eds), Elsevier Science Publishers.

34

Relationship between finite element and distinct element simulations

J. Martinez and S. Masson

34.1 INTRODUCTION

Two main scales can be considered for analysing the mechanical behaviour of bulk solids in relation to silo flow and wall pressure problems as illustrated in Table 34.1. At a microscopic scale, the material is a discontinuous set of a finite and often small number of individual particles. At this scale, the analysis focuses on the understanding of fundamental phenomena involved in bulk solids behaviour and on their consequences on silo flow and wall pressures. In this case the solutions, exclusively numerical, use discrete particle models among which the distinct element method is the most frequent. At a macroscopic scale, the material sample is considered to be continuous and homogeneous. This is the most traditional scale of analysis, as it is closer to the overall structure scale and more directly related to practical problems. The mathematical solutions at this scale can be analytical such as Janssen's methods or numerical such as the finite element method.

It must be pointed out that the differences between the above two scales are not only geometrical but also conceptual because of the opposition between a continuum and a discrete medium, which leads to the use of quite different mathematical quantities to represent each concept and makes the passage between these two scales difficult.

As seen in Fig. 34.1, this scale change is first necessary at the material sample level in order to derive the macroscopic behaviour of the continuous material from its microstructure. This operation, called material homogenization, is fundamental as it makes a link between the microscopic scale of the particles and the overall scale of the structure using the intermediate

Introduction

Table 34.1 Main scales of analysis of bulk solids behaviour in relation with silo problems

Scale of analysis	Microscopic	Macroscopic
Material definition	Discrete set of particles	Continuous, homogeneous
Purpose of analysis	Fundamental behaviour of bulk solid	Practical silo problems
Mathematical approach	Numerical	Analytical, numerical
Example of modelization	Distinct element method	Finite element method

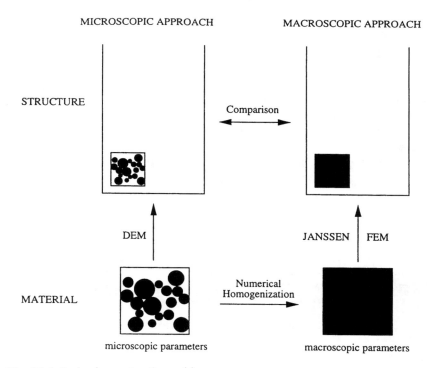

Fig. 34.1 Scale change in silo problems.

scale of the homogenized continuous material. At the same time, for small size problems, involving at most 10 000 particles, the distinct element method enables direct simulation of the whole boundary problem, and so gives wall forces and particle displacements anywhere within the silo from the discrete particle model. It is then possible to compare the solutions given by the two approaches, direct or indirect, and to validate each one with respect to the other.

This contribution presents the general principles and some useful relations which govern scale changes between distinct element and finite element simulations. More than presenting new results, the aim is to synthesize and discuss existing data and techniques relative to the necessary links to be established between these two approaches.

34.2 GENERAL PRINCIPLES OF SCALE CHANGE IN GRANULAR MEDIA

In the following, we will strictly limit our purpose to mechanical aspects of dry granular material submitted to purely mechanical actions, discarding contact or particle breaking and other factors such as thermal or chemical phenomena which can have important mechanical effects. From this mechanical point of view, four groups of parameters have to be considered at each of the two scale levels described above, as presented by Cambou (1993) and summarized in Table 34.2: the geometric, the kinematic, the static and the constitutive parameters will each be described in detail in the paragraphs below.

Two main 'scale change operations' can be defined which involve quite different mathematical techniques. The homogenization operation consists of finding the macroscopic quantities from the microscopic ones and can be considered as a mathematical integration or an averaging process. The localization operation consists of deriving microscopic quantities from macroscopic ones, which can be associated with a mathematical derivation.

Table 34.2 Main variables and governing relations for the analysis of bulk solids behaviour at microscopic and macroscopic scales

	Microscopic (discrete set of particles)	Basic relations (scale change process)	Macroscopic (homogenized material)
Geometry	Particle shape/size Contact distribution	(Averaging →)	Continuum
Kinematics	Particle displacement /rotation ↑	← Compatibility →	Strains ↑
Constitutive relations	Contact law ↓	(Homogenization → ← Localization)	Stress–strain law ↓
Statics	Contact forces	← Equilibrium →	Stresses

Each of these operations of homogenization or localization can affect either the kinematic or the static variables, but for solving a given problem, the sequence to follow is precisely determined. For instance, for simulating a macroscopic stress controlled test, we must first process an operation of static localization and then a kinematic homogenization. Inversely, a strain-controlled problem would imply kinematic localization followed by static homogenization.

As pointed out above, homogenization involves an averaging process which sets the problem of the statistical meaning of the group of particles. It is often considered that a ratio of the sample dimensions to the maximum grain diameter equal to 20 is sufficient. In fact, the scale length of heterogeneities seems different according to the quantity to homogenize and is higher for static than for geometrical parameters.

34.3 GEOMETRICAL PARAMETERS

34.3.1 Microscopic parameters

For a single particle of a real material, shape and dimensions are basic information but difficult to measure and to represent mathematically. Simplified shapes are often adopted, like spheres or ellipsoids, which permits defining characteristic lengths such as maximum, minimum, intermediate or mean diameter and different ratios between these quantities. For the sake of simplicity, most mechanical models adopt discs or spheres, some use ellipses (Rothenburg, Bathurst and Berlin, 1993; Ting, Rowell and Meachum 1993; Ng and Lin, 1993), but very few models consider more general shapes such as polygons (Hogue and Newland, 1993) or superquadric representations (Mustoe and de Poorter, 1993).

For a set of particles, simple statistical analysis gives mean parameters such as morphological ratios or grain size distributions. A difference must be made when defining the grading curve of an assembly from the number of particles or, more usually, from their cumulative weight. For well-graded materials, the corresponding curves can be very different because of the low relative weight of the smallest particles. Care must also be taken when deriving a grading curve of a three-dimensional assembly from measurements over a plane section or along a segment of the probe (Auvinet, 1989). A dual curve of the grain size distribution is the pore size distribution, the pore size being defined as the diameter of the biggest sphere which can be located in the interparticle space. From the comparison between a simulated material and experimental measurements, Auvinet and Bouvard (1989) have shown the limits of the usual technique of mercury porosimetry and that of the Kozeny formula giving the material permeability from the porosity.

A major geometrical feature of a dense assembly is its topology, that is the orientation of the particles and the contact distribution which are highly involved in kinematic compatibility and force transmission between particles. As shown in Fig. 34.2, the particle orientation can be characterized by the direction m of their maximum length. The contact orientation is given either by the contact vector r joining the mass centre of a particle to the contact point, or by the vector n normal to the contact plane. In the particular case of spheres or discs, the above vectors are reduced to a unique quantity, the contact normal n. These quantities are precisely defined in the case of hard, round-shaped particles, but their definition becomes more conventional in the case of very soft or angular shaped particles. For a bidimensional assembly, the radical axes of neighbouring particles (Fig. 34.3) allow the construction of a polygonal cell around each particle which produces a Voronoi tessellation of the plane. Annic *et al.* (1993) have shown that the mean number of polygon sides is equal to six in the case of monosized discs for a large range of packing fractions and equal to five for

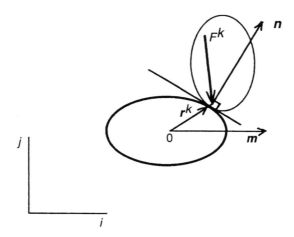

Fig. 34.2 Geometrical and force parameters at a contact.

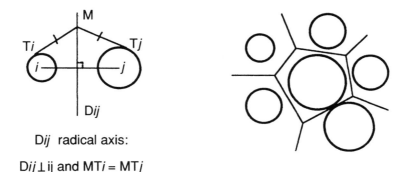

Dij radical axis:

$Dij \perp ij$ and $MTi = MTj$

Fig. 34.3 Radical axis and Voronoi cell.

Geometrical parameters

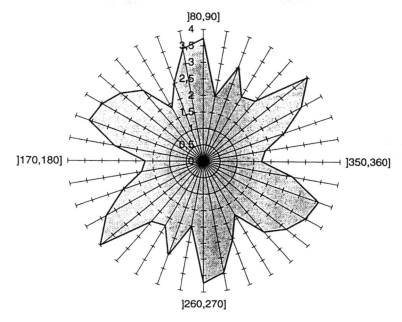

Fig. 34.4 Distribution of contact orientations (%) in the case of nearly uniform discs after gravity deposition.

a dense polydisperse packing. Considering the contacts, the coordination number, equal to the mean number of contacts per particle, quantifies the connectivity between particles. For dense random packings of monosized particles the coordination number is close to four in the case of discs (2D packing) and to six in the case of spheres (3D packing). Furthermore, the spatial orientation of the contacts is an interesting property as it is directly related to the material history. A simple illustration of the contact orientation in terms of the contact frequency versus the normal angle is given in Fig. 34.4, from the plane simulation of a gravity deposit of nearly uniform discs.

34.3.2 Macroscopic parameters

Simple global geometric parameters are defined from ratios between the particles and the pore volume such as compacity, porosity and voids ratio. Though these global parameters can be easily calculated from knowledge of the microstructure, they are often determined from the particle's specific weight and the global specific weight of the packing. The relations between these global volumetric parameters and the grading curve are well known and very useful in civil engineering for optimizing the material's composition. In the case of storage of bulk solids the compacity will be lower for a uniform material than for a well-graded one. Moreover, the compacity appears strictly related to the contacts density as shown by Oda (1977) who expresses the voids ratio as a decreasing function of the coordination number.

The influence of the assembly structure on the macroscopic mechanical behaviour of the material is particularly related to its anisotropy. Distinction is made between inherent (initial) and induced (by loading) anisotropy. A basic three-dimensional representation of particles orientation and of contacts distribution uses density continuous functions $E(m)$, $E(n)$ and second-rank fabric tensors A_{ij}, F_{ij} (Oda and Sudoo, 1993). The inherent anisotropy is thus represented by the tensor A_{ij} defined by

$$A_{ij} = \int_\Omega m_i m_j E(m) d\Omega(m) \qquad (34.3.1)$$

Ω being the unit sphere in three dimensions or the unit circle in two.

The induced anisotropy is represented by the tensor F_{ij} defined by

$$F_{ij} = \int_\Omega n_i n_j E(n) d\Omega(n) \qquad (34.3.2)$$

The above expressions are geometric homogenization formulae giving simple macroscopic continuous representations of the assembly structure and allowing definition of orthotropy directions and ratios. They may be insufficiently representative in some situations as in the case of a complex loading history (Cambou, 1987) or when large strains are developed (Rothenburg, Bathurst and Dusseault, 1989).

34.4 STATIC VARIABLES

34.4.1 Microscopic variables

At a given contact k, the basic microscopic static variable is the contact force F^k (Fig. 34.2) which, in the general case of a three-dimensional assembly, possesses three components F_i^k ($i = 1 \ldots 3$). Most often, the distinction is made between normal (F^N) and tangential (F^T) components, as each of them plays a quite different role regarding the particle behaviour. Because of the complexity and the heterogeneity of the individual contact forces field for a set of particles, the mean contact force value $\bar{F}(n)$ in a direction of contact n is often introduced and a statistical microscopic static variable $f(n)$ is defined (Cambou, 1987):

$$f(n) = E(n)\bar{F}(n) \qquad (34.4.1)$$

An example of the variation of the function $f(n)$ in a two-dimensional sample of discs deposited by gravity in a silo is shown in Fig. 34.5.

34.4.2 Macroscopic variables

The simplest representation of the macroscopic static variables is the usual symmetric stress tensor σ whose components σ_{ij} will be determined from the

Static variables

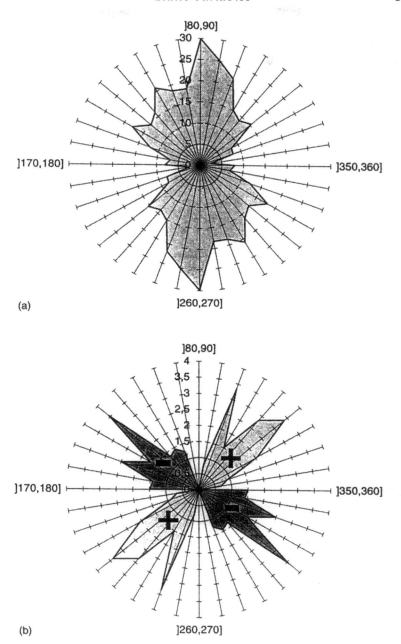

Fig. 34.5 Distribution of the static variable $f(n)$ in the case of an ensiled material after gravity deposition: (a) normal component, (b) tangential component.

microscopic forces according to the relationships mentioned below. A well-known expression of the homogenized macroscopic stress, for a set of particles occupying a global volume V, is derived from the individual contact forces F_i^k as follows:

$$\sigma_{ij} = \frac{1}{V}\sum_{k=1}^{N_c} F_i^k r_j^k \qquad (34.4.2)$$

In this formula, r_j^k is the j-component of the contact vector r^k and N_c the total number of contacts within the volume V. Given the discrete nature of the granular assembly, the above expression gives a continuous stress tensor only for a statistically homogeneous assembly which implies a large volume V (Rothenburg, Bathurst and Berlin, 1993). An alternative formulation consists in using the statistical homogenized variable $f(r)$ which gives:

$$\sigma_{ij} = \overline{N}\overline{R}\int_{\Omega} f_i(r) r_j \mathrm{d}\Omega(r) \qquad (34.4.3)$$

where $\overline{N}$ is the number of contacts per unit volume, r is the unit contact vector, r_j its j-component, $\overline{R}$ the mean contact vector length, $f_i(r)$ the i-component of $f(r)$, and the summation stands over a unit sphere (in three dimensions) or a unit circle (in two dimensions).

The above expressions are homogenization formulae giving the macroscopic stress from the microscopic contact forces. Inversely, localization expressions can be written which give microscopic variables such as $f(n)$ from the macroscopic stresses. As an example, for an isotropic material composed of an assembly of discs or spheres, the following expression gives the microscopic static variable $f(n)$ from the stress tensor σ:

$$f(n) = \mu \sigma n + \frac{1-\mu}{2}\left[(2+d)n\sigma n - \mathrm{tr}\sigma\right]n \qquad (34.4.4)$$

where d is the space dimension (2 or 3), $\mathrm{tr}\,\sigma$ is the trace of σ and μ an internal variable which characterizes the obliquity between $f(n)$ and n. For anisotropic materials similar relations can be found in Cambou (1993).

34.5 KINEMATIC VARIABLES

At the microscopic scale, the basic kinematic variables are the displacements and rotations of individual particles. At the macroscopic scale, for a set of particles, an average displacement gradient $\overline{u}_{i,j}$ can be defined by a dual expression of equation (34.4.2), which in the case of spheres or discs is written as follows:

$$\overline{u}_{i,j} = \frac{1}{N_c}\sum_{k=1}^{N_c} \frac{u_i^k}{l_j^k} \qquad (34.5.1)$$

in which, N_c is the number of contacts, u_i^k is the i-component of relative displacement at contact k and l_j^k the j-component of the vector l^k joining the centres of particle in contact. For the sake of consistency with tensorial properties, a variant of equation (34.5.1) is

$$\bar{u}_{i,j} = \frac{1}{N_c} \sum_{k=1}^{N_c} \frac{u_i^k l_j^k}{\|l^k\|^2} \qquad (34.5.2)$$

According to the definition of a continuous strain, an alternative approach leads to a definition of the mean displacement gradient within a volume V by

$$\bar{u}_{i,j} = \frac{1}{V} \int_V \frac{\partial u_i}{\partial x_j} dV \qquad (34.5.3)$$

Considering the perimeter Ω of the volume V, the volume integral can be transformed into a contour integral:

$$\bar{u}_{i,j} = \frac{1}{V} \int_\Omega u_i n_j \, d\Omega \qquad (34.5.4)$$

where n_j is the j-component of the unit normal to the perimeter Ω.

For a finite set of particles, simple techniques can be used to obtain a discrete evaluation of the above integral from the displacements of particles intersected by the perimeter Ω (Bardet and Proubet, 1989). Then a macroscopic strain tensor ε can be calculated using:

$$\varepsilon_{ij} = \frac{1}{2}\left(\bar{u}_{i,j} + \bar{u}_{j,i}\right) \qquad (34.5.5)$$

Following the logic of expression (34.4.1), Cambou (1993) proposes a mean displacement $u(n)$ for contacts of normal n as a basic microscopic kinematic variable. From energy considerations, a homogenization relation can be written giving the macroscopic strain rate tensor $\dot{\varepsilon}$ from the microscopic kinematic displacement rate $\dot{u}(n)$. As an example, for an isotropic assembly of discs or spheres the volumetric strain rate $\dot{\varepsilon}_{kk}$ is given by

$$\dot{\varepsilon}_{kk} = \frac{3}{(d+1)\pi \bar{D}} \int_\Omega n_k \dot{u}_k \, d\Omega \qquad (34.5.6)$$

where $\bar{D}$ is the mean diameter of particles and d the space dimension.

Inversely, localization relations can be written giving the displacement rate $\dot{u}(n)$ from the strain rate tensor $\dot{\varepsilon}$. For instance, for an isotropic assembly of discs or spheres, the normal component $\dot{u}(n)$ of the mean microscopic displacement in direction n is given by

$$\dot{u}^N(n) = \bar{D}\left[(n\dot{\varepsilon}n)n + \frac{\mu b}{d+2}(dn\dot{\varepsilon}n - \text{tr}\dot{\varepsilon})\right]n \qquad (34.5.7)$$

where b is an internal variable which governs the relative amount of normal to tangential components of displacement rate.

34.6 CONSTITUTIVE PARAMETERS

34.6.1 Microscopic parameters

As for a continuous material, it is usual to distinguish elasticity and plasticity as the two main behaviour modes for the contacts. Elastic behaviour of contacts usually uses the normal K^N and the tangential K^T stiffness which are coefficients of proportionality between the normal F^N and tangential F^T contact forces components and the corresponding normal u^N and tangential u^T relative displacements between the two particles in contact. Thus, for the normal components, we have the general relationship

$$F^N = K^N u^N \qquad (34.6.1)$$

and similarly, for the tangential components, we write

$$F^T = K^T u^T \qquad (34.6.2)$$

Simple linear contact models consider contact stiffness coefficients K^N and K^T as intrinsic contact parameters. More sophisticated contact models derive K^N and K^T from more fundamental solutions. This is particularly the case for the well-known Hertz–Mindlin model which expresses the normal secant stiffness between two spheres in contact with diameters d_1 and d_2 as follows:

$$K^N = \frac{2G}{3(1-v)}\sqrt{\frac{d_1 d_2}{d_1 + d_2}}\sqrt{u^N} \qquad (34.6.3)$$

and the tangential tangent stiffness by

$$K^T = \frac{2\left[3G^2(1-v)\right]^{1/3}}{(2-v)}\left[\frac{d_1 d_2}{d_1 + d_2} F^N\right]^{1/3} \qquad (34.6.4)$$

where G and v are the shear modulus and the Poisson's ratio of constituent spheres.

Plastic behaviour of contacts uses a Coulomb's criterion, which for non-cohesive contacts, defines a friction coefficient ψ such as

$$F^T \leq \psi F^N \qquad (34.6.5)$$

34.6.2 Macroscopic parameters

Derivation of macroscopic behaviour parameters from the macroscopic ones uses either empirical, analytical or numerical methods. An empirical relationship similar to equation (34.6.6) has been proposed by Biarez (1962) under the following form:

$$E = \alpha\, p^n \qquad (34.6.6)$$

where α and n are empirical parameters which can be precisely calculated for regular assemblies (Biarez and Hicher, 1987).

Theoretical calculations of the macroscopic elastic and plastic parameters presented by Emeriault (1993) using a statistical homogenization technique (Cambou, 1993), gives the secant Young's modulus $\overline{E}$ and Poisson's ratio $\overline{v}$ for an isotropic assembly of spheres with a Hertz–Mindlin contact law and submitted to an almost isotropic stress:

$$\overline{E} = \sqrt[3]{\sigma_{kk}} \, \overline{N} \overline{D}^3 f_E(G, v, b, \mu) \qquad (34.6.7)$$

and

$$\overline{v} = f_v(G, v, b, \mu) \qquad (34.6.8)$$

where $\overline{N}$ is the number of contacts per unit volume, $\overline{D}$ the mean diameter of particles, f_E and f_v are functions of the microscopic elastic parameters G and v and of the internal variables b and μ appearing in relations (34.4.4) and (34.5.7).

From these relations it can be seen that the Young's modulus is an increasing function of the spheric pressure while the Poisson's ratio is independent of the applied stress. By the same technique, the calculation of the macroscopic internal friction angle φ as a function of the microscopic friction angle ψ shows a horizontal asymptotic trend for high ψ values (Fig. 34.6). Similar results regarding the slight influence of high ψ values on the global friction angle have also been found from numerical simulations of multiaxial compression of spheres or discs (Thornton and Sun, 1993; Yemmas, 1993) and from experiments (El Hosri, 1984; Abriak and Mahboubi, 1992). This limiting effect seems to be emphasized by the spherical or circular shape of particles. Ting, Rowell and Meachum (1993)

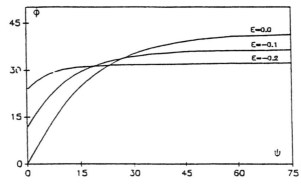

Fig. 34.6 Theoretical relation between the macroscopic internal friction angle ϕ and the microscopic friction angle ψ (from Cambou, 1993).

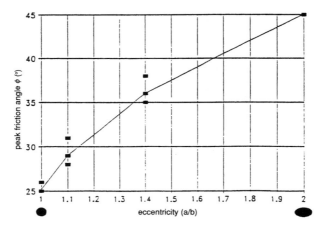

Fig. 34.7 Effect of elliptical particle shape on macroscopic peak friction angle from compression test simulations (from Ting, Rowell and Meachum, 1993).

have shown that the macroscopic peak friction angle increases with the length to width ratio of particles (Fig. 34.7).

34.7 EXAMPLE OF COMPARED DEM AND FEM SIMULATIONS

In order to compare the results obtained by the microscopic and the macroscopic approaches, an example of the stresses within a plane rectangular silo calculated both by the finite element and the distinct element methods is presented. The method followed is shown in Fig. 34.1. The microscopic parameters of the bulk solids are the following:

- mean particle diameter: 10 mm
- linear elastic stiffness: $k^N = 1\,\mathrm{MPa}$; $k^T = 0.1\,k^N$
- particle friction angle: $\psi = 23°$

The macroscopic parameters of the material have been determined by simulating loading and unloading biaxial compression tests on a set of 400 cylinders with the DEM code PFC2D (1995). The parameters obtained are the following:

- elastic parameters: $E = 0.125\,\mathrm{MPa}$; $\nu = 0.37$
- internal friction angle: $\varphi = 11°$

Calculations of internal stresses and wall pressures at the end of filling have then been processed with PFC2D and with Cesar, a finite element code available at the Ecole Centrale de Lyon. The results, plotted in Figure 34.8, show that the scatter of wall pressures is higher when using the microscopic approach but that both methods give quite close mean values of the macroscopic stresses.

Example of compared DEM and FEM simulations

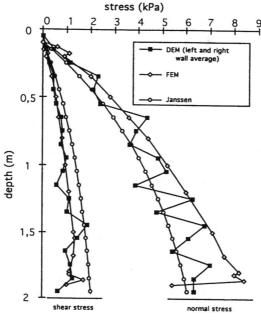

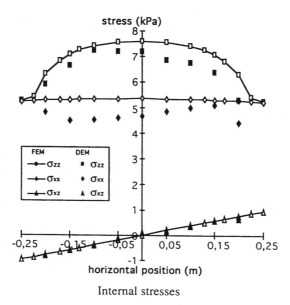

Fig. 34.8 Comparison between internal and wall stresses from DEM and FEM simulations (from Masson, 1996).

This example shows that homogenization techniques allow us to derive meaningful macroscopic mechanical parameters from microscopic ones. The simulation of the structure at the microscopic scale gives acceptable results compared to those given by the macroscopic approach, and moreover they enable us to take better account of the fundamental parameters of the bulk material.

REFERENCES

Abriak, N. and Mahboubi, A. (1992) *Influence du frottement local sur le frottement local*. GRECO Géomatériaux, Lyon.

Annic, C.; Bideau, D.; Lemaitre, J.; Troadec, J.P. and Gervois, A. (1993) Geometrical properties of 2D packings of particles. *Powders and Grains 93*, Thornton, C. (Ed.), Balkema, Rotterdam.

Auvinet, G. (1989) Plane sections and straight crossing of granular media. *Powders and Grains 89*, Biarez, J. and Gourvès, R. (Eds), Balkema, Rotterdam.

Auvinet, G. and Bouvard, D. (1989) Pore size distribution of granular media. *Powders and Grains 89*, Biarez, J. and Gourvès, R. (Eds), Balkema, Rotterdam.

Bardet, J.P. and Proubet, J. (1989) Application of micromechanics to incrementally non-linear constitutive equations for granular media. *Powders and Grains 89*, Biarez, J. and Gourvès, R. (Eds) Balkema, Rotterdam.

Biarez, J. (1962) Contribution à l'étude des propriétés mécaniques des sols et des milieux pulvérulents. Thèse d'Etat, Grenoble.

Biarez, J. and Hicher, P.Y. (1987) *Constitutive Equations for Granular Non Cohesive Soils*. Balkema, Rotterdam.

Cambou, B. (1987) Mécanique des matériaux granulaires; l'approche micro structurelle. *Manuel de rhéologie des géomatériaux*, Darve (Ed.), Presses de l'ENPC, France.

Cambou, B. (1993) From global to local variables in granular materials. *Powders and Grains 93*, Thornton, C. (Ed.), Balkema, Rotterdam.

El Hosri, M. (1984) Contribution à l'étude des propriétés mécaniques des matériaux. Thèse de doctorat d'Etat, Université de Paris 6.

Emeriault, F. (1993) Modélisation micromécanique des milieux granulaires. Thèse EC Lyon.

Hogue, C. and Newland, D.E. (1993) Efficient computer modelling of the motion of arbitrary grains. *Powders and Grains 93*, Thornton, C. (Ed.), Balkema, Rotterdam.

Masson, S. (1996) Simulations numériques discrètes de l'ecoulement de matériaux granulaires dans les silos. Utilisation de la méthode des éléments distincts. Elaboration de modèles de grains sur réseau. Thèse de doctorat, INSA Rennes, France.

Mustoe, G.G.W. and de Poorter, G. (1993) A numberical model for the mechanical behaviour of particulate media containing non circular shaped particles. *Powders and Grains 93*, Thornton, C. (Ed.), Balkema, Rotterdam.

Ng, T.T. and Lin, X. (1993) Numerical simulations of naturally deposited granular soil with ellipsoidal elements. *2nd Int. Conf. on DEM*, MIT.

Oda, M. (1977) Coordination number and its relation to shear strength of granular material. *Soils and Foundations*, **17**, (2).

Oda, M. and Sudoo, T. (1993) Fabric tensor showing anisotropy of granular soils and its application to soil plasticity. *Powders and Grains 93*, Thornton, C. (Ed.), Balkema, Rotterdam.

PFC2D (1995) *Particle Flow Code in 2 Dimensions*. Itasca, Minneapolis.

Rothenburg, L.; Bathurst, R.J. and Berlin, A.A. (1993) Micromechanical response of simulated granular materials under principal stress rotations. *Powders and Grains 93*, Thornton, C. (Ed.), Balkema, Rotterdam.

Rothenburg, L.; Bathurst, R.J. and Dusseault, M.R. (1989) Micromechanical ideas in constitutive modelling of granular materials. *Powders and Grains 89*, Biarez, J. and Gourvès, R. (Eds), Balkema, Rotterdam.

Thornton, C. and Sun, G. (1993) Axisymmetric compression of 3D polydisperse systems of spheres. *Powders and Grains 93*, Thornton, C. (Ed.), Balkema, Rotterdam.

Ting, J.M.; Rowell, J.D. and Meachum, L. (1993) Influence of particle shape on the strength of ellipse-shaped granular assemblages. *2nd Int. Conf. on DEM*, MIT.

Yemmas, R. (1993) Simulations numériques des milieux granulaires. Thèse de doctorat, Montpellier.

35

Evaluation of applications of FEM and DPM

P.J. Reuderink

35.1 INTRODUCTION

In an industrial research and development environment the question 'which approach is best' is irrelevant. Unfortunately, the 'state of the art' in solids flow modelling is such that, whenever possible, one will always perform experiments to get a comfortable feeling about new solids handling tools or process equipment prior to commercial application. Experimental results are backed up by modelling, using any available modelling approach, 'quick and dirty' if it has to be. The reliability of the design rather than the aesthetics or the general applicability and validity of a model is what counts.

The role of modelling is regarded as complementary to experiments, in three ways:

- Prior to, or between experiments: scouting. Modelling can quickly reveal which design is most promising, which design parameters are most important, and how parameters can be tuned to obtain improved behaviour.
- Supporting experiments: to get the maximum amount of information. Some data are difficult to obtain experimentally. Modelling can provide answers, e.g. by deriving the required data from data which can be measured.
- Translating experiments: scale up. Experiments are often carried out on a different, usually smaller scale than the commercially envisaged one. Models can help in estimating the effects of scale-up. In addition, models can be helpful in forecasting whether a design can be used for other applications, e.g. other solids.

Table 35.1 Strengths and weaknesses of different approaches

	Experiment	DPM	FEM
Particle effects:			
particle size distributions	0	0	−
shape	+	0	−
elasticity	0	+	0
friction properties	−	+	0
Forces:			
internally, in bed	−	0	+
on wall, on internals	+	0	+
Velocity distributions	0	0	+
Stagnant zones	+	0	+
Transient behaviour	0	0	−
Voidage distributions	0	+	0
Boundary layers	0	+	−
Effect of boundary layers	0	0	+
Free surfaces	+	0	−
Rapid fluctuations (e.g. quaking):			
in time	0	+	−
in space	−	+	−
Attrition	0	0	0
Segregation	0	0	−
Complicated geometries	+	−	+
Developing scaling rules	0	0	+

With the above in mind, experiments, discrete particle models (DPM) and finite element (FEM, continuum) models are assessed with respect to their capability to contribute to issues frequently encountered in research and development (Table 35.1).

35.2 DISTINCTIONS BETWEEN EXPERIMENTS, FEM AND DPM

By definition, the discrete particle method is suitable for the study of particle effects on solid flow. Accounting for broad particle size distributions and complicated shapes might be a little bit difficult, but mechanical properties such as elasticity and friction can be well accounted for. In experiments, some practical complications may be encountered. For instance, it is usually impossible to vary mechanical properties independently. An important effect of the particle size distribution, segregation, can be monitored only partly, as it is difficult to obtain information from the interior of the bed. FEM is largely unsuited to study particle effects as they use bulk properties as input.

In experiments, measuring forces is largely restricted to the walls and internals. Using a DPM only a relatively limited number of particles can be used. As a consequence fluctuations due to the discrete nature of the system are overemphasized. The FEM offers an excellent opportunity to obtain information on stresses, both in the bed and near the wall.

With respect to velocity distributions and related issues, each of the approaches has its advantages and disadvantages. In experiments it is difficult, though not impossible, to get information on velocities in the bed. Stagnant areas, however, can be easily detected, as they occur near walls. The DPM can be useful in many respects, although it might be hampered by too pronounced discrete effects, due to the fact that only a limited number of particles can be used. In any case, it is already difficult to model steady-state behaviour using the FEM: a description of transient phenomena will be even more complicated, requiring even more input parameters.

Boundary layers, such as shear layers near the bin wall, are usually related to discrete particle phenomena. Therefore, the DPM is a promising tool to predict boundary phenomena, while such phenomena will always be difficult to predict using the FEM. On the other hand, the effects of certain boundary phenomena can be accounted for in the FEM. One might think of a hybrid model combining the DPM to model the boundary effect and the FEM to predict its effects on bulk behaviour.

Rapid fluctuations, especially those in space, can be best monitored using DPM. Segregation will be difficult to account for in the FEM. The DPM would have been an excellent tool, but it might have problems when a very broad particle distribution is used.

There is usually too much optimism about the possibilities of modelling complicated geometries using the DPM. Especially in three dimensions, defining a complicated geometry implies that a large number of particles

Table 35.2 Strengths and weaknesses of experiment, DPM and FEM

	Experiment	DPM	FEM
+	Complicated geometries	Link particle parameters to bulk behaviour	Complex geometries Scaling
	Boundary phenomena	Boundary effects	In-bed phenomena
	Forces on wall	Rapid fluctuations	
	Stagnant zones	Voidage distributions	
	Free surfaces	Segregation	
−	In-bed phenomena	Larger complex geometries	Link with particle parameters
	Internal forces		Time-dependent effects
	Fluctuations in space		Free surfaces
	Segregation		Boundary layers

have to be dealt with in order to obtain a simulation which behaves realistically.

Undoubtedly, the ranking in each box is subject to debate: many researchers will have outspoken ideas on model approaches or modifications turning '−' into a '+'. In such detail the table is probably of limited value. But it does give a good first impression on the strong and weak points of the various techniques. These are rearranged in Table 35.2.

35.3 SUMMARY

Summarizing, experiments can deal well with complicated geometries, and near wall phenomena. The DPM is useful for discrete effects like particle properties, voidage distributions and segregation. The FEM is promising when dealing with complex geometries and to obtain in-bed information. It is clear that the three techniques are complementary. Research and development in solids flow will benefit most by pursuing a hybrid approach, where one technique provides input to another.

36

Challenges for the future in numerical simulation
J.M. Rotter

36.1 INDUSTRIAL PROBLEMS IN SILOS

36.1.1 Introduction

Before defining the challenges which face the numerical modelling of granular bulk solids in silos, it is desirable to identify the features of silos which make them difficult to design and operate, and which are industrially relevant.

Silos are not items for disinterested scientific study, as distant galaxies might be: they are practical structures of great industrial significance, and the shortcomings of silos lead to grave economic losses in all countries in the EU. The nature of industrial problems should be recognized before the tasks for computer modelling are defined.

Complex relationships exist between bulk solids material properties, the silo filling process, the flow patterns which occur during discharge, the wall pressures on filling and discharge, the stresses induced in the silo structure and the conditions which might cause distress or failure of the structure (Fig. 36.1).

The mechanical characteristics of the stored solids and the process by which they are filled into the silo determine the distribution of densities and particle orientations in the silo, which strongly affect the flow pattern (Nielsen, 1983). The filling process and the flow pattern on discharge are largely responsible for segregation of the solids. The solids packing and material characteristics also determine whether arching or ratholing occurs across the outlet (Fig. 36.2).

The flow pattern strongly influences the pressures on the silo wall during discharge, so these cannot be predicted with certainty unless the flow

Industrial problems in silos

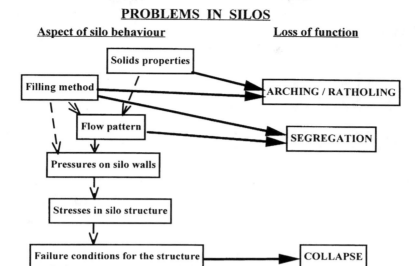

Fig. 36.1 Relationship between silo solids and handling and loss of function.

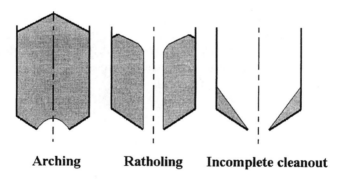

Fig. 36.2 Simple problems which arrest flow.

pattern itself can be predicted. The pressures on the silo wall both on filling and during discharge are, in general, unsymmetrical and non-uniform. The relationships between these pressures and the stresses which develop in the silo walls depend on shell bending phenomena (or coupled bending and stretching actions in flat walls), which can be very complex and are not easily understood, though they are predictable with finite element analyses.

Finally, the silo wall stress conditions which will induce structural failure are only understood for simple cases at present, and much work remains to be done. These failure strengths can be very dependent on trivially small imperfections in the wall geometry and also on the strengthening effect of the stiffness of the bulk solid. In addition, the structural failure strengths remain quite difficult to predict accurately even when the best nonlinear finite element analyses are used.

36.1.2 The key problems

Three key problems regularly arise in solids flow from silos (Fig. 36.1):

1. The structural integrity of the silo may be jeopardized by pressures which are too high or too low.
2. The stored solids may hang up in the container.
3. The flow pattern may cause segregation of the solids.

All three are related to flow patterns in the silo, but the three phenomena have different characteristics.

36.1.2.1 High or low wall pressures

High pressures are not in themselves necessarily a serious danger to the silo structure. High pressures must be seen in the context of the structural form and the way in which the structure carries loads. For this reason, local low pressures can be even more damaging than very high symmetrical pressures. This is a complex subject because the silo is a multi-segment shell structure, and is beyond the scope of this chapter, but is treated extensively elsewhere (Rotter, Pham and Nielsen, 1986; Rotter, 1986b, 1993, 1996a, b). If the silo collapses, the process which it feeds is arrested, and grave economic losses ensue.

36.1.2.2 Arching and ratholing

Arching over the outlet and ratholing are other means by which the solids flow is arrested. Arching over the outlet is generally attributed to the development of cohesion in the solid, though recent work suggests that the solids dilation requirement, which is often but not always related to the cohesion, must play a role too. Ratholing is the formation of a stable hole down the entire height of a silo, leading to major loss of effective storage capacity, and consequent serious economic losses. Both arching and ratholing are essentially static phenomena, so dynamic analyses are not necessary nor perhaps helpful in addressing these problems.

36.1.2.3 Segregation during filling and discharge

Segregation may arise from many different phenomena, but in the silo it can occur on filling or on discharge. On filling, segregation occurs in coarse solids principally by larger particles rolling down an inclined surface more readily than smaller ones, leading to large particle accumulations adjacent to the wall. In fine powders, the transport of finer particles by air to zones away from the natural gravitational trajectory leads to the opposite segregation pattern.

Once segregation has been established within a silo, it may be harder to eliminate. Mono-sized particles flow more easily than graded materials, and the flow may often be preferentially shifted towards the coarser zones of these segregated solids. If funnel or internal flow is used, the segregation which occurred on filling can lead to larger particles emerging early in the discharge, followed by finer fractions towards the end. If the silo is repeatedly part-discharged and refilled, the finer materials may be retained, develop cohesion and become very difficult to remove at all.

Segregation during discharge has largely been addressed by the adoption of mass flow geometries whenever segregation must be avoided. The criteria for mass flow were developed by Jenike and others in the 1960s (Jenike, 1961, 1964). Unfortunately, recent work has somewhat undermined the simplicity of that description (Drescher, 1992) and considerable doubt now exists as to whether current accepted knowledge is correct. Funnel flow silos inevitably lead to segregation of the stored solid, so they are only useful for solids where this is not a problem. The flow pattern in a funnel flow silo remains a topic of serious research because asymmetries in the flow pattern can endanger the structural integrity, but the complex form of the pressure distribution, including both low and high pressures, must also be defined here before progress can be made.

36.1.3 The role of computational models

Computational models present the very best opportunity to resolve many of the paradoxes of past research work, because they are not restricted by the simplistic assumptions which algebraic work had to accept. They offer the power to eliminate theoretical assumptions of all kinds; they provide a detail of description which cannot be obtained in experimental work; they provide the opportunity to make predictions relating to geometries and sizes which cannot be investigated in the field or in the laboratory; and they offer a vital source of new knowledge which can be used to devise new design guidance. However, few of these tasks have even been attempted to date.

In the context of the above discussion, a huge amount of work remains to be done in exploiting computational models to make useful predictions of silo pressures and flow, solid packing arrangements and anisotropy, behaviour associated with filling processes and wall irregularities, of the consequences of complex geometries, the effects of earthquakes and internal structures within the silo, of statistical variability and poorly understood deterministic phenomena. Computational models have barely begun their most valuable work.

36.2 MATERIAL MODELLING

If computational models are to achieve the large goals set out above, they must be able to model simple phenomena which have been shown by existing experiments to affect solids flow and silo pressure regimes. To this end, the material models used in computational models cannot be regarded as adequate for all tasks unless they model the following features.

36.2.1 Cohesion in solids

When fine granular solids or granular solids with fine components are compressed, they develop cohesion. This is normally related either to interstitial water (as in soils) or interstitial air (as in fine dry powders). In some solids, such as coal, fine particles (clay) with small amounts of water present too, make the solid quite cohesive, leading to serious practical handling problems in silos.

The models used to predict flows in silos cannot hope to be of practical use in addressing problems of either fine powders or moist sticky solids unless a cohesive mechanism is included. The above examples illustrate the fact that a single physical mechanism for this phenomenon will not cover all industrially relevant cases. Thus, the inclusion of interstitial fluid in a discrete element model will not be adequate to address this problem. Finite element analyses address this problem empirically.

36.2.2 Flow function of the solid

The flow function of the solid describes the development of cohesion as a consequence of previous stress history. It is usually defined in terms of the results of a Jenike shear cell test, and is widely used to characterize solids of all kinds and a lot of data on solids flow functions have been collected by laboratories all over the world in the last three decades. Comparable results are obtainable in other apparatuses, but no significant data base exists for any of these. Thus, any computational model which wishes to predict in advance the behaviour of an industrially relevant solid should first be able to predict the progressive development of cohesion in a Jenike shear cell. This challenge has not been taken up very widely by either discrete element or finite element analysts: both have some difficulties in modelling particulate solid behaviour in a shear cell.

36.2.3 Anisotropy and the filling process

The effect of the filling process on flow patterns in silos has been known to experimentalists for many years (Sugden, 1980; Moriyama, Hayano and Jokati, 1983; Nielsen, 1983; Munch-Andersen and Nielsen, 1986, 1990). However, the mechanism which causes a flow to be affected by the filling process is not fully identified. In some cases, it is clearly a consequence of anisotropy in the solid caused by long particle packing arrangements (Nielsen, 1983), but in others (Zhong, Ooi and Rotter, 1996), it is evidently related to the packing density. Sometimes the sensitivity is acute, with a minor change in filling procedure causing a major change in flow pattern with a consequential dramatic change in the pressures exerted on the silo walls (Zhong, Ooi and Rotter, 1996).

Discrete element analyses have the potential to address this matter, but do not appear to have succeeded in demonstrating the causes yet. Finite element analyses appear to have the potential too, but the material characterization must include anisotropy, and some method must be developed to model the filling process itself, instead of taking the filled solid geometry and 'initial conditions' as given.

36.2.4 Complex force–displacement histories

The solid stored in a silo is subjected to a complex stress history after placement in the silo. An example might be given of a rectangular silo with flexible walls, where solid in the corners develops very high triaxial compressive stresses on filling, whilst that at the mid-side experiences low stresses and a well-developed active failure state (Lahlouh, Brown and Rotter, 1995). On discharge, the principal stresses change orientation radically, and the stress levels reduce sharply. As the solid passes to the outlet, the stress falls to close to zero and dramatic dilation occurs.

Most continuum models can follow simple stress histories, but are less successful with these more complex ones (Dunstan *et al.*, 1994). Discrete element models should be better at representing this behaviour.

36.3 GUARANTEED FLOW

The first practical problem which silo operators face is that of guaranteeing flow. The most elementary requirement is for flow rather than no flow, but certainty of a maximum attainable flow rate is also critically important in many industrial applications. This section is concerned only with avoiding no-flow conditions. Three separate cases are found.

36.3.1 Arching over the outlet

The simplest case is that of solid arching across the outlet of a silo. This can be caused by mechanical arching or by cohesive arching (Fig. 36.2).

Mechanical arching is well understood and generally avoided by very simple measures. As a result, computational models which endeavour to predict it appear to be of little practical interest, though some anecdotes suggest that solids containing small proportions of long fibres or strings may need study.

Cohesive arching is much more serious and more difficult to predict. Cohesive arching depends on the stress history of the solid before it reaches the outlet, and where the cohesion is developed partly as a consequence of moisture present in the solid, it may also depend on the moisture history. Chemical changes in a stored solid during storage can increase cohesion by adding chemical bonds. Vibrations can also cause consolidation and increase cohesion. Even without these additional complications, prediction of the stress history of a mass of solid near the outlet is not simple, as the difference between the filling and discharge stress states can be very great in this small area, and any small solids displacement may induce the reduced stresses associated with discharge. A plant may thus fortuitously operate successfully for a long period, but later have difficulties when the small displacements fail to occur for special reasons.

The modelling of cohesive arching is thus a considerable challenge. Discrete element models have little chance of success until they are able to reproduce the development of cohesion. Finite element continuum models have a better chance, but the reliable prediction of arching will depend very much on the ability to model the filling process, and this still presents considerable difficulties. Thus, neither of these models looks likely to make greatly improved predictions for cohesive arching in the near future.

36.3.2 Stable ratholes

The second reason for cessation of flow is the formation of a stable rathole. This is a narrow tall hole down the middle of the stored solid, caused by an initial internal narrow pipe flow which ceases when it is emptied. The natural sloughing of surface material into the pipe is arrested by cohesion in the solid. This is a serious and common industrial problem, depriving many storage facilities of effective volume and incurring additional costs if the solid is to be removed.

Discrete element modelling of ratholes presents the same difficulties as arching: a good cohesion model is needed. In addition, it should be noted that arching and ratholing are commonly but not always three-dimensional phenomena. This means that a satisfactory discrete element model must be three-dimensional, and correspondingly expensive. Continuum models offer a much better chance of addressing these problems.

36.3.3 Incomplete clean-out

Although much of the solid in a silo may discharge naturally by gravity, where the hopper is rather shallow the flow may be arrested when a stable natural slope develops on the surface of the solid. A casual observer might imagine that this will only occur where the hopper has a slope shallower than the angle of repose which can be observed in a free-standing heap, but this is not the case, again because of the stress-history dependence of the granular solid's response. Incomplete clean-out has been studied much less than arching and ratholing, but it remains a major problem in some industries. Again, continuum models have a much better chance of addressing these problems than discrete elements, but good stress-path-dependent constitutive models are needed to provide reliable predictions in advance of the problem occurring.

36.4 FLOW RATES, FLOW PATTERNS AND SEGREGATION

A solid which flows with certainty may still present materials handling problems. The flow rate through the outlet may be inadequate, the pattern of flowing solid may cause overstressing of the silo walls, or segregation may occur.

36.4.1 Flow rate

Most numerical and experimental studies of flow rate are concerned with solids falling freely from an unimpeded outlet. However, most silos do not operate in this manner, but have the flow from them regulated by a feeder, rotary valve, plough or similar device. Thus predictions of flow rate should be recognized as predictions of the maximum flow attainable for the given solid subject to the geometric and frictional constraints.

Discrete element models have been relatively successful at predicting free-fall flow rates (e.g. Langston, Heyes and Tüzün, 1995). This is probably attributable to the flow rate's minor dependence on particle size. Finite element attempts to predict flow rates are much rarer, as they are dominated by attempts to predict the first few instants of the discharge process, when the flow may be incompletely developed. No calculations are known which include the effect of a feeder on the pattern and magnitude of the flow, though this is a question of considerable industrial importance. Continuum models appear to be unlikely to succeed in solving this problem quickly, and discrete elements should have a better chance.

36.4.2 Flow patterns

The flow patterns in silos have been the focus of an enormous body of experimental, empirical, approximate theoretical and practical work for the last three decades. The flow pattern is critically important in determining the pressure distributions on the silo walls, the wear of the silo, the reliability of the flow, potential difficulties such as silo quaking, and many other phenomena.

The criteria by which mass flow (all the solid in the silo moving when the outlet is opened) may be distinguished from other flows were quite well established by Jenike (1961, 1964) and have been widely adopted since. These do not appear to have been reproduced by either finite element or discrete element calculations, despite the fact that they present a relatively simple challenge problem with a strong record of experimental background and practical interest. Both schools of computational modellers should attempt to reproduce the mass flow limits as evidence of their predictive capacity. Recent investigations by Drescher (1992) suggest that these bounds may prove a greater test than might have been supposed.

However, the principal difficulties arise when attempts are made to predict funnel flow channel boundaries. If the silo does not flow in mass flow, some material remains static and a boundary develops between a flowing core and the stationary solid. This boundary is important for several reasons. First, if the flow is entirely symmetric, the boundary may reach to the surface (Fig. 36.3) in an internal pipe flow. Where this happens, the pressures on the silo walls are relatively benign during discharge and much of the literature on silo wall pressures is not needed. If the flow is symmetric and the flow channel boundary intersects the wall, the zone where the intersection occurs experiences high and variable pressures (Fig. 36.3) which may cause serious problems. In most silos, even though the conditions appear to be symmetric, a small element of asymmetry in the flow creeps in, and this has consequences out of all proportion to its scale in a circular silo.

Where the outlet causes eccentric discharge, or where other factors (segregation or a feeder) make the flow systematically unsymmetrical in an otherwise symmetrical configuration (Fig. 36.4), very serious structural problems arise because of the high unsymmetrical pressures.

Current models of both the discrete element and finite element type should be able to address the question of the intersection of the flow channel

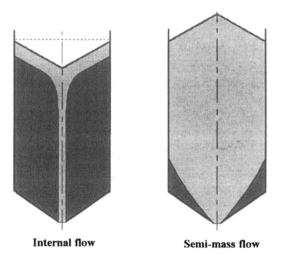

Internal flow **Semi-mass flow**

Fig. 36.3 Funnel flows: internal and semi-mass.

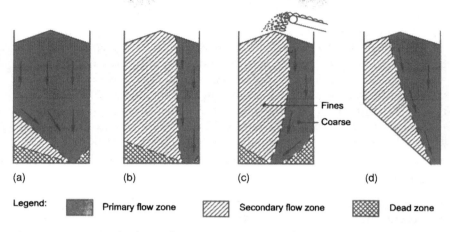

Fig. 36.4 Eccentric discharge flow patterns: (a) Mixed or semi-mass flow; (b) pipe flow; (c) segregation; (d) unsymmetrical hopper.

boundary with the silo wall. However, the finite element models appear to have difficulty in making accurate predictions for flow channel boundaries, and have not yet reproduced the sensitivity to filling procedure, described above. A study of the sensitivity of these predictions to constitutive model parameters would be most helpful, both in identifying key elements of the solid's behaviour which govern the flow channel geometry and in identifying the physical parameters which need careful measurement or control in practice if the boundary is to be reliably controlled.

Discrete element models generally have other difficulties. The images produced by discrete element models are qualitatively good, reproducing the general characteristics of flow patterns well. However, difficulties arise when the solid whose flow pattern is to be predicted in advance is identified. How does the flow in crushed granite differ from that in wheat? The experimentalists answer these questions with some assurance because the differences are very marked, but much work remains to be done to relate measurable characteristics of practical solids to the parameters used in discrete element models.

36.4.3 Segregation

Where the filling process permits segregation of the solids into particles of different sizes, the segregation may have a strong influence on the flow pattern (Fig. 36.4). The segregation itself may influence product quality, and the changed flow pattern may endanger the structure. The segregation process is thus worthy of study in its own right, as well as the effects of different degrees of segregation on the flow pattern.

594 *Challenges for the future in numerical simulation*

Such studies are quite difficult using finite element calculations, as the effects of changing particle size distributions on the constitutive model must be discovered experimentally, and this is likely to prove a long task. Discrete element models have a much better chance of modelling these phenomena, since they can, in principle, reproduce segregation behaviour, and the degree of segregation can be accurately defined in a mass of discrete particles. The resulting flow patterns can easily be related to the measures of segregation, without the need to identify the precise characteristics of the solid involved. This is therefore an excellent application for discrete element studies.

36.5 PRESSURES ON SILO WALLS

Silo structures must be designed to resist the worst loading conditions that may occur during their lives, and the difficulties of predicting these loads and designing structures to resist them have caused and continue to cause many serious problems in all countries in the world. The pressures on silo walls from stored solids can be classed into five simple groups: 'symmetrical' filling pressures, storing pressures, 'symmetrical' discharge pressures, eccentric filling pressures and eccentric discharge pressures.

36.5.1 Symmetrical filling pressures

The wall pressures arising from symmetrical filling are almost always taken as the reference pressures in considering any other pressure condition. They are therefore a very important starting point for all numerical simulations. The simplest pattern is that defined by Janssen's theory (1895), and it is possible to reproduce these pressures with very simple continuum analyses, provided that wall friction is modelled properly (Ooi and Rotter, 1990). Some finite element analyses have considerable difficulty in obtaining converged solutions for the stress state, especially adjacent to the boundaries, and this is a result of the algorithms used for wall friction, rather than a result of the chosen constitutive model.

Janssen's theory is clearly in error near the silo base and near the highest solids/wall contact. Even the simplest finite element analyses obtain much improved predictions in these locations, and these are valuable in the design of large squat silos, despite the disparaging remarks sometimes made in ignorance by academic researchers (Chapter 26).

Unfortunately discrete elements often have considerable difficulties in reproducing this simple filling pressure distribution. Since not all individual particles will have a wall contact in which the full particle–wall friction coefficient is developed, and none may exceed this limit, most discrete particle models using circular disc particles underestimate the wall friction phenomenon considerably. Unrealistically high individual particle frictional coefficients are required if the known experimental response is to be reproduced. This is again a difficulty in choosing appropriate parameter values for discrete elements in order to reproduce macroscopic experimental phenomena in solids with different particle shapes from those adopted in the computational model.

A major feature of real filling pressure distributions which is widely overlooked in predictions is the unsymmetrical pressures which arise under notionally symmetrical conditions. A silo which is quite symmetrically filled often develops significantly unsymmetrical pressures on filling (Hartlen *et al.*, 1984; Nielsen, 1983; Schmidt and Stiglat, 1987; Ooi, Rotter and Pham, 1990; Ooi and Rotter, 1991; Zhong, Ooi and Rotter, 1996). If only the mean pressure at any level is reported, these asymmetries are eliminated and the Janssen distribution is found, but the asymmetries are generally present. Experimentalists with limited instrumentation capacity have often assumed that the pressures are symmetric and adopted an instrumentation strategy which cannot detect asymmetry. However, these asymmetrical pressures are very important in structural design and their prediction presents challenges to both the discrete element and continuum analysts.

36.5.2 Storing pressures

Pressures during storage are usually thought of as identical to those at the end of filling. However, in experiments, it is often found that the pressures vary somewhat during a storing period following filling. Several phenomena are responsible: time settlement and consolidation, slip–stick phenomena against the wall and thermal or hygral changes. Of these, the thermal and moisture content changes are probably the most important. Both thermal changes and increasing moisture contents have been responsible for serious silo failures (Andersen, 1966; Rotter, 1983), and a number of experimental studies have been conducted. However, quality predictions of the mechanics of these increased pressures are rare.

36.5.3 Discharge pressures

Most of the effort in predicting discharge flow pressures using finite elements has been put into the case of mass flow, where all the solid is in motion. This case is the simplest, and reasonable qualitative predictions may now be made by a number of different programs for somewhat idealized conditions.

It is commonly held that the pressures which occur during discharge are always larger than those after filling. From an experimentalist's viewpoint, this is not true, and the increase in pressure from filling to discharge is sensitive to the point on the silo wall which is being considered. In many experiments, it can be shown that any increase in pressure in one location is counterbalanced by a decrease elsewhere. Structural design considerations suggest that the peak pressures are often not particularly important, but the difference between the highest and lowest pressures and their separation are critical. Where these high and low pressures are at the same level, the resulting non-symmetric pressures are very important to the design.

Most finite element models of discharge assume symmetry in the conditions. The analysis may attempt to model the dynamics of the solids flow (Eibl *et al.*, 1982; Eibl and Rombach, 1987; Häußler and Eibl, 1984; Ruckenbrod and Eibl, 1993), or may make assumptions about the flow pattern and adopt a quasi-static analysis to determine pressures. Where the conditions are truly symmetric (Fig. 36.5), these analyses successfully predict the early stages of flow and the high pressures associated with a hopper/ cylinder transition zone. The best time-domain analyses have difficulty following more than the first second of discharge of a large silo (Rombach, 1991), though this may be adequate to capture the key moments for the structural design.

The discrete element models are well suited to capture the dynamics of the problem, and are not restricted to an early part of the discharge. However, the problems described above in the context of filling pressure predictions are not overcome. While these analyses can make good predictions of flow patterns in the solid for an idealized solid, it is extremely difficult to relate the properties of the particles to those of a real solid. In particular, the challenge of deducing the properties which should be chosen for discrete elements to represent a known solid (e.g. plastic pellets or coal) remains a serious stumbling block to quantitative predictions.

The unsymmetrical conditions more commonly seen in experiments (Fig. 36.5) do not appear to have been predicted by finite elements to date,

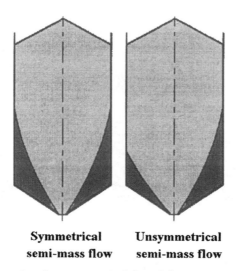

Symmetrical   **Unsymmetrical**
semi-mass flow   semi-mass flow

Fig. 36.5 Symmetrical and unsymmetrical funnel flow patterns.

leaving the experimenters speculating on the attributable causes: rupture planes developing in the solid, anisotropy of the solid's properties, segregation, non-uniform wall friction, geometric imperfections in the wall, etc. Discrete element analyses find different pressures on different walls, but this is caused by random packing differences which are not reproduced from one calculation to another: the experimental phenomena are often systematically repeatable (Ooi, Rotter and Pham, 1990) and require a different explanation. Many more studies of these effects are urgently needed.

It is now well established that there are significant scale effects in silo experiments (Nielsen and Askegaard, 1977; Nielsen and Kristiansen, 1980; Munch-Andersen and Nielsen, 1986; Munch-Andersen, 1986). Observations at full scale often do not match those of a good model, for a variety of reasons, some associated with particular solids and others with particular flow patterns. Thus, the results of laboratory model tests must be used with considerable caution. The capacity of numerical models to reproduce these scale effects in free-flowing solids and to show that full scale silos should differ from models does not appear to have been properly tested yet, but available indications (Rotter *et al.*, 1996) suggest that this is another challenge to be addressed.

The above discussion has suggested that there are 'discharge pressures' which need to be predicted: actually the pressure pattern on the silo wall varies in time and space continuously, and is difficult to describe in a simple summarized manner. The worst set of pressures from a structural design viewpoint is not easily identified, and analyses are really needed which can present many sets of possible pressure patterns changing in time, so that studies of the sensitivity of the structure to different alternatives can be identified. This is a problem which will take many years to solve.

36.5.4 Eccentric filling

In squat silos (height to diameter ratio less than perhaps 1), any asymmetry in the filling process can lead to very large differences in wall pressures from one side of the silo to another. Very few studies have examined the pressures which arise, and the only known studies use simple theories rather than quality mechanics (Bervig, Wiley and Sutton, 1977; Rotter, 1983), together with experiments which have shown the structural failure mechanisms (Eccleston, 1987). Both finite element and discrete element analyses could usefully be applied to identify simplifications with a more rigorous basis.

36.5.5 Eccentric discharge

Eccentric discharge is sometimes adopted intentionally for the purpose of simplifying or extending the materials handling system. At other times it arises accidentally as a result of segregation, malfunction of handling equipment or asymmetries of geometry or wall friction. Whatever the cause, it is the commonest source of disastrous and expensive failures in silos, and deserves much more study than has been undertaken to date.

Mass flow silos are not normally affected by eccentric discharge, but malfunctioning of the handling system can easily induce eccentric ratholing flow in a silo which otherwise meets all the mass flow criteria.

Recent finite element studies of the problem have made enormous progress (Rombach, 1991), identifying the stages of development of the characteristic pressure patterns and probably covering the critical times during flow channel development where the most serious pressures occur. However, this work has only studied a few example problems, so generalization to other materials and geometries is not easy. The key material properties which control the flow channel shape must be identified, the manner in which this shape affects the pressure distribution (e.g. Rotter, 1986a), the form of the pressure distribution (Rotter *et al.*, 1995) and the most critical instant for design all need clarification.

Discrete element analyses have the potential to provide a better understanding of the mechanisms leading to eccentric discharge development: segregation, inhomogeneities arising from filling trajectories, etc. These are matters to which finite element analyses are unsuited.

36.5.6 Needs

The aim of these studies of wall pressures is the structural reliability of the silo. Their final goal should therefore be the development of excellent rules for standards, which combine quality mechanics with simplicity and lead to safe and economic structures.

The European standard for silo pressures (EC1 Part 4, 1992) is currently in its draft ENV form and must be transformed into a true European Norm EN within the next couple of years. Its provisions are very limited compared with many other standards (Wilms, 1990), and much work is needed to improve our current understanding of silo pressures. Other standards committees (e.g. ACI-313, 1989) have had very long drawn out debates about the manner in which silo pressures should be defined, principally because there is insufficient evidence to determine how widespread is the liability to unforeseen eccentric discharge after several years of successful service. Numerical models have the potential to answer these questions by identifying the key features of the mechanics of filling and flow which govern the pressure distributions.

Existing rules in standards are derived from empirical interpretations and fits to experiments, coupled with traditional simplified continuum mechanics treatments. Numerical models have, to date, effectively had no impact on the standards development, placing this field at odds with most other structural engineering activities.

36.6 STRUCTURAL FAILURES AND SOLIDS INTERACTION

Structural failures in silos are relatively common, with a higher incidence than most other forms of construction. The types of failure are varied, and only some relate to pressures from bulk solids. In general, where bulk solids are implicated, the design usually has shortcomings associated with misunderstandings of bulk solids pressure, misunderstandings of structural response, and inadequate assessments of structural resistance (Fig. 36.1). These misunderstandings are principally caused by the current incapacity to predict the phenomena well.

The simple conceptual model which is commonly adopted is that of an infinitely deformable bulk solid applying pressures to a rigid container. However, the work on pressure cells and wall imperfections indicates that the pressures are themselves very sensitive to local deformations of the wall, and the silo structures are often far from rigid. As a result, interactions occur between the solid and the structure. The real required structural strength can only be found by including these interactions in the assessment of bulk solids pressures and the response of the structure. For this purpose, numerical simulations of solids flow and pressures need to be coupled to structural analyses. Key items of this type are defined here.

36.6.1 Cylindrical walls

Concrete silo walls often suffer cracking due to circumferential bending. This is caused by high and low differential pressures at a single level in the silo and is covered by the standards using the 'patch load' concept. However, the pressures reduce where the silo deforms, and the stiffness of the silo may significantly affect the pressure patterns. Because concrete silos are typically rather stiff, this is a lesser effect, but it does appear to have influenced the pressures observed in the Karpalund silo (Hartlen *et al.*, 1984).

Metal silos are much more deformable than concrete silos, so a really high pressure may be relieved by the deformation of the silo. However, it appears that high pressures arising from different causes can be either sustained during wall deformation or dissipated by wall deformation. In turn this idea, derived chiefly from experimental studies, gives rise to the idea of 'stiff' and 'flexible' patches of pressure: the former can be dissipated and is similar to imposed deformations, the latter is governed chiefly by equilibrium and independent of the silo deformation. Much work is needed to identify the conditions under which each arises.

The commonest failure mode for cylindrical steel silos is by buckling under axial compression (Rotter, 1985, 1993). The strength is reduced by geometric imperfections in the wall, but increased again by internal pressure from the granular solid (Rotter, 1985). The stiffness of the solid has a considerable additional strengthening effect, which has been explored in a number of studies (Rotter, Trahair and Ansourian, 1980; Trahair et al, 1983; Rotter and Zhang, 1990; Knödel and Schulz, 1992). However, the most difficult part of this assessment is to determine the appropriate stiffness of bulk solid which can be relied upon.

Where experiments are conducted on the buckling of cylinders under bulk solids loading (Jumikis, 1987; Rotter *et al.*, 1989; Fitz-Henry, 1986), when a buckle forms in the silo wall, the loading is often redistributed back into the solid, so that the silo failure may be severe, but does not lead to total destruction of the silo. Evidence that this is common in practice is clear from the many available images of buckled silos which are still standing. Sometimes the redistribution leads to a local 'elephant's foot' failure at the silo base (Rotter, 1990) if the internal pressure in the granular solid is large enough to prevent a buckling failure. However, one feature of modern safety assessments is the need to distinguish between 'benign' and 'catastrophic' failures: numerical models for the post-buckling response of a shell wall containing bulk solid with finite stiffness are needed.

Where eccentric discharge occurs in a funnel flow pattern against the silo wall, the low pressures in the channel and high pressures at the edge of the channel deform the wall into a non-circular shape (Rotter, 1987; Rotter *et al.*, 1989). This deformation is certainly resisted by the remaining stationary solid in the rest of the silo, but determining the extent of this effect is very difficult. It was formally introduced as part of the alternate design procedure of ACI-313 (1989), but needs much numerical verification.

36.6.2 Hoppers

The structural failure of conical hoppers has not been studied very much, though there have been many studies of the pressures on hopper walls. It is clear from the existing studies (e.g. Teng and Rotter, 1989, 1991, 1993) that large deformations of the hopper may precede collapse. Where the hopper is part of a funnel flow silo, it may be that considerable strength gains arise from pressure redistribution before total collapse. This problem does not appear to have ever been studied.

The deformations of a hopper before collapse may also give rise to changes in the flow pattern, so interactions between the solid and structure may either ameliorate or exacerbate the failure.

36.6.3 Needs: Eurocode on silo structures

The new Eurocode 3 Part 4.1 (EC3 Part 4.1, 1996) for the design of steel silos is likely to be the first large standard in the world dealing with the many and varied problems of structural design of steel silos. Many structural problems have no satisfactory researched solution, and current practice often has weak foundations in approximate mechanics of improbable validity. Some of the problems which need to be addressed relate to finite element and discrete element modelling of the solid.

The most important effect which is worth codifying is the strengthening effect of stored solids on the buckling of cylindrical walls. This effect has been studied for more than two decades, and is exploited in many designs. Good numerical modelling is urgently needed to relate measurable simple bulk solid properties to the stiffness offered to resist buckling failures.

REFERENCES

ACI-313 (1989) Alternate design procedure, Discussion document before ACI Committee 313 on Concrete Bins, Silos and Bunkers for Storing Granular Materials, ACI, Detroit.

Andersen, P.F. (1966) Temperature stresses in steel grain storage tanks, *Civil Engineering, ASCE*, 36(1), 74–76.

Bervig, D.; Wiley, A.; and Sutton, T. (1977) *Influence of Static and Dynamic Asymmetric Loading Conditions on Silo Design*, American Society of Mechanical Engineers, Paper No. 77-Det-145, Sept. 1977, 8 pp.

Drescher, A. (1992) On the criteria for mass flow in hoppers, *Powder Technology*, 73, 251–260.

Dunstan, T., Jamebozorgi, M. and Akbarian-Miandouab, S. (1994) Powder strength after changes in principal stress direction, *Powder Technology*, 81, 31–40.

EC1 Part 4 (1992) *Eurocode 1: Basis of Design and Actions on Structures Part 4: Actions on Silos and Tanks*, ENV 1991-4, CEN, Brussels.

EC3 Part 4.1 (1996) *Eurocode 3: Design of Steel Structures: Silos*, ENV 1993-4-1, committee working drafts, CEN, Brussels.

Eccleston, P.A. (1987) The buckling of squat silos after eccentric filling, BE Thesis, Department of Civil Engineering, University of Sydney, Australia.

Eibl, J.; Landahl, H.; Haußler, U. and Gladen, W. (1982) Zur Frage des Silodrucks, *Beton und Stahlbetonbau*, 77(4), Apr., 104–110.

Eibl, J. and Rombach, G. (1987) *Stress and Velocity Fields at Discharging of Silos*, NUMETA, Swansea.

Fitz-Henry, J.O.D. (1986) Buckling failure of eccentrically discharged silos, BE Thesis (Hons), University of Sydney.

Hartlen, J.; Nielsen, J.; Ljunggren, L.; Martensson, G. and Wigram, S. (1984) *The Wall Pressure in Large Grain Silos*, Swedish Council for Building Research, Stockholm, Document D2:1984.

Häussler, U. and Eibl, J. (1984) Numerical investigations on discharging silos, *Jnl Eng. Mech. Divn, ASCE*, 110, (EM6), June, 957–971.

Janssen, H.A. (1895) Versuche über Getreidedruck in Silozellen, *Zeitschrift des Vereines Deutscher Ingenieure*, 39(35), 1045–1049.

Jenike, A.W. (1961) *Gravity Flow of Bulk Solids*, Bulletin of the University of Utah, 52 (29), Bulletin No. 108 of the Utah Engineering Experiment Station, October, Salt Lake City, Utah, 309 pp.

Jenike, A.W. (1964) *Storage and Flow of Solids*, Bulletin of the University of Utah, 53(26) Bulletin No. 123 of the Utah Engineering Experiment Station, November, Salt Lake City, Utah, 197 pp. (Revised Nov. 1976).

Jumikis, P.T. (1987) Stability problems in silo structures, PhD Thesis, University of Sydney.

Knödel, P. and Schulz, U. (1992) Buckling of cylindrical bins – recent results, *Proc., International Conference: 'Silos – Forschung und Praxis'*, University of Karlsruhe, October, pp. 75–82.

Lahlouh, E.H.; Brown, C.J. and Rotter, J.M. (1995) *Loads in Rectangular Planform Steel Silos*, Research report R95-027, Department of Civil and Environmental Engineering, University of Edinburgh, Nov., 170 pp.

Langston, P.A.; Heyes, D.M. and Tuzun, U. (1995) Discrete element simulation of granular solid flow in hoppers: discharge rate and wall stress predictions in 2 & 3 dimensions, *Proc. Partec 95, 3rd European Symposium on the Storage and Flow of Particulate Solids*, Nurnberg, pp. 357–366.

Moriyama, R.; Hayano, N. and Jokati, T. (1983) The effect of filling method on the flow pattern in a bin, *Proc., Second International Conference on the Design of Silos for Strength and Flow*, Stratford-upon-Avon, Powder Advisory Centre, Sept., pp. 317–331.

Munch-Andersen, J. (1986) The boundary layer in rough silos, *Proc. Second Int. Conf. on Bulk Materials Storage, Handling and Transportation*, Instn Engrs, Aust., Wollongong, July, pp. 160–163.

Munch-Andersen, J. and Nielsen, J. (1986) Size effects in large grain silos, *Bulk Solids Handling*, 6, 885–889.

Munch-Andersen, J. and Nielsen, J. (1990) Pressures in slender grain silos, *CHISA 1990, Second European Symposium on Stress and Strain in Particulate Solids*, Prague, 26–31 August, 9 pp.

Nielsen, J. (1983) Load distribution in silos influenced by anisotropic grain behaviour, *Proc., Int. Conf. on Bulk Materials Storage, Handling and Transportation*, I.E. Aust., Newcastle, August, pp. 226–30.

Nielsen, J. and Andersen, E.Y. (1982). Loads in grain silos. *Bygningsstatiske Meddelelser*, 53(4), 123–135.

Nielsen, J. and Askegaard, V. (1977) Scale errors in model tests on granular media with special reference to silo models, *Powder Technology*, No. 1.

Nielsen, J. and Kristiansen, N.O. (1980). Related measurements of pressure conditions in full scale barley silo and in model silo. *Proc., Int. Conf. on Design of Silos for Strength and Flow*, Univ. of Lancaster, Sep.

Ooi, J.Y. and Rotter, J.M. (1990) Wall pressures in squat steel silos from finite element analysis, *Computers and Structures*, 37(4), 361–374.

Ooi, J.Y. and Rotter, J.M. (1991) Measured pressures in full scale silos: a new understanding, *Proc., International Conference: Bulk Materials – Towards the Year 2000*, Institution of Mechanical Engineers, 29–31 October, London, pp. 195–200.

Ooi, J.Y.; Rotter, J.M. and Pham, L. (1990) Systematic and random features of measured pressures on full-scale silo walls, *Engineering Structures*, 12(2), April, 74–87.

Rombach, G.A. (1991) Schuttguteinwirkungen auf Silozellen – Exzentrische Entleerung, Dr-Ing dissertation, University of Karlsruhe, Feb., 291 pp.

Rotter, J.M. (1983) Structural effects of eccentric loading in shallow steel bins, *Proceedings, Second International Conference on the Design of Silos for Strength and Flow*, Stratford-upon-Avon, Nov., pp. 446–463.

Rotter, J.M. (1985) Buckling of ground-supported cylindrical steel bins under

vertical compressive wall loads, *Proc., Metal Structures Conf.*, Instn Engrs Aust., Melbourne, May, pp. 112–127.
Rotter, J.M. (1986a) The analysis of steel bins subject to eccentric discharge, *Proc., Second International Conference on Bulk Materials Storage, Handling and Transportation*, Institution of Engineers, Australia, Wollongong, July, pp. 264–271.
Rotter, J.M. (1986b) Recent advances in the structural design of steel bins and silos, *Pacific Steel Structures Conference*, Auckland, Aug., Vol. 4, pp. 177–194.
Rotter, J.M. (1987) Bending theory of shells for bins and silos, *Transactions of Mechanical Engineering*, Institution of Engineers, Australia, ME12(3) Sept., 147–159.
Rotter, J.M. (1990) Local inelastic collapse of pressurised thin cylindrical steel shells under axial compression, *Journal of Structural Engineering*, ASCE, 116(7), July, pp. 1955–1970.
Rotter, J.M. (1993) The design of circular metal silos for strength, *Proc., International Symposium: Reliable Flow of Particulate Solids II*, EFChE Publication Series No. 96, Oslo, 23–24 August, pp. 217–234.
Rotter, J.M. (1996a) Shell structures: design standards, recent progress and unsolved problems, Invited plenary paper, *Proc., International Conference on Structural Steelwork*, Hong Kong, Dec., 20 pp.
Rotter, J.M. (1996b) Patch load effects in unstiffened steel silos, *Proc. CA-Silo Project on the Effect of Patch Loads on Metal Silos*, Edited by J.M. Rotter, CA-Silo, Edinburgh, pp. 5–195.
Rotter, J.M.; Jumikis, P.T.; Fleming, S.P. and Porter, S.J. (1989) Experiments on the buckling of thin-walled model silo structures, *Journal of Constructional Steel Research*, 13(4), 271–299.
Rotter, J.M.; Ooi, J.Y.; Chen, J.F.; Tiley, P.J.; Mackintosh, I. and Bennett, F.R. (1995) *Flow Pattern Measurement in Full Scale Silos*, British Materials Handling Board, Ascot, UK, 230 pp.
Rotter, J.M.; Pham, L. and Nielsen, J. (1986) On the specification of loads for the structural design of bins and silos, *Proc., Second International Conference on Bulk Materials Storage, Handling and Transportation*, Institution of Engineers, Australia, Wollongong, July, pp. 241–247.
Rotter, J.M.; Trahair, N.S. and Ansourian, P. (1980) Stability of Plate Structures, *Proc., Symposium on Steel Bins for the Storage of Bulk Solids*, Australian Institute of Steel Construction/Australian Welding Research Association Joint Symposium, Sydney and Melbourne, Sept., pp 36–40.
Rotter, J.M. and Zhang, Q. (1990) Elastic buckling of imperfect cylinders containing granular solids, *Journal of Structural Engineering*, ASCE, 116(8), Aug., pp. 2253–2271.
Ruckenbrod, C. and Eibl, J. (1993) Numerical results to discharge processes in silos, *Proc., International Symposium: Reliable Flow of Particulate Solids II*, EFChE Publication Series No. 96, Oslo, 23–24 Aug., pp. 503–516.
Schmidt, K.H. and Stiglat, K. (1987) Anmerkungen zur Bemessungslast von Silos, *Beton und Stahlbetonbau*, 9, 239–242.
Sugden, M.B. (1980) Effect of initial density on flow patterns in circular flat bottomed silos, *Proc., Int. Conf. on Design of Silos for Strength and Flow*, University of Lancaster, Sept., pp. 11–28.
Teng, J.G. and Rotter, J.M. (1989) The strength of silo transition rings and hoppers,

Transactions of Mechanical Engineering, Institution of Engineers, Australia, **ME14**(3), 170–177.

Teng, J.G. and Rotter, J.M. (1991) The strength of welded steel silo hoppers under filling and flow pressures, *Journal of Structural Engineering*, ASCE, **117**(9), 2567–2583.

Teng, J.G. and Rotter, J.M. (1993) Structural consequences of filling and flow pressures in steel hoppers, *Transactions of Mechanical Engineering*, Special Edition on Bulk Materials Handling, Institution of Engineers, Australia, **ME18**(1), March, pp. 75–89.

Trahair, N.S.; Ansourian, P. and Rotter, J.M. (1983) Stability Problems in Axisymmetric Steel Silos, *Proc., Second International Conference on the Design of Silos for Strength and Flow*, Stratford upon Avon, Nov., pp 434–445.

Wilms, H. (1990) Criteria for evaluation of silo design codes, *Proc., 2nd European Symposium on the Stress and Strain Behaviour of Particulate Solids – Silo Stresses*, Prague, Aug., 12 pp.

Zhong, Z.; Ooi, J.Y. and Rotter, J.M. (1996) The sensitivity of silo flow and wall pressures to filling method, *Proc., 12th International Congress of Chemical and Process Engineering, CHISA '96*, Prague, Aug., 10 pp.

37

Concluding comments
J. Martinez

By presenting a large set of examples of the work carried out in different research institutions, this Part has illustrated the abundance and the diversity of European activity in the field of numerical simulation of silo problems. The contributions show how numerical simulation addresses different complex phenomena occurring in silos and that it is undoubtedly a helpful tool for their understanding.

In terms of research goals, the presentations cover a large variety of problems such as flow, pressures and dynamic loading. The various approaches developed expand from microscopic to macroscopic observation scale, including stochastic variations of input parameters. The calculation methods and the corresponding numerical programs can vary from quite sophisticated and general research codes to simpler and more restrictive tools focusing on particular design problems.

This diversity is proof of the vitality of research in silo modelling and at the same time, it may be misinterpreted as a lack of coordination between European research institutions. The CA-Silo project has undoubtedly contributed to improving this coordination by giving research people the opportunity of knowing each other's work better and by giving rise to several collaborative research projects.

In spite of this research vitality, there remain open several difficult problems for which close collaborative research would be fruitful, providing a precise definition of the problems and the methods from the beginning. Another priority is to continue and enlarge the evaluation and validation of different codes by comparing the results with experimental data from well-documented full-scale tests.

Finally, it is well known that by nature research activity needs some space and freedom to allow expression of the investigator's imagination which is particularly true in the area of modelling and simulation. However, as research on silos is in direct relation to economic preoccupations and industrial applications, great effort must be made to transfer research results to current design. Moreover, the importance of informing and involving industrialists in the elaboration and the evaluation of the research programmes must be emphasized.

Part Five

Silo Tests

38

Introduction and scope
H. Stoffers

'Silo tests' represent silo experiments carried out at model or full scale. Silo tests seem a natural approach, as flow and pressures from particulate materials, and the effect of the action on the silo structure, are strongly interrelated. Since Janssen applied his tests on wooden model scale silos in 1895 numerous silo tests have been carried out, and several others will follow because the behaviour of stored materials is very complex and not yet understood. No theoretical models have been developed which give a completely reliable description of the behaviour of particulate materials in silos. Silo tests are therefore in many cases the most effective way of improving knowledge on silos and the materials stored inside.

As the behaviour of stored materials depends on both the properties of the material itself and on the properties of the silo structure, careful attention to these influencing factors is a necessity when applying and reporting silo tests. Reports of silo tests very often only provide information with respect to the main activities in the tests; this limits their contribution to the improvement of knowledge. Often this situation is related to the two main fields of interest in silo research, i.e. flow behaviour of the solid and the structural consequences of wall pressures. Flow experts therefore report extensively on properties and behaviour of the solid while civil engineers are more interested in the silo structure in which the tests have been applied. In the same way civil engineers report in detail on the silo structure while they often only mention the name of the solid which was stored in the silo.

When it is decided that experiments should be carried out in a test silo the choice of the kind of test silo is still open. Which silo is most suited depends on the objectives of the study (study of flow mechanism, determination of wall pressures, test of devices). Tests in full-scale (industrial) silos have the advantage that no scale factors influence the test results. However, full-scale tests are usually very expensive and the properties of the test silo cannot easily be changed when one is interested in the influence of such changes on the test results. Several institutions and laboratories have test silos on model scale which are provided with a set of instrumentation. These are the facilities that are mostly used in the field of silo research. However, as for example with the flow behaviour of stored materials dependent on gravity forces, scale factors have to be used for the translation of results on scale models to full-scale results. Tests on model-scale silos placed in a centrifuge offer another possibility, but with other scale errors.

Evaluation of the results from silo tests requires sufficient information on the properties of the test silo and on the material stored in the test silo. Regarding the test silo it is clear that information on the shape, dimensions and the number, dimensions and positions of inlets and outlets must be available. However information should also be provided for example on imperfections and the structural integrity (buckling, cracks). Samples of the stored material must be taken in the right way and at the right time, and storage of the samples and tests on them have to be done in such a way that broad acceptance of the results is assured.

Measuring equipment used in silo tests can influence the results of the tests in a decisive way. Sensitivity and range of measuring devices must be in accordance with the level of the signals that will be measured. It may be a problem that an integral part of the tests concerns the range of the signal of the phenomena studied.

It is clear that the measuring devices should be calibrated before using them in a test. However, what is the best test procedure for the calibration? When wall pressures are to be measured it also has to be decided in which positions on the wall the devices should be placed. This requires knowledge of the type of flow that will happen in the silo and the relation between this flow and the wall pressures.

Results of silo tests are always influenced by the test conditions. Several of them are introduced as part of the objectives of the tests, while others appear spontaneously. In this respect temperature of the stored material, air temperature and air humidity are relevant. It is important to report on all test conditions, as comparison with other tests might be difficult or even meaningless if some of the test conditions are unknown. Further, interruptions during the tests caused for instance by defects in the measuring equipment or by other sources should be reported.

Today's modern data acquisition technology permits enormous quantities of readings to be taken during the tests. This can cause practical problems as data files become too big to be handled by computer hardware or software. Such situations should be prevented by sampling methods carefully chosen in advance. Continuously recorded signals can be processed later. However, it is important to be informed constantly during the tests about magnitude and variation in these signals. They can justify

Introduction and scope 611

additional readings or even changes in the measuring approach. Before the measurements even start it should be clear what kind of results are expected from the measurements. This provides a basis for examining data coming in during the tests and to conclude whether unexpected occurrences are happening. If the phenomena studied show a random behaviour then the collected data have to be processed to find out the statistical characteristics of their behaviour. Spectral analysis of signals is a helpful tool to find probability density functions and correlations between phenomena occurring at different places. Again it is important to report in detail what processing methods have been used.

This Part provides further detailed information on some of the matters introduced above.

39

Classification of silo tests
J. Garnier

39.1 INTRODUCTION

Several reasons explain the considerable difficulties encountered in the theoretical study of the behaviour of materials stored in silos, during both filling and discharge. First of all, the rheology of ensiled materials is very complex, very poorly understood, and affected by many parameters. For example, the response of a granular material to a given loading depends on the intensity of the applied stresses, their orientation and direction, the rate of loading, and even the stress history. It also varies with the density of the material and with the arrangement of the particles. In addition, the strains are very often concentrated in narrow shear bands, which are difficult to model. Again, the problem of silos is most often three-dimensional, which makes the numerical calculations longer and more difficult. Finally, inertial phenomena cannot be neglected because of the relatively high displacement speeds that can occur in silos.

The experimental programmes must be conceived in terms of precise objectives, defined in advance, that may be quite varied (study of flow mechanisms, determination of pressures, tests of devices or equipment, response to an earthquake). Furthermore, different experimental approaches can be considered, each having advantages and limitations that must be taken into account (observation of actual silos in operation, test station, pilot-scale models, small-scale models – centrifuged or not).

A double classification of the problems and methods is therefore necessary to determine the approaches best suited to the problem at hand, before the conditions under which these experiments should be performed are examined.

39.2 CLASSIFICATION OF THE VARIOUS TYPES OF STUDIES

The classification proposed here of the various experimental investigations is based on an examination of their objectives. It is limited to application on pre-standardization research works.

39.2.1 Type 1: Tests of equipment

This category contains tests of equipment, technical devices, and constructive arrangements (examples: effectiveness of vibrators, comparison of different extraction screws). The results are used directly by the designers and the builders of silos to improve the equipment.

39.2.2 Type 2: Determination of pressures

The basic objective of these tests is to determine the forces exerted on the walls and bottom of the silo during filling and discharge. These data can be undertaken for:

- direct study of pressure distributions
- the development of design methods
- the validation of theoretical models

Two methods are available for the determination of the forces:

1. Local direct measurement of the normal and tangential stresses applied by the ensiled material, using total pressure cells. These measurements are rather difficult and the cells must satisfy very strict conditions (see Part Six on experimental techniques).
    Because of the asymmetry of the pressures, the number of measurement points must also be sufficient to allow determination of the distribution over the whole wall.
2. Measurement of the strains and therefore of the forces in the walls by strain gauge. Two main problems can be encountered:
    (a) effects of temperature variations and gradients that can induce strains of the same order of magnitude as those due to the internal pressures;
    (b) problems in deriving the pressures acting on the structures from the measured strains (since this reverse problem has an infinite number of solutions, see Chapter 45).

39.2.3 Type 3: Study of flow mechanisms

This category includes experiments performed to study flow mechanisms and the conditions of formation of stable arches, and to determine paths and velocity fields. The studies often concern the effects of the various parameters controlling the flows (shape, height and diameter of silo, roughness of walls, dimensions and position of outlets, presence of a hopper, type of ensiled materials).

39.2.4 Type 4: Response to exceptional stresses (earthquake, explosion)

Silos must sometimes withstand exceptional stresses, for which they must be designed accordingly. In particular, research must be done on their response to these stresses, notably earthquakes and explosions.

Two special features set silos apart from other civil engineering structures.

- Their earthquake behaviour is substantially different, because of their large masses and the presence of granular materials, themselves sensitive to seismic stresses.
- Under some conditions and with some ensiled materials, there are risks of spontaneous explosions, the effects of which must be taken into account in the design of the silos.

39.2.5 Type 5: Structural failure

Silo tests may be undertaken to determine failure loads or buckling conditions.

39.3 CLASSIFICATION OF TEST SILOS

Different classes of test silos, with very different characteristics and domains of application, can be distinguished.

39.3.1 Class A: Industrial silos in operation

It is sometimes possible to make observations on actual silos in operation. These observations and measurements constitute an unchallengeable reference, because they are made on full-scale structures in which actual materials are stored.

This approach, however, has many limitations. The actual structures are often complex (geometry, component material, adjacent cells) and modelling them is difficult. The boundary conditions and the state of the ensiled material (distribution of densities, anisotropy) are not well known.

It is, in addition, almost impossible to control the experimental conditions, because the silo is in operation (the filling and discharge sequences cannot be freely chosen). Parametric studies are impossible because practically all of the test conditions are frozen.

Finally, these actual silos in operation can often only be partially instrumented, making interpretation of the results more difficult.

39.3.2 Class B: Experimental station, full-scale silos

Full-scale test stations exist for the study of silos and hoppers. They are most often installed in technical centres (silos of the CTICM's Chartres experimental base) or in research laboratories (silos of the universities of Kaiserslautern and of Karlsruhe, hoppers at LCPC Nantes).

A list of silo test facilities is given in Chapter 53. These test stations are designed for research work and have the following benefits and advantages:

- reference tests on full-scale structures containing actual materials may exist;
- complete instrumentation possible;
- complete control of experimental conditions.

The limitations are concerned with the high cost of designing and building the test station rather than the costs of the tests themselves. As in class A above, the experiments are performed on actual structures that are so relatively complex that analysis of their behaviour is often difficult (geometrical imperfections, for example, may have large effects on pressure distributions).

It is, furthermore, difficult to vary some parameters, in particular those that concern the geometry of the silo (shape, height, diameter), the mechanical characteristics of the walls (rigidity, roughness), the presence of a hopper.

Finally, visualization and study of the flows during the emptying operations is difficult.

39.3.3 Class C: Pilot-scale models

Pilot-scale models of silos are often used because they have many advantages (cf. the list of such installations in Chapter 53).

It is, however, essential to clearly define the limit between pilot-scale models and small-scale models (class D). The definition involves analysis of the similarity conditions for the phenomena to be studied.

In most physical phenomena and systems, a change of the dimensions (or of the scale) of the structures leads to a difference of behaviour, known as a 'size effect' or 'scale effect' (Galilei, 1638). The smaller the scale, the larger these effects; they disappear when the scale is close to unity.

Therefore, there exists a scale above which it may be assumed that size effects are negligible, i.e. that the behaviour of the model will be identical to that of the full-scale structure (qualitatively and quantitatively).

The following denominations are therefore proposed:

- *Pilot-scale models (class C)*, in which size effects are negligible; the results of tests on these models can be applied directly to full-scale structures;

- *Laboratory small-scale models (class D)*, in which the scale is too small; size effects modify the response of the model and make it impossible to transpose the results directly to actual structures.

Theoretical and experimental study of similarity conditions, and in particular of scale effects, is therefore capital, because it is the only way to know whether the results obtained can be applied to actual structures (Munch-Andersen and Nielsen, 1986, and Part Six).

When the similarity conditions are satisfied (class D models), tests on models have the same advantages as tests on actual silos in experimental stations (the results can be transposed to full-scale structures, thorough instrumentation, control of experimental conditions). They have, in addition, with respect to tests in a test station, the following advantages, which extend their domain of application:

- lower cost of installations and of tests;
- parameters easier to change;
- models of specially designed silos (simpler structures, easier to model, built-in instrumentation).

39.3.4 Class D: Laboratory small-scale models

These silo models are widely used because they cost very little. They make it possible to multiply the number of tests and easily vary all parameters likely to influence the response of the silo.

They may, however, lead to a very severe problem of interpretation. The similarity conditions are often not satisfied, because the mass forces and therefore the stresses due to the self-weight of the ensiled material are much smaller than in actual silos.

It is well known, for example, that the behaviour of cereals and of granular materials generally is highly dependent on the level of stresses to which they are subjected. The response of the small-scale laboratory model may therefore be, quantitatively and even qualitatively, very different from that of the corresponding full-scale silo.

The same material at the same density may prove to be dilatant (increase in volume) if loaded at low mean stress, and contractant (reduction of volume) otherwise. This difference can have an effect on the flow modes.

Furthermore, the ensiled materials are often slightly cohesive. In a full-scale silo (classes A and B) or pilot-scale silo (class C), or in a centrifuged model (class E), the effect of cohesion is small with respect to the friction forces, which then almost completely govern the pressure on the walls. In a small-scale laboratory model (class D), this is no longer the case, and the pressure, during both filling and discharge, will depend as much or even more on the cohesion than on the friction.

For all these reasons, many of these laboratory models, the results of which cannot be transposed to actual silos, are of practically no value to applied research. They may be useful in more fundamental studies of the mechanical behaviour and flow of granular media.

39.3.5 Class E: Centrifuged small-scale models

As noted above, the similarity conditions must be satisfied for the behaviour of the small-scale model to be identical to that of the full-scale silo. The similarity conditions for tests on silos are presented in detail in Part Six.

For continuous media, the relations between scale factors that the model must satisfy (identical stresses and strains in the model and in the prototype) are the following:

$$\rho^* g^* L^* = 1 \quad \text{and} \quad \xi^* = g^* t^{*2}$$

where L^* is the scale factor on the length (L^* = model dimensions/prototype dimensions), ρ^* the scale factor on density, t^* the scale factor on time, ξ^* the scale factor on displacements and g^* the scale factor on the acceleration of gravity.

These relations can be satisfied under the following two conditions:

- the same materials are used in the model and in the actual structure (so that $\rho^* = 1$) and,
- earth's gravity is replaced, in the model, by an acceleration n times as great ($g^* = n$).

Tests on $1/n$ scale models must then necessarily be performed in a centrifuge under an acceleration of ng.

However, the ensiled materials cannot be regarded as continuous media, and other conditions of similarity must be added to the foregoing. The most restrictive, in granular materials, concerns the possible effect of the particle size, which must remain small enough with respect to the characteristic dimension of the structure not to introduce a size effect.

When experiments are planned on a new type of structure, an experimental investigation must be performed to determine the minimum value of the ratio between the characteristic dimension of the model and the diameter of the grains. The method used for these preliminary studies (modelling of models) consists of simulating the same actual structure by smaller and smaller models, under the corresponding centrifugal accelerations, while keeping the same granular material in all the models.

In the absence of a particle size effect, the results obtained on the different models, converted to prototype values, are identical. When a size effect occurs, discrepancies appear, indicating that the limiting value of the ratio (model dimension)/(grain diameter) has been reached. To avoid any particle size effect, the later experiments must therefore be performed on models of which the scale is larger than this limiting value.

In the case of a shallow foundation resting on a sand mass, the limiting value of the ratio of the diameter of the foundation to that of the coarsest grains is well known and close to 35. In the case of silos, tests have been performed to study the effect of the grain size on the discharge flow rate in a centrifuged model (Lepert, Ranaivoson and Gourdon, 1989). The study showed that discharge flow rate Q was related to grain diameter d, outlet diameter D, and the centrifugal acceleration G to which the model is subjected, by the following equation:

$$Q = Ad^{-0.5}D^3G^{0.5}$$

This expression can be used to reproduce a correct flow rate on the model while keeping the actual ensiled materials.

Up to now, centrifuge tests on silos and hoppers have been carried out at the Technical University in Denmark, Manchester University and LCPC in France (see references of the installations in Part Six).

Table 39.1 Domains of use of test silos for applied or pre-standardization research

Type of study	Class of silo				
	Class A Industrial site in operation	Class B Experimental station actual size	Class C Pilot-scale model	Class D Laboratory small-scale model	Class E Centrifuged small-scale model
Type 1 Tests of equipment	**	**	*/o according to equipment to be tested	†	o
Type 2 Determination of pressures	†	** with local measurement of pressures	*	×	*
Type 3 Study of flows	†	o	**	o	**
Type 4 Earthquakes	×	×	* (using a shaking table)	×	**
Explosions	×	*	*	×	o

** = Recommended test method, because well suited to the objectives of the study, or the only effective approach that can be considered.
* = Use of this class of test silo generally possible.
o = Method that can be used if absolutely necessary, in some special cases, provided that its feasibility has been demonstrated.
† = Method generally ill suited, posing problems of experimental design or interpretation (measurements difficult, complexity of the structures, failure to preserve similarities).
× = Method totally inappropriate.

39.4 DOMAINS OF USE OF TESTS ON SILOS

Before any experimental programme on silos can begin, it is essential to define its objectives clearly. It is in effect never possible to obtain, from a single test silo, all responses concerning the various aspects of silo behaviour.

The choice of type of test silo will therefore depend on the objectives of the research; Table 39.1 presents the possibilities and limitations of the various classes of test silos. It is important to recall that this table concerns only applied or pre-standardization research programmes.

For more fundamental studies, for example on the rheology or flow of granular media, laboratory models may turn out to be useful. In this case, direct transposition of the results to full-scale structures is not an objective of the work.

39.5 CONCLUSIONS AND FUTURE RESEARCH

It was found necessary to establish a double classification, on the one hand, of test silos according to their utility and their limitations, and on the other, of types of experimental investigations according to their main objective. The analysis, limited to the case of applied and pre-standardization research, led to five classes of test silos and four types of experimental programmes.

A summary table has been prepared to facilitate choosing the experimental approach best suited to the silo problem to be dealt with. In all cases, the first phase of the analysis consists of defining, as precisely as possible, the objective of the experimental programme. Further studies were found to be necessary to:

- determine the limit of pilot-scale tests (class C) such that the results obtained can be applied directly and without correction to full-scale silos;
- determine the limiting ratio of grain diameter to model dimensions and the smallest reduction scale for centrifuged small-scale models (class E).

REFERENCES

Galilei, G. (1638), *Discorsi e dimonstrazioni matematiche interno a due nuove scienze*. Leida 1638.

Lepert, P.; Ranaivoson, D. and Gourdon, J.L. (1989), Centrifuge modelling of the flow of a granular medium, *Powders and Grains*, Balkema, Clermont-Ferrand, September, pp. 477–484.

Munch-Andersen, J. and Nielsen, J. (1986), Size effects in slender grain silos, *Bulk Solids Handling*, 6(5), 885–889.

40

Test design

40.1 Tests for pressures
H. Stoffers

40.1.1 Introduction

Tests on full-scale silos mostly concern wall pressure measurements and the structural behaviour of the test silo. However, tests related to the development or improvement of technical devices for extraction of material from silos are also carried out in full-scale test silos. Full-scale test silos have the disadvantage that modifications, for example shape and dimensions of the bin or the hopper part, are difficult to realize and such changes are very expensive. An interesting question, however, is whether this disadvantage should still be preferred to uncertain translations of results from model scale tests to full scale.

Full-scale tests can be applied to both a silo situated on an industrial plant or a silo specially designed and built for test purposes. Which of these two possibilities should be used depends on several factors. If information is sought on the combined behaviour of specific materials stored in a specific silo on an industrial plant then full-scale tests on the site may be the best approach. If some general study is intended on, for example, factors influencing flow behaviour and wall pressures, then tests in a special purpose full-scale test silo may be a good choice.

When full-scale tests are planned, careful attention should be given to the establishment of relevant data for the test silo. Many publications on silo tests found in the literature provide little information about the test silo. Often information is only given on the shape, the main dimensions and the kind of structural material of the silo. This is not always enough for readers who want to study the published test results thoroughly, and may wish to make a comparison with other test results. Civil engineers have special interest in structural aspects so sufficient information on the silo structures should be given. In some cases more background information on the test silo is available and can be provided by the people who carried out the tests. However, in other cases no more additional information on the test silo is available. The contribution of such silo tests to the general improvement of knowledge in the field of silos is very doubtful. Detailed information on the test silo should therefore be established and provided.

40.1.2 Required information on the test silo

The information on the silo should start with a brief description of the place of the silo, its main shape and dimensions, the structural material, its storage capacity, the material stored in the silo during the tests and the methods of filling and emptying. If the test silo is part of an industrial storage plant the owner should be asked to give information on its history. It is important, for example, to know the age of the silo, the type of materials that have been stored and if structural problems have happened in the past. If this is the case information should be obtained about the circumstances, and the location and amount of any damage. Also information on the method of repair should be requested. Further, it is of importance if the silo is free standing or part of a silo block. In the latter case the position of the silo in the block should be given precisely. It must also be clear if during the tests filling and/or discharge activities took place in the silos adjacent to the test silo. If so a description in detail of every parallel activity should be included in the report of the measurements in the test silo.

It is of special importance to give information on the type of foundation of the test silo. In case of a steel silo, information on the support structure of the silo should also be given. Dynamic behaviour of stored materials can be strongly influenced by the support structure and/or the kind of foundation. With respect to the foundation, information should be given on soil properties, on dimensions and positions of concrete foundation blocks and on positions, number and dimensions of foundation piles.

40.1.2.1 Bin section

Information on the shape of the cross-section of the bin should be given using one of the words out of the set 'circular, square, rectangle, regular n-shape'. In other cases a sketch of the shape should be given including the nominal inner dimensions in millimetres. The real inner dimensions of the cross-section should be measured at several levels. In this way information is obtained on the mean inner dimensions and the variation in it. The inner height of the bin should be measured in millimetres at four uniformly distributed places along the circumference of the bin.

40.1.2.2 Flat-bottomed silo

For a flat bottom the number, shape and positions of the outlets should be given on a sketch which should include measured distances and dimensions in millimetres. The thickness of the bottom (in mm) and positions of supporting columns should be provided and the type of structural material of the bottom should be given.

40.1.2.3 Hoppers

For each hopper a sketch should be given showing the shape, the outlet and the dimensions of the hopper in millimetres. Further information about the structural material and the wall thickness provisions (in millimetres) should be provided. If the hopper is provided with a lining or coating, information should be given on the material used for it. Further, some indication on the roughness of the lining or coating is needed.

40.1.2.4 Structural condition of the silo

The condition of the silo in terms of location of damage, cracks or local buckling can influence the results of the tests that are carried out in the silo. In case of a concrete silo the existence of cracks in the wall should be investigated. If cracks are found their positions and crack widths should be reported. For each crack it should be established if it is ongoing through the wall or only exists on the inner or outer surface of the wall. It is advised to make recordings of the crack widths during the silo tests.

40.1.2.5 Imperfections

Deviations in dimensions and disruptions of wall surfaces influence flow velocity and flow profiles of the stored material and will as a consequence also influence wall pressures. If these imperfections occur in the vicinity of measuring devices then the readings can be strongly influenced. It therefore is of importance to report on such so-called imperfections. Imperfections of greater dimension can be discovered during a visual inspection of the silo. Smaller imperfections are also of importance and can only be discovered through measurements in the silo on a fine mesh of measuring lines. It is advised to carry out such measurements.

40.1.2.6 Wall roughness

Roughness of the silo wall is of ever-increasing interest for understanding the behaviour of particulate materials stored in silos. Wall roughness predominantly characterizes a boundary condition that influences the flow and as a consequence influences the pressures on the wall. Therefore, some indication on the roughness of the wall should be given. Particularly in slip-formed concrete silos, wall roughness can vary to a great extent. Information on this variation should be given.

If the wall is provided with a lining or special coating information should be given on the kind of material used for it and on the roughness of it.

40.1.2.7 Instrumentation

Most full-scale silo tests aim to improve the understanding of the wall pressures exerted by the stored material. Planning such measurements implies that many aspects must be considered and choices have to be made. Important questions, for example, concern the type of pressure cell to be used, the calibration of these cells, the position of the cells on the wall, conditions for taking measurements and the method of processing the measured data.

Wall pressures have a stochastic nature (Fig. 40.1.1). Readings of pressures taken at the same place on the wall will show scatter even under static conditions. The observed variation is caused by randomly distributed differences in local densities and is also influenced by rates of filling. During discharge pressures will change continuously due to the flowing material.

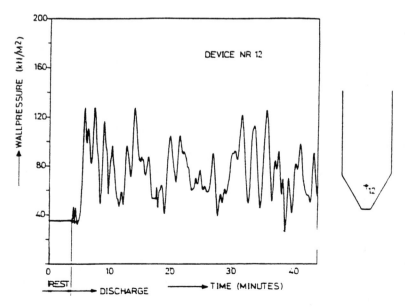

Fig. 40.1.1 Example of recorded wall pressures (Stoffers, 1983).

Peak values of pressures and pressure variation depend on the properties of the stored material and on the type of flow. Peak values and variation will normally be higher in mass flow silos than they are in funnel flow silos.

Because of the stochastic nature of wall pressures, a large number of readings have to be taken in order to gain reliable conclusions on the subject. Modern electronic equipment makes it easy to take readings very frequently, for example 100 readings per second, and to store great amounts of data. Special computer software is available for processing the data. Collecting lots of data, however, easily creates the risk of an overflow of data storage capacity. Often a better approach is to first check the reading on the basis of chosen criteria and then decide if it should be stored or not.

40.1.2.8 Pressure cells

Several types of pressure cells have been developed for the measurement of these pressures. Examples of these are piston-type cells, plate-type cells filled with a fluid and plate-type cells provided with strain gauges or with a vibrating wire. The cells are mainly made of steel and must be installed in the silo wall in such a way that the diaphragm of the cell is flush with the wall surface. Errors caused by improper installation of a cell can cause serious errors. Pressure cells can be designed for measuring normal stresses only or for shear stresses or for both. The diameter of the cells varies between 50 mm and more than 300 mm. The cell diameter should be at least 50 times the diameter of the biggest particle of the stored material.

Pressure cells can be suitable for doing only single readings of the pressure at a time. Others can be used for both single readings and continuous registration of the stresses. If it is planned to make calculations of the correlation between pressures occurring at different places then continuous registrations of the pressures are an advance. However, this also depends on the electronic equipment connected to the cells. If this equipment is suitable for making very fast single readings in small time steps then the readings can also be used for correlation calculations. Fast readings are necessary if a number of cells have to be read during discharging of the silo. In that circumstance pressures are changing continuously due to the flow of the material. Comparison of pressures occurring at the same time at different places then requires that all the readings have been taken within hundredths of a second.

40.1.2.9 Sensitivity and pressure range of the cells

Important items in the choice of pressure cell are the required sensitivity of the cell and the pressure range that must be covered. Both requirements are very often not fulfilled to the same extent because high sensitivity is mostly connected to a relatively small pressure range. Cells which can measure high pressures often have robust bodies and become, as a consequence, insensitive to low pressure levels. This circumstance is not easy to handle because one has to make assumptions about the level of pressures that can be expected to be able to choose a type of cell. The planned pressure measurements, however, were meant to find out about these pressures.

40.1.2.10 Calibration of pressure cells

The calibration of pressure cells is mostly performed by the company who produced the cells. The calibration figures are included in the specifications of the devices. It is advisable, however, to check if the provided information is sufficient for the tests that are to be applied. Calibrations should be carried out at universities or institutions with much experience in this field. One should be aware of the possibility that the calibration figures are sensitive to the way the device is fixed in the calibration apparatus. If so then the device will probably act in a different way when it is fixed to the silo wall.

40.1.2.11 Position of the cells on the silo wall

Pressure cells and shear cells are costly instruments. The number of cells to be applied will therefore be limited for reasons of economy. On the other hand, sufficient information on pressure levels and pressure distributions over the wall must result from the measurements. Both requirements ask for a carefully chosen distribution of the cells over the silo wall (Fig. 40.1.2). Decisions on positions of pressure cells on the wall should in the first place be based on information about the expected type of flow in the silo. Consultation of experts on flow may therefore be necessary. Places of interest are those where peak values of pressures can be expected. However, these places are not necessarily of interest from a structural point of view. When peak pressures are acting in massive concrete hoppers for example, the structural consequences will mostly be limited. 'Weak places' of the structure should therefore preferably be chosen for measuring the pressures.

If the horizontal cross-section of the test silo has one or more axes of symmetry then the possibility exists of placing cells in only one of the symmetrical parts of the wall. However, the flow pattern of the material must in addition be symmetrical otherwise pressure levels and pressure distributions on symmetrical parts of the wall will differ. It is advised even for axially symmetrical silos and flow patterns to check symmetry by placing at least a small number of cells on positions opposite to the main instrumentation.

40.1.2.12 Distance between the cells

For what area of the wall is a pressure, measured with a certain device, valid? That question is repeated whenever results of wall pressures are

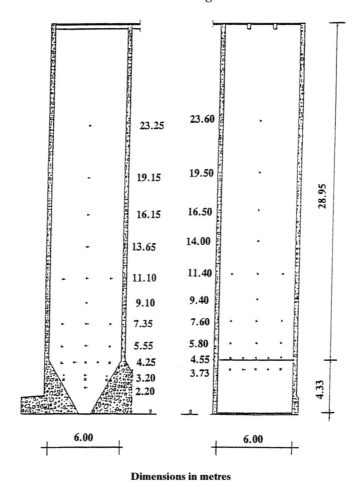

Fig. 40.1.2 Positions of pressure devices in a full-scale industrial silo (Stoffers, 1983).

discussed. Pressure devices in principle only provide information with respect to their own cross-sectional area. The application of a lot of devices could solve the problem, but this is not a realistic approach because most pressure devices are rather expensive. From a scientific point of view detailed information on the pressure distribution would be nice. However, from a structural point of view it may be sufficient to have a more global insight into the pressure distribution. It seems to be wise to combine information on the expected type of flow in the silo and the sensitivity of the silo structure for pressure differences as a basis for decisions on the distances between the measuring devices. In areas where higher and varying pressure levels can be expected and where the impact of these pressures on the structure could be serious, the distance between the devices should be for example twice the diameter of the devices. In less important areas four or five times the diameter or even more could be sufficient.

References

Askegaard V. The pressure cell problem *Silos – Forschung und Praxis* Karlsruhe, Germany, 1988

Askegaard V.; Nielsen J. Probleme bei der Messung des Silodruckes mit Hilfe von Druckzellen *Die Bautechnik* 3, 1972

Hartlen J. *et al. The Wall Pressure in Large Grain Silos* Swedish Council for Building Research, 1984

Munch-Andersen J. A probabilistic approach to silo loads *Silos – Forschung und Praxis* Karlsruhe, Germany, 1988

Stoffers H. Pressure measurements in a silo for soya meal *Second International Conference on Design of Silos for Strength and Flow* Stratford-upon-Avon, 1983

Stoffers H. Safety of silos and silo research. What are the difficulties? *Silos – Forschung und Praxis* Karlsruhe, Germany, 1988

40.2 Tests for flow
H. Stoffers

Flow behaviour of granular solids is by far the most studied subject in silo research. This is because of the direct relevance of the issue for the silo industry. Bad or uncertain flow behaviour of solids can cause enormous financial losses if the flow of the solid is interrupted every time that it is extracted from the silo. Such uncertainties are very frustrating because additional flow-promoting measures are constantly needed, promised deliveries of the solid to customers are delayed, and production processes by end users of the solid are possibly endangered. Tests for flow are therefore very important in the field of silo research.

40.2.1 Flow tests in small-scale models

Most tests for flows are applied in small-scale models. Such tests are much easier to apply than flow tests in full-scale silos. This makes model tests very interesting and they are in addition much cheaper than full-scale tests. However, results of flow tests in small-scale models have limited and uncertain relevance to real installations. This is mainly due to the lower stress level in the solid because they are a direct function of gravity forces acting on the solid. Another uncertainty concerns the influence of the shear zone along the wall on the flow because this zone has more influence in a small-scale model than it has in a real scale silo. Further, the possible effect of the particle size on the test result has to be mentioned. The particle size has to remain small in comparison with the dimensions of the model. These and other factors influence the flow behaviour of the solid, and because of this the chance of arching (flow–no flow), and the segregation of the solid is influenced.

In theory results of model tests can be translated to full-scale results. However, the reliability of such translations is still uncertain. Nevertheless it has to be stated that small-scale model tests have contributed greatly to the knowledge of the behaviour of bulk solids in silos. A big advantage of tests in small-scale models, for example, is that factors influencing flow can be more readily investigated. Many tests can be completed within a short time and it is quite easy to modify the model (e.g., another overall height, wall roughness changed, new hopper) and study the effects on the flow. Last but not least, flow tests in small-scale models are much cheaper to apply than full-scale tests.

In the literature very different dimensions of small-scale models used for studies on flow (and pressures) can be found. Models have been used consisting of a small tube and models have been used with dimensions comparable with those of a small size real silo. Kaminski (1988) for example used a circular model made of steel with a diameter of approx. 515 mm and a height of approx. 1000 mm. Strusch et al. (1995) used two models for their studies on insert loads and wall stress distributions. One was made of Perspex plates and had a rectangular cross-section of 400 × 800 mm, the height was approx. 3 m. The second model was made of steel and had a rectangular cross-section of 600 × 1200 mm. The height of the model was approx. 6 m. As already stated, other model silos have been used with dimensions more or less equal to small real scale silos, for example silos for

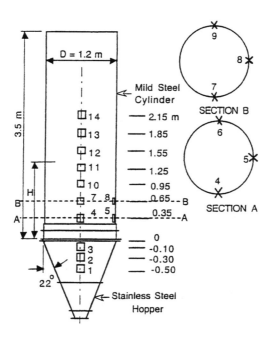

Fig. 40.2.1 Model scale silo used by Roberts (1995).

632 Test design

the storage of animal feed at a farm. Figure 40.2.1 shows a silo used by Roberts (1995).

40.2.2 Flow observations

Flow behaviour of solids in small-scale models is mostly observed on a visual basis. The models are therefore provided with windows or they have one or more walls made of transparent material. The flow is observed via these windows or via the transparent walls as a whole. In addition the upper surface of the solid is observed. This provides valuable information on the main flow type (mass flow, funnel flow), on the starting point of rat-holing and on the main movement of particles near and in the hopper (dead zones) when the silo is emptied to that level.

A very commonly used method for flow observations from the outside is to fill the model with layers of the solid which are alternately coloured and non-coloured (Fig. 40.2.2). The movements of the layers during (filling and) discharge provide information on the movements of these layers and on the velocities of these movements. Further, it can show the build-up of dead zones in the silo. If the model is emptied by means of a belt conveyor the pattern of coloured and non-coloured material on the belt provides some indication on the internal flow in the model. Video cameras are in this respect a very useful tool for registration of the movements of the layers and on their appearance on the belt conveyor (if used). Measurements of the changes of weight of the model will deliver additional information on the amount of solid that has been extracted from the model.

Modern techniques make it possible to digitize video images of the moving coloured layers of the solid. The digitized images can be enhanced

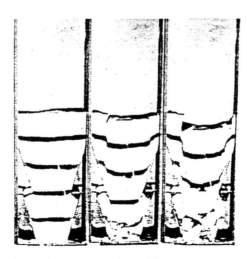

Fig. 40.2.2 Flow observations using coloured layers.

to increase the contrast between coloured and non-coloured layers and also between the particles. Then the digital images are cross-correlated to determine the vertical and the horizontal shift of the particles. Averaging the shifts of the particles within chosen areas finally results in figures regarding the directions of the shifts and the velocity and velocity fluctuations of the particles within the areas considered.

In spite of this modern approach, such observations only provide information on the outside behaviour of the solid. The inside movement of the particles, the process of dilatancy between the particles and the segregation of the material is still unknown.

Other modern observation techniques, some of them based on nuclear sources, exist or are in progress. However, their importance for flow observations of particulate materials in silos is not clear. With these methods it seems possible to take observations inside the solid. However, sufficient information on this subject is not yet available.

Several attempts have been made to collect information on the internal flow of the solid. Markers have been inserted in the solid to measure residence time, paraffin has been added to freeze and study the flow and photographic and tracer techniques using X-rays and radio pills have been used. From these methods the insertion of markers seems to be the simplest to apply. However the shape, the elastic properties and the weight of inserts have to be chosen very carefully because such inserts can easily influence the stress field in the solid at the position of the insert. This can result in other residence times of the insert in the silo and it is possible that the insert influences the flow profile. This is a risk in particular connected with flow tests in small-scale models.

40.2.3 Full-scale tests for flow

The problems described with respect to flow observations in small-scale silo models are not unique to these models. Granular solids cannot be directly observed at full scale either: the silo walls are opaque, the solids are opaque and the flows are very often internal. Visual observations therefore provide the same limited information as mentioned in relation to small-scale models.

For flow studies in full-scale silos the insertion of radio tag markers already mentioned seems a promising solution to this problem. Chen *et al.* (1995) used up to 300 of such markers for flow observations in a full-scale silo. Up to eight layers of markers were placed in the solid. Flow profiles were calculated on the basis of residence times of the markers combined with information regarding the remaining volume of solid in the silo.

40.2.4 Additional measurements

The interpretation and useful reporting of flow observations are impossible without having additional information regarding the tests. For example, the height of fill of the silo, the filling method and the rate of discharge have to be known. Further, the properties of the silo such as the shape, the dimensions and also the wall roughness of the bin and the hopper part of the silo must be known. Very important, of course, is information on the properties of the solid itself. This concerns information at least on:

- particle size including its distribution
- particle shape
- particle surface structure
- particle density
- density of the solid
- angle of internal friction
- wall friction angle
- lateral pressure ratio

In many cases it can be of interest to apply in addition measurements on the silo structure itself. Wall pressure measurements can probably be a help in explaining the observed flow of the solid. For such measurements strain gauges can be fixed on the silo (model) or pressure devices can be used. If dynamic behaviour of the solid is expected displacement and acceleration devices should be used.

References

Chen J.F. *et al.* (1995) Visualisation of solids flow in a full scale silo *3rd European Symposium Storage and Flow of Particulate Solids (Janssen Centennial)* Nuremberg, Germany, 1995

Kaminsky M. (1988) Wanddrucke von Silos in Abhängigkeit von Beschickung und Entleerungsgeschwindigkeit *Silos – Forschung und Praxis*, Karlsruhe, Germany, 1988

Roberts Alan W. (1995) Shock loads in silos due to flow pulsations *Particulate Solids (Janssen Centennial)* Nuremberg, Germany, 1995

Strusch J. *et al.* (1995) Insert loads and wall stress distributions in silos with inserts *Particulate Solids (Janssen Centennial)* Nuremberg, Germany, 1995

40.3 Tests for vibrations
H. Stoffers

40.3.1 Introduction

Several stored bulk solids show dynamic effects when they are extracted from the silo. More or less rhythmic pulsations of the material are very common. Pulsation frequencies up to 10 Hz have been reported (Franz, 1967). Pulsation seems to result from repetitive dilation within the bulk solid during flow and the 'slip–stick' characteristics of internal and boundary friction (Roberts, 1995). It does not cause problems in the extraction of the material from the silo. Certain combinations of material properties and silo geometry result in periodic shocks of high energy. In particular, coarse solids with little fines such as cement clinker and coal are reported to show these effects (Pieper, 1973).

Vibrations and shocks cause dynamic loads on the silo structure. These loads can endanger the safety of the structure, for example by fatigue of the structural material. However, vibrations and shocks can also disturb sensitive apparatus used in the handling of the bulk solid. If the shocks are transmitted via the silo foundation to buildings in the vicinity of the silo the comfort of people living or working in these buildings can be disturbed.

Vibration measurements on the silo structure can provide answers to questions with respect to the cause of the vibrations, the safety of the structure and on measures to limit the vibrations. Vibration measurements, however, require very special measuring equipment and only experienced people in this field of measurements are able to set up and carry out such measurements properly.

In the following sections, some guidelines are given for vibration and shock measurements on silo structures.

40.3.2 Information required

Many vibration and shock measurements in silos aim to answer the question of the safety of the silo structure. The cause of the vibrations and shocks is of no question because, without taking any measurement, it is clear that the bulk solid is responsible for the dynamic behaviour of the silo. However, it always appears that information on the flow behaviour and on material properties of the bulk solid can provide very valuable explanations and answers while analysing results from vibration measurements. For example, observed vibration frequencies and intensities of shocks can be connected with particular properties of the bulk solid such as the moisture content or the particle size distribution. Changing these properties (if possible and acceptable) can then probably solve the vibration problems and no further steps are necessary. Detailed information on bulk solid properties and on test conditions should therefore be collected parallel to the application of the vibration measurements. Items in this respect are filling rate, surface level, surface shape, inlet pattern, height of fall, discharge rate, flow pattern, times of filling and/or discharge, particle distribution, moisture content and temperature of the bulk solid. Further, the total weight of the bulk solid and the outside climate (temperature, humidity) have to be known. Visual observation of the surface of the bulk solid in the silo during the vibration measurements is highly recommended.

To answer the question of the safety of the silo structure, acceleration, strain and displacement measurements at particular points of the structure will provide the information required on load and stress variations in the structure. Based on this information conclusions can be drawn on the safety of the structure.

Displacement and acceleration measurements, applied at several points of the silo structure and in surrounding buildings (if necessary), will provide information needed for conclusions on the transmission of vibrations and shocks through the structure and through the soil.

It is clear that detailed information on the silo structure itself must be available. This concerns information on the kind of structural material and the shape and dimensions of the silo and its supporting structure. The type of foundation of the silo and the geotechnical properties of the soil should also be known.

If attention is paid to the above-mentioned items it will be possible to handle questions with respect to:
- the cause of the vibrations and shocks;
- the load and stress levels in the structure;
- the transmission of vibrations and shocks through the structure and through the soil.

40.3.3 Preparation of vibration measurements

When considering measurements on a vibrating silo structure it is necessary to construct a somewhat simplified model of the structure. This helps to draw conclusions on places where vibrating forces are introduced into the structure, which masses are brought into motion and how loads from these motions are transmitted to other parts of the structure. Such information is a must for decisions on the kind of measurements to be carried out and on places where the measuring devices should be positioned. It is common to build a mechanical model consisting of combinations of masses, springs and dampers (Fig. 40.3.1). One of the masses of the model represents, for example, the dead weight of the bulk solid and another, the dead weight of the bin and the hopper. Another mass in the mechanical model could represent the mass of a foundation block. The springs represent, for example, the supporting structure of the silo such as steel columns and/or the concrete piles of the foundation. Finally the damper represents the natural ability of the structure to return to the rest position when the vibrating force is no longer acting.

In certain cases the silo vibrations are not only caused by the bulk solid but in addition by machinery in the vicinity of the silo. In such situations, assumptions have to be made about the combined influence of both vibration sources on the silo structure, in order to decide on types and places of measurements to be carried out.

40.3.4 Frequency range

Vibrations of silo structures can be considered to be within the frequency range of 1–50 Hz. Frequencies higher than 50 Hz may be filtered out of the measuring signal. Sometimes frequencies lower than 1 Hz can be of importance.

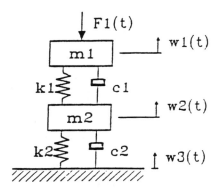

Fig. 40.3.1 Two-degree-of-freedom mechanical system.

Table 40.3.1 Recommended device measuring ranges

Type of measurement	Frequency range (Hz)	Dynamic range	
		Lowest	Highest
Accelerations	1–50	$100\,\mu m\,s^{-2}$	$30\,m\,s^{-2}$
Velocities	1–50	$200\,\mu m\,s^{-1}$	$50\,mm\,s^{-1}$
Displacements	1–50	$250\,nm$	$10\,mm$

40.3.5 Measuring range of devices

The measuring range of the devices should be in accordance with Table 40.3.1.

40.3.6 Measuring equipment

Measuring equipment in general consists of a number of measuring devices, conditioning apparatus and registration instruments. In order to calibrate the whole system calibration apparatus will often also be needed.

The measuring device should, within the required frequency range, generate an electrical signal which is linearly dependent on the acceleration, velocity or displacement component of the vibration in the chosen measuring direction. The sensitivity of the device to vibration components perpendicular to the chosen measuring direction should be lower than 5% of the main component.

40.3.7 Conditioning of the measuring signal

Measuring signals from a measuring device have to be conditioned in order to get a signal that is suitable for instruments displaying results and for instruments storing the data. The conditioning of the measuring signals can include filtering, integration, differentiation and amplification.

40.3.8 Registration instruments

Registration of measuring signals is a must for thorough evaluation of the measuring data. The registration has to be such that the complete frequency domain is covered. The registration error in amplitude or frequency of the signal should be less than 5% of the real value. Analogue or digital band recorders (FM) can fulfil these requirements. Also digital analysers with sufficient storage capacity can be used. The sample frequency of digital instruments should be at least 10 times the highest frequency in the required frequency interval.

Tests for vibrations

In order to prevent the storage of enormous amounts of data it is often wise to allow the measurements to start automatically by a trigger signal produced by one of the installed measuring devices. The trigger level can be defined after taking a number of pre-measurements and defining the kind and level of information that is required.

40.3.9 Calibration

Measuring instruments need to be calibrated. The method of calibration depends on the types of measuring devices and the registration instruments used in the measurements. The calibration should consist of a so-called level calibration and a frequency response calibration. The calibration should be carried out on the measuring system as a whole and not on each single part of the system.

40.3.10 Fixing of the devices

Measuring devices have to be fixed to the structure in order to measure the response of the structure. The fixing must be in such a manner that the behaviour of the structure or that particular part of the structure is not influenced by the device. An important requirement in this respect is that the mass of the device and its fixing parts can be neglected in comparison with the dynamic mass of the structure or its part on which the device is fixed. The devices should be fixed to the structure by means of screws, glue, wax or by magnetic aids. Cables must be positioned and fixed in such a manner that no forces are introduced into the devices and motion of the cables is prevented.

40.3.11 Positions of the devices

Devices should be fixed to those parts of the structure which, because of their natural frequency and their position in the structure, are sensitive to vibrations or shocks. The devices should at least be fixed to stiff parts of the structure at ground level. The measuring direction should be vertical and horizontal in two directions perpendicular to each other. Measuring devices should, further, be fixed at a high level of the structure at stiff points. These measuring points should preferably be positioned in a vertical line with the measuring points on ground level. Measuring directions should again be vertical and horizontal in two directions perpendicular to each other. Figure 40.3.2 shows as an illustration a displacement response of a shock load measured on a support structure of a ring beam of a silo (Stoffers, Staalduinen and van Halderen, 1995).

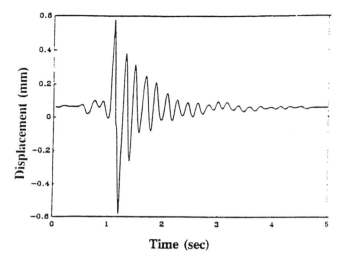

Fig. 40.3.2 Response (displacements) on a shock load measured on a ring beam of a silo (Stoffers *et al.*, 1995).

40.3.12 Duration of the measurements

The duration of the measurements should cover at least a representative number of periods, for example 1000 times the lowest important frequency for the silo structure.

40.3.13 Processing and analysing measuring data

Vibration measurements produce data of a complex nature. In order to interpret their meaning the data have to be processed. If the measurements are aimed at assessing whether or not the vibrations constitute a nuisance for people living or working in the neighbourhood of the silo, the processing can consist of the establishment of peak values and connected dominant frequencies within a frequency spectrum. The peak value is the greatest value in the absolute sense of the measured displacement, velocity or acceleration. The dominant frequency is the frequency connected with the maximum value of the spectral density of the vibrations. Figure 40.3.3 shows an example of dominant frequency within a density spectrum. In this example three local spectral maxima exist. The highest peak value appears at 71 Hz. A second (lower) peak exists at $f = 37$ Hz and a third peak exists at $f = 17$ Hz. Although the peak value at 71 Hz is the highest of the three peaks calculations showed that the real dominant frequency is the one at 17 Hz.

If the vibrations and shocks are caused by two sources, for example by the bulk solid and, in addition, by machinery in the vicinity of the silo, then a frequency analysis of vibrations from both sources could be necessary.

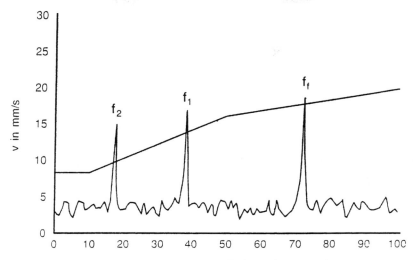

Fig. 40.3.3 Velocity–frequency spectrum with three dominant frequencies.

If the safety of the silo structure has to be assessed information on stress and load levels and on stress and load variations in several parts of the structure is required. Conclusions regarding the safety of the structure have to take into account the expected number of stress and load cycles within the whole (intended) lifetime of the structure. Vibration and shock measurements on the silo structure are a very useful way of drawing conclusions with respect to structural safety.

References

Franz, K. (1967) *Die Seitendrücke in Getreidesilos.* Vortragsverband des Betontages, Germany.
Pieper, K. (1973) Über das 'Schlagen' in SiloZellen. *Aufbereitungstechnik* **4**.
Roberts, Alan. W. (1995) Shock loads in silos due to flow pulsations. *3rd European Symposium Storage and Flow of Particulate Solids* (Janssen Centennial). 21–23 March, Nuremberg, Germany.
Schade aan bouwwerken. Meet- en beoordelingsrichtlijn. SBR, 1993 (in Dutch).
Stoffers, H.; Staalduinen, P. and van Halderen, M.W.A.M. (1995) Dynamic effects due to flow in silos. *Partec 95*, Nuremberg, Germany.

40.4 Tests for structural buckling
P. Knoedel

40.4.1 Scope

Structural tests with thin-walled metal silo structures are very delicate and require special skills and experience. The aim of such tests is to gain information on the structural behaviour of the silo rather than gaining information on features of the bulk solid, such as wall pressures or flow rates. Usually a test involves strain gauge readings under different loading conditions. Also, loading the structure to failure gives some information on ultimate states, bearing capacity and failure mechanisms (Knoedel, 1995; Ummenhofer, 1996).

40.4.2 Model shell

The properties of the shell must be recorded carefully. Special regard is to be paid to:

- Distribution of wall thicknesses.
- Distribution of Young's modulus in meridional and circumferential direction.
- Distribution of the yield limit in meridional and circumferential direction.
- Geometrical shape deviations. These should be recorded in a grid, which should be small enough to enable detection of the smallest permissible imperfections specified in the structural buckling codes.
- Smoothness/roughness of the wall. It is recommended to perform friction tests with the wall material and the bulk solid.

40.4.3 Instrumentation

Thin-walled structures should be strain gauged at both surfaces of the wall in order to be able to separate membrane and bending components of the stress resultants. The difficulty with silo tests is that strain gauges on the inside surface disturb the motions, flow and consolidation of the granular solid, and might lead to erroneous results as a consequence. This shortcoming can be overcome by using so-called sandwich strain gauges, which consist of two measuring grids attached to each side of a piece of plastic of defined thickness, e.g. 1 mm. The sandwich gauge is attached to the outer surface of the silo, and is subjected to axial strain and bending like the parent material. From the readings of the two measuring grids and the thicknesses of the piece of plastic and the metal wall the strain at the inner surface of the silo can be calculated. Before using a sandwich gauge technique, it is highly recommended to have the gauges tested on a dummy strip with the original thickness.

40.4.4 Test set-up

In most cases the tests are performed on model silos of reduced scale. The test is then set up inside a laboratory and should allow realistic loading of the silo.

Well-defined boundary conditions are important. These should be described in such a way that:

- the tests can be repeated uniquely by other researchers;
- the tests can be simulated numerically.

In cases where the edges of the shell are planned to be evenly loaded/supported, the model shell as well as the adjacent parts of the test set-up need to be machined. The supporting structure must have sufficient stiffness to transfer the loads evenly into the shell. It is recommended to have the actual distribution of the loads along the circumference documented by strain gauge readings.

40.4.5 Loadings

The loading with the bulk solid must be done in a way that allows the tests to be repeated. Further advice is given in the section on testing the bulk solid.

40.4.6 Results

Storage and handling of data from dynamic measurements are described in the section on data processing. For buckling tests it is desirable to have the stress state immediately before failure is recorded. Also, the state of the bulk solid should be described exactly. If possible, the beginning of failure should be assigned to a certain locus of the structure.

40.4.7 Interpretation

When the shell has failed, the mean meridional compression stress in the shell wall at failure, σ_u^{exp}, has to be determined. The compression stress results from the wall friction loads of the bulk solid as well as from additional longitudinal loading of the shell, e.g. by dead load and prestressing by a hydraulic jack. In usual cases the compression stress increases from top to bottom, so the shell will fail near the bottom edge. The failure stress in the experiment σ_u^{exp} will be determined for the bottom edge of the shell.

Depending on the distribution of the hoop stresses along the shell axis, shells can fail distinctly above the bottom edge. In this case the failure stress σ_u^{exp} is to be determined for the locus of the failure.

The results obtained are related to theoretical values. If the shell is very thin-walled (e.g. $R/T > 500$ with mild steel) the failure is predominantly elastic. The failure stress σ_u^{exp} is then compared to the 'classical buckling stress' $\sigma_{cr} = 0.605 ET/R$. $\alpha = \sigma_u^{exp}/\sigma_{cr} < 1$ is called the 'elastic buckling coefficient'. Typically α is plotted versus R/T in order to compare the experimental findings with the predictions of the shell codes. If the shell is of medium wall thickness (e.g. $R/T < 500$ with mild steel) the failure is elasto-plastic. The mean meridional compression stress in the shell wall at failure σ_u^{exp} is then compared to the 'yield stress' f_y of the shell wall material. $\kappa = \sigma_u^{exp}/f_y < 1$ shows the effectiveness of the invested shell material. Typically κ is plotted versus the normalized shell slenderness $\lambda = \sqrt{(f_y/\sigma_{cr})}$ in order to compare the experimental findings with the predictions of the shell codes.

A thorough survey of the shell surface is needed to obtain realistic results with numerical simulation. In this case the relation of the experimental failure stress and the bifurcation stress or limit stress of the numerical model, $\alpha = \sigma_u^{exp}/\sigma_u^{num}$, gives hints to the quality of the numerical model.

References

Knoedel, P.: Stabilitaetsuntersuchungen an kreiszylindrischen staehlernen Siloschuessen. PhD thesis, University of Karlsruhe (Germany) 1995.

Ummenhofer, T.: Stabilitaetsverhalten imperfekter zylindrischer Stahlsiloschalen – experimentelle und numerische Untersuchungen. PhD thesis, University of Karlsruhe (Germany) 1996.

41
Test documentation

41.1 Test conditions
J. Munch-Andersen

41.1.1 Introduction

All silo tests involve numerous test conditions many of which are unchangeable. It is important to report not only on those which have been chosen or specifically studied, but also to report on those other test conditions without which comparison with other tests might be difficult or even meaningless. A list of test conditions that ought to be reported is given below. Dust or similar problems might call for an extra test where for example filling (or discharge) is interrupted a number of times to allow for the dust to settle, so that the required information can be obtained.

41.1.1.1 Filling rate

The best way to obtain the filling rate (mass per time) is by sampling the total mass of the stored material along with the pressures, etc. The rate will often be very constant as the flow rate for a free-flowing material through a hole is practically constant as long as some head of material is present above the hole. Knowledge of the total mass and the time for filling will, therefore, in many cases be sufficient.

41.1.1.2 Surface level

The surface level should be observed regularly during the test, preferably simultaneous to observations of the total mass, as this enables calculation of the unit weight as a function of level. It must be stated which point of the cross-section the level refers to or if the value corresponds to surface level. This applies for filling as well as for discharge.

41.1.1.3 Surface shape (filling)

Most filling methods will cause a cone-shaped surface with a tip to appear where the inlet stream hits the surface. The level and the horizontal position of the tip should be observed together with the level of material along the wall at a number of positions. If distributed filling is aimed at, it should be described how the distribution is arranged and how well the particles are distributed.

41.1.1.4 Inlet pattern

The pattern of the inlet stream from the inlet gate to the surface is helpful when interpreting non-symmetric pressures or flow. It should also be observed if the stream tends to spread. If the inlet stream hits the wall the reflection of the particles should be described. The inlet pattern is probably best estimated from the position of the tip of the surface cone.

41.1.1.5 Height of fall

The height of fall influences the forces and stresses at the impact of the inlet stream as it hits the surface of the bulk material. A reservoir at the top of the silo from which the material falls freely ensures a well-defined height of fall. When a reservoir is not present details of the conveying system and chutes near the inlet should be given. Some measure of velocity can be obtained by observing the cross-section of the flowing material in a chute near the inlet when the filling rate is known.

41.1.1.6 Particle movements on the surface

The particles have to distribute themselves over the cross-section (except in the case of a perfectly distributed filling). At least two types of movements are possible. One is where the slope of the cone increases for a while, followed by a sudden slide of particles down the surface, normally not covering the entire surface at each slide. The other results in a sort of plastic cone with layers of particles that become larger and thinner until they reach the wall. Also a type where the particles slide continuously down the surface can be imagined, together with any sort of combination of the basic types described. These movements can give rise to segregation (section 41.1.1.12).

41.1.1.7 Consolidation effects

The surface level should be observed immediately after completion of filling and just before the start of discharge. If large consolidation effects are expected more observations might be advisable.

41.1.1.8 Discharge rate

The rate can be obtained similarly to the filling rate. It should be stated if the discharge takes place as a free gravity flow or if the rate is determined by some discharge equipment or possibly a narrow section of a chute after the silo outlet. In the latter case the principle of the equipment must be described.

41.1.1.9 Surface shape (discharge)

During discharge observation of the shape of the surface is very helpful for determining the flow type. An undisturbed surface proves the existence of a plug flow zone (also referred to as semi-mass flow). In the case of a rough wall in combination with plug flow, a bank of particles will form along the wall due to the reduced velocity of the particles in the boundary layer next to the silo wall. The volume of the bank can be used to estimate the thickness of the boundary layer if a velocity profile of the boundary layer is assumed. Changes of the surface shape (apart from the bank) prove the presence of internal flow.

A narrow pipe flow will quickly 'invert' the surface cone and particles will slide down the cone towards the pipe. If the flow zone is wider the surface shape can become quite complicated and difficult to interpret. Further, the flow type could change during discharge, and occasionally two flow types might coexist in the silo. An example of this is shown by Munch-Andersen, Askegaard and Brink (1992). It is important to note that an inverted cone with particles sliding down towards the apex can also develop for other flow types besides pipe flow. A simple example is if the bank due to the boundary layer eventually covers the entire surface. The number of particles sliding down will, however, be much smaller than in the case of pipe flow.

A hint for interpreting surface shapes: the ridges might be rounded off and consequently difficult to identify when the surface is inspected from the top of the silo. The valleys will usually be sharp and more easily spotted.

41.1.1.10 Samples

The time of and the method used for taking samples of the stored material should be described.

41.1.1.11 Time

The time for start of filling, end of filling, start of discharge and end of discharge should be recorded. The time elapsed from when the outlet is opened until the surface starts to move or change its shape can be considerable and should therefore be recorded too. The time for any disturbance or disruption of filling and discharge should be recorded as well. The reason for disturbances, etc. should also be reported.

41.1.1.12 Segregation

If the particle size distribution is not measured by analysing samples taken from different positions at the cross-section, a description of the visual impressions should be given.

41.1.1.13 Temperature

Relevant temperatures to record are the temperature of the bulk material, the silo wall, the transducers and the air, all probably at several positions. For outdoor facilities the solar conditions should be reported, along with the position and aspect of the silo.

41.1.1.14 Others

For some materials the moisture content and even the humidity of the air could influence the test. The atmospheric pressure could also be of interest, especially if the pressure transducers used are is sensitive to it.

Reference

Munch-Andersen, J., V. Askegaard, A Brink: *Silo Model Tests with Sand*. SBI Bulletin 91. Danish Building Research Institute. Hørsholm. 1992.

41.2 Properties of the stored granular solid

J.M. Rotter, J. Munch-Andersen and J. Nielsen

41.2.1 Introduction

It is widely accepted that the mechanical behaviour of the stored material has a strong effect on the pressures and flow of the solid. The behaviour of granular solids is often very complex and appears to involve many different factors. Unless the material properties are adequately defined, the results of silo tests cannot be properly interpreted. This section is therefore concerned with the mechanical properties of the stored material which are relevant for the evaluation of silo tests on pressures and flow. Its goal is to define the matters which should be addressed in a materials report as part of the technical report on a silo test.

Several important material properties which should be measured in a silo test have been discussed elsewhere. These include silo wall roughness, moisture content and experimental techniques and density measurement.

41.2.2 Purposes of the material characterization

A description of the stored material is a vital part of any description of a silo test. This material description may serve the following important purposes:

1. It should characterize the material in such a way that, in principle, the tests can be repeated.
2. It should characterize the material so that standard design or similar calculations relating to the test conditions can be made for comparative purposes (e.g. Janssen, Jenike).
3. It should characterize the material so that advanced computer numerical simulations of the test can be conducted.

Properties of the stored granular solid

It is normal scientific practice to fulfil condition 1. Fulfilment of condition 2 is critical to permit other experimental researchers and standards drafters to make use of the results. Condition 3 permits the results to be fully exploited in further research without additional material testing being necessary (sometimes impossible to perform later when the material specification is partly lost).

41.2.3 Introductory ideas

41.2.3.1 Properties and parameters

In the following, the aim is to measure and document the properties of the solid in such a way that the material is well defined for all useful purposes. The following definitions are used here to clarify the use of terms in the later sections.

- A 'property' of a solid is a behaviour in response to external influences (stress, packing, etc.).
- The properties of the solid are generally represented by mathematical models of varying accuracy and efficacy.
- A 'parameter' is a mathematical constant which appears in the mathematical model and attempts to describe the property or a part of it.

Several alternative mathematical models may be used to try to represent the same property, so several alternative parameters may be used to capture the same behaviour. It is possible that parameters measured for one model may be translated into a different set of parameters in another, perhaps with some approximation. Thus, failure to measure all the parameters described for one model does not mean that the material properties have not been captured.

In addition, many parameters can be determined in different ways, so it is important that the materials report on a silo test states how the parameters were determined, possibly by referring to a standard which defines the test.

41.2.3.2 Completeness

A full description of all relevant properties of a granular material is currently impossible, as we do not yet know all the parameters which should be measured, nor how some of the known properties should be measured. What is known is that, in total, a huge number of parameters will be needed, and that many of these will be very difficult to measure.

41.2.3.3 Test characterization and design measurements

Material tests for practical industrial silo design purposes are not the same as those for the characterization of scientific research silo tests. Material tests for design purposes attempt to identify the worst conditions which may occur during the operating life of the silo, and so safe assumptions may be implied within the test and sampling procedures. Tests for characterization of materials used in experiments should be as representative as possible of the actual conditions. Mean values of parameters should be reported, with the addition of standard deviations wherever possible.

41.2.3.4 Powders, coarse-grained particles and fines contents

Particle size has an important influence on the behaviour of a bulk solid in a silo. Fine particles (powders) have such closely spaced particles that the interstitial air between the particles develops significant pressures and flow characteristics of its own, and a two-phase (solid and air) treatment of the material is generally necessary. Powders also contain many contacts in which electrical or hydroscopic forces may influence the behaviour. In particular, cohesion can be developed in powders by compaction alone.

In free-flowing coarse materials without fines, these factors are generally absent. Thus a simpler characterization is possible in coarse solids. However, coarse solids present problems for materials tests of particle assemblies, because the large particles often mean that very large materials testing apparatus is needed to obtain a large enough sample to be treated as a continuum.

Most coarse solids contain a proportion of fine particles. These may be made of identical material to the coarse particles (as with plastic pellets), or they may be completely different (as a clay content in coal). Because of the special role of fine particles in developing cohesion in the solid, it is a common practice in tests for practical silo design purposes to extract the fine material and use it to characterize the whole solid. Often this is the only practicable method, since a cohesion apparatus cannot include the larger particles.

However, in the following, it is the complete solid used in the silo tests which must be characterized. Only a few of the following measures can be usefully performed on the fines extracted from the complete solid. Wherever fines alone are used, the materials report should clearly state that the test refers only to the fines, and should include the particle size distribution of the truncated sample.

41.2.3.5 Changes with time and usage

A key part of all material testing should be checks to see if the properties of the material change during the course of the experiments. Commonest among these is probably an increase in fines content through damage in handling. These changes may lead to changing stress and flow conditions in the test silo.

Material properties may change with time, both during an experiment and during storage in other containers between the time of the experiment and the materials test. Great care should be taken to try to perform materials tests at approximately the same time as the silo experiments, and to store samples under conditions which are representative of the material at the time of test.

Most important of the potential changes with time, which deserves special mention because of the role of water in our planet's atmosphere, is the moisture content. Some properties of solids are very sensitive to the moisture content, so the moisture content at the time of test should be measured and the materials tests performed under the same conditions, wherever possible.

41.2.3.6 Segregation

During silo experiments, it is not uncommon for segregation of the material to occur, even if the effect is slight. Some attempt should be made in all tests to identify the level of segregation and, where appropriate, to characterize the different properties of the different segregated samples. The traditional 'representative sample' of materials testing, with no segregation, is not the only information needed if significant segregation has occurred during the filling or discharge of the silo test.

41.2.3.7 Necessary parameters

Among the most common parameters are those which appear in the Janssen and Jenike equations. These may be adequate for most standard methods for predicting stresses and flow but they are far from sufficient for others (e.g. numerical simulations). Similarly, they may be inadequate for inferring changes in the material properties during a test series or as part of a production control. Information on these matters may also be found in Parts One and Six.

41.2.3.8 Division of parameters: particle and assembly

The measurable material parameters can be divided into two groups: single particle parameters and particle assembly parameters. Parameters relating to particle assemblies may be referred to as 'continuum parameters' in that they are usually used in analyses which consider the material to be a continuum without internal boundaries.

The single particle parameters (e.g. particle shape, size distribution and solid density) are independent of the particle packing or embedment. The assembly parameters (e.g. pressure ratio, unit weight and friction angles) depend on the particle packing structure and the stress state and history.

Laboratory tests are sometimes difficult to use for determining the assembly parameters because granular materials form different particulate packing structures or embedments under different conditions, and reproduction of these in a control test is not straightforward. Even spherical particles of uniform size can be packed in different ways so that significantly different densities and anisotropic behaviour is obtained. The packing affects the unit weight, elastic properties, yield properties, dilation, and many other behaviours.

The packing naturally depends on the filling conditions, but it may also change with time during storage and with discharge, so the parameters which should be measured can be expected to change during time. This means that laboratory tests aimed at determining material properties should not only reflect the properties of the material in the silo just after filling, but also those changes in packing structure that might occur later on.

41.2.4 Parameters which should be considered for characterization

Since the full set of parameters needed to characterize a granular bulk solid is not yet known, a material must currently be characterized by an appropriate subset of this full set of parameters. In the following description, three levels are suggested:

- *Level A: Minimum characterization*: Needed to make any use of the test at all.
- *Level B: Desirable characterization*: For general use by the research community, but not complete.
- *Level C: Specialized characterization*: The most complete characterization known at present.

The features of the solid which the measured parameters must attempt to capture include those shown in Table 41.2.1, which also contains an indication of the recommended level of characterization, with distinctions between coarse-grained particulates and powders.

For all types of characterization it is of utmost importance that the researcher describes very precisely how the parameters have been obtained. As long as there are no agreed standards for these measurements, this is the only way to ensure that other researchers can benefit from the test results.

The conditions pertaining in the silo test cannot be accurately known. Indeed the conditions vary from one part of the silo to another, so the possible range of each particle assembly parameter should be sought, rather than simply a single value.

The simplest approach to this range within the silo is to determine the parameters for loose and dense packing arrangements, but also to measure the sensitivity to other conditions (moisture content, temperature, pressure level, etc.), which may be relevant for some parameters.

Properties of the stored granular solid

Table 41.2.1 Features for different levels of characterization

Parameter	Minimum level A	Desirable level B	Specialized level C
Single particle parameters			
Particle size distribution	✓		
Particle (solid) density		✓	
Typical particle geometry	Coarse	Powders	
Particle angularity and sphericity		Coarse	
Particle surface roughness			✓
Particle internal voidage (associated with absorbed moisture content)			✓
Photograph of typical particles		✓	
Particle assembly (continuum) parameters			
Bulk density (under different conditions) γ	✓		
Moisture content and temperature	Fine	Coarse	
Wall friction coefficient μ	✓		
Lateral pressure ratio k	✓		
Internal friction angle ϕ	✓		
Angle of repose ϕ_r		✓	
Cohesion c	Powders	Coarse	
Jenike parameters: flow function	Powders		
Häußner ratio of bulk densities		✓	
Compaction with stress (Jenike cell)	✓		
Porosity			✓
Dilation angle (volume change during failure)			✓
Elastic material parameters		✓	
Volumetric response parameters (consolidation)			✓
Stress–strain relationships			✓

41.2.5 Single particle parameters

In the following, most of the above parameters are discussed in more detail.

41.2.5.1 Particle size distribution

41.2.5.1.1 Level A

The particle size distribution should be determined by sieving and/or sedimentation as appropriate. Coarse solids should be sieved. Fine particles should be measured by sedimentation.

For coarse particles, the type of mesh sieve should be described. Several standards exists for sieving (e.g. BS 1377: 1990). The one used should be stated.

For fine powders, sedimentation methods should be used (e.g. BS 1377: 1990).

The particle size distribution should be tabulated in the report.

Several measures may be used to characterize the grading curve, and it is helpful if these are included. Useful parameters include the effective particle size, the uniformity coefficient (C_u), and the coefficient of curvature (C_z) (Scott, 1980; Craig, 1992). These are defined in terms of the particle sizes at which proportions by weight pass through a sieve: the sieve size for only 10% is termed D_{10}, 60% is D_{60} and 30% is D_{30}. The 'effective particle size' is defined as D_{10}.

The coefficient of uniformity is given by

$$C_u = \frac{D_{60}}{D_{10}} \qquad (41.2.1)$$

The coefficient of curvature is given by

$$C_z = \frac{D_{30}^2}{\left(D_{10} \times D_{60}\right)} \qquad (41.2.2)$$

41.2.5.1.2 Level C

Segregation may affect the outcome of the silo test. Samples of the solid should be taken from different parts of the silo after filling, and the grading separately measured. Differences between the gradings should be tabulated in the report.

41.2.5.2 Particle (solid) density

41.2.5.2.1 Level B

The particle density is the mass of a particle divided by its volume, including open and closed air-filled pores. This density is sometimes referred to as the 'effective particle density' or the 'aerodynamic particle density'. It is also inaccurately called the 'solid density'. It is not easily determined for small particles. Knowledge of this density permits the void ratio to be calculated from the bulk density. It is therefore quite important.

41.2.5.3 Particle geometry

41.2.5.3.1 Level B

A close-up photo of a sample of particles spread in a single layer should be included. For fine particles, a microscopic image of a sample of particles should be included.

Relevant measures of the geometry of a typical particle should be given where the particles are very similar (e.g. agricultural grains, plastic pellets).

For simplicity, these may treat the particle as an approximate ellipsoid and define the typical geometric parameters.

These may be chosen as:

- the maximum diameter
- the minimum diameter
- the intermediate diameter

41.2.5.3.2 Level C

Measures of typical particle angularity and sphericity should be used where possible (King and Dickin, 1972).

41.2.5.4 Particle surface roughness

41.2.5.4.1 Level C

The local surface roughness of typical particles is not easy to measure. However, it may be important in using discrete particle models of the mechanics of assemblies of particles.

41.2.5.5 Particle absorbed moisture content and internal voidage

41.2.5.5.1 Level C

The moisture content (an assembly parameter noted later) consists of two parts: internal moisture and interstitial moisture. The interstitial moisture is the dominant water in affecting particle interactions and material behaviours. The internal absorbed moisture is driven off during the process of measuring total moisture content. Thus the internal absorbed moisture, which is found when the internal voids are filled with water but the solid is otherwise dry, is an important parameter.

Measurement of the internal voidage is not simple. No recommendation is offered.

41.2.5.6 Statistical measures

41.2.5.6.1 Levels B and C

All the above properties and parameters vary considerably through the particles which make up the stored solid. It is desirable that as many of the tests are repeated on different samples of material and the scatter in each parameter reported, especially for level B and C characterizations. For brevity, it is a reasonable assumption that each parameter is normally distributed: the mean and standard deviation should be reported. However, in a complete report all measurements should be given.

41.2.6 Particle assembly (continuum) parameters

41.2.6.1 Bulk density

41.2.6.1.1 Level A

The bulk density of the solid is a vital parameter if the tests are to be interpreted at all. However, it is not a single simple value, so as soon as very precise measurement of this parameter is sought, the question of how it should be measured arises. For the simplest characterization, the unstressed bulk density should be measured in a manner that bears some relation to the silo test. Usually the solids have been dropped through a significant height on to a pile of existing material. The energy of impact leads to a denser structure than the loosest packing, but not so large as the densest packing possible. The test should be generally in line with Annex B to the Eurocode (EC1 Part 4, 1992).

41.2.6.1.2 Level B

Accurate laboratory determination of the unstressed bulk density in the silo cannot be achieved. For a better characterization, the bulk densities for very loose and very dense packings of the bulk solid should be measured. The materials report should state how the packing arrangements were established.

41.2.6.1.3 Level C

Some solids have bulk densities which are very sensitive to packing arrangements for the particles. For these solids, changes in the bulk density will usually mean changes of principal directions and anisotropic behaviour, both in the laboratory apparatus and in the silo.

Really thorough measurement of bulk density, which may be appropriate for very sensitive solids, should involve *in situ* measurement of bulk density. Where this rather onerous procedure is undertaken, it is most desirable that distinct samples should be taken at different heights in the silo during filling (different particle drop heights) and at different points in the plan section (segregation and different energies of impact).

In the absence of *in situ* measurements, a range of laboratory measurements of density using different packings, or possible drop heights or formation techniques, would be a beneficial set of measurements.

41.2.6.2 Moisture content and temperature

41.2.6.2.1 Level A

The moisture content of the granular solid may have a very marked effect on its behaviour. Even in solids for which this is not commonly recognized

Properties of the stored granular solid

(e.g. agricultural grains), the effect can be very great. Measurement of the moisture content of the solid is therefore a vital part of the test documentation.

The temperature of the materials test has less influence, but may be important. It is such a simple matter to document, that it should always be recorded.

The documentation of temperature variations in silo tests is much more important but is not considered here.

41.2.6.2.2 Level C

The thermal expansion coefficient and the hygral expansion coefficient of a granular solid are not commonly measured. However, where temperature or moisture changes may occur during a silo test, these probably should be found if the test is to be properly interpreted in the future. No recommendations are offered here for a procedure.

41.2.6.3 Wall friction coefficient

41.2.6.3.1 Level A

The wall friction coefficient μ of the solid against a typical piece of wall is a vital parameter if the tests are to be interpreted at all. Several devices for measuring the wall friction coefficient exist. The common principle is that an amount of the granular material is retained within a ring or a square. A normal load is applied and the force necessary to slide the material along a sample of the wall material is measured. The tests are easily carried out at different load levels.

However, the wall friction coefficient μ is not a single simple value, and comparisons of fitted Janssen parameters to measured silo pressures (Ooi *et al.*, 1990) demonstrate clearly that the control test is sometimes far from the mark in identifying the real developed wall friction in the silo test.

For the minimum characterization, wall friction should be measured on what is deemed to be a representative piece of the silo wall in the manner defined for the Jenike shear cell (Jenike, Elsey and Woolley, 1960; Arnold, McLean and Roberts, 1978; BMHB, 1987; EFCE, 1989) or a similar test (EC1 Part 4, 1992), at several different normal load levels.

41.2.6.3.2 Level B

The sensitivity of the measured wall friction to the condition of the wall, which may vary from point to point, deserves investigation by changing the wall sample to alternative wall surfaces in different representative conditions. It may also be found that the wall friction varies considerably with the proportion of fines in the material sample, and minor segregation can so easily lead to variations in fines content near the wall that several tests to explore the sensitivity of the wall friction to the proportion of fines present are worth while.

The effect of non-uniform wall friction on the pressure distribution in silos has not been studied very much (Blight, 1991; Rotter and Ooi, 1991), so the significance of its variation is not well understood. However, it seems likely that it can be responsible for many experimental phenomena which are poorly explained at present. This parameter is therefore well worth careful documentation in tests.

41.2.6.3.3 Level C

Close attention should be paid to slip–stick behaviour, and the possibility of adhesion to the wall. At each load level, there might be two coefficients, one static and the other during motion (dynamic) (van der Kraan, 1996). If the static coefficient is larger than the dynamic value, it will appear as a peak in the shear load, reached before the material starts to slide along the wall sample. The measured wall friction coefficients should be reported as a function of the normal stress.

The wall sample is normally horizontal, which means that the particles cannot be packed into the apparatus in a fashion similar to the packing structure achieved in a silo against a vertical wall. Usually, the wall friction coefficient is not very dependent on the load level, but elongated particles may have different friction properties depending on the orientation of the majority of particles relative to the wall surface. As the long axis of elongated particles tends to pack horizontally, the wall friction measured in a horizontal shear apparatus may be smaller than the real value.

If the wall is very rough, as a concrete silo wall can be, or if the wall is corrugated, the particles may not slide along the wall and the effective shear will then take place in a boundary layer forming next to the wall (Munch-Andersen, 1986; Munch-Andersen and Nielsen, 1990). The devices which are commonly used do not allow this boundary layer to form but compel the sliding to occur at the wall surface. This leads to an overestimate of the effective wall friction coefficient. For corrugated walls, the global wall friction coefficient can be estimated (AS 3774, 1990), but more careful tests are appropriate (Haaker and Scott, 1983).

For a full characterization of the wall friction effects, it is desirable that measures of surface roughness are conducted since these reveal more about the nature of the wall friction contact (Ooms and Roberts, 1983; Roberts, Ooms and Wiche, 1988).

Where very low stress levels are encountered and important in the tests, special provision may need to be made for low stress wall friction measurements (Roberts, 1996).

41.2.6.4 Lateral pressure ratio

41.2.6.4.1 Level A

The initial post-filling stress state in a silo with vertical walls depends significantly on the lateral pressure ratio, k (or λ). Where the test has been performed in a silo with relatively squat proportions, this parameter is very important, and should be given level B characterization.

The lateral pressure ratio k is defined from Janssen's equation as the ratio between the (assumed uniform) horizontal wall pressure and the mean vertical stress at any section in the silo. This cannot be deduced directly, but the material constant related to it, the ratio of horizontal to vertical stress in a laterally contained solid sample subjected to one-dimensional stress, can be assessed more easily.

For simple characterization, the ratio is commonly inferred from the angle of internal friction ϕ by means of mathematical expressions of uncertain accuracy. Measurement of the effective angle of internal friction ϕ is described below.

The expression used to infer k from ϕ depends on the assumptions made about the state of stress which will develop. Simple versions can be written as follows. At rest value k_0 (Jaky, 1948):

$$k = 1 - \sin\phi \qquad (41.2.3)$$

Modified at-rest value (EC1 Part 4, 1992):

$$k = 1.1(1 - \sin\phi) \qquad (41.2.4)$$

Active value (assumes the wall to expand away from the solid) (Rankine, 1857):

$$k = \frac{1 - \sin\phi}{1 + \sin\phi} \qquad (41.2.5)$$

Active value accounting for variation in the stress ratio in the silo and the wall friction condition against the wall (Walker, 1966; Arnold, McLean and Roberts, 1980; Hartlen et al., 1984; Rotter, 1986; AS 3774, 1990):

$$k = \frac{1 + \sin^2\phi - 2\sqrt{\sin^2\phi - \mu^2\cos^2\phi}}{4\mu^2 + \cos^2\phi} \qquad (41.2.6)$$

Ideally rough wall active value as a special case of equation (41.2.6) (Hartmann, 1966):

$$k = \frac{1 - \sin^2\phi}{1 + \sin^2\phi} \qquad (41.2.7)$$

More complicated expressions can also be devised, involving the cohesion c of the solid or the adhesion of the wall, but there is little evidence that these estimates are any more accurate than the above.

For values of the internal friction angle ϕ around 30° (and a typical μ value), the above expressions all yield similar values, with the exception of equation (41.2.5).

The above expressions are listed, so that the experimenter following these guidelines may see the variety of potential values which could be considered.

41.2.6.4.2 Level B

In soil mechanics, three key values for the parameter k exist: the active k_a, passive k_p and at-rest k_0 values. The most relevant for the filling condition in a silo is the at-rest value k_0. Development of the active stress state demands that some horizontal expansion of the solid occurs, whereas the stresses may move towards a passive state if there is considerable horizontal constriction, as perhaps at the transition to a hopper. Discharge of a mass flow silo permits expansion in the vertical direction, but this does not mean that a passive stress state is achieved.

The at-rest lateral pressure ratio for the solid k_0 is better determined directly by compressing solids vertically into a relatively stiff ring. The ring is instrumented to obtain the normal stress acting on the ring when a normal load is applied to the free surface. A simple version of this apparatus is described in Annex B to Eurocode 1 (EC1 Part 4, 1992), using long strain gauges around the circumference of the ring. Several apparatuses of this type have been developed by different researchers. A recent well-designed device was described by Kwade, Schulze and Schwedes (1994).

The disadvantage of this apparatus is the difficulty in achieving a uniform sample, so that the lateral pressure varies around the ring. When the ring is made deeper, greater uniformity is achieved, but the results begin to be affected by wall friction developed between the solid and the ring casing. In some apparatuses, this is recognized directly and assessed during the interpretation of the results (Lohnes and Lui, 1985; Zachary and Lohnes, 1988).

41.2.6.4.3 Level C

It might be supposed that the best value of lateral pressure ratio would be derived from a sophisticated constitutive model (see below) which has been carefully calibrated against triaxial or biaxial test results. However, great care should be taken with this approach, as the stress paths often used in these better tests may not have focused well on the stress condition of zero lateral expansion without wall friction. Such a condition is necessary to obtain an accurate measure of k_0. It is recommended that experiments of the level B type be conducted as part of any constitutive model calibration, because this parameter is so important in defining the initial stress state in the silo.

41.2.6.5 Angle of internal friction

41.2.6.5.1 Level A

The angle of internal friction ϕ is widely used to characterize the behaviour of granular solids for all purposes, so it is vital that it is measured as part of the documentation of any test.

For coarse-grained particulates the friction angle can be determined in different ways. The crudest measure is obtained by measuring the angle of repose ϕ_r of a free pile of the solid, but this is unreliable and has been widely criticized in the past. It is not recommended, except for conditions where extremely quick and rough assessment is needed.

If k_0 is determined at level B, the friction angle can be estimated from equation (41.2.3). The simplest satisfactory method of assessing the angle of internal friction is using a shear cell (Jenike or similar). For solids which do not develop cohesion readily when overconsolidated, no distinction is needed between the simple and effective angles of internal friction. Shear tests at different normal stress levels rapidly lead to the angle of internal friction ϕ (e.g. as described in Annex B to Eurocode 1 (EC1 Part 4, 1992)).

For powders and coarse-grained solids containing fines, the complete Jenike flow function should be obtained by a series of Jenike shear cell tests (see below). From the flow function, the effective angle of internal friction may be deduced.

41.2.6.5.2 Level C

Comprehensive exploration of the strength of the solid, represented crudely by the internal friction angle, is best done using either low stress triaxial or biaxial tests (see below).

41.2.6.6 Angle of repose

41.2.6.6.1 Level B

The angle of repose ϕ_r of the solid is closely related to the angle of internal friction ϕ, and for this reason, it is listed here as a level B characterization when it is to be separately measured. The angle of repose is important in the assessment of silo tests on squat silos, where the total mass of solid in the silo depends considerably on the shape of the top surface.

Measurement of the angle of repose is notoriously sensitive to the condition in which the solid is resting and the manner of formation of the particle assembly (planar conditions differ from axisymmetric ones, a slope formed by dropping particles from above is different from that formed by removing particles from below, etc.). Thus, the conditions under which the angle of repose is measured should be closely related to those in which it is to be used.

41.2.6.6.2 Level C

For a full characterization, three angles are particularly useful. The first ϕ_{rh} (heap) is the angle formed on a heap when it is filled from above in the manner of the silo test: this is best measured *in situ* in the silo after filling, possibly by using plumb-bob depth measurements from above.

The second ϕ_{rf} (flow) is the angle which forms on any sloping surface which is in motion during the course of the test: where solids slough off the surface and pass down a funnel flow of some type.

The third ϕ_{rd} (dead) only occurs in tests where dead material remains in the silo after the discharge is complete: the final angle of dead solid depends on the cohesion which has developed in the material during the course of the test and is an important repose angle for assessing the test.

41.2.6.7 Cohesion

41.2.6.7.1 Level A for powders, level B for coarse-grained particles

When solids are compressed and the stress is then reduced, they commonly develop a strength independent of the normal applied stress. In all silo tests in which arching, ratholing or incomplete clean-out are involved, some measure of the development of cohesion with stress is needed. The most widely used method is the Jenike shear cell, from which the flow function of the solid can be derived (see below).

Other shear cells may also be used (Carr and Walker, 1968; Peschl, 1989; Schulze, 1994), though the measures of cohesion deduced from them are not quite identical. The cell defined in Annex B to the Eurocode (EC1 Part 4, 1992) is a generic representation of the Jenike cell.

Direct cohesion tests may also be conducted, giving quicker and more direct measures for relatively cohesive solids (Levorson *et al.*, 1996; Maltby and Enstad, 1995; van der Kraan, 1996).

Less direct cohesion tests have been developed to address hopper design directly. These are less useful for silo test materials characterization. They include the tests of Gerritsen (1986) and Bates (Bell *et al.*, 1995) and the Johanson indicizer (Johanson, 1992).

41.2.6.7.2 Level C

Comprehensive exploration of the strength of the solid, involving the cohesion, is best done using either low stress triaxial or biaxial tests (see below).

41.2.6.8 Jenike flow function

41.2.6.8.1 Level A for powders, level B for coarse-grained solids

The Jenike flow function is very important for any good documentation of a silo test, and is vital for all materials which contain fines or high moisture contents.

The flow function is determined using the Jenike shear cell (Jenike, Elsey and Woolley, 1960; Jenike, 1961). This apparatus is well defined, widely described and much effort has been put into ensuring operating procedures which lead to reproducible results (EFCE, 1989) and how to interpret the results (Jenike, 1961; Arnold, McLean and Roberts, 1980; BMHB, 1987). Nevertheless, the outcome of the test is a little sensitive to the cell operator, and great care is needed to ensure the data are representative of the solid.

Improved shear testers operating on effectively the same principle, but with many of the disadvantages eliminated, are still being developed (Schulze, 1994, 1995).

It is important to recognize the value of the Jenike flow function: because of the special characteristics of the test, the parameters determined are not directly usable for purposes other than the design of hoppers for flow using the Jenike theory. Nevertheless, a documented flow function certainly gives a widely recognized and clearly documented measure of the development of cohesion in the solid as a result of stress.

Where the silo test has been undertaken over a significant time-scale, and there is reason to believe that the flow function may be time-sensitive (e.g. with coal or solids with high moisture contents), the Jenike time flow function should be documented for the solid.

41.2.6.9 Triaxial tests

41.2.6.9.1 Level C

The classic triaxial test, developed in the field of soil mechanics (Craig, 1992), is one in which three-dimensional uniform compressive stress is applied to a sample, and a uniaxial compression can be added until the sample fails. The test has the potential to give very extensive information about the behaviour of a solid, and modern computational constitutive models have been developed from information derived from this test. It is therefore a very valuable test for granular bulk solids.

This test, or a similar one, is absolutely vital if the silo test results are to be modelled using modern finite element computer programs which attempt to predict flow and pressures. Thus, any experiment which is intended to serve as a classic benchmark must have the solids properly characterized using a triaxial or biaxial test. Where the solid contains coarse particles, it is generally necessary to use a triaxial test, as the elimination of coarse particles from the sample is not acceptable for tests which aim to calibrate a constitutive model.

Researchers who have developed special versions of the triaxial test for use with dry granular bulk solids include Hartlen (1980), Smith and Lohnes (1981), Bokhoven and Lohnes (1986), Bradfield and Lohnes (1988), Ooi, Rotter and Hull (1988, 1989), Ooi and Rotter (1991), Bock, Puri and Manbeck (1989) and Kolymbas (1989).

However, there are a number of disadvantages to the triaxial test applied to granular solids:

1. In the test, two principal stresses are always equal, so the number of stress paths is limited.
2. The stress levels for which the test was developed are larger than those needed for silo tests, so modifications to the test rig are desirable to permit low stress testing (e.g. Ooi, Rotter and Hull, 1988).
3. It was developed for tests in which the granular solid is fully saturated with interstitial water: modifications to use interstitial air with low stresses make precise results more difficult to obtain on dry granular solids (e.g. Ooi, Rotter and Hull, 1988).

The triaxial test can reveal many features of the response of the solid, captured in the following parameters:

- elastic properties (E and v) and their variation with stress condition;
- dilation angle ψ at large strains;
- failure properties for normally consolidated stress conditions (angle of internal friction ϕ);
- failure properties for overconsolidated stress conditions (e.g. apparent cohesion c);
- volumetric response parameters for different stress paths;
- stress–strain relationships.

The equivalent of the Jenike flow function can also be derived, though the triaxial test is more onerous to perform than a Jenike shear cell test.

Conventional triaxial tests are carried out by first consolidating a cylindrical sample (typically 100 mm diameter and 200 mm high) to a chosen isotropic stress state, then increasing the vertical stress until failure occurs (the sample becomes very seriously distorted from its original shape).

Because the properties are generally very sensitive to the stress level at which the testing is conducted, the test should be carried out at stress levels to be found in the silo test. This means that relatively small confining stresses (e.g. ≈ 30 kPa) should be used. It may be easier to achieve these using air pressure rather than water (or oil), as the hydrostatic component of the water pressure can be quite significant compared to the relevant stress (100 mm of hydrostatic pressure equals 1 kPa). For coarse-grained granular solids, membrane penetration destroys any chance to determine the volume changes from changes in the air volume within the membrane (Ooi, 1990).

Instead, direct measurements of the specimen circumference must be made (Kolymbas, 1989; Ooi and Rotter, 1991). This requires measurements at several levels. Tests needed for silo test characterization have been discussed by Nielsen and Kolymbas (1988).

The tests which should be used if the test is to be useful for silo predictions include:

- isotropic consolidation, monitoring the change in volume, and using unloading and reloading to explore the quasi-elastic stiffness produced at several different stress levels;
- isotropic consolidation to a chosen stress, followed by deviator stress increase to failure (this should be done for several different isotropic stress levels);
- isotropic consolidation to a chosen stress (as above), reduction of the isotropic stress to a much lower value, followed by deviator stress increase to failure (for each initial isotropic consolidation stress, several different levels of stress reduction should be performed). This test series is the one which most closely models the Jenike shear cell flow function test series.

Even with the limitation that the two horizontal principal stresses must be equal, several other stress patterns can be investigated in a triaxial test. The vertical stress can be reduced until failure occurs (with an appropriate small change to the apparatus), which may be taken to model the vertical expansion of solid in a silo during discharge (discharge of a mass flow silo permits expansion in the vertical direction, but this condition is not normally covered in standard triaxial tests (Ooi, 1990; Ooi and Rotter, 1991)). Alternatively, failure can be obtained by reducing the horizontal stresses whilst keeping the vertical stress (or the vertical deformation) constant.

The triaxial test may be used to explore anisotropic properties of dry granular solids (Hartlen et al., 1984; Ooi, 1990), together with anisotropic particle assemblies. These will probably become increasingly important in future years.

The reporting of a triaxial test should include:

- a description of the preparation process for the sample;
- the initial unit weight of the sample (indicating packing density);
- diagrams showing the stress paths used in the tests;
- diagrams showing the isotropic uniform stress consolidation behaviour and swelling after its release (under conditions $\sigma_1 = \sigma_2 = \sigma_3$; plot $(\sigma_1 + \sigma_2 + \sigma_3)/3$ against volumetric strain ε_v);
- diagrams showing the deviatoric behaviour (under conditions $\sigma_1 \neq \sigma_2 = \sigma_3$; plot $\sigma_1 - \sigma_3$ against deviator strain ε_1).

Only if this information is fully documented can other researchers gain the full benefit of the effort spent in performing the tests.

41.2.6.10 Biaxial tests

41.2.6.10.1 Level C

A biaxial cell is one in which two principal stresses or strains can be governed, but the third principal strain is fixed at zero ($\varepsilon_z = 0$). This cell type is more expensive and more complicated to operate than the triaxial cell.

The biaxial cell is a relatively recent development (Arthur, Dunstan and Enstad, 1985), because techniques to introduce uniform displacement to the sample without significant end platen friction were not easily devised. Different biaxial cells have been reported by a number of researchers (Arthur *et al.*, 1991; Maltby, 1993; Nowak, 1993; van der Kraan, 1996).

Most research carried out in biaxial cells has been aimed at replacing the Jenike cell, because of the latter's limitations and sensitivity to operator variation. In the biaxial cell, one test can replace several tests undertaken in the Jenike cell, so the repeatability of formation of samples is not such an important issue. In addition, the serious shortcomings of the Jenike cell that failure occurs in an undefined zone and that the displacements have little or no significance are overcome in the biaxial cell.

The biaxial cell can be used to determine the internal friction angle ϕ and the cohesion c, or the effective angle of internal friction δ, but the tests can also be carried out following stress and strain paths of greater variation than in the triaxial cell. This means that biaxial tests can be used to achieve a better description of the complete response of a granular material in the three-dimensional space, and to deduce the parameters needed for modern computational constitutive models (Feise, Lyle and Novak, 1993), though these possibilities are not commonly used.

The chief advantages of the biaxial cell are:

- For silos work, the zero lateral strain condition ($\varepsilon_z = 0$) is a better constraint condition than the equality of the second and third principal stresses ($\sigma_2 = \sigma_3$) used in the triaxial test. This is because the constraint of silo walls is relatively close to a zero strain condition.
- Observations of volumetric change can be made directly.
- Great control can be exercised over stress and strain paths in the two-dimensional operating plane.

The chief disadvantages of the biaxial cell are:

- It is expensive to construct and instrument.
- Great care is needed to introduce the sample displacements without boundary shears.
- The cell generally cannot be used for materials which include any coarser particles.
- For observations on anisotropic solids, the natural particle packing assembly is wrongly oriented relative to the direction of stress and strain changes in the silo.

- It is not as well suited to the study of solids with large particles as a triaxial test.
- The triaxial test has a very much larger literature, and most modern constitutive models are based on observations made using triaxial cells.

The reporting of a biaxial test should include:

- a description of the preparation process for the sample;
- the initial unit weight of the sample (indicating packing density);
- diagrams showing the strain or stress paths used in the tests;
- diagrams showing the uniform stress consolidation behaviour and swelling after its release (under conditions $\sigma_1 = \sigma_2$; plot $(\sigma_1 + \sigma_2)/2$ against volumetric strain ε_v);
- diagrams showing the deviatoric behaviour (under conditions $\sigma_1 \neq \sigma_2$; plot $\sigma_1 - \sigma_2$ against deviator strain ε_1).

Only if this information is fully documented can other researchers gain the full benefit of the effort spent in performing the tests.

41.2.6.11 True triaxial tests

41.2.6.11.1 Level C

A true triaxial cell is one in which all three principal stresses or strains can be governed independently (Wood, 1975). These cells are very expensive and rare and the test results which are obtained are so voluminous that their interpretation is a significant challenge. To these writers' knowledge, no tests on dry bulk solids have ever been conducted in a true triaxial cell, but it does, in principle, represent the best possible test for characterizing the mechanical responses of granular solids.

References

Arnold, P.C.; McLean, A.G. and Roberts, A.W. (1978) *Bulk Solids: Storage, Flow and Handling*, Tunra Bulk Solids Handling Research Associates, University of Newcastle, Australia (second edition 1980).

Arthur, J.R.F.; Dunstan, T. and Enstad, G.G. (1985) Determination of the flow function by means of a cubic plane strain tester, *International Journal of Bulk Storage in Silos*, 1(2), 7–10.

Arthur, J.R.F.; Dunstan, T.; Dalili, A. and Wong, R.K.S. (1991) The initiation of flow in granular solids, *Powder Technology*, 65, 89–101.

AS 3774 (1990) *Loads on Bulk Solids Containers*, Australian Standard with Commentary, Standards Association of Australia, Sydney, August.

Bell, T.A.; Grygo, R.J.; Duffy, S.M. and Puri, V.M. (1995) Simplified methods of measuring powder cohesive strength, *Proc. Partec 95, 3rd European Symposium on the Storage and Flow of Particulate Solids*, Nuremberg, pp. 79–88.

Blight, G.E. (1991) Defects in accepted methods of estimating design loading for silos, *Proc. Institution of Civil Engineers*, London, Part 1, Vol. 90(3), Paper 9593, 1077–1088.

BMHB (1987) *Silos: Draft Design Code for Silos, Bins, Bunkers and Hoppers*, British Materials Handling Board and British Standards Institution, London.

Bock, R.G.; Puri, V.M. and Manbeck, H.B. (1989) Modelling relaxation response of wheat en masse using triaxial test, *Trans. ASAE*, 32(5), 1701–1708.

Bokhoven, W.H. and Lohnes, R.A. (1986) Strength and stress–strain characteristics of soybean meal as determined by triaxial testing, *Proc. 11th Annual Powder and Bulk Solids Conference*, Rosemont, Illinois, May, pp. 49–57.

Bradfield, B.E. and Lohnes, R.A. (1988) Triaxial testing of coal: influence of gradation and moisture on flow characteristics, *Proc. 13th Annual Powder and Bulk Solids Conference*, Rosemont, Illinois, May, pp. 437–447.

BS 1377: 1990 (1990) *Methods of Test for Soils for Civil Engineering Purposes*, British Standards Institution, London.

Carr, J.F. and Walker, D.M. (1968) An annular shear cell for granular materials, *Powder Technology*, 1, 355–368.

Craig, R.F. (1992) *Soil Mechanics*, 5th edition, Chapman & Hall, London.

EC1 Part 4 (1992) *Eurocode 1: Basis of Design and Actions on Structures Part 4: Actions on Silos and Tanks*, ENV 1991-4, draft, CEN, Brussels.

EFCE (1989) *Standard Shear Testing Technique for Particulate Solids using the Jenike Shear Cell*. European Federation of Chemical Engineers, The Institution of Chemical Engineers, London.

Feise, H.; Lyle, C. and Nowak, M (1993) Calibration of a hypoplastic constitutive model from biaxial tests, in *Modern Approaches to Plasticity*, Ed. D. Kolymbas, Elsevier, Amsterdam, pp. 259–276.

Gerritsen, A.H. (1986) A simple method for measuring powder flow functions with a view to hopper designs, *PARTEC 1986, Preprints*, Nuremberg, pp. 257–279.

Haaker, G. and Scott, O. (1983) Wall loads on corrugated steel silos, *Proc., International Conference on Bulk Materials Storage, Handling and Transportation*, Newcastle, I.E. Aust., Aug., pp. 218–225.

Hartlen, J. (1980) The strength parameters of grain, *European Symposium on Particle Technology*, 3–5 June, Amsterdam, 9 pp.

Hartlen, J.; Nielsen, J.; Ljunggren, L.; Martensson, G. and Wigram, S. (1984) *The Wall Pressure in Large Grain Silos*, Swedish Council for Building Research, Stockholm, Document D2:1984.

Hartmann, F. (1966) Berechnung des Fulldruckes in einem Silo, *Beton und Stahlbetonbau*, No. 7, 177–183.

Jaky, J. (1948) Pressures in silos, *Proceedings, 2nd International Conference on Soil Mechanics and Foundation Engineering*, Rotterdam, 21–30 June, Vol. 1, pp. 103–107.

Jenike, A.W. (1961) *Gravity Flow of Bulk Solids*, Bulletin No. 108, Utah Engineering Experiment Station, Vol. 52, No. 29, October 1961, University of Utah, Salt Lake City, Utah, 309 pp.

Jenike, A.W.; Elsey, P.J. and Woolley, R.H. (1960) Flow properties of bulk solids, *Proceedings of the American Society for Testing and Materials*, 60, 1168–1181.

Johanson, J.R. (1992) The Johanson Indicizer system vs. the Jenike shear tester, *Bulk Solids Handling*, 12(2), 237–240.

King, G.J.W. and Dickin, E.A. (1972) The evaluation of grain shapes in silica sands from a simple flow test, *Matériaux et Constructions*, 5(26), 85–92.

Kolymbas, D. (1989) Stress strain behaviour of granular media, *Proc., Third Int. Conf. Bulk Materials Storage, Handling and Transportation*, I.E. Aust., Newcastle, June, pp. 141–149.

Kwade, A.; Schulze, D. and Schwedes, J. (1994) Determination of the stress ratio in uniaxial compression tests: Part 2, *Powder Handling and Processing*, 6(2), 199–203.

Levorson, S.M.; Lohnes, R.A. and Treiber, B.S. (1996) An apparatus for the direct measurement of unconfined yield strength of crushed coal, *Trans. Soc. Mining, Metallurgy and Exploration*, 298, 1811–1815.

Lohnes, R.A. and Lui, J.C. (1985) Experimental determination of Ko stress ratios in grain, *Proc. 10th Annual Powder and Bulk Solids Conference*, Rosemont, Illinois, May, pp. 231–237.

Maltby, L.P. (1993) Investigation of the behaviour of powders under and after consolidation, PhD thesis, Telemark Institute of Technology, Porsgrunn, Norway.

Maltby, L.P. and Enstad, G.G. (1995) Uniaxial tester for quality control and flow property characterisation of powders, *Bulk Solids Handling*, 13(1), 135–139.

Munch-Andersen, J. (1986) The boundary layer in rough silos, *Proc. Second Int. Conf. on Bulk Materials Storage, Handling and Transportation*, Instn Engrs, Aust., Wollongong, July, pp. 160–163.

Munch-Andersen, J. and Nielsen, J. (1990) Pressures in slender grain silos, *CHISA 1990, Second European Symposium on Stress and Strain in Particulate Solids*, Prague, 26–31 August, 9 pp.

Nielsen, J. and Kolymbas, D. (1988) Properties of granular materials relevant for silo loads, *Proc., International Conference: 'Silos – Forschung und Praxis'*, University of Karlsruhe, October, pp. 119–132.

Nowak, M. (1993) Spannungs-/Dehnungsverhalten von Kalkstein in der Zweiaxialbox, PhD thesis, Technical University of Braunschweig, Germany.

Ooi, J.Y. (1990) Bulk solids behaviour and silo wall pressures, PhD Thesis, University of Sydney.

Ooi, J.Y. and Rotter, J.M. (1991) The mechanical behaviour of wheat under storage stress histories, *Proc., International Conference: Bulk Materials – Towards the Year 2000*, Institution of Mechanical Engineers, 29–31 October, London, pp. 181–186.

Ooi, J.Y.; Rotter, J.M. and Hull, T.S. (1988) Triaxial testing of dry granular solids at very low stresses, *Proc., Eleventh Australasian Conference on the Mechanics of Structures and Materials*, Auckland, New Zealand, Aug., 8 pp.

Ooi, J.Y.; Rotter, J.M. and Hull, T.S. (1989) *Triaxial Testing of Dry Granular Solids at Very Low Stresses*. School of Civil and Mining Engineering, the University of Sydney. Research Report No. R588.

Ooi, J.Y.; Rotter, J.M. and Pham, L. (1990) Systematic and random features of measured pressures on full-scale silo walls, *Engineering Structures*, 12(2), April 1990, 74–87.

Ooms, M. and Roberts, A.W. (1983) Hopper surface finish and friction interrelation with respect to bulk solids flow from storage bins, *Proc., International*

Conference on Bulk Materials Storage, Handling and Transportation, IE Aust., 22–24 August, Newcastle, Australia.
Peschl, I.A.S.Z. (1989) Equipment for the measurement of mechanical properties of bulk materials, *Powder Handling and Processing*, 1, 73–81.
Rankine, W.J.M. (1857) On the stability of loose earth, *Phil. Trans. Roy. Soc., London*, 147, 9.
Roberts, A.W. (1996) Feeding of bulk solids, *Proc., 12th International Congress of Chemical and Process Engineering*, CHISA'96, Prague, 25–30 August, 18 pp.
Roberts, A.W.; Ooms, M. and Wiche, S.J. (1988) Concepts of boundary friction, adhesion and wear in bulk solids handling operations, *3rd International Conference on Bulk Materials Storage, Handling and Transportation*, Newcastle, June, pp. 349–358.
Rotter, J.M. (1986) Recent advances in the structural design of steel bins and silos, *Pacific Steel Structures Conference*, Auckland, Aug., Vol. 4, pp. 177–194.
Rotter, J.M. and Ooi, J.Y. (1991) Discussion of 'Defects in accepted methods of estimating design loading for silos' by G.E. Blight, *Proc. Institution of Civil Engineers*, London, Part 1, 90(3), Paper 9593, Oct. 1991, 1077–1088.
Schulze, D. (1994) A new ring shear tester for flowability and time consolidation measurements, *Proc., First International Particle Technology Forum*, Part III, AIChE, Denver, Colorado, pp. 11–16.
Schulze, D. (1995) Appropriate devices for the measurement of flow properties for silo design and quality control, *Proc., 3rd European Symposium: Storage and Flow of Particulate Solids, PARTEC 1995*, Nuremberg, 21–23 March, pp. 45–56.
Scott, C.R. (1980) *An Introduction to Soil Mechanics and Foundations*, 3rd edition, Applied Science Publishers, London.
Smith, D.L.O. and Lohnes, R.A. (1981) Frictional and stress–strain characteristics of selected agricultural grains as indicated by triaxial testing, *Proc. 6th Annual Powder and Bulk Solids Conference '81*, Chicago, Illinois, May, 8 pp.
Van der Kraan, M. (1996) Techniques for the measurement of the flow properties of cohesive powders, PhD thesis, Technical University of Delft, 165 pp.
Walker, D.M. (1966) An approximate theory for pressure and arching in hoppers, *Chemical Engineering Science*, 21, 975–997.
Wood, D.M. (1974) Some aspects of the mechanical behaviour of kaolin under truly triaxial conditions of stress and strain, PhD thesis, Cambridge University.
Wood, D.M. (1975) Explorations of principal stress space with kaolin in a true triaxial apparatus, *Geotechnique*, 25(4), 783–797.
Zachary, L.W. and Lohnes, R.A. (1988) A confined compression test for bulk solids, *Proc. 13th Annual Conf. Powder and Bulk Solids Handling*, Powder Advisory Centre, London, pp. 483–494.

41.3 Data presentation
J. Munch-Andersen

41.3.1 Introduction

The data to be sampled during a silo test should naturally be chosen to fulfil the purpose of the test, but the value of the test will be increased considerably if the data can be used to study phenomena other than those presently in question. However, the ideal data sampling method does not exist, as fast reading means either less accurate readings or calls for individual amplifiers for each channel. Further, current data acquisition technology permits taking so many readings during a single test that the size of the data file easily becomes a practical problem.

41.3.2 Data acquisition

There are two main decisions to be taken when planning the data acquisition. The first is the resolution of the data acquisition system, i.e. how accurate the readings need to be. The second is the sample rate, i.e. how frequently the readings should be taken.

A silo pressure (or any other measure of silo loads) can be considered as being composed of a mean value (like the Janssen pressure) and one or more zero-mean processes, which might include both slow and fast pressure variations. What is 'slow' and what is 'fast' cannot be described generally. A constructed example of a pressure and its different components is given in Fig. 41.3.1.

Fourier transforms and power spectrum analysis of a typical pressure are a helpful tool when planning data acquisition. The power at each frequency can be obtained as the summed square of the Fourier coefficients

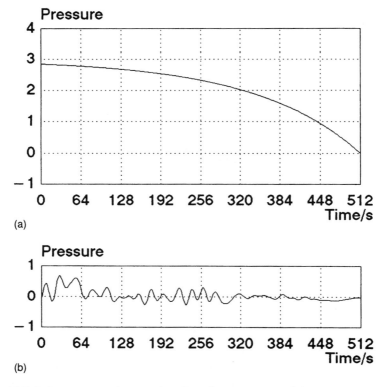

Fig. 41.3.1 A constructed example of a silo pressure and its components. The sample distance, s, is also used as time unit. Only the first half of the period will be used in the following examples: (a) the Janssen component; (b) the slow zero-mean process; (c) the fast zero-mean process; (d) the silo pressure.

for that frequency. The total power is equal to the covariance of the pressure if the mean value has been subtracted. The power spectrum reveals at which frequencies the major variations take place. The fastest frequency for which the power spectrum can be estimated is the so-called Nykvist frequency, which is half the sample rate or $1/(2s)$, where s is the sample distance.

Estimation of the power spectrum requires readings taken at a 'sufficiently' high rate, that is faster than all significant pressure variations. A severe problem is that major decisions regarding the hardware of the acquisition system usually have to be taken long before it is possible to run a preliminary test, which can provide the necessary data for a power spectrum analysis.

The analysis should not be extended over sudden changes of the pressure characteristics, for example due to change of flow pattern. Instead the analysis should be carried out separately for the data before and after the change.

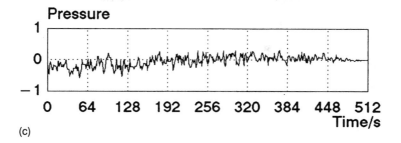

(c)

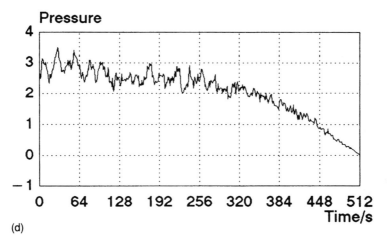

(d)

Fig. 41.3.1 *Continued*

Figure 41.3.2 shows the power spectrum of the first half of the pressure from Fig. 41.3.1, presented in different ways. When significant trends are present, as the underlying Janssen mean value, this trend will cause large power at low frequencies. Using a period where the trend is small makes the interpretation simpler.

Assume a situation where a power spectrum analysis of the pressure reveals a frequency at which the power characteristics change significantly, for example seen as a sharp bend of the summed spectral density. This could define what should be regarded as fast and slow variations for the actual test. The bend might indicate that variations at frequencies above the bend are due to a separate physical phenomenon that can be ignored, for instance, noise or very local phenomena.

If the power of the fast variations are small compared to the power of the slow variations, it will for many purposes be sufficient to choose a sample rate high enough to catch the slow variation, that is twice the highest frequency appearing in the slow variation part. The fast variation will then appear as noise.

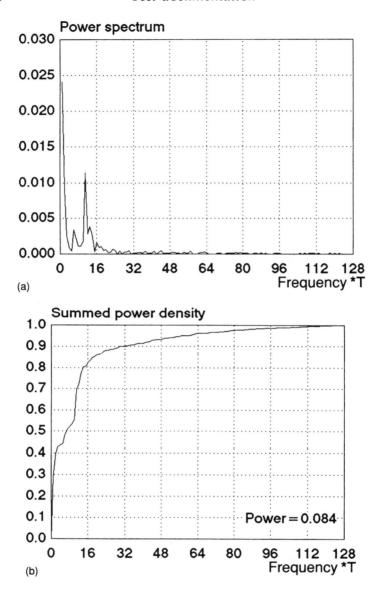

Fig. 41.3.2 The power spectrum of the first half of the pressure in Fig. 41.3.1 T is the length of the data stretch, $T = 256$ s. (a) A simple plot, from which it can mainly be seen that the power of the lower frequencies are by far the most significant. Plotting the logarithm of the power instead of the power is often useful, especially when combined with averaging over a few frequencies. (b) Summing the power starting from the low frequencies is often very useful. The sum is divided by the total power, thus obtaining a spectral density.

Data presentation 677

A simple way to get an idea of the introduced noise for a considered sampling rate is to calculate the Fourier transform of the stress, and transform back to stresses after having zeroed all the coefficients for the frequencies below half the considered sampling rate. Figure 41.3.3 shows an example of such noise.

If the fast pressure variations are not negligible, but considered uninteresting for some reason, their contribution to the signal can be eliminated by using an acquisition device which can integrate over a period equivalent to the sampling rate.

Instead of integration, all channels can be read less accurately at a high rate m times. The average of the m readings for each channel is then estimated and stored. The averaging time can be adjusted by changing the number of times the group is read before the average is estimated.

A sampling strategy, applicable for all situations, is to sample the signal at a rate sufficient for the fast variations as well. The major problem of that strategy is the enormous amount of data sampled from each test.

A simple way to reduce the amount of data is to use different sample rates for different types of observation, that is, for example, temperatures are read less frequently than stresses. Another method is to sort the sampled data before they are stored. This requires the definition of a threshold level such that only if the latest sampled value of a channel deviates more than the specified threshold value from the last stored value will the latest value be stored.

The price to be paid for this method is that the stored values must be accompanied by the channel number in the data file, whereby each reading takes up more disk space. The experience is, however, that the net saving

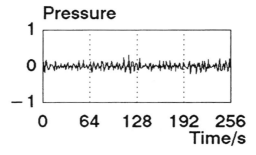

Fig. 41.3.3 From Fig. 41.3.2 it can be seen that the power characteristic changes at 32/T, thus a sampling rate of 64/T could be considered. This figure shows the noise that would be introduced to the pressure in Fig. 41.3.1 if it was sampled at $64/T = 1/(4s)$ ($T = 256s$). The variance (or power) of the noise is 0.0083.

is very significant. Another price is that the processing becomes more complicated.

The threshold value can be appropriately chosen in the same order as the square root of the variance of the noise estimated in Fig. 41.3.3. (This variance can also be determined from Fig. 41.3.2(b). It equals the power of the frequencies above $32/T$ which is about 0.1×0.084.)

As a safe mixture of these sampling methods, it can be considered as an alternative (if the computer and especially the speed of the hard disk permits it) to store all sampled values and then sort them afterwards to obtain files with the significant information only. The original files can then be erased from the hard disk, perhaps after being copied on to tape which enables sorting by other criteria at a later stage, if necessary.

41.3.3 Data storage and processing

Independent of the sampling strategy it is always advisable to store 'raw' data, i.e. the direct readings which are usually in mV. The experience is that the ASCII format is almost a 'must' for the raw data file, as measuring errors and perhaps their reasons are much more easily found and corrected when the data file can be inspected directly.

Storing the readings in mV instead of scaled to the relevant physical unit not only makes it simpler to track errors, it also means that the principles or constants used for estimating the physical values from the raw data can be changed more easily if later experience tells that a different interpretation or further correction would be appropriate.

For documentation and easy processing, all relevant information about the test should be stored in the data file or in a separate file, uniquely attached to the data file. The information should include the choice of test conditions for the particular test, the date, the sampling rate(s) and all factors necessary to estimate the physical values from the raw data, e.g. scaling factor and temperature sensitivity for each channel. Also the threshold level should be stored for documentation.

As the test set-up is likely to change over time, for example because the number of transducers is increased, it is preferable to keep the computer programs as general as possible. This means that further information should be stored in the data file or the attached file. For each channel it would be relevant to store the numbers of the channels to which the supply voltage and the representative temperature are attached, if the reading is absolute or if it should be referred to a zero-reading, fixed off-set constants, if the channel readings should be compared to a threshold level before storage, and at which of the specified rates the channel should be sampled.

A format similar to the data exchange format suggested below can be used for storing the raw data if keywords and blocks with the necessary factors are added.

41.3.4 Exchange format

Even though the data ought to be stored as they are read (usually in mV) this format is not very attractive for the exchange of data. The algorithms that should be used to transform the readings to physical values might be complex and difficult to use with sufficient confidence by researchers other than those who had carried out the tests. It is, therefore, recommended that data are exchanged in physical values. This enables a safe exchange even when the complete documentation is not yet available. An agreed standard for exchange of data will ease comparative studies of data from several sources.

The format needs to allow for all sample methods without taking up too much disk space. Further, ASCII format seems to be the safest as transmission errors, etc. are easy to detect and any programming language can read it.

A format that will be sufficient for all sample methods will be a block for each sampling time that contains the time and several pairs of channel numbers and observations. In the beginning of the file, information that enables identification of the test, such as place and date of the test, the choice of those test conditions that can be changed, and reference to a documentation report should be included. If the documentation report is not completed, more information should be provided in the file.

The processing of data becomes easier if a few conventions are agreed upon. A most useful one is that if the first character of a line is not a space or one of two specified characters, then the line is regarded as a comment. The characters specified could be '*' and '.' (full stop), as these are most unlikely to appear as the first character of a comment line.

- '*' indicates the start of a block containing time and observations at that time;
- '.' means a block containing some set-up values. A block is the lines from a line starting with '.' or '*' up to the next line starting with '.' or '*'. Within each block, only lines starting with a space are considered as data.

The use of the conventions is illustrated by the suggestion of a format shown below. The first part is any number of lines with identification and documentation. (All lines until the first line starting with '.' or '*' should be assumed to be comments, also if the first character is a space.)

```
1990.11.30
Technical University of Denmark
Department of Structural Engineering
Medium Scale Model
Leighton-Buzzard Sand
Rough Wall
Centric Inlet 40mm, controlled fall
```

```
Centric Outlet 56mm
Test no 13 in: J. Munch-Andersen, V. Askegaard, and
A. Brink: Silo Tests with Sand. SBI-Bulletin 92.
Danish Building Research Institute. Hørsholm. 1992.

.Units (1992.06.11)
   1 Volts  2 kPa  3 kPa  4 kPa
 . . .
  58 mV  59 mV  60 C  61 kN
.Decimals
   1  1  2  1  3  1  4  1  5  2
 . . .
  58  0  59  0  60  1  61  2
* 0 10 38 50 384
   1 850  2 484  3 -32  4 800
 . . .
  58 -695  59 -875  60 63  61 -999
* 0 10 38 52 980
   3 -26  10 122  59 -850
Reading 0 10 38 52 150 deleted due to error
* . . .
```

'.' in the first column means that the next word is a set-up keyword and the rest of the line should be ignored (i.e. comments). In the example two keywords are used, 'Units' and 'Decimals'. The 'Units' block contains the physical unit of the observation for each channel and the 'Decimals' block defines how many digits of the integer number representing the observations below that should be regarded as decimals. (This enables all numbers to be integers.) Other keywords can be added. A helpful sub-convention could be that only the first three letters of the keywords need to be checked to identify the content of the block.

'*' in the first column means that the next numbers are the time of a reading and that the rest of the block is pairs of channel numbers and observations.

The advantages of each data line starting with a space in both types of blocks is that the first character can be read as a character that identifies the type of information that follows, permitting numbers to be read directly as numbers. Without this convention all lines must be read as strings and then converted into numbers, a simple but time-consuming task. The convention also allows comments to be put everywhere in the file. The comments could regard correction of errors as documentation, or enable easy tracing of for example 'start of discharge'.

The format of the time following '*' could perhaps be allowed a few different formats as the time-scale of silo tests can be very different. A complete time would contain number of days since the start of the experiment, hours, minutes, seconds, and ms (milliseconds). This format is used in the example. Days or ms might be irrelevant in some cases, but the potential savings by permitting more than one format are small.

Alternatively, it could be considered if the time should be represented in decimal hours or seconds. Hours are presumably most convenient as the relevant time-scale for most tests are hours or tenths of hours. (24 hours are less than 10^8 ms, thus eight significant digits should be sufficient for storage of the time in decimal hours in most cases.)

42

Concluding remarks
H. Stoffers

This Part summarizes methods appropriate for carrying out silo tests and the information which should be provided when these tests are reported. The Part aims to get silo tests to be applied in such a manner that the results will have optimum chances of being understood and accepted within the field of silo research and in the silo industry.

In the past, pressure measurements have been applied using rather poor measuring equipment. Often only a few readings with limited accuracy have been taken and the processing of data required a lot of time. This situation has changed completely. Modern electronic measuring equipment and computer facilities are now available, and make possible greater accuracy and quantity of data.

It is generally agreed that wall pressures may be treated as stochastic phenomena. It is therefore relevant to process and interpret data in accordance with this stochastic nature. Measurements reported from silo tests should present information in such a manner that conclusions regarding the probability of certain wall pressure distributions can be drawn from it.

Part Six

Experimental Techniques

43

Introduction
J. Garnier

This Part presents the current state of development of techniques for use in silo experiments. The work described has been developed by recent or current research programmes and describes techniques for determination of many of the states of the stored granular material (pressure, moisture content, density and so on) as well as the application of existing techniques to particular silo problems in novel ways.

This state-of-the-art report does not attempt to be exhaustive or to make value judgements on the merits of different techniques, but aims to give the reader an overview of some of the techniques in use by research practitioners.

For each of the topics discussed, sources of published literature are listed at the end of each chapter.

Areas of current research and problems known to be in need of further research are emphasized in Chapter 54.

44

Normal and shear stress on a silo wall, and stress and strain state in a silo medium
V. Askegaard

44.1 INTRODUCTION

Pressure cells are used to measure stresses in the fields of soil mechanics, road research, silo research and structural engineering. The design bases for pressure cells are the same in the different fields, whereas the practical problems of using them may differ, leading to variations in geometry and stiffness.

The subject can be subdivided in the following way:

- interface (wall) problem with no relative displacements
- interface problem with relative displacements
- embedded cell problem (stress and strain state in silo medium)

Design bases for pressure cells measuring normal stress in an interface or being embedded have been proposed by several authors. A comprehensive review of these approaches up to 1972 is given by Hvorslev (1976). A bibliography on silos from 1857 to 1983 is given by Walli and Schwaighofer (1979).

44.2 INTERFACE PROBLEM WITH NO RELATIVE DISPLACEMENT

44.2.1 Normal stress

The analytical solution for a fluid-filled, membrane-type cell, assuming linear elasticity, is given by Gravesen (1959). The same author also gave the numerical solution for the piston-type cell. These results, together with the expressions for the plate-type cell with or without fluid behind it (Fig. 44.1), are discussed by Askegaard (1961). The error expression has the form (44.2.1) and can be used when errors are small.

$$\frac{\Delta p}{p} = K \frac{E}{(1-v^2)a} \frac{\Delta w_{\text{aver}}}{p} \qquad (44.2.1)$$

Here, p is the uniform pressure on the undisturbed wall, and $p - \Delta p$ is the mean pressure transmitted to the pressure cell. $p - \Delta p$ depends on the average displacement Δw_{aver} of the cell's front surface under the load p. It also depends on the modulus E and Poisson's ratio v for the compressible medium, and the radius a of the pressure cell. K is constant depending on the cell type (about 1.9 for the stiff piston, 1.2 for a plate with fluid behind it and 0.7 for a plate with no fluid behind it).

Expression (44.2.1) can also be used to evaluate error signals caused by temperature changes when materials with different coefficients of expansion are used in the cell–wall arrangement. Large errors due to temperature changes may, in particular, occur in fluid pressure cells unless the fluid volume is kept to a minimum.

The requirements for stiffness of the pressure cell are rigorous if small measuring errors are to be obtained. Underestimation of these requirements still seems to be a major cause of errors in pressure cell work. For example, in the case of a pressure level $p = 50\,\text{kPa}$, if $a = 50\,\text{mm}$, $E = 100\,\text{MPa}$ (sand), and $v = 0.3$, then even such a small displacement of the piston as $10^{-3}\,\text{mm}$ (for $p = 50\,\text{kPa}$) will give a measuring error of about 10% when the pressure cell is of the rigid-piston type.

By making a suitable choice of cell stiffness $\Delta w_{\text{aver}}/p$, a small error, say less than 2%, can be obtained for a range of values of E, indicating that the assumed value of E need not be very precise. The material need not even be linear elastic, as assumed, if a reasonably good guess of the stiffness can be made and small errors are aimed at. It is thus justifiable to talk about the measurement of stress.

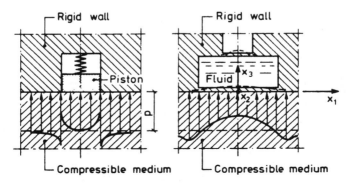

Fig. 44.1 Measuring principles for stress cells at an interface (Askegaard, 1961).

The design basis has been tested with the central bottom cell in a calibration chamber similar to the one shown in Fig. 44.6 but without the oil-filled rubber bag. It is essential that the stress distribution over the bottom area is known. In this set-up a uniform normal pressure is produced because the radial strain in the particulate medium is very nearly zero and the friction between particulate medium and the calibration chamber's cylindrical wall is negligible.

A finite element calculation of the stress distribution in a calibration chamber with a cylindrical steel wall is given by Askegaard (1978a, App. F) and compared with bottom pressure cell measurements. A mean deviation of 1% was found between the calculated and the measured sensitivity. The coefficient of variation was 0.02.

44.2.2 Shear stress

The design basis for a shear cell has been developed by making a limit analysis of the case where an ellipsoidal inclusion is placed in a matrix (silo medium) under external load, as illustrated in Fig. 44.2 (Askegaard, 1984).

The following expression was obtained for a cell type having a front plate of constant thickness and fixed along the edge:

$$\frac{\sigma_{23}}{\sigma_{23}^A} = \frac{8(1-v^2)}{\pi(2-v)U + 8(1-v^2)} \qquad (44.2.2)$$

where

$$U = \frac{Eu_2}{\sigma_{23}a} \qquad (44.2.3)$$

σ_{23} is the shear stress on the cell surface, σ_{23}^A is the shear stress in the matrix, which is to be measured, E and v are the modulus of elasticity and Poisson's ratio respectively, of the matrix, a is the cell radius, and u_2 is the displacement in the x_2 direction of the front plate centre caused by σ_{23}. For example, using the values $E \sim 100\,\text{MPa}$ (sand), $v \sim 0.3$, $a = 75\,\text{mm}$, and $\sigma_{23} \sim 0.1\,\text{MPa}$, it can be seen that to obtain a measuring error of less than 5%, the displacement u_2 for the stress $\sigma_{23} \sim 0.1\,\text{MPa}$ should be less than $5 \times 10^{-3}\,\text{mm}$.

Calibration tests have been carried out with a cell of this type in the calibration set-up shown in Fig. 44.3. The shear cell was placed in the interface between a rigid wall and a sand layer with a thickness of 150 mm and a diameter of 1200 mm. The sand was encapsulated in a 0.3 mm thick rubber membrane and evacuated. The shear load was obtained by 90° rotation from the horizontal, as shown in the figure. In this way a uniformly distributed shear stress over the cell area is produced, corresponding to the weight of the volume of the column of sand over a unit of surface area. Good correspondence between the calculated and measured error of the shear cell was found, being 7 and 9% respectively (Askegaard, 1984).

A shear cell type, where the front plate is not fixed along the edge but

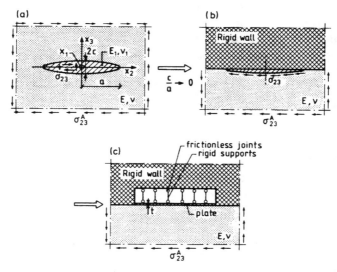

Fig. 44.2 Transference of ellipsoid in infinite medium into a plate fixed along the edge in an interface.

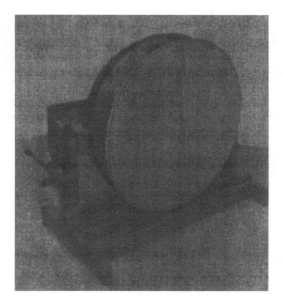

Fig. 44.3 Calibration equipment with shear cell in an interface.

moves in the plane as a whole, has also been calibrated. Expression (44.2.2) seems to give a good idea of expected error in this case too.

Cells of that type are mounted in two medium-scale model silos (Askegaard, 1987; Askegaard, Nielsen and Wiche, 1990). Equilibrium checks were carried out to evaluate the shear cell behaviour. The correspondence seemed to be good, giving 3–7% difference between expected and measured shear load during filling at nearly full silo and early emptying. It is important that the coefficient of friction between wall surface and particulate medium is the same as between pressure cell surface and particulate medium and that the roughness is the same. The influence of single and multiple surface grooves on the coefficient of friction is treated by Blight (1990).

44.2.3 Reinforcing effect of the pressure cell installation

A typical normal stress cell installation in a reinforced concrete wall is shown in Fig. 44.4. The layers of epoxy-mortar are kept as thin as possible, and the free surface is given a roughness comparable with that of the surrounding concrete, even though the measuring signal from a normal stress cell is almost insensitive to deviations in roughness. For shear cells this is only true if wall friction and friction between shear cell and silo medium are bigger than internal friction in the silo medium.

Tests with a pressure cell installed in a concrete specimen subjected to a strain state of the order of magnitude that can be expected in full-scale silos has shown only small changes in sensitivity and zero shift when thin front plates (0.3 mm) are used. In the case of thicker front plates, as the one in Fig. 44.4, which are necessary in the case of coarse grains in the particulate medium, non-negligible changes must be expected. Such changes may also occur when curved front plates are used – in small-diameter model silos, for instance.

Askegaard, Nielsen and Wiche (1990) discusses errors that may occur when pressure cells installed in thin-walled silos deviate in stiffness and

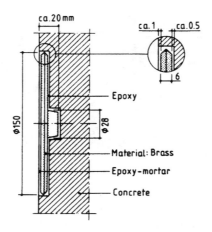

Fig. 44.4 Installation of normal stress cell in a concrete wall.

thickness from the undisturbed wall. The results show that these deviations should be small, particularly for model silos made of low modulus materials (e.g. Perspex, epoxy) and for full-scale steel silos.

44.3 INTERFACE PROBLEM WITH RELATIVE DISPLACEMENTS

Large relative displacements between wall and medium occur during emptying in mass flow silos. The requirements to normal pressure cells used under these conditions have been investigated by Askegaard, Bergholdt and Nielsen (1971).

Tests showed that serious errors could occur if the cell was not mounted flush with the wall. An angle of 1° between the cell's front surface and the wall surface thus showed a change of about 50% in the measured stress.

The tests also indicated that the relatively rapid variations in pressure about a slowly varying mean value, which are characteristic of pressure cell measurements during the discharge of barley, were caused by local irregularities in the geometry of the wall or in the compactness of the silo medium. These rapid variations, in contrast to the slower ones, were thus presumed to represent only the condition in an area of the wall that is not much larger than the measuring surface of the pressure cell itself and should not normally cause serious bending moments in the silo wall. Piston-type pressure cells as described by Arthur and Roscoe (1961) and Schulze, Lyle and Schwedes (1989) can also give information about the area represented by the cells because the change of position of the resulting force on the cell surface can be measured. Measurements carried out in a fly-ash silo (Nielsen, 1984) have shown that pressure cells, when in contact with powder materials, represent a wall area much bigger than their own.

Pressure cells designed for measuring normal and shear stress on corrugated surfaces are described by Buisson, Gabriel and Serriere (1989).

When measuring shear stresses and when the relative displacements occur in the interface itself, it becomes important to ensure that the coefficient of friction of the pressure cell is the same as that of the surrounding wall. The equilibrium check carried out with friction cells in a model silo with barley (Askegaard and Munch-Andersen, 1985) mentioned previously, was also done in the discharge situation, where semi-mass flow occurs, leading to large relative displacements near the wall. The deviations in the two situations were measured as 6 and 10%.

44.4 EMBEDDED CELL PROBLEM (STRESS AND STRAIN STATE IN SILO MEDIUM)

If a stress cell is made flat and thin enough, the measuring error can be made arbitrarily small, if the matrix material around the cell remains homogeneous, whatever the material properties of the matrix and the cell. When errors are small, therefore, an almost free choice of the material properties is acceptable when establishing a design basis. A design basis has, therefore, been formulated (Askegaard, 1963; 1978a, b) based on linear (isotropic, homogeneous) elasticity and on cells with axially symmetrical, ellipsoidal geometry.

$$\sigma_{33} = C\sigma_{23}^A + D(\sigma_{11}^A + \sigma_{22}^A) \quad (44.4.1)$$

is found for a normal stress cell and

$$\sigma_{23} = F\sigma_{23}^A \quad (44.4.2)$$

for a shear stress cell. Here σ_{11}^A, σ_{22}^A and σ_{33}^A are normal stress components in the surrounding medium with the shear stress σ_{23}^A acting on the plane of the flat stress cell and with the normal stress σ_{33}^A perpendicular to this plane. σ_{23} and σ_{33} are the corresponding stress components in the homogeneous ellipsoid. C, D and F are factors containing Poisson's ratio, the thickness–diameter ratio of the ellipsoid, and the ratio between the moduli of elasticity of the homogeneous ellipsoid and the surrounding medium.

By careful design and under certain restrictions, the almost ideal situation where $C \sim 1.0$ and $D \sim 0.0$ can be obtained, even up to large deformations. A load-history-dependent sensitivity will be encountered when stress cells are designed in such a way that C differs substantially from 1.0.

Expressions describing the situation where stress-free strain (shrinkage and differences in thermal expansion) occur, are also given by Askegaard (1978a, b). It is, of course, possible to refine the calculations by using better approximations of geometry and material properties and by using FEM techniques, but very little seems to be achieved by doing so when small errors are aimed at. Nor do these more rigorous approaches render calibration tests superfluous.

The 150 mm diameter pressure cells shown in Fig. 44.5 have been used in calibration tests described by Askegaard (1988, 1995) to get an idea of the overall accuracy that can be expected when using pressure cells. Similar

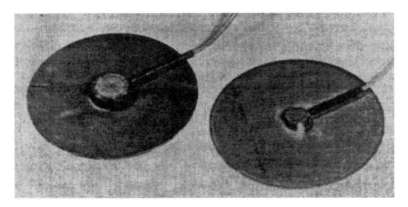

Fig. 44.5 Shear stress cell (left), normal stress cell (right).

tests with a 75 mm diameter pressure cell are also described by Askegaard (1987). These tests were performed in the calibration equipment shown in Fig. 44.6 with the pressure cell embedded in wheat and in sand. Compressibility of the calibration chamber in the vertical direction was obtained by making the cylinder of silicone rubber, while steel reinforcement in the hoop direction made the cylinder stiff in the radial direction.

When evaluating results from the calibration experiments, it is important to have obtained homogeneity in the stress state of the particulate medium contained in the cylinder. From Fig. 44.7, this appears to be the case with very good accuracy when using wheat. The same is true when a sand mass is used.

In practice, pressure cells are used under load conditions which are only poorly known. Therefore, to get an idea of the overall accuracy of the pressure cell under such conditions, calibration tests must be performed in such a way as to obtain greatly differing load situations.

Figures 44.8 and 44.9 show the three types of loading histories used in the tests. They all involve the 1st and 10th load cycles. Each cell has been tested at three different tilting angles θ; 0, 45 and 90° for the normal stress cell and 20, 45 and 70° for the shear stress cell. For each cell nine different tests are thus carried out representing very varied conditions. The stress ratio $\sigma_{11}^A/\sigma_{33}^A$ seen from the point of view of the cell varies between 1:2 and 2:1, very different stiffnesses of particulate media occur and a permanent

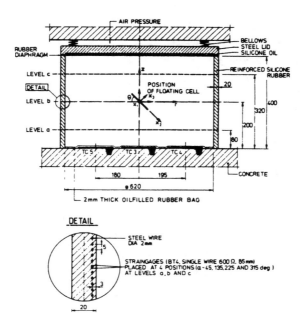

Fig. 44.6 Set-up for calibration tests.

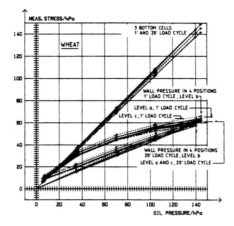

Fig. 44.7 Stress state in wheat-filled calibration chamber.

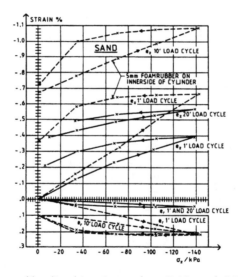

Fig. 44.8 Two types of loading histories used on G-12 sand. Maximum value of σ_z during shear cell tests was only 100 kPa.

strain of up to 4% is observed. All tests are pooled for each stress cell and the results are shown in Figs. 44.10 and 44.11.

The test results for the normal stress cell correspond to an estimate for the coefficients in (44.4.1) of $C \sim 0.91$ and $D \sim 0.04$ to be compared with the predicted values: $C \sim 0.91$ and $D \sim 0.10$. The agreement is considered to be good, and the scattering between the nine tests representing very varied conditions seen from the point of view of the stress cell, is small; it

Embedded cell problem

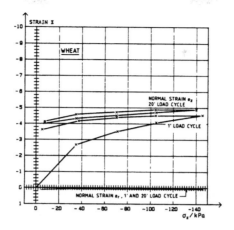

Fig. 44.9 Loading history used on wheat. Maximum value of σ_z during shear cell tests was only 100 kPa.

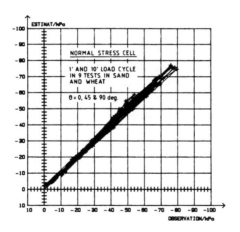

Fig. 44.10 True versus estimated normal stress. Nine tests in sand and wheat at $\theta = 0°$, $45°$ and $90°$. 1st and 10th load cycle used.

corresponds to a coefficient of variation on the slope of about 0.04. The design expression (44.4.1), therefore, seems to be justified.

Other loading histories would be of interest but cannot be produced in the calibration set-up used here. The accuracy, however, during an arbitrary loading history is expected to be of the same order of magnitude as mentioned above.

Accuracy is less for the shear cell as can be seen from Fig. 44.11. There is zero shift after the first load cycle corresponding in average to about 5% of the maximum stress. The average slope corresponds to $F \sim 0.85$, as

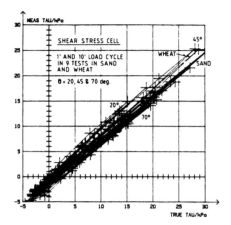

Fig. 44.11 True versus measured shear stress. Nine tests in sand and wheat at $\theta = 20°$, $45°$ and $70°$. 1st and 10th load cycle used.

expected somewhat lower than the design value of about 1.00. The slope is a little bigger for tests in wheat than for sand, again as expected, but changes systematically with the tilting angle. A qualitative explanation of this phenomenon is given by Askegaard (1995). The explanation is based on the assumption that the cell which is stiff changes the homogeneity of the matrix material locally depending on the ratio $\sigma_{33}^A/\sigma_{11}^A$ resulting in lower stiffness near the cell than further away from it. The effect of such a local change will be more pronounced for the shear cell than for the normal stress cell.

The results show that the cell responds to shear in an almost linear way and that the design expression can be used to give a rough estimate of cell behaviour.

Taking the nine loading tests to present arbitrary load histories in materials with a stiffness lower than $\sim 10^2$ MPa, the results indicate that the maximum shear stress in a test can be determined with an accuracy corresponding to a coefficient of variation of about 0.15. That may be enough to give useful information in practice.

Normal stress cells made of low stiffness materials for use in a low stiffness matrix are described by Askegaard (1978; 1981). The cells' low stiffness leads to values of C and D (expression (44.4.1)), very near the ideal of 1 and 0. The personal factor, when mounting the cells in sand, is also described by Askegaard (1981). It shows very little difference in results for a skilled and unskilled person.

Shear cells mounted in sand seem to be much more dependent on the mounting procedure.

An expression similar to (44.4.1) is established between the normal strains for a long thin axially symmetric ellipsoid (Askegaard, 1978a, b).

Calibration tests with such a strain cell in sand are described in the same references. Very good accordance is found between calculated and measured normal strain for the strain cell placed in sand and externally loaded, and also in sand in a stress-free strain state.

44.5 CONCLUSION

Design expressions are described for normal and shear stress cells in an interface (silo wall) and for normal and shear stress cells embedded in a particular medium. Reference to similar expressions for strain cells is given. The medium may be externally loaded or a stress-free strain state (shrinkage, temperature differences) may appear.

Calibration tests have shown that these design expressions will give a good estimate of cell behaviour and can, therefore, be used to evaluate planned or existing cells and cell installations. The necessary information to make an evaluation include:

- geometry of pressure cell;
- geometry of silo wall near the cell;
- compressibility of pressure cell or stiffness of cell materials and type and volume of fluid used in the cell;
- approximate stiffness of wall and particulate materials;
- temperature coefficients of cell, wall and particulate materials;
- stress and temperature range;
- friction coefficients of silo wall and cell surface.

44.6 FUTURE WORK

There seems to be a need for further work in the following areas:

1. Development of calibration set-ups where bigger strains and more varied load histories can be produced.
2. Behaviour of normal and shear stress cells:
   (a) when used embedded in cohesive materials;
   (b) when used embedded under high strain values;
   (c) when used embedded under loading histories close to those met in silos during filling, rest and emptying cycles.
3. Investigation of the personal factor when mounting normal and shear stress cells; if necessary, standardization of the mounting procedure also.

REFERENCES

Arthur, J.R.F. and Roscoe, K.H. (1961) An earth pressure cell for the measurement of normal and shear stresses. *Civil Engineering and Public Works Review*, **56**, (659), 765–770.

Askegaard, V. (1961) Measurement of pressure between a rigid wall and a compressible medium by means of pressure cells. *Acta Polytechnica Scandinavica*, Ci, 11.

Askegaard, V. (1963) Measurement of pressure in solids by means of pressure cells. *Acta Polytechnica Scandinavica*. Ci, 17.

Askegaard, V. (1978a) *Stress and Strain Measurements in Solid Materials*. Department of Structural Engineering, Technical University of Denmark, Lyngby. Report No. R 92, 92 pp.

Askegaard, V. (1978b) Stress and strain measurements in solids. *VDI-Berichte No. 313*, pp. 259–268.

Askegaard, V. (1981) Design and application of stress and strain cells with small measuring errors. *NDT International*, pp. 271–277.

Askegaard, V. (1984) Design basis for cells measuring shear stresses in an interface. *Geotechnical Testing Journal*, 7, (2), 94–98.

Askegaard, V. (1987) Consequence of loading history on the measuring error of embedded stress cells. *Transactions of the Institution of Engineers, Australia*, ME 12, (3), 191–196.

Askegaard, V. (1988a) The pressure cell problem. *Proc. Tagung 88, Silos – Forschung und Praxis*. Karlsruhe, pp. 339–361.

Askegaard, V. (1988b) Accuracy of normal and shear stress measurements in particulate media. *Proc. 6th Congress on Experimental Mechanics*, Portland, pp. 480–484.

Askegaard, V. (1995) Applicability of normal and shear stress cells embedded in cohesionless materials. *Experimental Mechanics*, pp. 315–321.

Askegaard, V.; Bergholdt, M. and Nielsen, J. (1971) Problems in connection with pressure cell measurements in silos. *Bygningsstatiske Meddelelser* No. 2.

Askegaard, V. and Munch-Andersen, J. (1985) Results from tests with normal and shear stress cells in medium-scale model silo. *Powder Technology*, 44, (2), 151–157.

Askegaard, V.; Nielsen, L.O. and Wiche, S. (1990) Measurement of contact stresses on a thin silo wall. *2nd European Symp. on the Stress and Strain Behaviour of Particulate Solids–Silo Stresses*. Prague, 26–31 Aug.; also in *Proc. 9th Int. Conf. on Exp. Mech.*, Copenhagen, 20–24 Aug., pp. 59–66.

Blight, G.E. (1990) Silo wall friction and wall roughness. *Powder Handling and Processing* 2 (3), 235–238.

Buisson, R.; Gabriel, S. and Serriere, C. (1989) Capteur d'action 'Grain-parois' à grande raideur. *Construction Métallique* No. 2, 19–30.

Gravesen, S. (1959) Elastic semi-infinite medium bounded by a rigid plate with a circular hole. *Bygningsstatiske Meddelelser* No. 3.

Hvorslev, M.J. (1976) *The Changeable Interaction between Soils and Pressure Cells. Tests and Reviews at the Waterways Experiment Station*, Technical Report S-76-7, US Army Engineering Waterways Experiment Station, Vicksburg, MS.

Nielsen, J. (1984) Pressure measurements in a full-scale fly ash silo. *Particulate Science and Technology*, 2, (3), pp. 237–246.

Schulze, D.; Lyle, C. and Schwedes, J. (1989) A new load cell for measuring normal and shear stresses. *Chem. Eng. Techn.*, 12, 318–323.

Walli, G.; and Schwaighofer, J. (1979) *A Bibliography on Silos (1857–1979) Addendum 1899–1983*. University of Toronto, Dept. of Civil. Eng. Publication No. 79-05.

45

Strain in a silo wall

J.Y. Ooi, J.F. Chen and J.M. Rotter

45.1 INTRODUCTION

The pressures on silo walls are often measured using pressure cells mounted in the wall. Recent research has shown that the patterns of pressure are often very complex (e.g. Munch-Andersen and Nielsen, 1990; Ooi, Pham and Rotter 1990), so a comprehensive picture can only be obtained with very many instantaneous measurements. The cost of making and installing reliable cells is relatively high, and the number of cells needed to characterize a complex pressure distribution is large.

Strain gauges have sometimes been used to measure the strains in the silo walls. Attempts have been made to deduce the pressure distribution acting on the silo walls from simple strain readings (e.g. Blight, 1990a, b; Bishara, 1992). Since, in general, the silo structure is a thin shell under unsymmetrical loading, both stretching and bending deformations of comparable magnitudes occur in the wall. Strains measured on the outside of the wall are thus considerably affected by local bending. Huge errors of interpretation can occur (Rotter and Ooi, 1991) if it is assumed that the local value of the wall pressure p is simply related to the circumferential stress in the wall as $\sigma_\theta = pR/t$, or through two-dimensional plane stress elasticity relations (e.g. Bishara, 1992). Instead, the strains and stresses at every point in the structure are affected by the normal pressure and frictional traction everywhere on the wall (Rotter, 1986).

This chapter principally describes a new rigorous statistical technique for inferring pressures from strain measurements, which was developed at the University of Edinburgh recently. The requirements for the measurement and interpretation of wall strains are also discussed. The technique has been successfully used to infer the wall pressures in a highly instrumented full-scale silo (Rotter et al., 1995; Chen, 1996).

45.2 MEASUREMENT OF STRAIN IN A SILO WALL

45.2.1 Installation of strain gauges

There are various strain measurement techniques which are in use, for example photoelasticity, grid system, extensometers and electrical gauges. For electrical strain gauges, many different types are available such as vibrating wire, semiconductor gauge, capacitance gauge and wire or foil gauge. The discussion on strain measurement in this section is confined to only the wire or foil electrical resistance strain gauge.

Proper gauge installation procedures are vital for reliable and high quality measurements. Consideration must be given to surface preparation, gauge bonding to the base metal, leadwire connections, and gauge protection against moisture, mechanical forces, electrostatic noise, electromagnetic noise, thermal changes, and finally inspection and checking. The correct installation procedures and the characteristics of electrical resistance strain gauges are often provided by the strain gauge manufacturers and suppliers, and are also described in detail elsewhere (e.g. Pople, 1979; BSSM CP1, 1992).

45.2.2 Metal silo

If the measured strains on an unsymmetrically loaded shell are to be accurately translated into inferred wall pressures, the complete state of strain at any point on the wall must be considered. The complete state of strain at any point may be described in terms of six components (three membrane strains and three curvatures; or alternatively three strain components on each of the two surfaces). Unfortunately, measurement of these six components normally means that gauges must be placed on both the inside and outside surfaces of the silo wall (e.g. Bishara, 1992). This arrangement inevitably leads to an imperfection over which stored bulk solid must slide inside the silo, which in turn may dramatically affect the local value of pressure, causing a serious misinterpretation of the real pressure regime.

In very thin shells, the local values of pressure are strongly correlated to the membrane strains in the wall (not necessarily at the same point on the wall), so a good estimate of the membrane strains is often adequate to give a moderate accuracy in the inferred pressures. However, the membrane strains are strains at the middle surface of the shell, which are not easily measured directly. The strains which can easily be measured (surface strains on the outside and inside) are strongly affected by bending strains, which can be very large wherever local bending occurs. In unsymmetrically loaded silos with fabrication imperfections, plate thickness changes, stiffeners, etc., local bending occurs in a great many places (Trahair *et al.*, 1983), often in the very zones where the most dramatic pressure peaks are observed (e.g. near the hopper transition). Thus it is important that six measures of strain are made at any measuring station even if the membrane strains alone are to be used to infer the pressure distribution.

The measurement of strains on the inside surface presents considerable difficulties as noted above. One remedy to the dilemma is to use 'sandwich' or 'double deck' strain gauges (Fig. 45.1(a)) (Itoh, 1975; Kyowa, 1977), which can be placed on one surface but which measure both the local surface strain, and by extrapolation, the bending strain or curvature (Fig. 45.1(b)). A rosette of sandwich strain gauges can be set up at each measuring site to obtain the six measures of strain (Fig. 45.1(c)).

These six strain measures are here represented by the vector

$$\{\bar{\varepsilon}\}^T = \{\varepsilon_m, \varepsilon_b\}^T \qquad (45.2.1)$$

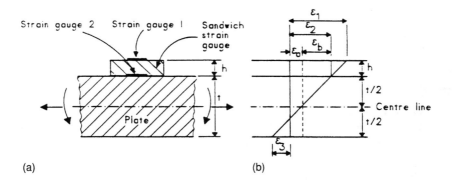

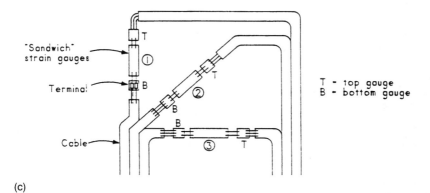

Fig. 45.1 'Sandwich' strain gauge: (a) bonded on a plate subjected to tension and bending; (b) assumed strain distribution; (c) rosette formation.

in which the membrane strains $\{\varepsilon_m\}$ are given by the vector

$$\{\varepsilon_m\} = \{\varepsilon_{m\phi}, \varepsilon_{m\theta}, \varepsilon_{m\phi\theta}\}^T \qquad (45.2.2)$$

and the bending curvatures by the vector

$$\{\varepsilon_b\} = \{\kappa_{b\phi}, \kappa_{b\theta}, \kappa_{b\phi\theta}\}^T \qquad (45.2.3)$$

The values $\varepsilon_{m\phi}$, $\varepsilon_{m\theta}$ and $\varepsilon_{m\phi\theta}$ are the middle surface strains in the meridional, circumferential and shearing directions and $\kappa_{b\phi}$, $\kappa_{b\theta}$ and $\kappa_{b\phi\theta}$ are the meridional, circumferential and twisting curvatures respectively.

The complete set of measured strains at all measuring stations on the wall is then represented by the vector $\{\bar{\varepsilon}\}_{6M}$ (there being six strain measures at each of M stations). Although it is expected that six strain components would normally be used in the present analysis, the influence of the twisting curvature is almost always small, and that of the bending curvatures may be minor. Thus, there may be occasions in which only five strain measures, or possibly only the three membrane strains, are used in the pressure inference procedure. In the rest of this chapter, the number of strain measures at a point is therefore written as β, where β can take values of 1, 2, 3, 4, 5 or 6 as appropriate (a distinct set of special practical circumstances can be identified for each of these possibilities).

45.2.3 Concrete silo

Strain gauges have also been used on concrete silos to measure the strains in the concrete and the reinforcement (Askegaard and Nielsen, 1986). Knowledge of the strain field at a limited number of positions could give an indication on the structural integrity of the concrete structure. If the wall is uncracked, the strains in the circumferential direction, which are of particular interest, will be very small and thus not easy to measure accurately. If the wall is cracked, the concrete strains will still be small, while the strains in the reinforcement near the crack will be large; modelling of a cracked concrete structure is not straightforward. In either case, it is very difficult to infer the wall pressure distribution from these observed strain values reliably.

45.3 TRANSFORMATION OF STRAINS INTO INFERRED PRESSURES

This section describes an analytical process by which the measured strains at a number of points on the silo wall at a given time can be transformed into inferred pressures, not necessarily at the same point.

45.3.1 Assumed pressure distribution

When strain gauge readings are used to deduce the pressure pattern on the silo wall, there may or may not be a strong correlation between the strain

Transformation of strains into inferred pressures

observation at a point and the pressure at that point (e.g. Rotter, 1986). Thus, in interpreting the observations, it is better to make a clearly defined assumption about the nature of the pressure distribution. The assumption for the vertical distribution could be, for example, a piecewise linear variation between observation stations (comparable with usual interpretations of pressure cell readings), or a polynomial distribution down the wall (an obvious mathematical distribution, but not particularly well suited to silo pressures), or a cubic spline function, or a Janssen (1895) expression with additional terms to display the departures from the best-fit Janssen curve (often the most useful description for silos).

The assumed variation of pressures around the circumference of the silo has received less attention, partly because it is often assumed to be invariant, as in most theories. Here, it is probably best described by a harmonic decomposition (e.g. Ooi, Pham and Rotter, 1990), giving constant pressure as one term of the calculated set.

All the above possibilities and many others are available in the present formulation: the key concept is that the pressure distribution is formally assumed to take a particular form, and that the complete pressure distribution is characterized by the values of a limited number of relevant parameters.

To implement this procedure, the pressure distribution in the silo is first characterized as

$$p_n(\theta, z) = \sum_{i=1}^{N} a_i f_i(\theta, z) \quad (45.3.1a)$$

$$p_v(\theta, z) = \sum_{i=N+1}^{2N} a_i f_{i-N}(\theta, z) \quad (45.3.1b)$$

$$p_\theta(\theta, z) = \sum_{i=2N+1}^{3N} a_i f_{i-2N}(\theta, z) \quad (45.3.1c)$$

in which the variables p_n, p_v and p_θ represent the normal wall pressure, the vertical wall frictional traction and the circumferential wall frictional traction at any point. The functions $f_1, f_2, \ldots, f_N$ are used to represent the assumed variation of normal pressure and the loading coefficients $a_1, a_2, \ldots, a_N$ define the magnitude of each normal pressure term. The coefficients $a_{N+2}, \ldots, a_{2N}$ define the local vertical component of the wall frictional traction while $a_{2N+1}, \ldots, a_{3N}$ define the horizontal (circumferential) frictional component.

Where this analysis is applied to a problem in which there is no wall friction, only the terms of equation (45.3.1a) are required. Similarly, in a silo with completely axisymmetric wall loads, only the terms of equations (45.3.1a) and (45.3.1b) are needed. Thus, in the remainder of this chapter, a generality of description is retained by defining the number of unknown parameters a_i as αN, where α can take the value of 1, 2 or 3 as appropriate. It may be noted that the loading terms represented by equation (45.3.1c) do not appear to have been included in any previous theoretical or experimental work on silo pressures. It must be present for the sake of completeness, and probably takes significantly non-zero values under conditions of funnel flowing eccentric discharge.

The assumption that wall friction is fully mobilized is not used in the present technique. Instead, the complete wall friction at each point is broken into two parts, which may or may not make a vector sum equal to the real wall friction μ. The description as a wall friction coefficient makes the characterization more transparent, and means that the traction follows the normal pressure in a naturally controlled manner. The coefficients $a_{N+1}, \ldots, a_{2N}$ and $a_{2N+1}, \ldots, a_{3N}$ are treated as separate unknown parameters. Thus the extent of mobilization of wall friction at each point in the silo can be found as an outcome of the interpretation.

45.3.2 Structural analysis of the silo

Since the strains measured on the silo wall are not direct measures of the wall pressure, a structural analysis is needed to relate the measured strains to the inferred pressure distribution. If the structural behaviour is assumed to be very simple, with pressures related to wall stresses through $\sigma_\theta = pR/t$, a structural analysis is still being used, though this analysis is trivially simple and is almost always in serious error.

The possible forms of structural analysis which could be applied in the present work include the membrane theory of shells (Rotter, 1987a) and the linear bending theory of shells (Rotter, 1987b). If the membrane theory of shells is applied to shells under non-symmetric loads, it yields only membrane strains for a given pressure distribution, and ignores the membrane strains arising from bending of the shell; nevertheless it may be adequate if all the strain observations are distant from sources of local bending (e.g. there are no rapid changes in the pressure distribution). The bending theory of shells is much more complicated, and algebraic solutions of practical relevance to unsymmetrical loading distributions cannot, in general, be obtained. However, it does include all the phenomena of local bending.

The structural analysis consists of several steps: first the load must be defined as in equation (45.3.1), which indicates the target pressure distribution. The parameters $a_1, a_2, \ldots, a_{\alpha N}$ each define the amplitude of a pressure distribution of a certain shape. For each of these αN pressure distributions, a separate structural analysis must be conducted to determine the complete state of strain which that distribution would induce at each of the locations in the shell at which the strains have been measured. To achieve this using the bending theory of shells, it is easiest to use a finite element analysis, which can include all necessary boundary conditions, stiffeners, adjacent structural elements, etc. The wall stress resultants (three membrane stress resultants and three bending moments) are calculated at each gauge location by finite element analysis. These must then be transformed into stretching

Transformation of strains into inferred pressures

and bending strains at the gauge location using the constitutive equations for the shell.

The αN structural analyses produce M sets of up to six strains $\{\varepsilon\}$ (there being M gauge locations), induced by each of αN pressure distributions, giving the equation set

$$\{\varepsilon\}_{\beta M} = [S]_{\beta M \times \alpha N} \{a\}_{\alpha N} \qquad (45.3.2)$$

in which $[S]$ is termed here the sensitivity matrix, and the element S_{ij} is the value of the strain ε_i which is caused by the load equation (45.3.1) when $a_j = 1$ and all other load parameters equal zero. Equation (45.3.2) is the foundation of the following process for deducing pressures from the strain gauge readings.

45.3.3 Inversion of pressure–strain relations with error minimization

The above analyses produce a total of M sets of β strain measures on the silo walls. The vector of observed strains in the silo test $\{\bar{\varepsilon}\}$ is given by

$$\{\bar{\varepsilon}\}_{\beta M} = [\bar{\varepsilon}_1, \bar{\varepsilon}_2 \ldots \bar{\varepsilon}_{\beta M}]^T \qquad (45.3.3)$$

The goal of the present analysis is to find the load parameter vector $\{a\}$ which has minimum errors in predicting the observations. To obtain this vector, a related vector of strains associated with $\{a\}$ is defined as the vector of expected strains $\{\varepsilon\}$. The discrepancies between the strain observations vector $\{\bar{\varepsilon}\}$ and the expected strain vector $\{\varepsilon\}$ may then be expressed as an error vector $\{e\}$

$$\{e\} = [S]\{a\} - \{\bar{\varepsilon}\} \qquad (45.3.4)$$

The statistical processing of the observations seeks to minimize the error vector $\{e\}$. This is achieved in a least squares manner by first expressing the errors as a target function

$$E = \{e\}^T [W]\{e\} \qquad (45.3.5)$$

in which $[W]$ is a weighting matrix. If the weighting matrix is set as a unit matrix $[I]$, the target function becomes simply the sum of the squares of the individual errors. The use of the weighting matrix permits different emphasis to be placed on different observations. The vector $\{a\}$ can now be found by minimizing equation (45.3.5) as

$$\frac{\partial E}{\partial \{\varepsilon\}} = 0 \qquad (45.3.6)$$

which leads to

$$\{a\} = \left([S]^T [W][S]\right)^{-1} [S]^T [W]\{\bar{\varepsilon}\} \qquad (45.3.7)$$

which can be written more succinctly as

$$\{a\} = [U]\{\bar{\varepsilon}\} \qquad (45.3.8)$$

in which the projection matrix [U] is given by

$$[U] = \left([S]^T[W][S]\right)^{-1}[S]^T[W] \qquad (45.3.9)$$

45.3.4 Outline of the pressure inference method

A general procedure, using the above calculations, may be described as follows:

1. Assume a set of functions with a finite set of unknowns to characterize the load distribution. This results in αN unknown load coefficients (equation (45.3.1)). The loads may be generalized loads which could include base settlements or temperature changes.
2. Calculate the sensitivity matrix [S] (equation (45.3.2)) through a series of structural analyses of the shell. The structural calculations can only rarely be performed algebraically: finite element analysis is required in most useful applications.
3. Calculate the projection matrix [U] using equation (45.3.9). The weighting matrix [W] may be set to be equal to the unit matrix [I] if no weighting of data is desired or needed, but it may be modified to reflect the different reliability or significance of different strain readings.
4. Calculate the load parameter vector $\{a\}$ using the observed strain vector $\{\bar{\varepsilon}\}$ as in equation (45.3.8).
5. Calculate the magnitude of the fitting errors, which are given by $\{e\}$ in equation (45.3.4). Explore the sensitivity of the errors to the assumptions made about the load distribution. If necessary, repeat the procedure with a different assumed load distribution or a different weighting matrix [W].

To illustrate the procedure, a simple example considering an on-ground cylindrical silo with a fixed base under axisymmetric loading is given in Appendix 45.A. An example of the use of the method in unsymmetrical loading conditions can be found in Chen, Ooi and Rotter (1996b).

45.4 CONSIDERATIONS IN THE MEASUREMENT AND INTERPRETATION OF STRAIN

45.4.1 Assumptions concerning the load distribution

When pressure cells are used to measure the pressure distribution, the pressure is deemed to have been reliably measured at each cell site, and the pressure between cells is inferred either by connecting observations with straight lines (Hartlen et al., 1984; Ooi, Pham and Rotter 1990; Blight, 1990) or, where the data permit it, with smooth curves. Both interpretations imply assumptions about the complete pressure distribution, though these are rarely stated. In the present process, the assumed pressure distribution is seen more as an assumption, and is more clearly defined. However, since this assumption must be made at the outset of an interpretation, some comments on its form should be noted.

Any component of the assumed load distribution $\{a_i\}$ (equations (45.3.1)) which lead to small strains induced in the wall will not be determined reliably. This may be stated alternatively as follows: if a column in the matrix $[S]$ (equations (45.3.2) and (45.A.4)) contains only small entries, the load parameter a to which it corresponds will be poorly defined by the strain observations represented by the rows in $[S]$. If the strains are measured near all points at which the structural integrity is in question, then the unreliability of the load parameter evaluation is perhaps not important, since this parameter clearly influences the wall stresses very little, but the assumed load distribution should be designed so that all terms in the vector $\{a\}$ are well conditioned. A comprehensive discussion on the selection of load functions is given in Chen (1996).

45.4.2 Measurement of the strain components

A total of six strain gauges are required at each point to measure the complete strain state. The relative magnitude of each of the six strain components depends on the silo geometry, the boundary conditions, the choice of strain gauge sites and the loading conditions. Again, a proper understanding of the shell structural behaviour is needed to ensure that reasonable assumptions are made about the strain state.

If the loading is symmetric, as assumed in the example in Appendix 45.A, the only non-zero strains were the membrane and bending strains in the meridional and circumferential directions $\varepsilon_{m\phi}$, $\varepsilon_{m\theta}$, $\kappa_{b\phi}$ and $\kappa_{b\theta}$. Under such conditions, the circumferential strains are highly correlated with the normal pressures, while the meridional strains are sensitive to the frictional traction (Fig. 45.A.3). These simple connections become much weaker when the loading is non-symmetric, but a much more complicated example is needed to illustrate this, so it falls outside the scope of this chapter.

45.4.3 Number of strain observations

Where simple symmetrical pressure distributions occur on silo walls, the need for a large number of observations is not so pressing. However, both experimental (Hartlen et al., 1984; Rotter, Pham and Nielsen, 1986) and theoretical (Rotter, 1986; ACI313, 1989) studies indicate that the pressure patterns occurring in eccentrically discharging silos or silos with even minor unsymmetrical features are highly unsymmetrical. In these circumstances, the number of observations required to characterize the pattern sufficiently even to give an understanding of the qualitative behaviour (Rotter, Pham and Nielsen, 1986) is very large.

For the inference procedure, the total number of strain readings βM must be equal to or greater than the number of unknown load parameters being sought αN. In general, a larger number of strain observations and/or gauge positions may be expected to produce a better definition of the loading distribution.

Each complete time scan of the measured strains gives an inferred pressure distribution at a fixed time. With many scans of strains, the inferred pressure distribution may be treated as time-varying stochastic process. Simple theoretical study (Chen, Rotter and Ooi, 1993; Chen, Ooi and Rotter, 1996a) has indicated that the inferred pressure distribution can be determined with progressively increasing accuracy as the total number of strain measurements increases. The standard deviation of the deduced pressures σ was found to be approximately inversely proportional to the square root of the number of strain readings $\sqrt{\beta M}$:

$$\sigma \sqrt{\beta M} = \text{constant} \qquad (45.4.1)$$

45.4.4 Quality of the strain observations

The quality of the source strain data (i.e. the accuracy of the strain measurements) naturally has a strong influence on the inferred pressures. This depends on the gauges and experimental equipment as well as the data acquisition system.

Chen, Ooi and Rotter (1996a) explored the effects of measurement noise in a theoretical study by perturbing the theoretical strains with a randomly varying evenly distributed scatter. Each of these complete strain scans is then subject to the strain–pressure inference procedure outlined above. It was found that for a large number of scans (say greater than 20), the mean deduced pressure distribution is very close to the theoretical 'real' distribution. However, the inferred frictional traction distribution is always worse than the inferred normal pressure distribution. This is because, under axisymmetric loading, the strain observations for the former arise from the integral of the pressure distribution whereas the latter arise directly from the pressures.

The work by Chen, Ooi and Rotter (1996a) has also indicated that the relationship between noise level in the strain readings and the standard deviation in the inferred pressures is approximately linear and can be expressed as

$$\frac{\sigma}{e} = \text{constant} \qquad (45.4.2)$$

in which e is the noise level in the strain measurements and can be expressed as a percentage of the magnitude of the mean absolute strain.

45.4.5 Location of the measurement stations

The location of the measurement stations also affects the accuracy with which the load parameter vector can be evaluated. The influence may be explained using equation (45.3.2) which shows that each strain to be measured is a linear function of the load parameters: the proportionality factors are the sensitivity functions given in $\{S\}_{\beta M}$. Thus measurements made in the zone where larger strains are to be expected should result in a larger signal-to-noise ratio.

However, a strain gauge should not be mounted too close to the boundary, because it will be subject to significant local bending (Rotter, 1987a). This phenomenon is illustrated in Fig. 45.A.3 which shows that the sensitivity functions can change dramatically with height near the bottom. Thus a small deviation from the intended position of a strain gauge may result in exaggerated interpretation errors in the evaluation of the sensitivity matrix $[S]$. Furthermore, minor differences between the experimental and analytically assumed boundary conditions can lead to very serious errors.

In general, the best locations for strain measurements can only be determined from a careful study of the structural response of the test silo under a variety of expected load distributions: positions in the structure which display a poor sensitivity should not be used as gauge sites.

45.5 CONCLUSIONS

The requirements for the measurement of strain on a silo wall have been discussed. A rigorous procedure has been described for inferring the silo wall pressure distribution from measured strains on a silo wall. A simple axisymmetrically loaded silo subject to Janssen normal pressures and frictional tractions has been used to illustrate the procedure.

The considerations to be given for the measurement and interpretation of wall strains have been discussed. The number of strain observations and the level of noise in the strain measurements can have very significant effects on the inference process. The standard deviation of the inferred pressures can be reduced linearly by either reducing the level of noise or increasing the square root of the number of strain observations.

When planning the experiment, it is important that a thorough structural analysis of the test silo should be made, followed by an investigation of the sensitivity of the loading parameters to the measuring station locations and data accuracy. Both the measuring station locations and the number of strain components measured at each location have a significant bearing on the usefulness of the data in inferring the pressures acting on the silo walls.

APPENDIX 45.A
AN EXAMPLE ON INFERRING THE PRESSURE DISTRIBUTION ON A SILO WALL

In this appendix, a simple example is used to illustrate the strain–pressure inference procedure. Consider an on-ground cylindrical silo with a fixed base under axisymmetric loading from the stored solid (Fig. 45.A.1). Because the loading is taken to be axisymmetric, only two strain observations are made at each station. For simplicity, the normal pressure loading and the meridional traction on the silo walls (equation (45.3.1)) are here approximated by a piecewise linear variation with six segments of equal heights, which can be represented by six triangular loading functions f_i as shown in Fig. 45.A.2. The normal pressure p_n and the vertical frictional traction p_v are then given by

$$p_n(z) = \sum_{i=1}^{6} a_i f_i(z) \tag{45.A.1a}$$

$$p_v(z) = \sum_{i=7}^{12} a_i f_{i-N}(z) \tag{45.A.1b}$$

The load parameter vector with $\alpha N = 12$ ($N = 6$) is then defined by

$$\{a\} = \{a_1, a_2, \ldots, a_{12}\}^T \tag{45.A.2}$$

For this illustration, the silo was given a height $H = 12$ m, radius $R = 2$ m, wall thickness $t = 5$ mm, Young's modulus $E_w = 2 \times 10^5$ MPa, Poisson's ratio

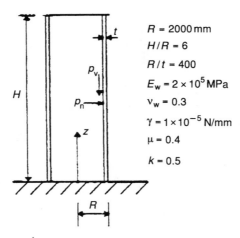

$R = 2000$ mm
$H/R = 6$
$R/t = 400$
$E_w = 2 \times 10^5$ MPa
$\nu_w = 0.3$
$\gamma = 1 \times 10^{-5}$ N/mm
$\mu = 0.4$
$k = 0.5$

Fig. 45.A.1 Silo example.

$v_w = 0.3$ and the wall was assumed to be isotropic. Suppose that pairs of gauges are installed at the heights of $z_1 = 9.25$, $z_2 = 7.25$, $z_3 = 5.25$, $z_4 = 3.25$, $z_5 = 1.25$ and $z_6 = 0.60$ m. At each pair only the circumferential and longitudinal strains on the outer surface of the shell wall are measured ($\beta = 2$, $\beta M = 12$). The strain vector $\{\varepsilon\}$ is given by

$$\{\varepsilon\} = [\varepsilon_1,\ \varepsilon_2,\ \varepsilon_3,\ \varepsilon_4,\ \varepsilon_5,\ \varepsilon_6,\ \varepsilon_7,\ \varepsilon_8,\ \varepsilon_9,\ \varepsilon_{10},\ \varepsilon_{11},\ \varepsilon_{12}]^T \quad (45.A.3)$$

The numbering of the gauges is arranged so that strain observation $2i - 1$ represents the circumferential strain at $z = z_i$ and strain observation $2i$ represents the longitudinal strain at $z = z_i$ (e.g. ε_5 presents the circumferential strain in the gauge at height z_3).

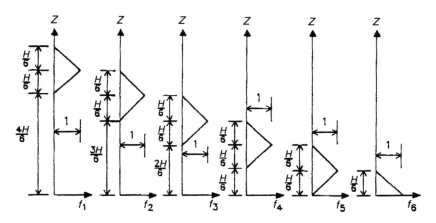

Fig. 45.A.2 Load functions.

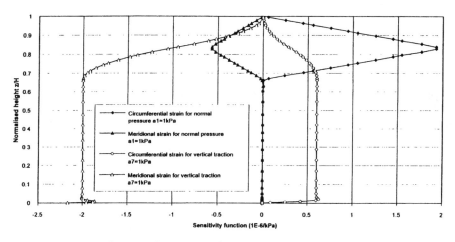

Fig. 45.A.3 Distribution of sensitivity functions.

The measured strain at each gauge is a linear function of the load parameters (equation (45.A.2)), and the coefficients in the matrix of these linear relationships are known as the sensitivity functions (for each strain with respect to each loading parameter). These sensitivity functions were evaluated using the FELASH suite of finite element programs for the analysis of axisymmetric shells (Rotter, 1989) with 12 load cases as shown in Fig. 45.A.2 (with $p_n = f_i$ for $i = 1 \ldots 6$ and $p_v = f_{i-6}$ for $i = 7 \ldots 12$). The calculated strains or sensitivity functions for two loading functions, f_1 and f_7, are plotted in Fig. 45.A.3.

The sensitivity matrix is given by

[S] =

1.25	0.0749	−5.46E-04	−3.27E-06	−1.96E-08	−1.19E-10	0.483	0.0422	−2.21E-06	−1.32E-08	−7.93E-11	−4.80E-13
−0.376	−0.225	7.99E-05	4.79E-07	2.87E-09	1.74E-11	−1.61	−0.141	3.24E-07	1.94E-09	1.16E-11	7.02E-14
−1.97E-03	1.25	0.749	−5.46E-04	−3.27E-06	−1.98E-08	0.600	0.483	0.0422	−2.21E-06	−1.32E-08	−8.01E-11
2.85E-04	−0.376	−0.225	7.99E-05	4.79E-07	2.90E-09	−2.00	−1.61	−0.141	3.24E-07	1.94E-09	1.17E-11
−1.18E-05	−1.97E-03	1.25	0.749	−5.46E-04	−3.31E-06	0.600	0.600	0.483	0.0422	−2.21E-06	−1.34E-08
1.72E-06	2.85E-04	−0.376	−0.225	7.99E-05	4.84E-07	−2.00	−2.00	−1.61	−0.141	3.24E-07	1.96E-09
−7.04E-08	−1.18E-05	−1.97E-03	1.25	0.749	−5.52E-04	0.600	0.600	0.600	0.483	0.0422	−2.23E-06
1.03E-08	1.72E-06	2.85E-04	−0.376	−0.225	8.08E-05	−2.00	−2.00	−2.00	−1.61	−0.141	3.27E-07
−3.95E-10	−6.60E-08	−1.10E-05	−1.85E-03	1.25	0.748	0.600	0.600	0.600	0.600	0.483	0.0422
5.87E-11	9.81E-09	1.64E-06	2.71E-04	−0.376	−0.225	−2.00	−2.00	−2.00	−2.00	−1.61	−0.141
−4.82E-12	−8.05E-10	−1.35E-07	−2.25E-05	0.600	1.40	0.600	0.600	0.600	0.600	0.573	0.147
−9.28E-12	−1.55E-09	−2.59E-07	−4.33E-05	−0.180	−0.420	−2.00	−2.00	−2.00	−2.00	−1.91	−0.490

(45.A.4)

Following a concentric filling of a silo, the normal pressure distribution on the wall is close to that predicted by Janssen theory (1895):

$$p_n(z) = \frac{\gamma R}{2\mu}\left(1 - e^{-2\mu k(H-z)/R}\right) \quad (45.A.5a)$$

in which R is the radius of the silo, μ is the wall friction coefficient and γ is the unit weight of the stored solid. The parameter k is the ratio of the normal wall pressure to the mean vertical stress in the solid (lateral pressure ratio) and is assumed to be a material constant.

The meridional traction when friction is fully mobilized against the wall is

$$p_v(z) = \mu p_n(z) \quad (45.A.5b)$$

The technique of pressure interpretation can be further illustrated by studying an example in which it is supposed that the real load distribution is represented exactly by equation (45.A.5) with $\gamma = 10\,\text{kN/m}^3$, $\mu = 0.4$ and $k = 0.5$. The exact strains which would be observed at each gauge location may be calculated numerically as

$$\{\bar{\varepsilon}\} = 10^{-6} \times [23.06,\ -12.69,\ 35.71,\ -26.04,\ 46.18,\ -41.57,\\ 55.17,\ -58.58,\ 63.17,\ -76.58,\ 65.58,\ -82.56]^T \quad (45.A.6)$$

which are here treated as the observed strains. The above technique may now be applied to these 'observed' strains to see how satisfactory the procedure is in predicting the 'known' Janssen distribution.

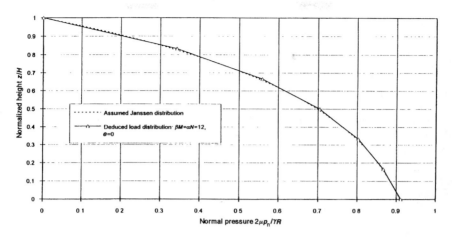

Fig. 45.A.4 Normal pressure distribution: Janssen and deduced.

The load parameter vector $\{a\}$ (which describes the load distribution as piecewise linear) was found by applying equation (45.3.8) to $\{\bar{\varepsilon}\}$, and resulted in

$$\{a\} = \begin{bmatrix} 8.54, & 13.97, & 17.60, & 20.06, & 21.66, & 22.78, \\ 3.46, & 5.56, & 7.02, & 8.01, & 8.68, & 9.05 \end{bmatrix}^T \text{kPa} \quad (45.A.7)$$

These load coefficients were substituted into equations (45.A.1) to produce the predicted pressure and traction distributions. Figure 45.A.4 shows that the predicted piecewise linear normal pressure distribution is in very close agreement with the 'real' Janssen pressures. The slight differences are due to the multi-linear representation of the exponential relationship. Naturally, these differences can be further reduced by increasing the number of loading functions and the number of strain measures.

Since theoretical strains were used as observed strains in the above calculations and the number of unknown load parameters is equal to the number of 'observed' strains, a null error vector $\{e\}$ (equation (45.3.4)) is obtained. In real situations, discrepancies will arise between the expected and observed strains.

REFERENCES

ACI313 (1989) *Alternate Design Procedure*, Discussion document before ACI Committee 313 on Concrete Bins, Silos and Bunkers for Storing Granular Materials, ACI, Detroit.

Askegaard, V. and Nielsen, J. (1986) Instrumentation of reinforced concrete silos, *Bulk Solids Handling*, 6(5), 893–897.

Bishara, A.G. (1992) Moments and axial forces in circular silo walls during eccentric discharge (test data versus finite element analysis results), *Silos – Forschung und Praxis, Tagung '92*, Karlsruhe, Oct., pp. 41–50.

Blight, G.E. (1990a) Defects in accepted methods of estimating design loading for silos, *Proc. Instn Civ. Engrs*, Part 1, 88, Dec., 1015–1036.

Blight, G.E. (1990b) Lateral pressures and frictional wall loads in corrugated steel silos as revealed by strain measurements, *10th Int. Congr. of Chem. Engng, Chem. Equipment Design and Automation*, Prague, Czechoslovakia, Aug.

BSSM CP1 (1992) *Code of Practice: for the Installation of Electrical Strain Gauges* British Society for Strain Measurement.

Chen, J.F. (1996) Interpretation of solids flow and pressures in full scale silos, Ph.D. thesis, the University of Edinburgh, 678 pp.

Chen, J.F.; Rotter, J.M. and Ooi, J.Y. (1993) A technique for the interpretation of silo wall pressures from strain measurements, *Proc., International Symposium on Reliable Flow of Particulate Solids II*, Oslo, Aug., EFChE Pub. No. 96, pp. 255–267.

Chen, J.F.; Ooi, J.Y. and Rotter, J.M. (1996a) A rigorous statistical technique for inferring silo wall pressures from wall strain measurements, *Engineering Structures*, 18(4), 321–331.

Chen, J.F.; Ooi, J.Y. and Rotter, J.M. (1996b) A method for determining unsymmetrical pressures in circular silos using wall strain measurements, *Proc., International Conference on Advances in Steel Structures (ICASS'96)*, 11–14 Dec., Hong Kong.

Hartlen, J.; Nielsen, J.; Ljunggren, L.; Martensson, G. and Wigram, S. (1984) *The Wall Pressure in Large Grain Silos*, Swedish Council for Building Research, Stockholm, Document D2:1984.

Itoh, F. (1975) *On the Characteristics of the Bending Strain Gauge*, translation of the report presented at 1975 Spring Meeting of NDI (The Japanese Society for Non-Destructive Inspection).

Janssen, H.A. (1895) Versuche über Getreidedruck in Silozellen, *Zeitschrift des Vereines Deutscher Ingenieure*, 39(35), 1045–1049.

Kyowa (1977) Characteristics of new series 'double deck' strain gauges, *Engineering News*, Internal Publication, Kyowa Electronic Instruments Co. Ltd, No. 2/221, June.

Munch-Andersen, J. and Nielsen, J. (1986) Size effects in large grain silos, *Bulk Solids Handling*, 6, 885–889.

Munch-Andersen, J. and Nielsen, J. (1990) Pressures in slender grain silos, *CHISA 1990, Second European Symposium on Stress and Strain in Particulate Solids*, Prague, Aug., 9 pp.

Nielsen, J. (1983) Load distribution in silos influenced by anisotropic grain behaviour, *Proc., Int. Conf. on Bulk Materials Storage, Handling and Transptn*, I.E.Aust., Newcastle, Aug., pp. 226–230.

Ooi, J.Y.; Pham, L. and Rotter, J.M. (1990) Systematic and random features of measured pressures on full scale silo walls, *Engng Struct.*, 12(2), 74–87.

Ooi, J.Y. and Rotter, J.M. (1991) Measured pressures in full scale silos: a new understanding, *Proc., Bulk Material Handling – Towards the Year 2000*, London, Oct., pp. 195–200.

Pople J. (1979) *BSSM Strain Measurement Reference Book*, British Society for Strain Measurement.

Rotter, J.M. (1983) *The Effect of Increasing Grain Moisture Content on the Stresses in Silo Walls*, Investigation Rpt S444, Sch. of Civil and Mining Engng, University of Sydney, March.

Rotter, J.M. (1986) The analysis of steel bins subject to eccentric discharge, *Proc., 2nd Int. Conf. on Bulk Materials Storage, Handling and Transptn*, Institution of Engineers, Australia, Wollongong, July, pp. 264–271.

Rotter, J.M. (1987a) Membrane theory of shells for bins and silos, *Trans. Mech. Engrg*, I.E. Aust., **ME12**(3), Sept., 135–147.

Rotter, J.M. (1987b) Bending theory of shells for bins and silos, *Trans. Mech. Engrg*, I.E. Aust., **ME12**(3), Sept., 147–159.

Rotter, J.M. (1989) The FELASH suite of programs for the analysis of axisymmetric shells, *Proc., Fourth Int. Conf. on Civil and Structural Engrg Computing*, London, Vol. 1, pp. 323–328.

Rotter, J.M. and Ooi, J.Y. (1991) Discussion on 'Defects in accepted methods of estimating design loading for silos', *Proc. Instn Civ. Engrs*, Part 1, **90**, Oct., 1077–1088.

Rotter, J.M.; Ooi, J.Y.; Chen, J.F.; Tiley, P.J.; Mackintosh, I. and Bennett, F.R. (1995) *Flow Pattern Measurements in Full Scale Silos*, British Materials Handling Board publication, 230 pp.

Rotter, J.M.; Pham, L. and Nielsen, J. (1986) On the specification of loads for the structural design of bins and silos, *2nd Int. Conf. Bulk Materials Storage, Handling and Transptn*, Institution of Engineers, Australia, Wollongong, July, pp. 241–247.

Trahair, N.S.; Abel, A.; Ansourian, P.; Irvine, H.M. and Rotter, J.M. (1983) *Structural Design of Steel Bins for Bulk Solids*, Australian Institute of Steel Construction, Nov.

46
Displacements, crack openings and total volume
J. Nielsen

46.1 INTRODUCTION

This chapter deals with the observation of three secondary parameters in silo testing: wall displacements, crack openings, and total volume of stored materials. These parameters are discussed in three separate sections.

46.2 DISPLACEMENTS

In many cases silos are considered stiff and the pressure distribution independent of wall displacements. However, it has been reported how especially metal silos can support uneven load distributions by membrane forces activated partly through wall displacements and their related changes of wall curvatures. Also the evaluation of stress state, i.e active or passive state, involves evaluation of wall displacements.

These, and similar situations, lead to a need for instrumenting a silo wall for the determination of wall displacements. For laboratory models the most commonly used method is to instrument an independent test rig with displacement transducers. The test rig must be designed for stiffness, and changes in temperatures have to be considered. Dependent on the size of silos (models) an accuracy of up to 0.001 mm can be achieved with standard laboratory equipment.

For full-scale silos it will normally be almost impossible to construct a rig for transducers. In such cases the photogrammetric monitoring technique may be considered. The best result is obtained with clearly marked target points fixed to the silo wall and photographs taken from different fixed points. The three-dimensional coordinates of the displacements can then be found by standard equipment. This technique has been used for the observation of a 36 m diameter sugar silo (Langsø, 1981). The accuracy was about 7 mm.

With the better equipment which is available today, an estimate of the accuracy which can be achieved would be 1–2 mm. This is based on the assumptions that a resolution of 5–10 μm can be achieved in the photograph and that the photo is scaled 1:200. The accuracy is thus scaled linearly with the size of the silo.

46.3 CRACK OPENINGS

Cracks are mapped and changes in crack openings are monitored on damaged concrete silos. Crack patterns may indicate where large pressures have been located at previous loadings and are best observed when the silo is full. Crack widths may be estimated with an accuracy of about 0.1 mm.

Measurements of changes of crack openings have been taken in order to follow their magnitude during filling and discharge of concrete silos, as reported by Askegaard and Nielsen (1986). Such measurements cannot be used to calculate the pressure distribution in the silo, but they can be used to compare situations before and after certain changes such as a shift from eccentric outlet to central.

The measurements may be misleading if the crack opening is not found at a point in the wall corresponding to the neutral axis of the reinforcement. Therefore displacement transducers must be fixed at two distances from the wall surface so that rotation and translation of the wall parts may be separated.

Changes in crack openings may in this way be measured at an accuracy of between 0.01 and 0.001 mm. The devices on the wall should be protected from direct sun and rain by some kind of cover to improve the zero point stability (Askegaard and Nielsen, 1986).

46.4 TOTAL VOLUME

The density of stored materials may vary considerably. The volume of stored materials – or the filling height – has therefore to be measured even in cases where the weight is known.

Such measurements are normally made by measuring the distance from the ceiling to a point on the surface of the stored material. This can be done automatically by a so-called silo pilot which lowers a weight until the surface is touched. Then the weight is pulled up again and the distance registered at an accuracy of about 1 cm.

This information has to be completed by information about the shape of the surface. Such information may be collected by using more silo pilots or by visual observations combined with some more careful observations made while the filling or discharge has been stopped.

REFERENCES

Askegaard, V. and J. Nielsen, Instrumentation of reinforced concrete silos. *The International Journal of Storing and Handling of Bulk Materials*, 6(5), 893–897, 1986.

Langsø, H. Overvågning af melissilo på Nakskov sukkerfabrik [Survey of a sugar silo at the Nakskov Sugar Company] (In Danish). COWI consult., Copenhagen, 1981.

47

Local density measurements
J. Garnier

47.1 INTRODUCTION

The mechanical characteristics of a granular material depend significantly on the arrangement of the particles and on the number and condition of contacts between grains, and therefore on the compactness of the material. This compactness, which can be expressed by the density, itself depends on the mode of placement of the material and the stress condition to which it is subjected.

It is obvious that, in a silo several tens of metres high, the stresses at the top and bottom of the ensiled material are very different. The mechanical properties of the material (deformability and shear strength) therefore themselves vary considerably from one point to another.

In current design methods, this inhomogeneity of the density and mechanical properties of the material in the silo is not taken into account because it is very poorly understood. The material is assumed to be homogeneous throughout the silo, which is probably very far from the truth.

In researches in progress, on the other hand, theoretical models that are more representative of the behaviour of the material are being used, in particular with the help of numerical methods. It is no longer necessary to assume that the material is homogeneous everywhere, and variations of density should be known and taken into account for the results of tests on silos to be interpreted.

Methods must therefore be imagined to allow local measurement of the densities at different points in the ensiled material and at different stages of filling and emptying.

47.2 CHARACTERIZATION OF ARRANGEMENT OF PARTICLES

Many parameters are involved in the arrangement of the particles in a granular material and may affect its mechanical behaviour, for example:

- the shape of the grains;
- the dimensions of the grains;
- their surface condition (roughness);
- the type of material constituting the grains;
- the arrangement of the grains (distribution, orientation, anisotropy of deposit).

For a given material, however, the decisive parameter is the compactness of the material, which must therefore be the object of the first investigations. This compactness reflects the quantity of solid (volume, weight, number of grains) contained in a given volume.

The easiest measurement to make is obviously that of the weight, and the compactness of a granular material is therefore most often quantified by its density (t/m^3) or unit weight (kN/m^3).

It is, however, important to note that a material, in a given arrangement of grains, will have different wet unit weights depending on the quantity of water it contains. The dry unit weight or dry density therefore better represents the compactness of the material and will provide more information about its mechanical properties. It then becomes important to define precisely what is meant by 'dry condition'. The water molecules surrounding a particle may be free water, adsorbed water at the surface, or water that is part of the material. A procedure is therefore necessary for determination of the conventional dry conditions corresponding to a water content of zero (Chapter 50 on water content).

47.3 RANGE OF VARIATION OF DENSITIES

The dry density or dry unit weight γ_d of a granular material varies between two extreme values γ_{dmin} and γ_{dmax} characterizing a very loose condition and a very dense condition. These extreme values are conventional and depend in part on the procedure used to measure them. In soil mechanics, this procedure is totally standardized, reducing but not totally eliminating the differences between the results obtained by different laboratories on the same material.

These measurements are important because the behaviour of the material depends primarily on the position of the unit weight γ_d with respect to the two extreme values γ_{dmin} and γ_{dmax}. For example, if the material is in a rather dense state it will swell (increase in volume) when sheared. The same material will on the contrary contract (reduction in volume) if it is in a looser condition. It is easy to imagine that the mechanism of failure and the shear strength mobilized may then be totally different. Orders of magnitude

Table 47.1 Example of minimum and maximum unit weights of granular materials and procedures used for their determination

Type of material	Minimum unit weight (kN/m³)	Maximum unit weight (kN/m³)	Procedure used
Wheat	8.1	9.0	Oedometer
Barley	6.9	7.7	Not specified
Cement	13.7	16.8	Electron microscope
Fontainebleau sand	13.9	16.6	ASTM
Fontainebleau sand	13.6	16.4	Japanese Soil Mechanics Society

of the minimum and maximum unit weight, recorded in the literature, together with examples of the procedures followed, are given in Table 47.1.

A primary stage of the researches must therefore concern the standardization of tests, appropriate to the materials that may be ensiled, for the determination of their minimum and maximum unit weights. An additional difficulty for this standardization work arises from the fact that while standardized procedures already exist for sands and gravels, they may be unsuitable for fine powders and for materials of agricultural origin (French standard AFNOR NF P 94-059, German DIN standards, American standards ASTM D 2049-69, 4253-83 and 4254-83, procedures recommended by the Japanese Soil Mechanics Society).

The situation of the material with respect to its two extreme states can be characterized by its relative density (or density index I_D, by analogy with the conventions used in soil mechanics), expressed by

$$\text{Density index} \quad I_D = \frac{\gamma_{max}}{\gamma} \times \frac{\gamma - \gamma_{min}}{\gamma_{max} - \gamma_{min}} \qquad (47.3.1)$$

This density index therefore varies from $I_D = 0$ when the material is in its loosest state ($\gamma = \gamma_{min}$) to $I_D = 1$ when it is very dense ($\gamma = \gamma_{max}$).

47.4 VARIATION OF DENSITIES IN A SILO

Along with the mode of deposition, the main parameter governing the density of a granular material is the maximum stress it bears. Increasing the mean stress tends to increase the density of the material.

In a silo, the stresses in the material are very different between the top and bottom of the deposit. For example, in cereals, the vertical stresses due to self-weight are less than 10 kPa in the first metre and can exceed 100 or 200 kPa at the bottom of the silo.

Table 47.2 Change of unit weight with mean stress for wheat and barley

Mean stress (kPa)	Barley Unit weight (kN/m³)		Wheat Unit weight (kN/m³)	
	Horizontal particles	Inclined particles	Horizontal particles	Inclined particles
0	77.5	69.6	82.4	76.5
10	82.4	72.6	90.2	85.3
20	85.3	75.5	93.2	90.2
40	89.3	78.5	97.1	96.1

This difference in stresses is inevitably reflected by differences in the compactness of the material. Table 47.2 shows, as an example, the variations of density observed on samples of wheat and barley versus mean applied stress for two different grain orientations (Hartlen et al., 1984). This table shows that when the mean stress increases merely from 0 to 40 kPa, the densities can increase more than 20%.

47.5 INFLUENCE OF DENSITY ON MECHANICAL PROPERTIES

The densities of the ensiled material and therefore its mechanical characteristics will vary considerably between the top and bottom of the deposit. As already reported, the density in fact has a very large influence both on the deformability of granular materials and on their strength.

The case of sands is better known than that of cereals and can illustrate this influence of density and mean stress on the mechanical response of the material. An approximate but simple law, relating for example the angle of internal friction ϕ of the granular materials to their voids index e, is expressed by

$$e \tan \phi = \text{constant} \tag{47.5.1}$$

where the value of the constant depends on the type of material. For Fontainebleau sand, this constant is 0.46. The dry density γ_d is furthermore related to the voids index e by the relation

$$\gamma_d = \gamma_s / (1 + e) \tag{47.5.2}$$

where γ_s is the unit weight of the material constituting the grains. These equations (47.5.1) and (47.5.2) finally lead for Fontainebleau sand to

$$\tan \phi = 0.46 \gamma_d / (\gamma_s - \gamma_d) \tag{47.5.3}$$

This equation shows, for example, that when the unit weight changes by 10% (γ_d increasing from 15 to 16.5 kN/m³), the angle of internal friction changes from $\phi = 31.5°$ to $\phi = 38°$, or more than 6° difference. If the material is at its equilibrium limit, the active coefficients of pressure on a vertical wall are $k_a = 0.315$ and $k_a = 0.235$, respectively. They therefore differ by more than 30%.

The deformability of granular materials is even more sensitive to the density and the mean stress. To continue with the example of sands, a relation has been found, by triaxial tests, between the modulus of axial strain E and the confinement stress σ_3 (Le Tirant, 1964):

$$E = C\sigma_3^\alpha$$

For Fontainebleau sand, under a first loading cycle, constants C and α are 270 and 1, respectively. The modulus is therefore in this case proportional to the confinement stress σ_3.

$$E = 270\sigma_3$$

For moduli measured after several cycles, the constants take the values $C = 16.5$ and $a = 0.55$, if E is in MPa and σ_3 in kPa, hence the relation

$$E = 16.5\sigma_3^{0.55}$$

with E in MPa and σ_3 in kPa. These relations show the very large influence of the mean stresses on the deformability of granular materials. The strain modulus of the ensiled material can, therefore, substantially vary between the top and bottom of the silo. These differences must be taken into account in analysing the results of tests on silos.

47.6 DETERMINATION OF DENSITIES OF ENSILED MATERIAL

As already reported, current engineering methods assume that the density of the material is homogeneous throughout the silo. Different values of this mean density are proposed for the calculation, depending on the design method; for example:

- $\gamma = (\gamma_{min} + 2\gamma_{max})/3$, but the procedure for determination of the extreme values γ_{min} and γ_{max} of the unit weight is not always specified;
- γ measured by oedometer under a pressure of 100 kPa;
- γ set equal to values fixed a priori for each type of material (cf. Table 47.3).

From the standpoint of silo operation, the true mean density must also be determined to determine the weight of material contained in the silo at any given time.

The various methods of measuring the volume and weight of ensiled material have been analysed by Ooms (1981). The errors have also been evaluated and, according to a study by McLean and Arnold mentioned by Ooms, the hypothesis of a constant density in the silo led to overestimating the quantity stored by about 4%.

Table 47.3 Examples of unit weights recommended by the French SNBATI rules for concrete silos (Règles professionnelles, 1986)

Product	Unit weight (kN/m^3)
Wheat	8.35
Barley	8.1
Maize	7.85
Rape-seed	7.0
Cement	14.7

47.7 LOCAL DENSITY MEASUREMENTS

A local density measurement could therefore be useful for silo operation; it becomes absolutely necessary for the interpretation of tests performed on silos in the research context.

The theoretical methods now being developed make use of rheological models that are more representative of the true behaviour of granular materials for which the assumption of homogeneous density is no longer acceptable. The distribution of densities in the silo will have to be determined and taken into account.

The means of local density measurements mentioned below apply only to experiments performed in the research context, on full-scale silos or on scale models. The problems are, moreover, different in the two cases.

47.7.1 Tests on actual silos

Given the volume of material and the depths to be investigated, the techniques that can be considered are analogous to those used in soil mechanics.

47.7.1.1 Taking of samples

Samples could, for example, be taken in the silo, either by vertical boring from the free surface or by horizontal boring through openings in the walls.

The difficulty of taking intact samples (necessary for measurement of the volume) in granular materials is well known in soil mechanics. Special core drills must be used, which themselves require rather heavy boring equipment. Techniques in which the material is frozen are sometimes proposed to facilitate the taking of intact samples of the materials most sensitive to remoulding.

This approach to determining local densities would therefore seem to be very cumbersome and unsuitable for tests on actual silos.

47.7.1.2 *Gamma densitometers*

Another technique, also used in site investigations, would probably be more effective. It is based on the scattering of gamma radiation in matter. A radioactive caesium-137 source placed in the material emits a flux of photons; these gamma rays undergo a certain number of Compton scatterings. A detector at a known distance from the source collects the scattered radiation. The number of photons detected is related to the density of the material by an exponential law. The test is interpreted using nomographs obtained in the laboratory on blocks of reference materials placed at known densities.

In experiments on silos, direct use of the probes developed for soil mechanics, placed in casings arranged vertically (or horizontally) in the silo, can be considered. Some probes use two detectors to reduce perturbations of the measurement (effect of the chemical composition of the material, surface effect due to the irregularities of the casing walls).

It must, however, be checked in advance that the presence of these casings in the material, about 10 cm in diameter, has little or no effect on the densities, especially in the case of horizontal tubes. For this purpose, comparative measurements must be made between casing installed in the silo before filling and casing placed after filling, in a borehole. This method can determine the vertical and radial variations of the density of the material, during or after filling. Measurements during discharge are more delicate and the orientation of the tubes should be chosen so as to minimize the perturbations of the flows.

47.7.2 Tests on scale models of silos, in the laboratory or in the centrifuge

Tests on models are often used for research on the behaviour of silos because they have many advantages (lower cost, control of experimental conditions, easier instrumentation, ease of changing parameters including the geometry of the models). On the other hand, they are never more than an approximate simulation of the full-scale structure. In the case of silos, the mass forces due to the self-weight of the ensiled material are decisive.

Scale models in normal gravity do not reproduce the mass forces and the stresses in them are much smaller than in the full-scale structure. Because of this, they can provide only qualitative information, which is sometimes difficult to transpose to the actual structure. Determination of the densities in the ensiled material is therefore not useful for tests of this type.

To give quantitative results concerning the behaviour of the silo and of the material, the mass forces must be correctly simulated in the reduced scale model. The tests must then be performed in a centrifuge, at an acceleration such that similarity conditions are satisfied. In this case, for the same reasons as in tests on actual silos, determination of the distribution of densities in the material may prove necessary for the detailed analysis of the results (use of more representative rheological models, fitting of numerical models). Several methods can be considered.

47.7.2.1 Taking of samples

This technique is much easier to use than in the case of full-scale silos, but requires stopping the centrifuge. It can therefore be used only with materials that swell relatively little.

Measurement of the density on the intact samples taken is still rather delicate on the most sensitive materials, but the freezing technique (Clayton, Bica and Moore, 1994) or a laboratory gamma densitometer (Kus, 1992) can be used.

It is also possible to conduct special tests with the only objective of determining the distribution of densities in the silo.

47.7.2.2 Gamma densitometry

The probes developed for site investigations are unsuitable because of their size and the volume of material concerned. On the scale of the model, the measurement would no longer be local. The principle remains valid, but smaller probes must be designed; this might pose technological problems. In addition, the energy of the source must be limited so as to avoid effects on the environment. If this is not possible, the measurements must be made in a special room, with no operator present, and this would make the method much less useful.

47.7.2.3 Calibrated boxes

A simpler method, already very widely used in soil mechanics tests in the centrifuge, consists of placing calibrated boxes in the silo. At the desired stage of the test, these boxes, the volume of which is very precisely known, are extracted from the soil mass and weighed. By optimizing the shape and size of the boxes and standardizing the testing procedure, it is possible to attain a precision better than 0.5% (Garnier and Kus, 1993). This method is therefore effective but it sometimes requires that tests be specially performed to study the distribution of the densities (Kus, 1992). In silos, it can be applied only to the filling stage.

47.7.2.4 Impregnation

This method, first used to study the variations of density of samples of sand, consists of injecting a liquid chemical that sets and gives the sample a high cohesion. It can then be cut, allowing highly localized measurements of densities.

This technique is perfectly transposable to the case of tests on scale models of silos. The impregnation is done using hypodermic needles, after the centrifuge has stopped. However, if the material is likely to swell when the centrifuge stops, it is possible to inject during rotation, using an on-board device and needles placed in the silo in advance.

Many products have been tested, such as plaster, sodium silicate, acrylamine cement, agar–agar (Kus, 1992), and various resins (Clayton, Bica and Moore, 1994). The injection product must be easy to separate from the material tested. The last two products (agar–agar and resin) are probably the most useful and the easiest to use. With agar–agar, in two successive series of measurements on specimens of fine sand, the deviation was less than 2% (Kus, 1992). With an epoxy resin, the method was calibrated by comparison with the results of direct measurement of the density of a sand placed in a CBR mould (Clayton, Bica and Moore, 1994). This study showed that 95% of the measurements by impregnation lay within ±1.5% of the true value.

47.7.2.5 Numerical image processing

This method could be used in the study of flow mechanisms on centrifuged models. In this case, the problem treated must be plane or axisymmetrical and the flow is filmed by an on-board camera, through the transparent side of the silo. The images are then digitized and a computer program performs an automatic search for markers (coloured material, special particles) and determines their centre of gravity and their positions at various times. Velocity or displacement fields can easily be obtained in this way. The technique has already been applied to silos and hoppers (Ranaivoson, 1991). It would undoubtedly be possible to run another interpretation of the digitized images to deduce the density of the material at different places, but preliminary tests are necessary.

47.8 CONCLUSIONS AND FUTURE RESEARCH

In current silo design methods, the density is assumed to be homogeneous. This simplifying assumption ceases to be acceptable in research, especially when theoretical models more representative of the true behaviour of the material are used. The density in fact varies considerably between the top and bottom of a silo, and the mechanical properties of granular materials are highly dependent on their compactness, in particular their relative density.

Methods must therefore be developed to allow local measurement and so make it possible to determine the distribution of densities in the silo. However, the first stage concerns the standardization of laboratory tests for measurement of the minimum and maximum densities, which can then be used to situate the compactness with respect to the two reference limit states (density index). Measurements should therefore be undertaken, to constitute a data base on the extreme densities, of the most common materials:

- For the local measurement of densities in tests on full-scale silos, the techniques could be derived from those of site investigations (taking of samples or gamma densitometers). Existing gamma densitometer probes should be adapted to the case of in-silo measurements and the perturbations caused by tubes left in place for them should be studied.
- For tests on centrifuged scale models, various local density measurement techniques can be considered (taking of samples, gamma densitometers, calibrated boxes, impregnation, digital image processing).

Some are already in common use for tests in the centrifuge in the field of soil mechanics (taking of samples, calibrated boxes). Others might be suited to the problem of silos but require additional research.

Application of the impregnation technique should be studied. It is already used occasionally in soil mechanics and can, for example in sands, attain precisions of the order of 2%. On the other hand, image processing has so far been used, in tests on centrifuged models, only for the determination of velocity and displacement fields. It would be interesting to examine the feasibility of digital image processing for the local measurement of densities.

REFERENCES

Clayton, C.R.I.; Bica, A.V.D. and Moore, S.R. (1994) A resin impregnation technique for the determination of the density variations in completed specimens of dry cohesionless soil, *Géotechnique* **44**(1), 165–173.

Garnier, J. and Kus, B. (1993) Cartographie des densités de massifs de sable reconstitués par pluviation, *VI Colloque Franco-Polonais de Mécanique des Sols*, Douai, 8 pp.

Hartlen, J. et al. (1984) *The Wall Pressure in Large Grain Silos*, Swedish Council for Building Research, Stockholm, 66 pp.

Kamgueu, V. (1979) Contribution à l'étude de l'écoulement gravitaire des matériaux pulvérulents ensilés, Thèse de doctorat, INSA de Rennes, 251 pp.

Kus, B. (1992) *Pluviation des sables*, DEA Génie Civil, Université de Nantes, 56 pp.

Le Tirant (1964) Contribution à l'étude des relations contraintes-déformations dans les milieux pulvérulents, *Bulletin de Liaison LPC*, No. 6, March–April, 1–32.

Ooms, M. (1981) Determination of contents in storage bins and silos, *Bulk Solids Handling*, 1(4), Dec., 439–453.

Ranaivoson, D. (1991) Dosage des granulats: étude des phénomènes d'écoulement et de voûte. Application à la conception des trémies doseuses. *Etudes et Recherches LPC*, Série Géotechnique, GT46, 280 pp.

Règles professionnelles de conception et de calcul des silos en béton armé ou précontraint (1986) *Annales ITBTP*, No. 446, July–Aug., 1–47.

48

Interstitial and atmospheric air pressure measurement
G. Dau

48.1 INTRODUCTION

In a filled silo, some time after filling and while the bulk material remains at rest, pressure on the silo walls arises mainly from the bulk material. It is presupposed that:

- local pressure differences arising from local compression of the air have been levelled by air flow through the pores of the material, and
- equalization of air pressure from inside the silo to the atmosphere is possible.

During filling or while emptying, or when flow aids are used (such as air cannons or fluidization), some additional pressure effects may arise leading to under- or overpressure within the bulk solid or at the walls. Figure 48.1 shows the nomenclature in this case.

To measure the air pressure at the wall or inside an air-filled but otherwise empty vessel or duct is not a new problem and can be done by means of well-known measurement devices. Likewise, the equipment to measure the atmospheric pressure is also well known.

A greater problem arises where there is a need to know and measure the static pressure inside a bulk material or at the wall of a silo filled with more or less fine granular material. To measure the interstitial pressure in the voids of the bulk material is of interest in cases where the material is passed by an air or gas flow to combine storage of bulk solids with other unit operations such as drying or adsorbing.

730 *Interstitial and atmospheric air pressure measurement*

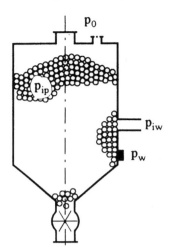

Fig. 48.1 Nomenclature of pressures: p_0 = atmospheric pressure; p_{ip} = interstitial pressure in voids; p_{iw} = interstitial pressure at wall; p_w = wall pressure.

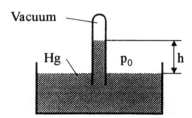

Fig. 48.2 Mercury barometer.

48.2 ATMOSPHERIC AIR PRESSURE

The most common device to measure the absolute pressure of the air in the atmosphere is the mercury barometer (Fig. 48.2). The mercury barometer indicates directly the absolute pressure in terms of height h of the mercury column.

$$p_0 = \rho g h \qquad (48.2.1)$$

Normal (standard) barometric pressure is 760 mmHg (at 0°C) by definition. Equivalents in other units are 1 atm, 29.921 inHg or (and especially) 1.01325 bar.

48.3 INTERSTITIAL AIR PRESSURE MEASUREMENT

48.3.1 Description of general measurement needs

In general, a complete pressure measurement system to measure the static pressure of air or a gas at a wall of a containment consists of a pressure tap, a pressure line and the pressure gauge (Fig. 48.3). The pressure to be measured p_{iw} is transported by the pressure line to the pressure gauge, where it is indicated. This may be accompanied by measuring faults and a lag in instrumentation of the pressure value. Therefore, there is a need not only to choose an appropriate pressure gauge, but also to connect the pressure gauge in a convenient way to the tap. Especially in conditions when fluctuations of the pressure exist, shape and magnitude of pressure taps as well as cross-section and length of the pressure line play an important role. Reliable measuring arrangements are described, for example in VDE, VDI-standard 3513 sheet 3 (VDE, 1971).

It is somewhat more complicated when the air or gas is moving in a containment. In this case, the local static pressure is equal to the pressure on a surface which moves with the fluid or equals the normal pressure on a stationary surface which parallels the flow. According to VDE (1971) or Perry and Chilton (1973) the pressure on such a surface is measured by providing a small hole perpendicular to the surface. The location for the hole has to be chosen in such a way that there exists an undisturbed flow. If this is not possible, then it is recommended to install several taps in the same cross-section and to connect them by a ring line. The cross-section of the ring line should be greater than the sum of inner cross-sections of the pressure taps. An important fact is that the necessary bore holes in the wall of the containment or duct have to be perpendicular to the flow direction of the gas, flush with the surface, without burrs, and not exceed a certain dimension. Recommendations for pressure tap dimensions are summarized in Table 48.1 (Perry and Chilton, 1973).

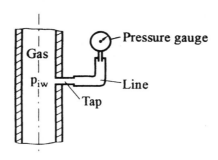

Fig. 48.3 Static pressure measurement device at a wall of a gas-filled containment.

Table 48.1 Pressure-tap holes

Nominal inside pipe diameter		Maximum diameter of pressure tap		Radius of hole-edge rounding	
in	mm	in	mm	in	mm
1	25.4	1/8	3.2	<1/64	<0.4
2	50.8	1/4	6.4	1/64	0.4
3	76.2	3/8	9.5	1/64–1/32	0.4–0.8
4	101.6	1/2	12.7	1/32	0.8
8	203.2	1/2	12.7	1/32–1/16	0.8–1.6
16	457.2	3/4	19.1	1/32–1/16	0.8–1.6

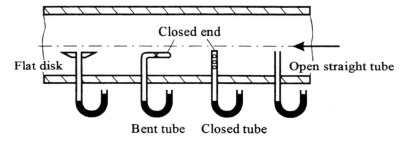

Fig. 48.4 Measurement of static pressure inside a containment or duct.

Sometimes it is necessary to measure the static pressure inside a containment or duct. Some solutions are shown in Fig. 48.4. If the flow is in straight lines, aside from the fluctuations of normal turbulence, the flat disc and the bent tube give satisfactory results when properly aligned with the stream (Perry and Chilton, 1973). Small misalignments can cause serious errors.

When measuring the static pressure of air or gas at the wall of a filled silo, one has to prevent the bulk material plugging the pressure tap. Therefore pieces of porous material may be inserted into a pressure tap to overcome this problem if the diameter of the particles is smaller than or equal to the inner tap diameter. In critical cases, a possibility for cleaning the porous inserts may exist.

When the holes of the pressure taps are reduced by use of porous materials, the recommended hole diameters may not be reached. In this case, it is usual to connect several holes by a ring line as mentioned before. Nevertheless there is uncertainty concerning the measuring error.

There is little published about this kind of problem. Solutions are found empirically by researchers or customers. Systematic investigations are lacking.

Fig. 48.5 Open U-tube, draft gauge.

48.3.2 Overview of pressure gauges

To measure static pressures, a lot of gauges are in use (Dubbel, 1983). The measuring principle of most pressure gauges consists of comparing the force produced by the pressure and a counteracting force, being either the weight of a liquid column or the action of a spring. Well-known devices are the open U-tube or the draft gauge (Fig. 48.5).

To measure very high or very low pressures, or pressures that fluctuate with high frequencies, pressure gauges which make use of electric effects are convenient, e.g. the piezoelectric effect, change of the resistance of wires and semiconductors, change of the capacity of a condenser, inductive measuring transduction or use of a strain gauge device. According to Goldstein (1983), Fig. 48.6 shows schematic representations of the leading types of pressure transducers.

As can be seen from Fig. 48.6 the application of these pressure transducers in filled silos suffers from one problem: the transducer has to be installed as a part of the wall. In this case the air as well as the bulk material will exert a pressure on the transducer, but the transducer cannot distinguish between the two pressure components. Therefore if only the air pressure component has to be measured, these types of pressure gauges can only be used if the bulk material is prevented from touching the transducer area. One possible way to avoid contact between the bulk solid and the transducer wall is shown in Fig. 48.7.

An interesting new technique to measure air or gas pressures at the wall of a filled silo is shown in Fig. 48.8. Similar to the electric effect systems, this new technique measures pressure in an indirect manner. According to over- or underpressure in the containment in question, here a silo, air will be blown out of, or sucked into, the containment through a hole in the wall (Neubert and Petry, 1990). The flow rate through the hole and through a connected flow chamber depends on the pressure difference between the inside and the outside. Depending on the flow direction, the gas velocity is either high on the left-hand sensor and low on the right, or low on the left and high on the right. Thus the flow direction, and hence the sign of the pressure difference, can be measured. Additionally, the height of the pressure can be measured by measuring the flow velocity at the sensors. This can

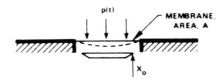 Capacitance device

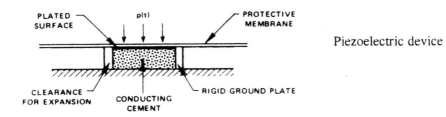 Piezoelectric device

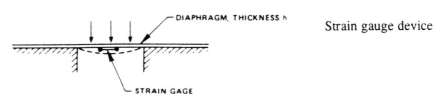 Strain gauge device

Fig. 48.6 Schematic representation of pressure transducers.

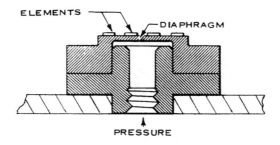

Fig. 48.7 Strain gauge pressure element.

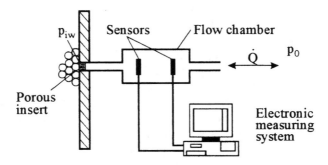

Fig. 48.8 Thermoanemometric pressure gauge.

be done by thermoanemometry. Such a system has been tested at the University of Kaiserslautern in connection with a normal, unfilled duct (Stengel, 1991). It can be applied to a filled silo, because penetration of small particles into the connecting hole and the chamber can be prevented by a porous insert, the pores of which are adapted to the fineness of the particles. The influence of the porous insert on flow velocity and hence on the pressure measurement can be eliminated by the calibration of the system which, in any case, has to be done.

48.3.3 Interstitial air pressure in voids

There may be different reasons why air or gas flows through the voids of a bulk material which is loaded into a silo or silo-type device. Some are already mentioned above. Others include:

- during filling or emptying, air gets displaced or sucked by some pressure gradients originating from these events;
- air is blown into the silo by overpressure to help the bulk material to discharge;
- the silo or silo-type device may have additional tasks besides storing, e.g. drying, absorbing or performing a chemical reaction. In these cases air or gas is blown into the device leading to locally different overpressures in the voids.

A great deal of information exists on how to calculate the static pressure loss across a fixed bed of bulk solids (Ziolkowska and Ziolkowski, 1988), but little is known about how to measure the static pressure inside a bulk solid, especially if the diameter of the particles is small causing even smaller void dimensions. Each measuring device or probe (Fig. 48.4) inside the bulk solid disturbs the assembly of particles unless these are very large compared with the dimensions of the probe. Thus it seems that measurement of local static pressures inside bulk solids can only be performed if one uses large-scale geometrical models of beds (Ziolkowska and Ziolkowski, 1988). Then

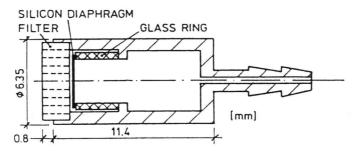

Fig. 48.9 Pore pressure transducer.

it is possible to install several pressure taps from inside the stored materials. Another question is the value of such measurements, because a tap for static pressure measurement has to be perpendicular to the flow direction. In a randomly filled silo the flow channels have very complicated shapes so the above condition normally will not be fulfilled.

In cases where the dimensions of a silo are large and the local pressure is of interest in a restricted area of the voids (not in a single pore), a special pore pressure transducer (König et al., 1994) may be used for measurement (Fig. 48.9).

48.4 GAS VELOCITY DISTRIBUTION

There is a lot of knowledge about the fluid flow inside bulk solids, in many cases referred to as packed beds. An enlarged review of important papers, which have dealt with the problems of the geometry of porous systems as well as with its influence on the characteristics of fluid flow and, in consequence, on the course of the transport process within such systems, is given by Ziolkowska and Ziolkowski (1988). They report upon fluid flow investigations distinguishing between investigations inside ideal porous systems, real infinite systems and real semi-infinite systems. Most of the existing technical systems are real semi-infinite systems. They are infinite in the direction of the flow and finite in the perpendicular direction. Experimental methods to describe the flow inside such systems or beds are similar for all cases.

The axial flow through a porous or bulk material is frequently characterized by a general variable, referred to as 'mean effective velocity' or as the 'theoretical pore velocity'

$$u_p = \frac{u_L}{\varepsilon} \qquad (48.4.1)$$

and is defined as the ratio of the superficial gas velocity u_L and the mean volumetric porosity ε. The superficial gas velocity

$$u_L = \frac{\dot{V}}{A} \qquad (48.4.2)$$

is defined as the ratio of the gas flow rate $\dot{V}$ and the cross-sectional area A of the empty device perpendicular to the main flow direction. Since the local porosity within a porous system is subject to permanent changes, it is obvious that the velocity of a fluid in the voids of such a system cannot attain a constant value and that it must be subject to a non-uniform distribution. According to Tsotsas and Schlünder (1988), three types of non-uniform distribution can be distinguished: the microscopic, the mesoscopic and the macroscopic (Fig. 48.10).

Microscopic non-uniform distribution is determined by the non-slip condition for the fluid on the surface of the bulk material and by changing

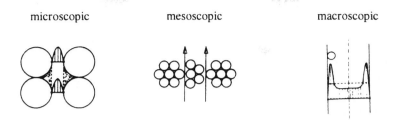

Fig. 48.10 Types of non-uniform flow distribution.

of the individual channel cross-sections. Mesoscopic non-uniform distribution occurs where the flow bypasses relatively dense and compact particle agglomerates in channels, whereby no or only a comparatively small flow exists within the agglomerates themselves. The macroscopic non-uniform distribution is caused by the increase in the bulk material porosity at the walls of the containment, in particular with diameter ratios $D/d > 20$ (Kast and Otten, 1987) and at the walls of installations.

In view of these non-uniform distributions alone, a comprehensive description of the fluid flow at any point within the pore void of a bulk solid is a hopeless undertaking (Kast and Otten, 1987). On the other hand, in technical applications information on local flow conditions is frequently required, going beyond the information content of the theoretical pore velocity. Such cases exist, for example, when in tower driers, the drying air is to be charged using relatively large installations and distributed uniformly in the bulk material.

Other cases of interest are the influence of gas velocities on the type of solids flow (mass flow or funnel flow) or the influence of gas velocities locally exceeding the minimal fluidization velocity on gas distribution, bridge formation and distribution of the porosity in the solid.

48.4.1 Pressure gradient and flow velocity

Besides local gas velocities the pressure gradient across fixed beds built from bulk solids is often of interest. Normally, to calculate the pressure gradient, it is assumed that semi-infinite systems can be treated as real infinite systems. From this it is further assumed that the velocity distribution inside a porous system does not depend on the macroscopic geometrical parameters of the system, nor on the space coordinates.

Inside a porous system the fluid flow at small velocities is laminar, the flow resistance increases linearly with the velocity, and the instantaneous velocities within the layers adjacent to the particles are stable. As the fluid velocity increases the laminar flow inside the bed changes dependent on the local porosity from laminar to turbulent. Because there exist several definitions for the Reynolds number:

$$Re = \frac{u_L d_p}{\nu} \tag{48.4.3a}$$

$$Re_\varepsilon = \frac{u_L d_p}{(1-\varepsilon)\nu} \tag{48.4.3b}$$

$$Re^* = \frac{u_L}{(1-\varepsilon)\nu S_v} \tag{48.4.3c}$$

considerable disagreement is observed between various expert opinions concerning the critical range of Reynolds numbers. This uncertainty also affects the range of application of the pressure gradient equations.

According to Darcy (1856) the pressure gradient for ($Re < 1$) can be written as:

$$\Delta p = \frac{u_L \mu \Delta L}{B} \tag{48.4.4}$$

where μ is the dynamic viscosity of the fluid, ΔL the length of the bed and B the permeability of the system.

A second well-known equation is the Carman (1956) and Kozeny (1927) equation:

$$\Delta p = \frac{u_L k (1-\varepsilon^2) \mu S_v^2}{\varepsilon^3} \Delta L \tag{48.4.5}$$

where ε is the mean porosity of the system, S_v the volumetric specific surface of the particles and k a matching parameter, experimentally determined to a value of 5.

The most important equation, valid from the laminar to the turbulent region of Reynolds numbers, has been developed by Ergun (1952), based on experimental data:

$$\Delta p = u_L \left\{ 4.16 \frac{(1-\varepsilon)^2}{\varepsilon^3} \mu S_v^2 + 0.292 \frac{1-\varepsilon}{\varepsilon^3} \rho_f S_v u_L \right\} \Delta L \tag{48.4.6}$$

with the Reynolds number defined as in equation (48.4.3c). This equation is valid for Reynolds numbers $Re^* < 400$. Because of the difficulty in defining a characteristic velocity inside the bulk material in all equations the superficial gas velocity is used as characteristic velocity. The equations allow estimates, within their range of application, of the pressure in a distinct height of the bed, presupposing steady flow of the gas.

48.4.2 Experimental techniques

To get a more or less detailed picture of the velocity distribution inside packed beds several methods have been developed or used. Some older methods include the adsorption technique, the sublimation technique, the electrochemical method and the electroconductometric method (Ziolkowska and Ziolkowski, 1988). The results of these measurement techniques had a more qualitative character but revealed that:

- fluid flow inside the pores is inhomogeneous;
- in the region near the wall a preferential flow exists;
- velocity oscillations arise in the bed, being greater near the wall than in the core;
- inlet effects are restricted to a zone smaller than two diameters of the apparatus.

In more recent times, some thermoanemometric, pneumatic and laser techniques have been applied. Most of the techniques are used for measurements above the bed using the Depuit–Forchheimer hypothesis, which relates the velocity within the pores u_p to the apparent local velocity u above the bed.

Pneumatic methods consist in using small Pitot tubes for velocity measurement. Their disadvantage is that they are not very exact because the apparent fluid velocity just above the bed is three-dimensional, but the Pitot tube reacts only to the velocity component perpendicular to the plane of the opening.

From a variety of thermoanemometric techniques the most popular device is hot-wire anemometry, because the wires are small and from this do not disturb the velocity field very much (Mickley, Smith and Korchak, 1965; van der Merve and Gauvin, 1971). Thermistor probes are less popular, because of their strong sensitivity to temperature variations (Ziolkowska and Ziolkowski, 1988).

In two cases, laser anemometry was applied to measure velocities inside packed beds (McGreavy, Foumeny and Javed, 1986; Johnston, Dybbs and Edwards, 1975). Some precautions have to be taken with this method, making particles invisible by giving them the same optical characteristics as the fluid. The advantage of this method is the possibility of non-contact gauging.

Another method to measure flow velocities inside a bed was presented by Dau (1991), who also used a thermoanemometric sensor, but located it within a perforated cylindrical probe which could be placed across various planes inside a bulk solid. An extensive example study with this technique was performed with a tower drier filled with plastic pellets (Fickinger, 1990).

Except for the investigation described (Fickinger, 1990), all other investigations have been conducted in devices where the bulk material is supported by a grid. According to Ziolkowska and Ziolkowski (1988), the investigations of the velocity distribution in the cross-section perpendicular to the main gas flow direction in packed bed apparatus were performed over rather broad ranges of geometrical and dynamic parameters:

$$45 < D < 500 \text{ mm} \qquad 0.25 < d_p < 25 \text{ mm},$$
$$3 < D/d_p < 500, \qquad 0.01 < u < 30 \text{ m/s}$$

The following main conclusions can be drawn from the various investigations: as long as the gas is introduced axially into the packed bed, the radial velocity profile before the bed is axially symmetric and almost flat. When the gas is laterally introduced into the bed, the velocity radial profile is deformed. The deformation depends on the ratio of the cross-sectional area of the column to that of the supplying duct. An inlet zone exists, its height being an increasing function of D/d and Re, tending asymptotically to the value $(L/D)_\infty = 1$. Some further parameters which influence the dimensions of the inlet zone are the ratio D/d_p, Re and the porosity of the grid supporting the bed.

Detailed measurements of flow velocities inside the porous media were made by only a few researchers (Mickley, Smith and Korchak, 1965; van der Merve and Gauvin, 1971; McGreavy, Foumeny and Javed, 1986; Johnston, Dybbs and Edwards, 1975; Dau, 1991; Fickinger, 1990; Lamberty, 1991). With the exception of Fickinger (1990), all investigations were made inside regular packings of relatively large, monodisperse spheres ranging from 6 to 70 mm in diameter. In two cases, (Mickley, Smith and Korchak, 1965; van der Merve and Gauvin, 1971) hot-wire anemometry, in two further cases (McGreavey, Foumeny and Javed, 1986; Johnston, Dybbs and Edwards, 1975) laser anemometry, and in the remaining cases (Dau, 1991; Fickinger, 1990; Lamberty, 1991) thermoanemometry were used.

In hot-wire anemometry, experimental work required spheres with diameters as large as 38 mm (Mickley, Smith and Korchak, 1965) or 70 mm (van der Merve and Gauvin, 1971). Though laser anemometry seems to be the best method to obtain detailed information of the flow inside bulk solids, performance of experiments is not easy and requires some precautions, e.g. adequate optical paths, and restriction of the number of elements in the packing.

The investigations by Dau (1991) were performed with the main aim of detecting irregularities of the flow in tower driers, where air is introduced into the bulk material in a special way.

The applied probe technique allows for the velocities to be measured inside a bed of bulk solids. Contrary to laser anemometry, no special precautions have to be provided. From the results it can be concluded that the method is suitable for bulk material with particle sizes above 3 mm and allows measurement of axial pore velocities greater than 0.3 m/s belonging mainly to the mesoscopic scale.

Figure 48.11 shows the cylindrical flow probe (diameter 10 mm) which was used for the measurements. The sensor inside the probe is a platinum resistor wire mounted on a plate-shaped ceramic support (cross-section $2 \times 2 \text{ mm}^2$). In contrast to hot-wire anemometry the sensor is very robust and not affected by soiling.

Gas velocity distribution

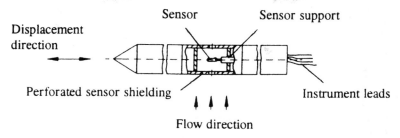

Fig. 48.11 Cylindrical flow probe.

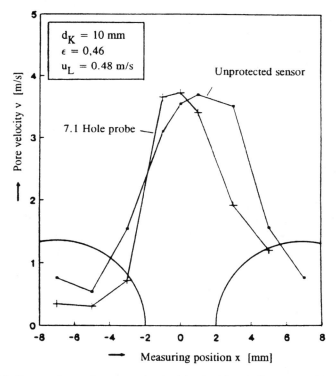

Fig. 48.12 Comparison of measured velocities in 10 mm diameter spheres packing for protected and unprotected sensor.

Figure 48.12 shows an example where the probe-protected and the unprotected sensor was comparatively used to measure pore velocities in a cubic packing of 10 mm diameter spheres (Lamberty, 1991). Application of the new technique to a tower drier filled with plastic pellets revealed zones of inhomogeneity causing non-uniform drying conditions for the pellets (Fickinger, 1990). By changing the method of introducing the air into the drier, satisfactory distribution of the air in all cross-sections over the height of the drier was performed.

48.5 CONCLUSIONS

48.5.1 Pressure measurement

- Measurement of the atmospheric pressure is no problem.
- Measurement of the static air pressure at the wall of a silo becomes increasingly problematic with particle diameters less than about 1 mm. Systematic investigations of the effect of porous wall taps on pressure measurement with special emphasis on pressure fluctuations are lacking.
- Measurement of interstitial air pressure in bulk solids is very difficult, especially when the bulk material, the air, or both, are in motion. For materials staying at rest the new pore pressure transducer may give rise to new possibilities.

48.5.2 Velocity measurement

- Velocity measurement in bulk solids may be performed for microscopic, mesoscopic or macroscopic length scales dependent on the purpose of the measurement being pursued.
- Different measuring techniques have been developed for all three cases.
- Often velocity measurements on the surface of a porous system are performed and conclusions are drawn on the velocities inside the voids.
- For detailed velocity information, laser anemometry and hot-wire anemometry are applicable but need regular bed models with relatively large elements.
- For velocity information in the mesoscopic range – often sufficient for technical purposes – thermoanemometry with a protected sensor is suitable at least for particles greater than 3 mm diameter.

48.6 FUTURE WORK

There seems to be a need for further work in the following areas.

48.6.1 Pressure measurement

- Further development of devices for static pressure measurement for solids with particles less than 1 mm diameter at silo walls. Investigation of the effect of porous wall taps on measured pressures, especially when pressures are fluctuating. Standardization of calibration procedures.
- Further development and testing of devices for static pressure measurement inside bulk solids.

48.6.2 Velocity measurement

- Classification of application needs for velocity measurement in the microscopic, mesoscopic and macroscopic length scale.
- Investigation of non-steady-state flow effects.
- Development of velocity measuring systems for particle diameters less than 3 mm and the mesoscopic range.

REFERENCES

Carman, P.C. (1956) *Flow of Gases through Porous Media*. Butterworth, London.

Darcy, H.P.G. (1856) *Les Fontaines Publiques de la Ville de Dyon*. Dalmont, Paris.

Dau, G. (1991) Experimental determination of the local flow velocities in gas-flow through bulk materials. *Aufbereitungs-Technik*, 32(3), 105–112.

Dubbel, (1983) *Taschenbuch für den Maschinenbau* (Handbook of mechanical engineering) Springer, 15th edition.

Ergun, S. (1952) Fluid flow through packed columns. *Chem. Engng. Progr.*, 48, 49ff.

Fickinger, H. (1990) Experimentelle Bestimmung der Geschwindigkeitsverteilung in einem Versuchstrockner (Experimental determination of flow velocity distribution in an experimental dryer) Diplomarbeit, University of Kaiserslautern.

Goldstein, R.J. (1983) *Fluid Mechanics Measurements*. Springer.

Johnston, W.; Dybbs, A. and Edwards, R. (1975) Measurement of fluid velocity inside porous media with a laser anemometer. *The Physics of Fluids*, 18, 913–914.

Kast, W.; Otten, W. (1987) Der Durchbruch in Adsorptions-Festbetten: Methoden der Berechnung und Einfluß der Verfahrensparameter (Breakthrough in adsorption beds: Methods of calculation and influence of operation parameters) *Chem.-Ing. Technik*, 59(1), 1–12.

König, D. et al., Bolton, M. et al., Bagge, G., Renzi, R. and Garnier, J. (1994) Pore pressure measurement during centrifuge model tests – experience of five laboratories to be published on the Centrifuge 94 Conference, September.

Kozeny, J. (1927) Sitzungsberichte, Akad. d. Wissenschaften. Wien, math.-naturwiss. Klasse, Abt. II a 136, 271ff.

Lamberty, T. (1991) Zur Genauigkeit der thermoanemometrischen Sonden-Geschwindigkeitsmessung (On the accuracy of the thermoanemometric velocity measurement by means of a probe) Diplomarbeit, University of Kaiserslautern.

McGreavy, G.; Foumeny, E.A. and Javed, K.H. (1986) Characterization of transport properties for fixed bed in terms of local bed structure and flow distribution. *Chemical Engineering Science*, 41, 787–794.

Mickley, H.S.; Smith, K.A. and Korchak, E.I. (1965) Fluid flow in packed beds. *Chemical Engineering Science*, 20, 237–246.

Neubert, J. and Petry, M. (1990) Indirekter Drucksensor zur Messung kleiner Druckdifferenzen (Indirect pressure sensor to measure small pressure differences) *Luft- und Kaltetechnik*, 26(1), 22–24.

Perry, R.H. and Chilton, C.H. (1973) *Chemical Engineers Handbook* McGraw-Hill Book Company, 5th edition.

Stengel, F. (1991) Weiterentwicklung eines Meßverfahrens zur Ermittlung kleiner

Über- oder Unterdrücke (Further development of a measuring system to measure small over or under pressures) Studienarbeit, University of Kaiserslautern.

Tsotsas, E. and Schlünder, E.U. (1988) On axial dispersion in packed beds with fluid flow. *Chem. Eng. Process.*, **24**, 15–31.

Van der Merve, D.F. and Gauvin, W.H. (1971) Velocity and turbulence measurements of air flow through a packed bed. *AIChE Journal*, **17**(3), 519–528.

VDE/VDI (1971) Richtlinien 3512, Blatt 3 Meßanordnungen für Druckmessungen (Measuring equipments for pressure measurements) *VDE/VDI Handbuch Meßtechnik*, September.

Ziolkowska, J. and Ziolkowski, D. (1988) Fluid flow inside packed beds. *Chemical Engineering Processing*, **23**, 137–164.

49

Flow visualization

J.Y. Ooi and J.M. Rotter

49.1 INTRODUCTION

The study of the pattern of solids flow out of a silo is an important area of silos research. Much of the research undertaken so far has been concerned with axisymmetric mass flow silos and hoppers. Such flow pattern measurements are of lesser interest now since mass flow is reasonably well understood. However, many industrial silos do not exhibit mass flow and a significant number discharge eccentrically. There is a need to study the much more complex flow patterns which arise from these more realistic silo configurations.

The current view is to classify the flow pattern into three main classes: mass flow, funnel flow and expanded flow, as shown in Fig. 49.1 (e.g. ISO Draft, 1993). Recent experimental observations have shown that flow pattern in full-scale silos can be very complicated and often has three-dimensional features (e.g. Munch-Andersen and Nielsen, 1990; Rotter *et al.*, 1993).

This chapter is principally concerned with the measurement and interpretation of flow pattern in non-mass flow silos. The measurement of the flow pattern is difficult because the solid is opaque and movement cannot be easily detected from outside the structure. This chapter first describes the various techniques for flow pattern measurement which have been employed in previous studies. The experimental observations from these techniques often give fairly limited information, so the task of inferring the flow pattern from the data is not straightforward. The interpretation of the experimental observations is also discussed.

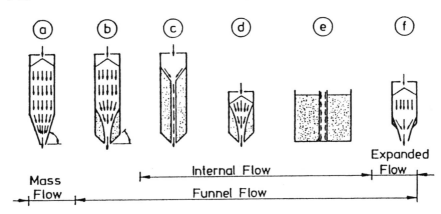

Fig. 49.1 Symmetric flow patterns (after ISO Draft, 1993).

49.2 FLOW PATTERN MEASUREMENT TECHNIQUES

Many different techniques have been used to investigate the flow of granular solids in silos. Most flow pattern studies have used laboratory models, since the scale is small enough to permit special techniques to be used. However, extrapolation of model silo flow observations to full-scale silos is only possible if similitude laws are satisfied (Nielsen and Askegaard, 1977). When self-weight factors are a relevant factor, they can be simulated using reduced scale models in a centrifuge (Nielsen, 1984). The challenges of extrapolating from model tests to full scale are discussed separately (Chapter 51).

Most of the techniques in use are not suited to the full-scale structure because of the limitation of the methods; for example, X-rays can only penetrate a short distance and radio aerials have fairly limited range. The flow pattern measurement in full-scale silos is discussed further in section 49.3

49.2.1 Residence time technique

The most common flow pattern measurement technique in use is by seeding the solid with markers and observing the time taken by each marker to exit the silo, i.e. the residence time. The key data of this technique are the location of each marker when the silo is filled and the time it takes to reach the outlet during solids flow. Inferring solids flow pattern from these data is clearly not straightforward and is discussed in section 49.4.

Various types of markers have been used such as radio tags, steel particles, colour or number coded glass or wooden beads but the technique remains the same (Brown and Richards, 1959; van Zanten, Richards and Mooij, 1977; Graham, Tait and Wadmore, 1987; Dau and Ebert, 1990;

Ranaivoson, 1991; Gourdon *et al.*, 1992; Rotter *et al.*, 1993; Ebert and Dau, 1993).

This technique assumes that the path of each marker represents the actual path taken by the bulk solid which it replaces. However, the markers used are often different in size, shape, density and surface roughness to the bulk solid, which may affect the flow pattern. To avoid these problems, it may be possible to use the bulk material itself for making the markers. Ranaivoson (1991) developed a method which involves pouring a radioactive substance at different locations and depths on the bulk material. During discharge, several radioactive detectors are used for tracking the markers at the outlet.

In addition, the markers need to be placed either through a placing tube, or by stopping the filling, and levelling the solids surface for seeding. The extent to which these procedures affect the flow pattern is not totally clear.

49.2.2 Tracer technique

Tracing the movement of specific particles during silo discharging is another method which has been used before. Perry, Rothwell and Woodfin (1976) used radio pills, the signals of which were picked up by loop aerials wound round the bin at several intervals. Lead shots have also been used as tracers with X-rays exposures of the model (e.g. Bransby and Blair-Fish, 1974).

Similar to the residence time technique, tracer technique also makes use of foreign objects and assumes that the path of each tracer represents the actual path taken by the bulk solid which it replaces. Thus, the comments in section 49.2.1 also apply here. In addition, there is considerable difficulty in determining the location of each marker to a satisfactory precision (Perry, Rothwell and Woodfin, 1976).

49.2.3 Boundary observation technique

Another common technique is to observe the boundary movement of the solid, either on the top surface profile of the solid or through transparent walls or transparent sections of wall. Johanson (1964) used coloured sand layers in plane sections with transparent walls to study the development of flow pattern. Other common features include following movement of some particles at the wall and observing the transition between flowing and non-flowing solid at the wall (e.g. Rotter *et al.*, 1989; Munch-Andersen and Nielsen, 1990; Carson, Goodwill and Bengtson, 1991).

Photographic techniques were used to record the movement of particles through the transparent wall (e.g. Bosley, Schofield and Shook, 1969). Successive photographs can be used to track the movement of the particles as they flow through the silo. Flow images can also be recorded using a CCD camera which can then be digitized and processed (e.g. Lepert and Corte, 1989). Garnier et al. (1991) used such a technique in a centrifuge model and images produced were processed using a computer program to provide horizontal and vertical displacement of each marker.

This method is often used to measure the flow patterns in two-dimensional plane strain hoppers and silos, which are useful for validating two-dimensional numerical and theoretical models. Apart from that, the method offers limited information which, on its own, is normally not sufficient for inferring the flow pattern of the solid. However, no foreign objects are involved and so the observations though limited are usually reliable. Thus, coupled with other techniques, this method gives useful independent checks on the flow pattern deduction.

49.2.4 Freezing technique

Arresting the flow pattern has also been attempted. This is normally done by freezing the solid with a setting agent such as paraffin wax and then dissecting the mould to observe the pattern of the flowing solid at a certain instant (e.g. Chatlynne and Resnick, 1973; Nielsen and Askegaard, 1977). Another method, used by Giunta (1969), is to use a split-mould model and remove the solid in one half of the model which was laid horizontal to expose the flow pattern. The freezing method is obviously only applicable for small models.

49.2.5 Others

Other techniques include inserting sticks through a hole in the wall and measuring the rotation of the stick; using X or gamma rays to study the variations of porosity of the solid; observing the signs of abrasion and polishing of the internal walls.

49.3 FLOW PATTERN MEASUREMENT IN FULL-SCALE SILOS

Measurements of flow patterns in full-scale silos are rarely done, and most observations rely on visual records of the top surface profile together with signs of abrasion, scouring and polishing of the walls. From these, the regions of flowing solid are approximately deduced, though often it is not easy to ascertain whether the same flow pattern always occurs and whether it changes from time to time during a discharge.

As noted in section 49.2, most of the techniques are not suitable for measuring flow pattern in full-scale silos. One current method used to investigate solids movement in a full-scale industrial installation is to drill a series of holes in the silo wall at different heights, and to insert a bar through the wall into the solid (Levison and Munch–Andersen, 1993). During discharge, the bar is seen to move if the solid inside is moving, and in careful studies, the rotational velocity of the bar about the hole can be used to estimate the local velocity of the moving solid. By placing such bars at many heights, the boundary between the moving and stationary material in a semi-mass flow silo can be detected. However, the technique has several disadvantages. The movement does not measure a real velocity since the bar's rotation means slow translation near the wall, but more rapid translation further inside. Second, the bar must be repeatedly reinstalled as the flow progresses, involving much human interaction with no potential for automation. Third, the movement of the bar only indicates the flow of solids against the wall, so events deeper in the silo are undetectable. Fourth, many penetrations must be made into the wall to achieve the goal.

Another technique that has been used at full scale is the residence time technique: placement of markers and automated measurement of residence times of the markers. Rotter, Ooi and their co-workers (1993, 1995) conducted a series of experiments in which a massive quantity of residence time observations were made in two full-scale silos: a 250t industrial steel silo with circular planform storing gypsum powder (Fig. 49.2) and a $100 \, m^3$

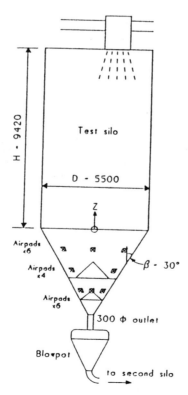

Fig. 49.2 British Gypsum silo.

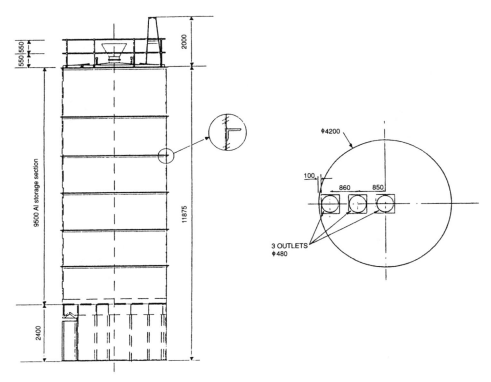

Fig. 49.3 BMHB instrumented test silo.

fully strain-gauged flat-bottomed steel silo with three outlets (Fig. 49.3). The silos were seeded with radio frequency tags which were placed in a systematic pattern using a specially designed deployable seeding device. Up to 300 radio frequency tags were placed in known positions at up to nine levels of fill. The 'residence time' was assessed in terms of the amount of solid remaining in the silo at the instant when each marker passed through the outlet. This is a more useful measure than the actual time to achieve discharge, since it is independent of both varying rates of flow and intermittent flow as controlled by discharging device in the plant.

The chief challenges in full-scale flow pattern measurement lie in making direct observations, the expense of conducting full-scale studies, the constraints of operational needs of the plant, and the critical importance of making reliable observations.

The location of each marker is very important, since there is no independent means of verifying where the marker was placed once it has been covered by additional bulk solid. Thus the chosen technique had to lend certainty to the fact that (a) the marker was correctly identified at the time

Analysis and interpretation of experimental data 751

of placement, and (b) it was placed in exactly the intended location. Rotter *et al.* (1993) used markers which were carefully identified by colour and number coding, and which were precisely placed by using a placement template within the silo.

49.4 ANALYSIS AND INTERPRETATION OF EXPERIMENTAL DATA

Naturally, the task of inferring the flow pattern of the solid from the experimental data depends on the technique used. Whatever the technique, the task is often not straightforward and is further complicated by the complexities of the flow pattern which can occur. This section is confined to discussion relevant to the interpretation of residence time observations.

As noted earlier, the key data of the residence time technique are the location of each marker when the silo is filled and the time it takes to reach the outlet during solids flow. If the silo exhibits mass flow, a relatively small number of markers can be used to characterize the entire flow regime, because the variations in velocity are smooth and discontinuities in flow (flow channel boundaries) do not occur. By contrast, where funnel flows and narrow channel pipe flows occur, a very large number of observations are required, since the flowing channel may be missed entirely by a wide placement of markers. In addition, it has been noted that the accuracy of flow pattern inference from residence time observations depends on a large body of data being available (Rotter *et al.*, 1995).

49.4.1 Marker residence times

The simplest interpretation of the residence time observations involves simply plotting the residence time as a function of the position of the marker in the silo. Some typical contour plots of the remaining volume of solid in the full-scale silo experiments (as a measure of the residence time) undertaken by Rotter, Ooi and their co-workers (1995) are shown here. Figures 49.4(a) and (b) show a vertical section and a horizontal section at the third layer through the silo for a concentric discharge experiment. Another set of corresponding plots for an eccentric discharge experiment are shown in Fig. 49.5. For each experiment, different vertical sections and as many horizontal sections as there are seeded layers, can be drawn. In each sectional plot shown, a pair of figures giving the individual measured values and contours of the remaining volume V at each marker position are shown.

The contouring was performed by forcing the solid at the outlet to discharge immediately and the solid at the silo bottom to remain in the silo indefinitely. This was effected by prescribing the appropriate boundary conditions for the values of V, which is required to constrain the residence time field. The extrapolation beyond the real data area in the plots is clearly

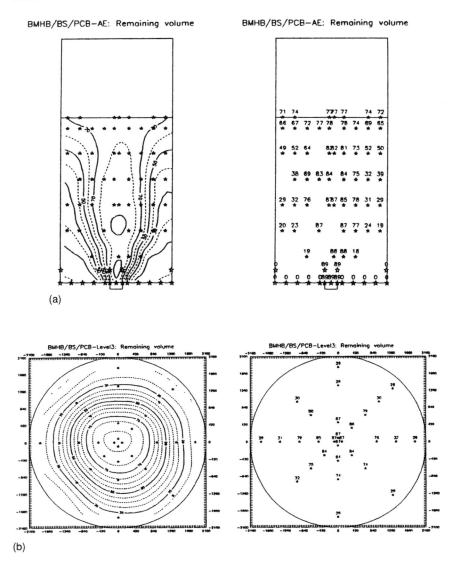

Fig. 49.4 Typical contours of remaining volume of solid in the silo (test PCB: concentric discharge): (a) vertical diametrical section A–E; (b) horizontal section at level 3 ($z = 2.60$ m).

of doubtful validity. The contours were drawn using the Kriging interpolation technique (Ripley, 1981) and must be treated as speculative in the zones where insufficient data are available.

Studying the contours at many different levels can give limited informa-

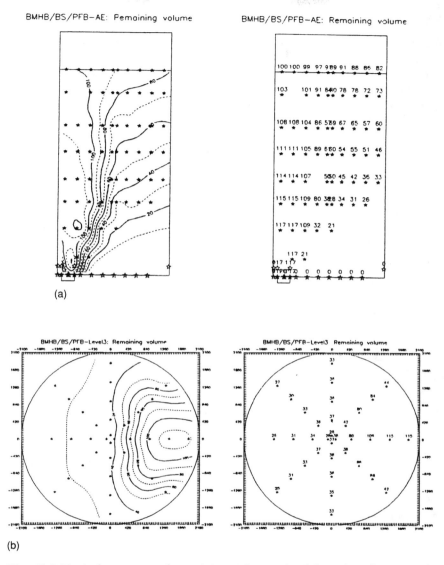

Fig. 49.5 Typical contours of remaining volume of solid in the silo (test PFB: eccentric discharge): (a) vertical diametrical section A–E; (b) horizontal section at level 3 ($z = 2.89$ m).

tion on the overall flow pattern of the solid. Since the residence time is an integral of the time over an unknown path with an unknown particle velocity variation, it is difficult to infer a certain pattern of flow conclusively.

49.4.2 Marker mean velocities

A clearer picture of the overall flow pattern may be obtained by determining the mean velocity of discharge of each marker. An assumption on the particle path is required. The corresponding mean velocity contours of the

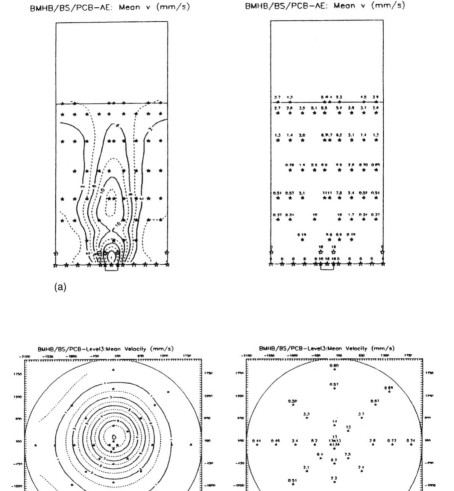

Fig. 49.6 Typical contours of mean velocity in mm/s (test PCB: concentric discharge): (a) vertical diametrical section A–E; (b) horizontal section at level 3 (z = 2.60 m).

Analysis and interpretation of experimental data 755

same data presented in Figs 49.4 and 49.5 were obtained by dividing the shortest distance from the marker position to the centre of the outlet with the residence time. Figures 49.6 and 49.7 show the mean velocity values and contours for the same horizontal and vertical sections as shown in Figs 49.4 and 49.5.

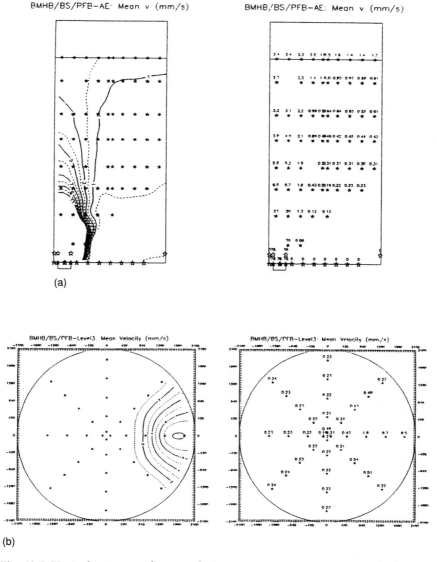

Fig. 49.7 Typical contours of mean velocity in mm/s (test PFB: eccentric discharge): (a) vertical diametrical section A–E; (b) horizontal section at level 3 ($z = 2.89$ m).

The mean velocity is not quite the same as the flow velocity, since it assumes that each marker has moved at constant speed towards the outlet and followed the shortest path. Nevertheless, it does provide a better picture of the flowing material, since solids which must move quickly from the top of the silo to the outlet in the same time as a slower particle near the bottom are identified as involved in very different flow rates. Because the fast flow in the flowing regions is so distinct from the much slower movement in the more stationary parts, the image is sometimes clearer (compare Fig. 49.4(b) with Fig. 49.5(b)).

49.4.3 Further analysis

Further methods of processing the residence time data have recently been undertaken to give more information on the solids flow pattern. These

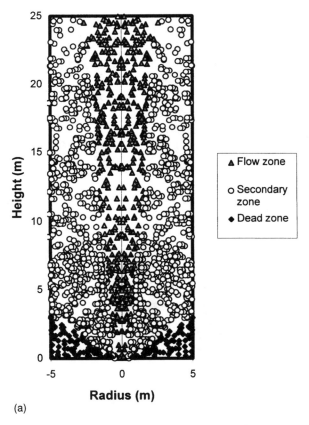

Fig. 49.8 Flow pattern recognition using residence time plot: (a) randomly placed markers in an internal funnel flow silo; (b) characteristics pattern for internal flow mode.

Analysis and interpretation of experimental data 757

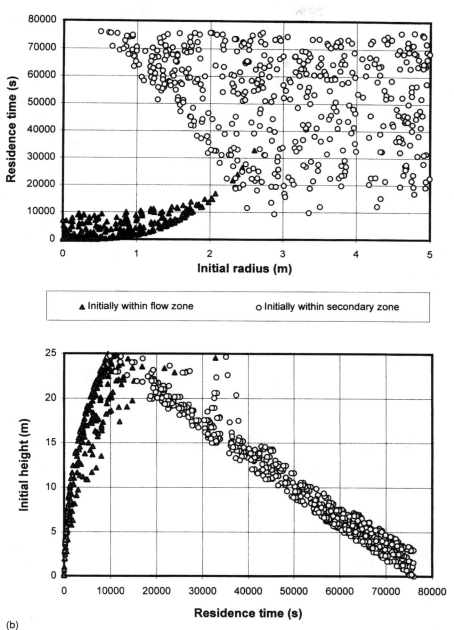

(b)

Fig. 49.8 *Continued*

include studying the statistical measures of the residence time observations and studying the characteristic pattern in residence time plots. An example of the latter is shown in Fig. 49.8 which shows the characteristic patterns expected for an internal funnel flow mode. Further details can be found in Rotter et al. (1995). In addition, development of computational algorithms to transform residence time data into a time-dependent velocity field using some basic assumptions is currently being undertaken by the Edinburgh University Silo Research Group. A computer program which can display two- and three-dimensional images of the moving markers as the markers move towards the outlet has been developed. Several simple flow algorithms have been implemented. The graphics program can be used for displaying the results of any residence time experiments.

49.4.4 Flow channel boundaries

The main aim of flow pattern experiments is to define the flow pattern which occurs, i.e. the flow channel boundaries. For semi-mass flow (Fig. 49.1(b)), this principally means finding the transition between mass flow against the wall and internal flow against the solid. For internal flow (Figs 49.1(c)–(e)), the shape and size of the flow channel need to be determined. However, flow channels develop and change in shape and size from the beginning of discharge, and do not always have steady-state flow boundaries. This further complicates the issue. Many studies have been conducted in an attempt to measure or predict the shape and size of the flow channels in funnel flow silos (e.g. Giunta, 1969; Carson, Goodwill and Bengtson, 1991; Rotter et al., 1995). The analyses of measured residence time data described above can give a good estimate of the position of the flow channel. However, further work is needed to improve the techniques for interpreting the flow measurements so that the flow channel boundaries can be predicted reliably and accurately.

49.5 CONCLUSIONS

A discussion of the techniques for flow pattern measurement has been presented. With the current state of the art, none of the techniques have been proven to be able to fully define the flow pattern which occurred in an experiment. Therefore, two or more techniques must be employed simultaneously to give independent checks on the deductions made concerning the flow pattern.

The experimental observations from these techniques often give fairly limited information, so the task of inferring the flow pattern from the data is not easy. The interpretation of the experimental observations has been discussed. Much work is currently in progress to advance the technique of inferring flow patterns from residence time observations.

REFERENCES

Bosley, J.; Schofield, C. and Shook, C.A. (1969) An experimental study of granular discharge from model hoppers, *Trans. I.Chem.E.*, **47**, 147–153.

Bransby, P.L. and Blair-Fish, P.M. (1974) Wall stress in mass flow bunkers, *Chem. Engng Sci.*, **29**, 1061–1074.

Brown and Richards (1965) Kinematics of flow of dry powders and bulk solids *Rheol. Acta*, 163–164.

Carson, J.W.; Goodwill, D.J. and Bengtson, K.E. (1991) Predicting the shape of flow channels in funnel flow bins and silos, *ACI Spring Convention*, Boston, March.

Chatlynne and Resnick (1973) Determination of flow patterns for unsteady-state flow of granular materials, *Powder Technology*, **8**, 177–182.

Dau, G. and Ebert, F. (1990) A method to determine the flow behaviour of moving granular materials, *Powder Handling and Processing*, **2**(1), 7–11.

Ebert, F. and Dau, G. (1993) Residence time measurements in bulk solids handling devices, *Proc., Int. Symp. Reliable Flow of Particulate Solids II*, Oslo, Aug., EFChE Pub. No. 96, pp. 897–908.

Garnier, J.; Chambon, P.; Ranaivoson, D.; Charrier, J. and Mathurin, R. (1991) Computer image processing for displacement measurement, *Centrifuge 91*, Boulder, Balkema, pp. 543–550.

Gourdon, J.L.; Ranaivoson, D.; Torchet, B. and Lepert, P. (1992) Ecoulement des matériaux granulaires dans les trémies de dosage: modelisation, vérification, perspectives. *Bulletin de Liaison des Laboratoires des Ponts et Chaussées, No. 180*, July–Aug., pp. 5–9.

Graham, D.P.; Tait, A.R. and Wadmore, R.S. (1987) Measurement and prediction of flow patterns in granular solids in cylindrical vessels, *Powder Technology*, **50**, 66–76.

Giunta, J.S. (1969) Flow patterns of granular materials in flat-bottom bins, *Trans. ASME, J. Engng for Industry*, Series B, **91**(2), 406–413.

ISO Draft (1993) *Loads due to Bulk Materials* Draft International Standard, ISO/DIS 11697, Geneva.

Johanson, J.R. (1964) Stress and velocity fields in the gravity flow of bulk solids, *Jnl of Appl. Mech.*, Series E, **31**, Sept., 499–506.

Lepert, P. and Corte, J.F. (1989) Etude d'un silo métallique en centrifugeuse, *Construction Métallique*, No. 2, 97–104.

Levison, B. and Munch-Andersen, J. (1993) Shocks in coal silos: a case study, *Proc., Int. Symp. Reliable Flow of Particulate Solids II*, Oslo, Aug., EFChE Pub. No. 96, pp. 1015–1021.

Munch-Andersen, J. and Nielsen, J. (1990) Pressures in slender grain silos, *CHISA 1990, Second European Symposium on Stress and Strain in Particulate Solids*, Prague, Aug., 9 pp.

Nielsen, J. (1984) Centrifuge testing as a tool in silo research, *Proc., Symp. Application of Centrifuge Modelling to Geotechnical Design*, Ed. W.H. Craig, Manchester, pp. 475–483.

Nielsen, J. and Askegaard, V. (1977) Scale errors in model tests on granular media with special reference to silo models, *Powder Technology*, **16**, 123–130.

Perry, M.G.; Rothwell, E. and Woodfin, W.T. (1976) Model studies of mass flow bunkers II: Velocity distributions in the discharge of solids from mass flow bunkers, *Powder Technology*, **14**, 81–92.

Ranaivoson, D. (1991) Dosage des granulats: étude des phénomènes d'écoulement et de voûte, Application à la conception des trémies doseuses. *Etudes et Recherches LPC*, GT46, 273 pp.

Ripley, B.D. (1981) *Spatial Statistics*, Wiley, New York.

Rotter, J.M.; Jumikis, P.T.; Fleming, S.P. and Porter, S.J. (1989) Experiments on the buckling of thin-walled model silo structures, *Journal of Constructional Steel Research*, 13(4), 271–299.

Rotter, J.M.; Ooi, J.Y.; Chen, J.F.; Tiley, P.J.; Mackintosh, I. and Bennett, F.R. (1995) *Flow Pattern Measurement in Full Scale Silos*, British Materials Handling Board, 230 pp.

Rotter, J.M.; Ooi, J.Y.; Lauder, C.; Coker, I.; Chen, J.F. and Dale, B.G. (1993) A study of the flow patterns in an industrial silo, *Proc., Int. Symp. Reliable Flow of Particulate Solids II*, Oslo, Aug., EFChE Pub. No. 96, pp. 517–524.

Van Zanten, Richards, P.C. and Mooij (1977) Bunker design – Part 3, *J. Eng. Ind., Trans. ASME*, Series B, Nov., 819–823.

50

Measurement of moisture in silos
J.M. Fleureau

50.1 INTRODUCTION

Experience shows that moisture can drastically change the conditions of gravity flows in granular materials, and even prevent the discharge of silos (Johanson, 1975; Ranaivoson, 1988). For instance, flow measurements were made at the Ecole Centrale de Paris in conical hopper models (Biarez *et al.*, 1989). The models were filled with slightly moist sand at different water contents. In each test, the diameter of the outlet was progressively increased until a flow was observed: Fig. 50.1 represents the minimum diameter of the outlet for which the discharge occurred versus the corresponding water content of the sand. This experiment points out the extreme sensitivity of flow to water content, as a 1% change results in a diameter eightfold larger. Such problems happen with many kinds of products (carbon, chemicals, food products, etc.).

Generally, in industry, the admissible range of water contents varies from zero to a few per cent, depending on the type of materials, its affinity for water, etc. Thus, their measurement requires extremely sensitive devices, which implies the use of a destructive method, as the sensitivity of all non-destructive methods presently existing is insufficient.

Clearly, the mechanism responsible for this behaviour is the formation of bonds between the particles, due to the presence of water menisci. Within the menisci, the water pressure u_w is negative (i.e. lower than the pressure in the air phase, u_a, which is assumed to be the continuous phase, usually atmospheric) and can reach values up to several MPa or more. A small change in water content will produce a large change in the negative

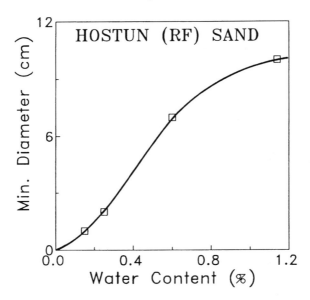

Fig. 50.1 Minimum diameter of the silo hopper outlet for which the discharge of the wet material was observed vs. the water content of the material (Hostun RF sand: $100\,\mu m < D < 600\,\mu m$).

pressure. This results in strong attractive forces between the particles and the existence of a 'capillary' cohesion in the granular medium.

50.2 INTERGRANULAR FORCES DUE TO MENISCI

In the most elementary model, the intergranular force due to the water meniscus between two particles in contact is calculated as the product of the negative pressure $(-u_w)$ by the area of the cross-section of the meniscus (Σ):

$$f_u = -u_w \Sigma$$

This relation shows that the force increases with the pressure, but more slowly than the pressure itself as the area of the meniscus decreases when $-u_w$ increases. When the particles are no longer in contact and their distance increases, f_u decreases and the bond may eventually be broken (Taibi, 1994). This phenomenon is likely to happen during the discharge of a silo when the material is submitted in some parts of the hopper to large deformations that often result in dilatancy.

If the material is not dry, the particles tend to agglomerate in aggregates, the diameter of which is closely related to the negative pressure of the medium. In fact, the diameter of the aggregates also depends on other parameters, e.g. their position in the silo, the rheological behaviour of the material, so that their distribution is not uniform within the material. The

Relation between water content and negative pressure

discharge of the silo will stop when the ratio of the diameter of the aggregates to the diameter of the outlet becomes larger than a threshold value. Thus, the negative pressure appears as the mechanical parameter directly responsible for stopping the flow of material, and it is therefore particularly relevant to the problem of silos to try to measure it.

50.3 RELATION BETWEEN WATER CONTENT AND NEGATIVE PRESSURE

Two examples are shown in Fig. 50.2, for sand and glass balls respectively. The results of the controlled-pressure tests are shown as pF, which is the logarithm of the negative pressure (in centimetres of water height) versus the material water content. These characteristics of the materials are obtained in the laboratory by submitting small samples to given negative pressures and measuring the state of the samples when the equilibrium is reached. Different techniques are used to control the negative pressure, depending on its value (Biarez et al., 1988):

- between $-u_w = 1\,\text{kPa}$ and $30\,\text{kPa}$: tensiometric plates;
- between $-u_w = 10\,\text{kPa}$ and $1500\,\text{kPa}$: air overpressure or osmotic technique;
- between $-u_w = 1\,\text{MPa}$ and $1000\,\text{MPa}$: desiccators with salt solutions.

When the water content decreases from 5% to 0, the increase in negative pressure is considerable, especially between 2% and 0:

- between $w = 5\%$ and $w = 2\%$, the pF varies from 1.3 to 1.9 ($-u_w$ from 2 to 8 kPa) for the sand and from 3 to 4 ($-u_w$ from 100 to 1000 kPa) for the glass balls;
- between $w = 2\%$ and $w = 0$, the pF varies from 1.9 to 4 ($-u_w$ from 8 to 1000 kPa) for the sand and from 4 to 6 ($-u_w$ from 1 to 100 MPa) for the glass balls.

The relation between the water content and the negative pressure depends on many parameters: the surface properties of the grains (their affinity for the liquid), the dimension of the particles, the density of the granular material, etc.

A simple approach developed by Taibi (Biarez, Fleureau and Taibi, 1993) can be used to predict the relation between water content and negative pressure for quasi-undeformable media composed of isodiametral spheres. In this approach, several regular packings are considered and the water content is derived from the calculation of the volume of the menisci corresponding to given values of the contact angle and of the negative pressure. The predictions of this model are in general agreement with the results of tests, as shown on Fig. 50.3

For the same water content and void ratio, the model shows that the negative pressure is inversely proportional to the diameter of the particles

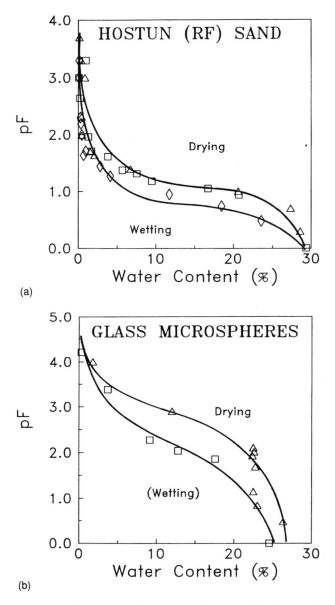

Fig. 50.2 Drying–wetting curves of two granular materials (Hostun RF sand and glass balls: $4\,\mu m < D < 40\,\mu m$).

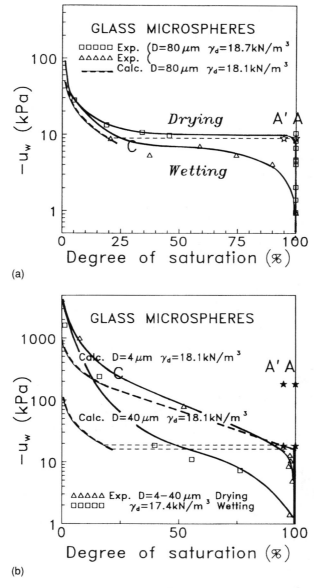

Fig. 50.3 Comparison between the predictions of the model and the experimental results for two samples of glass microspheres: (a) with a uniform particle size of 80 μm; (b) with a non-uniform distribution of particle sizes between 4 and 40 μm.

Table 50.1 Correspondence between diameter of grains and negative pressures for $0 < w < 5\%$

d (d_{10})	0.4 μm	4 μm	40 μm	400 μm
$-u_w$ for $w = 0.1\%$	5 MPa	500 kPa	50 kPa	5 kPa
$-u_w$ for $w = 5\%$	1500 kPa	150 kPa	15 kPa	1.5 kPa

(i.e. multiplied by 10 when the diameter is divided by 10), which is verified in practice. When the distribution of grain sizes is not uniform, experience shows that the representative dimension to be taken into account in the model is d_{10}, the diameter corresponding to 10% of particles passing through the corresponding sieve. This leads to the correspondence indicated in Table 50.1 between the diameter of grains and the range of negative pressures for water contents between 0 and 5%.

50.4 MEASUREMENT OF WATER NEGATIVE PORE PRESSURE

The devices used to measure the water negative pressure are quite different according to the range of pressures concerned:

- From 0 to 1500 kPa, the measurement can be made by tensiometers, the principle of which is based on the use of semi-permeable porous plugs, permeable to water but impermeable to air. It is thus possible to measure a negative pressure ($u_w < 0$; $u_a = 0$) with an absolute pressure transducer without desaturating the measurement circuit. For proper functioning of the device, it is necessary that there is continuity between the water phases in the material and in the porous plug, which is sometimes difficult to obtain in some coarse materials with large particles. Until recently, these devices were limited to negative pressures below 70 kPa. A new apparatus developed at the Imperial College of London in recent years allows measurements to be carried out up to 1500 kPa. Unfortunately, this apparatus tends to desaturate after some time, randomly varying from 10 minutes to 10 hours.
- From 200 kPa to several hundreds of MPa, psychrometers can be used to measure negative pressure. In this method, the apparatus measures the relative humidity of the air within the material. The value is derived from the measurements made by two thermometers: the first one is dry (dry bulb) and measures the temperature T_0 of the sample; the second one is constantly maintained wet (wet bulb) and measures the evaporation temperature T_e in the atmosphere of the sample. The difference $T_0 - T_e$ is a function of the relative humidity of the air phase in the material. The relative humidity (RH) is related to the curvature of the water–air interfaces and thus, to the negative pressure by the following

Measurement of water negative pore pressure

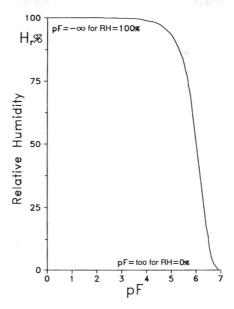

Fig. 50.4 Relationship between pF and RH at 25°C.

thermodynamic relationship derived from the Kelvin–Goodrich law (Verbrugge, 1974):

$$\text{pF} = \log(-u_w)_{\text{cmWC}} = 4.035 + \log T_0 + \log(2 - \log \text{RH})$$

This relation is plotted in Fig. 50.4.

The measurement of the temperatures T_0 and T_e is made by means of either thermocouples, thermistors or transistors, each technique presenting advantages and drawbacks. In all the cases, it is necessary to calibrate the device using salt solutions. The negative pressure is determined by relating the generated output to the calibration curve.

These devices are extremely sensitive to temperature changes. It is therefore necessary to measure precisely the temperature of the material (±0.1°C) in the vicinity of the probe and to carry out the calibrations at different temperatures.

Other devices are used to measure the air relative humidity in the range from 10 to 95% (5 < pF < 6.5), based on the measurement of electric parameters related to moisture (dielectric constant, resistivity, capacity, etc.). Usually, these devices have an accuracy of ±1 RH, or ±0.1 pF in this part of the curve (Fig. 50.4), which is somewhat lower than that of the psychrometers but may be sufficient for control.

A few very accurate devices have been developed in recent years (with an accuracy of 0.1 RH or 0.01 pF, similar to that of the psychrometers), which are not well adapted to use in granular materials, due to their bulk and fragility. Among these devices, those measuring the dewpoint using an optical method appear very promising; however, their present state of development seems to prohibit their use in an industrial context. A great deal of research will be necessary to miniaturize the systems and make them more durable.

50.4.1 Thermistor psychrometers

The thermistor psychrometer apparatus (Fig. 50.5) measures the negative pressure in the range of 3.0–5.5 pF with an accuracy of ±0.01 pF. The device includes both dry bulb and wet bulb carefully matched thermistors. The main drawback of the device is the relatively long time necessary to attain equilibrium (about 3 hours) after the deposition of a drop. A model was developed at CSIRO in Australia, but is no longer available as the matched thermistors are no longer manufactured. The thermistor psychrometer is currently replaced by the transistor psychrometer which presents improved characteristics.

50.4.2 Transistor psychrometers

The transistor psychrometer (Fig. 50.6) is similar to the thermistor psychrometer, but the two thermistors are replaced by two carefully

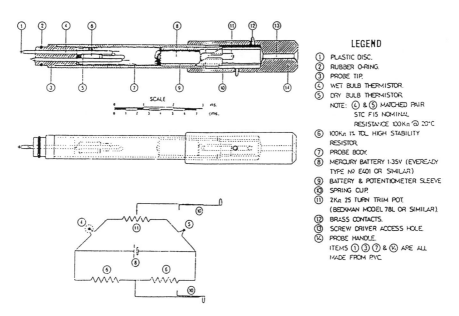

Fig. 50.5 The thermistor psychrometer.

Fig. 50.6 The transistor psychrometer.

matched (in terms of gain) transistors to measure the dry bulb and wet bulb temperatures. Like the other psychrometers, this apparatus is sensitive to temperature changes and must be used in a temperature-controlled environment.

The pF range of the apparatus developed at CSIRO, Australia, is the same as that of the thermistor psychrometer (3–5.5), and the accuracy is ±0.01 pF above a pF of 3.3 and ±0.05 pF below 3.3. The apparatus is more reliable than the thermistor one and easier to operate. The time necessary to reach equilibrium is also shorter: approximately 1 hour instead of 3 hours.

An important drawback of both the thermistor and the transistor devices is the fact that the water necessary to wet one of the bulbs must be supplied from the outside, generally using a micrometric syringe. This leads mainly to two problems:

- When the operation is repeated often, and especially in the case of small quantities of material, it may result in a local change in the moisture condition of the material; however, in silos, this should not cause too much trouble.
- The probe must be taken away after each measurement and the placement of a small quantity of water appears very difficult to automate.

50.4.3 Thermocouple psychrometer

The main difference, compared to the two other devices, is the ability to create the water drop directly in the material by condensation of water on the measurement probe. In that case, the temperature measurements are made by means of thermocouples (generally Chromel–Constantan). The condensation of water is obtained when a small current runs through the junction, producing the cooling of the junction by the Peltier effect. The second phase of the measurement consists in measuring the temperature change due to the evaporation of the drop.

Two very similar devices were commercially developed in the USA (by Wescor: Fig. 50.7) and in Australia. Both employ two modes: the wet bulb mode, identical to that of the thermistor and transistor devices, and the dewpoint mode, which helps to reduce the sensitivity experienced with the measurement of soil suction while undergoing temperature variations, and delivers a stronger signal than the wet bulb mode; the dewpoint technique relates to the measurement of the dewpoint depression temperature. Initially, the thermocouple is cooled below the dewpoint temperature by passing a current through the junction. Once the instrument is cooled, the thermocouple is controlled solely by the evaporation or condensation of the water on the junction. The temperature of the thermocouple then converges to the dewpoint whereby evaporation ceases and the temperature remains

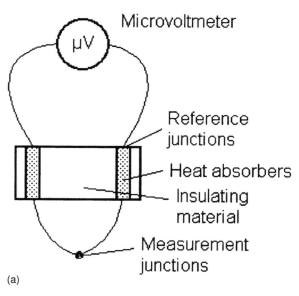

Fig. 50.7 (a) Schematic description of a thermocouple psychrometer; (b) the Wescor thermocouple psychrometer probe.

constant. The current necessary to obtain this result is related to the relative humidity.

With the thermocouple psychrometers, the pF range is reduced compared to the other psychrometers, due to the difficulty of condensing water on the junction in very dry environments: the pF range is from 3.5 to 4.7, with an accuracy between ±0.1 and ±0.01 pF, depending on the pF value. On the other hand, the time to reach equilibrium is smaller, approximately half an hour. The apparatus is more difficult to operate, as the signal is

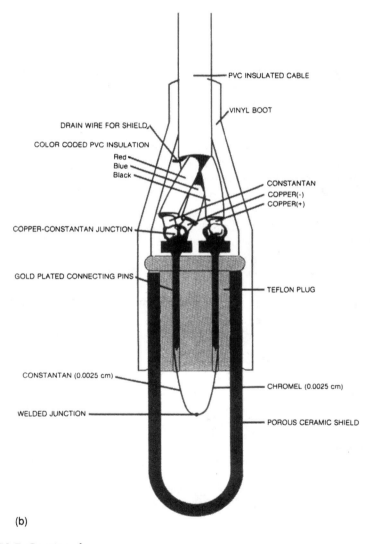

(b)

Fig. 50.7 *Continued*

weaker than with thermistors or transistors. The problems related to temperature and the complexity of the calibration stages are the same in the three cases.

50.5 APPLICATION TO SILOS

The measurement of moisture in granular materials in the range from 0 to 5% water content is therefore complex. Among the different devices presented, the easiest to operate and the most reliable are probably the transistor psychrometer for pressures greater than 500 kPa, and the Imperial College tensiometer for pressures smaller than 1500 kPa. In the second case, the apparatus does not require further substantial improvements to be used in silos. It only needs to gain some ruggedness for industrial use.

Conversely, in the first case, important work must be done to automate the process. The main improvement is to devise a way of placing the water bubble at the tip of the probe in very reproducible conditions, as the shape and surface of the bubble play a part in the result of the measurement. This operation must be carried out, without removing the probe from the material, with a small capillary tubing placed at the end of an automatic syringe. Careful testing of the influence of the water added on the local value of the water content and negative pressure must then be done. As for the tensiometer, adaptation of the apparatus for industrial use in silos appears feasible.

A few other devices, based on different principles, also appear promising, but their use in industrial applications requires substantial research and developments.

Whatever the method used to measure the negative pressure, important information will be derived from the determination of the relationship between the water content and the negative pressure of the material. This calibration must be carried out prior to the measurement of the *in situ* pressure, and in the same conditions of density and stresses and at least in the range of water contents considered.

REFERENCES

Biarez, J.; Fleureau, J.M.; Zerhouni, M.I. and Soepandji, B.S. (1988) Variations de volume des sols argileux lors de cycles de draînage-humidification, *Revue Française de Géotechnique*, 41, 63–71.

Biarez, J.; Fleureau, J.M.; Indarto; Taibi, S. and Zerhouni, M.I. (1989) Influence of the negative pore pressure on the flow of granular materials in silos, *Proceedings 1st Int. Conf. on Micromech. Granular Media*, Clermont-Ferrand, Sept., ed. by J. Biarez and R. Gourves, Balkema, Rotterdam, pp. 385–392.

Biarez, J.; Fleureau, J.M. and Taibi, S. (1993) Constitutive model for unsaturated granular media, *Proceedings 2nd Int. Conf. on Micromech. Granular Media*, Birmingham, July, ed. by C. Thornton, Balkema, Rotterdam, pp. 51–58.

References

Briscoe, R.D. (1984) Thermocouple psychrometers for water potential measurements, *Proc. NATO Advanced Study Institute on 'Advanced Agricultural Instrumentation'*, Il Ciocco (Pisa), May–June.

Dimos, A. (1991) Measurement of soil suction using transistor psychrometer, Vic Roads, Melbourne, Internal report No. IR/91-3, Sept.

Johanson, J.R. (1975) Why bulk powders flow or don't?, *Chemical Technology*, 5(9), 572–576.

Ranaivoson, D. (1988) Le phénomène d'écoulement, *Bulletin de liaison des Ponts et Chaussées*, **15**, 38–43.

Taibi, S. (1994) Comportement mécanique et hydraulique des sols non saturés, Doctorate thesis, Ecole Centrale de Paris.

Verbrugge, J.C. (1974) Contribution à la mesure de la succion et de la pression interstitielle dans les sols non saturés, Doctorate thesis, Université Libre de Bruxelles, 212 pp.

Woodburn, J.A. (1993) Soil suction measurement with the transistor psychrometer, *Proceedings of the International Symposium on Arid Soils*, City University, London, July, ed. by J. Atkinson, Balkema, Rotterdam, pp. 321–324.

51
Model laws and scale errors
J. Nielsen

51.1 INTRODUCTION

Silo tests are performed in silos within a wide range of sizes. This reflects partly that silos in practice do exist within a wide range of sizes and partly that researchers want to perform tests at reduced scales.

Tests at reduced scales are made to have better control of the working conditions, to be able to control secondary parameters as temperature, moisture, etc., or to save money on instrumentation and time in running a test.

Such tests may in principle be understood in three different ways:

- as a measure to explore silo phenomena to be able to form hypotheses for a theoretical description;
- as a measure to calibrate computer models;
- as a model which can be used to predict conditions in full-scale silos.

For the first two groups the scale errors (or size effects) are not important as long as the phenomena which are seen in full-scale silos are also observed at reduced scales and as long as phenomena which do not play any role at larger scales do not dominate the observations. As an example even small amounts of cohesion may prevent wet sand from flowing in very small models subject to the natural field of gravity.

For the calibration of computer models size effects may be built into the theoretical model and tested with results from silos at different scales. Provided this is the case, no specific requirements concerning a model law have to be met to perform these tests.

However, when the test is considered a model of a full-scale silo aiming at predicting quantitative results for full-scale conditions the test has to be carried out according to a set of specific model requirements which lead to certain model conditions and transformation laws or scale factors. The model conditions and the transformation laws are together called the model law or the scale factors.

The remaining part of this chapter is devoted to a discussion of model laws and the related question of scale errors.

51.2 GENERAL CONSIDERATIONS

Model laws may be developed based on different sets of assumptions. In general, the fewer the assumptions, the wider the range of silos covered and the more complicated the model law. In some cases with very few assumptions, which means they are almost universally valid, the model laws are not only complicated but also contain contradicting model conditions or transformation laws which indicate that scale errors may appear.

Model laws can be developed from many different starting points. However, the influential parameters always have to be determined. One way is simply to do so by intuition and use the standard technique of non-dimensional parameters as the tool to arrive at the model law. Another method is to take a theory as the starting point. This method has the advantage that general experience from applications of the theory can be taken into account in estimating the scale errors.

To illustrate the fundamental question about the choice of influential parameters two extreme cases are considered. If the Janssen description of silo pressure is assumed to contain all relevant parameters, it is simple to arrive at a set of model conditions stating that the geometry of the model has to be made geometrically similar at a scale which can be chosen without restrictions, the stored material can be substituted by any material with the same wall friction coefficient and the same relation of horizontal to vertical stress (k-factor). Strictly, the model does not even have to have the same cross-sectional shape as long as the relation between the periphery and the cross-sectional area satisfies the geometrical scaling. The transformation law is equally simple. Pressures are scaled linearly with the product of the chosen geometrical scale and the (arbitrary) scale of stored materials density.

At the other extreme, a case is taken where it is considered essential to model the cohesive forces as they vary with pressure and time, the dynamic stresses acting at discharge, the interaction between stresses in the stored material, the deflections of the wall, and a buckling phenomenon in the wall. Even in much less complicated cases (Nielsen, 1977) it can be seen that if such phenomena take place at the same time it is not possible to devise a consistent model law. Again this implies that only if the test is performed at full scale can the risk of serious scale errors be avoided.

The first case shows that if very restrictive assumptions are made (very few stored materials are realistically described by the wall friction coefficient and the horizontal–vertical stress coefficient) then the model law is simple but scale errors appear as soon as these assumptions are not valid. The other case indicates that less restrictive assumptions (more realistic) very soon lead to inconsistencies in the model law so that scale errors have to be expected. However, model laws based on realistic assumptions have the advantage of pointing out where the problems are so that special studies may be carried out.

51.3 MODEL LAWS

As indicated above, model laws may be established based on many different sets of assumptions. No specific universal model law has been (and probably cannot be) developed. The model law has to be developed for the specific case (set of phenomena) with an experienced evaluation of the parameters of importance. However, some general guidance is given below. More details may be found in the literature (see list of references).

51.3.1 Particle size/continuum

Since it is very difficult to ensure the same or similar behaviour of different stored materials the substitution of one material for another is in practice not possible except for some coarse-grained industrially produced particles. In cases where continuum mechanics may be considered applicable, the particle size may be disregarded. Since continuum mechanics has proved to be an efficient tool in soil mechanics as well as in solid mechanics this is in many cases an acceptable assumption. For silo applications the modelling of rupture planes and the related volumetric changes and the modelling of conditions around the outlet represent the main reasons for scale errors.

51.3.2 Stiffness/modulus of elasticity

The stiffness of the stored material plays an important role in cases where the wall deflection influence on loads is to be studied. In such cases the strains of the stored material and the deflections of the wall have to be scaled in a controlled way. The strains may originate from changes in pore pressure which may put requirements on the time-scale or they may originate from particle deformations which may put restrictions on the stiffness (or modulus of elasticity) of the stored material as well as on the wall material.

51.3.3 Load–structure interaction

Models laws for load–structure interaction problems have only been developed in a few cases. Normally the wall is considered stiff and a model law for the study of flow and loads is developed. However, the model at the Danish Technical University described by Nielsen and Kristiansen (1980) models the load–structure interaction of a full-scale concrete structure. More attention has been given to structural aspects in the model studies on buckling (Fleming, 1985; Fitz-Henry, 1986; Rotter et al., 1989). These experiments were designed according to model laws for the silo structure with special attention to buckling.

51.3.4 Tests in centrifuges or in the natural field of gravity

Centrifuge testing has been successfully applied to a number of soil mechanics problems (Craig, James and Schofield, 1988; Corté, 1988). In principle there is only one serious assumption to be made. That is the assumption of continuum mechanics. In practice there are two more problems to overcome. They are related to the centrifuge technique as the method to achieve a controlled field of gravity. One set of problems is caused by the Coriolis forces which occur in the inhomogeneous field of gravity and which disturb the filling process. Since the filling process for many stored materials controls the inhomogeneity and anisotropy of the stored materials serious scale errors may occur. The other problem is that the size of the centrifuge model is more limited than the model for tests in the natural field of gravity. Even a large centrifuge has a radius of about 5 m only, and if 10% of inhomogeneity is accepted the height of the model will be about 0.5 m. For a slender silo this may mean a diameter of about 0.1 m. A 10 m diameter silo may thus typically be modelled at a scale 1:10 in the natural field of gravity and at a scale of 1:100 in the centrifuge. In fact the centrifuge models are so small that it is often rather costly to meet the necessary tolerances in instrumentation and control of geometrical imperfections.

This illustrates how one is faced with a dilemma in the choice of model type for a certain case: in principle centrifuge testing is better, but is it so much better that errors due to particle sizes in the smaller models, the inhomogeneous field of gravity, and other errors do not exceed the errors in models at the natural field of gravity, especially if the centrifuge models have to be kept an order of magnitude smaller than models in the natural field of gravity? No general answer can be given to this question, as it depends on the scale errors in the specific cases.

51.4 SCALE ERRORS

Determination of the magnitude of scale errors has mainly been left to experimental investigations. References on general scale errors can be found in numerous textbooks and Conference Proceedings in soil mechanics.

Special reference to scale errors for silo models has been given in a number of cases (see list of references: Nielsen and Askegaard, 1977; Molerus and Schoneborn, 1977; Nielsen and Kristiansen, 1980; Craig and

Wright, 1981; Munch-Andersen, 1983, 1987, 1989a, b; Nielsen, 1984; Kristiansen, 1984; Munch-Andersen and Nielsen, 1984, 1986, 1990; Fleming, 1985; Fitz-Henry, 1986; Kristiansen, Munch-Andersen and Nielsen, 1988; Lepert and Corté, 1988, 1989; Corté and Lepert, 1990; Rotter et al., 1989; Lepert, Ranaivoson and Gourdon, 1989; Munch-Andersen, Askegaard and Brink, 1992; Gourdon et al., 1992; Munch-Andersen and Askegaard, 1993; Scott, 1989; Altaee and Fellenius, 1994; Garnier, 1995). Most studies have dealt with loads and flow which have been studied in centrifuges and in the natural field of gravity. A few studies have dealt with stresses in the silo structure (buckling) (Fleming, 1985; Fitz-Henry, 1986; Rotter et al., 1989).

It is a general conclusion that flow is easier to model than loads and that very small models (table models) in the natural field of gravity in general are affected by serious scale errors.

51.5 CONCLUSIONS

It can be concluded that:

- Different model laws should be developed for different problems to be studied.
- Standard techniques to develop such model laws do exist.
- Scale errors play an important role in silo applications.
- Our knowledge about scale errors is not sufficient to ensure a rational choice of model for specific cases.

REFERENCES

Altaee, A. and Fellenius, B. (1994) Physical modeling in sand, *Canadian Geotechnical Journal*, 31, 420–431.

Corté, J.F. (ed). (1988) *Centrifuge 88*. Balkema, Rotterdam.

Corté, J.F. and Lepert, P. (1990) Pertinence d'essais sur modèle réduit en centrifugeuse pour l'étude du comportement d'un silo métallique céréalier. *Revue Française de Géotechnique*, no. 52.

Craig, W.H.; James, R.G. and Schofield, A.N. (eds) (1988) *Centrifuges in Soil Mechanics*. Balkema, Rotterdam.

Craig, W.H. and Wright, A.S.C. (1981) Centrifuge modelling in flow prediction studies for granular materials. *Proceedings of the 1981 Powtech Conference*, EFCE pub. series No. 16, pp. D3/U/1–14.

Fitz-Henry, J.O.D. (1986) Buckling failures of eccentrically discharged silos. BE (Hons) Thesis, Univ. Sydney.

Fleming, S.P. (1985) The buckling and collapse of silos under eccentric discharge. BE (Hons) Thesis, Univ. Sydney.

Garnier, J. (1995) Modèles réduits en mécanique des sols. *Les modèles rèduits en génie civil*, AUGC, pp. 21–44.

Gourdon, J.-L.; Ranaivoson, D.; Torchet, B. and Lepert, P. (1992) Écoulement des

matériaux granulaires dans les trémies de dosage: modélisation, vérification, perspectives. *Bull. Liaison Lab. Ponts et Chaussées*, no. 180.
Ko and McLean (eds), (1991) *Centrifuge 91*. Balkema, Rotterdam.
Kristiansen, N.Ø. (1984) Tryk- og strømningsforhold i siloer med kohœsive medier. Pressure and flow conditions in silos with cohesive media. In Danish. Ph.D. Thesis, R 179. Department of Structural Engineering, Technical University of Denmark, Lyngby.
Kristiansen, N.Ø.; Munch-Andersen, J. and Nielsen, J. (1988) A centrifuge study of load and flow conditions in silos with cohesive media. In: *Centrifuge 88* (ed. J.-F. Corté), Balkema, Rotterdam, pp. 593–600.
Lepert P. and Corté, J.F. (1988) Etude de la vidange d'un silo céréalier métallique. *Centrifuge 88*. (ed. J.F. Corté) Balkema, Rotterdam, p. 607.
Lepert, P. and Corté, J.F. (1989) Étude d'un silo métallique en centrifugeuse. *Construction Métallique*, No. 2.
Lepert, P.; Ranaivoson, D. and Gourdon, J.L. (1989) Centrifuge modelling of the flow of a granular medium. *Powders and Grains*. Balkema, Rotterdam.
Luong, Lu and Tan (eds), (1994) *Centrifuge 94*. Balkema, Rotterdam.
Molerus, O. and Schoneborn, P.R. (1977) Bunker design on experiments in a bunker centrifuge. *Powder Technology*, 16, 265–272.
Munch-Andersen, J. (1983) Scale errors in model silo tests. *2nd Int. Conf. on Design of Silos for Strength and Flow*, Stratford-upon-Avon, UK, 7–9 Nov., pp. 230–241.
Munch-Andersen, J. (1987) The boundary layer in rough silos. *Mechanical Engineering Transactions*, The Institution of Engineers, Australia, ME12(3), 167–170.
Munch-Andersen, J. (1989a) Trykfordelinger og skalaeffekter i høje kornsiloer (Pressure distributions and scale effects in slender grain silos). Ph.D. thesis. Dept. of Structural Engineering, Technical University of Denmark, Lyngby.
Munch-Andersen, J. (1989b) Silomodelforsøg med byg, hvede og raps (Silo model tests with barley, wheat and rape-seed). Dept. of Structural Engineering, Technical University of Denmark, Lyngby.
Munch-Andersen, J. and Askegaard, V. (1993) Silo model tests with sand and grain. *Symp. Reliable Flow of Particulate Solids II*. Oslo, Norway. 23–25 Aug.
Munch-Andersen, J.; Askegaard, V. and Brink, A. (1992) *Silo Model Tests with Sand*. Danish Building Research Institute, SBI-Bulletin 91. Hørsholm, Denmark.
Munch-Andersen, J. and Nielsen, J. (1984) Use of physical silo models. *Seminar Design of Concrete Structures – the Use of Model Analysis*. BRE, Watford, UK, 29–30 November.
Munch-Andersen, J. and Nielsen, J. (1986) Size effects in slender grain silos. *The International Journal of Storing and Handling of Bulk Materials*, 6(5), 885–889.
Munch-Andersen, J. and Nielsen, J. (1990) Pressures in slender grain silos. Measurements in three silos of different sizes. Presented at *CHISA '90*, Prague. 26–31 Aug.
Nielsen, J. (1977) Model laws for granular media and powders with a special view to silo models. *Archives of Mechanics*, 29(4), 547–560. Warsaw.
Nielsen, J. (1984) Centrifuge testing as a tool in silo research. In *Application of*

Centrifuge Modelling to Geotechnical Design (ed. W.H. Craig). Balkema, Rotterdam, pp. 475–483.

Nielsen, J. and Askegaard, V. (1977) Scale errors in model tests on granular media with special reference to silo models. *Powder Technology*, **16**, 123–130.

Nielsen, J. and Kristiansen, N.Ø. (1980) Related measurements of pressure conditions in full-scale barley silo and in model silo. *Int. Conf. on Design of Silos for Strength and Flow*, Lancaster, UK, 2–4 Sept, pp. 1–23.

Rotter, J.M.; Jumikis, P.T.; Fleming, S.P. and Porter, S.J. (1989) Experiments on the buckling of thin-walled model silo structures. *Journal Constructional Steel Research*, **13**(4), 271–299.

Scott, R. (1989) Essais en centrifugeuse et technique de modelisation, *Revue Française de Géotechnique*, **48**, 15–34.

52

Gamma-ray tomographic techniques in granular flows in hoppers

U. Tüzün and M.S. Nikitidis

52.1 INTRODUCTION

Mass discharge of single or multi-component granular systems from large-scale silos is one of the major areas of interest in process industries. Filling methods of the silos and flow behaviour of granules during discharge play a very important role in the quality of the final product and therefore all research in this area has been focused on the prediction of the flow behaviour of granules within the silo, using various theoretical methods based either on continuum mechanics principles or on empirical correlations resulting from model experiments and computer simulations.

Alongside the experimental and numerical simulation efforts the need for reliable three-dimensional flow measurement and flow quality control has grown, and a considerable amount of the research pursued during the last 10 years in the bulk solids technology area has been focused on the investigation and application of these methods. The main consideration in choosing the appropriate method for characterizing the bulk voidage profiles in a granular system is the need for achieving the necessary spatial resolution, and in the case of dynamic events the appropriate temporal resolution is also important.

Various non-invasive methods based on a variety of physical principles (nuclear emission, magnetic resonance, electrical impedance), already in use in other fields like medicine, chemistry and biology, found significant application in particulate systems from the early 1980s.

Positron emission particle tracking (PEPT) has been successfully applied in the investigation of flow characteristics in multiphase granular systems by monitoring the trajectories of single radio-labelled particles as they move in the system, using the intersection points of the lines formed from the coincident positional events of the two gamma photons emitted in opposite directions during annihilation of the positrons (Parker *et al.*, 1993; Beynon *et al.*, 1993).

Non-ionizing methods like electrical impedance and nuclear magnetic resonance (NMR) are also in current use in the study of granular systems. Electrical imaging has found wide application in multiphase systems and especially in fluidized beds (Halow *et al.*, 1993) and pneumatic conveying

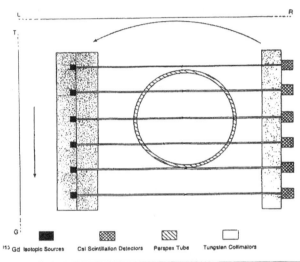

Fig. 52.1 The parallel beam scanner.

Introduction

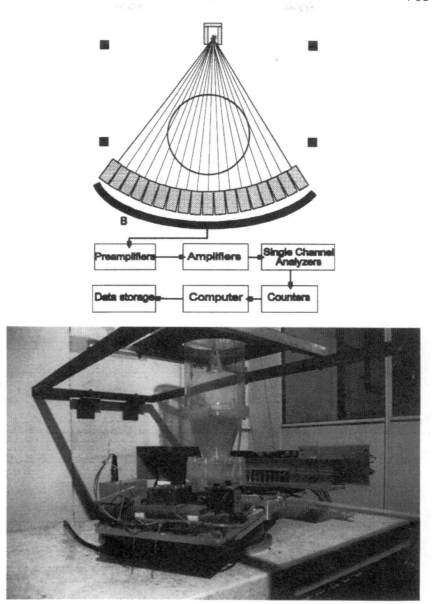

Fig. 52.2 The fan beam scanner.

(McKee *et al.*, 1995). Nuclear magnetic resonance imaging has also been used in flow studies of multiphase systems like rotating silos of particles (Nakagawa *et al.*, 1993) or diffusion through porous media studies (Gladden, 1993). Based on the excitation and relaxation of the magnetization of a medium it provides images with high spatial resolution.

52.2 GAMMA-RAY TOMOGRAPHIC METHODS

Gamma ray tomography was one of the first non-invasive techniques used to investigate the flow behaviour of single or multicomponent granular systems (MacCuaig et al., 1985; Seville, Morgan and Clift, 1986; Bosley, Schofield and Shook, 1969; Fickie, Mehrabi and Jackson, 1989; Hosseini-Ashrafi and Tüzün, 1993a, b). Based on the absorption of the incident photons of a finely collimated beam on the object of interest, it provides information about the interstitial voidage in a granular system more accurately than any other technique while at the same time it can be optimized to give us additional information about flow properties as well.

Two gamma-ray scanners (Figs 52.1 and 52.2) of different geometrical arrangement for data acquisition (a parallel arrangement of 6 finely collimated beams and a fan beam arrangement of 18 finely collimated beams) are used to set up the experiments.

52.2.1 Experimental methods

52.2.1.1 Full tomographic imaging

The scanner gantry translates laterally to sample the object to the appropriate extent and repeats this procedure for several angular projections around the object. The data acquired are fed into a reconstruction algorithm which filters the data to remove unwanted frequencies and projects them back to the plane of scan for all the acquired projections, to produce an array of linear attenuation coefficients at any point of the slice (Brooks and Di Chiro, 1976). A grey level image is produced by assigning a grey scale to the array of reconstructed attenuation coefficients. The solids fraction content η at a certain location is given by

$$\eta(x) = \frac{x - x_{air}}{x_{sol} - x_{air}} \qquad (52.2.1)$$

x_{air}, x_{sol} are the linear attenuation coefficients of pixels fully filled with air and solid respectively. Figure 52.3 shows an evaluation for the solids fraction content measurement precision by means of a binary test object (air and solid).

52.2.1.2 Single profile absorptiometry

This technique allows faster scan times to be obtained (<5s) while the scanner gantry translates laterally at a fixed angular projection. Therefore, linear attenuation coefficients are obtained integrated along the scanned lines and the solids fraction content at any position is given by

$$\eta(x) = K \frac{F_m(x) - F_b(x)}{F_m(x) - F_w(x)} \qquad (52.2.2)$$

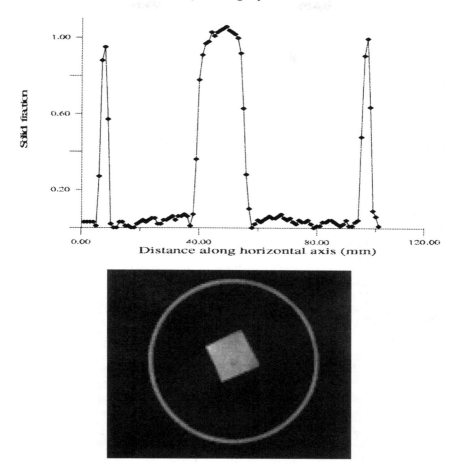

Fig. 52.3 Accuracy of 1–2% in solids fraction calculation from a tomograph using a test object.

where $F_m(x)$, $F_b(x)$, $F_w(x)$ is the amount of the beam attenuation from the bed matrix (gas or liquid), the bed (matrix and particles) and the walls of the vessel respectively. The system is calibrated against known solids fraction contents and a constant K is extracted which is characteristic of the particles and does not depend on hopper geometry.

The radial variation of the solid fraction content $F(r)$ can be obtained by applying a transformation formula (from Cartesian to polar coordinates) on the measured linear data (Fig. 52.4)

$$F(r) = -\left(\frac{1}{\pi}\right) \int_r^R \frac{F'(x)\,dx}{\left(x^2 - r^2\right)^{1/2}} \qquad (52.2.3)$$

where $F'(x)$ is the derivative of the linear solid fraction function and R is the radius of the object.

52.2.1.3 Dual photon measurements

The individual components of a binary mixture can be determined by using the technique of dual photon tomography which is based on the principle that the attenuation coefficient of a substance at low energies depends primarily on the elemental constitution, and therefore materials with different elemental constitutions but almost equal densities can be distinguished by scanning them with gamma-ray energies lower than 100 keV (Kouris, Spyrou and Jackson, 1982).

Two energy levels are enough to examine an air-based binary mixture (Fig. 52.5) since the changes in the mixture occur within a fixed boundary volume, which enables us to close the system of the two equations resulting from attenuation data at the two energies, with a third equation expressing

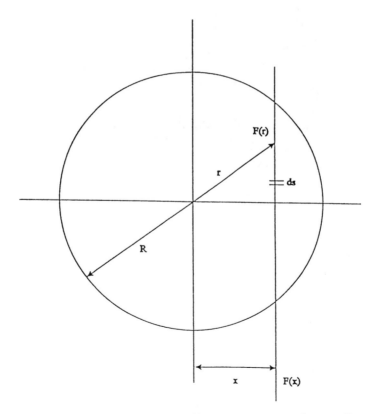

Fig. 52.4 Transformation of linear data from Cartesian to polar coordinates.

Monodisperse systems

the normalization of changes in the system, as can be seen in equation (52.2.4):

$$\mu^{low} = \varepsilon_A \mu_A^{low} + \varepsilon_B \mu_B^{low} + \varepsilon_C \mu_C^{low}$$
$$\mu^{high} = \varepsilon_A \mu_A^{high} + \varepsilon_B \mu_B^{high} + \varepsilon_C \mu_C^{high} \qquad (52.2.4)$$
$$\varepsilon_A + \varepsilon_B + \varepsilon_C = 1$$

where ε_A, ε_B, ε_C are the volume fractions occupied by each component in the examined volume and μ_i^j (j = low, high; i = A, B, C) are the linear attenuation coefficients for each component of the mixture at each one of the two energy levels. More information about the dual photon technique can be found in Nikitidis *et al.* (1994).

52.3 MONODISPERSE SYSTEMS

A series of experiments were performed using experimental methods described in sections 52.2.1.1 and 52.2.1.2 on a mono-sized bed of particles 5–7 mm in diameter (Canadian maple peas) in a 30° half-angle hopper with orifice diameter of 34 mm attached to a 150 mm diameter cylindrical section during static and flow conditions.

The experimental results are compared with simulation results obtained using the Hertz model of interaction. Both qualitative and quantitative comparison is possible since the gamma-ray techniques mentioned above can provide images for direct visual comparison as well as solid fraction profiles.

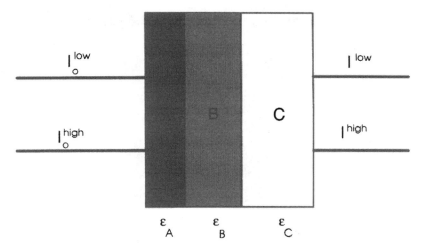

Fig. 52.5 All three phases of an air/liquid binary granular system can be determined using dual photon measurements.

Figure 52.6 shows a reconstructed image of the bed at 20 mm above the orifice together with a simulation scan. There is clearly a strong similarity in the nature of these packings in particle–wall alignment, maximum gap size and number of large particles. Figure 52.7 shows a comparison between linear and radial profiles at 60 mm above the orifice for both static and flowing cases. There is very good agreement in terms of fluctuation and absolute values of the solid fraction. In some instances the simulation peaks slightly higher which is due to the infinitesimal width of the simulation beam in the calculation of solid fraction content in opposition to the experimental beam which has considerable size (2×4 mm).

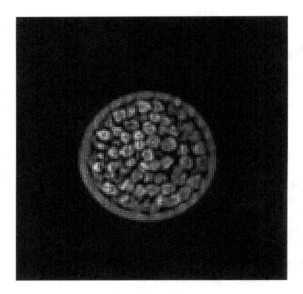

tomography

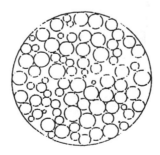

simulation

Fig. 52.6 Comparison between a simulated and a tomographic slice at 20 mm above the orifice.

Monodisperse systems

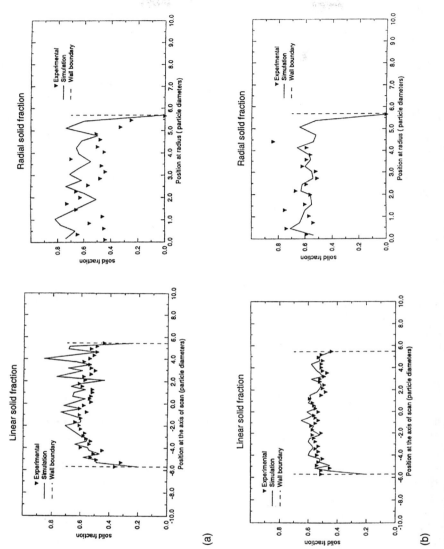

Fig. 52.7 Comparison between experimental and theoretical linear and radial profiles for a mono-sized mixture at 60 mm above the orifice: (a) static; (b) flow.

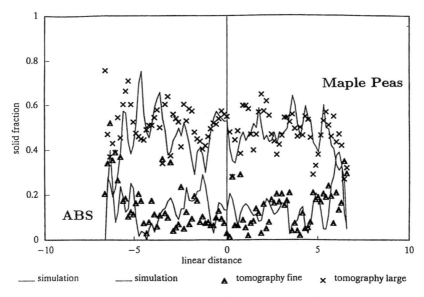

Fig. 52.8 Comparison between experimental and theoretical linear and radial profiles for a binary mixture of size ratio 2:1 and 80% coarse and 20% fines by weight at 60 mm above the orifice.

52.4 POLYDISPERSE SYSTEMS

The investigation of the properties of a binary mixture consisting of two components of different elemental constitution is possible using experimental method of section 52.2.1.3. A binary mixture consisting of Canadian maple peas and ABS particles of size ratio 2:1 and weight fraction 80% of coarse and 20% of fine particles in a 20° half-angle hopper of 50 mm orifice diameter attached to a cylindrical section of 150 mm in diameter has been scanned.

Figure 52.8 shows a comparison between simulated profiles for each of the two components together with experimental ones extracted using the novel dual photon technique during flow conditions at 60 mm above the orifice. Generally, there is good agreement in terms of absolute values and fluctuation. The same factor of beam width is also present in these measurements with the only difference that the experimental beam size has been reduced (2 × 2.5 mm) but still remains of considerable size.

52.5 CONCLUSIONS

Gamma-ray transmission methods like tomography and absorptiometry (single and dual energy) can prove very powerful tools for the experimental investigation of granular media properties. Voidage determination is a routine procedure for those techniques and flow information can also be obtained by the appropriate optimization of the system (e.g. volume reconstruction of various parts of a vessel to define the residence times of tracers participating in the flow).

Both quantitative and qualitative information provided by these methods can be used for inter-comparison with voidage and flow patterns simulated using various theoretical models of molecular dynamics.

REFERENCES

Beynon, T.D.; Hawkesworth, M.R.; McNeil, P.A.; Parker, D.J.; Bridgwater, J.; Broadbent, C.J. and Fowles, P. (1993) Positron-based studies of powder mixing. *Powders & Grains 93*, Thornton, C. (Ed.), Balkema, Rotterdam, p. 377

Bosley, J.; Schofield, C. and Shook, C.A. (1969) An experimental study of granule discharge from model hoppers. *Trans. Instn. Chem. Engs*, 47, 147

Brooks, R.A. and Di Chiro, G. (1976) Principles of computer assisted tomography (CAT) in radiographic and radioisotopic imaging. *Phys. Med. Biol.*, 21, 689

Fickie, K.E.; Mehrabi, R. and Jackson, R. (1989) Density variations in a granular material flowing from a wedge-shaped hopper, *AIChE*, 35(5), 853

Gladden, L.F. (1993) Nuclear magnetic resonance studies of porous media. *Chem. Engng. Res. Des*, 71, 657

Halow, J.S.; Fasching, G.E.; Nicoletti, P. and Spenik, J.L. (1993) Observations of a fluidized bed using capacitance imaging. *Chem. Eng. Sci.*, 48, 643

Hosseini-Ashrafi, M.E. and Tüzün, U. (1993a) A tomographic study of voidage profiles in axially symmetric granular flows. *Chem. Eng. Sci.*, 48, 53

Hosseini-Ashrafi, M.E. and Tüzün, U. (1993b) Quantification of flowing bed porosity near the outlet of an axially symmetric hopper using single photon absorptiometry. *Meas. Sci. Tech.*, 4, 1394

Kouris, K.; Spyrou, N.M. and Jackson, D.F. (1982) *Imaging with Ionizing Radiations*. Surrey University Press, UK

MacCuaig, N.; Seville, J.P.K.; Gilboy, W.B. and Clift, R. (1985) Application of gamma-ray tomography to gas fluidized beds. *Appl. Opt.*, 24, 4083

McKee, S.L.; Dyakowski, T.; Williams, R.A.; Bell, T.A. and Allen, T. (1995) Solids flow imaging and attrition studies in a pneumatic conveyor. *Powd. Tech.*, 82, 105

Nakagawa, M.; Altobelli, S.A.; Caprihan, A. and Fukushima, E. (1993) Non-invasive measurements of granular flows by magnetic resonance imaging. *Powders and Grains 93*, Thornton, C. (Ed.), Balkema, Rotterdam, p. 383

Nikitidis, M.S.; Hosseini-Ashrafi, M.E.; Tüzün, U. and Spyrou, N.M. (1994) Tomographic measurements of granular flows in gases and in liquids, *KONA Powder and Particle*, 12, 53

Parker, D.J.; Broadbent, C.J.; Fowles, P.; Hawkesworth, M.R. and McNeil, P. (1993) Positron emission particle tracking – a technique for studying flow within engineering equipment. *Nucl. Instr. Meth. Phys. Res.*, A326, 592

Seville, J.P.K.; Morgan, J.E.P. and Clift, R. (1986) Tomographic determination of the voidage structure of gas fluidized in the jet region. *Fluidization V*, Ostergaard, K. and Sorensen, A. (Eds), Engineering Foundation, New York, p. 87

53

Silo test facilities in Europe
C.J. Brown

53.1 INTRODUCTION

This chapter provides information to serve as a basis for future collaborative work, and particularly for experimental work in Europe. The use of existing testing facilities may reduce the costs of experimental work significantly. Not only are the physical facilities expensive, but often access to the expertise associated with such facilities is most important. The information on available experimental facilities is abstracted from the research reviews which were submitted following the CA-Silo Workshop held in Delft in 1993. Where updates are available they have been added. The initial compilation was completed in October 1994. The data provide a 'snapshot' of ongoing experimental work in Europe, and are to some extent indicative of where research funding and interest have been identified.

53.2 EXPLANATION OF DATA

The information has been produced in tabular form (Table 53.1). The data initially provided by each establishment have not, in themselves, been sufficient to provide all the information which would be ideally required for a more thorough survey.

The information which has been tabulated has not been modified in any way. Where there is the possibility that experiments refer to silos of sufficiently significant dimensions then these data have been included. Experiments on very small-scale models are not intended for this survey. Addresses are listed so that contact may be established by interested readers, and it is assumed that those interested will contact the appropriate institutions identified to obtain further information.

Table 53.1 Experimental facilities: contacts and comments

Organization	Contact	Nationality	Details of experimental facility
LMSCG	Dr F. Chevoir Laboratoire Central des Ponts et Chaussées BP19 F-44340 Bouguenais France Other contacts: C. Weill	F	2-D hopper for granular flow through an orifice Comments: Has good links to existing French groups. European links with H. Hermann, J. Hinch
INSA, Rennes	Dr Deserable 20 Avenue des Buttes de Coesmes F-35043 Rennes France	F	2-D hoppers with transparent walls, cylindrical bin with truncated cone base. '1 axisymmetric device, 2 two-dimensional devices' Comments: Objective to continue small scale experimentation with image analysis. Looking for access to experimental data base
Ecole Centrale de Paris	Professor J.M. Fleureau Laboratoire de Mécanique Grande Voie des Vignes F-92295 Chatenay Malabry France Other contacts: Dr P. Evesque	F	2-D experiments of flow using Schneebeli duralumin cylinders. Video observations Comments: Interested in large deformations. General interest in collaboration for complex flow patterns and pressure fluctuations

Table 53.1 *Continued*

Organization	Contact	Nationality	Details of experimental facility
LCPC	Dr J. Garnier Laboratoire Central des Ponts et Chaussées Route de Pornic BP19 F-44340 Bouguenais France	F	Large centrifuge, radius 5.5 m, payload mass 2000 kg. Has associated digital image processing for flow velocity measurement Comments: Has existing links in France and contacts with other centrifuge groups (e.g. Copenhagen, Cambridge, Bochum, Delft)
Ecole Polytechnique	Dr M.P. Luong F-91128 Palaiseau France	F	Centrifuge testing under dynamic and seismic loadings Comments: Also interested in materials testing and has a proposed collaboration with Prof. J. Schwedes at Braunschweig and Dr Jin Ooi at Edinburgh
University of Nancy	Professor Roth Le Montet F-54601 Villers les Nancy France Other contacts: Professor Khelil Dr Baraka	F	CTICM. Large-scale testing facility at Chartres. Full-scale tests. 4 silos in total. Steel structures research programme Comments: Some results have been published (*Construction Métallique*) but if I understood correctly, the work was industry funded and the publication and sharing of results was restricted. This may now be less of a restriction. Has some proposed/agreed collaborations

Explanation of data

University of Poitiers	Professor Texereau 40 Avenue du Recteur Pineau F-8600 Poitiers France	F	Some experimental work is described. Small-scale model of cylindrical and conical silos, strain gauges
Ceten – Apave Int	Dr J. Trinh 191 Rue de Vaugirard F-75015 Paris France	F	No facility, but may be able to provide experience of failures due to on-site conditions. Site monitoring experience
University of Kaiserslautern	Dr G. Dau Postfach 3049 Erwin-Schroedinger Strasse D-67653 Kaiserslautern Germany or Daimler Benz Strasse D-67663 Kaiserslautern Germany	D	Silo experiments; 5 m high steel silo – 1 m^3 volume. Diameters of 0.6 and 0.8 m. Air injection and inserts 3 m high steel 'half-silo' with Perspex front plate. Several hoppers and inserts Rectangular lab. scale with wedge hopper. Demonstration units for flow visualization experiment and mixing Comments: Residence time measurement. Flow velocity measurement. On line particle concentration measurement. For references see list

Table 53.1 Continued

Organization	Contact	Nationality	Details of experimental facility
University of Karlsruhe	Dr S. Hochst PO Box 6980 D-776128 Karlsruhe 1 Germany Other contacts: W. Leuckel	D	$50\,\text{m}^3$ reinforced concrete silo for dust explosions. Other explosion vessels. Measurement of pressure, flame detection, etc. Measurement of strains in silo shell Comments: Existing collaboration with Prof. Eibl, Dr Radant and Dr Pfoertner (all Germany)
University of Karlsruhe	Dr Karcher Address as above	D	Multi-cell silos; model scale for three cells and four cells. Full scale on existing structures. 'Measurements under internal pressure'; FE calculations, parameter studies Comments: Dr Karcher recommended collaboration with Prof. Rotter (pressure distribution in multi-chamber silos) and Prof. Greiner (buckling and non-linear problems). Also involved with FE calculations and parameter studies
University of Karlsruhe	Dr P. Knoedel Address as above Other contacts: T. Licht	D	Cylindrical model ($D = 1250\,\text{mm}$, $H = 1000\,\text{mm}$) for investigation of buckling strength of silos Comments Interest in imperfections. Has already formed links with Rotter, Chryssanthopoulos. (The response for Thomas Licht from the same institution, I think, refers to the same group.) I know there is a large steel silo at Karlsruhe. This is referred to by Licht as height 6.00 with strain gauges

Explanation of data

Martin Luther University of Halle	Dr J. Runge Institut für MVT/UST D-06217 Merseburg Germany	D	Cylindrical model ($D = 1000$ mm, $H = 2500$ mm) for investigation of discharge function and rate. Stainless steel test silo can be fitted with different outlets and discharge aids (e.g. bin activator, porous bottom, mixing hopper). Details of facilities and instrumentation available
TU Braunschweig	Professor J. Schwedes Volkmaroder Strasse 4–5 D-38104 Braunschweig Germany	D	Eight silos from 1.00 to 4.00 m in height from transparent material plus two steel silos, 0.6 m in diameter and 0.6×0.8 m, and 7 and 6 m tall with inserts. Measurement of wall stresses and loads on inclined walls, plus gas pressure for some models. Has equipment for the determination of material properties Comments: Measurement devices developed and described in open literature. See references
KAI Berlin	Dr D. Hohne Chemnitzer Strasse 40 D-9200 Freiberg Germany Other contacts: Dr Schunemann	D	Model bin 0.6×4 m with variable inclination angle of hopper and opening width. Measurement of air and gas pressure on aerated walls
University of Karlsruhe	T. Ummenhofer Kaiserstrasse 12 D-76128 Karlsruhe Germany	D	Experiments at nearly full scale on buckling of cylindrical shells filled with bulk solid. Strain measurement and determination of shell geometric imperfections Comments: See Knoedel, Licht, etc.

Table 53.1 Continued

Organization	Contact	Nationality	Details of experimental facility
Brunel University	C.J. Brown Department of Mechanical Engineering Uxbridge UB8 3PH Middlesex Great Britain	UK	Square planform steel silo, 3.5 m high. Pressure cells from Prof. Askegaard, plus strain gauges. Sited at BRE, Watford in thermally controlled environment. Also some small-scale Perspex models Comments: Collaborative project with University of Edinburgh and BRE. See references
Imperial College	Dr M. Chryssanthopoulos Exhibition Road London SW7 Great Britain	UK	Experimental rig for shell buckling/silo tests. Imperfection measurement Comments: Has developed links with C. Poggi, Milan
University of Edinburgh	Professor J.M. Rotter Department of Civil and Environmental Engineering Edinburgh EH9 3JN Great Britain Other contacts: Dr J.Y. Ooi Dr A.S. Usmani Dr C.B. York Dr J.F. Chen Dr J.M.F.G. Holst Dr Z. Zhong	UK	Full-scale test silo (4.2 m dia. ×12 m high, 100 m^3) designed for flow patterns and wall pressures Hopper test facility: 2 m dia. × 8 m high Pilot scale silo (3 t: 1.05 m dia. × 4.1 m high) for wall pressures Scale models (~1 m high) for structural failure observations Comments: Link with C.J. Brown for square planform tests. Link with INSA Lyon on structural tests

Explanation of data

University of Edinburgh	Dr J.Y. Ooi Department of Civil and Environmental Engineering The King's Buildings Edinburgh EH9 3JN Great Britain Other contacts: Prof. J.M. Rotter Mr P.A. Berry Dr H. El-Lahlouh Mr K.F. Zhang	UK	Half-silo model (0.65 m dia. × 1.5 m high) for flow pattern observations Small models (0.30–0.45 m dia.) for flow pattern measurements Low stress triaxial testing Jenike, confined compression, unconfined compression and novel tests on dilation
University of Twente	Dr G. Haaker Department of Mechanical Engineering PO Box 217 NL-7500 AE Enschede The Netherlands	NL	Experimental work on the effect of stiffness of test equipment on pressure measurements. Various adjustable laboratory-scale silos. In collaboration with *Bulk Solids Engineering*
AKZO	Dr J.A.H. de Jong Dept CRP Velperweg 76 PO Box 9300 NL-6800 Arnhem The Netherlands	NL	Test silo, 1.2 m square, 2.5 m height. Adjustable hopper angles and outlet size. Small silos up to 1000 t volume
Shell Research	Dr P. Reuderink PO Box 3800 Badhuisweg 3 NL-1031 Amsterdam The Netherlands	NL	Various bunker test facilities (dia. 0.1–1.0 m, height up to 3.0 m Perspex, steel, aluminium). Ultrasonic level measurement, load cells

Table 53.1 *Continued*

Organization	Contact	Nationality	Details of experimental facility
Technical University of Denmark	Professor V. Askegaard Bygning 118 DK-2800 Lyngby Denmark Other contacts: Dr J. Nielsen Dr J. Munch-Andersen	DK	Centrifuge facility, silos 80 mm diameter, 300 mm height with normal and pore pressure. Normal gravity model, 0.7 m diameter, 5.0 m height. Instrumentation normal and shear cells, force transducers Comments: Calibration of pressure cells has been carried out for many years – 'full size' calibration rig in use. Work carried out in collaboration with SBI. See references
POSTEC	Dr G. Enstad Kjolnes Ring N-3914 Porsgrunn Norway	N	Plane flow silo with variable geometry equipped with stress transducers and data acquisition system Comments: Many powder test facilities are also available
ATB Potsdam	Dr C. Furll Institut für Agrartechnik Bornim Max Eyth Allee Bornim D-14469 Potsdam Germany	D	Four large bins (24–120 m^3) used for determination of segregation; varying discharge angles Comments: No indication of pressure measurement, etc.

There is little consistency between the information provided. For example, in some cases precise data are given for the dimensions, and in other cases only the total volume of the silo is described. No attempt has been made to standardize the output. Similarly, there is little or no description of instrumentation, although it is again recognized that this is mainly because of the way information has been acquired. Much of the additional information that might be required is available in the open literature; a readily available key reference(s) describing the experimental facility has been provided by those who have updated their information.

Information about materials testing facilities has not been collated; further information on the work relating to silo flow may be obtained from Part One.

REFERENCES

Askegaard, V. (1984) Design basis for cells measuring shear stresses in an interface, *Geotechni. Testing Journ*, 7(2), June, 94–98.

Askegaard, V. (1987) Consequence of loading history on the measuring error of embedded stress cells, *Transact. of Mechanical Engineering (Australia)*, ME12(3) Sept., 191–195.

Askegaard, V. and Brown, C.J. (1995) Influence of personal factor on cell response when mounting embedded pressure cells, *Bulk Solids Handling*, 15(2, 5), 221–224.

Askegaard, V. *et al.* (1991) *5m Tall Silomodel* (in Danish), report S8728, August 1991, Dept. of Structural Eng, TU of Denmark.

Dau, G. (1991) Experimental determination of the local flow velocities in gas-flow through bulk materials, *Aufbereitungs-Technik*, 32(3), 105–112 (in German and English).

Dau, G.; Ebert, F. and Hahner, F. (1994) On-line analysis of discharge concentration in solids mixers, *Aufbereitungs-Technik*, 35(6), 281–289 (in German and English).

Ebert, F. and Dau, G. (1993) Residence time measurements in bulk solids handling devices, *Proceedings of the RelPowFlow II*, Oslo, pp. 897–909.

Jarrett, N.D.; Brown, C.J. and Moore, D.B. (1992) Obtaining accurate pressure measurements in a stored granular medium, *Canadian Geotechnical Journal*, 29.

Nielsen, J. and Askegaard, V. (1977) Scale errors in model tests on granular media with special reference to silo models, *Powder Technology*, 16, 123–130.

Rotter, J.M.; Ooi, J.Y.; Chen, J.F.; Tiley, P.J.; Mackintosh, I. and Bennett, F.R. (1995) *Flow Pattern Measurement in Full Scale Silos*, British Materials Handling Board, 230 pp.

Runge, J. (1993) *Powder Handling and Processing*, 5(2), 156–157.

Schulze, D.; Lyle, C. and Schwedes, J. (1989) A new load cell for measuring normal and shear stresses, *Chem. Eng. Technol*, 12, 318–323.

Zhong, Z.; Ooi, J.Y. and Rotter, J.M. (1996) The sensitivity of silo flow and wall pressures to filling method, *Proc., 12th International Congress of Chemical and Process Engineering, CHISA '96*, Prague, Aug., 10 pp.

54

Concluding comments and research requirements

J. Garnier

New non-trivial experimental techniques will be needed in future research on silos. More parameters must be measured to better understand the behaviour of silos and stored materials during filling and discharge. These experimental data are also needed for validating theoretical and numerical models.

Pressures applied on the walls are obviously the first parameters to be determined since they lead directly to the design of silos. Although significant progress has been made in the theoretical design of pressure cells, it is still difficult to find cells suitable for silo tests. The existing cells are self-made devices developed by one laboratory for very specific silo tests and not usually available to others. Calibration of such pressure cells presents a further difficulty since it must be done in contact with the stored materials themselves, in special chambers or possibly in geotechnical centrifuges if only normal stress is considered.

Application of the theoretical expressions to design new pressure cells or evaluate existing ones needs data such as stiffness of the stored material or compressibility of the cell that is difficult to collect. The drastic influence of personal factors when mounting embedded cells has again been demonstrated.

One other method to determine pressures on the walls is to try to derive them from strain measurements. This may be done through strain gauges installed on the surface of the walls of steel silos. Measurement of strain on the inside surfaces is very difficult and 'sandwich' strain gauges must be used. On the other hand, strains measured on the outside may be considerably affected by local bending moments due to wall imperfections. When inferring the wall pressure distribution from measured strains, the number of strain observations and the measuring station locations can have very significant effects. The application of this method is more difficult in full-scale silos than in laboratory models. However, the method is more direct for problems related to structural design.

Study of flow pattern is another area of research and several flow visualization techniques have been discussed. None have proved to be able to fully define flow pattern except in two-dimensional (plane strain or axisymmetric) conditions where direct observations can be made through transparent walls. This method has been successfully used in laboratory and centrifuge models, with CCD camera and numerical image processing techniques providing horizontal and vertical displacements of each marker. In full-scale silos, residence time technique is the most common method. Various types of markers have been tested (radio tags, steel particles, glass or wooden beads, radioactive bulk material). The main difficulty remains inferring flow patterns from the data.

In future research, more attention must be paid to the real state of materials placed in silos. Distribution of density must be studied since unit weight of the stored materials can vary widely and have strong effects on their behaviour. Local measurements of density are possible at rest, with techniques and probes similar to those developed for site geotechnical investigations. However, they are much more difficult during filling or discharge except perhaps in special model tests.

Similar problems arise with air pressures inside the bulk material or at the wall of the silo. Measurements at rest are possible with thermoanemometric pressure gauges and pore pressure transducers. They are very difficult when the bulk material, the air or both are in motion.

Moisture may have very strong effects on pressures acting on the walls and on flow patterns. The reason is the development of bonds and high forces between particles due to negative pressures. A few per cent change in water content may multiply negative pore pressures by more than 100 times as shown by results obtained in unsaturated soils. A similar relationship must be investigated in materials stored in silos, especially if particles are small (powders). Moisture measurement requires extremely sensitive devices such as psychrometers or tensiometers. They are possible in laboratory tests but need adaptations for industrial silos.

Most of the experimental research will, however, continue to be done on reduced-scale or pilot models and herein arises the problem of similitude conditions. In physical systems, a change in the dimensions may lead to a difference in behaviour, known as scale or size effects. Therefore models must satisfy conditions or laws to avoid or reduce these scale errors. The difficulty is that these model laws depend on the problem to be studied. For example, they may be different if the model is designed to investigate flow patterns or wall pressures or response to earthquakes.

When models are used to predict the quantitative response of full-scale silos, the corresponding scaling laws must be known and satisfied entirely.

As is now commonly done in soil mechanics, scale errors may be studied experimentally by comparing results from silos at different scales (modelling of models). However, one condition is usually essential: the state of stresses and body forces into the bulk materials must be similar in the model and in the full-scale silo since the behaviour of granular materials is mainly dependent on the stress level. This can be easily achieved in centrifuge models, and the large geotechnical centrifuges installed in Europe offer new possibilities for silo tests.

This similitude condition on self-weight is only met in small models in the natural field of gravity if specific conditions for the stored materials behaviour can be met. This is often not the case, which explains why such models are affected by serious scale errors. For example, in such models, contrary to centrifuge models or full-scale silos, a small amount of cohesion will drastically reduce the wall pressures and may prevent the bulk material from flowing.

This Part has provided an overview of some of the problems outlined, and given an outline of the state of the art and of recent developments. It has identified deficiencies in knowledge and provides a basis for future research requirements.

Part Seven

Research for Industry

55

Industrial requirements
C.J. Brown and J. Nielsen

55.1 INTRODUCTION AND BACKGROUND

The CA-Silo programme was established with several objectives, one of which was to enhance links between existing European research activity and the industry using or producing silos. This is already an important element of most ongoing research activity in engineering and applied science at a national level, and many research funding organizations link projects to industrial requirements. An alternative strategy is to establish research programmes in which industry is the lead player – as with programmes such as Brite-EuRam. CA-Silo was funded by Brite-EuRam, and determining the state of the art, and future research requirements has been an important element of the project.

The programme was initially advertised quite widely, and has subsequently been well supported by coverage from national data bases, and from journals. Nevertheless, the contributors from industry have been self-selecting. Those elements of industry who have been willing to invest some time and effort for their own current interests, and for possible future advantage are included; those who do not perceive any benefit did not become involved.

The nature of the industry also affects the potential interactions. The silo industry has some special features, particularly with reference to research activity. Silos are used in many industrial sectors. A questionnaire (Appendix 55.A) identified the chemical, agricultural, food and mining industries specifically, as well as some general bulk handling requirements. The recycling industry is now a significant element of bulk solids handling. Producers of silos are not a homogeneous group. They vary from industrial producers of mass produced rather small silos with special applications, to owners who require a unique large facility – produced like other civil engineering structures.

The silo 'industry' is thus made up of individual businesses of different sizes. There are large pan-European and international businesses but there are also many small and medium-sized enterprises which may have insufficient in-house research expertise either to design or to specify the design requirements. In large organizations, in-house expertise can be justified on the grounds of market edge and the facility to fulfil the requirements of key potential customers quickly. In smaller units, a permanent research capability would be a luxury, and any specialist expertise will be acquired on an *ad hoc* basis to satisfy individual customer requirements. This latter feature is common to many industries, but combined with the wide sectorial interest has led to disparate silo research effort in the past.

Industry funds research. It can do this either directly – through payment of employees or through research contracts let to external agencies – or indirectly through payment of taxes and disbursement of the subsequent income by national research agencies. There are other mechanisms, but these are the two principal ways in which research funding is generated. It is therefore important that research is focused to ways in which income for industry can be maximized in both the short and long term.

The survey reported below aims at determining the direction of basic research and to establish the wider state of the art, based on industrial needs.

55.2 DESCRIPTION OF THE SURVEY

This survey seeks to obtain views from different elements of silo producers, designers and users. While engineering consultancies and structural designers can be large organizations, they can also be small businesses established around one individual. Similarly contractors can be large or small; end users can vary from individual farmers to large conglomerates.

The survey was set up by sending out a copy of the questionnaire to all industrial addresses available on the CA-Silo data base. Furthermore, the questionnaire was published in an edition of the journal *Bulk Solids Handling*. The respondents are evidently self-selecting, in that they have replied out of interest.

A copy of the questionnaire and accompanying letter are given in Appendix 55.A. The accompanying letter, and the table were written in English, French or German and sent as appropriate. A key aim was to make it as straightforward as possible for respondents, and so a tick-box approach was used.

55.3 RESULTS OF THE SURVEY

Thirty-six replies were received. Of these, four were from exclusively researchers, and their results have not been analysed further. One reply from India (through *Bulk Solids Handling*) has not been included.

The results are produced directly in Tables 55.1 and 55.2. Table 55.1 shows the interests of the respondents, while Table 55.2 shows the problems perceived by the respondents. Names of respondents have been removed to ensure the confidentiality of the replies. The results are presented by country, and in no particular order.

One possibility which should be considered is that those who have not responded do not see any problem, and their perception is that no further research is needed; this premise is considered unlikely.

55.4 SUMMARY OF RESULTS

55.4.1 Range of results

The survey incorporates response from designers, constructors and end-users. It is highly skewed to response from northern European nations, because of the involvement of those nations in silo research.

The number of respondents does not justify an extensive statistical analysis of the data, but it is interesting to note that there is a good range of industries represented, and a good range of size of silo; the data are neither restricted to very small silos, nor to a small number of large industrial installations.

There is a preponderance of metal silos for most users, although concrete silos are more widely used in the UK.

Only a small proportion of the respondents were involved with feeders and discharge aids.

5.4.2 Problems/research requirements

The survey asked where respondents had problems and/or where there was an identified research need.

1. *Flow problems* (e.g. arching, ratholing, hang-ups, dead zones, segregation) Nearly all respondents answered positively, and so it is clear that silo flow still presents major challenges. Because the survey was designed to elicit maximum response, little detail has been included. It is therefore difficult to identify specific problems in more detail, but challenges for the future have been identified in Part One.
2. *Poor feeder performance* (e.g. non-uniform feed rates, flooding, asymmetric discharge) Again, nearly all the respondents identified this problem. Because only a limited number of respondents were involved with feeders and discharge aids, it might be reasonably supposed that most of the respondents refer to problems arising from asymmetric discharge. In the authors' experience, this is not surprising given the paucity of published work on the effects of eccentric inlet and outlet.
3. *Structural failures* A much smaller number responded here. Possible reasons for the small response might be that there was a restricted number of respondents concerned with structural design, but alternatively, the fact that so many responded in an area so critical to structural integrity and safety is somewhat alarming. For such problems,

Table 55.1 Experience base of respondents

No.	Type of industry	Type of business	Silos A	Silos B	Feeders A	Feeders B	D. Aids A	D. Aids B	Others A	Others B	SGEO	MATC
FRANCE												
1.	vi	a	–	2.68–32 m	–	–	–	–	–	–	c	M
2.	ii, iii, iv, v	a, d, e, f	2000	50–80 000 t	various	5–2000 t/h	3	to 100 t/h	–	–	c, r	M
3.	iv	f	various	–	–	–	–	–	–	–	c	C, M
4.	vi (all solids)	f	–	–	–	–	–	–	–	–	–	–
5.	i, ii, v	a, d, f	–	10–700 m³	–	–	–	–	–	–	c, r	M
6.	iii (food), iv (cement), v (bulk handling)	f	–	–	–	–	–	–	–	–	r	M, O
7.	vi	f	–	–	–	–	–	–	–	–	–	–
8.	vi	g	–	–	–	–	–	–	–	–	–	–
GERMANY												
9.	vi (recycling)	b, e	11	to 600 m³	–	–	–	–	–	–	r	O
10.	i, iii, v	a, c, d, e	–	to 70 m³	various	–	–	–	–	–	r	M

Summary of results

#												
11.	–	a, d, e	100	10–1000 m³	–	–	yes	–	–	–	r, c	M
12.	i	b, d, f	–	–	–	–	–	–	–	–	–	–
13.	i	e	ca. 120	5–250 m³	–	–	ca. 90	–	–	–	r	M
14.	i	a, d	–	–	–	–	–	–	–	–	–	–
15.	i, iv	e	–	–	–	⌀3500	–	–	–	–	r	M
16.	i	a, d, e, f	–	–	–	50–100 t/h	–	10–100 t/h	–	–	–	–
17.	i, iv, v, vi (waste and recycling)	a, d, f	–	–	–	–	–	–	–	–	–	–
18.	vi	a, d, f, h (bulk solids testing)	–	–	–	–	–	–	–	–	–	–
19.	v	a, c, d, e	–	100–1000 m³	Rotary feeder	0.5–80 t/h	Vibratory	600–1800 mm ⌀	Bottom air cannon	–	r	M
20.	vi	h (design and construction)	–	–	–	–	–	–	–	–	r, c	C
21.	iv, v	a, d, f	–	–	–	–	–	–	–	–	–	–
THE NETHERLANDS												
22.	i	b, f	–	–	–	–	–	–	–	–	c, r	M
23.	i	d, f	750	0.5–1000 m³	Screw vibratory	0.001–120 t/h	Various	–	–	–	c, r	C, M FRP
DENMARK												
24.	ii	a, c	–	–	–	–	–	–	–	–	r	M
GREECE												
25.	–	d, f	–	–	–	–	–	–	–	–	–	–
BELGIUM												
26.	vi	d	–	–	–	–	–	–	–	–	–	–

Table 55.1 Continued

No.	Type of industry	Type of business	Silos			Feeders			D. Aids			Others			SGEO	MATC
			A	B		A	B		A	B		A	B			
SWITZERLAND																
27.	i, ii, iii, iv, v	a, c, d, e, f, g, h	Various	Various		Various	Various		Various	Various		Conveyors	Various		c, r, sq	C, M, FRP, O
UNITED KINGDOM																
28.	i, ii, iii, iv, v	a, d	–	–		–	–		–	–		–	–		–	–
29.	vi	f	None	None		None	None		None	None		None	–		–	–
30.	i, ii, iii, iv, v	a, d, e	100s	1–8000 m³		100s	–		100s	–		–	–		c, r	C, M
31.	ii, iii, v, vi	d	Various sites	–		–	–		–	–		–	–		–	–
32.	i, iii	a, b, f	Many	10–1000 m³		Many	0.1–50 t/h		Many	–		–	–		c, r	C, M, FRP
33.	vi	a, d, f	–	–		–	–		–	–		–	–		–	–
34.	ii, iv	a, d, e	–	–		–	–		–	–		–	–		–	–
35.	i	b	100s	5–2500 m³		Many	100 kg–100 t/h		Many	–		–	–		c	M

Type of industry: (i) Chemicals, plastics; (ii) agriculture, grain; (iii) food, dairy; (iv) minerals, cement, coal, steel; (v) bulk handling/logistics; (vi) other.
Type of business: (a) Silo design; (b) silo/plant operation; (c) equipment manufacturing; (d) consulting; (e) contract engineering; (f) research; (g) control and inspection; (h) other.
Type of equipment: Silos – (A) number/type (B) capacity/volume/size; Feeders – (A) number/type (B) capacity/volume/size; Discharge Aids – (A) number/type (B) capacity/volume/size; Others – (A) number/type (B) capacity/volume/size.
SGEO – Silo geometry: (c) Circular; (r) rectangular; MATC – Material of construction: (C) Concrete; (M) metal; (FRP) FRP; (O) other, e.g. Al, etc.

Table 55.2 Problems perceived by respondents

No.	Problems/experiences requiring further research *							General information yes/no				
	A	B	C	D	E	F	G	a	b	c	d	e
FRANCE												
1.	*		*	*	*	*		y	n	n	n	y
2.	*	*		*	*	*		y	y	y	y	y
3.	*	*						y			n	y
4.	*		*		*			y	y	y	y	y
5.	*	*		*	*	*		y	y	y	y	y
6.	*	*						y	y	y	y	y
7.									y		n	y
8.		*			*			y	y	y		n
GERMANY												
9.	*	*						y	n	y	y	y
10.		*			*			y			n	y
11.	*	*		*				y	n	n	n	n
12.	*	*		*				y	y	y	y	y
13.	*	*		*				y	y	y	n	n
14.	*	*				*		y	n	n	y	y
15.	*	*		*		*			n	n	y	y
16.	*	*		*				y	n	n	n	n
17.	*	*	*			*		y	y	y	y	y
18.	*	*				*	*	y	y	y	y	n
19.	*	*	*		*		*	y	y	y	y	y
20.								y	y			
21.	*	*	*		*	*		y	y	y	y	y
THE NETHERLANDS												
22.	*	*					*	y	y	n	y	y
23.	*	*					*	n	y	y	y	y
DENMARK												
24.	*		*	*	*			y			y	
GREECE												
25.	*							y	y	y	y	y
BELGIUM												
26.	*					*	*	y	y	y	y/n	n
SWITZERLAND												
27.	*	*	*	*	*	*	*	y	y		y	y

Table 55.2 *Continued*

No.	Problems/experiences requiring further research *							General information yes/no				
	A	B	C	D	E	F	G	a	b	c	d	e
UNITED KINGDOM												
28.	*		*					y	n	n	n	n
29.								n	n	n	n	y
30.	*	*	*	*		*	*	y	y	y	y	n
31.			*	*		*		y	y	y	y	n
32.	*					*		y		y	y	y
33.	*		*			*		y	y	y	y	y
34.						*		y	y	y	y	n
35.	*		*		*	*		y	y	y	y	

Problems/experiences requiring further research
A: flow problems (e.g. arching, ratholing, hang-ups, dead zones, segregation); B: poor feeder performance (e.g. non-uniform feed rates, flooding, asymmetric discharge); C: structural failures (e.g. buckling, cracking, collapse); D: dust explosion hazards; E: vibrations, noise emissions, shocks, seismic loads; F: lack of suitable design procedure; G: others.
General information
(a): Would you like to receive more information about our project (CA-Silo)? (b): Are you interested in participating in our project? (c): Are you interested in participating in a future research programme or project? (d): Do you regularly receive information on silo and bulk solids technology/research? (e): Are you a member of an industrial or research organization?

responses to such a question would be small in other areas of structural design (e.g. frames). This supports the statement that silo failures are more common than for any other type of structure.

4   *Dust explosion hazards*   Again this result is surprising and alarming. It is clearly still an area where research, and possibly dissemination of research results, are needed. Part Two includes a significant section on dust explosions.

5   *Vibrations, noise emissions, shocks, seismic loads*   This remains a specific problem. Seismic loading of silos has been addressed by ENV 1991-4. Vibrations and noise is the subject of much debate, and is discussed in Part One.

6   *Lack of suitable design procedure*   Overall, about half of the respondents felt there was a lack of suitable design procedures, while the percentage of UK respondents rose to 75%. This may reflect the fact that codified design has often been based on DIN 1055 or other codes. Again the introduction of ENV may provide an improvement, although the limited scope may not be acceptable to industry.

7   *Others*   A number of other problems were specifically identified. They were: aeration, trickle flow problems, design procedures for inserts, de-aeration (as opposed to aeration) and feeding fibrous materials. Again, some of these problems are addressed in Part One.

55.5 CONCLUSION

The survey has highlighted the problems of flow and feeding that remain to be solved. This combined with an alarming number of structural safety problems and a lack of suitable design procedure are the main areas where this survey of industry has revealed that future research is required.

APPENDIX 55.A LETTER TO INDUSTRY AND QUESTIONNAIRE

Concerted Action Silo Research

December 1995

Safe Economic SILOS

The improvement of silo performance, safety and cost requires your input. Many companies report silo problems. Such problems might include:

 Flow problems
 Structural problems
 Process disruption
 Unacceptable noise emission
 Collapse

If you use, design or construct silos we need your contribution. On behalf of the European Union we are compiling data to include your needs in future research programmes.

Please complete the attached form and return it to me.

If you want further information about the EC-funded CA-Silo programme, please indicate on the form.

Many thanks in advance.

C.J. Brown
CA-Silo Project Coordinator

Industrial Silo Research Needs

Your Company/Organization		Your Industry	
Name		Chemicals, Plastics	
Attn of		Agriculture, Grain	
Address		Food, Dairy	
City		Minerals, Cement, Coal, Steel	
Country		Bulk handling/Logistics	
Phone/Fax		Other	

Your Business		Your Profession	
Silo Design		Civil/Structural Engineer	
Silo/Plant Operation		Chemical/Process Engineer	
Equipment Manufacturing		Mechanical/Electrical Engineer	
Consulting		Plant Operator	
Contract Engineering		Maintenance Technician	
Research		Sales	
Control and Inspection			
Other		Other	

Your Equipment (Use or Fabrication)	Number/ Type	Capacity/ Volume/Size	Silo Geometry		Material of Construction	
Silos			Circular		Concrete	
Feeders			Rectangular		Metal	
Discharge Aids					FRP	
Others					Other	

Your Problems or Experiences which require further Research	
Flow Problems (for example: arching, ratholing, hang-ups, dead zones, segregation)	
Poor Feeder Performance (for example: non-uniform feed rates, flooding, asymmetric discharge)	
Structural Failures (for example: buckling, cracking, collapse)	
Dust Explosion Hazards	
Vibrations, Noise Emissions, Shocks, Seismic Loads	
Lack of suitable design procedure	
Others	

General Information	yes	no
Would you like to receive more information about our project (CA-Silo)?		
Are you interested in participating in our project?		
Are you interested in participating in a future research programme or project?		
Do you regularly receive information on silo and bulk solids technology/research?		
Are you a member of an industrial or research organization?		

Thank you for your assistance!

56

Prenormative research

J. Nielsen

56.1 INTRODUCTION AND SCOPE

Storage structures are significantly different from many other structural forms, and are subject to the full design load many times during their existence. There is a strong linkage between their working conditions and their structural safety. This has for a long time presented both designers and standards drafting committees with challenges; the rate of failures of silos has been higher than for other types of structures.

Following the European tradition concerning standards, it is an agreed objective to mainly cover the design of common types of structures. For such structures simple rules or requirements are given in the standards without much explanation. Agreement to such rules is facilitated by well documented research presented and discussed in the international society of researchers.

More advanced structures, often those for which very little experience exists, have to be designed without reference to standards – and with more responsibility put on the designer. Specialist companies have gradually developed experience each for a limited set of silos. At the European level there has been an increasing demand for documentation on the structural safety of these silos. Again, well-documented research results form an important basis for the designer's final decisions when dealing with such silos and in presenting the documentation of structural safety.

56.2 CURRENT STATE

The work in ISO and CEN committees on standards for loads or structural design of silos has revealed that, although many valuable research projects have been carried out in many countries, the number of phenomena which have been observed, the number of parameters which are involved, the difficulties in using complicated experimental equipment, and the difficulties in introducing realistic material models for theoretical simulations have led to many open questions. This has resulted in codes with scope that does not include many types of silos which are often constructed.

Unsatisfactory code limitations are highlighted by resolution 52 (1992) from the Standards Committee CEN/TC250/SC1 stating that rules for silos with large eccentricities and silos with tie rods should be developed and included in a future revised standard.

For loads, the load model for filling is the only one to some extent based on a theoretical approach. Load models for discharge are as yet empirically based, while waiting for a consensus to be formed concerning the accuracy of computer simulations.

The fact that silo structures include shell structures, some of which are subjected to buckling, means that some of the most difficult types of structural analyses are involved. That makes it a challenge to present simple design rules, which may even require a reformulation of the load models given in the actions code.

Special attention has to be paid to interaction between loads and structures. This is a delicate question to deal with in codes for structures which deal with structural actions and structural design separately.

In general, it is a major problem that we know about or have descriptive models for many important phenomena but cannot give satisfactory objective data or design rules. We have to devise and prove models that make adequate predictions for these phenomena.

56.3 THE TRANSFORMATION OF RESEARCH INTO STANDARDS

The fundamental processes for the transformation of research into standards and into practical design are:

- well-documented research
- international presentation and evaluation
- transformation of results into application rules

Researchers work for – and standards committees and designers encourage – this process to become complete. Only then does research serve practical needs. Unfortunately, it cannot be claimed that this process works well with respect to silo research. This can be explained by the mismatch of the complexity of this field and the limited research funds which are available world-wide.

There are therefore a number of unanswered questions to be addressed by research and a considerable gap between current knowledge and industrial needs still exists. CA-Silo has addressed these problems, and worked for effective use of research funds to reduce the gap between knowledge and industrial needs; a considerable task still remains.

56.4 RESEARCH NEEDS

Part of the philosophy behind CA-Silo has been to identify high priority needs for prenormative research, and a Working Group has identified 10 topics based on requests to standards committees. They are:

- wall pressures in silos with extreme eccentric outlet or inlet
- silos with internal ties
- calibration of parameters for stored materials
- loads in squat silos
- seismic actions in silos
- calibration of patch loads with measured pressures
- dust explosions in silos
- loads in silage silos
- loads due to differential temperatures
- buckling strength of metal silos under eccentric loads

For each of these topics, a research Assessment Sheet has been completed. These are shown in Appendix 56.A. The other members of the Working Group who have made the major contribution to this work are: D. Briassoulis (GR), J. Eibl (D), J.C. Leray (F), J.M. Rotter (UK), and their efforts are gratefully acknowledged.

APPENDIX 56.A

> **Shortcomings of the silo standards Assessment sheet**
>
> **Topic: Silos with internal ties**
>
> *Existing standards regulation*: CEN/ENV, excluded. ISO, excluded. DIN 1055, ignored. French code, limited rule. BMHB guideline, ignored.
>
> *Standard for which work is needed*: Loads, concrete structures, steel structures.
>
> *Relevant resolutions*: CEN/TC250/SC1/1992/Resolution 52.
>
> *Description of structure*: Internal ties are used in rectangular silos to limit bending effects in the corners and the panels.
>
> *Description of problem*: The forces in the ties and the pressures on the walls are known from current commercial designs, but only for a very limited range of conditions. Many parameters affect these actions: silo shape, flow pattern, tie cross-section, arrangement of ties, etc. Many failures of the ties and the walls have occurred.
>
> *Range/scope of problem*: Widely used in agricultural silos in France; also in Germany. Potential for wider use in other countries since it is an economic structure.
>
> *Reasons why a rule cannot be formulated yet*: Very few tests have been performed and the complexity of the problem does not allow rules to be formulated within the scope of the existing codes.
>
> *Restricted classes of problem for which a rule could be drafted*: Current commercial designs have very restricted geometries; a prescriptive rule for these could be written.
>
> *Work needed: class of problem*: Fundamental and standards related.
>
> *Work required to formulate a standards recommendation*: Evaluation of existing research; collection of knowledge from companies with experience, followed by a test programme on about five medium scale silos of different geometries. At a later stage, more basic research leading to a better understanding should be performed to support a more general rule.
>
> *Probable time-scale for this work*: Medium scale test: 2–3 years.
>
> *Urgency/seriousness/priority for this project*: Very urgent, see Relevant Resolution.
>
> *Existing relevant literature*:
>
> See Chapters 20 and 21.

Shortcomings of the silo standards Assessment sheet

Topic: Wall pressures in silos with extreme eccentric outlet and/or inlet

Existing standards regulation: CEN/ENV, effectively excluded. ISO, excluded. Australian, empirical method. ACI standard, subject of prolonged committee debate.

Standard for which work is needed: Loads, concrete structures, steel structures.

Relevant resolutions: CEN/TC250/SC1/1992/Resolution 52.

Description of structure: Problem most severe for circular silos with unsymmetrical flow patterns.

Description of problem: Severe action-effects are induced by extreme unsymmetrical flow. Unsymmetrical flow patterns arise for many reasons, the most obvious of which is an eccentric outlet. The resulting flow pattern and unsymmetrical pressures cause many failures, but cannot in general be defined simply yet.

Range/scope of problem: Widely occurring in agricultural and industrial silos, sometimes intentional, sometimes inadvertent (e.g. screw feeder biases flow).

Reasons why a rule cannot be formulated yet: Flow channels cannot be predicted with confidence. Wall pressures cannot be predicted well, even if flow is known.

Restricted classes of problem for which a rule could be drafted: Guaranteed cylindrical pipe flow channel. Simplified rules for a number of silo types such as small farm silos, small silos for aggregates, etc.

Work needed: class of problem: Fundamental and standards related.

Work required to formulate a standards recommendation: Evaluation of past research with formulation of rules for restricted classes of problems. Experiments on eccentric discharge, observing flow channels and unsymmetrical wall pressures. Theoretical studies to relate solids properties to resulting flow channels.

Probable time-scale for this work: 3–5 years.

Urgency/seriousness/priority for this project: Urgent.

Existing relevant literature:

See Chapters 8, 14, 16, 23 and 26.

Shortcomings of the silo standards Assessment sheet

Topic: Loads in squat silos

Existing standards regulation: CEN-ENV, simplified rules.

Standard for which work is needed: Loads.

Relevant resolutions:

Description of structure: Large circular silos with a height to diameter ratio less than 1.5.

Description of problem: Centrally unloaded squat silos are not subject to large redistributions of pressures during discharge which makes the filling pressure be the design pressure. Loads in squat silos are very much affected by the shape of the surface of the stored material. This is not to the same extent the case for slender silos which is why most codes do not introduce the complications which are necessary for giving more precise and more economic rules.

Range/scope of problem: This type of silos is widely used and is expected to become even more popular to match the future demand for storage.

Reasons why a rule cannot be formulated yet: Theories for loads related to curved and inclined surfaces of limited extension have not been developed.

Restricted classes of problem for which a rule could be drafted: Two-dimensional (plane) silos. Circular silos with plane or cone-shaped surfaces.

Work needed: class of problem: Fundamental and standards related.

Work required to formulate a standards recommendation: Transfer of knowledge from the field of soil mechanics. A study of existing experimental data. Further development of the theoretical background and numerical simulations.

Probable time-scale for this work: 2 years.

Urgency/seriousness/priority for this project: Urgent.

Existing relevant literature:

See Parts Two, Three and Four.

Shortcomings of the silo standards Assessment sheet

Topic: Seismic actions in silos

Existing standards regulation: CEN, oversimplifying situation.

Standard for which work is needed: Loads, concrete structures, steel structures, seismic actions.

Relevant resolutions:

Description of structure: All types of silo structures including foundations.

Description of problem: Very few national or international standards include explicit requirements concerning the design of silos against earthquakes. Existing knowledge is poor concerning dynamic displacements of stored materials and the influence of soil–structure interaction at the foundations as well as at the walls.

Range/scope of problem: For very large silo structures as they are seen today it is considered an oversimplification to base the design on existing rules, especially when taking into account the extensive effects of a collapse of such silos on property and lives.

Reasons why a rule cannot be formulated yet: Research in this area, both analytical and experimental, is rather limited and the problem is complicated due to the interaction of the structure with the stored material and the foundation.

Restricted classes of problem for which a rule could be drafted: Cylindrical silos used to store specific granular materials.

Work needed: class of problem: Fundamental and standards related.

Work required to formulate a standards recommendation: Critical literature review. Evaluation of today's practice and national standards dealing directly or indirectly with this problem. Basic research with analytical and experimental work.

Probable time-scale for this work: 3–4 years.

Urgency/seriousness/priority for this project: Serious.

Existing relevant literature:

See Chapters 8, 18 and 29.

Shortcomings of the silo standards Assessment sheet

Topic: Calibration of patch loads with measured pressures

Existing standards regulation: CEN/ENV patch loads used, ISO also, DIN 1055 also. Patch loads proposed for ACI 313.

Standard for which work is needed: Loads.

Relevant resolutions:

Description of structure: Patch loads are a simple way of ensuring that a structure can support unsymmetrical pressures.

Description of problem: Many silos experience unsymmetrical pressures in complex patterns. The design process allows for this by requiring a 'patch load' to be used. The size, shape, and amplitude need to be verified against silo experiments.

Range/scope of problem: Most large silos are required to support the patch load. How should the magnitude vary with silo geometry and stored solid properties?

Reasons why a rule cannot be formulated yet: Rule is already formulated, but not scientifically based.

Restricted classes of problem for which a rule could be drafted: Range of applicability currently uncertain.

Work needed: class of problem: Standards related.

Work required to formulate a standards recommendation: Theoretical work to calibrate the effect of alternative patch load descriptions against the effect of experimentally measured pressures.

Probable time-scale for this work: 2 years.

Urgency/seriousness/priority for this project: Required before next revision of the code.

Existing relevant literature:

See Chapters 16 and 23.

Shortcomings of the silo standards Assessment sheet

Topic: Calibration of parameters for stored materials

Existing standards regulation: Figures are given in all standards.

Standard for which work is needed: Loads.

Relevant resolutions:

Description of structure: All structures.

Description of problem: Properties of stored materials are given in standards for silo loads. However, the present CEN/ENV is the first standard which introduces parameters with reference to test methods. Traditionally safety considerations have influenced the figures given in the standards.

There is a need to calibrate the new design rules and evaluate the figures in the ENV.

Range/scope of problem: The problem exists for all silos and means that the safety margin may be larger or smaller than intended.

Reasons why a rule cannot be formulated yet: Lack of data from controlled testing.

Restricted classes of problem for which a rule could be drafted: The most common stored materials.

Work needed: class of problem: Standards related.

Work required to formulate a standards recommendation: Round robin tests of a selected number of materials. Four or five institutes in different countries should be involved.

Probable time-scale for this work: 1 year.

Urgency/seriousness/priority for this project: Serious, and should be done before the end of the ENV period.

Existing relevant literature:

See Chapters 2 and 41.

Shortcomings of the silo standards Assessment sheet

Topic: Dust explosions in silos

Existing standards regulation: A draft German guideline exists.

Standard for which work is needed: Loads, concrete structures, steel structures.

Relevant resolutions:

Description of structure: All types of silo structures.

Description of problem: If dust explosion is a possibility that loading case is the critical one and has to be followed up by technical measures such as vent openings, retaining structures, etc.

Range/scope of problem: Silos for storage of organic materials, metal powders and others subject to dust explosions. Several people have been killed by such accidents.

Reasons why a rule cannot be formulated yet: Sufficient research has not yet been performed, especially concerning the technical measures.

Restricted classes of problem for which a rule could be drafted: The most common cases can be covered.

Work needed: class of problem: Fundamental and standards related.

Work required to formulate a standards recommendation: Review of literature and existing guidelines. Further research, theoretical and experimental concerning technical measures.

Probable time-scale for this work: 2 years.

Urgency/seriousness/priority for this project: Urgent.

Existing relevant literature:

See Chapters 8 and 18.

Shortcomings of the silo standards Assessment sheet

Topic: Loads in silage silos

Existing standards regulation: CEN, no rules. DIN 1055, Canadian Farm Building Code, ISA recommended practice, Australian Standard.

Standard for which work is needed: Loads.

Relevant resolutions:

Description of structure: Silos for various types of silage material, unloading conditions, support conditions.

Description of problem: A significant proportion of silos are used for storing silage for agricultural purposes. The determination of pressures induced by silage on silo walls is more complicated and involves more parameters than it does for granular materials. Available methods for estimating lateral pressure, average vertical pressure, and capacity in farm silos give results which vary within a wide range. In most countries there is no standard concerning calculation of wall loads in slender silos.

Range/scope of problem: Recent developments in the technology of production and handling ensiled farm products have led to the construction of large farm silos. A rational method for determining (or evaluating) silage-induced lateral and vertical pressures in farm silos, as well as silo capacities, is now needed.

Reasons why a rule cannot be formulated yet: Farm structures were not given a high priority in the first generation of the Eurocodes. Research work in this area, both analytical and experimental, is limited. Furthermore, this work has not been organized systematically and exploited accordingly, partly due to the complex characteristics of the various silage materials.

Restricted classes of problem for which a rule could be drafted: Cylindrical silos and squat plane silos used to store specific categories of silage materials.

Work needed: class of problem: Fundamental and standards related.

Work required to formulate a standards recommendation: Critical literature review. Evaluation of today's practice and of national standards dealing directly or indirectly with this problem. Basic research, analytical as well as experimental.

Probable time-scale for this work: Rules for restricted classes of problems: 2 years. Duration of basic research: 3–4 years.

Urgency/seriousness/priority for this project: Serious.

Existing relevant literature:

See Chapter 18.

Shortcomings of the silo standards
Assessment sheet

Topic: Loads due to differential temperatures

Existing standards regulation: CEN, oversimplifying situation, referring to thermally induced loading with no suggested analytical procedure. An exception may be found in the ACI code, which, however, does not cover the subject adequately.

Standard for which work is needed: Loads, concrete structures, steel structures.

Relevant resolutions:

Description of structure: Circular silo structures, support conditions, hot stored material.

Description of problem: Circular silo structures do not have the flexibility to avoid serious action effects from hot infill or rapid changes of external temperatures. The effect is complicated by stored material structure interaction.

Range/scope of problem: Collapses have been reported and actions from temperatures are for some types of design very important at the serviceability limit state.

Reasons why a rule cannot be formulated yet: Research in this area, both analytical and experimental, is limited and the problem is complicated due to the interaction of the structure with the stored material and due to the need for specification of the working conditions in the case of hot infill.

Restricted classes of problem for which a rule could be drafted: Cylindrical silos used to store specific granular materials.

Work needed: class of problem: Fundamental and standards related.

Work required to formulate a standards recommendation: Critical literature review. Evaluation of today's practice and of national standards dealing directly or indirectly with this problem. Collection of temperature data as a basis for analytical and experimental research.

Probable time-scale for this work: 2–3 years.

Urgency/seriousness/priority for this project: Serious.

Existing relevant literature:

See Chapters 8, 14 and 18.

Shortcomings of the silo standards Assessment sheet

Topic: Buckling strength of metal silos under eccentric loads

Existing standards regulation: None.

Standard for which work is needed: Steel structures.

Relevant resolutions: CEN/TC250/SC1/1992/Resolution 52.

Description of structure: Circular metal silos under eccentric discharge.

Description of problem: Eccentric discharge leads to serious buckling problems in metal silos, and has caused many catastrophic failures. The stresses in the wall are locally very high. Little is known about buckling under local high stresses.

Range/scope of problem: Widely occurring in agricultural and industrial silos. Failure often attributed to another cause because flow pattern is not recognized.

Reasons why a rule cannot be formulated yet: No calculations or tests of buckling strength under local high stresses. Existing tests on eccentric discharge buckling are difficult to interpret.

Restricted classes of problem for which a rule could be drafted: Only a speculative rule is possible.

Work needed: class of problem: Fundamental and standards related.

Work required to formulate a standards recommendation: Calculations and tests of cylindrical shells under unsymmetrical loads leading to buckling.

Probable time-scale for this work: 2 years.

Urgency/seriousness/priority for this project: Prediction on eccentric discharge pressures is of no use to metal structures if this study is not undertaken.

Existing relevant literature:

See Part Three.

Index

Abrasion, *see* Wear
Actions, *see* Differential settlement, Dust explosion, Loads, Pressures, Seismic action, Temperature, Wind load
Aeration 88
   flow properties 91
   packed beds 89
   rotary viscometer 92
   see also Discharge aids, Fluidization
Air pressure measurement
   adsorption technique 739
   electroconductometric method 739
   electromechanical technique 739
   gas velocity distribution 736
   laser technique 739
   pneumatic technique 739
   pore pressure transducer 735
   pressure – atmospheric 729, 730
   pressure – interstitial 729, 731, 735
   pressure gauges – overview of 733
   sublimation technique 739
   thermoanemometric technique 739
Angle of internal friction, *see* Flow property measurement, Material characterization for silo tests
Angle of repose, *see* Flow property measurement, Material characterization for silo tests
Anisotropy, *see* Flow property testing
Arches 134, 180, 200
   see also Flow patterns

Blending
   arrangements 134–139
   blending quality 154
   gravity blending 130, 140
   homogenizing 130, 134, 143
   inserts for 130, 132
   layer model 145
   mixing 130
   multiple compartment tubes 138
   multiple intake openings 137
   multiple pipe blender 144
   pneumatic pellet blender 136, 143
   recirculation 131, 145
   residence time 130, 144, 157, 185
   retrofitting 134
   simulation of 142, 150
   velocity profile 130
   see also Inserts
Buckling
   bulk solids restraint 360
   circumferentially corrugated cylinders 362
   cylinders with circumferential welded joints 350
   eccentric discharge 373
   flow channel 374
   lap-jointed cylinders 349
   local buckling 369
   pressurized cylinders 355
   strengths 336, 372
   unstiffened cylinders 346
   see also Hoppers, Rectangular silos, Wind load
Bulk density 724
   gamma densitometry 726
   impregnation technique 726

Index

numerical image processing 727
see also Flow property testing, Material characterization for silo tests
Bulk solids handling, *see* Flow patterns
Bulk solids properties
 classification 107
 identification 105
Bulk solids testing, *see* Flow property measuring techniques/equipment, Flow property testing

Centrifuge technique, *see* Model laws, Test classification
Code of Practice, *see* Standards
Cohesion, *see* Flow property measurement, Moisture measurements
Collapse, *see* Hoppers, Metal silo structures
Column support, *see* Hoppers, Metal silo structures
Concrete silo construction
 reinforcement cover 318
 slipform problems 317
Concrete wall design
 abrasion 318, 320
 chemical attack 319
 corrosion protection 318
 crack control 312
 interaction of shear and tension 314
 minimum reinforcement 312
 prestressing 313
 reinforcement 312
 see also Concrete silo construction, Dust explosions, Seismic action, Wear
Conical roofs, *see* Metal silo structures
Consolidation, *see* Documentation of silo tests, Flow property testing
Constitutive laws, *see* Constitutive models
Constitutive models 528
 Boyce–Wilde model 496
 calibration of 543
 choice of 539
 creep model 536
 deformation mechanisms 70
 elastic models 529
 elastic–plastic models 530
 Kolymbas model 543
 Lade model 543
 non-elastic models 530
 polar models 535
 rate-type models 534
 rheology 72
 stress–strain histories 540
 see also Finite Element analysis, Flow property testing, Metal silo structures, Software for numerical simulation
Construction, *see* Concrete silo construction, Metal silo construction
Control 221
 see also Discharge systems, Level control

Conveyors, *see* Discharge systems
Cylindrical shell, *see* Shell structures
Cylindrical silos, *see* Shell structures

Data presentation for silo tests 673
 data acquisition 673
 data exchange format 679
 data processing 679
 data storage 678
 power spectrum analysis 675
 sample rate 673, 675, 767
 spectral density 675
 time format 680
Design, *see* Concrete silo construction, Metal silo structures
Differential settlement, *see* Foundation
Discharge aids
 aeration pads 202
 air cannon 202
 Binsert© 204
 emptying tubes 451
 flow agent 204
 flow promoting devices 200, 221
 inflatable pads 203
 operation of 210
 pneumatic 88, 202
 rotary screws 446
 rotary valve 203
 rotating plough 202
 stirrers 203
 vibrating hopper 202
 see also Discharge systems, Inserts
Discharge systems 221
 assessment criteria 222
 see also Discharge aids
Discrete particle models, *see* Numerical simulation – discrete particle models
Documentation of silo tests
 consolidation 647, 678
 discharge rate 648
 filling rate 646
 geometry 623–625
 height of fall 647
 inlet pattern 647
 instrumentation 625–629
 sampling 648
 segregation 649
 surface level 646
 surface particle movement 647
 surface shape 647, 648
 temperature 649
 time 648
 see also Data presentation for silo tests, Material characterization for silo tests
Dust explosions
 design 276, 407
 explosive dust 274
 guideline for design 277
 ignition source 275

protective measures 276
venting system 276

Earthquakes, *see* Seismic action
Eccentric (filling or discharge), *see* Buckling, Numerical simulation – finite element models, Pressures
Embedded cell, *see* Stress and pressure measurements
Equipment, *see* Discharge systems
Experimental techniques for silo tests 685
   crack openings 717
   sandwich strain gauges 643, 701
   strain cell 697
   volume of stored material 717
   wall displacements 716
   see also Air pressure measurement, Bulk density, Flow visualization, Gamma-ray tomography, Moisture measurements, Numerical simulation – finite element models, Stress and pressure measurements, Wall strain

Failures, *see* Hoppers, Metal silo structures
Feeders 200, 257
   design 211–19
   hopper/feeder interface 211
Feeding 231
   belt weigher 234
   continuous weighing 234
   flow meter 234
   gravimetric feeding 237
   see also Feeders
Finite element analysis of metal structures
   imperfection models 455
   modelling of bulk solids 455
   stability of plates 454
   stability of shells 453
   stress state 452
Finite element methods, *see* Finite element analysis of metal structures, Numerical simulation – finite element models
Finite element models, *see* Numerical simulation – discrete particle models
Fixed bed reactors, *see* Purge bins
Flow function, *see* Flow property testing, Material characterization for silo tests
Flow in silos, *see* Flow patterns
Flow patterns 112, 116, 192, 256
   measurement techniques 746
   radial stress field 115
   residence times 193
   simple analytical model 195
   velocity distributions 192
   see also Buckling, Flow visualization, Wall friction
Flow promoting devices, *see* Discharge aids
Flow property measurement techniques/equipment

angle of repose 35
biaxial shear tester 9, 56
compressibility tester 38
flowability test 39
funnel 34
Hang-up Indicizer© 30, 44
ideal bulk solids tester 99
Imse test 36
Jenike shear tester 7, 22, 46, 53, 99
Lambdameter 13
monoaxial shear test 42
penetration test 40
powder bed tester 43
powder tester 37
quality control tester 45
ring shear tester 25, 48, 99
stirrer 38
torsional shear tester 47
triaxial test 65, 66
uniaxial compression test 41, 54
see also Flow property testing
Flow property testing 6, 254
   anisotropy 29, 60
   applications 12
   consolidation procedures 10, 19, 27, 32, 59
   flow function 6, 24
   flowability 19, 21, 65, 73
   industrial application 98
   Mohr stress circle 24, 114
   preshear 23, 26
   quality control 15
   relaxation 61
   simplified procedure 27
   stationary flow 23, 27
   steady-state shear 23, 60
   time consolidation 20, 24, 26
   unconfined yield strength 8, 20
   uniaxial compression 27
   yield locus 23, 114
   see also Flow property measurement techniques/equipment
Flow visualization
   boundary observation technique 747
   contour plot 751
   flow pattern 748
   freezing techniques 748
   photographic techniques 747
   residence time technique 746, 751
   tracer technique 747
Flowability, *see* Flow property measurement techniques/equipment, Flow property testing
Fluidization 88
   properties 90, 94
   see also Aeration
Foundation
   differential settlement 268, 344, 387, 408
   pile foundation 272

Index 833

Frictional traction 337, 346, 439
  see also Hoppers
Funnel flow 116, 172, 192
  see also Flow patterns

Gamma-ray tomography 781
  application to monodisperse systems 787
  application to polydisperse systems 790
  dual photon measurement 786
  full tomographic imaging 784
  single profile absorptiometry 784
Geometric imperfections 335, 347, 350
  see also Finite element analysis of metal structures, Metal silo structures

Homogenizing, see Blending
Hoppers
  buckling 421, 422
  column support 422
  conical shell 415
  frictional traction 415
  loads on 341
  membrane yielding 419
  meridional rupture 420
  plastic collapse 419
  pressures 415
  ring beam 424
  transition junction 420
  see also Feeders, Numerical simulation – discrete particle models, Numerical Simulation – finite element models, Pressures – switch, Rectangular silos

Imperfections, see Geometric imperfections
Industry
  fabricator's and supplier's view 250
  problems 584–7
  survey of research requirements 807
  see also Flow property testing, Test classification
Inserts 118
  arrangements 125, 126
  loads on 124, 126, 128
  wall loads 120, 122
  see also Blending
Instrumentation, see Documentation of silo tests, Experimental techniques
Internal ties 436, 443
  structural design 444
Interstitial air pressure, see Air pressure measurement

Jenike tester, see Flow property measurement techniques/equipment

Level control 240, 248
  alarms 245
  continuous 241
  empty volume 240
  instruments 243
  inventory control 240
  radar 246
  ultrasonic 246
Loads
  bottom pressure 262
  discharge pressure 337
  filling pressure 337
  non-symmetrical loads 339
  patch loads 373
  silage 409
  unsymmetrical loads 373
  see also Dust explosions, Frictional traction, Inserts, Material properties for load models, Metal silo structures, Pressures, Purge bins, Rectangular silos, Seismic action, Wall friction, Wind load

Mass flow 76, 115, 172, 192, 485
  see also Flow patterns
Material characterization for silo tests 650, 655
  angle of internal friction 663, 665
  angle of repose 663
  bulk density 660, 720
  changes with time and usage 652
  cohesion 664
  continuum parameters 658
  flow function 665
  lateral pressure ratio 661
  moisture content and temperature 658
  particle density 656
  particle geometry 656, 720
  particle moisture content 657
  particle size distribution 655
  particle surface roughness 657
  properties and parameters 651, 654
  segregation 653
  single particle parameters 655
  stress–strain relations 665
  variation of bulk density 721
  wall friction coefficient 659
Material models, see Constitutive models
Material properties for load models 13, 68
Material property testing, see Flow property testing, Material characterization for silo tests
Metal silo construction
  out-of-plumb 343
  tolerances 343
Metal silo structures 325, 327
  buckling strength 347, 355, 373, 388, 421, 456
  bursting failure 346
  column support 343, 367
  design 330, 432
  design guides 331
  effective transition 362
  elephant's foot failure 357
  engaged columns 367

failure modes 368
failures 327
loads 331
local forces 343, 367
plastic collapse 360, 363
review 325
ring beam 367
standards 331
see also Buckling, Dust explosions, Finite element analysis of metal structures, Hoppers, Internal ties, Rectangular silos, Seismic action, Shell structures, Structural forms, Wear, Wind load
Mixing, see Blending
Model laws 774
centrifuge testing 777
load/structure interaction 776
particle size/continuum 776
scale errors 777
Moisture measurements 761, 766
cohesion from moisture 763
menisci 762
psychrometer 766, 768–72
relative humidity 767
tensiometer 766

Non-symmetric, see Eccentric
Norm, see Standards
Numerical simulation – comparison between finite element and discrete particle models 564, 580
applicability 580
constitutive parameters 574
contact distribution 564
contact forces 570
geometrical parameters 567
kinematic variables 572
macroscopic parameters 569, 570
macroscopic scale 564, 566
microscopic parameters 567, 570
microscopic scale 564, 566
static variables 570
strengths and weaknesses 582
Numerical simulation – discrete particle models 551, 556
characteristics of lattice grain models 557, 558
hopper flow 552
simulation of flow 559
see also Numerical simulation – comparison between finite element and discrete particle models
Numerical simulation – finite element models 471, 481, 497
bulk solids behaviour 472
dynamic finite element model 481
eccentric discharge 488
Eulerian formulation 482
flow predictions 503
hoppers 485

interaction 472, 484, 486
rate-dependent formulation 483
rate-independent formulation 483
relation to experimental testing 473
relation to practical design 473
seismic loading 518–26
silo geometry 471
smoothed transition 502
stochastic behaviour 509–16
temperature effects 487
velocity field 491
see also Constitutive models, Numerical simulation – comparison between finite element and discrete particle models, Software for numerical simulation

Particulate material, see Material characterization for silo tests
Patch loads, see Metal silo structures – design, Research needs – metal structures
Pipe, see Flow patterns
Piping, see Flow patterns
Plastic collapse, see Hoppers, Metal silo structures
Pneumatic, see Blending, Discharge aids
Powders 53, 90, 130
see also Material characterization for silo tests
Prenormative research 819–29
buckling strength 829
calibration of parameters for stored materials 825
calibration of patch loads 824
dust explosions 826
loads due to differential temperatures 828
loads in silage silos 827
loads in squat silos 822
pressures in silos with extreme eccentricity 821
seismic actions 823
silos with internal ties 820
see also Research needs
Pressure cells, see Stress and pressure measurements
Pressures
eccentric discharge 262, 263, 340
eccentric filling 339
FE-methods 262
switch 263, 415
see also Hoppers, Loads, Numerical simulation, Prenormative research, Rectangular silos
Purge bins 183
aeration requirements 187
aeration ring 185
aeration systems 185
cross bars 186

Index

invert cone 185
loads 189

Rathole 179, 590
Rectangular silos
  buckling 437
  buckling mode 439
  functional design 429
  pyramidal hoppers 440
  structural form 426
  wall pressures 429
Research needs
  buckling strength 462
  concrete silos 322
  discrete particle models 562
  experimental techniques 802
  finite element analysis of metal structures 457
  flow promoting devices 221
  flowability testing 49, 62
  imperfections 462
  internal ties 446
  interstitial air pressure and velocity measurements 743
  measurement of local density 727
  metal structures 461
  numerical modeling 466
  pressures for design 463
  rectangular silos 441, 465
  standards 461, 600
  stress and pressure measurements 697
  see also Standards, Industry; Survey of research requirements
Research needs in numerical simulation 584, 587
  anisotropy 588
  arching 589
  cohesion 588
  discharge pressures 595
  eccentric discharge 597
  eccentric filling 597
  filling process 588
  flow function 588
  flow patterns 591
  flow rate 591
  hoppers 600
  incomplete clean-out 590
  industrial problems 584
  ratholes 590
  segregation 593
  solid interaction 599
  storing pressures 595
  stress history 589
  symmetrical filling pressure 594
Residence time, see Blending, Flow patterns, Flow visualization
Ring beam, see Hoppers, Metal silo structures

Scale errors, see Model laws

Segregation 160
  displacement 162
  fluid 162
  heap 161
  impact 163
  modelling 167
  percolation 162
  testers 165
  see also Material characterization for silo tests
Seismic action 272, 400
  see also Numerical simulation – finite element models, Prenormative research, Standards
Settlement, see Foundation
Shell structures
  axial compression 338
  textbooks 330
  see also Buckling, Metal silo structures
Silage, see Loads
Silo batteries 268
Silo flow 3
  design 12
Silo quaking 171
  collapsing arches 180
  excitation by feeding 179
  pulsating flow 179
  silo noise 180
  slip–stick wall friction 179
  unstable stagnant zones 174
Silo test design 609
  tests for flow 630–4
  tests for pressures 622, 623–9
  tests for structural buckling 642–4
  tests for vibration 635–41
Software for numerical simulation 500
  comparison of programs 476
  computer programs 477, 495
  material models 479, 495
Standards 817
  seismic action 400
  transformation of research into 818
  wall friction 79
  wind loading 378
  see also Research needs
Steady-state flow, see Flow property testing – stationary flow
Strain/pressure transformation, see Wall strain
Strengths, see Buckling, Concrete wall design, Metal silo structures, Shell structures
Stress and pressure measurements 686
  calibration 688, 693
  design basis 688, 697
  embedded cell 691
  interface problem 686, 691
  mounting procedure 690, 691, 696
  normal stress 686, 692
  shear stress 688, 692

Structural analysis 704
  see also Concrete wall design, Finite element analysis of metal structures, Hoppers
Structural design, see Buckling, Concrete wall design, Metal silo structures, Shell structures
Structural forms 327, 334
  corrugated sheeting 335
  rolled steel plate construction 334
  spirally wound silos 335
  stiffened plate construction 334
  see also Metal silo structures, Rectangular silos, Shell structures
Swelling of stored solid 343
Switch, see Pressures

Temperature
  differential 343, 405
  effects of temperature 266
  solar radiation 343
  see also Numerical simulation – finite element models
Test classification 612, 618
  centrifuge models 617
  equipment 613
  experimental station 615
  explosions 614
  flow 613
  industrial silos 614
  laboratory-scale 616
  pilot-scale 615
  pressures 613
  seismic actions 614
  structural failure 614
Test facilities in Europe 792

Unit weight, see Bulk density

Venting systems, see Dust explosions
Vibrations, see Silo quaking

Wall cell, see Stress and pressure measurements
Wall design, see Concrete wall design, Metal silo structures – design
Wall friction
  angles of 78
  influence on flow pattern 76
  influence on load 77
  influence on wear 77
  parameters affecting 84
Wall friction testing
  Jenike shear tester 80
  Newcastle large diameter tester 83
  Newcastle–Twente tester 82
  rotational shear tester 81
  van den Bergh and Scarlett tester 82
Wall strain 700, 707
  error minimization 705
  strain–pressure inference method 706, 708, 710
  strain/pressure transformation 702
Wear 85
  see also Concrete wall design – abrasion, Wall friction
Wind buckling 334
Wind load
  anchorage of silos 386
  buckling mode 391
  cylindrical shell 378
  empty silo 339, 378, 382
  ring stiffening 394
  roofs 380
  structural analysis 382
  wind buckling 388
  wind pressure variation 378, 379

Printed in the United States
by Baker & Taylor Publisher Services